A Review of the Events of 1990

The 1991 World Book Year Book

The Annual Supplement to The World Book Encyclopedia

World Book, Inc.

a Scott Fetzer company

Chicago London Sydney Toronto

World Book, Inc.
525 West Monroe
Chicago, IL 60606

ISBN 0-7166-0491-4
ISSN 0084-1439
Library of Congress Catalog Card Number: 62-4818

Staff

Editor in Chief
Robert O. Zeleny

Executive Editor
A. Richard Harmet

Editorial
Managing Editor
Wayne Wille

Associate Editor
Sara Dreyfuss

Senior Editors
David L. Dreier
Carol L. Hanson
Jinger Hoop
Barbara A. Mayes
Jay Myers
Karin C. Rosenberg
Margaret Anne Schmidt
Rod Such

Contributing Editors
Joan Stephenson
Darlene R. Stille

Cartographic Services
H. George Stoll, Head
Wayne K. Pichler

Head, Index Services
Beatrice Bertucci

Senior Indexer
David Pofelski

Statistical Editor
Richard S. Bready

Editorial Assistant
Ethel Matthews

Art
Art Director
Alfred de Simone

Senior Artist, Year Book
Lisa Buckley

Senior Artists
Cari L. Biamonte
Melanie J. Lawson

Photography Director
John S. Marshall

Senior Photographs Editor
Sandra M. Dyrlund

Photographs Editor
Geralyn Swietek

Production
Director of Manufacturing
Henry Koval

Manufacturing, Manager
Sandra Van den Broucke

Pre-Press Services
Jerry Stack, Director
Barbara Podczerwinski
Madelyn Underwood

Proofreaders
Anne Dillon
Marguerite Hoye
Daniel Marotta

Research Services
Director
Mary Norton

Researchers
Karen McCormack
Kristina Vaicikonis

Library Services
Mary Ann Urbashich, Head

Publisher
William H. Nault

Contents

Page 28

Page 47

Page 68

Page 98

Page 215

Page 537

The Year in Brief

1990

January
February
March
April
May
June

July
August
September
October
November
December

A pictorial review of the top news stories of 1990 is followed by a month-by-month listing highlights some of the year's significant events.

See pages 28 and 29 ▶

The Year's Major News Stories

From the reunification of Germany to the crisis in the Persian Gulf, 1990 was an eventful year. On these two pages are the stories that *Year Book* editors picked as the most memorable, the most exciting, or the most important of the year, along with details about where to find information about them in the book.   *The Editors*

Animation: Livelier than ever in 1990
The popularity of TV's "The Simpsons" was just one example of a growing enthusiasm for animated entertainment. In the Special Reports section, see **Once Again, "Toons" Are Tops,** page 134. In the Year Book News Update section, see **Groening, Matt,** page 313; **Television,** page 448.
▼

"Iron Lady" out
After 11½ years in office, British Prime Minister Margaret Thatcher, known as the "Iron Lady," resigned in November. In the Year Book News Update section, see **Great Britain,** page 310.

Troubles in the U.S.S.R.
The Soviet Union struggled throughout the year with a crumbling economy, typified by the bread line shown below, and growing demands for independence from its 15 republics. In the Year Book News Update section, see **Union of Soviet Socialist Republics,** page 460.
▼

The Persian ▶ Gulf crisis
Iraq invaded and annexed Kuwait in August. In response, the United States and many Arab nations sent forces to the Persian Gulf to discourage further aggression by Iraq. In the Year Book News Update section, see **Armed forces,** page 170; **Middle East,** page 366.

◀ German reunification
East and West Germany merged in October to form a single nation. In the Year Book News Update section and in the World Book Supplement section, see **Germany,** pages 307 and 508**.**

NASA problems
The U.S. National Aeronautics and Space Administration (NASA) had problems in 1990. The agency announced in June that the $1.5-billion *Hubble Space Telescope* did not work properly and that the agency's three shuttles must be grounded until fuel leaks could be corrected. In the Year Book News Update section, see **Space exploration,** page 431.
▼

Human gene therapy
Scientists in September began the first gene therapy on a human patient, inserting missing genes into the cells of a child with an inherited immune-system disorder. In the Year Book News Update section, see **Medicine,** page 362.

▲
Mandela's release
South Africa released black nationalist leader Nelson R. Mandela in February, after more than 27 years in prison. In the Year Book News Update section, see **Mandela, Nelson,** page 360; **South Africa,** page 430.

			January			
S	M	T	W	TH	F	S
	1	2	3	4	5	6
7	8	9	10	11	12	13
14	15	16	17	18	19	20
21	22	23	24	25	26	27
28	29	30	31			

2 The Dow Jones Industrial Average (the Dow) closes above 2,800 for the first time ever, ending the day at 2,810.15.

3 Ousted Panamanian dictator Manuel Antonio Noriega surrenders to U.S. authorities.

9-20 The space shuttle *Columbia* carries out a nearly 11-day mission, the longest shuttle flight ever, during which it launches a communications satellite and retrieves a science satellite.

15 Bulgaria's parliament ends the Communist Party's monopoly on power.

18 Mayor Marion S. Barry, Jr., of Washington, D.C., is arrested on drug charges. After a two-month trial, he is convicted on August 10 on one charge of cocaine possession. The jury acquits him of another charge and deadlocks on 12 charges. He is sentenced on October 26 to six months in prison.

The longest and costliest criminal trial in United States history ends in California with the defendants in the McMartin Pre-School case found innocent of child molesting.

20 Soviet troops storm Baku, the capital of the Soviet republic of Azerbaijan, to quell ethnic violence that erupted there on January 13 between Azerbaijanis and Armenians.

Clashes break out between Indian troops and Muslim separatists in India's Kashmir region.

20-29 Haiti's government imposes a state of siege under which it suspends civil liberties, censors news broadcasts, and arrests dozens of political opponents.

22 The Yugoslav Communist Party votes to give up its monopoly on power.

24 A federal judge sentences retired Air Force General Richard V. Secord to two years probation for lying to Congress about the Iran-contra affair.

William Lozano, a Hispanic police officer in Miami, Fla., is sentenced to seven years in prison for a 1989 shooting that caused the death of a black motorcyclist and passenger and triggered three days of rioting.

25 A Colombian jetliner runs out of fuel and crashes on Long Island, New York, killing 73 people.

Pakistan's Prime Minister Benazir Bhutto gives birth to a girl, becoming the first modern head of government to bear a child while in office.

Pope John Paul II begins an eight-day visit to the African nations of Cape Verde, Guinea-Bissau, Mali, Burkina Faso, and Chad.

28 The San Francisco 49ers win football's Super Bowl XXIV, defeating the Denver Broncos 55-10.

Poland's Communist Party votes to dissolve itself and reorganize as a socialist party.

29 Scientists at American Telephone and Telegraph (AT&T) Bell Laboratories in Holmdel, N.J., unveil a digital optical processor, a device that could lead to superfast computers using pulses of light rather than electric currents to make calculations.

31 President George Bush delivers his first State of the Union address and proposes that the United States and the Soviet Union make deep cuts in their military forces in Europe.

▲
Panama's former dictator Manuel Antonio Noriega is booked on federal drug charges in Miami, Fla., one day after his January 3 surrender to United States authorities in Panama City.

Investigators inspect the wreckage ▶ of a Colombian jetliner that crashed on Long Island, New York, on January 25. The airplane ran out of fuel while circling Kennedy International Airport; 73 people were killed.

Quarterback Joe Montana leads the San Francisco 49ers to their second consecutive Super Bowl victory on January 28. The 49ers defeated the Denver Broncos 55-10.

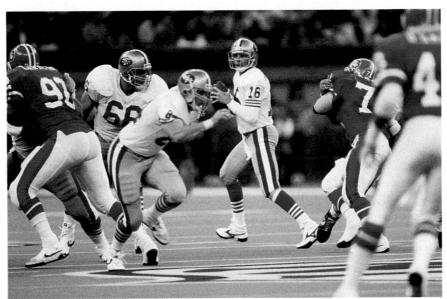

| February |||||||
S	M	T	W	TH	F	S
				1	2	3
4	5	6	7	8	9	10
11	12	13	14	15	16	17
18	19	20	21	22	23	24
25	26	27	28			

2 South Africa lifts a 30-year ban on the African National Congress (ANC), a black opposition group fighting white minority rule.

7 The Soviet Communist Party votes to surrender its monopoly on power, clearing the way for a multiparty system.

The tanker *American Trader* spills an estimated 395,000 gallons (1.5 million liters) of crude oil into the Pacific Ocean near Huntington Beach, Calif.

9 Major league baseball owners announce a lockout, calling off the opening of spring training because of salary disputes with the players' union.

11 South Africa releases black nationalist leader Nelson R. Mandela after more than 27 years in prison.

Boxer James (Buster) Douglas knocks out heavyweight champion Mike Tyson in one of the greatest upsets in boxing history.

Riots break out in the Soviet republic of Tajikistan against resettlement of Armenian refugees there.

12 The "Open Skies" conference between the Warsaw Pact and the North Atlantic Treaty Organization (NATO) opens in Ottawa, Canada. It results in unexpected agreements on German reunification and superpower troop levels in Europe.

15 Bush attends a summit in Cartagena, Colombia, with the presidents of Bolivia, Colombia, and Peru. The four leaders pledge increased cooperation to fight illegal drug trafficking.

18 Despite political scandals and an unpopular sales tax, Japan's long-governing Liberal-Democratic Party wins a majority in the powerful lower house of parliament in elections.

19 Coal miners of the United Mine Workers of America vote to accept a new contract with the Pittston Company. Most miners return to work on February 26, ending a strike that began on April 5, 1989.

22 The U.S. Food and Drug Administration approves the first low-calorie substitute for fat, the NutraSweet Company's Simplesse.

24 The Soviet republic of Lithuania holds the first multiparty election in Soviet history. Nationalist or independent candidates win more than half the seats in the republic's parliament.

25 Newspaper publisher Violeta Barrios de Chamorro is elected president of Nicaragua, defeating President Daniel Ortega of the left wing Sandinistas.

A smoking ban takes effect on all domestic U.S. airline flights of less than six hours.

Demonstrations calling for economic reform and more democracy draw an estimated 100,000 people in Moscow and smaller crowds in at least 20 other Soviet cities in the most widespread antigovernment protest ever in the Soviet Union.

26 Soviet troops begin withdrawing from Czechoslovakia, which they have occupied since 1968.

28 After five delays, the space shuttle *Atlantis* lifts off from Cape Canaveral on a secret military mission that includes the launch of a spy satellite.

Nicaragua's President Ortega declares a cease-fire with the U.S.-backed *contra* rebels.

After more than 27 years of ▶ imprisonment, African National Congress leader Nelson R. Mandela celebrates his release in Cape Town, South Africa, on February 11.

Violeta Barrios de Chamorro flashes the victory sign after defeating Daniel Ortega in Nicaragua's presidential elections on February 25.

◄ James (Buster) Douglas delivers a knockout punch to Mike Tyson during a heavyweight title bout in Tokyo on February 11.

March						
S	M	T	W	TH	F	S
				1	2	3
4	5	6	7	8	9	10
11	12	13	14	15	16	17
18	19	20	21	22	23	24
25	26	27	28	29	30	31

1 The U.S. Nuclear Regulatory Commission approves an operating license for the Seabrook nuclear plant in New Hampshire, begun in 1976 but delayed by safety concerns.

2 Greyhound bus drivers strike for higher pay.

3 The International Trans-Antarctica Expedition, a group of six explorers from six nations, completes the first dog-sled crossing of Antarctica.

10 Haiti's President Prosper Avril resigns after a week of protests. He is replaced on March 13 by Supreme Court Justice Ertha Pascal Trouillot, Haiti's first woman president.

11 Lithuania declares its independence from the Soviet Union.

12 Soviet soldiers begin leaving Hungary as part of an agreement to remove all Soviet troops from the country by June 1991.

13 The Soviet parliament approves constitutional amendments to create a strong U.S.-style presidency, abolish the Communist Party's monopoly on power, and allow ownership of private property. Mikhail S. Gorbachev is elected to a five-year term in the new presidency on March 15.

15 Fernando Collor de Mello takes office as Brazil's first popularly elected president since 1961. The day after taking office, he announces a sweeping anti-inflation plan that creates a new currency and freezes large bank accounts for 18 months.

18 Two thieves dressed as police officers steal 12 paintings worth at least $200 million from the Isabella Stewart Gardner Museum in Boston in what may be the largest art theft in history.

Major league baseball owners and players agree to a new four-year contract, ending a lockout that began on February 15.

East Germany holds the first free parliamentary elections in its history. The Alliance for Germany, a three-party coalition favoring reunification with West Germany, wins about 48 per cent of the vote.

21 Namibia, formerly known as South West Africa, becomes independent from South Africa.

22 An Anchorage, Alaska, jury convicts *Exxon Valdez* skipper Joseph J. Hazelwood of misdemeanor negligence in connection with a 1989 oil spill. He is sentenced to pay $50,000 in restitution and spend 1,000 hours cleaning oily beaches.

24 In Australian parliamentary elections, Prime Minister Robert Hawke's Labor Party clings to power with a reduced majority.

25 Hungarian voters elect a new parliament in their nation's first competitive elections since 1948. The center-right Hungarian Democratic Forum wins the most seats.

A fire at a social club in the Bronx section of New York City kills 87 people. A Cuban refugee is charged with 174 counts of murder in the case.

26 *Driving Miss Daisy,* a film about a white Southern widow and her black chauffeur, wins Academy Awards for best picture, best screenplay, best make-up, and best actress (Jessica Tandy).

▲
Jessica Tandy and Morgan Freeman star in *Driving Miss Daisy,* which won the Academy Award for best picture on March 26.

Explorers on skis and dog ▶ sleds on March 3 complete the International Trans-Antarctica Expedition, the first crossing of Antarctica without motor vehicles.

◀ Jubilant Namibians celebrate their nation's independence from South Africa on March 21.

April						
S	M	T	W	TH	F	S
1	2	3	4	5	6	7
8	9	10	11	12	13	14
15	16	17	18	19	20	21
22	23	24	25	26	27	28
29	30					

1 A per capita tax on all adults—called the community charge or poll tax—takes effect in England and Wales amid widespread protests.

2 The University of Nevada, Las Vegas, wins the National Collegiate Athletic Association (NCAA) men's basketball championship, defeating Duke University 103-73, the largest-ever margin of victory in an NCAA title game.

7 A federal jury convicts retired Rear Admiral John M. Poindexter, a former national security adviser to President Ronald Reagan, of five felonies in the Iran-contra affair. He is sentenced on June 11 to six months in prison.

Fires break out aboard the *Scandinavian Star* ferry in the North Sea, killing at least 166 passengers and crew members. Authorities suspect arson.

8 Nepal's king, after violent protests demanding more democracy, lifts a ban on political parties.

Greece's conservative New Democracy party wins the most seats in parliamentary elections, falling just one short of a majority. Party leader Constantine Mitsotakis becomes prime minister on April 11.

The Yugoslav province of Slovenia holds Yugoslavia's first free multiparty elections since 1938. A center-right coalition wins a majority and forms the first non-Communist regional government in Yugoslavia since 1945.

9 Comet Austin, the brightest comet seen from Earth since 1975, makes its closest approach to the sun at about 32 million miles (51 million kilometers).

12 Lothar de Maizière becomes prime minister of East Germany, heading a coalition of three conservative parties favoring reunification of the two Germanys.

17-18 Bush meets with representatives of 17 nations and 2 international organizations at a White House conference on global warming and environmental issues.

18 The Supreme Court of the United States rules that judges may order school boards to raise taxes to achieve desegregation.

22 Kidnappers in Lebanon free U.S. educator Robert Polhill, a hostage since January 1987.

Earth Day observances draw millions of people worldwide to marches and rallies calling for preservation of the environment.

24 Financier Michael R. Milken pleads guilty to six felonies and agrees to pay $600 million in fines and restitution, the largest criminal settlement ever.

Zaire's President Mobutu Sese Seko lifts a 20-year ban on opposition parties.

25 The space shuttle *Discovery* launches the $1.5-billion *Hubble Space Telescope*, the most expensive and advanced scientific satellite ever built. On June 27, the National Aeronautics and Space Administration (NASA) announces that at least one of the telescope's mirrors is faulty and will not perform as expected.

28 *A Chorus Line,* Broadway's longest-running show, closes after 6,137 performances.

30 Kidnappers in Lebanon free the second U.S. hostage in eight days—Frank H. Reed, an educator held captive since September 1986.

Robert Polhill, an American educator held hostage by Lebanese kidnappers for more than three years, waves to well-wishers after being released on April 22.

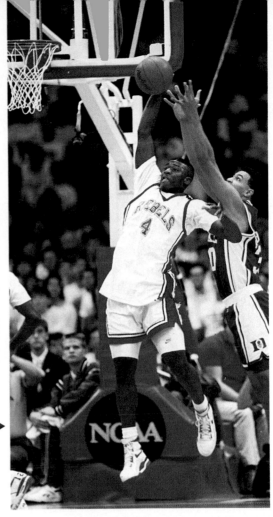

Larry Johnson scores 2 of ▶ his eventual 22 points toward an NCAA basketball championship for the University of Nevada, Las Vegas, on April 2. The Runnin' Rebels defeated Duke University 103-73.

Fire fighters struggle to ex- ▶ tinguish blazes aboard the North Sea ferry *Scandinavian Star.* At least 166 passengers and crew members died in the April 7 fires.

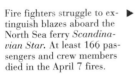

◀ Proclaiming their concern for the environment, New Yorkers rally in New York City to observe Earth Day, April 22.

17

			May			
S	M	T	W	TH	F	S
		1	2	3	4	5
6	7	8	9	10	11	12
13	14	15	16	17	18	19
20	21	22	23	24	25	26
27	28	29	30	31		

2-4 **The South African government holds** its first formal talks with the once outlawed ANC. The two sides discuss future negotiations on ending apartheid.

4 Latvia declares its independence from the Soviet Union.

6-13 **Pope John Paul II visits** Mexico.

8 Rafael Angel Calderón Fournier of the Social Christian Unity Party, the son of a former president of Costa Rica, takes office as president of the nation.

9 South Korean police battle antigovernment protesters in Seoul and other cities.

13 Gunmen kill two United States airmen near Clark Air Base in the Philippines on the eve of talks between the U.S. and Philippine governments on the future of U.S. military bases in the Philippines.

15 A Japanese businessman buys Dutch painter Vincent van Gogh's *Portrait of Dr. Gachet* (1890) for $82.5 million, a record price for art, and on May 17 buys *Au Moulin de la Galette* (1876) by Pierre Auguste Renoir of France for $78.1 million.

18 East and West Germany sign a treaty to merge their economies and social systems. The pact is ratified by the parliaments of both nations on June 21 and takes effect on July 1.

19 The United States and the Soviet Union agree to end production of chemical weapons and to destroy most of their stockpile of such weapons.

20 An Israeli gunman kills 7 Palestinian laborers with an assault rifle and wounds at least 10 others. The killings trigger bloody riots in the Israeli-occupied Gaza Strip and West Bank.

Romania holds its first free elections since 1937. Interim President Ion Iliescu, a Communist, becomes president, and the National Salvation Front, dominated by former Communists, wins a majority in parliament.

21 A Kashmiri Islamic leader is assassinated in India's disputed Kashmir region, and Indian security forces open fire on mourners carrying the slain leader, killing at least 47 people.

22 Yemen (Aden) and Yemen (Sana) merge to form a single nation, the Republic of Yemen.

Lucien Bouchard, Canada's environment minister, resigns because of differences with the government over Quebec's status within Canada.

24 The Edmonton Oilers win hockey's Stanley Cup, defeating the Boston Bruins four games to one.

27 Burma, also known as Myanmar, holds its first multiparty elections in 30 years. The National League for Democracy, a prodemocratic opposition party, wins by a landslide, but Burma's military government ignores the election results.

César Gaviria Trujillo of the Liberal Party is elected president of Colombia. He takes office on August 7.

29 Gorbachev arrives in Ottawa, Canada, for a 29-hour visit.

Boris N. Yeltsin, Gorbachev's main political rival, is elected president of the largest Soviet republic, the Russian Soviet Federative Socialist Republic.

30 Bush and Gorbachev begin a four-day summit meeting in Washington, D.C.

▲

Vincent van Gogh's *Portrait of Dr. Gachet* is sold on May 15 for $82.5 million, the highest price ever paid for a work of art.

The Edmonton Oilers defeat the Boston Bruins four games to one in Stanley Cup finals on May 24.
▼

▲
Pope John Paul II walks across a carpet of flowers in a Mexico City plaza before celebrating a Mass during a May visit to Mexico.

June						
S	M	T	W	TH	F	S
					1	2
3	4	5	6	7	8	9
10	11	12	13	14	15	16
17	18	19	20	21	22	23
24	25	26	27	28	29	30

Black smoke pours from burning crude oil after a June 9 explosion ripped the Norwegian oil tanker *Mega Borg* in the Gulf of Mexico.

1 The Dow closes above 2,900 for the first time ever, ending the day at 2,900.97.

Bush and Gorbachev sign major trade and disarmament pacts and several other agreements.

4 Violence breaks out in the Soviet republic of Kirghiz between the Kirghiz majority and the Uzbek minority over the distribution of homestead land.

The U.S. Supreme Court rules that public schools must give religious and political clubs the same access to facilities that other extracurricular activities have.

8 South Africa lifts a four-year-old state of emergency except in Natal Province, site of fighting between rival black groups, where the state of emergency lasts until October 18.

Israel's Prime Minister Yitzhak Shamir ends 88 days with only an acting government by forming a coalition of his Likud bloc and several far right and religious parties.

8-9 Czechoslovakia holds its first free elections since 1946. The prodemocracy Civic Forum wins the most seats in parliament but falls short of a majority.

9 The Norwegian oil tanker *Mega Borg* explodes in the Gulf of Mexico off Galveston, Tex.

10 Alberto Fujimori, an agricultural engineer, is elected president of Peru in a runoff with novelist Mario Vargas Llosa. Fujimori takes office on July 28.

10, 17 The Bulgarian Socialist Party, made up of former Communists, wins a majority in the National Assembly in Bulgaria's first free elections since 1932.

11 Nolan Ryan of the Texas Rangers pitches his sixth career no-hitter, a major league record.

The Supreme Court overturns a 1989 federal law that made it a crime to burn the American flag.

12 Algeria's fundamentalist Islamic Salvation Front wins control of more than half the nation's municipal councils and 32 of the 48 provinces in Algeria's first multiparty elections since 1962.

14 The Detroit Pistons win the National Basketball Association championship, defeating the Portland Trail Blazers four games to one.

17-30 Mandela visits three Canadian and eight U.S. cities on a 14-day North American tour.

21 A devastating earthquake rocks northwestern Iran, killing an estimated 40,000 people.

22 The U.S. Fish and Wildlife Service declares the northern spotted owl a threatened species, making it illegal to harm the bird or destroy its habitat.

23 Canada's opposition Liberal Party elects Jean Chrétien, a former finance minister, as its new leader.

The Meech Lake Accord, a 1987 pact designed to secure Quebec's full participation in Canada's constitution, expires after 2 of the 10 provinces fail to ratify it.

26 Bush abandons his campaign pledge of "no new taxes," conceding that "tax revenue increases" will be needed to reduce the deficit.

29 NASA grounds its three space shuttles after discovering a fuel leak on the shuttle *Atlantis*.

Bush vetoes a bill that would have required large companies to give employees unpaid leave to care for newborn or adopted children or ill family members.

Surrounded by reporters, Alberto Fujimori celebrates his June 10 victory in Peru's presidential runoff elections.

◀ An Iranian bewails the destruction caused by a June 21 earthquake that killed about 40,000 people and left 10 times as many homeless in northwestern Iran.

July						
S	**M**	**T**	**W**	**TH**	**F**	**S**
1	2	3	4	5	6	7
8	9	10	11	12	13	14
15	16	17	18	19	20	21
22	23	24	25	26	27	28
29	30	31				

1 East and West Germany merge their economies.

2 A U.S. District Court jury acquits former Philippine first lady Imelda Marcos on racketeering and fraud charges. Her codefendant, Saudi financier Adnan M. Khashoggi, is also acquitted.

5 Riots against single-party rule erupt in Kenya.

6 Bulgaria's President Petur Toshev Mladenov resigns over charges that he ordered tanks to disperse an antigovernment protest in December 1989.

7-8 Tennis players Martina Navratilova of the United States and Stefan Edberg of Sweden win Wimbledon singles championships, Navratilova for a record ninth time.

8 West Germany wins the World Cup soccer championship in Rome, defeating Argentina 1 to 0.

9-11 Leaders of the world's seven major industrial democracies hold an economic summit in Houston.

12 Nicaragua's President Chamorro agrees to wage hikes and other concessions to end a strike by pro-Sandinista unions that began on July 2.

13 Congress passes a civil rights act outlawing discrimination against disabled people in employment, government services, transportation, and access to public facilities. Bush signs the bill into law on July 26.

16 A deadly earthquake kills at least 1,650 people in the Philippines.

19 Pete Rose, former Cincinnati Reds manager and player, is sentenced to five months in prison after he pleads guilty to filing false tax returns.

20 A federal appeals court overturns one of the three 1989 Iran-contra convictions of former Marine Lieutenant Colonel Oliver L. North.

Justice William J. Brennan, Jr., 84, retires from the Supreme Court for health reasons.

22, 29 Mongolia holds its first multiparty elections. The ruling Communist Party wins by a wide majority.

23 Bush nominates U.S. Appeals Court Judge David H. Souter to replace Brennan on the Supreme Court.

25 Bishop George L. Carey of Bath and Wells is named to succeed Robert K. Runcie as archbishop of Canterbury, head of the Church of England.

The U.S. Senate votes to denounce Senator David F. Durenberger (R., Minn.) for improper financial dealings and orders him to pay restitution.

26 The U.S. House of Representatives votes to reprimand Representative Barney Frank (D., Mass.) for conduct stemming from his relationship with a male prostitute.

27 Muslim radicals in Trinidad and Tobago capture Prime Minister Arthur Napoleon Raymond Robinson, some 40 other hostages, the Parliament building, and a television station. The militants surrender on August 1 after releasing their hostages.

28 Two barges and a tanker collide in the Houston Ship Channel, spilling an estimated 700,000 gallons (2.6 million liters) of oil into Galveston Bay.

A fire at a generating plant knocks out electric power for about 40,000 homes and businesses on Chicago's West Side. Power is restored to almost all customers by July 31.

Federal appeals court Judge David H. Souter, at left, is nominated for the Supreme Court on July 23. Souter was confirmed in October.

▼

◀ In Rome on July 8, West Germany becomes the 1990 World Cup soccer champion by defeating Argentina 1 to 0, the lowest score ever in a World Cup final.

President George Bush, Great Britain's Prime Minister Margaret Thatcher, and their spouses watch a lariat-twirling rodeo showman in Houston before an international economic summit July 9 through 11.
▼

August						
S	**M**	**T**	**W**	**TH**	**F**	**S**
			1	2	3	4
5	6	7	8	9	10	11
12	13	14	15	16	17	18
19	20	21	22	23	24	25
26	27	28	29	30	31	

1 Bulgaria's parliament elects Zhelyu Zhelev as the nation's first non-Communist president in more than 40 years.

2 Iraq invades Kuwait.

The U.S. government indicts Representative Floyd H. Flake (D., N.Y.) and his wife, Elaine, on 17 counts of conspiracy, fraud, and tax evasion. The couple deny the charges.

6 Pakistan's President Ghulam Isaq Khan dismisses Prime Minister Bhutto, accusing her of corruption and abuse of power.

The South African government and the ANC begin talks to prepare for formal negotiations on ending white minority rule.

7 Bush orders United States combat planes and troops to Saudi Arabia to guard against a possible attack by Iraq.

India's Prime Minister Vishwanath Pratap Singh announces a plan to reserve 49 per cent of all civil service jobs for lower-caste Hindus. The plan triggers riots and suicides that take at least 70 lives by the end of September.

8 Iraq declares that it has formally annexed Kuwait.

Peru's government announces huge increases in the price of gasoline and food as part of an austerity plan. The plan sets off several days of rioting and a nationwide strike on August 21.

9 Yosemite National Park is temporarily closed due to forest fires.

10 The *Magellan* spacecraft reaches an orbit of Venus on a mission to map the planet's surface.

Egypt, Syria, and 10 other Arab nations vote to send military forces to Saudi Arabia to discourage aggression by Iraq.

12 Fighting breaks out between South Africa's Xhosa and Zulu ethnic groups. By the end of August, more than 500 people have been killed.

18 A New York City jury finds three teen-agers guilty of raping and assaulting a woman jogger in Central Park in April 1989. On Sept. 11, 1990, the three receive sentences of 5 to 10 years in prison.

21 Five West African nations—Gambia, Ghana, Guinea, Nigeria, and Sierra Leone—send a peacekeeping force to intervene in Liberia's eight-month civil war.

22 President Bush calls up U.S. military reservists for service in the Persian Gulf crisis.

23 Armenia declares its independence from the Soviet Union.

26 Protesters set fire to the headquarters of the governing Socialist Party in Sofia, Bulgaria.

26-28 Police in Gainesville, Fla., find five college students murdered, apparently by a serial killer.

28 A deadly tornado rakes northern Illinois, killing 29 people.

29 Canadian soldiers and Mohawk Indians begin to tear down barricades that the Mohawks had erected at the Mercier Bridge near Montreal on July 11 to block expansion of a golf course onto what the Indians regard as ancestral land. The bridge reopens on September 6.

◀ South African Zulus rush into conflict with a rival group of Xhosas in August. Ethnic violence in South Africa killed at least 500 people that month.

A fire fighter in Yosemite ▶ National Park battles one of several blazes that closed the park from August 9 to 20.

American combat troops arrive in Saudi Arabia after President Bush on August 7 dispatched U.S. forces to guard against an invasion by Iraq.

▼

September

S	M	T	W	TH	F	S
						1
2	3	4	5	6	7	8
9	10	11	12	13	14	15
16	17	18	19	20	21	22
23	24	25	26	27	28	29
30						

1-10 Pope John Paul II visits the African nations of Tanzania, Burundi, Rwanda, and Ivory Coast.

4 New Zealand's Prime Minister Geoffrey Palmer resigns and is succeeded by Foreign Minister Michael K. Moore.

4-6 North Korea's Premier Yon Hyong-muk meets with South Korea's President Roh Tae Woo and other officials in the highest-level contact between the two Koreas since the country was divided in 1945.

6 Ontario's socialist New Democratic Party (NDP) defeats the ruling Liberal Party in elections in that Canadian province. NDP leader Robert K. Rae becomes premier on October 1.

The military government of Burma (Myanmar) arrests the acting opposition leader and five other political dissidents.

9 Bush and Gorbachev meet in Helsinki, Finland, to discuss the Persian Gulf crisis.

United States tennis player Pete Sampras, 19, becomes the youngest champion in U.S. Open history.

Ellis Island, a former U.S. immigration center in New York Harbor, reopens as a museum of immigration history after a six-year renovation.

9-10 Liberian rebel forces led by Prince Yormie Johnson capture and kill President Samuel K. Doe.

12 Premier John Buchanan of Nova Scotia resigns to take a seat in Canada's Senate. Deputy Premier Roger S. Bacon succeeds him.

14 Scientists at the National Institutes of Health in Bethesda, Md., begin the first gene therapy on a human patient, inserting missing genes into the cells of a 4-year-old girl with an immune disorder.

17 Secretary of Defense Richard B. Cheney fires Air Force Chief of Staff General Michael J. Dugan for talking publicly about plans to bomb Iraq.

18 The International Olympic Committee awards the 1996 Summer Olympic Games to the city of Atlanta, Ga.

Financier Charles H. Keating, Jr., is indicted and jailed on criminal fraud charges in connection with the 1989 failure of Lincoln Savings & Loan Association of Irvine, Calif.

24 South Africa's State President Frederik Willem de Klerk meets with President Bush at the White House, becoming the first South African head of government to visit the United States since 1945.

The Soviet parliament grants Gorbachev special economic powers for the next 18 months to direct the Soviet Union's transition to a market economy.

26 The Motion Picture Association of America replaces its X rating with a new NC-17 rating intended to exclude all viewers under 17 years of age.

29 Builders set the final stone on Washington Cathedral, a Gothic-style Episcopal church in Washington, D.C., that was begun in 1907.

29-30 The United Nations World Summit for Children draws more than 70 world leaders to UN Headquarters in New York City.

▲

Young people from many nations hold a candlelight vigil in New York City as leaders of more than 70 countries gather for the United Nations World Summit for Children on September 29-30, the first global meeting devoted to improving the lives of children.

26

Scientists at the National Institutes of Health in Bethesda, Md., display equipment used on September 14 in the first human gene therapy, an attempt to cure an inherited immune disorder in a 4-year-old girl by genetically altering some of her cells.

▼

October

S	M	T	W	TH	F	S
	1	2	3	4	5	6
7	8	9	10	11	12	13
14	15	16	17	18	19	20
21	22	23	24	25	26	27
28	29	30	31			

1 The African nation of Rwanda is invaded from Uganda by rebel forces, exiled members of Rwanda's Tutsi minority group.

2 The Senate confirms Souter to the Supreme Court. He takes his seat on October 9.

3 East and West Germany unite.

A jury in Fort Lauderdale, Fla., convicts a record store owner of obscenity for selling an album by the rap group 2 Live Crew. On October 20, another jury in that city acquits 2 Live Crew of obscenity charges stemming from a performance in June.

4 Philippine rebels seize two military posts on the island of Mindanao before surrendering on October 6, ending the seventh uprising in four years against President Corazon C. Aquino.

5 A Cincinnati, Ohio, jury finds an art museum and its director innocent of charges that they broke obscenity laws by displaying sexually explicit photographs by Robert Mapplethorpe.

6 The space shuttle *Discovery* lifts off and launches the European-built *Ulysses* spacecraft on a mission to study the sun.

6-8 The U.S. government temporarily halts all but essential services after Congress fails to enact a new budget and Bush vetoes a stopgap spending bill.

8 A stone-throwing attack by Palestinians at the Temple Mount, a holy site in Jerusalem, sets off shooting by Israeli police that kills at least 17 Palestinians.

13 Renegade Lebanese General Michel Awn (also spelled Aoun), the leader of Christian militias, surrenders after resisting President Ilyas Harawi's government since November 1989.

15 Soviet President Gorbachev wins the Nobel Peace Prize for his efforts to ease global tensions.

South Africa ends segregation of libraries, trains, buses, toilets, swimming pools, and other facilities.

20 The Cincinnati Reds sweep the World Series, defeating the Oakland Athletics in four straight games.

22 Bush vetoes a major civil rights bill that would have strengthened federal protection against job discrimination, arguing that it will lead employers to use quotas based on race and sex.

A judge in Orange County, California, denies the request of a surrogate mother for parental rights to the child she bore for another couple.

24 Secretary of Labor Elizabeth H. Dole announces her resignation.

The center-left Pakistan People's Party, headed by former Prime Minister Bhutto, loses in Pakistan's parliamentary elections to a right wing alliance.

25 Boxer Evander Holyfield knocks out Douglas to become the new heavyweight champion.

27 Congress passes the Clean Air Act of 1990, crime and immigration bills, and a $492-billion deficit-reduction bill that raises taxes and cuts spending.

New Zealand's conservative National Party wins parliamentary elections, and party leader James B. Bolger becomes prime minister.

29 The coalition government of Norway's Prime Minister Jan P. Syse collapses.

▲ Israeli police detain suspects near the Dome of the Rock in Jerusalem following an October 8 conflict in which the police shot and killed at least 17 Palestinian Arabs after a stone-throwing attack by the Palestinians.

A crowd at the Brandenburg ▶ Gate in Berlin celebrates the reunification of East and West Germany on October 3.

► Cincinnati Reds pitcher José Rijo, voted the Most Valuable Player in the World Series, pitches against the Oakland Athletics on October 20 in the final game of the series, won by Cincinnati in a four-game sweep.

November						
S	M	T	W	TH	F	S
				1	2	3
4	5	6	7	8	9	10
11	12	13	14	15	16	17
18	19	20	21	22	23	24
25	26	27	28	29	30	

3 Gro Harlem Brundtland of the Labor Party becomes prime minister of Norway, replacing Syse.

5 Israeli militant Meir Kahane is assassinated in New York City. The police take an Egyptian-born repairman, El Sayyid A. Noasair, into custody.

6 Nawaz Sharif is sworn in as prime minister of Pakistan, heading a rightist coalition.

Democrats increase their majority in both houses of Congress in U.S. elections.

Democrat Sharon Pratt Dixon is elected mayor of Washington, D.C.—the first black woman to head a major U.S. city. She will take office on Jan. 2, 1991.

7 India's Prime Minister Singh resigns after losing a vote of confidence in Parliament, having lost the support of Hindus who want a Muslim mosque in Ayodhya torn down to build a Hindu temple.

8 William J. Bennett resigns as director of the U.S. Office of National Drug Control Policy.

9 A new constitution takes effect in Nepal, establishing multiparty democracy and a constitutional monarchy.

10 Chandra Shekhar, a leftist, becomes prime minister of India, heading a minority government.

12 Emperor Akihito of Japan is formally enthroned as Japan's ruler.

15-20 The space shuttle *Atlantis* **carries out** a secret military mission, reportedly launching a satellite that will spy on Iraq.

16 Bush leaves on a trip to Europe and the Middle East, where he spends Thanksgiving Day with U.S. troops in Saudi Arabia.

17 Soviet President Gorbachev proposes a radical restructuring of the Soviet government, including expanded powers for the Federation Council made up of the heads of the 15 Soviet republics.

19-21 Leaders of Canada, the United States, and 32 European nations hold a summit meeting in Paris to formally mark the end of the Cold War.

21 Milken is sentenced to 10 years in prison for the securities violations to which he pleaded guilty in April.

22 Britain's Prime Minister Margaret Thatcher announces her resignation after more than 11 years in office. John Major succeeds her on November 28.

25 Poland's Prime Minister Tadeusz Mazowiecki finishes third in the first round of voting for president, and he resigns the next day.

27 The National Football League fines three New England Patriots players a total of $22,500 and the team $50,000 for the alleged sexual harassment of reporter Lisa Olson in the team's locker room.

28 Singapore's Lee Kuan Yew steps down after 31 years as prime minister. Goh Chok Tong succeeds him.

29 The United Nations Security Council authorizes the use of force against Iraq unless Iraq withdraws from Kuwait by Jan. 15, 1991. The vote is the UN's first approval of military action since 1950, when the Korean War began.

Bulgaria's Prime Minister Andrey K. Lukanov and his government of former Communists resign under pressure from strikes and street protests.

▲
Margaret Thatcher holds a farewell press conference in London after her November 22 resignation as prime minister of Great Britain.

Japan's Emperor Akihito formally begins his reign in a ceremony in Tokyo on November 12. ▶

President Bush accepts a trophy from a United States soldier at a Thanksgiving dinner in Saudi Arabia on November 22.

December

S	M	T	W	TH	F	S
						1
2	3	4	5	6	7	8
9	10	11	12	13	14	15
16	17	18	19	20	21	22
23	24	25	26	27	28	29
30	31					

▲

Lech Walesa addresses his supporters from a window after winning Poland's presidential election on December 9.

1 British and French workers digging a tunnel under the English Channel meet after knocking out a passage large enough to walk through.

Ty Detmer, a quarterback at Brigham Young University in Provo, Utah, wins the Heisman Trophy as the outstanding U.S. college football player.

Chad's President Hissein Habré flees after a series of victories by rebel guerrillas. Rebel leader Idriss Deby declares himself president on December 4.

2 German Chancellor Helmut Kohl and his center-right coalition win by a large margin in Gemany's first elections as a unified nation since 1932.

The space shuttle *Columbia* lifts off carrying an astronomical observatory. *Columbia* lands on December 10, a day earlier than planned, ending a mission plagued by computer and plumbing problems.

2-8 President Bush visits Brazil, Uruguay, Argentina, Chile, and Venezuela.

3 Two jetliners collide on a runway at Detroit Metropolitan Airport, killing eight people.

Mary Robinson, an independent backed by the Labour Party, becomes Ireland's first woman president.

4 Bangladeshi President Hussain Mohammad Ershad resigns, bowing to demands for his ouster. Shahabuddin Ahmed becomes interim president of Bangladesh on December 6.

6 Iraq's President Hussein says he will release all foreign hostages. The first freed hostages arrive home on December 10.

7 International trade talks in Brussels, Belgium, fail because of a dispute between the United States and the European Community over farm export subsidies.

Bulgaria's parliament elects Dimitar Popov, a political independent, to succeed Lukanov as prime minister.

9 Lech Walesa wins a landslide victory in Poland's first-ever direct presidential election. He takes office on December 22.

13 Canada's Senate approves the highly unpopular goods and services tax (GST), a 7 per cent sales tax that will take effect on Jan. 1, 1991.

14 Bush names Representative Lynn M. Martin (R., Ill.) to replace Dole as secretary of labor.

16 Jean-Bertrand Aristide, a Roman Catholic priest, wins Haiti's first free presidential election since it gained independence from France in 1804. He is scheduled to take office on Feb. 7, 1991.

17 Bush chooses former Tennessee Governor Lamar Alexander as secretary of education, replacing Lauro F. Cavazos, who resigned on December 12.

20 Soviet Foreign Minister Eduard A. Shevardnadze announces his resignation.

22 A ferry capsizes off Haifa, Israel, drowning at least 20 U.S. sailors from the aircraft carrier U.S.S. *Saratoga.*

24 A military coup overthrows Suriname's President Ramsewak Shankar.

25 *The Godfather Part III* opens at motion-picture theaters throughout the United States and Canada.

British and French workers digging a tunnel under the English Channel exchange flags after the tunnelers digging from both sides meet near the middle on December 1.

Jean-Bertrand Aristide, a Roman Catholic priest, campaigns for the presidency of Haiti, which he won in elections on December 16.

Special Reports

1990

Planets
Memory
Ellis Island
Pacific rim
Puerto Rico

Animation
African elephants

Seven articles give in-depth treatment to subjects of current importance and lasting interest.

See page 74 ▶

By Eugene J. Walter, Jr.

The African Elephant: Saved from Extinction?

An international ban on the ivory trade and crackdowns on illegal hunting have curbed—for now at least— the slaughter of African elephants.

Preceding pages: Against the backdrop of Mount Kilimanjaro, a herd of elephants in Kenya's Amboseli National Park make their way across the savanna.

The author: Eugene J. Walter, Jr., is director of publications at the New York Zoological Society and editor in chief of *Wildlife Conservation* magazine.

Pale reddish hues in the eastern sky silhoutte distant hilltops as the first light of dawn filters across the savanna. All is quiet at this early hour in the sweeping grassland in a remote corner of an African national park. The rains have been plentiful this year, and the grass is lush. It is much to the taste of a family of 12 elephants, rousing themselves lazily in the morning coolness. All are females except one of the two babies, born just a month before. The little ones—small only by elephant standards—suckle eagerly at their mothers' breasts. The leader, or *matriarch*, of this tribe, a middle-aged "grandma," strolls toward a nearby river to quench her thirst. The others follow.

Suddenly the matriarch pauses as she hears a distant sound: the growl and whine of automotive engines. Three Land Rovers soon come into view, bouncing across the rutted plains. Warily, the family bunches together in a defensive formation, the adults surrounding the youngsters. The leader faces the danger.

The arriving vehicles sweep around the group at a safe distance, their tires churning up a billowing cloud of dust. Abruptly, they grind to a stop, and their occupants—men armed with high-powered automatic rifles—leap to the ground. The elephants, trumpeting loudly, toss their heads and flap their ears in a display of menacing defiance. The grandmother begins a mock charge as further warning to the intruders, but it is a futile gesture. A barrage of steel-clad bullets rips through her hide and flesh, and she topples. The other elephants huddle closer together; terrified though they are by the rattling gunfire, they are too tightly bonded to one another to respond by trying to escape.

One of the matriarch's daughters prods the dying leader, trying to lift her with trunk and tusks. Moments later, she too is cut down. One by one, the great beasts are slaughtered until only the little male remains alive. Screeching in confusion and terror, he pushes frantically at his mother, begging her to rise and help him. Another burst of gunfire ends his misery.

Flinging their weapons into the vehicles, the efficient crew grab gasoline-powered chain saws and begin an even more grisly operation. The screeching saws spit blood and bits of bone and tissue into the air as the killers slice away the front of each elephant's head to remove the animals' valuable ivory tusks. When they have completed their butchery, the men load the tusks into the vehicles and roar away as swiftly as they came, lest they be caught in their crime. But despite their haste, the men are not especially worried. They know the park rangers have no parts to repair their single aging, broken-down Land Rover and so must patrol the park on foot.

It is now well past daybreak. As the sun climbs higher in the sky, it warms patches of grass stained the color of rust by pools of drying blood from the huge, faceless corpses. The earth is littered with empty bullet casings and scarred by tire tracks. Overhead, vultures are already beginning to circle.

Elephant life

A mother elephant shepherds her young calf. Female offspring stay with the family into which they were born for their entire life, but males are expelled from the group when they reach puberty at about 13 years of age.

Seeking relief from the heat, an elephant prepares for a roll in the mud. Elephants often cool off in this way or by bathing in rivers, lakes, or water holes.

The mass slaughter of a species

Scenes like the one just described have occurred thousands of times in Africa in recent years. Between 1979 and 1989, the elephant population on the continent plummeted from about 2 million to fewer than 700,000 (fewer than 650,000, by some estimates). Although some of that decline has been due to the loss of elephant habitats, most of the deaths have been caused by *poachers* (illegal hunters) killing elephants for their tusks.

In 1973, the Kenya Game Department estimated that Kenya's elephants numbered about 167,000. Today, there are fewer than 20,000, a drop of nearly 90 per cent. The neighboring country of Uganda has lost a comparable percentage, and in Tanzania's Selous Game Reserve, Africa's largest animal park, 50 per cent of the elephants have died in the past 10 years. Biologists estimated in 1989 that at the rate elephants were being slaughtered by poachers, there would be no more than 100,000 of the great beasts remaining on the continent within 15 to 20 years.

But fortunately for elephants, millions of people love them and are determined to save them from destruction. Because of that commitment, there is now hope that the outlook for these magnificent creatures may be brightening. In late 1989, most of the world's nations agreed to prohibit ivory imports, and within months that ban seemed to be taking effect. Ivory trading—and elephant killing—had declined markedly. Moreover, several African nations have shown a new resolve to protect their remaining elephant herds.

The natural wonder of elephants

The African elephant is the largest land-dwelling animal on earth, and in the entire animal kingdom only a few species of whales attain a greater size. A mature male elephant is typically about 11 feet (3.4 meters) in height at the shoulder, with a weight of approximately 12,000 pounds (5,400 kilograms). Females are smaller, averaging about 9 feet (2.8 meters) in height and 8,000 pounds (3,600 kilograms) in weight. Yet despite its colossal bulk, an adult elephant can, when necessary, run 25 miles per hour (40 kilometers per hour), easily outracing a swift human runner over short distances.

Although the ancestors of modern elephants once roamed over most of the globe, the only other elephant in the world today is the Asian elephant, found in India and Southeast Asia. This species is shorter, weighs less, and has smaller ears than its African cousin. Only male Asian elephants have tusks that protrude past the lips, and the tusks are usually smaller than those of the African elephant.

African elephants are divided into two subspecies: the savanna or bush elephant and the forest elephant. The latter is a somewhat smaller animal, with smaller ears, a domed back, and longer, narrower tusks. Although the forest elephant is found mostly in the rain forests of western and central Africa, the

ranges of the two subspecies frequently overlap, and it is not unusual for them to interbreed.

The bodies of these huge creatures are marvels of specialized function. The enormous ears, for instance, serve as air conditioners in the African heat. Just under the thin skin covering the back of the ears is an intricate network of blood vessels. When an elephant fans its ears, it cools its blood by evaporation. Often it speeds up the process by spraying water, dust, or mud over this area with its trunk.

An elephant's trunk—a nose like no other on earth—is one of the most remarkable adaptations evolved by any animal. Whereas other animals must bend or crouch to lap up water, its trunk enables an elephant to drink while standing upright. After sucking water up the nasal tubes, the elephant curls its trunk inward and squirts a drink into its mouth. The trunk has other uses as well. For feeding, it serves as a hand, grasping clumps of grass or leaves, tugging them loose, and transferring them to the mouth. The trunk is also a sensory organ, used to both feel and smell objects—including other elephants—and it is a highly sensitive scanner of the environment, enabling the elephant to "sniff out" enemies when they are still distant.

The trunk also makes a potent weapon in a fight with other elephants or in subduing enemies such as lions or snakes. But an elephant's most dangerous weapons are its tusks. A well-aimed thrust with one of those ivory sabers can be lethal to an attacker. As effective as they are for defense or aggression, though, that is just one of their functions. More often, an elephant uses its tusks while feeding to dig for roots or to strip the bark from trees.

The tusks are actually elongated upper incisor teeth. They grow throughout the elephant's lifetime—more than 4 inches (10 centimeters) a year for males. Record-length tusks have exceeded 11 feet (3.3 meters). Relatively few elephants' tusks reach

Slaughter on the savanna
The carcasses of four elephants killed by poachers in Uganda decay under the harsh tropical sun. In the 1980's, poachers in Africa killed an average of 80,000 elephants a year for their valuable tusks.

41

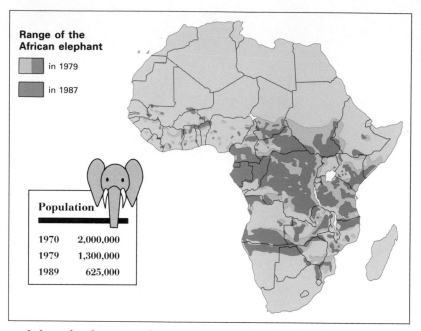

Range of the
African elephant

in 1979

in 1987

Population	
1970	2,000,000
1979	1,300,000
1989	625,000

such lengths, however, because they get broken in fights or worn
down through everyday use.

Elephant society

Whatever they are doing, most elephants do it as part of a
group. Except for adult males, elephants are members of stable
families of up to 25 related individuals. A large herd of elephants, which can number in the hundreds, is an association of
these family units. Each family is ruled by a matriarch, the oldest mother in the group.

When a calf is born, several females become "aunties" and assist the mother in rearing the youngster. If the new arrival is a
female, she will be a permanent member of the group. If it is a
male, his time with the family will be limited; when he reaches
puberty—about 13 years of age—he will be expelled by the other adults. After leaving the family circle, some males form loose,
temporary associations with other males, while others lead a
largely solitary life.

Group ties within an elephant family are very close, and members look after one another's welfare. They are especially atten-
tive to the babies. If a youngster gets stuck in a mud hole, the
other elephants work frantically with their trunks and feet to
free it. And should a calf falter when a herd is on the move, its
relatives rush to its aid.

Elephants seem to experience feelings of joy. When wandering
groups of elephants encounter one another, they engage in
"greeting ceremonies" marked by a variety of excited sounds
and body movements. Many of the sounds made by elephants
are apparently part of a complex vocal language. A research

Elephants versus people

Africa's elephants face an array of human pressures. Across the continent, elephant habitats have been destroyed, and elephants have been hunted down by poachers. Without protection, the African elephant may be doomed.

Africa's exploding population in this century has made life hard for elephants. The cutting and burning of forests, *above*, has shrunk the habitat available to many elephants. Likewise, the expansion of rural towns, *right*, and the conversion of large tracts of wild land to agriculture have crowded elephants into ever-smaller areas, where they often have trouble finding enough to eat.

The clamor for ivory has been the most critical factor in the elephant's decline. Customers at a Hong Kong ivory shop, *left*—and at others like it throughout the world may not have thought about it, but their desire for ivory products pushed the price of tusks to about $100 a pound ($220 a kilogram) in the 1980's, keeping poachers busy.

43

team at Cornell University in Ithaca, N.Y., reported in 1986 that these giants communicate through infrasonics, low-frequency sounds below the range of human hearing. The calls, produced in the forehead area, are used for various purposes—for example, to locate each other when out of sight or as a mating call by a sexually receptive female to distant males.

The elephant versus humanity

In ancient times, elephants ranged across the whole of Africa, from the Mediterranean Sea in the north to the Cape of Good Hope, 5,000 miles (8,000 kilometers) to the south. But even then, elephants were being hunted down. The Romans killed elephants for their ivory and captured them for display in the empire's amphitheaters. By the Middle Ages, elephants were extinct in northern Africa.

Still, as late as the 1400's, there may have been 10 million elephants south of the Sahara. At that time, Africa had only about 16 million people, so human pressures on elephant herds were minimal. Since then, the population of Africa has soared to more than 600 million, with the rate of increase in recent decades averaging 3 per cent a year. This relentless expansion of human habitation has reduced the original range of Africa's elephants by more than 75 per cent.

As a result, elephants in many parts of the continent are finding themselves increasingly cut off from food, water, and shelter from the broiling tropical sun. Malnutrition and heat stress are becoming the common lot of many herds. Periods of drought—always difficult for elephants, with their need for large quantities of water—can now be devastating, bringing death to many females of breeding age. The consequence of that is that fewer babies are being born.

Elephants that are hemmed in by human settlements can transform forest or savanna into desert as they devour trees, shrubs, and grass to satisfy their huge appetites. And when natural vegetation has been exhausted, they will not hesitate to look beyond their usual habitat for food. In recent years, as farms have spread across the land, elephants have turned to cultivated crops for sustenance. Even strong fences won't keep hungry elephants out of a vegetable patch. Farmers retaliate, and, inevitably, the elephants lose.

The vastly increased logging of Africa's forests to meet a growing world demand for timber has compounded the elephant's woes. As the trees fall, the forest elephants are crowded into ever-smaller areas, and conflicts with human beings become more frequent. Again, it is the elephants who are the losers.

The incessant shrinking of their habitats is clearly a serious problem for the elephants, but not a fatal one. The phenomenon that has decimated elephant herds over the centuries and that now threatens to exterminate the species is the international trade in ivory.

Ivory: the white gold

Ivory has been a valuable material for at least 2,000 years. It is prized for its natural beauty and its "feel" and as a medium for artists. It has always been largely a luxury commodity, a raw material to be transformed into jewelry and fine carvings. More recently, ivory has also been shaped into tourist baubles, piano keys, and in Japan, carved name seals used to sign checks and correspondence.

During the 1700's and 1800's, the ivory trade expanded, usually carried out by the same traders who dealt in what was sometimes called "black ivory": human slaves. Elephant hunting was so intense in southern Africa that the species was nearly annihilated in that region. Western Africa's elephants suffered as well. During the entire history of the ivory trade, the Africans themselves have usually done the hunting, but the demand for tusks has come principally from Europe, the Far East, and the Arab nations.

In the late 1800's and early 1900's, several African nations tightened controls on the ivory trade, which helped curb the slaughter. World War I (1914-1918) disrupted international trade in general, and after the war the demand for ivory dropped substantially. In subsequent years, elephants made so strong a recovery that several African countries began culling programs, shooting "surplus" elephants to prevent the animals from overpopulating their increasingly restricted habitats. The tusks from culled elephants are sold on the international market and have long been a major source of legally traded ivory.

In the 1970's, a period of financial uncertainty and rising inflation, ivory became a safe, desirable investment, much like gold or old-master paintings. As a result, the demand for ivory soared. From about $3 a pound ($6.60 a kilogram) in 1970, the price of ivory skyrocketed within just three years to $30 a pound ($66 a kilogram). The 1980's saw the easing of inflation, but the world demand for ivory—fueled by consumers' increasing desire for ivory jewelry, trinkets, and artworks—continued to grow. By 1989, the price of the substance stood at about $100 a pound ($220 a kilogram). Throughout the 1980's, poachers killed an average of 80,000 elephants each year to satisfy the international clamor for ivory.

The people guilty of this carnage have been driven by a single motive: money. A villager who killed an elephant could sell the tusks to a black-market buyer for a few hundred dollars. In many African countries, that is equal to the average annual income. But rural folk trying to augment their meager incomes by selling a few tusks have not been the major problem. More often, poaching is carried out by highly organized, well-financed gangs, equipped with not only automatic assault rifles and four-wheel-drive vehicles but even helicopters and airplanes.

These all-too-efficient killing squads have long since eradicated most of the larger male elephants, which had the biggest

tusks. In the 1980's, the gangs began killing progressively smaller males to acquire enough ivory to meet the market demands.
Then, when most of the males had been wiped out, the poachers
turned their gunsights on breeding-age females, especially the
older herd leaders. By the early 1980's, about 50 per cent of
those animals were also gone.

Poachers have operated with relative ease because the soldiers
and park rangers charged with apprehending them are typically
underpaid and poorly equipped. Some of them have reportedly
taken bribes from poachers to ignore their operations, and a few
have been accused of killing elephants themselves. But the situation began to improve in the late 1980's as the governments of
some African countries came to the realization that tourism—an
important part of their economies—would dry up if there were
no elephants for people to see. In Kenya and Tanzania, antipoaching patrols have been beefed up and supplied with better
equipment. Kenya's President Daniel T. arap Moi ordered patrols
to shoot poachers on sight, and in July 1989 he personally set
fire to a huge pile of confiscated tusks as a symbol of his determination to stop the illegal ivory trade. Nevertheless, in Kenya
and elsewhere, the killing continued.

Out of Africa: the international ivory trade

Ivory is traded on world markets in two forms: raw, the tusks
as they come from an elephant; and worked, or carved, ivory.
Although there are no controls on the commerce in worked ivory,
the export of raw ivory is regulated by the Convention on International Trade in Endangered Species of Wild Fauna and Flora
(CITES), established in 1973. This treaty, which has been
signed by 108 countries, including the United States, Australia,
Canada, and Great Britain, governs the trade in all types of
wildlife products, from crocodile hides to turtle eggs. Its aim is
to prevent extinctions while allowing countries to exploit their
wildlife resources for economic gain. In the case of ivory, CITES
requires African countries to specify the yearly quota of tusks
they can "harvest" without depleting their elephant populations,
a concept known as *sustainable yield*.

While this quota system did curb ivory imports by consumer
countries, it failed to firmly regulate the trade. The rate of elephant slaughter continued unabated, largely because so much of
the traffic in ivory occurred outside official, controlled channels.
Enormous quantities of tusks were "laundered," falsely certified
as legally harvested ivory by unscrupulous traders and corrupt
government officials.

One common method for evading CITES regulations was to
ship tusks to Middle Eastern countries that placed no restrictions
on the importation of raw ivory. Carvers in those countries
worked the tusks into semifinished pieces to be shipped as "legal" ivory to Hong Kong, for years the global crossroads of the
ivory trade. At Hong Kong's factories, the pieces were made into

Stopping the slaughter

In 1989 and 1990, the outlook for Africa's elephants improved considerably. Several countries, including Kenya, where a huge pile of tusks was burned in 1989 as a symbolic gesture, *left*, have shown a determination to protect their remaining elephant herds. They have beefed up antipoaching patrols—such as the one shown *below*, also in Kenya. An international agreement, in effect since January 1990, banned trade in ivory.

finished articles that were sent to markets around the world. Burundi, a small east African nation, was regarded as one of the worst offenders in this law-evading commerce. Despite having no elephants of its own, Burundi was conducting a thriving ivory trade. In 1988, after Burundi was found to be stockpiling more than 100 short tons (90 metric tons) tons of illegal tusks, the United States banned all ivory imports from that country. Burundi was far from unique, however. Conservationists contend that Zaire has also been a major source of poached ivory, and that in the 1980's Kenya and Tanzania—their recent get-tough stance notwithstanding—were notorious for the participation of high-level officials in the illegal ivory trade.

"Save the elephants!"—an international cry

Worldwide sentiment against the deadly traffic in illegal ivory began to build in the 1970's and gathered momentum through the 1980's. The United States and other non-African nations launched movements to protect Africa's elephants. In September 1988, when the U.S. Congress renewed the Endangered Species Act, a new piece of legislation called the African Elephant Conservation Act was incorporated into the law. Among other things, the Elephant Conservation Act barred imports of raw ivory into the United States from any country without a native population of elephants. It also imposed a moratorium on imports of both raw and worked ivory from any country that was not a party to CITES.

One of the first actions taken under the new law was a ban on ivory from Somalia. That east African country's elephant population numbered fewer than 4,500 in 1987, yet the Somali government had sold or stockpiled 25,000 tusks over the previous three years. Clearly that ivory was coming from somewhere else, most of it probably poached in neighboring Kenya.

In May 1989, Tanzania proposed a change in the CITES classification for elephants, from *threatened* to the more critical classification *endangered*, a change that would end all commercial trade in ivory between CITES members. Kenya, Zaire, Gambia, and several other African states—including even Somalia—pleaded for a worldwide ban on sales of ivory. That same month, the Ivory Trade Review Group—an international body made up of elephant experts, trade specialists, and economists—announced after a lengthy study of the situation that nothing short of a total ban on ivory trading would enable elephant populations to recover.

Largely on the basis of that report, the United States and the 12 countries of the European Community (Common Market) halted all ivory imports on June 9, 1989. A few days later, Japan, the biggest consumer of ivory, announced a partial ban prohibiting the import of any ivory that did not come directly from producer nations in Africa. In response to international criticism, it later stopped all ivory imports. Hong Kong, too, de-

clared an import ban—an attempt to clean up its reputation as a center of the illegal ivory trade.

The main opponents to a total prohibition on ivory trading were several nations in southern Africa, notably Zimbabwe, Botswana, and South Africa. All have elephant populations that, unlike those in other parts of Africa, are better protected from poachers and are stable or increasing in size. Those countries regularly cull their herds, giving the meat to local villagers and selling the tusks and hides. The sale of those commodities has made an important contribution to the nations' economies. For instance, it has earned Zimbabwe, with some 50,000 elephants, about $4.75 million annually in recent years. Zimbabwe and the other countries opposed to an outright ban on ivory trading did not want this source of revenue cut off. They accused nations whose elephant populations were dwindling—such as Kenya and Tanzania—of poor management.

That was the view they presented to CITES, first at a meeting in Botswana in July 1989 and then at an October conference in Lausanne, Switzerland. After long and heated debate, 76 of the

Hope for the future?

Perhaps this mother elephant and her calf will live out their days naturally rather than dying from poachers' bullets. The international ban on ivory imports is a positive development, but the desire for ivory remains strong in many areas of the world. The next few years should tell the story.

49

member nations (then numbering 103) voted at the Lausanne meeting to shift the African elephant from the threatened category to endangered, thereby prohibiting all ivory trading among member nations. The ban became effective on Jan. 18, 1990.

Under CITES bylaws, members are allowed to take out *reservations* to the endangered classification—exemptions, subject to approval by two-thirds of CITES members, that enable them to continue trading ivory. Five African countries that rely on income from legally harvested ivory—Botswana, Malawi, South Africa, Zambia, and Zimbabwe—claimed that exemption. So did China, which has many ivory-carving workshops. In addition, Britain in January 1990 reversed its long-time opposition to the ivory trade and took out a reservation, limited to six months, on behalf of its Hong Kong colony. The British government hoped that Hong Kong's ivory-working factories could dispose of their stock of 700 short tons (630 metric tons) of ivory during that period and so avoid severe economic losses.

A diminished trade raises cautious optimism

A study released in June 1990 by the World Wildlife Fund, an international conservation organization, proclaimed a dramatic decline, if not quite a disappearance, of the ivory trade. The United States market had all but vanished, even for items that were imported before the June 1989 U.S. ban and discounted by 40 to 70 per cent. Prices and demand for ivory products in most of Europe, Asia, and the Middle East were also falling or were at least stable. And poachers in Africa were reportedly getting no more than $2.25 a pound ($5 a kilogram) for tusks.

The CITES ban seemed to be working well in China and Japan. Although China had taken out a reservation to the CITES action, its carving industry had virtually closed down by mid-1990. In September, the country withdrew its reservation and accepted the ban.

Japan, which had been the world's largest consumer of ivory with nearly 40 per cent of the market, will be a major factor in making the ivory-trading ban stick. A member of CITES, Japan halted all imports of ivory in 1990, and that move seems to have been largely accepted by merchants and the general public. The price of ivory that had been stockpiled in Japan before the ban went into effect, however, has risen by one-third. Japanese authorities have intercepted small shipments of smuggled ivory, but so far smuggling has not been a big problem there or in other countries.

Some conservationists are concerned that an ivory trade might develop in Asian countries that are not parties to CITES. South Korea, for example, imported more worked ivory in 1989 than it had in the previous five years. Some observers speculate that South Korea is positioning itself to become a way station for ivory goods bound for illegal markets in Japan, Europe, and North America. Also worrisome are two other non-CITES Asian nations, Laos and Vietnam, both of which have sizable ivory markets developing in their large cities. To supply those markets, poachers in Laos and Vietnam are shooting Asian elephants, only a few thousand of which survive there.

In Africa, the illegal hunting of elephants has continued despite the plummet in black-market prices, but the rate of killing has declined dramatically. Nevertheless, conservationists worry that the African ivory trade, and thus intensive poaching, could revive in a few years. The governments of the southern African nations that took reservations against the CITES reclassification of elephants appear to be just biding their time, retaining existing stocks of ivory in the hope that the legal market for it will be restored. They also hope that their elephant populations will be transferred back to the "threatened" category, allowing them to resume trading ivory from culled herds. Ivory traders in several African countries are also betting that the legal international trade will be restored at the next CITES meeting, in 1992. Hence, they continue to buy ivory, which encourages poaching. Per-capita incomes in most African countries are so low that even at the current low price for raw ivory, poachers can earn more money by hunting elephants than from any other activity.

If CITES does lift its ban on the ivory trade, it will be up to the countries of Africa to prevent a resumption of the wholesale slaughter of their elephants. The dedicated efforts that Kenya, Tanzania, and several other African nations have made in the past few years to fight poaching give cause for hope. They have mobilized their armies and police forces in their campaigns to put an end to the illegal ivory trade.

Kenya has been in the forefront of this conservation battle. To emphasize his commitment to protecting Kenya's elephants, President Moi in April 1989 named the famed anthropologist Richard E. F. Leakey director of the national wildlife service. With Moi's blessing, Leakey has been rooting out corruption in the wildlife agency and aggressively pursuing poachers. Leakey thinks the rest of Africa will be watching Kenya closely to see whether saving the elephants is a goal that can really be achieved or just an elusive dream. "If we go wrong here," he said in 1989 after assuming his new post, "hope will be lost in many parts of this continent. If we go right here, there is a chance for things to happen elsewhere much more rapidly than any of us would have dared to believe."

For further reading:

Bosman, Paul, and Hall-Martin, Anthony. *Elephants of Africa.* Safari Press, 1988.

Douglas-Hamilton, Iain and Oria. *Among the Elephants.* Viking Press, 1975.

Moss, Cynthia. *Elephant Memories: Thirteen Years in the Life of an Elephant Family.* Morrow, 1988.

"Trail of Shame." *Time* 134 (Oct. 16, 1989): 66-69.

By Pamela S. Falk

Puerto Rico— The 51ˢᵗ State?

Whether Puerto Rico joins the Union as a state, becomes an independent nation, or remains a commonwealth, great changes lie ahead for this former Spanish colony.

Sometime early in the 1990's, the people of Puerto Rico will walk into polling places and cast a vote that will determine the island's future. They will vote on whether Puerto Rico should seek independence, become the 51st state, retain the current commonwealth status, or modify that status. President George Bush gave his support to Puerto Rican statehood in a February 1989 message to Congress, and Puerto Rico's Governor Rafael Hernández Colón suggested Congress give the island the choice. Hernández Colón himself favors an improved commonwealth status. When the vote is held, Puerto Ricans will cast their ballots against a background of history that has seen the island evolve from a Spanish colony to a U.S. territory to its present status as a commonwealth—an arrangement that permits the island's 3.3 million residents some say in how they are governed, but not as much as full statehood.

Puerto Rican life displays a rich ethnic heritage

From Columbus to self-rule

Christopher Columbus claimed Puerto Rico (Spanish for *rich port*) for Spain in his second voyage to the New World in 1493. The island then was home to almost 30,000 Taino Indians, part of the Arawak tribe, who lived throughout the West Indies. Spaniards under Juan Ponce de León established the first European settlement on the island in 1508. The Indians rose against the settlers a number of times, but the revolts failed, and by the mid-1500's most of the Indians were dead or enslaved. During this period, the Spaniards introduced sugar cane to the island, established plantations, and imported slaves from Africa to work on them.

Spain permitted its colony almost no self-government. Power centered in a governor who was not only the colony's chief executive and financial officer, but also the supreme judge and religious authority.

In the 1800's, immigration rapidly increased the population. By 1898, more than 953,000 people of many ethnic groups— particularly Spanish, but also Corsican, Irish, and South American—inhabited the island. This influx of immigrants gave rise to demands by Puerto Ricans for increased participation in their own government. Partly as a result, in 1812 Spain granted Puerto Rico a constitution and gave islanders Spanish citizenship and the right to name a deputy to the Spanish parliament.

Previous pages: The view from Puerto Rico's historic El Morro Fortress, built in Spanish colonial days.

The author:
Pamela S. Falk edited *The Political Status of Puerto Rico* (1986). She has taught U.S. foreign policy and Latin-American politics at Columbia University.

Puerto Rican markets, *previous page*, sell goods that show the influence of African slaves who worked plantations until the 1800's. Puerto Ricans in traditional costumes, *left*, dance to folk music that blends African and Spanish rhythms.

Laws still were either enacted in Spain or decreed by the governor, however, and only people who met rigid educational and property qualifications could vote or hold public office.

Major rebellions against Spanish rule broke out in 1835, 1838, 1867, and 1868. In response, Spain signed the Autonomic Charter of 1897, giving the island an elected house of representatives and a partly elected senate, along with the right to establish the budget and to determine tariffs and taxes.

Commonwealth government under U.S. rule

Puerto Rico had little opportunity to govern itself. In 1898, the Spanish-American War, a brief conflict between the United States and Spain over the liberation of Cuba, broke out. The December 1898 Treaty of Paris forced Spain to withdraw from Cuba and ceded Puerto Rico to the United States.

As residents of a U.S. territory, Puerto Ricans had no citizenship, constitutional guarantees, or legislative process. Just as they had once been under the absolute power of Spanish nobles, now they were controlled by U.S. military commanders. An outcry was immediate. At hearings in Washington, D.C., Puerto Ricans asked for free trade and eventual statehood.

In response, Congress in 1900 passed the Organic Act, or Foraker Act. The act established a civilian government with executive authority belonging to a governor and an executive

Facts in brief about Puerto Rico

Population: 3,282,000.

Area: 3,515 square miles (9,103 square kilometers).

Gross domestic product: $20.1 billion in 1989—62 per cent from manufacturing.

Official name: Commonwealth of Puerto Rico or Estado Libre Asociado (ELA) de Puerto Rico.

Climate: Tropical. Average temperature 73°F. (23°C) in January and 80° F. (27°C) in July.

Capital: San Juan (population 434,849).

Chief crops: Sugar cane, coffee, tobacco.

Chief industries: Manufacturing, especially medicines and electronics; agriculture; tourism.

Unemployment rate: 14 per cent in 1989 compared with 6 per cent for the rest of the United States.

Poverty: 60 per cent of the population live below the official U.S. poverty line.

Monetary unit: United States dollar.

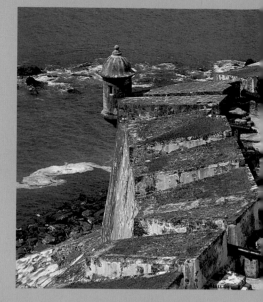

Workers harvest sugar cane, *below*. Puerto Rico's sugar cane industry was established in the mid-1500's, when sugar was the backbone of the island's economy. Sugar is still a leading export. ▼

▲ More than 2,000 plants in Puerto Rico produce export items, such as electronic components, *above*, medicines, machinery, and textiles.

Tax breaks have been granted to attract U.S.-based firms such as the drug company Abbott Laboratories, *below*, to Puerto Rico.

▼

▲ Puerto Rico's historic sites attract many tourists. Spanish conquerors began building the huge fortress of El Morro, *above*, in 1539 to protect San Juan from invasion.

Puerto Rico lies southeast of the United States mainland, *left*, between the Atlantic Ocean and the Caribbean Sea.

▼

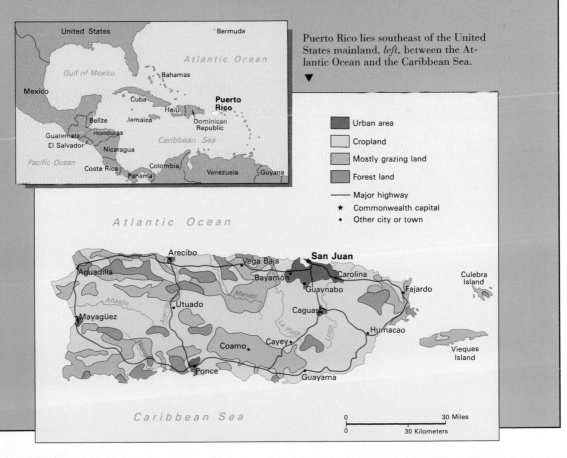

Urban area
Cropland
Mostly grazing land
Forest land
— Major highway
★ Commonwealth capital
• Other city or town

council appointed by the U.S. President. Puerto Rican residents voted in local elections. The island's legislative assembly consisted of the executive council and a locally elected house of delegates. The governor could veto laws, however, and the U.S. Congress could annul them. Judicial power rested in a presidentially appointed Puerto Rican supreme court and a district court, which the Supreme Court of the United States could overrule. An elected resident commissioner spoke on behalf of Puerto Rico in the U.S. House of Representatives but could not vote.

The Foraker Act said that all U.S. laws not specified as locally inapplicable—except for federal tax laws—pertained to Puerto Rico. The United States promised to defend Puerto Rico and to provide its currency, postal, and customs services. Most goods imported into Puerto Rico were subject to U.S. tariffs, but the proceeds would be remitted to the island. Likewise, duties and taxes on goods shipped between Puerto Rico and the United States would be returned to the Puerto Rican treasury.

On balance, the Foraker Act gravely disappointed Puerto Rico's leaders because it did not provide as much *autonomy*, or self-government, as the 1897 Spanish charter. In 1909, the Puerto Rico House of Delegates complained to Congress that the Foraker Act made it "impossible for the people's representatives to pass the laws they desire." In response, President William H.

Milestones in Puerto Rico's history

1493
Christopher Columbus sails to Puerto Rico and claims it for Spain.

1508-1509
The Spanish explorer Juan Ponce de León arrives in Puerto Rico and establishes the first European colony there.

1830's
Puerto Rico develops an economy based on sugar cane, coffee, and tobacco.

1898
Spain cedes the island to the United States after the Spanish-American War.

1900
The Foraker Act makes Puerto Rico an unincorporated territory of the United States. Military government is replaced by civilian government. The island is exempted from taxes.

1917
Puerto Ricans become U.S. citizens without the right to vote for President.

1930's
Puerto Rico's political parties divide over the question of possible U.S. statehood.

1932
The island's name is changed from Porto Rico to Puerto Rico.

Taft sent officials to the island to assess the situation. One reported, "It is clear that there is a general and almost universal desire and demand of all classes, interests, and political parties for American citizenship."

Congress listened and, in 1917, passed the Second Organic Act, or Jones Act, granting U.S. citizenship to Puerto Ricans. Citizenship, however, was not clearly defined. The act authorized an elected senate in the Puerto Rican legislature, gave the executive council an advisory rather than legislative role, and provided for council members to be appointed by the Puerto Rican governor rather than the U.S. President.

The Jones Act angered many Puerto Ricans because a governor appointed by and answering only to the U.S. President still headed the island. The President also appointed Puerto Rico's attorney general, commissioner of education, auditor, and members of the supreme court. Congress could veto Puerto Rican-passed laws. And, the act made Puerto Ricans eligible for the draft in World War I (1914-1918).

By the mid-1900's, Puerto Ricans were as dissatisfied with their economy as they were with their political status. The United States had tried to deal with economic problems early in the century, when islanders had an average income of only $122 per year, by instituting programs to encourage industrial growth. In

1952
Puerto Rico becomes a self-governing U.S. commonwealth with its own Constitution.

1967
Puerto Ricans vote to remain a commonwealth.

1989
Hernández Colón proposes a referendum on whether Puerto Rico should become a state, an independent nation, or remain a commonwealth.

1949
Luis Muñoz Marín, who favored a commonwealth link with the United States, is inaugurated as the first elected governor of Puerto Rico.

1950's
Puerto Rico's economy changes from one based on agriculture to manufacturing.

1984
Rafael Hernández Colón, who favors commonwealth status, is elected governor. He is reelected in 1988.

1990
The Puerto Rico Self-Determination Act dies in the U.S. Congress.

the 1940's, hydroelectric power and irrigation were developed. The Puerto Rican economy nevertheless lagged far behind the U.S. economy. Economic imbalance became a rallying cry for Puerto Ricans demanding greater self-rule.

In 1947, Congress passed the Crawford-Butler Act, which permitted islanders to elect their own governor, who then appointed executive officials. Luis Muñoz Marín became the first elected governor of the island. He called for a Puerto Rican constitution separate from that of the United States.

In 1951, Congress authorized Puerto Ricans to write a constitution that would be consistent with the United States Constitution and would outline a commonwealth status based on common currency, defense, and markets. At the same time, provisions of the Foraker Act that had given the United States responsibility over local matters on the island were repealed. Congress could no longer veto Puerto Rican laws, though the Supreme Court of the United States could still declare them invalid. After a year of debate, the Constitution was approved by Puerto Ricans. On July 25, 1952, the island became the Commonwealth of Puerto Rico.

If Puerto Rico were a state, it would rank…

1st in number of hot, sunny days (average daily high temperature 86°F. [30°C] in 1987).

1st in percentage of Hispanic population (99.9 per cent).

1st in population density (909 people per square mile [351 people per square kilometer]).

1st in unemployment (14 per cent in 1989).

1st in percentage of population receiving food stamps (43.5 per cent in 1990).

1st in percentage of population employed in government (though Washington, D.C., is higher).

2nd in infant mortality (only North Dakota is higher).

3rd in birth rate (Utah and Alaska are higher).

9th in violent crime.

24th in percentage of population employed in manufacturing (18 out of 100 people).

43rd in gross state product ($18.4 billion estimated in 1990).

49th in land area (larger than Delaware and Rhode Island).

51st in per capita income ($5,700 in 1989—less than half that of Mississippi, which is 50th).

Demonstrations demanding independence and others calling for statehood draw many supporters among Puerto Ricans both on the U.S. mainland, *above left*, and on the island, *above*.

Subsequently, portions of the Foraker Act were reaffirmed in the Puerto Rican Federal Relations Act, including Puerto Rico's exemption from certain U.S. tax laws. Since the Puerto Rican Constitution and Federal Relations Act took effect, Puerto Ricans have been electing their own governor and legislature, appointing judges, cabinet members, and lesser officials in the executive branch; setting their own educational policies; determining their own budget; and amending their own civil and criminal code. The U.S. Congress, however, can pass laws relating to Puerto Rico without consulting the island.

The economy and culture of Puerto Rico today

During the 1950's, Puerto Rico's economy changed from agricultural to industrial. Once an exporter of farm products, the island became an importer of most of its own food. Overall, its gross domestic product—the total value of goods and services produced on the island—stood at $28 billion in 1989, up from $724 million in 1950.

Industry helped make Puerto Rico the richest of the Caribbean islands. Per capita income today is about $5,700, compared with $370 in Haiti. Only 14 per cent of Puerto Ricans are unemployed, compared with 50 per cent of Haitians.

If Puerto Rico were a state, however, it would be the least prosperous. In 1989, when per capita income in Puerto Rico was about $5,700, it was $11,700 in Mississippi, the state with the lowest personal earnings. Moreover, the cost of living in Mississippi is about half what it is in Puerto Rico.

Culturally, Puerto Rico has an identity that is a mixture of Taino Indian, African, Spanish, and U.S. influence. Words such as *hamaca*, referring to the Indian hammock-style bed, are part of everyday speech. Spanish and English are both official languages, though schools are taught in Spanish. Some Puerto Rican music blends African rhythms with Spanish melodies, but U.S. hit tunes also are popular.

Puerto Ricans look at the alternatives

Under both Spanish and U.S. sovereignty, Puerto Ricans have steadfastly pursued greater political responsibility. The current debate over status centers on the fact that island residents have almost—but not quite—achieved full U.S. citizenship. A person born and living in Puerto Rico, for instance, may vote in a presidential primary—but not in the presidential election itself. Puerto Ricans may travel to the mainland without a passport. There, they may take up residence and vote for President and

How statehood would affect Puerto Ricans

As citizens of a commonwealth, Puerto Ricans...

❑ Vote for governor of Puerto Rico and for local officials. Are represented in Congress by a nonvoting delegate.

❑ Enter their own teams in the Olympic Games and other international sporting events.

❑ Receive time off from work to celebrate holidays in memory of Puerto Rican patriots, such as Eugenio Maria de Hostos and José de Diego.

❑ Attend public schools taught in Spanish.

❑ Pay taxes to local government.

❑ Qualify for limited food stamps and other welfare benefits.

As citizens of the 51st state, Puerto Ricans would...

❑ Vote for U.S. President, state, and local officials. Be represented in Congress by two senators and possibly seven representatives.

❑ Compete for places on U.S. teams.

❑ Possibly receive time off for U.S. national holidays only.

❑ Attend public schools taught in possibly both English and Spanish.

❑ Pay federal income taxes in addition to state and local taxes.

❑ Qualify for the same welfare benefits as all other citizens. (A person who now gets $90 in food stamps would receive about $130 after statehood.)

members of Congress. But if they move back to Puerto Rico, they lose these voting rights.

While working on the mainland, Puerto Ricans pay federal income tax, but they are exempt from the tax while working in Puerto Rico. If poor, Puerto Ricans receive food and health-care help from the U.S. government, but the amount of these benefits is lower than for mainland recipients. The U.S. Medicaid program, for example, which provides medical care to low-income individuals, caps payments at 50 per cent of cost in Puerto Rico—lower than the ceiling in any state. Puerto Ricans are ineligible for some forms of U.S. welfare, such as Supplemental Security Income (SSI), assistance for needy adults who are elderly, disabled, or blind.

Although Puerto Ricans have consistently sought increased political powers, they are divided about how to continue the island's political evolution. But all of the island's major political parties want a change from the current status. Today, the debate has moved to center stage in Washington, D.C. A bill called the Puerto Rico Self-Determination Act, outlining the island's choices, was passed by the House of Representatives in October 1990, but the Senate failed to act. The bill's supporters vowed to reintroduce the legislation in Congress in 1991.

Only one plebiscite has ever been held on the island—in 1967. Then, 60 per cent of the voters favored commonwealth status, 39 per cent statehood. Independence leaders boycotted the election, but their cause received 1 per cent of the vote. A public opinion poll taken in June 1990 showed 48 per cent in favor of statehood, 44 per cent for modified commonwealth, 7 per cent for independence, and 1 per cent undecided.

A modified commonwealth?

Those in favor of modified commonwealth status say Puerto Rico's present form of "free association" is advantageous to the island. They note that Puerto Ricans receive many of the benefits of citizenship, such as U.S. welfare payments, without some of the burdens, such as paying federal income taxes. Commonwealth proponents say that given the island's lack of natural resources and its large population, the present level of U.S. aid is necessary to sustain the island's economy and encourage economic growth.

Besides shoring up the economy, commonwealth status gives the island considerable control over internal affairs. It leaves the door open to statehood or independence should those options ever become something that nearly all Puerto Ricans desire. Furthermore, procommonwealth Puerto Ricans believe the current status permits a mutually beneficial cultural interchange with the United States.

Modified commonwealth status, proponents say, would maintain present basic arrangements with the U.S. government, including common currency, duty-free access to U.S. markets, and

Puerto Ricans hope that any change in the island's status will alleviate the poverty typified by these slums in the capital, San Juan.

tax exemptions. But the island would gain increased authority over its own affairs. For example, Puerto Rico would be able to set minimum wage and other labor policies, and to offer up to 100 per cent exemption from income taxes to a firm locating on the island. Puerto Rico also could establish shipping rates, negotiate air rights, collect tariffs on goods coming to the island, enter into foreign trade agreements, and participate in international organizations. United States payments now targeted for specified programs could be replaced with huge block grants that could be used to fund almost any activity the island government chose. Finally, commonwealth proponents say the island should elect voting delegates to both houses of the United States Congress.

The main advocates of a modified or enhanced form of commonwealth are the members of the Popular Democratic Party (PPD), or *populares*, headed by Governor Hernández Colón. In trying to help Puerto Ricans feel they have their own identity though a part of the United States, the PPD in recent years has been instrumental in entering Puerto Rican teams in the Olympic Games and island contestants in international beauty pageants. In 1990, the party introduced a bill in the Puerto Rican House of Representatives that would make Spanish the only language used in government on the island. More of these pride-building endeavors could be encouraged, PPD members say, under continued commonwealth.

The main argument opponents of modified commonwealth raise is that its measures may not be enough to restore the sense of pride that Puerto Ricans say they have lost under United States rule.

What statehood would mean

The supporters of statehood for Puerto Rico argue that a shift to that status is the logical course to continue the island's political and economic development. Puerto Ricans would gain greater influence over issues affecting the island by voting for President and sending voting representatives to Congress—two senators and six or seven members of the House. In a broader sense, advocates contend, statehood would fulfill a promise implied in Puerto Ricans' U.S. citizenship. Over time, it would add to political stability on the island, increase Puerto Ricans' sense of dignity, and assure long-term economic security.

The New Progressive Party is statehood's chief advocate. In addition to achieving long-term political goals, according to the party, statehood would give more than half of all Puerto Ricans added welfare benefits. These include increased payments under Medicaid, Aid to Families with Dependent Children, and nutritional aid programs; and new benefits under such programs as SSI. Party leaders point to a U.S. Congressional Budget Office (CBO) study that says Puerto Rico will receive $1.8 billion through social service programs in 1992. Under statehood, advocates say, benefits would jump to $5.1 billion—one-third of the island's income—by 1995.

Opponents argue that statehood would cause Puerto Rico to lose some of its current economic benefits. The U.S. Constitution requires the states to be treated similarly with regard to income taxes, duties, and excise taxes. Puerto Rico, therefore, would forfeit existing exemptions and rebates.

The island's biggest tax exemption results from Section 936 of the U.S. tax code. So-called 936 exemptions excuse Puerto Rican-based U.S. subsidiaries from paying U.S. taxes. In the manufacturing sector during 1989, such firms accounted for about $10 billion of the island's $28-billion gross domestic product.

Under statehood, opponents insist, the island's gross domestic product would drop by 10 to 15 per cent and unemployment would double within a few years because some companies would find it more economical to relocate than to stay on the island and pay taxes. A CBO study estimates that as much as one-half of the investment in Puerto Rican manufacturing by U.S. corporations—and as many as 150,000 jobs—might be lost.

In addition to the 936 exemptions, U.S. companies would lose exemptions on interest earned when profits are reinvested in Puerto Rico. Withdrawal of these funds, currently about $15-billion, could seriously hurt the island's banking industry.

With statehood, Puerto Ricans whether living on the mainland or on the island would pay personal income taxes. One study says that under statehood Puerto Ricans in 1994 would pay some $650 million in federal income taxes.

Puerto Rico now receives about $374 million annually in rebates from excise taxes collected on Puerto Rican products sold in the United States, such as rum, and from customs duties. To make up for losing this money under statehood, local government probably would have to raise personal taxes above what Puerto Ricans already pay in local income taxes, property taxes, municipal taxes, sales taxes, and inheritance taxes.

Statehooders say that most of these economic difficulties can be avoided if Puerto Rico is given financial assistance over a transition period of 20 years or more. During this time, new taxes would be phased in and business incentives phased out. If unusual aid proves necessary to sustain the island's economy, say statehood advocates, Congress should make special grants-in-aid and continue welfare payments.

Puerto Rico as an independent country

Puerto Ricans who favor independence—the *independentistas*—contend that the island is entitled to complete separation from the United States. They say that Puerto Rico's basic problem is its dependence on the United States politically, economically, and culturally. According to the *independentistas*, such dependence is humiliating and has kept the island from protecting and developing its unique cultural identity.

As a sovereign nation, Puerto Rico would possess authority over all governmental matters. The island's government would establish its own foreign and economic policies, including strategies for promoting business development. For the first time, it would set its own monetary policy, establish wage rates and labor policies, apply tariffs, and negotiate foreign trade.

Two political parties lead the independence movement, the Puerto Rican Independence Party and the Puerto Rican Socialist Party. Independence advocates are more loosely organized than those who favor the commonwealth or statehood options, but they are highly vocal.

One of the main arguments by opponents of independence is that the island would lose all U.S. funding. At hearings recently, Congress was told that one source of funding alone, federal payments to individuals for such things as welfare and unemployment insurance, accounted for about one-fifth of Puerto Rico's personal income in 1988—$1,700 for every resident. These payments would be lost with independence. As with statehood, furthermore, businesses would forfeit incentives to locate in Puerto Rico—almost $640 million in tax exemptions—and the nation would lose rebates from excise taxes and customs.

While it was incurring all these losses, an independent Puerto Rico would face the tremendous expenses of setting up welfare, postal, and defense systems. It would have to take over the expensive maintenance of roads, ports, sewage treatment plants, and telecommunications systems put in place by the United States. Those who argue against independence say Puerto Rico would need sustained generous amounts of aid from the United States and other nations to prevent economic disaster.

Some independence advocates, however, do not see a need for continued large-scale U.S. funding, mainly because they would not make manufacturing the primary sector of the economy. They would promote agriculture so that Puerto Rico could produce most of what it consumes. They argue that an agricultural economy tends to provide full employment, and so welfare would be less necessary than now. The island would no longer import food, and the cost of living would decrease.

Because Puerto Rico, under independence, would lose duty-free access to U.S. markets, *independentistas* say treaties would be negotiated with the United States to continue free access to the mainland market. Some foresee the island establishing a wide network of foreign investment and trading partners and becoming—they hope—the Hong Kong of the Caribbean. To help solve initial economic problems, they say, an independent Puerto Rico would apply for aid to the International Monetary Fund and the World Bank, agencies of the United Nations that assist developing countries.

As do statehood advocates, *independentistas* propose that the United States phase out existing tax exemptions gradually to ease the nation into a new status. They want the U.S. government to contribute to a special economic reconstruction fund to help finance essential government activities until new revenue sources are developed. In addition, they hope the United States will donate existing judicial, military, and postal facilities to the new nation and temporarily maintain certain defense, communications, and transportation arrangements.

Any choice means change

No matter what outcome the proposed vote brings—a modified commonwealth, statehood, or independence—it is certain that Puerto Rico will undergo cultural, economic, and political changes. Not as certain are the scope and impact of each change. Still, for all the uncertainty, polls indicate that most islanders favor some kind of alteration from their current status of not a country but not quite a state either. Their feelings are perhaps expressed in the words of Puerto Rican writer Luis Rafael Sánchez, who has said that the current situation makes Puerto Ricans feel their island is "only a locality in the patio of the United States."

For further reading:

Morales Carrión, Arturo. *Puerto Rico: A Political and Cultural History.* Norton, 1983.

Puerto Rico: Information for Status Deliberations. General Accounting Office, March 1990.

The Political Status of Puerto Rico. Ed. by Pamela S. Falk. Lexington Bks., 1986.

By Richard J. Terrile

A Hitchhiker's Current Guide to the Planets

From the volcanic furnace of Venus to Neptune's icy moons, astronomers are making unexpected discoveries about our neighboring planets.

These are exciting times for me and every other planetary astronomer—and for everybody who is intrigued by the planets. During the past 20 years, scientists have seen almost all of the planets in our solar system close-up for the first time in history. Since 1979, United States and Soviet spacecraft have visited Mars, Venus, Jupiter, Saturn, Uranus, and Neptune, along with dozens of their moons. And in August 1990, the U.S. spacecraft *Magellan* began returning the most detailed images yet of the surface of Venus, revealing startling evidence of extensive volcanic activity. The findings from these expeditions have rewritten the textbooks on the planets, and astronomers have gained a far deeper understanding of the nature of the planets and of the origins of our own world.

The remarkable photographs and scientific data returned from these planetary missions have startled scientists and awak-

Opposite page:
A composite photograph shows Jupiter and its four largest moons. The discovery of these moons in 1610 by the Italian astronomer Galileo led to the realization that the planets are separate worlds.

ened us all to the marvels that exist within our solar system. We have seen erupting volcanoes on Io, a moon of Jupiter, and active geysers on Triton, a moon of Neptune. We have seen violent storm systems covering areas the size of Earth with winds greater than hurricane force on Saturn and Neptune. On Mars, we have seen mountains that dwarf Mount Everest and canyons almost 3 miles (5 kilometers) deeper than the Grand Canyon. Scientists have discovered intricate ring systems surrounding four planets. And they have observed evidence of cataclysmic collisions with asteroid-sized objects, including one that may have tilted Uranus on its side and caused its moon Miranda to break up and re-form.

Since ancient times, people have recognized the planets as special objects. Without the aid of telescopes, early astronomers could only wonder why a handful of "stars" seemed to wander about the sky in odd patterns while all the other stars remained fixed relative to one another. That fact led the ancient Greeks to name those moving objects *planetae*, meaning *wanderers*.

With the aid of the newly invented telescope, the Italian astronomer Galileo in 1610 discovered four moons orbiting Jupiter and recognized that Jupiter and the other known planets were separate worlds. Like Earth, the planets orbit the sun and are made visible by reflected sunlight. This understanding, along with the gradual realization that the sun is a star and that stars are suns, gave us our first clear picture of the nature of the solar system. A much clearer understanding of each individual planet, however, had to wait until the age of space exploration.

Empty space and vast distances

Our solar system is mostly empty space with vast distances separating the planets. To get a better idea of the size and position of the planets, imagine that Earth is the size of a pinhead. Then, the moon would be about the size of the period at the end of this sentence, and it would be about 1 inch (2.5 centimeters) from Earth. The sun would be about the size of a grapefruit and would be about 50 feet (15 meters) away—representing an actual distance of 93 million miles (150 million kilometers). The planets Mercury, Venus, and Mars range in size from slightly larger than the moon (Mercury) to the same size as Earth (Venus) and would be 19, 36, and 76 feet (6, 11, and 23 meters) from the sun, respectively.

The other planets all lie at much greater distances from the sun. Jupiter, represented by a marble (11 times larger than Earth), would be about 260 feet (80 meters) from the sun. Saturn, only slightly smaller than Jupiter, would be 475 feet (145 meters) away and would have a ring about 1 inch across. Uranus and Neptune, both the size of peas, would be 960 and 1,500 feet (290 and 455 meters) away. Finally, Pluto, another period-sized world, would be nearly 2,000 feet (600 meters) from the sun, though for part of its orbit, Pluto is closer to the

The author:
Richard J. Terrile is a planetary astronomer at the Jet Propulsion Laboratory in Pasadena, Calif.

How our solar system formed

Many scientists believe our solar system formed from a huge rotating cloud called a *solar nebula*. The way this nebula evolved explains why the planets nearest the sun are small rocky bodies with thin atmospheres and the outer planets, except Pluto, are giant balls of gas surrounding cores of rock and ice.

According to theory, the solar nebula consisted of gas and small grains of ice and rock. The rotation of the cloud caused it to take the shape of a flattened disk with a bulge at the center.

The force of gravity caused a dense core of matter to form at the center of the cloud. Temperatures at the core became so hot that nuclear reactions ignited, and a star—our sun—began to shine.

Heat from the sun evaporated the gas and ice grains in the inner region, leaving only rocky grains. These grains collided and merged with each other to form larger bodies called *planetesimals*. In the cold outer region, planetesimals formed from both rock and ice.

In the inner region, the rocky planetesimals continued to collide and merge, forming even larger bodies, while in the outer region, the gravitational force of the ice-and-rock planetesimals began to attract gas, forming atmospheres.

The inner planetesimals became the small rocky planets of Mercury, Venus, Earth, and Mars. The outer planetesimals became Jupiter, Saturn, Uranus, and Neptune, which have huge atmospheres. The nature of Pluto is still a mystery.

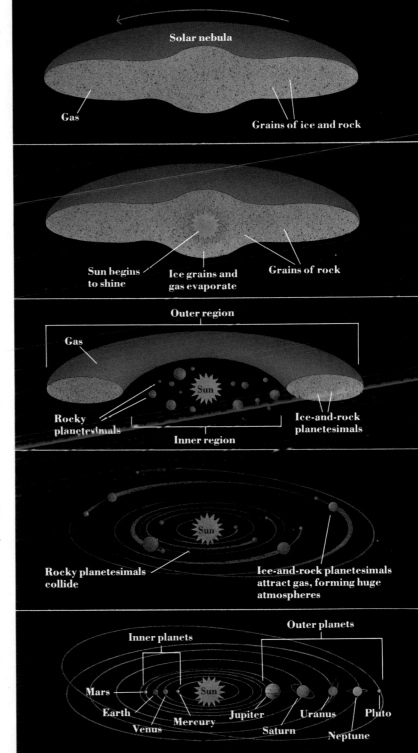

Solar nebula

Gas

Grains of ice and rock

Sun begins to shine

Ice grains and gas evaporate

Grains of rock

Outer region

Gas

Sun

Rocky planetesimals

Ice-and-rock planetesimals

Inner region

Rocky planetesimals collide

Ice-and-rock planetesimals attract gas, forming huge atmospheres

Inner planets

Outer planets

Mars

Earth

Venus

Mercury

Sun

Jupiter

Saturn

Uranus

Neptune

Pluto

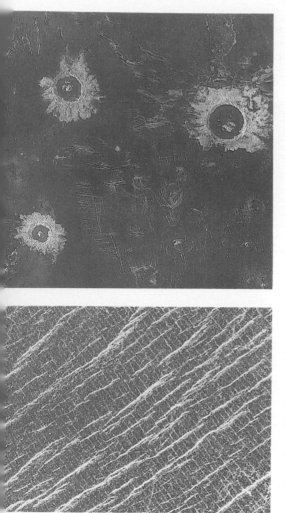

New views of Venus
In September 1990, the U.S. spacecraft *Magellan* returned detailed radar images of the surface of Venus, showing three impact craters and evidence of fault lines and volcanic activity, *top*. Another image, *above*, revealed an unusual regular pattern of nearly parallel lines that intersect brighter lines almost at right angles, puzzling scientists. The false color added to the images approximates what scientists think the surface of Venus looks like.

sun than is Neptune. On this scale, the entire solar system would fit into 1 square mile (2.6 square kilometers).

How the solar system formed

The sun is the largest and most important component of our solar system. Indeed, without the energy provided by the sun in the form of heat and light, life on Earth—or anywhere else in the solar system—would not be possible. At about 109 times the diameter of Earth, the sun is so massive that its outer layers exert tremendous pressure on the gas at its center. This pressure allows the center to be so hot that nuclear reactions occur, producing the sun's energy. The sun has given off heat and light ever since it and the solar system formed about 4.6 billion years ago. Scientists know that the solar system is at least this old because they have been able to date the oldest unchanged objects known to exist—meteorites that have fallen to Earth and rock samples from the moon.

Astronomers believe that the solar system formed from a collapsing, rotating cloud called a *solar nebula*, composed of gas, grains of ice, and rocky particles. The nebula gradually contracted, increasing its rotation, until it flattened into a disk. The dense core of the disk formed the sun, and concentrations of material farther out eventually formed the planets, moons, asteroids, and comets. All of the planets lie in a plane around the sun's equator because they originally formed from this flattened disk.

The differences between the inner planets—Mercury, Venus, Earth, and Mars—and the outer planets—Jupiter, Saturn, Uranus, Neptune, and Pluto—can be explained by the way the solar system formed. The inner planets are small rocky bodies, and the outer planets are gigantic balls of gas with inner cores of rock and ice—with the exception of Pluto, which is a small, solid planet. As the sun finally became massive enough to ignite its nuclear reactions, the high temperatures near the sun burned away most of the gases and ice grains from the inner region of the original solar nebula, leaving only the rocky particles. These particles gradually clumped together, forming asteroid-sized objects called *planetesimals*. These objects collided with one another as they orbited the sun, and the collisions resulted in ever-larger objects. Finally, they became the rocky inner planets.

In the outer regions of the solar nebula, far from the sun's heat, gases and ice grains remained along with rocky material. Ice and rocks in this region merged to form the cores of planets. Their gravity attracted and retained light gases, mostly hydrogen and helium with some methane and ammonia, and these outer planets developed into huge balls of mostly gas. Jupiter's rocky core, for example, is about the size of Earth, but Jupiter has an atmosphere about 11 times larger than Earth. The atmospheres of Jupiter, Saturn, Uranus, and Neptune are so thick that we cannot observe their surfaces.

By pooling the knowledge of the planets gathered from many spacecraft missions, astronomers can put together a comprehensive guided tour of the planets. Our itinerary begins with the planet closest to the sun:

Mercury: A cratered, shrunken world

In 1974 and 1975, an *elliptical* (oval-shaped) orbit around the sun enabled the *Mariner 10* spacecraft to fly by the planet Mercury three times, photographing about half the planet's surface at close range. The photographs showed Mercury to be heavily cratered, indicating little geologic activity since the solar system was formed. Geologic activity, such as volcanic eruptions or quakes, can modify a planet's surface by erasing or covering over the craters that form when meteoroids, comets, or other debris strike the planet. The less geologic activity there is, the more craters remain. The pockmarked surface of Mercury shows evidence of a vast number of collisions, dating back to the time when the planet was still forming.

The surface also has long ridges that scientists believe developed as the molten core of Mercury solidified and shrank. The shrinking core caused the solid outer crust to shrink, but not without breaking. These breaks now appear as ridges.

One important surprise from the *Mariner 10* mission was finding a weak magnetic field around Mercury. This was unexpected because scientists think magnetic fields around planets are generated by the rotation of a molten core in a planet's interior. Scientists had assumed that because of its small size, Mercury had long ago lost all of its internal heat and had become a solid cinder. The presence of a magnetic field may indicate that part of the interior of Mercury is still molten.

Venus: Overheated twin of Earth

In size and density, Venus is practically a twin of Earth. As demonstrated by the *Mariner 10* and *Pioneer Venus* spacecraft in 1974 and 1978, however, the two planets' surface conditions are very different. The atmosphere of Venus consists mainly of carbon dioxide, causing a phenomenon called the *greenhouse effect*. The atmosphere allows sunlight to reach the planet's sur-

Mercury

Venus

Earth

Mars

Jupiter

Sun

The planets at a glance

If all of the planets and their moons were put together, they would represent no more than 0.2 per cent of the entire mass of the solar system. The sun accounts for the rest. The sun has a diameter of 865,000 miles (1.4 million kilometers) and is 1,047 times more massive than Jupiter, the largest planet in the solar system.

Mercury

Average distance from sun: 36,000,000 miles (57,900,000 kilometers).
Diameter at equator: 3,031 miles (4,878 kilometers).
Number of satellites: None.
Highlights: Tiny Mercury does not have enough gas in its atmosphere to reduce the amount of heat and light it receives from the sun. So daytime temperatures can reach as high as 648°F. (342°C) and nighttime temperatures as low as −315°F. (−193°C). With scant atmosphere, Mercury's sky is black both day and night.

Jupiter

Average distance from sun: 483,700,000 miles (778,400,000 kilometers).
Diameter at equator: 88,700 miles (142,700 kilometers).
Number of satellites: 16.
Highlights: Jupiter's upper atmosphere has multicolored clouds that form a complex banded pattern. The U.S. spacecraft *Galileo* is expected to begin a 22-month orbit of Jupiter in December 1995. It will drop a probe containing scientific instruments into the atmosphere to determine if the banded pattern extends to the lower atmosphere.

Saturn

Average distance from sun: 885,200,000 miles (1,424,600,000 kilometers).
Diameter at equator: 74,600 miles (120,000 kilometers).
Number of satellites: 17.
Highlights: The second-largest planet in the solar system, Saturn has a beautiful ring system that was discovered by Galileo in the early 1600's, though he did not recognize them as rings. The United States and the European Space Agency plan to launch an unmanned spacecraft in 1996 to explore Saturn's moon Titan, which has an atmosphere rich in nitrogen.

Saturn **Uranus** **Neptune** **Pluto**

Venus

Average distance from sun: 67,230,000 miles (108,200,000 kilometers).
Diameter at equator: 7,520 miles (12,100 kilometers).
Number of satellites: None.
Highlights: Scientists had long suspected that Venus had volcanoes, but they were unprepared for the evidence of extensive geologic activity, including faults and volcanoes, revealed by the *Magellan* spacecraft in 1990. As *Magellan* continues to orbit the planet, scientists expect to learn if there are currently active volcanoes.

Earth

Average distance from sun: 92,960,000 miles (149,600,000 kilometers).
Diameter at equator: 7,926 miles (12,756 kilometers).
Number of satellites: 1.
Highlights: Probing the other planets has given scientists many insights about Earth. Scientists have warned that increasing levels of greenhouse gases in Earth's atmosphere, for example, could lead to the runaway greenhouse effect that occurred on Venus. A planned "Mission to Planet Earth" would monitor Earth's environment from space.

Mars

Average distance from sun: 141,700,000 miles (228,000,000 kilometers).
Diameter at equator: 4,200 miles (6,790 kilometers).
Number of satellites: 2.
Highlights: Features on Mars's surface that resemble river valleys and flooded terrain on Earth indicate that Mars may have once had a warmer climate with a thicker atmosphere that supported running water. Future space missions to Mars plan to search for fossils to learn if there was life on Mars when the planet was warmer.

Uranus

Average distance from sun: 1,781,000,000 miles (2,866,900,000 kilometers).
Diameter at equator: 31,570 miles (50,800 kilometers).
Number of satellites: 15.
Highlights: Uranus is the only planet tilted on its side. First one pole, then the other, faces the sun as Uranus completes a rotation around the sun every 30,685 Earth days. *Voyager 2* revealed a relatively quiet atmosphere with few cloud features and no evidence of storm systems. The planet's tilt may have been due to a collision with a large object early in its history.

Neptune

Average distance from sun: 2,793,000,000 miles (4,495,000,000 kilometers).
Diameter at equator: 30,800 miles (49,500 kilometers).
Number of satellites: 8.
Highlights: Neptune is a frigid planet with a temperature in the upper atmosphere of −370°F. (−220°C), but its atmosphere is extremely turbulent, with storm systems comparable to those on Jupiter. Scientists got their best look at Neptune in August 1989 when *Voyager 2* flew by. No future space missions are planned.

Pluto

Average distance from sun: 3,660,000,000 miles (5,890,000,000 kilometers).
Diameter at equator: 1,420 miles (2,285 kilometers).
Number of satellites: 1.
Highlights: The only planet not visited by spacecraft remains mysterious and probably will be so for a long time because no missions to this tiny outer world are planned. Some scientists think Pluto resembles Neptune's moon Triton.

face and heat it. But carbon dioxide, like the glass in a greenhouse, prevents *infrared* (heat) radiation from escaping into space. The trapped heat raises the surface temperature on Venus to about 850°F. (455°C), higher than any other planet.

While analyzing the high surface temperature of Venus in the early 1970's, scientists created the first climate model showing that a similar process was responsible for the global warming that appears to be occurring on Earth. Even small increases in the tiny amount of carbon dioxide in our atmosphere can cause temperatures to rise by measurable amounts.

Earth has not become the inferno that Venus is, however, because our oceans have removed most of the carbon dioxide from our atmosphere and turned it into limestone, a carbonate rock. Carbon dioxide in the atmosphere dissolves in ocean surface water and is also taken up by algae, other plantlike organisms, and shellfish. The decayed remains of carbon-containing ocean life eventually settle to the ocean floor as sediments. Heat and pressure turn these sediments into limestone.

On Venus, closer to the sun and without an ocean, almost all of the planet's original carbon dioxide remains in the atmosphere. If Venus ever had an ocean, it lost its water quickly. Scientists have calculated that the strong sunlight striking Venus' upper atmosphere would have broken apart evaporated water molecules into oxygen and hydrogen atoms. The oxygen would have eventually circulated back to the surface to combine with rocks, while the lighter hydrogen atoms—too light to be held by Venus' gravity—would have escaped into space.

A thick layer of clouds prevents direct photography of Venus' surface. By using radar to bounce radio signals off the surface, however, and by recording how long it takes for those signals to return, scientists can measure surface elevations and create an elaborate map of the surface that would otherwise be hidden below clouds. Radar images from *Pioneer Venus* and *Soviet Venera* spacecraft hinted at vast smooth plains, mountain ranges, some craters, and perhaps even recently active volcanoes.

The U.S. *Magellan* spacecraft began a more detailed mapping of Venus in August 1990. Using a radar mapper capable of resolving images 10 times more sharply than previous radar mappers, *Magellan* revealed that Venus has a much more complex geology than scientists previously thought. The spacecraft returned images of volcanic *calderas* (the craters that form at the summits of volcanoes) and solidified flows of volcanic lava. In September and November, *Magellan* sent back pictures of features never seen before on any planet, including extremely regular crisscrossed fault lines and pancake-shaped domes.

Mars: Cold and dry

In 1971 and 1972, the *Mariner 9* spacecraft orbited Mars and mapped its entire surface. In 1976, two U.S. *Viking* spacecraft sent landers down to the surface of Mars. The main objective of

Nuclear power generators: Provide continuous source of power in deep space.

Science boom: Contains video cameras and scientific instruments for recording images and collecting data.

Magnetometer boom: Isolates an instrument for measuring magnetic fields from metal on the spacecraft; 40 feet (12 meters) long.

Radio antenna: Sends and receives radio signals to communicate with Earth; 12 feet (3.7 meters) in diameter.

the *Viking* mission was to search for evidence of life on Mars. Although the two spacecraft found no life on this cold, dry world, they revealed a startling story of climatic change. Etched into the surface of Mars's cratered plains are huge drainage channels. All over the planet is evidence that in the past Mars had flowing water and perhaps even ancient lakes and seas.

These surface features must be extremely old because they are marked by numerous craters and probably date back to the first billion years of Mars's history. During this time, Mars had a thicker atmosphere that could retain liquid water on the surface. Because Mars is only half the size of Earth, its weak gravity was not strong enough to hold onto light gases that made up its original atmosphere. These gases, particularly hydrogen—which combines with oxygen to make water—escaped into space. As this happened, surface pressures decreased, and the planet began to dry.

Today, because of low surface pressures and cold temperatures, liquid water cannot flow on Mars's surface. Most of the surface water that Mars once had either has escaped into space or is frozen in the planet's polar icecaps or is underground in the form of permafrost.

Mars's former thick atmosphere and abundant water may be related to another surprise found on the surface of the planet. *Mariner 9*'s cameras discovered several huge volcanic mountains resembling the sloping, dome-shaped volcanic mountain Mauna Kea on Hawaii. One of the Martian volcanoes, Olympus Mons, is three times higher than Mount Everest. Gases that escaped from the interior of the planet during the volcanic eruptions that formed these mountains would have made the atmosphere thicker and increased the amount of carbon dioxide. The result-

Space age explorer Cameras and scientific instruments on the *Voyager 2* spacecraft revealed unknown worlds and phenomena as the spacecraft explored the outer planets of Jupiter, Saturn, Uranus, and Neptune. *Voyager 2* is now hurtling toward the outermost regions of our solar system.

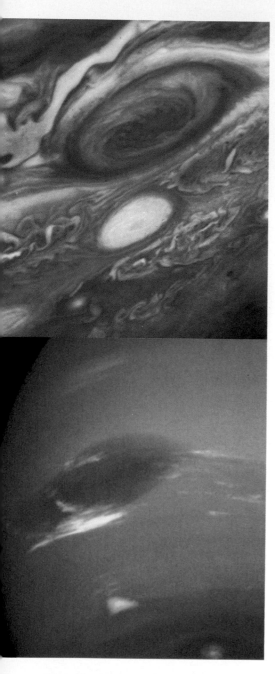

ing warmer temperatures and higher surface pressure would have allowed liquid water to form and flow.

Scientific interest now focuses on this early Martian climate and on whether life could have developed on Mars during this time. Both the Soviet Union and the United States plan to send sample recovery missions to Mars in the late 1990's to scoop up Martian soil and return it to Earth for analysis. Perhaps waiting to be discovered somewhere on the surface are fossils indicating the past existence of life on Mars.

Jupiter: The gassy giant

Voyager 1 and *2* encounters in 1979 revealed details of the Jupiter system. Jupiter is comprised mainly of hydrogen and helium gas. These light gases were mostly lost from the planets of the inner solar system but, along with water ice, are major components of the outer planets. Jupiter's multicolored clouds form a complex banded pattern consisting of dark lines called *belts* and light-colored areas called *zones*. Swirls and eddies within these bands are actually huge storms and reveal a dynamic weather system. The largest storm—the Great Red Spot—is bigger than Earth and has raged for at least 300 years.

The most surprising discovery at Jupiter, however, was on Io, one of its four large moons. About the same size as our moon, Io was found to have the most volcanic activity in the solar system. Cameras on *Voyager* spacecraft captured images of at least nine erupting plumes spewing material hundreds of miles above the surface. The photographs revealed no impact craters, but an abundance of volcanoes. So active is the volcanism on Io that during the four months between the *Voyager 1* encounter in March 1979 and the *Voyager 2* encounter in July, large areas on Io's surface had been altered by the flow of volcanic material.

The volcanic material is mainly sulfur and sulfur dioxide, and the volcanism apparently is caused by strong tidal forces acting on Io by Jupiter and two of its other moons. These tidal forces resemble the tidal tug that the moon's gravity exerts on Earth, but they are much more powerful. In fact, their pull is so strong that they cause Io to change shape. When Io's orbit brings it closest to Jupiter, Jupiter's gravity causes a

Gigantic storms
The oval-shaped Great Red Spot on Jupiter, *top*, is so large that Earth could fit inside it. Astronomers believe the spot is a huge storm system resembling a hurricane, though it has raged for an estimated 300 years. *Voyager 2* unexpectedly discovered a similar storm system on Neptune, *above*, which was dubbed the Great Dark Spot.

tidal bulge on Io as high as 300 feet (90 meters). In contrast, the land bulge caused by the moon's gravity on Earth is only 6 inches (15 centimeters) high. When Io's orbit takes it to its farthest point from Jupiter, the bulge on Io flattens out. The effect is like that of squeezing and then releasing a rubber ball, and the resulting friction created in the interior of Io generates the heat that powers Io's volcanism.

Scientists also found a geologically altered surface on Jupiter's moon Europa. Only a handful of small impact craters marred the extremely smooth surface of Europa, indicating that geologic processes had occurred to erase the impact craters that Europa must have collected during its early history. Europa's major features are a series of intersecting lines that may be cracks in an ice crust floating on a mantle of water.

Saturn: Surprises in its rings

Voyager 1 and *2* used the gravity of Jupiter to change their paths so they could visit Saturn— the second-largest planet in the solar system—in 1980 and 1981. Saturn's diameter is about 10

Rings around the planets
As *Voyager 2* sped past Saturn, its cameras captured the planet's shadow falling on part of the disklike ring system, *top*. Until *Voyager*, astronomers were unaware that Saturn's rings have small gaps and other unusual features. They knew that Neptune has a ring system but did not know that it completely encircles the planet, *above*.

Volcanoes: Past and present

Evidence abounds of past and current volcanic activity throughout the solar system. Scientists studying pictures of Olympus Mons on Mars, *below*, have determined that this huge volcano—three times higher than Mount Everest—was probably active about 1 billion years ago. *Voyager* found evidence of volcanoes that extrude ice on Neptune's cold moon Triton, *above*, along with an active geyser and dark streaks that may be material deposited on the surface by now inactive geysers (arrows). Perhaps the most dramatic finding was the erupting plume of an active volcano on Io, a moon of Jupiter, *opposite page*. The plume (arrow), probably composed of sulfur, soars hundreds of miles above Io's surface.

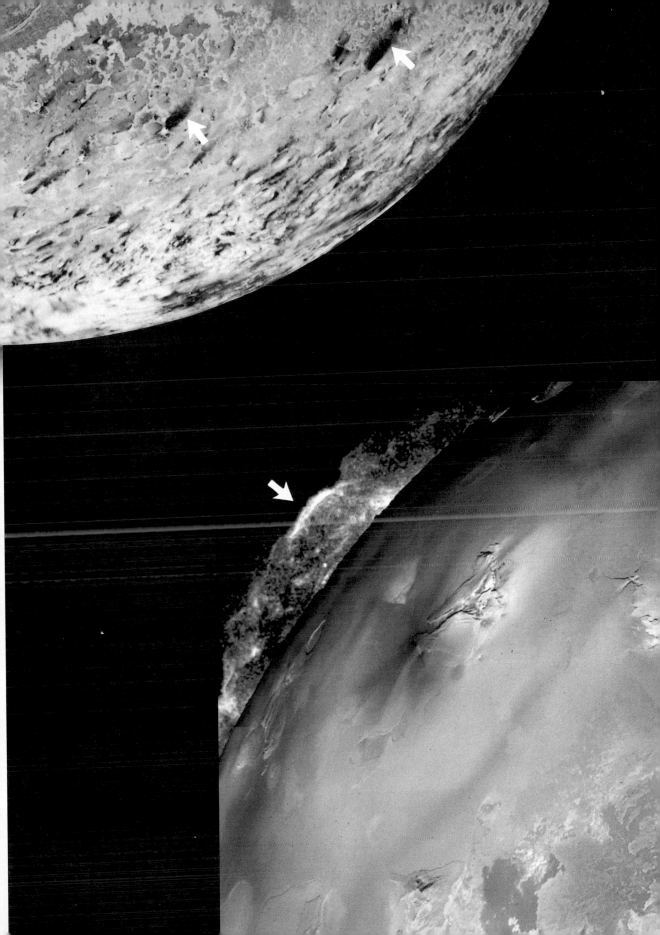

times that of Earth. Like Jupiter, Saturn has a banded pattern of clouds. But because Saturn is almost twice as far from the sun and receives less heat, the temperature at which clouds condense is reached at a lower altitude in the atmosphere. Although layers of haze make Saturn appear more subdued than turbulent Jupiter, Saturn has similar but smaller oval storm patterns. Winds in the equatorial region blow easterly at up to 1,100 miles (1,800 kilometers) per hour, more than twice as fast as winds on Jupiter.

Saturn's most familiar feature, its rings, turned out to be the most puzzling and held the most surprises. The rings are made up of rock and ice chunks that range in size from dust to mountain-sized masses. These particles orbit Saturn individually, but collectively they form the broad rings. Seen from Earth, the rings appear as three broad areas with one large gap.

The *Voyager* images, however, revealed that the rings had the grooved appearance of a phonograph record. Among the peculiar discoveries were small gaps in the rings with confined narrow "ringlets" within them. There were also tightly wound spiral features, wavelike patterns that changed with time, kinks, and other unusual features. Most of these characteristics probably result from the gravitational influence of moons orbiting outside the rings, pulling on ring particles and creating the patterns. Some patterns, however, could be explained only if there are unseen moons as large as 6 miles (10 kilometers) in diameter orbiting within the ring. And in 1990, astronomers tentatively identified one such moon in the *Encke division*—a large gap in an outer ring.

Many of Saturn's 17 known moons appear as small irregular shapes and could have been fragments broken off from larger bodies. This could also explain the origin of the rings, which may be debris left over from the destruction of one or more of these irregular moons. The total amount of material in Saturn's rings would form a moon a few hundred miles in diameter. In fact, some astronomers are starting to believe that all the ring systems around the outer planets were formed from material that broke off from moons.

The largest of Saturn's moons is Titan, with a diameter greater than that of Mercury. One of the few moons in the solar system with an atmosphere, Titan's surface is obscured by a dense haze of nitrogen and methane. Some scientists believe the atmospheric and chemical conditions on Titan are a frozen version of conditions that existed on Earth before life evolved.

Uranus: The tilted planet

Voyager 2 reached Uranus in 1986. Unlike the turbulent atmospheres visible on Jupiter and Saturn, Uranus' atmosphere was relatively calm with barely discernible cloud features. An unusual aspect of Uranus is that its *rotation axis* (an imaginary line around which the planet rotates) and those of its 15 moons

Bizarre moons

The surfaces of the solar system's moons take bizarre forms. The smooth surface of Jupiter's Europa, *below*, with its mysterious crisscrossing lines, contrasts with the craggy, jumbled terrain of Uranus' moon Miranda, *above*. Astronomers speculate that a huge collision may have caused Miranda to break up and re-form and in the process created a cliff (inset) several miles deep. A collision not quite great enough to shatter Saturn's Mimas, *right*, left a crater more than 100 miles (160 kilometers) in diameter.

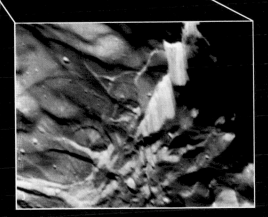

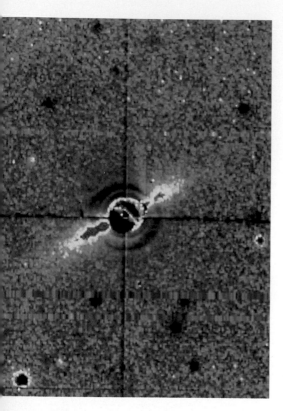

Other solar systems?
Using a special filter to blot out the image of the star Beta Pictoris, astronomers have detected a disk of material (seen edge on) surrounding the star. The orbiting disk may represent planets in the process of forming. Planets around other stars may be commonplace, astronomers believe.

are tipped on their side so that the axes are almost level with the planet's path around the sun. Most planets' rotation axes are almost perpendicular to the planet's path around the sun.

Some astronomers think that Uranus' unusual orientation may have resulted from a collision with another planet-sized body during the final stages of the planet's formation. Scientists searched for evidence of major collisions on the surfaces of the moons, and close-up images of the moon Miranda showed a startling history of major changes to its surface. Concentrically grooved features resembling oval racetracks have partially replaced older cratered terrains on Miranda. Faults with cliffs 12 miles (20 kilometers) high cut through this fractured world. Miranda may have broken apart and reassembled late in its formation period, giving rise to its peculiar grooved ovals.

Neptune: The windiest world

The last planetary encounter *Voyager 2* made was with Neptune in 1989 at a distance 30 times farther from the sun than Earth. Neptune was found to have a giant oval storm system similar to Jupiter's Great Red Spot. Called the Great Dark Spot, the system is as large as Earth. It wanders across the surface of Neptune and varies in shape in a cyclical manner, returning to its original shape every eight Earth days. With westward blowing winds of 1,200 miles (2,000 kilometers) per hour, Neptune is the windiest planet in the solar system. *Voyager* also revealed an unusual ring system that contains clumps of material embedded within faint narrow rings. Why this material does not spread out in its orbit remains unexplained.

One of the greatest surprises was finding evidence of geologic activity on Neptune's largest moon, Triton. Scientists did not expect to find much of interest on Triton because it receives so little sunlight and is the coldest object in the solar system with a temperature of −391°F. (−235°C), only 60 Fahrenheit degrees above absolute zero, the lowest temperature possible. But they found terrain on Triton that resembled terrain observed on Venus, Mars, and Jupiter's moon Europa.

The surface has many volcanic features with several geyserlike plumes shooting 5 miles (8 kilometers) into Triton's thin air of nitrogen and methane. Winds carry material from these plumes, forming long, thin cloud trails several hundred miles long. Scientists are still unclear about what powers these geyser eruptions. It may be that nitrogen ice trapped under a surface layer of ice is heated by sunlight. As heat changes the ice into a gas, the resulting pressure becomes too great for the surface ice to withstand, and the gas blows out as a geyser.

Dark streaks that fan out from small dark areas on Triton's surface also may be evidence of past volcanic eruptions. At the extremely cold temperatures on Triton, however, this volcanic material is not made up of molten rock, as on Earth, but probably consists of liquid water mixed with ammonia.

Triton's high density of rock and ice and the fact that it orbits in a direction opposite to that of Neptune may mean that the moon did not originally form around Neptune. Triton may have been in an orbit around the sun that brought it close to Neptune, and the planet's stronger gravity captured Triton.

Pluto: The unexplored planet

Pluto, the only known planet in our solar system not visited by spacecraft, appears similar in size and composition to Triton. Pluto has a moon called Charon, which orbits close enough to share Pluto's extremely thin atmosphere of methane gas. Scientists can only speculate about these outer bodies.

The discoveries made about the planets not only have given scientists a perspective on the origins of our solar system but also have convinced many of them of the possibility that planets exist around other stars. Researchers have begun to find evidence of material orbiting nearby stars. In 1984, astronomer Bradford A. Smith of the University of Arizona in Tucson and I photographed a disk around the nearby star Beta Pictoris. This disk, a flattened collection of dust and particles, could be the beginnings of a young planetary system or the remains of such a system. Astronomers have also found dusty disks around several other nearby stars. It seems likely that planet formation is a common part of star formation. It would not be surprising if most of the stars in the sky had planets orbiting them.

Our galaxy, the Milky Way, contains about 200 billion stars. Representing each star by a grain of sand, that is enough sand to fill half of an Olympic-sized swimming pool. Our sun is but one grain in this vast collection. We can only wonder what marvels exist around the billions of others.

For further reading:

"Exploring Space" (special issue). *Scientific American*, 1990.

Littmann, Mark. *Planets Beyond: Discovering the Outer Solar System.* Wiley, 1988.

Murray, Bruce C. *Journey into Space: The First Thirty Years of Space Exploration.* Nelson, 1989.

By James B. Bell

Ellis Island, Museum of Memories

In a historic U.S. immigration center—restored and reopened as a museum—exhibits, films, and tapes re-create the immigrants' experience.

Ellis Island—the portal through which millions of men, women, and children from other countries passed to begin a new life in the United States—itself took on new life on Sept. 9, 1990. On that day, a refurbished Ellis Island opened as a museum of United States immigration. From 1892 to 1954, the island served as the immigration center for the Port of New York and the chief U.S. reception center for immigrants. More than 12 million people first touched U.S. soil on Ellis Island during that time. About 40 per cent of all living Americans have a parent, grandparent, or great-grandparent who came through the immigration center there.

The primary function of the center was to screen out newcomers who were ineligible to enter the United States. Physicians examined would-be immigrants for lameness, infectious diseases, heart ailments, mental illness, and other conditions. Officials questioned the newcomers to de-

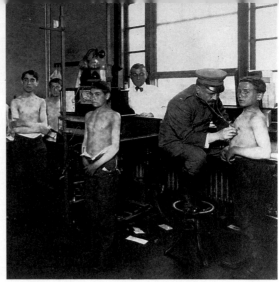

Processing included a mental test, *above*, and a physical examination, *above right*. If retardation was suspected, an *X* was chalked on the person's shoulder, meaning more tests were required. Insanity, indicated by an *X* within a circle, meant deportation. Having heart disease or tuberculosis also meant rejection.

In November 1954, the government moved the immigration center to Manhattan. Ellis Island bade farewell to its last immigrant and lapsed into neglect.

The immigrant experience on Ellis Island

The medical and legal examinations in the Great Hall, also known as the Registry Room, were an experience that immigrants dreaded—and which they remembered vividly long afterward. The doctors examined each immigrant's face, hair, neck, and hands. Through an interpreter, the doctors asked questions about the individual's age or work to test alertness. All immigrants, even children, were asked their names to determine whether they could hear and speak.

Suspected heart trouble, mental illness, skin infection, tuberculosis, physical disabilities, or trachoma (an eye disease often resulting in blindness) could cause the immigrant to be deported. Family members could be separated—some accepted, others rejected. As a result, many families had to make painful decisions on the spot whether to stay or to return to the homeland with a rejected family member.

After the medical examination, each immigrant was asked 29 questions, including:

- Who paid for your ship's fare?
- Do you have a job waiting for you?
- What kind of work do you do?
- Is anyone meeting you?
- Where are you going?
- Can you read and write?
- Have you ever been in prison?
- How much money do you have?

Many of the questions were designed to catch people who came as contract laborers in violation of United States law. So it was "incorrect" for an immigrant to say, for example, that a company had paid the ship's fare, or that a particular job was waiting for him or her.

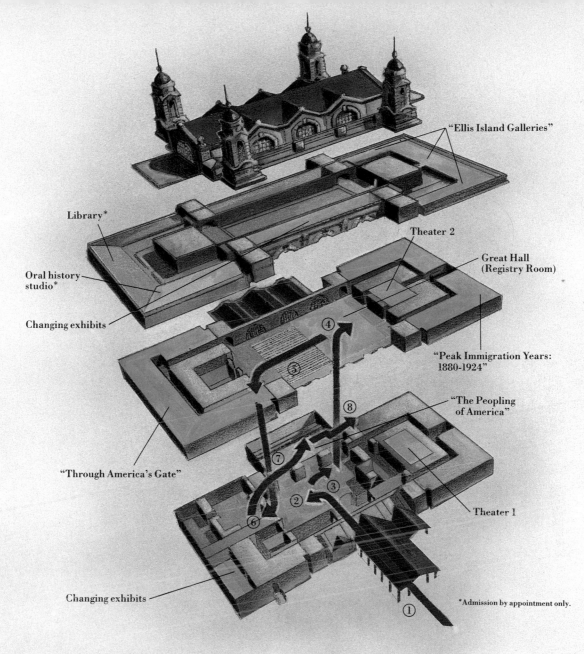

"Ellis Island Galleries"

Library*

Oral history studio*

Changing exhibits

Theater 2

Great Hall (Registry Room)

④

⑤

"Peak Immigration Years: 1880-1924"

⑧

"The Peopling of America"

"Through America's Gate"

⑦

②

③

Theater 1

⑥

Changing exhibits

*Admission by appointment only.

①

Pathway to a new life

This floor plan shows both the present-day features of the Ellis Island Immigration Museum (shaded in blue) and the historic route the immigrants followed (indicated by red arrows). Immigrants stepped from the ferry at the entrance (**1**) to the main building. Leaving their belongings in the baggage room (**2**), they walked east to ascend the stairs (**3**) under the watchful eyes of inspectors looking for signs of ill health. On the second floor (**4**), they entered the Great Hall (**5**), where the formal admission process began, and then crossed to the "stairway of separation" leading to Manhattan ferries, the railroad office, or detention rooms. Finally, they descended the staircase (**6**), picked up their belongings, bought railroad tickets (**7**), and departed (**8**).

Newcomers generally were in good health, and most of them knew the "correct" answers. So, in spite of their anxieties, more than 98 per cent of the immigrants who set foot on Ellis Island received landing cards and were officially admitted into the United States. The average stay on Ellis Island was only about five hours.

The restoration of Ellis Island

When the immigration center on Ellis Island closed in November 1954, the island was turned over to the General Services Administration, a federal agency, for disposal. The General Services Administration tried to sell the island and facilities to a government agency, nonprofit organization, or business—but no one wanted to buy the property.

In 1962, the U.S. Senate formed a Subcommittee on Intergovernmental Relations to Dispose of Ellis Island. In 1963, the subcommittee chairman, Senator Edmund S. Muskie (D., Maine), recommended that the National Park Service consider using the island. The Park Service, in turn, recommended that the island be designated a national historic site. On May 11, 1965, President Lyndon B. Johnson declared the island part of an existing national historic site, the Statue of Liberty National Monument, which is administered by the National Park Service.

In 1976, a number of individuals formed an organization to improve the condition of Ellis Island. This Ellis Island Restoration Commission cleaned up the main building and opened a few of the old offices. For several years thereafter, the Park Service conducted public tours of the building.

Ellis Island attracted so many tourists that support grew for establishing a memorial there. In 1982, President Ronald Reagan asked Lee A. Iacocca, chairman of the board of Chrysler Corporation, to set up the Statue of Liberty-Ellis Island Foundation. The foundation was given the job of raising money and overseeing the restoration and preservation of the Statue of Liberty and Ellis Island and planning the centennial celebrations for those two monuments. The restoration of the Statue of Liberty was completed in 1986. The Immigration Museum is the first fruit of the Ellis Island restoration, which began in 1984.

The main building had fallen into a state of disrepair. It was restored from its foundation to the tips of its copper-domed corner towers. Workers replastered and repainted the structure and replaced its wiring and plumbing. They also installed a climate control system. The restorers removed 19 layers of paint from every exposed surface of the building to find the color that was applied in about 1918—a pale institutional green.

The Great Hall has been restored to the condition it was in from 1918 to 1929 and has been left almost empty. Only a few original benches are here. Benches replaced iron railings in 1911, enabling the immigrants to sit rather than lean as they waited to be processed. Above the visitor's head in the Great

An American legacy comes to life

After Ellis Island restoration began in 1984, the Great Hall gradually emerged to the condition of its peak years, 1918 to 1929.

Years of grime darken the Great Hall before the restoration. Time, more than vandalism, had worn away much of the room's grandeur. But human activity was also evident in 19 layers of paint.

Scaffolding helps restoration crews reach the vaulted ceiling, constructed in 1918 after the original ceiling collapsed. Cleaning and inspecting the 29,000 tiles took nearly a year.

Today, the Great Hall looks as it did in the 1920's, when hundreds of officials speaking 30 languages processed hundreds of thousands of newcomers into American life.

Restoring a public treasure

Copper domes, cookware, caulking—every aspect of the main building, inside and outside, was inspected.

Workers repair one of the copper-clad domes crowning each of the four corner towers.

A curator catalogs kitchenware left behind when the building closed. Other cooking equipment was found under leaves and fallen plaster in the kitchen. Sinks and beds were discovered as they had been left years ago.

Painters work outside an intricate window under an arch of the Great Hall. Finished in 1900, the limestone and red brick building was designed in the grand Beaux-Arts style and re-placed a simpler building destroyed by fire.

The present commemorates the past

Nearly half of all Americans living in 1990 are descendants of immigrants who came to the United States through Ellis Island.

More than 200,000 people sent names of their immigrant relatives to be inscribed on the Wall of Honor. A centennial edition of the wall is due to be completed in 1992.

These "Treasures from Home," exhibited in the museum's east wing, help bring to life the immigrants' experience for museum visitors.

Passports, such as these from Poland, Macedonia, Italy, and Sweden, were contributed by many families after an appeal by the National Park Service. Thousands of such personal items are on permanent display in the museum.

By Danny Unger

Riding a Wave of Prosperity on the Pacific Rim

A flood of foreign investment has helped sweep Thailand, Malaysia, and Indonesia toward industrialization.

In the Asian countries that border the Pacific Ocean, cities are bustling with the business of business. East Asian factory workers turn out tons of manufactured goods—from canned goods to computers to cars. Bankers and entrepreneurs plan new ventures in Hong Kong, Singapore, and South Korea. Cargo planes laden with goods zoom from Taiwan to Tokyo and beyond.

This region, which some economists call the *Asian Pacific rim*, is the site of one of the world's richest nations—Japan—as well as the robust economies of Hong Kong, Singapore, South Korea, and Taiwan. Here, too, are formerly poor nations tasting prosperity for the first time. Thailand—known to most Americans for little more than the setting of the musical *The King and I*—is a remarkable case in point. In the 1950's, Thailand ranked among the world's poorest countries. By 1988 and 1989, its economy was growing at the fastest rate in the world. Two other developing countries along the Asian Pacific rim—Malaysia and Indonesia—have also made impressive gains. For families living in these nations, the new wave of prosperity means improvements in the standard of living—better medical care, more nutritious food, the chance to send their children to college.

had the technology to exploit these resources, fertile croplands were a natural source of wealth. Since at least the 1300's, the Thai people have cultivated rice. By the late 1800's, the country grew so much rice that some could be exported for profit.

Clever diplomatic maneuvering enabled Thailand to maintain its independence throughout the 1800's, when many other non-industrial nations could not. As the only Southeast Asian nation never ruled by a Western country, Thailand avoided the struggles of newly independent nations. Discord of another sort marked the mid-1900's, however. After centuries of rule by absolute monarchs, Thailand in 1932 became a constitutional monarchy with a prime minister and a legislature as well as a king. (Seven years later, its name was changed to Thailand from Siam.) Although Thailand's underlying social stability was unchanged, decades of economic mishaps followed.

The situation began to improve in the 1960's, when the government encouraged individuals to invest in money-making enterprises. The United States helped fund projects to construct roads, which stimulated agricultural diversification. Thai farmers became able to export such crops as rice, corn, sugar, and tapioca products. Beginning in the 1970's, the government tried to ensure that banks gave poor farmers loans to finance agricultural improvements. Thailand also profited from American military spending during the 1960's and early 1970's, as the Thai government allowed the United States to use air and naval bases in Thailand during the Vietnam War (1957-1975).

But by the mid-1980's, growth had begun to slow again. The economy was unbalanced, with debts mounting and savings declining. The United States went into a recession in the early 1980's, and this hurt the economies of other nations as well. Soon, the entire world was mired in a recession, decreasing the demand for Thailand's exports and cutting their prices. By late 1985, after 20 years of steady growth, Thailand's economic outlook appeared bleak.

A lucky break

Thailand's recovery from these conditions might have been very slow were it not for an international event entirely beyond Thailand's control—a sharp change in the values of foreign currency. Currency—such as the U.S. dollar and the Japanese yen—is exchanged between nations as they import and export goods. If the relative value of a currency increases, goods and services from that country suddenly become more expensive. If the value decreases, they become cheaper.

In late 1985, the value of the Japanese yen increased, and later so did the currencies of Taiwan and South Korea. This made Japanese, Taiwanese, and South Korean exports more expensive to foreign customers. It also suddenly made it cheaper for citizens of these countries to use their money to buy foreign real estate and other assets.

At the same time, labor costs in Japan, Taiwan, and South Korea were rising. Manufacturing production increased so quickly that the supply of workers could not keep pace with demand. As a result, wages rose, cutting into business profits.

In addition, the United States government stopped designating Singapore, South Korea, and Taiwan as developing countries. Because of this, imports from these countries no longer received preferential access to the U.S. market in the form of low tariffs.

All these events encouraged many Japanese, Taiwanese, and South Korean businesses to move their manufacturing facilities to Thailand. There, labor and land were inexpensive, and businesses could take advantage of Thailand's status as a developing nation in sending exports to the United States. The Thai government was agreeable, realizing it would reap some of the benefits of industrialization without having to pay to build the factories or train the workers. Overnight, Thailand became an exporter of goods it had not previously produced in great quantity, if at all. Taiwanese makers of Christmas-tree ornaments, for example, simply moved their factories to Thailand while continuing to serve the same wholesaler in the United States.

Boom times in Thailand

Driven by this foreign investment, Thailand recorded breakneck levels of economic growth in 1988 and 1989. The amount of goods and services produced in Thailand increased by an average of about 12 per cent—compared with 3 per cent in the United States in 1989 and just under 5 per cent in Japan. A government budget deficit of some $2 billion in 1985 became a surplus almost as large by 1989. The share of Thailand's export earnings devoted to paying off foreign debts fell from almost 23 per cent in 1985 to about 10 per cent at the end of the decade.

The economic boom meant good times for Thai citizens, who earned an average of 35 per cent more money at the end of the 1980's than at the beginning. This money purchased not only consumer goods, but also better medical care and more nutritious food. Thus, as incomes have risen, so have average life expectancies—from 58 years for Thai children born in 1970 to 65 years for those born in 1988.

The wealth of nations

Thailand, Malaysia, Indonesia, Japan, and the United States enjoyed comparable levels of economic growth in the 1980's, *below*. But there were great differences in natonal incomes, *bottom*.

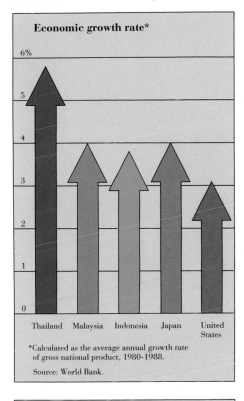

Economic growth rate*

Thailand   Malaysia   Indonesia   Japan   United States

*Calculated as the average annual growth rate of gross national product, 1980-1988.

Source: World Bank.

Gross national product* (U.S. dollars)	
Thailand	$54,550,000,000
Malaysia	$31,620,000,000
Indonesia	$75,960,000,000
Japan	$2,576,541,000,000
United States	$4,863,674,000,000

*1988, latest available data.
Source: World Bank.

The growth of manufacturing

For many countries, manufacturing is the engine of economic growth. Prosperity has come to Thailand, Malaysia, and Indonesia as workers have begun producing manufactured goods in addition to agricultural, forest, and mineral products.

Malaysian autoworkers assemble Protons, the first Malaysian-built make of car, in a Kuala Lumpur factory, *above*. Indonesians at an aircraft company in Bandung produce airplanes, *right*. Thai women, *opposite page*, *top*, assemble circuit boards at an electronics plant in Bangkok.

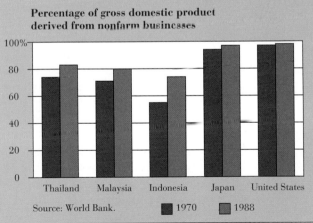

Percentage of gross domestic product derived from nonfarm businesses

Source: World Bank. ■ 1970 ■ 1988

The trend in all three nations is increased manufacturing, with more income derived from non-agricultural products than ever before, *above.*

Economists expect Thailand to continue its trajectory of rapid growth well into the next century. Problems remain, however. As foreign businesses have built hundreds of factories in the capital city of Bangkok, the city's system of roads and its telephone, sewerage, and electric power facilities have become overtaxed. The housing supply has become inadequate as workers from rural areas pour into the city to take jobs manufacturing clothing, motor vehicle parts, electrical appliances, electronic equipment, and other goods. Although the government encourages businesses to build factories in other regions, these areas also lack adequate roads and electric power facilities. Finally, even though many Thai factory workers earn relatively high wages, the majority of citizens still work on farms and are comparatively poor, particularly in the country's arid northeast. The government faces an urgent need to boost the skills and the incomes of Thailand's rural workers.

Riches and resentment in Malaysia

In contrast to Thailand, Malaysia—the southern part of the Malay Peninsula and the northern part of the island of Borneo—has the advantage of excellent transportation and communication facilities, which have been under government construction since the 1950's. Malaysia's nearly 18 million people live on the country's 127,000 square miles (329,000 square kilometers). Here, too, natural resources—primarily tropical forests and mineral deposits—are a source of wealth.

Unlike Thailand, Malaysia was once a colony. Through the centuries, Portugal, the Netherlands, Thailand, Great Britain, and Japan laid claim to some or all of the territory that today comprises Malaysia. The British regained control over the region after Japan was defeated in World War II (1939-1945), and in 1948 Great Britain allowed the islands to begin movement toward self-government. In 1963, the people established the Federation of Malaysia, a constitutional monarchy with the position of king rotating among the sultans of various states.

The new nation was racially and ethnically diverse. Thousands of immigrants from China and India had settled there to work in commerce, industry, and the professions. The native Malay population, most of whom lived on the peninsula, primarily farmed and fished. The Chinese and Indian citizens resented the political power of the Malays, who made up about half of the population and controlled the new government. The Malays in turn resented the other groups' wealth.

The dissatisfactions among the ethnic groups threatened to halt the drive toward prosperity. Worse, the tensions eventually triggered violence. In 1969, bloody riots in the midst of a closely fought election led to a declaration of a state of emergency and the suspension of the national legislature until 1971. After the riots, political leaders determined to improve the Malays' economic conditions. Malaysian officials launched new policies designed to achieve a better balance of wealth among the major racial groups.

Throughout the 1970's, the economy grew at a robust 8 per cent per year, but Malays still were not taking full part in the economic boom. To provide for their needs without sacrificing overall economic growth, the government in the 1980's helped set up such heavy industries as steel, cement, and automobile manufacturing. Some of these endeavors, particularly the production of motorcycle engines, were successful. But the world recession in the early 1980's forced the government to retrench its plans.

Officials then began to sell government-owned heavy industries to private investors. They allowed Malaysians of all ethnic groups and even foreigners to take over the management of state-owned enterprises. As with Thailand, the changing value of foreign currencies gave investors from other nations an incentive to move factories to Malaysia. Businesses from Japan, Taiwan, and other countries began to invest heavily in the nation, and by the late 1980's, economic growth was soaring. Workers produced processed foods, air conditioners, rubber goods, and semiconductors for computers. These products—in addition to exports of petroleum, tin, timber, and palm oil—made Malaysia's economy one of the strongest in Southeast Asia.

Nevertheless, ethnic tensions still limit the government's economic policy options. Malays still control Malaysia's political system, and officials must continually balance the desire for economic growth against the sensitivities aroused by the relative affluence of ethnic Indian and Chinese Malaysians.

Indonesia's economic roller coaster

Ethnic tensions were but one of the obstacles to prosperity in Indonesia. With more than 183 million people scattered over some 13,600 islands, Indonesia is the world's fifth most populous nation. Meeting the needs of this huge and ethnically diverse population has been difficult for Indonesia's leaders.

Fortunately, the country is rich in natural resources. Underground lie deposits of petroleum, tin, coal, bauxite, and nickel ore. The islands' fertile volcanic soil supports tropical forests of ebony, teak, rubber trees, and plants that yield

Citizens earn more money

Average personal incomes in Thailand, Malaysia, and Indonesia are so low that the nations are considered developing countries, according to the most common measure of standard of living, *below*. But the levels of income are rising, most dramatically in Thailand, *bottom*.

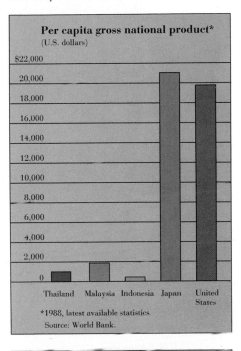

Per capita gross national product*
(U.S. dollars)

*1988, latest available statistics.
Source: World Bank.

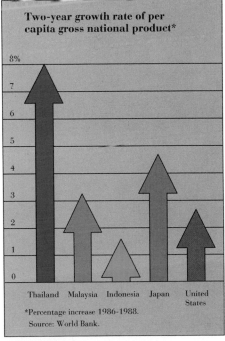

Two-year growth rate of per capita gross national product*

*Percentage increase 1986-1988.
Source: World Bank.

Spending increases

Consumer spending in Thailand, Malaysia, and Indonesia is increasing along with incomes. As workers earn money to buy more consumer goods, they create markets for new industries, further enhancing national prosperity.

Indonesian children, *above*, play Nintendo in an electronics store. Pinang, Malaysia, boasts new housing construction, *right*.

A Malaysian woman inspects a display of lighting fixtures in a Kuala Lumpur shopping center, *left*. Shoppers in Thailand enjoy a similarly dazzling array of choices in a jewelry store, *below*.

Prosperity can bring problems

Thailand, Malaysia, and Indonesia must now cope with the sweeping changes brought by industrialization. The nations' paths appear far from smooth.

With an ethnically diverse population, *above*, Malaysia has had to struggle to surmount widening economic divisions among its people. In Thailand, as business and workers have flocked to Bangkok, *right*, the city's roads and sewerage and power systems have become overtaxed—while the nation's rural areas remain underdeveloped.

Slums and high-rises
coexist in Indonesia, *above*.
Indonesia's newly acquired
wealth—like that of
Thailand and Malaysia—is
unevenly distributed.

By Jonathan W. Schooler

Why Do We Forget? What Can We Do About It?

Most everyday memory failures—like forgetting where we parked the car—are perfectly normal, but there are some ways to improve memory.

Words to remember about memory

Episodic memory: Long-term memory of specific events in our lives.

Interference: Forgetting that occurs when information learned at one time blocks the recall of information learned at another time.

Long-term memory: Memory that holds an unlimited amount of information for an indefinite time.

Motivated forgetting: Forgetting due to conscious or unconscious desire.

Procedural memory: Long-term memory for skills.

Prospective memory: Memory for things to be done at a future time.

Retrieval failure: The inability to recall something stored in memory.

Semantic memory: Long-term memory for word meanings and facts.

Sensory memory: Memory that holds a sense perception such as a sight or a sound for a split second.

Short-term memory: Memory that holds as many as seven items for as long as 30 seconds.

The author:
Jonathan W. Schooler is an assistant professor of psychology at the University of Pittsburgh and a research scientist at the university's Learning Research and Development Center.

Alan D. Baddeley, a British psychologist and expert on memory, was reading the paper at breakfast one morning when he had an awful realization: At that very moment, he was supposed to be at a radio station giving an interview on memory and its mysteries. Baddeley rushed to the station just in time to help wrap up the program with a few tips for remembering. Another memory expert was once asked the title of the book he was writing. To his dismay, he could not recall its title even though it was on memory improvement. No one, not even a memory expert, can avoid occasional memory lapses.

What causes memory to fail us? The full answer is not yet known, but scientists now understand that memory difficulties can have a variety of causes. Before discussing why memory fails, let's briefly take a look at what memory is and how it works. Knowing this should help in putting to use the ways for improving memory described from pages 131 to 133.

Understanding memory

The dictionary says memory is "the ability to remember or keep in the mind; capacity to recall that which is learned or experienced." There is no specific location in the brain, however, where remembering and forgetting take place. Many parts of the brain take part in the complex system for processing, storing, and retrieving information that makes up memory.

Psychologists find it useful to divide memory into three types: sensory, short-term, and long-term. Each type of memory holds information for a different span of time.

On many occasions, things happen so fast it's a wonder we perceive them at all. What we see as a bolt of lightning, for instance, is actually three or four separate bolts, each lasting about 1/1,000 second. We see them as a single bolt because of the highly detailed impressions that *sensory memory* provides. Yet most of what we are "seeing" is the sensory memory of each bolt. In this way, sensory memory enables us to perceive an extremely brief event such as lightning. Sensory memories disappear in half a second unless they are transferred into short-term memory.

How many times have you looked up a telephone number, remembered it long enough to dial, and then forgotten it completely? This is a classic example of the temporary storage—up to about 30 seconds—that *short-term memory* provides. Any information that enters memory must pass through short-term memory, much as incoming mail crosses a desk. Some of the information then shifts from short-term memory to long-term memory for use later, just as we file important documents that we receive. But much of the entering information is simply forgotten, just as we toss out unimportant mail after reading it.

Short-term memory can hold only a limited amount of information: about seven items at a time—just the number of digits in a telephone number. Fortunately, short-term memory has a trick, called *chunking*, for getting around this limitation. Look at the following letters, and then see how many you can recall:

FB IP HD IR ST WA UP SJ FK IB MN RA.

Now try

FBI PHD IRS TWA UPS JFK IBM NRA.

By chunking the letters into meaningful clusters, you remembered many more of them. In the same way, as your knowledge of a subject increases, you can pack more and more information into a single chunk.

Short-term memory, like a desktop, is where much of the sorting and shuffling of information occurs. For example, suppose you read the numbers 27 + 15. Short-term memory can both store the numbers temporarily and manipulate them to calculate the solution. Memory researchers believe that many basic mental skills, from reading to creative thinking, rely on the ability of short-term memory to reshuffle its contents.

Long-term memory is what most people think of as memory. It contains our factual knowledge—Rome is the capital of Italy—as well as recollections of our experiences—a fishing trip last July. Long-term memory, unlike short-term memory, can file away a virtually unlimited amount of information. Even though much information eventually gets lost or distorted, long-term memory can retain a considerable amount of data for decades.

If short-term memory is the mind's desktop, then long-term memory is its filing cabinet. Scientists are just beginning to understand the sophisticated system of storage and retrieval that keeps track of long-term memory's voluminous contents. One characteristic of this system seems particularly important: It tends to file similar memories together. Long-term memory stores new information most successfully by associating it with information it has stored previously. Learning a new concept— how memory works, for instance—is easier if you link it to a concept you already have, such as desktops and files. Similarly, it helps to recall links when you want to retrieve something from memory. To remember someone's name, it may help to recall everything else you can about the person.

Memory researchers classify long-term memories into three general types based on the kind of information they hold. These types are semantic, episodic, and procedural.

Semantic memory refers to our memory for facts, word meanings, and other information we can rapidly recall. The fact that George Washington was the first President of the United States, the meaning of the word *car*, and one's own telephone number are all examples of semantic memories. *Episodic memory* refers to our memory for specific events. Your 12th birthday party, what you ate for dinner last night, and where you were when the space shuttle *Challenger* exploded are examples of episodic memories. *Procedural memory* refers to our memory for skills. Remembering how to ride a bicycle, drive a car, or knit a sweater are procedural memories. We rarely forget these memo-

Types of memory

Psychologists distinguish between three types of memory: *sensory*, *short-term*, and *long-term*. Long-term memory, in turn, is divided into three types.

Short-term memory comes into play when we look up a phone number and remember it just long enough to dial.

Sensory memory enables us, as one example, to see the path traced by a sparkler after the point of light has moved on.

ries. Having learned to ride a bicycle, we still remember how even after not riding for many years.

We think of memory as holding the past, but it also enables us to make plans for the future. When we need to remember to pick up the groceries or keep an appointment, we are using another type of long-term memory called *prospective memory*. As we shall see below, lapses in prospective memory are some of the most common kinds of everyday memory failures.

Why we forget

We have all had a word on the "tip of the tongue," drawn a blank on a friend's name, mislaid our keys or umbrella, and had the awful feeling we should be somewhere else. Most of our forgetting, like the examples above, results from the normal workings of memory.

One of the simplest explanations of forgetting is the passage of time. During the 1880's, German psychologist Hermann Ebbinghaus used himself as a subject to examine memory loss over time. Ebbinghaus memorized lists of meaningless three-letter syllables, such as CAZ. He then tested himself on those syllables over several weeks. Ebbinghaus observed that forgetting initially occurred very rapidly and then slowed down. He concluded that memories decayed with the passage of time, much as an old newspaper fades.

Memory researchers after Ebbinghaus have found other explanations for forgetting, including interference, retrieval failure, motivated forgetting, and constructive processes.

Interference: intervening memories

Time not only takes away memories, it also adds them. Each day, we encounter new information. Information we learn at one

Procedural memory is our long-term memory for skills.

Columbus reached America in 1492.... H_2O is the formula for water.... George Washington was the first president ...there are 12 months in a year...

Semantic memory is our long-term memory for facts and word meanings.

Episodic memory is our long-term memory for specific events in our lives, such as the senior prom.

time may interfere with our ability to recall information learned at another time. This process is known as memory *interference*.

Imagine that Jane studies French in school and then goes to Japan. Jane may first have trouble remembering the Japanese words for things because the French words she learned earlier keep popping into mind. When her earlier memories interfere with her more recent memories, Jane is experiencing *proactive interference*. Jane may later have problems when she returns to her French class and finds that Japanese now interferes with her ability to recall French. In this case, called *retroactive interference*, Jane's more recent memories get in the way of her earlier memories.

Memory interference can have more serious consequences than Jane's inconvenience. Some exciting research on retroactive memory interference has examined how misleading questions can distort eyewitness recollections. For the past 15 years, psychologist Elizabeth F. Loftus and her associates at the University of Washington have used misleading questions to plant memories. In one study, people viewed a sequence of slides that included a red Datsun automobile at a stop sign. Some of the people were later asked, "Did another car pass the red Datsun when it was stopped at the yield sign?" Those who were asked about the nonexistent yield sign were much more likely to falsely remember it than were those who did not receive the misleading question. In later studies, Loftus demonstrated that misleading questions can cause people to remember falsely yet confidently any number of objects from barns to beards.

Our own recollections when put into words also can interfere with memory, as my colleagues and I recently demonstrated. In one study, we showed people a videotape of a bank robbery. We later asked some of them to describe the robber's face in as much detail as they could. Surprisingly, verbalizing the appearance of the robber—telling somebody what he looked like—greatly impaired the ability to recognize him later in a line-up. Researchers believe that this effect, called *verbal overshadowing*, occurs because an incomplete verbal description interferes with a superior visual recollection.

Retrieval failure: missing clues

Sometimes we cannot remember something because we lack enough clues to tell us where we have filed it in our memory. Psychologists call this kind of forgetting *retrieval failure*. If you mislay your keys, retracing your steps may remind you of what you were thinking and doing when you had them last. You may, for instance, see your umbrella, which reminds you that you left your keys in your raincoat. Failure to recall a word on the tip of your tongue is another example of retrieval failure. Often, you can cue your memory by remembering the letter the word starts with or a word it sounds like.

People also may experience retrieval failure when they try to recall information in a situation different from the one in which they learned it. Baddeley, the memory expert who forgot his radio interview, directs the British government's Applied Psychology Unit in Cambridge, England. Baddeley and a colleague found that divers who had learned word lists underwater had difficulty recalling the lists when they were tested on land. The divers did much better when tested underwater. Much other research supports the finding that context affects recall.

Failure to remember information learned in another context could help explain two classic types of forgetting. We may have difficulty remembering dreams because our states of mind differ so when we are awake and when we are dreaming. One reason for not remembering early childhood experiences may be that adults and young children view the world so differently.

Motivated forgetting: wanting to forget

We forget some things because we want to, a process called *motivated forgetting*. Memories of the past often grow more pleasant over time. We tend to remember best the good parts of vacations. Gamblers remember wins better than losses. Memory's ability to whitewash the past was demonstrated in 1986 by psychologist Willem Wagenaar at the Institute for Perception in the Netherlands. Wagenaar tested his memory for events he had recorded in a daily diary over six years. He discovered that he could recall the details of pleasant events substantially better than the details of unpleasant ones.

Constructive processes: filling gaps

Memory not only erases, it also fills in—especially the gaps left by forgetting. Psychologists use the term *constructive processes* for the invention of memories. You may, for example, be unable to remember exactly what you were doing last Friday at 8 a.m. But you can make some good guesses based on your activities other mornings. Memory research indicates that we often confuse what seems likely to have happened with what actually occurred.

In a 1986 study, psychologist Gordon H. Bower and his colleagues at Stanford University in California gave people a brief story about someone who goes to a restaurant. Some of the people later recalled statements about the person's eating and paying for the meal, even though those details were not in the story. Researchers now believe that our expectations influence many of our memories.

Everyday forgetfulness

Most research on normal forgetting has tested people's memory in laboratory situations. Such studies have revealed important clues about why we forget. But they cannot tell us what types of forgetting people most commonly experience in everyday life.

To find out, psychologist James Reason at the University of Manchester in England asked a group of young adults to record how often they experienced ordinary memory lapses. Two of the lapses they most often recorded were forgetting something they meant to do and forgetting the name of someone they knew. On average, respondents reported that both of these lapses occurred at least once a week. Other memory lapses that many respondents said occurred weekly were the inability to recall a well-known fact and remembering that they should be doing something but not what it was.

Many of Reason's participants also reported at times forgetting a step in a routine activity. Nearly half said that at least once a month they forget to complete a routine: "I walked out of the shop

Stress: Memory's enemy
Stress is a major cause of forgetting. Absent-minded forgetfulness occurs more often when we are under stress.

Causes of Memory Loss

We all fear losing our memory. Most of our everyday memory lapses, however, do not signal a breakdown in memory. But we can expect some memory impairment as we age. Other, often more serious, memory impairments result from disease, head injury, and alcohol.

Aging. As we grow older, we may find that we recall things more slowly than we once did and that things slip our mind more often. There is little question that some memory loss accompanies aging. But memory research indicates that not all types of memory are affected equally by aging, nor are all people.

Older people often remember early events in their lives quite clearly. Psychologist Harry P. Bahrick and his colleagues at Ohio Wesleyan University in Delaware, Ohio, tested how well adults of various ages recognized photographs of their high school classmates. The older people could attach names to more than 60 per cent of the faces, nearly as many as the young adults could.

Despite what Bahrick's study would seem to indicate, aging affects our long-term memory abilities the most. Sensory and short-term memory are least affected by age. How serious are the changes in long-term memory?

In testing how well people remember what they read, researchers found that older people can remember the substance as well as younger ones, though older people may not remember specific details as well. In addition, people can add to their vocabulary into their 60's, though they may recall words more slowly than they once did. Older people find it more difficult than young people to memorize lists of words if they are doing something else while hearing the words or if the words are presented rapidly. On the other hand, there is good evidence that elderly people can remember nearly as well as young people if they use one of the memory improvement techniques, such as visualization, described on pages 131 to 133.

Studies also show that older people report more everyday memory lapses, such as forgetting a name or leaving behind an umbrella. These lapses most often occur when the elderly vary their usual routines. Older people also worry a lot more than younger people about everyday memory failures. As a result, they are more likely to use calendars and other memory aids. Their greater reliance on aids may explain why older people are repeatedly more reliable than younger people in one area familiar to memory researchers: remembering to call a researcher at a set time.

Although some memory loss can be expected with age, many studies of aging and memory may paint an overly grim picture. Most of these studies compare college students with senior citizens. But the two groups may differ in ways other than age—for example, in the amount of mental activity they are accustomed to. A better method is to test and retest the same group over time. Psychologist K. Warren Schaie at Pennsylvania State University in University Park did this for seven years. Schaie observed little change in people's memory abilities up to age 60. And more than half his subjects had experienced only slight changes by the age of 81.

Many memory experts believe that how much people use their minds plays a role in how well they retain their memories as they age. Researchers at Concordia University in Montreal, Canada, have found less evidence of age-related memory loss among people who read and engage in other intellectual activities. In the case of memory, there may be some truth to the adage: "Use it or lose it."

Disease and injury. Many ailments can cause memory loss, including depression, abnormally low blood pressure, Hunting-

ton's disease, and Parkinson's disease. Drugs that treat these conditions can help restore memory function. At the same time, some prescription drugs used to treat chronic illnesses can cause memory problems as a side effect.

As yet, there is no drug to treat one dreaded destroyer of memory: Alzheimer's disease. Alzheimer's is probably the single greatest cause of major memory loss. The disease afflicts about 10 per cent of Americans over age 65 and nearly half those over 85, according to the Alzheimer's Association, a research organization. Alzheimer's produces a steady decline in memory and thinking abilities. If you forget where you put your keys, there is no reason to suspect Alzheimer's. If you forget how to use your keys, however, there is reason for concern.

Early symptoms of Alzheimer's disease include forgetting what occurred minutes ago; forgetting familiar routes; and regularly forgetting to carry out such routine chores as changing clothes or paying bills. As the disease progresses, victims become increasingly forgetful and confused, even forgetting where they are. Although Alzheimer's victims may still remember events from years ago, they become less and less able to store new information in long-term memory. Eventually, they may become completely disoriented.

Amnesia is a no less remarkable type of memory disorder. People with amnesia generally have great difficulty remembering what happened recently. Surprisingly, their memories may otherwise remain unaffected. For example, amnesiacs can learn a new skill yet not remember when they learned it.

Amnesia can follow a blow to the head or some other brain injury. If a person forgets what happened days or even weeks before the injury, the condition is called *retrograde amnesia.* In most cases, memory of this period gradually returns. Brain injuries also can leave people unable to remember what happened after the injury, a condition known as *anterograde amnesia.* Many people who experience anterograde amnesia regain their ability to store new events in long-term memory. But the events immediately following the injury are usually lost forever because they were never properly stored in long-term memory.

More severe brain injuries—resulting from tumors, strokes, and other causes—can damage the memory permanently. The type of memory loss depends largely on the area of the injury. Damage to one part of the brain can impair the ability to store new experiences. Damage to another part can impair the ability to use or understand words. A person may, for example, be unable to recognize faces but have an otherwise normal memory.

Alcohol and other drugs. Alcohol's effects on memory depend mainly on the amount consumed. After even moderate drinking, people may become less able to store information in long-term memory. In addition, people may find that information learned while drunk is difficult to remember when sober. Only after drinking again can they recall the information. This effect is known as *state dependency.*

Tobacco and marijuana can also have state-dependent effects on memory, as can drugs called *amphetamines* (in slang, "uppers") and *barbiturates* ("downers"). Like alcohol, marijuana and barbiturates can temporarily impair the ability to store information in long-term memory.

Heavy drinking can result in a memory failure known as a *blackout.* Blackouts range in severity from a partial inability to remember what happened while intoxicated to the complete inability to remember anything after a certain time. Prolonged heavy drinking can lead to permanent memory damage. After years of heavy drinking and careless eating, some alcoholics develop Korsakoff's syndrome, a disease caused by vitamin B deficiency. People with Korsakoff's syndrome may experience amnesia. [J.W.S.]

Memory boosters

Simple techniques like these can improve your memory.

without waiting for my change" or "I was just about to step into the bath when I discovered I still had my socks on." Often, when people engage in a routine activity such as shopping or taking a bath, they are thinking about something else entirely. Indeed, people in the study said they were distracted or preoccupied three-fourths of the time when they forgot a routine action. This suggests that we may well be thinking when we behave absent-mindedly; we just are not thinking about what we are doing.

Stress and forgetting

When our minds are elsewhere, they may be troubled. You may have noticed that stress makes you more likely to forget. For example, British researcher Gillian Kane found that university students experienced more absent-minded memory lapses, such as forgetting to pick up the groceries, as an upcoming examination grew closer.

When stress is extreme, it can block memory altogether. Ordeals such as the horrors of war and natural disasters are sometimes forgotten completely. People probably forget such traumatic experiences to protect themselves from painful memories. Hypnosis, drugs, and psychotherapy can help people remember. But attempts to recall traumatic experiences often produce great anxiety and a struggle to avoid remembering.

How to improve your memory

You can do a number of things to improve your memory. If you are concerned that your memory is getting worse, talk to friends and relatives to find out whether they share your perception. Many people, especially older people, overestimate how often their memory fails. You may want to keep a memory diary—actually, a forgetting diary—to record the types of memory problems you are having. If you conclude that your memory is getting worse, then try to identify possible reasons.

If you are under considerable stress, look for ways to relax, such as taking a vacation, developing an exercise routine, or meditating. If you drink, consider cutting back. If you take medications to treat a chronic illness, ask your doctor whether the drugs could affect your memory. If you suffer from depression or a major illness, speak with your physician about any possible

Mnemonic devices

Many people have favorite mnemonic devices to help them remember things. Here are some you may find useful.

Colors of the visible spectrum,
from longest to shortest wavelengths of light: Roy G. Biv (red, orange, yellow, green, blue, indigo, violet).

Layers of the earth's atmosphere,
from lowest to highest: *That Should Make It Easy* (troposphere, stratosphere, mesosphere, ionosphere, exosphere).

Notes on the treble clef:
Every Good Boy Does Fine (e, g, b, d, f).

Order of British hereditary titles,
in descending importance: *Did Mary Ever Visit Brighton Beach* (duke, marquess, earl, viscount, baron, baronet).

Order of the planets in the solar system,
from the sun: *Mary's Violet Eyes Make John Stay Up Nights Pacing* (Mercury, Venus, Earth, Mars, Jupiter, Saturn, Uranus, Neptune, Pluto).

Classification of plants and animals,
from the largest to the smallest units : *Kindly Put Clothes On For Goodness Sake* (kingdom, phyllum, class, order, family, genus, species).

Clock settings for daylight-saving time:
Spring forward, Fall back. (Set the time forward one hour in spring and back an hour in fall.)

The four sections of an orchestra:
Saints Will Be Praised (strings, woodwinds, brass, percussion).

To remember spellings:
No *ten* in lightning. Dessert has twice *s* because it is *so sweet*. Desert has one *s* because it is *so* dry. Nausea has a *sea* in it. Science has a con*science*. Connecticut *connects* New York and Rhode Island. Write a lett*er* on station*er*y. Station*ary* is where you *are*.

memory-related side effects. No matter what the cause, if memory problems are interfering with your life, you should talk to your physician about memory testing.

A number of things can help you overcome normal, everyday forgetting. First, focus on one or two areas in which you particularly want to improve your memory, such as remembering names or information for a test. Second, take full advantage of external memory aids such as calendars and datebooks, watch alarms, lists, pocket telephone books, and dated pillboxes. Third, recognize the situations in which you typically experience memory failures and make a practice of alerting yourself when you are in those situations. For example, if you have trouble remembering names, then remind yourself before meeting someone new: "I must pay attention when I am told this person's name." If you have trouble recalling names, you may want to review the names of the people you expect to see. If you forget to take things with you when you leave the house, get into the habit of thinking about everything you need before you go out.

The memory problem that most concerns students is remembering what they have studied. Good study habits will help. First and most important, space out your studying. You will remember more if you spread your studying over time than if you do it all in one sitting. So if you have a test coming up in a week, study an hour every day rather than seven hours the night before. Cramming may enable you to pass the test. But you are more likely to experience retrieval failure after cramming. And you will certainly forget what you learned much sooner than if you had distributed your study time.

A widely recommended technique for studying written material is called *SQR3*, which stands for *S*urvey, *Q*uestion, *R*ead, *R*ecite, and *R*eview. According to this technique, you should survey a chapter in a textbook before reading it. Study the outline; skim the material; and look at the headings, pictures, and graphs to gain an overview of the chapter. Next, ask some questions based on your survey: What is the chapter about? What does the author seem to emphasize? What themes or general points are presented? Asking such questions focuses your attention and makes you a more active learner. Then, read the chapter, keeping in mind the questions you have posed. Afterward, recite the chapter's subsections and main points without looking at the text. Now you are ready to review what you have read. See which points you recited correctly and which points you overlooked. Before going on to the next chapter, make sure you can answer all the questions you posed at the beginning.

In addition to these general approaches, there are also some helpful devices for remembering specific information. These memory aids are called *mnemonic devices*. The trick to most mnemonic devices is the creation of a meaningful association. Many of us have used mnemonics that take the first letter of a list of items and make a word or sentence. HOMES, for example, is a first-letter mnemonic for remembering the Great Lakes: *H*uron, *O*ntario, *M*ichigan, *E*rie, and *S*uperior.

First-letter mnemonics are especially useful if you need to re-member items in order. For example, the sentence *Every Good Boy Does Fine* has helped students who are learning to play a musical instrument remember the order of notes on the treble clef: e, g, b, d, f. A number of first-letter mnemonics are listed on page 131.

One mnemonic device dates back to ancient Greece. It calls for imagining the things you want to remember in familiar loca-tions, such as the rooms in your house. Take a mental walk through your house and pick out 10 or so locations in the order you reach them. Then if you wanted to memorize a shopping list, you would imagine an item in each location: milk on the couch, bread on a lamp, and so forth. To recall the information, you would mentally walk back through your house and pick up the items on the way.

The so-called *key-word mnemonic* has been developed for memorizing words in another language. The key word is an English word that sounds like the foreign word. To remember the French word *garçon*, meaning *boy*, you might pick *garden* as your key word. Next, visualize your key word (garden) interact-ing with the meaning of the foreign word (boy). You might, for example, imagine a boy playing in a garden. Then to remember what *garçon* means, simply recall your key word *garden* and the connecting image of a boy.

Vivid images aid memory. The ancient Greek method of places and the key-word mnemonic both rely on visualization. You can also use visualization to remember names. You might make a visual association between a person's name and a prominent fea-ture: for example, Mr. Goldstein wears gold-rimmed glasses. People might remember my name, Schooler, by visualizing my face in a school window.

There are many worthwhile techniques for improving memory. But don't get discouraged if your memory still fails from time to time. Most of us simply learn to live with our imperfect memo-ries. With so many reasons for forgetting, we should probably be grateful that our memories are as good as they are.

For further reading:
Baddeley, Alan. *Human Memory: Theory and Practice*. Allyn & Bacon, 1990.
Herrmann, Douglas J. *Supermemory*. Rodale Press, 1990.
Higbee, Kenneth L. *Your Memory: How It Works and How to Improve It*. Rev. ed. Prentice Hall, 1988.

By John Canemaker

Once Again, "Toons" Are Tops

No longer just kids' stuff, animated features are making an exciting comeback and drawing enthusiastic fans of all ages.

Bringing images to life

All animated films—whether created with drawings or puppets or by computer—consist of thousands of individual images that are run together at a fast speed to create an illusion of motion.

Cel animation is the most familiar form of animation. Most cartoons made for movie theaters and television, such as *The Little Mermaid*, are created from hand-drawn images using the cel animation process.

Computer animation can create images, such as the baby and toys in *Tin Toy*, that seem to be three-dimensional. Computers also can be used to develop special animated effects for live-action films.

Puppet animation creates an illusion of movement in three-dimensional objects, such as the snow walkers in *The Empire Strikes Back*, by photographing slight changes in the position of the objects.

Claymation, a form of puppet animation, uses figures or objects made of clay, which can be reshaped easily. The singing California Raisins may be the most famous Claymation characters.

1914

The development of the cel animation process, in which background drawings are reused, streamlines animation technology.

Gertie the Dinosaur stars as one of the first animated characters with a distinctive personality and naturalistic movements.

1919

Felix the Cat, the first international cartoon star, makes his initial film appearance.

1917

The Apostle, an Argentine political satire, premieres as the first feature-length animated movie.

By 1940 and the beginning of World War II, however, Disney films—with their storybook quality, slow pacing, and primary appeal to children—were becoming somewhat old-fashioned. The brash cartoons produced by the Warner Brothers studio starring Bugs Bunny, Daffy Duck, Elmer Fudd, and Porky Pig more accurately reflected the aggressive mood of the country during the war years. Bugs, Warner's biggest star, represented the little guy living by his wits and using extreme retaliation when his survival is threatened. In a 1969 interview, Warner cartoon director Bob Clampett described Bugs as "a symbol of America's resistance to [German dictator Adolf] Hitler and the fascist powers."

In the late 1940's and 1950's, the introduction of a technique called *limited animation* profoundly changed both the look and the production of cartoons. In this technique, used brilliantly by

1928

Mickey Mouse is a smash hit in his film debut, *Steamboat Willie*, the first cartoon with a sound track combining voice, music, and special effects.

1940

Bugs Bunny's film career is launched in *A Wild Hare*.

1937

Snow White and the Seven Dwarfs becomes the first feature-length animated cartoon produced in the United States.

United Productions of America (UPA), only certain simple movements of a character are animated, allowing portions of the figure to be reused. This process, which also features flat, bold colors, streamlined backgrounds, and modernistic styling, cuts production time and cost considerably. For example, cartoons created by limited animation usually have only 300 drawings per minute of film, compared with 1,000 drawings per minute in conventionally animated features.

The streamlined production process of limited animation led to a proliferation of inexpensive, quickly made Saturday morning TV cartoon series for children. The majority of these popular programs, including "Yogi Bear," "Quick Draw McGraw," and "The Flintstones," were produced by Hanna-Barbera Productions, Incorporated. In the mid-1960's, television networks began airing a new slate of children's cartoon series, nearly all

Late 1940's and 1950's

Limited animation, a technique in which only simple movements of a character are animated, gains in popularity.

1982

Tron is the first live-action feature film to make extensive use of imagery generated through computer animation.

1960

"The Flintstones" becomes the first animated series to appear on prime-time television.

produced by limited animation, each season. Although cartoons created by limited animation may be stylish and interesting, these Saturday morning cartoons often lacked detail, and the characters moved in stiff, unnatural ways. At this point, many people in the United States came to regard animation as entertainment suitable only for children.

A few animated features attempted to break through to adult audiences. One such crossover film was *Yellow Submarine* (1968), a showcase for the music of the Beatles and a visual time capsule of the psychedelic 1960's. Beginning in the early 1970's, animator Ralph Bakshi also created a number of animated features for adults, including *Fritz the Cat* (1971). But these had only limited success, mainly because they had so many scenes depicting drug use and sex that they received an X rating, and children and teen-agers were, officially, not allowed

1986

An American Tail becomes a box-office success and helps renew interest in feature-length animated films.

1990

"The Simpsons" becomes the first prime-time weekly animated series on U.S. network television in 20 years.

1989

Tin Toy becomes the first computer graphics project to win an Academy Award.

to see them. Even Warner releases, such as *1001 Rabbit Tales* (1982) and *Daffy Duck's Movie: Fantastic Island* (1983), failed to generate much excitement or profit. By the early 1980's, theatrical animation, except for Disney films, was considered box-office poison.

After Walt Disney's death in 1966, even his studio's animated films became, in the opinion of many critics, lackluster. Such films as *The Aristocats* (1970), *Robin Hood* (1973), and *The Fox and the Hound* (1981) generated only moderate enthusiasm. The bulk of the Disney company's earnings came from re-releasing old feature-length cartoons, such as *Snow White* or *Pinocchio* (1940), and from the company's theme parks, Disneyland in California and Walt Disney World in Florida.

In 1979, Don Bluth, one of Disney's most promising animation directors, resigned from Disney to start his own studio and

took a number of Disney's top young animators with him. Bluth has since been in the forefront of the recent renaissance of feature animation. Together with producer-director Steven Spielberg, he produced *An American Tail* and *The Land Before Time*, major box-office winners that each grossed more than $45 million on initial release. Like the Disney studio, Bluth uses full animation to simulate natural motion.

In 1984, after a reorganization, top management at the Disney studio decided to reestablish Disney's former stature in feature animation. That decision led to the production of the phenomenally successful *Who Framed Roger Rabbit*, starring one of the strongest cartoon personalities Disney has created in years, and *The Little Mermaid*, the first completely animated feature to win an Oscar since *Dumbo* in 1942.

What has triggered the cartoon craze? Some animation critics argue that rather than reviving interest in a neglected art, recent successful animated features have instead tapped into a waiting market. They suggest that the popularity of the old Warner cartoons, which have been a television mainstay for more than 30 years, is evidence that an adult audience for animation has actually been there all along. Says animation historian Charles Solomon, "There is an audience for more sophisticated animated cartoons, such as *Roger Rabbit* and *The Little Mermaid*, that don't talk down to audiences and aren't simple-minded."

That audience is composed largely of baby boomers, who grew up surrounded by animation on television and who have a great affection for the medium. Thus, their interest in animation is nostalgic as well as escapist, springing from a fondness for the past as well as a desire for laughs. *Roger Rabbit*, for example, has great nostalgic appeal. The cast has a variety of characters from classic animated features and cartoons, including Betty Boop and Pinocchio. And while *Roger Rabbit* contains enough silly slapstick, fast-paced action, and striking visuals to delight children, it also displays an adult-oriented attitude toward sex, humor, violence, and death.

Another suggested explanation for the animation boom is that baby boomers have started families of their own and are looking for entertainment that both they and their children will enjoy. Solomon says that many "young movie studio executives realized they are working in studios that may not be providing entertainment they can take their families to and they are doing something about it."

Undoubtedly, the possibility of making money has played a major role. The lingering interest in animation led a few movie studios to chance making new feature-length cartoons, such as *An American Tail*, *The Land Before Time*, and *Oliver & Company* (1988). The enormous box-office success of these and other features fueled the fire. "Anything that makes a lot of money gets attention in Hollywood and the press," says Solomon. "Economics caught up with the interest."

The economic appeal of animated features extends beyond the box office, however. Advances in video technology, including videocassettes, videocassette players, and cable television, have created a much wider market for motion pictures. The hefty profits earned by animated features on their initial release to movie theaters may be dwarfed by the money they bring in from videocassette sales and rentals.

Animation—this "lovely magic," as critic Gilbert Seldes described it in the 1930's—may be entering a new golden age. Although its popularity has risen and fallen over the years, it has never been a passing fad. Instead, animation has proved to be an enduring and beloved art form that continues to fascinate and charm audiences around the world.

For further reading:
Canemaker, John. *Winsor McCay—His Life and Art*. Abbeville Press, 1987.
Crafton, Donald. *Before Mickey—The Animated Film 1898-1928*. MIT Press, 1982.
Culhane, John. *Walt Disney's Fantasia*. Abrams, 1987.
Schneider, Steve. *That's All Folks! The Art of Warner Brothers Incorporated*. Henry Holt and Company, 1988.
Solomon, Charles. *Enchanted Drawings—The History of Animation*. Knopf, 1989.

Year Book News Update

1990

Iraq
Census
One Germany
The Simpsons

NASA problems
World Series

The major events of 1990 are summarized in nearly 300 alphabetically arranged articles—from "Advertising" to "Zoos." In most cases, the article titles are the same as those of the articles in **The World Book Encyclopedia** that they update.The writers' names appear at the end of the articles they have written, and a list of the writers is on pages 571 and 572.

Six News Update articles contain Close-Ups that focus on especially noteworthy developments of 1990:

"Bank"	196
"Canada"	220
"Census"	228
"Classical music"	243
"Deaths "	268
"Union of Soviet Socialist Republics"	462

See page 171 ▶

Riot police in Abidjan, Ivory Coast, head for a disturbance in April, as the nation is rocked by violent protests against strict economic measures.

Africa. South Africa continued to dominate the news from Africa in 1990, with the white-ruled republic producing an impact throughout the southern region of the continent and on the global stage as well. The lowering of the South African flag in Windhoek, Namibia, on March 21 brought independence to the continent's last colony, ending over 400 years of European rule in Africa. Coming after 23 years of civil war, Namibia's tranquil entrance into the community of nations raised hopes that peace negotiations in progress would also end civil wars in two other southern African nations—Angola and Mozambique. In Angola, and reportedly also in Mozambique, rebels opposing the central government have been supported by South Africa.

But the most dramatic news from South Africa in 1990 came on February 11 with the release from imprisonment of black leader Nelson R. Mandela. The name Mandela has been almost synonymous with opposition to South Africa's long-time system of *apartheid* (racial segregation). He had spent nearly 28 years in prison. See **Mandela, Nelson R.**

A week before Mandela's release, the government of State President Frederik Willem de Klerk indicated that it was charting a new political course for South Africa. The de Klerk government liberalized a number of restrictive policies and lifted long-standing bans on the African National Congress (ANC)—the opposition group that Mandela had led from his prison cell—and

other black political organizations. In addition, de Klerk promised that work would begin on the drafting of a multiracial constitution for South Africa.

Later in the year, Mandela was given a hero's welcome in the United States, Canada, and several European countries. Within South Africa, though, the government's proposed reforms received a mixed reception. Right wing whites mounted demonstrations and challenged de Klerk's National Party program for ending white supremacy. Mandela, moreover, seemed unable to bridge the political division between the ANC and the Inkatha party, a conservative Zulu political movement, and during the year there was extensive bloodshed between the two groups.

Civil wars. Seemingly endless civil wars continued in several African nations in 1990, preventing economic development and frustrating hopes for democratic reforms. The one conflict that appeared to be ending—the civil war in Chad, which began in the mid-1960's—erupted anew in 1990. President Hissein Habré, whose army had defeated Libyan-backed rebels in 1987, received surprising concessions from Libya's leader, Colonel Muammar Muhammad al-Qadhafi, in 1990. In May, Qadhafi agreed to stop aiding the rebels and to drop his claim to the Aozou Strip, a mineral-rich area in northern Chad. In November, however, a rebel force—presumably supported by Libya—under General Idriss Deby, the former commander of Habré's army, invaded Chad from Sudan. Deby's troops entered the capital, N'Djamena, on December 2. Habré had fled the country a day earlier.

There was optimism in 1990 that the 14-year-old desert war in Western Sahara might be resolved. In March, the Polisario Front, a rebel group fighting for Western Sahara's independence from Morocco, reached a cease-fire agreement with the Moroccan government. In June, the United Nations (UN) approved a peace plan, drawn up in 1988, for Western Sahara. The UN was also organizing a *referendum* (a direct vote of the people) in Western Sahara to decide whether the area should be independent.

In Angola, the government attempted early in the year to gain a decisive military victory over the rebel forces of Jonas Savimbi. Although a failure, the offensive came close to ruining the progress made by the leaders of several neighboring African nations to bring a negotiated peace to Angola. Unable to crush the rebels, the Angolan government returned to the negotiating table in April.

In Mozambique, guerrillas of the Mozambique National Resistance (Renamo) continued their assaults on government and civilian targets. During the 15-year-long war, an estimated 900,000 people have died from military action or famine. In July, at the urging of both African and Western leaders, representatives of the Mozambican government and Renamo sat down together for the first time to seek an end to the conflict. A breakthrough came in July when Mozambique's President Joaquím Alberto Chissano announced that the nation would hold multiparty elections in 1991 and that Renamo candidates could probably be on the ballot.

Wars in Ethiopia, Somalia, and Sudan were far from ending in 1990. In Ethiopia, guerrilla forces in the region of Eritrea achieved their greatest military advances since 1961, the year they launched their war for independence. A second rebellion—in the Tigre region—was also succeeding against great odds. The Tigre rebels are seeking self-rule and an end to the dictatorship of President Mengistu Haile-Mariam.

The civil war in Somalia, which pits the government of President Mohamed Siad Barre against the Somali National Movement (SNM), is related to the conflicts in Ethiopia. In retaliation for Somalia's long-standing claim to the Ogaden region of Ethiopia, Mengistu has given arms and sanctuary to the SNM. Barre, on the other hand, has armed Ethiopian refugees in Somalia. The human-rights organization Africa Watch reported in January that Ethiopians have aided the Somali army in poisoning wells, burning villages, and killing an estimated 50,000 Somali civilians.

The civil war in Sudan, which has been on-again, off-again since 1956 and which flared anew in 1983, dragged on for another year in 1990. In June, the government of Prime Minister Umar Hasan Ahmad al-Bashir rejected a U.S. offer to arrange a cease-fire with the Sudan People's Liberation Army.

Another simmering conflict roared back to life in September when an estimated 5,000 Rwandan rebels, members of the oppressed Tutsi ethnic group, left sanctuaries in Uganda to attack government forces in Rwanda. With the support of about 1,000 troops from Belgium, France, and Zaire, the Rwandan army stopped the invasion, and a cease-fire was arranged in mid-October. In November, Rwanda's President Juvénal Habyarimana promised to end racial and ethnic discrimination and allow multiparty elections in 1991.

Africa's newest civil war occurred in the continent's oldest independent country, Liberia. In December 1989, Liberian refugees from Ivory Coast invaded the country, determined to overthrow the regime of President Samuel K. Doe. By mid-1990, the rebels—by this time split into two factions—had pushed their way to the capital city, Monrovia. In September, one of the factions captured and executed Doe. To stop the bloodshed and help rebuild the shattered nation, a 6,000-troop peacekeeping force from five west African countries arrived in Liberia in August. In November, the task force installed a transitional government and arranged a cease-fire among the rebel leaders and the remnants of Doe's army.

Democratic reform. The move toward multiparty democracy in Africa, long blocked by single-party rule and military dictatorship, gained momentum in 1990. That became evident in July at a meeting in Addis Ababa, Ethiopia, of the Organization of African Unity (OAU), an association of 50 African nations. The leaders at the conference issued a statement endorsing democratic institutions and promising to further the growth of democracy in their respective countries.

The reasons for that new-found commitment to democratic reform varied widely. In Nigeria, for instance, it was part of the military government's step-by-step plan to launch a stable civilian political system by December 1992. In the case of Angola and Mozambique, government offers to establish multiparty systems were part of a strategy to end years of civil war and to bring rebel movements into the political process. In several countries—Zaire, for one—the move toward democracy was attributed to pressures from foreign nations and economic agencies that have linked assistance to evidence of democratic reform.

More than anything, however, Africa's tentative steps toward democracy in 1990 were related to the popular uprisings in eastern Europe the year before, which brought about the mass collapse of Communist one-party dictatorships. The example of "people power" in Europe emboldened students, labor unionists, religious leaders, and others in Africa to take direct action against governments that had long restricted freedoms and failed to deliver on economic promises.

In 1990, riots, strikes, and demonstrations occurred in Benin, Gabon, Ivory Coast, and a number of other countries. The beleaguered rulers of those nations saw the looming possibility of their political demise unless

Facts in brief on African political units

Country	Population	Government	Monetary unit*	Foreign trade (million U.S.$) Exports†	Imports†
Algeria	26,097,000	President Chadli Bendjedid; Prime Minister Mouloud Hamrouche	dinar (9.50 = $1)	9,100	7,800
Angola	10,302,000	President José Eduardo dos Santos	kwanza (29.9 = $1)	2,900	2,500
Benin	4,895,000	President Mathieu Kérékou	CFA franc (251.6 = $1)	226	413
Botswana	1,329,000	President Quett K. J. Masire	pula (1.85 = $1)	1,300	1,100
Burkina Faso	9,263,000	Popular Front President, Head of State, & Head of Government Blaise Compaoré	CFA franc (251.6 = $1)	249	591
Burundi	5,609,000	President Pierre Buyoya	franc (161.5 = $1)	128	204
Cameroon	11,550,000	President Paul Biya	CFA franc (251.6 = $1)	2,000	2,300
Cape Verde	391,000	President Aristides Pereira; Prime Minister Pedro Pires	escudo (64.55 = $1)	9	124
Central African Republic	2,987,000	President André-Dieudonne Kolingba	CFA franc (251.6 = $1)	138	285
Chad	5,822,000	President Idriss Deby‡	CFA franc (251.64 = $1)	432	214
Comoros	535,000	President Said Mohamed Djohar	CFA franc (251.6 = $1)	12	52
Congo	2,197,000	President Denis Sassou-Nguesso; Prime Minister Alphonse Poaty-Souchlaty	CFA franc (251.6 = $1)	912	494
Djibouti	418,000	President Hassan Gouled Aptidon; Prime Minister Barkat Gourad Hamadou	franc (177.72 = $1)	128	198
Egypt	54,673,000	President Hosni Mubarak; Prime Minister Atef Sedky	pound (2 = $1)	2,550	10,100
Equatorial Guinea	451,000	President Teodor Obiang Nguema Mbasogo; Prime Minister Cristino Seriche Bioko Malabo	CFA franc (251.6 = $1)	30	50
Ethiopia	47,986,000	President Mengistu Haile-Mariam; Acting Prime Minister Hailu Yimenu	birr (2.07 = $1)	418	1,100
Gabon	1,210,000	President Omar Bongo; Prime Minister Casimir Oye-Mba	CFA franc (251.6 = $1)	1,140	760
Gambia	881,000	President Sir Dawda Kairaba Jawara	dalasi (7.56 = $1)	133	105
Ghana	15,486,000	Provisional National Defense Council Chairman Jerry John Rawlings	cedi (344 = $1)	977	988
Guinea	7,051,000	President Lansana Conté	franc (620 = $1)	553	509
Guinea-Bissau	1,009,000	President João Bernardo Vieira	peso (650 = $1)	15	49
Ivory Coast	13,089,000	President Félix Houphouët-Boigny	CFA franc (251.6 = $1)	2,200	1,300
Kenya	26,160,000	President Daniel T. arap Moi	shilling (22.61 = $1)	1,000	1,800
Lesotho	1,824,000	King Letsie III; Military Council Chairman Justin M. Lekhanya	loti (2.51 = $1)	55	526
Liberia	2,637,000	disputed§	dollar (1 = $1)	550	335
Libya	4,708,000	Leader of the Revolution Muammar Muhammad al-Qadhafi; General People's Committee Secretary (Prime Minister) Abu Said Omar Bourda	dinar (0.27 = $1)	6,100	5,000

*Exchange rates as of Dec. 7, 1990, or latest available data. †Latest available data.
‡Deby declared himself president on Dec. 4, 1990, after President Hissein Habré had fled the country, but the United States and many other nations did not recognize Deby's claim to the presidency.
§President Samuel K. Doe was assassinated on Sept. 10, 1990. Two rival rebel leaders, Charles Taylor and Prince Yormie Johnson, both claimed the presidency, as did Amos Sawyer, who was installed as interim president in November by a group of five African nations.

Country	Population	Government	Monetary unit*	Foreign trade (million U.S.$) Exports†	Imports†
Madagascar	12,366,000	President Didier Ratsiraka; Prime Minister Victor Ramahatra	franc (1,125.27 = $1)	284	319
Malawi	8,708,000	President H. Kamuzu Banda	kwacha (2.60 = $1)	292	402
Mali	8,562,000	President Moussa Traoré	CFA franc (251.6 = $1)	260	493
Mauritania	2,081,000	President Maaouya Ould Sid Ahmed Taya	ouguiya (78.76 = $1)	424	365
Mauritius	1,116,000	Governor General Sir Veerasamy Ringadoo; Prime Minister Sir Aneerood Jugnauth	rupee (14.11 = $1)	1,000	1,300
Morocco	25,730,000	King Hassan II; Prime Minister Azzedine Laraki	dirham (8.04 = $1)	3,100	5,100
Mozambique	16,084,000	President Joaquím Alberto Chissano; Prime Minister Mário da Graça Machungo	metical (1022.3 = $1)	100	764
Namibia	1,934,000	President Sam Nujoma; Prime Minister Hage Geingob	rand (2.51 = $1)	935	856
Niger	7,952,000	Supreme Military Council President Ali Saibou; Prime Minister Aliou Mahamidou	CFA franc (251.6 = $1)	371	441
Nigeria	116,926,000	President Ibrahim Babangida	naira (8.5 = $1)	8,400	5,700
Rwanda	7,479,000	President Juvénal Habyarimana	franc (118.97 = $1)	118	278
São Tomé and Principe	128,000	President Manuel Pinto da Costa	dobra (150.7 = $1)	9	17
Senegal	7,461,000	President Abdou Diouf	CFA franc (251.6 = $1)	761	1,100
Seychelles	72,000	President France Albert René	rupee (5.03 = $1)	17	116
Sierra Leone	4,259,000	President Joseph Momoh	leone (170 = $1)	106	167
Somalia	7,734,000	President Mohamed Siad Barre	shilling (2,620 = $1)	58	354
South Africa	40,528,000	State President Frederik Willem de Klerk	rand (3.44 = $1)	21,500	18,500
Sudan	25,923,000	Prime Minister Umar Hasan Ahmad al-Bashir	pound (4.5 = $1)	550	1,200
Swaziland	816,000	King Mswati III; Prime Minister Obed Mfanyana Dlamini	lilangeni (2.51 = $1)	394	386
Tanzania	28,342,000	President Ali Hassan Mwinyi; Prime Minister Joseph S. Warioba	shilling (195.57 = $1)	394	1,300
Togo	3,563,000	President Gnassingbé Eyadéma	CFA franc (251.6 = $1)	344	369
Tunisia	8,331,000	President Zine El-Abidine Ben Ali; Prime Minister Hamed Karoui	dinar (0.83 = $1)	3,100	4,400
Uganda	19,095,000	President Yoweri Museveni; Prime Minister Samson Kisekka	shilling (505.94 = $1)	272	626
Zaire	37,145,000	President Mobutu Sese Seko; Prime Minister Lunda Bululu	zaire (648.44 = $1)	2,200	1,900
Zambia	8,769,000	President Kenneth David Kaunda; Prime Minister Malimba Masheke	kwacha (45.53 = $1)	1,184	687
Zimbabwe	10,022,000	President Robert Mugabe	dollar (2.57 = $1)	1,600	1,100

The Basilica of Our Lady of Peace in Yamoussoukro, Ivory Coast—the world's largest Roman Catholic church—was consecrated in September.

they responded positively to their citizens' angry demands for reform. In Ivory Coast, Africa's longest-ruling president—Félix Houphouët-Boigny, in office since 1960—responded to a wave of strikes and other disturbances by holding multiparty parliamentary elections in November 1990. Zambia's President Kenneth David Kaunda responded to rioting and an abortive coup by agreeing to hold multiparty elections in 1991.

In several countries, the leaders adamantly rejected political reform. Most notable among them were Kenya, Sudan, and Tanzania. In Kenya, once regarded as a model of democracy and a protector of human rights, the government of President Daniel T. arap Moi answered each new demand for reform with repression. Moi's crackdowns in 1990 included press censorship, police assaults on demonstrators, school closings, and the mysterious deaths of several prominent critics of the regime.

Economic crises. The escalating price of oil after Iraq's invasion of Kuwait in August dealt a devastating blow to Africa's fragile economies. The oil crisis compounded the economic impact on Africa of the earlier collapse of Communist governments in eastern Europe. As a result of the European upheavals, with a new emphasis on democracy and private enterprise, capitalists in Western nations and elsewhere now regarded Eastern Europe as more fertile ground than Africa for economic investment.

Another problem was a growing resistance in many countries to economic assistance programs for Africa. In the United States, long a major donor to struggling African nations, fears of a serious recession caused many development plans to be scrapped or scaled down. Still, the United States, France, and other creditor nations did cancel the debts of many African countries or at least rescheduled the payments on those loans.

African efforts at self-help, exemplified by regional economic cooperation, were also stalled in 1990. One such cooperative venture, the Economic Commission of West African States, was unable to significantly lower trade barriers between member countries or regulate the price and production of agricultural commodities grown in the region.

More famine, more refugees. In March, the Food and Agriculture Organization (FAO), an agency of the UN, reported that Africa's grain harvest was likely to be low in 1990 and that at least 2.3 million short tons (2.1 million metric tons) of food would be needed to avert massive famine. By November, the FAO's predictions were even more grim as diminished rainfall threatened to magnify continuing food crises in Ethiopia, Sudan, and Angola.

Weather was not the major factor causing famine in 1990, however. Rather it was Africa's unending civil wars. In war-torn countries, both government troops and their rebel opponents prevented emergency food

160

from reaching besieged cities or refugee camps in each other's stronghold areas. Food from donor nations and relief agencies was left to rot in warehouses, diverted to the military, or sold on the black market.

A major consequence of the civil wars has been a mounting refugee problem, with more and more mouths to be fed. The UN High Commissioner for Refugees estimated in August that civil strife in Africa has produced 4.4 million refugees. Most live in exile in neighboring countries, where they constitute an enormous drain on already weak economies.

The AIDS epidemic. AIDS continued to spread in Africa in epidemic proportions during 1990, particularly in the eastern and central regions of the continent. Public-health officials said that at least 5 million Africans were infected with the AIDS virus—transmitted in Africa mainly through heterosexual relations.

African governments tried to combat the AIDS epidemic with public-education programs and by distributing condoms free or at low cost at public clinics. But the clinics, the front line in the AIDS battle, often had poorly trained or poorly equipped staffs, and many public clinics actually spread the AIDS virus, unknowingly, through the use of unsterilized needles and syringes.   J. Gus Liebenow and Beverly B. Liebenow

See also the various African country articles. In the Special Reports section, see **The African Elephant: Saved from Extinction?** In *World Book,* see **Africa.**
Agriculture. See **Farm and farming.**

AIDS. The worldwide epidemic of infection with human immunodeficiency virus (HIV), the cause of AIDS, grew substantially worse during 1990. On July 31, the World Health Organization (WHO) raised its estimate of the number of HIV-infected people, reporting that at least 8 million to 10 million people were infected. WHO's previous estimate was 6 million to 8 million. Of particular concern were expected increases in Asia, Latin America, and parts of Africa. A conservative estimate was that in Africa alone, 5 million adults were infected with the AIDS virus.

U.S. cases. The U.S. Centers for Disease Control (CDC) in Atlanta, Ga., reported on Nov. 30, 1990, that 157,525 AIDS cases and 98,530 AIDS deaths had occurred in the United States since 1981, when the centers began keeping records. The CDC estimated that AIDS deaths could total 340,000 by 1993.

Lymphoma threat. The National Cancer Institute (NCI) in Bethesda, Md., on Aug. 15, 1990, reported that AIDS patients receiving the drug AZT (zidovudine) face a nearly 50 per cent chance of developing lymphoma after three years of drug treatment. AZT is the only drug licensed by the Food and Drug Administration (FDA) to treat AIDS patients, and lymphoma is a cancer of the lymphatic system. The NCI scientists could not determine whether the increased cancer risk resulted from AZT, from other drugs given to AIDS patients, or from other causes. They speculated that lymphoma occurs because AIDS patients are simply

Protesters unhappy with the pace of AIDS research and limited access to new drugs march in San Francisco during an AIDS conference in June.

Air pollution

living longer, and their weakened immune systems cannot prevent the development of cancer.

Vaccine progress. In June, scientists from 85 countries met at the Sixth International Conference on AIDS in San Francisco. About 30 AIDS vaccines were reported to be in various stages of development. Some of the vaccines are intended to protect uninfected people from the AIDS virus, and others would slow or prevent progression of the disease.

Pediatric AIDS treatment. On May 3, the FDA approved the use of AZT for children between the ages of 3 months and 12 years who show signs of impaired immune systems. AZT was approved in 1987 for patients aged 13 years and over.

New therapy. Researchers on Aug. 15, 1990, reported that an experimental therapy, *photopheresis*, appears to inactivate the AIDS virus and stimulate the patient's immune system. Each patient was given a drug called *8-methoxypsoralen;* two hours later, 1 pint (0.47 liter) of the patient's blood was removed, and the red and white cells were separated. The red cells were returned to the body. The white cells were exposed to ultraviolet light, then returned to the body in a four-hour procedure. Patients were given therapy for from 6 to 15 months.   Michael Woods

In *World Book,* see **AIDS.**

Air pollution. See **Environmental pollution.**

Alabama. See **State government.**

Alaska. See **State government.**

Albania departed in 1990 from the isolationism it has practiced since the Communists gained control near the end of World War II (1939-1945). It also moved away from the rigid Communist orthodoxy it has followed at home. The shifts indicated that the collapse of Communist governments in eastern Europe in 1989 had an impact on the regime of Ramiz Alia. In January 1990, Alia announced that eastern Europe's rejection of Communism would not be repeated in Albania. But the European political equilibrium had been altered, he added, and Albania must adapt.

In international relations, Albania said in April that it wished to renew diplomatic ties with the United States and the Soviet Union. The United States had broken relations with Albania after its occupation by Italy in 1939. Albania had severed ties with the Soviet Union in 1961 because of disagreements over Communist ideology. On July 30, 1990, Albania and the Soviet Union restored relations. The United States was expected to restore ties with Albania in 1991.

On June 6, 1990, Albania became an observer at the Conference on Security and Cooperation in Europe (CSCE), an organization that consists of nearly all European countries, the United States, and Canada. Albania pressed for full membership in the CSCE and was expected to receive it.

In a further move to develop international ties, Alia attended a session of the United Nations General Assembly in New York City—something his predecessor,

Albanian refugees cheer as their boat—which carries 3,915 men, women, and children seeking haven—arrives in Brindisi, Italy, on July 13.

Enver Hoxha, had not done in 41 years of rule. Alia addressed the General Assembly on September 28.

Albania also sought closer ties with the European Community (EC or Common Market). It already had trade agreements with 11 of the 12 EC members but showed increasing anxiety about being left out of the single market scheduled for western Europe in 1992.

A "new economic mechanism" introduced in 1990 freed state-owned industries from many central controls, making them largely self-managing and self-financing. The government also initiated bonuses for higher productivity, hikes in minimum wages, and un-employment benefits. In an effort to ease shortages of consumer goods, the government licensed small-scale private businesses and workshops. Self-management was also extended to Albania's collective farms. The government offered peasants more land of their own and distributed state-owned livestock.

A new penal code was adopted by the Albanian legislature on May 8. The code reduced outlawed "antistate activity" to acts specifically intended to overthrow the government. It excluded so-called "religious propaganda" from that category, leaving religious belief to "individual conscience." The turnabout was notable for a country that in 1967 had proclaimed itself the world's first atheistic state and had ruthlessly surpressed religious activity thereafter.

The new penal code also abolished domestic exile, a form of punishment in which thousands of suspected "troublemakers" had been sent to forced labor in remote areas. In addition, the code reduced fleeing the country from a severely punishable crime to a border violation. Albanians were guaranteed the freedom to travel and hold passports. The government restored the Ministry of Justice, which had been abolished in the 1960's; instituted safeguards for those accused of crimes; and created a legal bar of qualified, independent lawyers.

In spite of the reforms, thousands of Albanians jammed Western embassies in Tiranë, Albania's capital, in July seeking to escape the impoverished country. The Albanian government let them emigrate.

To speed the pace of reform, Alia in November called for changes in the Constitution that would curb the power of Albania's Communist Party of Labor and open the way for secret, multicandidate ballots in parliamentary elections scheduled for February 1991.

On Dec. 11, 1990, Communist leaders said they would permit formation of non-Communist political parties. Students and others promptly announced formation of the Democratic Party of Albania, the first opposition party in 45 years of Communist rule. Hard-line opposition to the reforms continued behind the scenes. But the reforms received popular approval. Alia consolidated his leadership by replacing "old guard" members of the Politburo with younger officials close to his own thinking.   Eric Bourne

See also **Europe** (Facts in brief table). In **World Book,** see **Albania.**

Britain's Queen Elizabeth II, also Canada's head of state, carries armloads of flowers after visiting a Red Deer, Alta., hospital in June.

Alberta. The Progressive Conservative government headed by Premier Donald R. Getty decided in 1990 to sell 60 per cent of province-owned Alberta Government Telephones, valued at $3 billion Canadian ($2.6-billion U.S.). An announcement on August 8 indicated that shares at a price of $12 to $13 Canadian ($10 to $11 U.S.) would be offered first to residents of the province. The sale is intended to enable the company to meet competition at home caused by changes in federal telecommunications policy and to pursue wider markets beyond the province.

Environment. Construction of a mammoth $1.3-billion ($1.1-billion U.S.) pulp mill on the Athabasca River in northern Alberta was approved by the provincial government in late December, following a report by an environmental review board. Environmental groups had opposed the project, calling for more scientific studies of the mill's effect on pollution levels in the river before Japanese interests sponsoring the project would be permitted to proceed.

Senate appointment. Alberta became the first province to nominate a federal senator chosen by voters. Prime Minister Brian Mulroney named Stanley Waters, who had won a special election, to the Senate on June 11 to fill an Alberta vacancy. In the absence of constitutional change making the Senate elective, Mulroney asked provinces to wait five years before holding further Senate elections.   David M. L. Farr

See also **Canada.** In **World Book,** see **Alberta.**

Muslim fundamentalists march in Algiers in April to protest gains in women's rights made by Algerian women since the 1960's.

Algeria. Algeria's economic picture remained bleak in 1990, despite attempts by President Chadli Bendjedid and the ruling National Liberation Front (FLN) party to institute economic reforms. Bendjedid began the reform process in 1988 after riots broke out, triggered by high food prices and other hardships resulting from Algeria's deteriorating economy.

In 1990, a population growth rate of about 3 per cent canceled gains from a 2.8 per cent rise in Algeria's *gross national product* (GNP), the value of all goods and services produced. By mid-1990, unemployment averaged 24 per cent and inflation had reached 14 per cent. Production stagnated and a black market flourished. Foreign trade remained static, so the government made little headway in reducing Algeria's $27-billion foreign debt. In addition, a housing scarcity worsened, and labor strikes occurred with greater frequency and intensity among professional groups, notably teachers.

The government responded by enacting measures designed to encourage joint ventures between Algerian and foreign firms and to increase foreign investment, especially in Algeria's rich natural gas reserves. The government also cut its own spending. New laws improved workers' rights by allowing them to form unions and engage in collective bargaining.

Elections. Partly in response to domestic pressures, the government on June 12 held its first free, multiparty elections since Algeria won its independence

from France in 1962. About 20 new political parties had formed by mid-1990. To the dismay of the government and many Algerians, numerous acts of political extremism occurred in the weeks before the local elections. Two major opposition parties boycotted the elections. They argued that the government's control of nearly all media and the use of FLN members to count the votes rigged the elections in favor of the ruling party.

The elections had surprising results. The fundamentalist Islamic Salvation Front (FIS) won control of 32 of Algeria's 48 regional assemblies and 853 of the 1,541 municipal councils. The FIS made an especially strong showing in Algiers, Algeria's capital, and other large urban areas. By contrast, the FLN was victorious in only 14 regional assemblies and 487 municipal councils. Smaller parties and independent candidates won control of the remaining assemblies and councils.

The success of fundamentalist candidates shocked many Algerians, who feared that the FIS would seek to establish Islamic law as the country's legal code. Many women, in particular, feared that Islamic laws would restrict their personal freedom. The election results also prompted some FLN members to call for reforms that would broaden the party's appeal, reduce government corruption, and increase government efficiency.   Christine Helms

See also **Middle East** (Facts in brief table). In *World Book,* see **Algeria.**

Angola. Efforts to end the 15-year-old civil war in Angola failed again in 1990. The military involvement of Cuba and South Africa was reduced as a result of a 1988 peace accord sponsored by the United States. Fighting continued, however, between the governing Popular Movement for the Liberation of Angola (MPLA) and the rebel National Union for the Total Independence of Angola (UNITA).

Eight African countries in January renewed an earlier offer to mediate a cease-fire, but Angola's President José Eduardo dos Santos rejected their proposal because it was linked to a UNITA demand for a multiparty political system. Dos Santos made a counteroffer: UNITA candidates could run in future elections as independents, if their leader, Jonas Savimbi, went into exile and UNITA troops joined the MPLA-controlled army.

Negotiations were delayed by each side's hope of gaining a decisive military advantage. Early in the year, UNITA increased its attacks on cities, railroads, and other facilities in areas held by the MPLA. Meanwhile, government troops continued a major offensive—begun in December 1989—against the UNITA stronghold of Mavinga in southeast Angola. In March, the MPLA forces claimed victory. But by mid-June, a combination of factors, including bad weather and the airlifting of U.S. military equipment to UNITA from Zaire, had turned the tide. With casualties mounting, the MPLA forces had to retreat.

Anticipating defeat in the Mavinga campaign, the MPLA in April accepted a mediation offer from Portugal, and on July 3 it agreed to abandon Angola's single-party political system. Several rounds of talks in Africa and Portugal brought no further progress, however. A breakthrough came on October 1 when the United States and the Soviet Union offered to police a cease-fire in Angola and monitor free elections. On December 13, Savimbi said that talks in Washington, D.C., had resulted in a tentative peace agreement between UNITA and the dos Santos regime.

The economy. The U.S.-Soviet action was hastened by reports that a major famine threatened Angola as a result of the war and two years of drought. The impending crisis was worsened in April by the dos Santos regime's refusal to permit food and medical supplies to be shipped to rebel areas. In July, yielding to foreign pressure, the MPLA relented and allowed United Nations relief efforts to begin.

The civil war has limited Angola's ability to exploit its vast mineral wealth. Oil was one exception in 1990, with the petroleum-rich Cabinda area bringing in more than $2 billion in revenues.

In accord with the decline of Communist regimes in much of the world, dos Santos said in March that his government was breaking away from Marxism.   J. Gus Liebenow and Beverly B. Liebenow

See also **Africa** (Facts in brief table). In *World Book,* see **Africa.**

Animal. See Cat; Conservation; Dog; Zoology; Zoos.

Anthropology. A fossil skull found in Greece and believed to be from 9 million to 10 million years old may be the oldest known hominid skull. That conclusion was reported in June 1990 by a team led by paleontologist Louis de Bonis of the University of Poitiers in France. (Hominids are modern human beings and their closest human and prehuman ancestors.)

The skull belongs to a species of apelike creatures called *Ouranopithecus macedoniensis,* known previously only from some teeth and part of a jaw. The newly discovered fossil includes much of the face, part of the skull, and almost all of the upper jaw. According to de Bonis, *Ouranopithecus'* teeth are similar in size and shape to those of *Australopithecus afarensis,* the earliest undisputed hominid species. The *A. afarensis* species, which lived about 3.5 million years ago in Africa, includes the fossil skeleton known as "Lucy."

Other anthropologists cast doubt on de Bonis' arguments, however. They argued that *Ouranopithecus'* upper face is similar to the faces of other ancient apes believed to be ancestors of orangutans. They also noted that dental features common to *Ouranopithecus* and *A. afarensis* are found in other ancient ape species not directly linked to hominids.

Scanning a fossil skull. An analysis of the fossilized remains of veins on the inner surface of an *Australopithecus africanus* skull has revealed new evidence supporting the theory that this hominid species was a direct human ancestor. The evidence was published in February by a team of scientists led by physical anthropologist Glenn C. Conroy of Washington University Medical School in St. Louis, Mo.

A. africanus, a delicately built apelike creature, lived from about 2 million to 3 million years ago. Most anthropologists believe this species was at least a close prehuman relative. But the scarcity of *A. africanus* fossils—only six reasonably complete skulls have been found—has made it difficult for scientists to establish a direct link with human beings.

To see inside the skull, which was clogged with stone, the scientists used an imaging technique called computerized tomographic (CT) scanning. The scans produced two- and three-dimensional images of the inner surface of the skull. Clearly visible in the images was a network of channels representing veins that had once drained blood from the brain. The scientists reported that the pattern of the channels is similar to that in modern human brains. Conroy suggested that the similarities in the patterns lend weight to the argument that *A. africanus* gave rise to larger-brained human beings.

Previous research had revealed a somewhat different pattern of veins in the skull of Lucy. This finding led some scientists to conclude that *A. afarensis* was not a direct human ancestor. Both patterns occur in modern human beings, however. As a result, some scientists advised caution in using venous drainage patterns to establish links between ancient hominid species and modern human beings

Anthropology

Gary Larson, "The Far Side"; reprinted by permission of Chronicle Features, San Francisco

"Yes, with the amazing new 'knife,' you only have to wear the SKIN of those dead animals."

Ancient diets. Microscopic stony particles found in some plants may help scientists determine what extinct animals, including ancient hominids, ate. That conclusion was reported in October by a team of scientists headed by anthropologist Russell L. Ciochon of the University of Iowa in Iowa City.

The stony particles, called *phytoliths*, are pieces of silica that form in and between plant cells from dissolved silica in water taken up by roots. When an animal eats a plant, some phytoliths become bonded to its teeth. Because phytoliths differ from species to species, they can serve as "fingerprints" to help scientists identify which plants an animal has eaten.

Ciochon and his colleagues used phytoliths to study the diet of *Gigantopithecus*, an extinct giant ape that lived in China and Southeast Asia several hundred thousand years ago. Scientists had assumed that the giant ape ate mainly bamboo, which is plentiful in that region. But when they examined four *Gigantopithecus* teeth using an advanced microscope called a scanning electron microscope, they found phytoliths from fruits and seeds as well as those from bamboo.

The scientists planned next to study teeth from ancient hominids to determine their diet. Such information may help scientists determine if diet played a role in the success of some types of hominids and the extinction of others.   Donald C. Johanson

In *World Book,* see **Anthropology; Prehistoric people.**

Archaeology. Native American tribes will be able to reclaim human remains and burial objects held by museums and other institutions under a law signed by United States President George Bush on Nov. 16, 1990. The measure is expected to end years of often-bitter debate over the ownership and fate of institutions' Indian collections.

The law requires all museums and other institutions receiving federal money to inventory their collections of Native American remains and burial objects. The museums must notify Indian tribes of any remains or burial objects linked to individual tribes, which may then take steps to reclaim the items.

Under the law, museums must also provide Indian tribes with general information about Indian artifacts other than burial objects in their possession. To reclaim these items, Indian tribes would have to establish that a museum was not the rightful owner. For example, they would have to prove that the objects had not been acquired in a legal sale.

Chinese tomb. A road crew working in central China near the city of Xi'an in March discovered a vast network of ancient underground vaults containing tens of thousands of terra-cotta sculptures. The 2,100-year-old vaults, which extend over an area about the size of 10 football fields, apparently are part of an imperial burial site.

The deceased emperor may be Jingdi, an emperor of the Han dynasty, who ruled from 157 to 141 B.C. The Han dynasty, which lasted from 202 B.C. to A.D. 220, represents one of the greatest eras in Chinese history. During this period, the Chinese invented porcelain. Art, education, and science also thrived during the Han dynasty.

The excavation at the newly discovered imperial tomb is the first modern exploration of a Han dynasty burial site. The finds at the Han tomb may surpass those made in 1974 at the tomb of Shi Huangdi, the first Qin dynasty emperor, about 25 miles (40 kilometers) away. At the Qin burial site, which is about 70 years older than the Han tomb, archaeologists found about 10,000 life-sized terra-cotta statues of warriors and horses.

Many details of the new discovery are unknown, because at year-end the Chinese government had released little information to foreign news media. According to reports in Chinese publications, however, the newly discovered terra-cotta statues depict men, boys, horses, and carts. The human figures, which have individualized facial features and expressions, are about 2 feet (60 centimeters) tall and are armless and painted red.

The tomb itself consists of a complex of at least 24 vaults, each about 13 feet (4 meters) wide and from 82 to 950 feet (25 to 290 meters) long. Not all the vaults contain male statues. Some vaults have only terra-cotta figures of carts and horses, while other chambers are empty, apparently plundered by grave robbers.

A 4,000-year-old statue of a dwarf, who was probably the companion of an ancient Egyptian king, was found with the dwarf's bones in 1990 in Egypt.

"Golden calf." A tiny 3,500-year-old statue of a calf found in June 1990 in Israel is the first known example of the religious images whose worship was denounced by the early Israelites. The figurine was discovered by a team of archaeologists from Harvard University in Cambridge, Mass., in the ruins of a Canaanite temple near the ancient port of Ashkelon. The temple that housed the statue was destroyed when the ancient Egyptians conquered Ashkelon in about 1550 B.C.

For at least 1,000 years, the golden calf was the central object of worship among the Canaanites, who were the chief inhabitants of ancient Palestine from about 3000 to 1200 B.C. Many archaeologists believe the early Israelites were Canaanites who established their own religious sect. A number of verses in the Bible condemn the worship of the calves, which were sometimes used to represent the Canaanite god Baal.

The calf figurine, which was found almost completely intact, is about 4¼ inches (11 centimeters) tall and about 4½ inches (11.4 centimeters) long. The body of the statue is made of bronze. The legs, head, horns, tail, and other parts of the statue, which were attached to the body in sockets, are made of other metals.

First riders. Human beings may have learned to ride horses about 6,000 years ago, 2,000 years earlier than archaeologists had believed, according to research reported in July. The finding, by archaeologists David W. Anthony and Dorcas R. Brown of Hartwick

167

Archaeology

A 3,500-year-old Canaanite statue, found in June in Israel, is the first known example of a "golden calf" whose worship was condemned by early Israelites.

College in Oneonta, N.Y., challenges the belief that the invention of the wheel was the first important development in human land transportation. The scientists argue that their research suggests that horseback riding predated the appearance of the wheel by about 500 years.

Archaeologists have long believed that horseback riding originated about 4,000 years ago in central Asia. This conclusion was based on figurines of riders on horses and of horse-drawn chariots discovered at sites dated to this period. Anthony and Brown, however, contend that horseback riding appeared first among a hunting people known as the Sredni Stog, who lived about 6,000 years ago in what is now the Ukraine, a region in the southeastern Soviet Union.

The archaeologists based their conclusions on their analysis of two cheek teeth from the skeleton of a horse discovered at a Sredni Stog site about 120 miles (190 kilometers) south of Kiev. The site has been dated to about 4000 B.C. An examination of the horse's teeth made with a scanning electron microscope, which uses electrons to illuminate specimens, revealed tiny scratch marks identical to those found on the cheek teeth of modern horses ridden with a metal bit. (A bit is the part of a bridle that goes into a horse's mouth. As a horse is ridden, the bit rubs against the cheek teeth.)   Barbara Voorhies

In *World Book,* see **Archaeology; Canaanites; Han dynasty; Shi Huangdi.**

Architecture grew increasingly international in scope in 1990. More than ever, American architects were designing buildings to be built in other countries. At the same time, architects from other places, especially Europe, were working in the United States.

A good example of such internationalism was the Walt Disney Company, which emerged in 1990 as perhaps the world's most important employer of major architects. The company was building a new theme park called Euro Disneyland in the Paris suburb of Marne-la-Vallée. Scheduled to open in 1992, Euro Disneyland will feature buildings by many of the most famous American architects, including Frank O. Gehry of Santa Monica, Calif.; Michael Graves of Princeton, N.J.; Antoine Predock of Albuquerque, N. Mex.; and Robert A. M. Stern of New York City. Graves also designed two fanciful new hotels, the Dolphin and the Swan, at Walt Disney World near Orlando, Fla.

The Osaka Aquarium, the world's largest aquarium, opened in Osaka, Japan, in July 1990. Designed by the Massachusetts firm Cambridge Seven Associates, the aquarium contains 2.9 million gallons (11 million liters) of water and 16,000 fish. And in Hong Kong came the completion of the spectacular 1,209-foot-tall (369-meter-tall) Bank of China by the Chinese-born American architect I. M. Pei.

Meanwhile, in the United States, the Museum of Modern Art in San Francisco in September unveiled a design for its new home by the Swiss architect Mario Botta. Construction of the $85-million museum was scheduled to begin in 1992. Italian architect Aldo Rossi, winner of the 1990 Pritzker Architecture Prize, designed a new school of architecture at the University of Miami in Coral Gables, Fla. The building was under construction in 1990.

The city of Paris continued to hold the architectural spotlight in 1990. Attention focused on Paris not only for Euro Disneyland but also for the so-called *Grands Projets* (Big Developments) that are being completed in that city, one after another, under the leadership of French President François Mitterrand. Opening in March 1990 was the Opéra de la Bastille, a new opera house in the Place de la Bastille, the former site of a hated prison. The opera house, designed by Uruguayan-born Canadian architect Carlos Ott, received generally bad reviews for its jumble of modern architectural elements.

Other notable buildings of 1990 included:
- Las Vegas Library/Discovery Museum, a branch library and children's museum in Las Vegas, Nev., by Predock.
- The 47-story corporate headquarters of the investment banking firm J. P. Morgan & Company in New York City, designed by Kevin Roche of that city.
- Carnegie Hall Tower, a 60-story skyscraper that also contains extra rehearsal rooms and backstage space for Carnegie Hall, the historic New York City concert hall. The tower was created by Cesar Pelli, an Argentine-born architect based in New Haven, Conn.

Light glows through the glass and steel walls of the Opéra de la Bastille in Paris, designed by Uruguayan-born Canadian architect Carlos Ott.

Historic preservation was in the news with the remarkable restoration of the main building of Ellis Island, a former U.S. immigration center in New York Harbor. Once the gateway to the New World for millions of immigrants, Ellis Island reopened in September as a national museum of immigration after a six-year renovation. Architects of the restoration were Beyer Blinder Belle of New York City and Notter Fine-gold + Alexander of Boston. In the Special Reports section, see **Ellis Island, Museum of Memories.**

Two houses by Frank Lloyd Wright, perhaps the most famous American architect, were restored and opened to the public: the Dana-Thomas House in Springfield, Ill., and the Zimmerman House in Manchester, N.H. In August, it was announced that a Taliesin Preservation Commission had been formed to preserve Wright's own home, Taliesin, near Spring Green, Wis. Taliesin is regarded as one of the greatest American buildings.

A preservation controversy during the year involved a proposed addition to Wright's Marin County Civic Center in California, which critics said would obscure views of the center's original buildings. After similar criticism, museum officials in February abandoned a plan to add new wings to Louis I. Kahn's Kimbell Art Museum (1972) in Fort Worth, Tex.

St. Bartholomew's Church, an Episcopal church in New York City, lost yet another round in a long struggle with the New York City Landmarks Preservation Commission. The commission has repeatedly refused to allow the church, which is designated a landmark, to replace its chapter house with a new office tower. The church argues that it needs the income from the proposed tower to help the needy and that landmark status interferes with its freedom of religion and its property rights. In September 1990, a federal Court of Appeals upheld the landmark designation of St. Bartholomew's. Lawyers for the church said they would take the case to the Supreme Court of the United States.

Architectural exhibitions included "The Art Museums of Louis I. Kahn" at the Yale University Art Gallery in New Haven, Conn.; "Frank Lloyd Wright Drawings: Masterworks from the Frank Lloyd Wright Archives" at the Phoenix Art Museum in Arizona; and "Sir Christopher Wren and the Legacy of St. Paul's Cathedral" at the American Institute of Architects in Washington, D.C. The Walker Art Center in Minneapolis, Minn., organized "Architecture Tomorrow: Domestic Arrangements," an exhibition of the work of New York City architects Tod Williams and Billie Tsien. After appearing at the Walker, the show traveled to the Whitney Museum of American Art in New York City, the Cleveland Center for Art, and the Wexner Center for the Visual Arts in Columbus, Ohio. It was scheduled to appear in 1991 at the Power Plant in Toronto, Canada.   Robert Campbell

In *World Book,* see **Architecture.**

Argentina

Argentina. For Argentine President Carlos Saúl Menem, 1990 was a year of unrelieved economic crisis, showdowns with his labor supporters, and trouble with his wife. The last caused him both political and domestic grief.

In seeking to reestablish Argentina's creditworthiness, Finance Minister Antonio Ermám Gonzáles unveiled an austerity program on March 4. It called for the shut-down of a state-owned bank and the elimination of 88 government departments, as well as increased export duties on Argentina's products.

Word of the unpopular measures leaked out in advance, causing the country's new currency, the austral, to lose more than two-thirds of its value. On March 5, an angry crowd of 2,500 workers occupied the bank targeted for the shut-down.

By June, Menem was comparing his situation to that of Soviet President Mikhail S. Gorbachev. Like Gorbachev, Menem said he was attempting to force the turnaround of an economy beset by excessive government spending, a bloated bureaucracy, and mismanagement—made worse in Argentina's case by declining world markets for its farm products.

State-run firms. Menem announced on July 1 that Argentina's national airline would be sold to a consortium led by Iberia Air Lines of Spain. Argentina's telephone company was sold on November 8 to a French-Italian firm and Telefónica of Spain.

The sale of state-run firms was opposed by Argentina's powerful labor union confederation, which had supported Menem in his campaign for the presidency. Menem was the candidate of the Justicialist Party, long identified as the champion of blue-collar workers. Labor's disenchantment with Menem was so deep that he was forced to curry favor with the nation's armed forces to maintain himself in power. In October and December, Menem pardoned officers—including two heads of previous military juntas—who were serving long prison terms for human-rights abuses. On December 3, two days before a visit by United States President George Bush, a revolt by dissidents in the army was harshly suppressed by officers loyal to Menem.

Mansion ban. On June 12, Menem barred his wife of 23 years, Zulema Yoma de Menem, from entering the presidential mansion. It was the latest chapter in a stormy marriage that included several separations. Ever since Menem took office in 1989, his wife publicly opposed his free-market reforms. She also began meeting with his political opponents.

Following a trip to Italy later in June, which included stops in Tahiti and elsewhere, Menem's critics charged that he had taken the trip "to mend a broken heart." They demanded that he repay the trip's cost of $217,750.   Nathan A. Haverstock

See also **Latin America** (Facts in brief table). In *World Book,* see **Argentina.**

Arizona. See **State government.**

Arkansas. See **State government.**

Armed forces. In August 1990, the United States undertook its most massive deployment of military forces since the Vietnam War. The deployment, dubbed Operation Desert Shield, was a response to Iraq's invasion of Kuwait on August 2 and Iraqi troop movement toward Saudi Arabia on August 3.

Operation Desert Shield began on August 7 as a purely defensive measure to protect Saudi Arabia. Like Kuwait, Saudi Arabia is an oil-rich nation whose petroleum exports are important to the economic well-being of the United States and other nations. When announcing the deployment of warplanes and several thousand troops to Saudi Arabia, President George Bush likened Iraq's aggression to the acts of Nazi Germany at the start of World War II.

By late August, the United States had sent troops from every branch of its military to the Persian Gulf region. The Navy deployed dozens of ships in four battle groups, with the Marines sending three expeditionary brigades and one expeditionary force. Army deployments included four divisions, and the Air Force sent three tactical fighter wings, including hundreds of bombers and fighters. To add to the build-up, Bush on August 22 ordered the mobilization of military reserve units. Most were involved in important combat-support functions such as cargo handling, water purification, and communications.

United States ships also spearheaded an international naval blockade to enforce United Nations (UN) sanctions halting Iraqi imports and oil exports (see **United Nations**). The blockade was designed to cripple Iraq economically in the hope of forcing Iraqi President Saddam Hussein to withdraw from Kuwait.

When Iraq refused to withdraw from Kuwait, the U.S. military expanded its contingency plans to include a possible invasion of Kuwait and air strikes against Iraq. As if to underscore the threat of hostilities, in September the Pentagon authorized "imminent-danger pay" for military personnel involved in the operation.

On September 17, Secretary of Defense Richard B. Cheney dismissed Air Force Chief of Staff General Michael J. Dugan after the general commented publicly on the military's contingency plans for air warfare in Iraq. Dugan had said that in the event of hostilities, Air Force bombers might target Baghdad in an attempt to kill Hussein and his associates.

In November, the Pentagon obtained authorization to call to active duty more than 125,000 reservists and members of the National Guard. During the month, the government began sending 150,000 U.S. troops to join the 230,000 U.S. troops already in place. The new deployment included three Army divisions, one Marine division, four Navy battle groups, and several Air Force units.

Joining the Americans in the Middle East were about 220,000 troops from more than 20 allied nations. They faced an estimated 680,000 Iraqi troops massed in Kuwait and southern Iraq.

On November 29, the UN Security Council authorized the use of force against Iraq unless Iraq withdrew from Kuwait by Jan. 15, 1991. On January 17, the United States and its allies launched an air strike against Iraq and Iraqi-held Kuwait. See **Middle East.**

Liberian evacuation. On Aug. 5, 1990, after a rebel leader in Liberia's civil war threatened to begin arresting foreigners, 230 marines in 11 transport helicopters flew into Liberia to evacuate American citizens. More than 100 American diplomats, their dependents, and citizens of other nations were evacuated. Later in August, marines evacuated another 800 people, most of them Lebanese.

Panama pullout. The last U.S. forces sent to Panama in the December 1989 invasion of that country returned to the United States in February 1990. They left behind the 13,500 troops stationed in Panama before the United States invaded the nation to topple the military government of General Manuel Antonio Noriega. The U.S. General Accounting Office estimated that the invasion cost $163.6 million.

Drug wars. The U.S. military continued to expand its involvement in the effort to reduce the flow of drugs into the United States. The Pentagon stepped up its technical assistance to Latin-American nations and assumed a larger role in the detection and prevention of drug trafficking along U.S. borders. But in January the Bush Administration hastily scrapped plans to station an aircraft carrier task force off the Colombian coast to monitor drug traffic. The plan met strong resistance from the government of Colombia, which considered it a threat to national sovereignty.

Defense scaled back. In an August speech, Bush pledged to continue modernizing strategic weapons programs as insurance against future regional conflicts. But because relations between the United States and the Soviet Union had significantly improved, the Bush Administration began preparing a major restructuring and reduction of U.S. military forces. Bush announced that the reduced Soviet threat would allow a 25 per cent cut in U.S. military strength by 1995.

Bush proposed slashing American troop strength by approximately 500,000, which would reduce the number of active forces to the lowest level since 1950. The reductions would allow cutting the Pentagon budget by 10 per cent over five years, resulting in savings of more than $100 billion.

Some members of Congress argued that even greater military cuts could be made without jeopardizing national security. But Pentagon officials warned that the crisis in the Persian Gulf required a reassessment of plans to reduce American military force and might result in fewer cuts than planned.

Arms control. The warming relations between the United States and the Soviet Union led to additional progress toward reducing strategic nuclear and conventional arsenals. In Washington, D.C., on June 1, Bush and Soviet President Mikhail S. Gorbachev signed a framework agreement for a strategic arms reduction

Operation Desert Shield begins in August as United States troops arrive in Saudi Arabia to repel a possible invasion by neighboring Iraq.

treaty (START). A precursor to a formal START treaty was expected to be completed in 1991. The agreement would limit each country to 1,600 strategic delivery vehicles—ballistic missiles or bombers—and a total of 6,000 warheads.

The negotiations failed to reach both leaders' goal of reducing total nuclear strength by 50 per cent, however, so Bush and Gorbachev agreed to begin a new round of talks "at the earliest practical date" to reach another START treaty. They also pledged to press for an early accord on the use of weapons in space and on the existing antiballistic missile treaty, a stumbling block to resolving differences over the U.S. program to develop a space-based missile defense system, the Strategic Defense Initiative (SDI).

In a companion agreement, the superpowers pledged to eliminate chemical weapons. Each side agreed to stop producing chemical arms immediately and begin destroying such weapons by 1992, according to an established timetable. The nations' last chemical weapons would be destroyed within two years after the signing of an international treaty sought by the United States to ban chemical weapons worldwide.

The United States and the Soviet Union—after several years of negotiations in Vienna, Austria—also agreed to significant reductions in the number of troops stationed in Europe. On November 19 in Paris, during the Conference on Security and Cooperation in

Armed forces

Trucks carry poison gas shells from American stock-piles in West Germany in July, as the United States begins destroying some of its chemical weapons.

Europe, Bush, Gorbachev, and leaders of 20 other nations signed a treaty hailed as the most important arms control agreement in history. Under the terms of the accord, the United States and the Soviet Union will each limit their forces in Europe to 195,000 troops. Each side also agreed to limits on its conventional weapons—13,300 main battle tanks, 20,000 armored personnel carriers, 13,700 artillery pieces, and 6,650 combat aircraft and helicopters.

Strategic weapons. Despite progress at the negotiating table, the Pentagon continued to work on a variety of strategic weapons systems. Development and testing proceeded on the MX land-based intercontinental missile, the Midgetman single-warhead mobile missile, the Trident II submarine-launched missile, the B-2 bomber, the ASAT system for destroying enemy satellites in outer space, and submarine-launched nuclear cruise missiles.

Research and development also continued on the SDI, a program designed to destroy enemy nuclear missiles in space. But critics in Congress and the scientific community insisted that the program was technologically dubious and prohibitively expensive.

Technical problems also continued to dog the B-1B strategic bomber. Air Force officials informed Congress in September that the bomber's device to detect enemy missiles did not work at low altitudes. Engine failures on two planes caused the entire fleet to be grounded on December 20.

Congress also pressured the Pentagon to scale back the scope of the B-2 bomber program because of escalating costs—estimated at well over $500 million per aircraft. In April, Cheney reduced B-2 production in the 1991 fiscal year from 5 planes to 2 and cut the total program from 132 to 75 planes.

Conventional weapons. Development proceeded on several conventional weapons systems, including an advanced tactical fighter plane, an experimental jet fighter, a light helicopter, a nonnuclear cruise missile, the SSN-21 Seawolf-class attack submarine, and a new family of armored vehicles. The Navy's 15th aircraft carrier, the nuclear-powered *George Washington*, was christened in July. Also in July, the last of 59 F-117 Stealth fighters was delivered to the Air Force.

In late November, the secretary of the Navy relieved three top naval officers of their duties for misrepresenting the status of the A-12 attack jet program. Plans were 18 months behind schedule and at least $1-billion over budget. Defense Secretary Cheney canceled the A-12 on Jan. 7, 1991. The $57-billion A-12 was the largest U.S. arms program ever scrapped.

***Iowa* investigation reopened.** On May 24, 1990, the Navy reopened its investigation of an April 1989 explosion aboard the battleship *Iowa* that killed 47 sailors. Scientific tests had cast doubts on the conclusions of a review panel, who in September 1989 had proposed that Gunner's Mate Clayton M. Hartwig was "most likely" responsible for the tragedy. But the *Iowa*'s former commanding officer rejected the conclusion, and independent laboratory tests found that the explosion could have been an accident.

Defense budget. The Bush Administration formally submitted its budget proposal for the Department of Defense to Congress on Jan. 29, 1990. The Pentagon asked for $295.1 billion in spending authority, a decrease of $3.7 billion from the preceding year and a 2.6 per cent decrease after adjusting for inflation. The total request for defense, including the defense activities of other government agencies, was $306.9 billion.

The $288.3-billion defense authorization bill approved by Congress in October reflected an $18.6-billion decrease in budget authority from what the Pentagon had sought. The budget did not include the expenses of Operation Desert Shield.

Personnel. United States military troop strength stood at 2,047,378 on October 31, a decrease of 79,709 from the previous year. The Pentagon announced in June that by 1995 it would reduce the number of generals and admirals on active duty by 78. In July, the Army announced plans to close Reserve Officer Training Corps (ROTC) programs at 50 colleges and universities by the end of the academic year.

Following allegations of sexual harassment, hazing, and grade tampering at the U.S. Naval Academy in Annapolis, Md., the Navy and Congress ordered several investigations. The Senate Armed Services Committee recommended in July that the Pentagon make military ethics a required course at each of the nation's service academies. In a related development, a study released by the Pentagon in September found that two-thirds of women in the military had experienced some form of sexual harassment.

The role of women in combat became the focus of new debate in 1990. At issue was the use of women soldiers in the invasion of Panama and their deployment in the U.S. build-up in the Persian Gulf region. Representative Patricia Schroeder (D., Colo.) in January introduced legislation requiring the Army to allow women to serve in combat jobs under a four-year test program. The plan drew little support.

The Supreme Court of the United States in February upheld the military's policy barring homosexuals from service in the armed forces. But in May, the Army and Navy decided not to require three ROTC students to repay their college scholarships after they were denied commissions because they were homosexual.

Foreign bases. On July 8, U.S. and Greek officials signed a defense agreement permitting American forces to retain two bases in Greece until 1998. The future of U.S. bases in the Philippines remained in doubt, however, and U.S. officials predicted that a major American installation in the Philippines might have to be closed in order to extend U.S. base rights beyond 1991.   Thomas M. DeFrank

In *World Book,* see the articles on the branches of the armed forces.

Art. A battle over federal funding for the arts continued to rock the United States art community in 1990. At issue was the continued existence of the National Endowment for the Arts (NEA), which provides artists with federal grants. Every five years, Congress authorizes the NEA to continue operating as a federal agency. With its authorization due to expire on Sept. 30, 1990, the endowment found itself under attack.

The NEA's problems had begun in 1989, when some legislators and conservative activists sharply criticized the endowment for funding artists whose work some considered obscene. In October 1989, Congress passed legislation to prohibit the endowment from funding artwork that was obscene as defined by a 1973 decision of the Supreme Court of the United States.

The NEA scrambled to meet the challenges. In response to the October 1989 law, NEA director John E. Frohnmayer began requiring grant recipients to sign a so-called loyalty oath, a pledge not to use NEA funds in the creation of obscene works of art. Many artists considered the pledge a restriction of their freedom of expression. As a gesture of protest, Joseph Papp, director of the New York Shakespeare Festival, in April 1990 refused to accept a $50,000 NEA grant awarded to his institution for the presentation of a Hispanic cultural festival. The action sparked a series of similar refusals from other grant recipients.

In May, the National Council on the Arts, a presidentially appointed group that advises the NEA, affirmed

Michelangelo's paintings in the Sistine Chapel in Rome glow with color after a 10-year project to clean and restore them is completed in March.

its support of the NEA's former policy—to make grants to artists without restricting the content of their work. At the same time, the council voted to deny two of three $40,000 grants recommended for the University of Pennsylvania's Institute of Contemporary Art. The vote was seen as a reprimand for the institute's role in organizing a controversial exhibition of photographs by Robert Mapplethorpe. The traveling exhibition, partially funded by the NEA, had provoked rancor in Congress because of the sexual content of a few of the photographs.

At the recommendation of the National Council of the Arts, Frohnmayer in June vetoed grants to performance artists Karen Finley, John Fleck, Holly Hughes, and Tim Miller, all of whose work dealt with nudity or sexuality. In August, the council voted to delay decisions on five grants to cultural institutions—including two that would support Finley and Hughes—until after Congress dealt with the NEA's reauthorization. At the same meeting, the council voted to eliminate the loyalty oath for future grants and to reinstate funds withdrawn from the Institute of Contemporary Art.

Politicians wrestled with the reauthorization issue throughout the year. The matter pitted some conservative legislators against President George Bush, who on March 23 said he opposed restrictions on the content of art funded by the NEA.

In September, a commission set up by President Bush to investigate the grant-making procedures of

both the NEA and the National Endowment for the Humanities issued its recommendation. Although the commission came out against new restrictions on the content of works supported by the endowments, it called for changes in the makeup of the peer-review panels that award the grants.

In October, Congress passed a bill reauthorizing the NEA for three years. The bill required that grants be made for work that is "sensitive to the general standards of decency." Some artists protested the bill, saying it was unduly restrictive.

Art in the courts. On October 5, an Ohio municipal court acquitted the Contemporary Arts Center in Cincinnati and its director, Dennis Barrie, of charges of obscenity in presenting the Mapplethorpe exhibition. NEA funds had not been used to pay for the showing.

On May 21, multimedia artist David Wojnarowicz filed a $5-million lawsuit against the American Family Association—a conservative activist group based in Tupelo, Miss.—and its director, Donald E. Wildmon. The artist charged the association with defamation of character, copyright infringement, and violation of a state law forbidding mutilation of an artist's work. In April, Wildmon's association had reproduced portions of Wojnarowicz' paintings in a mailing denouncing the NEA. In June, a federal district court awarded Wojnarowicz a symbolic $1 and ordered Wildmon to cease distribution of the mailing.

Auctions. The spring and fall art auctions indicated a cool-down in the overheated market for contemporary art. At the New York City auction houses Christie's and Sotheby's, several artworks failed to sell, though a few sales set record prices for their artists.

The most closely watched sale in May was the auction of Vincent van Gogh's *Portrait of Dr. Gachet* (1890). Offered at an estimate of $40 million to $50-million, the painting garnered the highest-ever auction price when it was sold for $82.5 million to Japanese businessman Ryoei Saito. Soon afterward, Saito paid the second-highest auction price for artwork, buying Pierre Auguste Renoir's *Au Moulin de la Galette* (1876) for $78.1 million.

The sale of the van Gogh painting—which had been on indefinite loan to the Museum of Modern Art in New York City before its owners put it up for auction—was seen as a poor omen for museums. Curators feared that reduced tax advantages for art donations and the record prices paid for classic works would make collectors less inclined to donate or loan artworks to museums.

Other sales. In March, the J. Paul Getty Museum in Los Angeles announced its purchase of van Gogh's *Irises* (1889) for an undisclosed price. In 1987, Australian businessman Alan Bond had purchased the painting for a record-breaking $53.9 million. Controversy dogged the purchase when Sotheby's, the auction house arranging the sale, revealed that it had financed Bond's purchase, using the painting as collateral. Bond could not pay off Sotheby's loan, and the

Vincent van Gogh's *Portrait of Dr. Gachet* sells for a record-breaking $82.5 million on May 15 at Christie's auction house in New York City.

auction house was criticized for its alleged role in helping inflate the painting's price. In January 1990, Sotheby's announced it would no longer finance purchases using artwork as collateral.

In April, Sotheby's and New York City art dealer William Acquavella announced their joint purchase of the contents of the Pierre Matisse Gallery in that city for $142.8 million. Through this move, Sotheby's entered the gallery scene.

On November 14, Acquavella purchased van Gogh's ink and pencil drawing *Garden of Flowers* (1888) for $8.4 million at auction at Christie's. It was the highest-ever auction price for a drawing.

Museum news. In February, New York City's Solomon R. Guggenheim Museum announced plans to purchase the artworks of Italian collector Giuseppe Panza di Biumo. Valued at between $24 million and $35 million, the Panza collection contained more than 200 paintings and sculptures from the 1960's and 1970's, most by American artists. To finance the acquisition, the Guggenheim sold three paintings from its modern collection. Meanwhile, the museum closed for expansion. Projected to be completed in 1991, the expansion plan included renovation of the existing building—designed by architect Frank Lloyd Wright—and the construction of a new building. The architect for the expansion was Charles Gwathmey.

At New York City's Whitney Museum of American Art, trustees in March 1990 voted to dismiss director Thomas N. Armstrong III. The trustees were reportedly dissatisfied with the museum's expansion plan and with Armstrong's direction of the museum's exhibition programs and its curatorial staff. The decision provoked sharp disapproval within the art community and led to the resignation of the museum's president, William S. Woodside, who was generally seen as the instigator of Armstrong's dismissal.

On March 18, an overnight theft from the Isabella Stewart Gardner Museum in Boston netted a dozen artworks, including paintings by Dutch artists Rembrandt and Jan Vermeer and French painters Edgar Degas and Edouard Manet. The value of the paintings—estimated at more than $200 million—made it one of the largest art thefts in history. Like many museums that cannot afford to pay insurance premiums, the Gardner Museum was not insured against theft.

French police on December 6 announced the recovery of nine impressionist paintings stolen in 1985 from the Marmottan Museum in Paris. The paintings, found in Corsica, included Claude Monet's *Impression, Sunrise* (1872), from which the impressionist movement got its name.

Exhibitions. Italy's prestigious Venice Biennale had its 44th showing from May 27 to October 1, with artists from some 30 nations represented. For the first time, the U.S. representative was a woman artist, Jenny Holzer. Holzer's striking electronic presentation of a collection of statements—such as "ABUSE OF

Demonstrators in Cincinnati protest the opening of an exhibition of Robert Mapplethorpe photographs at a local art center in April.

POWER COMES AS NO SURPRISE"—garnered the exhibition's much-coveted grand prize.

The eighth Sydney Biennale in Australia was on view from April 10 to June 3. The exhibition, called "The Readymade Boomerang: Certain Relations in 20th Century Art," included works by 140 artists from 30 countries.

"The New Sculpture 1965-75: Between Geometry and Gesture," organized by Whitney Museum curators Richard Armstrong and Richard Marshall, appeared from March 2 to June 3. The exhibition contained more than 90 works that traced the development of postminimalist sculpture from 1965 to 1975.

"Monet in the '90's: The Series Paintings" opened in February at the Boston Museum of Fine Arts before traveling to the Art Institute of Chicago and the Royal Academy of Arts in London. The exhibition presented nearly 100 series paintings created by Monet in the 1890's.

"High and Low: Modern Art and Popular Culture," Kirk Varnedoe's traveling exhibition highlighting the relationship of modern art and popular and commercial culture, opened at the Museum of Modern Art on October 7. Containing more than 250 works by some 50 artists, the exhibition presented modern works alongside pop-culture influences such as graffiti, comic strips, and advertising.   Eleanor Heartney

In *World Book*, see **Art and the arts; Painting; Sculpture.**

Asia

Holding candles in the dark, Hong Kong citizens gather on June 4 to mark the anniversary of China's 1989 Tiananmen Square massacre.

The rigid, often hostile relationships among Asia's nations began to change in 1990, as many of the countries improved their international ties. But old problems—such as the deluge of refugees from Vietnam—persisted, while a crisis in the Middle East caused new difficulties.

China improved relations with several neighbors. One was Vietnam, with which China has a 2,000-year history of hostility. But with Vietnam having officially withdrawn its army from Cambodia in 1989, Chinese and Vietnamese officials in 1990 engaged in several preliminary meetings. China's Premier Li Peng said on

October 1 that "China is ready gradually to improve its relations with Vietnam."

Indonesia had suspended diplomatic relations with China after accusing it of encouraging an unsuccessful effort by the Indonesian Communist Party to seize power in 1965. After preliminary talks, China's Premier Li visited Indonesia in August 1990, and the two nations signed an August 8 agreement to resume diplomatic relations.

In October, Indonesia's neighbor Singapore also established diplomatic relations with China. Singapore, which has an ethnic Chinese majority, had waited for

176

Japan's economic power also made it attractive to the Soviet Union, whose dealings with Japan had been limited by a dispute over the ownership of four islands in the Kuril Island chain. Japan had demanded that the Soviets return the islands, which the Soviet Union seized at the end of World War II (1939-1945). After Soviet officials suggested that they might discuss the islands, Japan announced that Gorbachev was scheduled to visit in April 1991.

Japan also took the lead among non-Communist economic powers in resuming loans to China. The powers had halted such loans after the Chinese government in June 1989 brutally crushed demonstrations in Beijing's Tiananmen Square.

Vietnam and the United States held their highest-level talks since the 1970's on Sept. 29, 1990. Vietnamese Foreign Minister Nguyen Co Thach and U.S. Secretary of State James A. Baker III in New York City discussed Vietnam's continuing support for the regime in Cambodia and efforts to account for Americans missing in action during the Vietnam War (1957-1975).

Outpouring of refugees. Another result of that war, the flight of refugees from Vietnam, troubled Southeast Asia throughout 1990. As of April 30, there were 107,800 Vietnamese "boat people" in refugee camps in nearby Asian countries, about half of them in Hong Kong. An additional 86,500 Vietnamese who had fled overland were encamped in Thailand.

Many of them were believed to be seeking better economic opportunities rather than fleeing political persecution. A number of countries, including the United States, helped finance the refugee camps and were willing to admit some political refugees. But the Asian countries that had granted the boat people first asylum were stuck with those Vietnamese considered economic refugees.

Both the United States and Vietnam opposed the forceable return to Vietnam of any of the refugees, who had typically spent their savings and risked their lives in their flight. But in June, Great Britain, which rules Hong Kong as a colony, along with Brunei, Indonesia, Malaysia, the Philippines, Singapore, and Thailand declared that they would feel free to force refugees to return to Vietnam unless the United States came up with a better plan.

Secretary of State Baker discussed the problem with Southeast Asian officials in Indonesia from July 27 to 29 but did not resolve it. Thailand and Malaysia tried to keep refugee boats from landing, pushing the problem on to Indonesia and Australia. Hong Kong kept its refugee population locked up, sometimes in defiance of its own courts. On September 21, Great Britain reached agreement with Vietnam and United Nations (UN) refugee officials to send home refugees who did not oppose repatriation.

Pakistan battled a politically less controversial refugee problem throughout 1990. As scattered warfare continued in Afghanistan, some 3 million Afghan ref-

decades to open formal diplomatic relations with China, though the two had trade dealings.

South Korea, with its booming economy, had become attractive as a trading partner for China and the Soviet Union despite their former support for South Korea's enemy, Communist North Korea. On June 4, Soviet President Mikhail S. Gorbachev met with South Korean President Roh Tae Woo in San Francisco. This, the first-ever meeting of top Soviet and South Korean leaders, led to the establishment of diplomatic relations on September 30. On October 20, China agreed to exchange unofficial trade offices with South Korea. Both the Soviets and the Chinese cooled their relations with North Korea, which in turn sought to improve ties to Japan.

Asia

ugees stayed in Pakistan. Only a few agreed to UN efforts to arrange their return home under conditions intended to ensure their safety.

Hong Kong fears. With Britain scheduled to relinquish control of Hong Kong to China in 1997, a record 62,000 people were expected to emigrate in 1990. Many were among the educated, skilled professionals needed to keep Hong Kong's highly sophisticated economy functioning. Some pregnant women left Hong Kong to give birth in foreign countries such as Canada, where the babies could acquire citizenship.

About one-fourth of the companies listed on the Stock Exchange of Hong Kong had by 1990 shifted their headquarters to other countries. The Tiananmen Square crackdown was blamed for Hong Kong's loss of business confidence and for a surge in sending investment money abroad.

The colony's authorities moved slowly toward giving Hong Kong its first elective government, and China tried to discourage such movement. China's 1984 promise to allow Hong Kong "a high degree of autonomy" after 1997 was thrown into doubt.

Singapore. Prime Minister Lee Kuan Yew—who had brought Singapore peace and prosperity since its independence in 1965—stepped down on Nov. 28, 1990. Lee voluntarily turned over the prime minister's post to Goh Chok Tong, his deputy, and became a senior minister in Goh's Cabinet. Goh named two deputy prime ministers of equal rank. One was Ong Teng Cheong, who had been Lee's second deputy. The other was Lee's 37-year-old son, Lee Hsien Loong, known as "B. G. Lee" because he had risen rapidly to the rank of brigadier general before leaving the army in 1984 for an equally fast-paced political career.

Before leaving office, Lee Kuan Yew had moved forcefully against any questioning of his rule. Several foreign publications were banned in 1990 because their reporting of Singapore affairs was officially termed interference.

Two Asian dictatorships were moderated in 1990. In Mongolia, the ruling Communist party allowed the first opposition parties to develop and in July held the country's first free elections. The Communist party won, but it began discussing policies with the opposition rather than just dictating them.

In Nepal, demonstrations in which scores of people were killed forced King Birendra Bir Bikram Shah Dev to yield to public pressure and give up absolute power. In November, he accepted a new Constitution providing for parliamentary democracy and guarantees of human rights.

Trouble loomed in Bhutan, a nearby kingdom in the Himalaya. In 1988, Bhutan's Buddhist ruler, King Jigme Singye Wangchuk, had begun enforcing the "Bhutanese way of life" by promoting Bhutanese clothing, language, and other ways favored by the Buddhists of the nation's high mountain valleys. But the plan worsened relations with the nation's ethnic Nepali Hindus, who make up the majority in the

lower, jungled foothills of southern Bhutan. The ethnic Bhutanese feared that their culture would be submerged by that of the quickly growing ethnic Nepali population.

In September, Nepalese organizations based in India charged that Bhutan was violating human rights and had killed hundreds of demonstrators. The government denied the charge, saying that armed militants from India had invaded the country to try to stir up trouble, and that only 2 had been killed and 36 kept imprisoned.

An old territorial dispute flared up over a small group of rocky islands northeast of Taiwan. China, Taiwan, and Japan all claim this uninhabited territory, which the Japanese call the Senkaku Islands. In addition to national pride, the dispute involves potentially lucrative offshore oil rights.

In 1978, a right wing Japanese political group built a lighthouse on one of the islands to assert Japan's ownership. Worried that the Japanese government might give official recognition to the action in 1990, a fishing boat full of Taiwanese athletes—accompanied by a press boat—tried in October to plant an Olympic torch on the islands. Japanese coastal patrol vessels repelled them. Both Taiwan and China protested, to no effect.

Asian economies were hurt by Iraq's August 2 invasion of Kuwait, though the subsequent rise in oil prices benefited Brunei, Indonesia, Malaysia, and a few other oil exporters. Some Asian countries—such as the Philippines—lacked significant domestic energy sources and were particularly vulnerable. Others—such as India—were simply ill-prepared to pay higher prices.

The invasion also destroyed the livelihoods of an estimated 535,000 Asian workers, who had been attracted to Iraq and Kuwait during the 1970's oil boom. Each Bangladeshi worker in the Persian Gulf region was estimated to support 11 people at home; each Sri Lankan or Pakistani worker supported 7; and each Indian, 3. Tens of thousands of these workers were stranded after the invasion of Kuwait, and many returned home penniless.

Asian nations also lost export markets in Kuwait and, because of UN sanctions, in Iraq. Both Middle Eastern countries had purchased substantial amounts of Asia's light industrial goods and foodstuffs, including tea. At the same time, Asian raw-material exports were on average earning lower prices on world markets, and the stock markets in most Asian countries experienced sharp drops.

The political changes in eastern Europe and the decline of the Soviet economy hit Indochina's Communist countries hard. Cambodia, Laos, and Vietnam all lost substantial amounts of badly needed aid from the Soviet bloc.   Henry S. Bradsher

See also the articles on the individual Asian nations. In the Special Reports section, see **Riding a Wave of Prosperity on the Pacific Rim.** In *World Book,* see **Asia.**

178

Facts in brief on Asian countries

Country	Population	Government	Monetary unit*	Foreign trade (million U.S.$) Exports†	Imports†
Afghanistan	17,666,000	President & People's Democratic Party General Secretary Najibullah; Prime Minister Fazil Haq Khaliqyar	afghani (55 = $1)	512	996
Australia	16,930,000	Governor General Bill Hayden; Prime Minister Robert Hawke	dollar (1.29 = $1)	43,200	48,600
Bangladesh	118,702,000	Interim President Shahabuddin Ahmed; Prime Minister Qazi Zafar Ahmed	taka (35 = $1)	1,300	3,100
Bhutan	1,550,000	King Jigme Singye Wangchuck	Indian rupee (18.09 = $1) & ngultrum (18.09 = $1)	71	138
Brunei	299,000	Sultan Sir Hassanal Bolkiah	dollar (1.71 = $1)	2,070	800
Burma (Myanmar)	42,546,000	State Law and Order Restoration Council Chairman Saw Maung	kyat (5.92 = $1)	311	536
Cambodia (Kampuchea)	7,147,000	People's Revolutionary Party Secretary General & Council of State President Heng Samrin (Coalition government‡—President Norodom Sihanouk; Vice President Khieu Samphan; Prime Minister Son Sann)	riel (460 = $1)	32	147
China	1,133,683,000	Communist Party General Secretary Jiang Zemin; Premier Li Peng; President Yang Shangkun	yuan (5.22 = $1)	52,500	59,100
India	871,208,000	President Ramaswamy Iyer Venkataraman; Prime Minister Chandra Shekhar	rupee (18.09 = $1)	17,200	24,700
Indonesia	183,258,000	President Suharto; Vice President Sudharmono	rupiah (1,880 = $1)	21,000	13,200
Iran	58,073,000	Leader of the Islamic Revolution Ali Hoseini Khamenei; President Ali Akbar Hashemi Rafsanjani	rial (64.21 = $1)	12,300	12,000
Japan	124,025,000	Emperor Akihito; Prime Minister Toshiki Kaifu	yen (131.63 = $1)	270,000	210,000
Korea, North	23,432,000	President Kim Il-sŏng; Premier Yon Hyong-muk	won (0.97 = $1)	2,400	3,100
Korea, South	44,018,000	President Roh Tae Woo; Prime Minister Ro Jai Bong	won (714.3 = $1)	62,300	61,300
Laos	4,167,000	Acting President Phoumi Vongvichit; Council of Ministers Chairman Kaysone Phomvihan	kip (685 = $1)	58	219
Malaysia	17,689,000	Paramount Ruler Azlan Muhibbuddin Shah ibni Sultan Yusof Izzudin; Prime Minister Mahathir Bin Mohamad	ringgit (2.70 = $1)	24,000	30,000
Maldives	227,000	President Maumoon Abdul Gayoom	rufiyaa (9.51 = $1)	47	90
Mongolia	2,295,000	President Punsalmaagiyn Ochirbat; Prime Minister Dashiyn Byambasuren	tughrik (3.35 = $1)	388	1,000
Nepal	19,591,000	King Birendra Bir Bikram Shah Dev; Prime Minister Krishna Prasad Bhattarai	rupee (29.61 = $1)	374	724
New Zealand	3,404,000	Governor General Dame Catherine Tizard; Prime Minister James B. Bolger	dollar (1.66 = $1)	8,900	7,500
Pakistan	122,666,000	President Ghulam Ishaq Khan; Prime Minister Nawaz Sharif	rupee (21.82 = $1)	4,500	7,200
Papua New Guinea	4,112,000	Governor General Sir Serei Eri; Prime Minister Rabbie Namaliu	kina (0.95 = $1)	1,400	1,200
Philippines	63,826,000	President Corazon C. Aquino	peso (28 = $1)	8,100	10,500
Singapore	2,728,000	President Wee Kim Wee; Prime Minister Goh Chok Tong	dollar (1.72 = $1)	46,000	53,000
Sri Lanka	17,639,000	President Ranasinghe Premadasa; Prime Minister D. B. Wijetunge	rupee (40.24 = $1)	1,500	2,300
Taiwan	20,923,000	President Li Teng-hui; Premier Hao Po-ts'un	dollar (27.27 = $1)	66,200	52,200
Thailand	56,454,000	King Bhumibol Adulyadej; Prime Minister Chatchai Chunhawan	baht (25.15 = $1)	19,900	25,100
Union of Soviet Socialist Republics	289,588,000	Communist Party General Secretary & President Mikhail S. Gorbachev	ruble (0.56 = $1)	110,700	107,300
Vietnam	67,290,000	Communist Party General Secretary Nguyen Van Linh; Council of State Chairman Vo Chi Cong; Council of Ministers Chairman Do Muoi	dong (6,450 = $1)	1,100	2,500

*Exchange rates as of Dec. 7, 1990, or latest available data. †Latest available data.
‡The coalition government, formed in exile in 1982, is recognized by the United Nations.

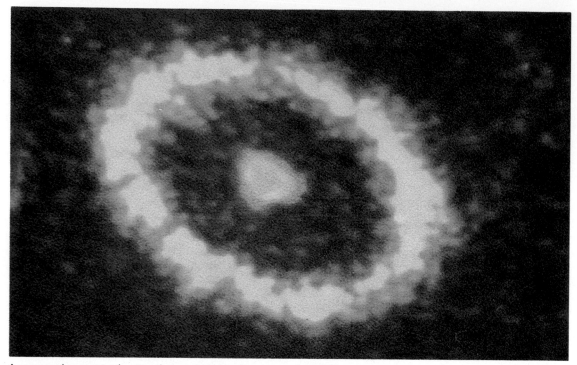

A gaseous ring surrounds a star that exploded as a supernova in 1987 in a photograph taken by the *Hubble Space Telescope* in August 1990.

Astronomy. Two major telescopic satellites were launched in 1990. A space probe reached the planet Venus in August, and, in June, astronomers found two extremely hot regions on Mercury.

Telescopic satellites. The United States National Aeronautics and Space Administration (NASA) launched the *Hubble Space Telescope* from Cape Canaveral, Fla., on April 24 on board the space shuttle *Discovery*. The *Hubble* is named for the American astronomer Edwin P. Hubble. *Discovery*'s robot arm deployed the telescope on April 25 in an orbit 381 miles (613 kilometers) above Earth.

The *Hubble*, with its 95-inch (2.4-meter) main mirror, was designed to produce the clearest views ever obtained of stars, nebulae, and galaxies. By late June, however, investigators concluded that the main mirror had been ground to the wrong optical prescription, causing the images from the telescope to be blurred. The blurring effect, called *spherical aberration*, occurs when light striking the outer parts of a mirror is focused at a greater distance from the mirror than light striking the inner parts. In a properly shaped mirror, all light is focused at the same distance.

Mathematicians came to the rescue with computer programs that restored much of the *Hubble*'s expected photographic clarity by a process known as *deconvolution*. The deconvolution programs measure the distortion in the image of an uncomplicated target, such as that of a single bright star, and then re-

move the corresponding distortions from the images of other objects in the photographs. On October 4, the Space Telescope Science Institute in Baltimore released deconvolved images of stars, star clusters, galaxies, and planets. These images revealed that, with help from the computer programs, the *Hubble* does obtain pictures in visible and ultraviolet light that are beyond the capabilities of telescopes on Earth.

X-ray telescope. An orbiting X-ray observatory known as *Rosat* was launched aboard an unmanned Delta 2 rocket from Cape Canaveral on June 1 as a joint project of Germany, Great Britain, and the United States. It is named for Wilhelm Roentgen, the German physicist who discovered X rays. *Rosat* began a sky survey that was expected to detect about 100,000 celestial sources of X rays and to find about 1,000 objects glowing in extreme ultraviolet radiation. Extreme ultraviolet radiation has wavelengths even shorter than those of ordinary ultraviolet light. X rays, extreme ultraviolet radiation, and ultraviolet light must be observed from space because the atmosphere blocks them from reaching the ground.

The *Magellan* spacecraft began orbiting the cloud-covered planet Venus on August 10. The probe is named for the Portuguese explorer Ferdinand Magellan. A radar instrument on board *Magellan* uses radar beams to penetrate Venus' thick cloud layer. The radar images enable geologists to obtain maps of the surface 10 times sharper than the best made with earlier spacecraft and ground-based radar telescopes.

In September, astronomer R. Stephen Saunders of NASA's Jet Propulsion Laboratory (JPL) in Pasadena, Calif., reported that *Magellan* had discovered sets of parallel, linear markings, perhaps fractures in the crust of Venus, that intersect almost at right angles. This crosshatched terrain is unlike any found on the other planets and moons of the solar system.

Hot spots. Astronomers studying the solar system with radio and radar telescopes on Earth found the long-theorized "hot poles" of Mercury. The hot poles are two regions that are alternately heated to the highest temperatures on the planet because of the relationship between the lengths of the orbital period, or year, of Mercury and its rotation period, or day. A year on Mercury is 1½ times longer than a Mercury day. Further, Mercury's orbit is noticeably *elliptical* (oval-shaped), bringing it much closer to the sun once per year, at *perihelion*, than at other times. When Mercury reaches perihelion, one of the hot poles faces the sun; one Mercurian year later, the other hot pole faces the sun.

On June 12, 1990, astronomers led by Jack O. Burns of New Mexico State University at Las Cruces and Michael J. Ledlow of the University of New Mexico in Albuquerque announced that the hot poles had been found in the first radio maps ever made of Mercury. The maps were obtained with the Very Large Array (VLA) radio telescope near Socorro, N. Mex.

Unlike the ordinary north and south poles of a planet, which mark the opposite ends of the planet's axis of rotation, the hot poles are located at opposite ends of a diameter through Mercury's equatorial plane, so that both hot poles are located on the equator. The VLA detected radio waves that came from depths of a few feet or more in the soil or bedrock of Mercury and revealed that the subsurface temperatures at the hot poles are as much as 1236°F. (669°C). At the surface, the temperature of the hot poles must reach about 1800°F. (980°C) during the day.

Dark dust in galaxies. Contrary to previous belief, the disks of spiral galaxies may be largely opaque, so that when astronomers look at these galaxies, they may be seeing only the stars in their outer layers. Astronomer Edwin A. Valentijn of the Kapteyn Astronomical Institute in Groningen, the Netherlands, reported this finding on July 12, 1990. A spiral galaxy is a huge system of hundreds of billions of stars arranged in a disk containing so-called *spiral arms*.

Valentijn surveyed 9,381 spiral galaxies photographed at the European Southern Observatory near La Serena, Chile. Valentijn found that the disks of most of the galaxies he surveyed are opaque, so that stars on the far side of a galaxy facing Earth cannot be seen. Astronomers have long thought that most parts of a galaxy are transparent. If the new finding is correct, then spiral galaxies contain much more dark interstellar dust than was previously believed. The visible stars are only a fraction of the total stars.

Largest galaxy. A giant elliptical galaxy at the center of a distant cluster of galaxies is the largest ever measured, according to an October 26 report by astronomers led by Juan M. Uson of the National Radio Astronomy Observatory in Socorro. An elliptical galaxy is a huge assemblage of stars with the cross-sectional shape of an ellipse. An ellipse is characterized by two perpendicular axes. The astronomers found that the longer axis of the central galaxy is at least 6.6 million light-years long. (A light-year is the distance light travels in one year, about 5.88 trillion miles [9.46 trillion kilometers].) Its shorter axis is one-half that length. By comparison, our Milky Way Galaxy's longer axis is 100,000 light-years long. The astronomers determined the size of the galaxy—which contains an estimated 100 trillion stars—by computer analysis of a mosaic of 16 photographs obtained with an electronic camera attached to an optical telescope at the Kitt Peak National Observatory, near Tucson, Ariz.

Milky Way. On January 12, astronomers announced results of a new study of the Milky Way that suggests it is not a normal spiral system, as previously thought, but rather is a *barred spiral galaxy*. In such a galaxy, the spiral arms do not start at the center but seem to begin at either end of an elongated collection of stars called a *galactic bar*.   Stephen P. Maran

In the Special Reports section, see **A Hitchhiker's Current Guide to the Planets.** In *World Book,* see **Astronomy.**

Australia. Prime Minister Robert Hawke and his Labor Party government retained power for a fourth consecutive term when the country went to the polls on March 24, 1990. With his reelection, Hawke became the longest-serving Labor prime minister in Australia's history. He had held the office since 1983.

After the election, the opposing Liberal Party replaced its leader of less than one year, Andrew Peacock, with John Hewson, a former economics professor at the University of New South Wales and a relative newcomer to politics. The small Australian Democrats Party was in tatters; its leader, Janine Haines, quit politics after losing her bid to move from the Senate to the House of Representatives.

Economy. In December 1990, Australia was officially declared to be in recession. Foreign debt, the high value of the Australian dollar, rising oil prices—which jumped 25 per cent after Iraq invaded Kuwait in August—and falling commodity prices, particularly for wheat and wool, were blamed for the declining economy. Australia is the world's largest exporter of wool. The Australian dollar fell to 77 U.S. cents by year-end. (Monetary amounts in this article are in Australian dollars.)

Australia continued to import more goods than it exported in 1990. The August deficit in the *balance of payments* (the value of goods exported compared with the value of goods imported) was just under $1.5 billion. Economic policy focused on reducing in-

Australia

In October in the opera *Les Huguenots,* Dame Joan Sutherland gives a farewell performance in her hometown, Sydney, Australia.

flation and interest rates. By late December, inflation, which had hovered around 7.7 per cent all year, fell to 6 per cent. Interest rates fell to the still high rate of 12 per cent.

Because of high interest rates, companies faced difficulties in raising money for investment, a reversal of the lending frenzy of the 1980's. A growing number of corporations collapsed, and—largely due to the lack of new jobs—unemployment grew to 8.2 per cent by December. In 1990, commonwealth spending was the lowest as a proportion of gross domestic product since 1974. Despite three years of budget surpluses and reduced government borrowing, the current account deficit rose to $18 billion by October.

On August 21, Treasurer Paul Keating issued his budget report for the 1990-1991 fiscal year. Keating stated that the budget would deliver a surplus of $8.11 billion, up from the $8.04-billion surplus of the previous year. Personal income taxes, which provide nearly half of all tax revenue in Australia, were cut as promised in the election campaign.

State news. Victoria's Labor premier, John Cain, resigned on August 7, after serving nearly nine years, because of the slumping economy. The sale of state-owned businesses to private investors to reduce state debt failed to bring as much revenue as expected, and financial institutions suffered big losses. Cain was replaced by Joan Kirner, deputy premier, who cut public-sector employment and raised taxes.

Financial institutions in Victoria suffered massive losses in 1990. In September, the government announced that a Royal Commission would investigate the collapse of Tricontinental, the merchant banking arm of the State Bank of Victoria. (A merchant bank, in Australia, is a banking firm that issues stocks for industry.) Corruption was not ruled out.

New South Wales had a big drop in business investment. In an unrelated development, Australia's biggest private-sector construction project, the World Square office and hotel complex in Sydney, closed because of union disruptions. As a result, an inquiry into the building industry began in November.

In Western Australia, Labor government agencies had invested more than $250 million to prop up Rothwells Bank in a scandal known as WA Inc. Loans remained unpaid after government projects with large corporations failed. Under pressure, Labor Premier Peter Dowding resigned on February 12, and Carmen Lawrence became premier.

Environment. The environmentalist momentum of 1989 slowed in 1990, though public concern over water pollution and the destruction of forests helped the Labor Party win 10 key seats in March elections. In September, federal and state environment ministers decided to issue guidelines for advertising "environmentally sound" products and for testing environmental claims by manufacturers.

In August, the federal government introduced tax incentives to encourage mine site rehabilitation, oil platform removal, and the erection of fences to prevent soil erosion. But it made a controversial decision in October to log forests in the national estate in southeastern New South Wales. The government decided to permit logging in 40 per cent of the forest region. Environmentalists wanted no more than 20 per cent opened to logging.

In Tasmania, a forestry agreement between the minority Labor government of Premier Michael Field and the five Green independent members of the state parliament ended in October. The Greens are environmental activists. The end of the pact paved the way for an increase in the export quota for wood chips.

In South Australia in September, Labor Premier John Bannon blamed environmentalists for the failure of several major projects. The state, nevertheless, was designated as the site for the $6-billion Multi-Function Polis, a high-technology city to be built over a 30-year period with Japanese investment.

Telecommunications. The shakedown in the television industry, which began in late 1989, continued into 1990. In August, Kerry F. B. Packer, the richest man in Australia and publisher of most of the country's magazines, bought back the television network channel 9 from brewing baron Alan Bond. Packer paid about one-fifth of the $1.1 billion that he sold it for two years previously.

On September 14, banks appointed a receiver for Northern Star Holdings Limited, the parent company of television channel 10. The company owed bankers $455 million.

On December 10, banks appointed a receivership for the 150-year-old John Fairfax Group newspaper company, which publishes *The Age* in Melbourne and *The Sydney Morning Herald.*

On September 24, the federal government decided to merge Telecom and OTC Limited, both government-owned telephone companies, and to sell Aussat, Australia's main communications satellite.

Corporate collapse. The year saw the collapse of many corporate giants and entrepreneurs, unable to repay their loans. Banks were censured for lending heavily to corporations and began tightening credit. September saw record losses, including a staggering $2.24-billion loss by Bond Corporation, the largest in Australia's corporate history. Just two days earlier, on September 25, Elders IXL Limited, a brewing conglomerate, announced losses of $1.31 billion.

Gulf crisis. Australia sent three ships to the Persian Gulf after Iraq invaded Kuwait in August. A United Nations embargo against Iraq cost Australia its second-largest wheat market.

Nobel laureate dies. On September 30, the novelist Patrick White died in Sydney, aged 78. He was the first Australian to receive the Nobel Prize for literature, in 1973.   Susan Williams

See also **Asia** (Facts in brief table). In *World Book,* see **Australia; White, Patrick.**

Austria, in 1990, remained eager to join the European Community (EC or Common Market) after the formation of a single market in western Europe, scheduled for 1992. Many Austrians, as a result, began to weigh internal developments against their probable impact on EC membership. In March 1990, for example, the government tightened restrictions on immigration to stem the influx of eastern European refugees, and it later was relieved to learn that some EC governments contemplated similiar curbs to prevent their welfare systems from being overwhelmed by the refugees. A number of Austrians also were heartened to see that the far-right, ultranationalist Freedom Party received fewer votes than forecast in October elections. The party's growth could have damaged Austria's image in Europe.

Wider role. Following the collapse of Communist governments in eastern Europe in 1989, Austria sought to play a role in stabilizing the region's emerging democracies. Austria expanded ties with neighboring Hungary and helped found a five-nation association called the Pentagonal with Czechoslovakia, Hungary, Italy, and Yugoslavia. Much of the Pentagonal's territory had belonged to Austria-Hungary through World War I (1914-1918). The new association planned to focus on practical steps that became possible with the lifting of the Iron Curtain. One example would be the creation of new roads linking central Europe with ports on the Adriatic Sea.

After Iraq invaded Kuwait in August 1990, Austria at first hoped to stay out of the conflict as a neutral nation. But the government agreed on August 11 to let United States warplanes use Austrian airspace, in accord with the actions of U.S. allies in Europe.

Austrian President Kurt Waldheim visited Iraq on August 25 and returned with 80 Austrians who had been held hostage. Waldheim's visit was the only such trip by a Western leader at a time of Iraq's political isolation. The visit drew criticism elsewhere in Europe. But a poll showed that 99 per cent of Austrians supported Waldheim's action.

In elections on October 7, the governing Socialist Party won 43 per cent of the vote, gaining 1 seat to give it 81 seats in the 183-member parliament. The Socialist leader, Chancellor Franz Vranitzky, again formed a coalition with the conservative People's Party. With 32 per cent of the vote, that party fell from 77 seats to 61. The lost seats were picked up chiefly by the far-right Freedom Party, which won 33 seats. The Freedom Party took 17 per cent of the vote, a big advance over its 1986 showing of less than 10 per cent. But it fell short of its target of 20 per cent. The Greens, an environmental party, won nine seats.

Bruno Kreisky, Austria's chancellor from 1970 to 1983, died on July 29, 1990. He did much to restore Austria's leadership in Europe.   Joseph Fitchett

See also **Europe** (Facts in brief table). In *World Book,* see **Austria.**

Automobile. The United States automobile industry settled slowly into a sales slump as 1990 drew to an end. The Big Three domestic automakers—General Motors Corporation (GM), Ford Motor Company, and Chrysler Corporation—announced layoffs, production cuts, and financial losses.

Japan-based firms continued to expand their sales and manufacturing presence in the United States at the expense of domestic companies. GM, the number-one domestic firm, fought back with Saturn, the first major new U.S. brand introduced since Ford launched its Edsel Division in 1958. Saturn's line-up of small, sporty, innovative coupes and sedans was well received by critics.

As the market became more crowded and competitive, all the major firms continued to seek refuge in joint ventures, cooperative alliances, or strategic partnerships with other automakers. Many experts predicted a worldwide shakeout in the 1990's, in which the number of independent automakers would shrink from about 40 to perhaps as few as 10.

Sales slump. For the Big Three, the most immediate and serious concern was a short-term sales slump that had all the earmarks of a classic automobile sales recession. Consumers who were worried about the weakening economy, rising oil prices, and the effects of the Persian Gulf crisis began to postpone automobile purchases. At the same time, rising oil prices hurt sales of big trucks and large family cars. Total U.S.

A junked Trabant, the largest-selling automobile in what was East Germany, symbolizes at least one owner's opinion of the quality of the cars.

sales of cars and trucks fell to 13.8 million in 1990 and were expected to slide further in 1991 before recovering slightly in 1992.

Lower earnings. Slower sales, coupled with cash rebates and other buyers' incentives averaging as much as $1,200 per car, cut deeply into profits. Ford, the worldwide automotive industry's profit leader in the mid-1980's, posted a $38-million loss in its international automotive business for the third quarter of 1990. That had not happened since the fourth quarter of 1982, when Ford lost $236 million.

The combined earnings of GM, Ford, and Chrysler for the first nine months of 1990 fell by 61 per cent, to $3.14 billion from $8.07 billion during the same period in 1989. In November, GM notified employees and shareholders that it planned to reduce December 1990 production schedules in North America by 110,000 vehicles. That came on top of a 181,000 cut in November resulting from slow sales. GM said it expected to post a worldwide loss in the fourth quarter—its first three-month deficit from ongoing operations in eight years.

Although the outlook was gloomy, virtually no experts felt the industry was in for a rerun of the sharp 1979-1982 slump, when sales plunged 32 per cent, from 15.4 million to only 10.5 million. In that downturn, long-term layoffs of U.S. hourly auto workers peaked at 350,000—more than half the industry's work force. Industrywide U.S. sales of 13.6 million in 1991 would represent a drop of 16.6 per cent from the

1986 peak of 16.3 million. Workers on indefinite layoff—workers sent home without a recall date—numbered a relatively modest 37,000 by the end of 1990.

New contracts. The downturn promised a severe test of the innovative labor agreements negotiated in 1990 by the domestic automakers and the United Automobile Workers (UAW), which represents most production workers. The new three-year agreement, reached without strikes at each of the Big Three companies, provided virtual lifetime job security for UAW members. The companies agreed that no worker could be laid off for more than 36 weeks per year. In return, the union allowed the firms to reduce their work forces through normal attrition and voluntary early retirements.

The UAW also gave GM a green light to close at least seven U.S. plants that had been idled previously or would not be making cars in the future. GM took a massive, $2.1-billion tax write-off in the third quarter of 1990 to cover the shutdown costs.

Japanese auto growth. By contrast, Japan-based automakers continued to show growth overall in the U.S. market. In April 1990, Honda Motor Company dedicated its second U.S. assembly plant at East Liberty, Ohio, a few miles from its car and motorcycle assembly complex at Marysville. The new plant had the capacity to build 150,000 Civic subcompacts per year, while the Marysville facility could pump out 360,000

Accord compacts annually. On November 27, Toyota Motor Corporation announced it will spend $800 million to construct a second auto assembly plant at Georgetown, Ky., where the company builds 220,000 Camry compacts per year. Camrys will also be built at the second factory.

Japanese automakers defied the sales slowdown. Toyota's share of the total U.S. car and truck market grew to 7.5 per cent in 1990 from 6.3 per cent the previous year. Honda's market share expanded to 6.1 per cent from 5.2 per cent. Despite a strategic withdrawal from the bottom end of the economy car market, Nissan Motor Company saw its share drop just slightly, to 4.5 per cent from 4.6 per cent. Chrysler's share shrank to 12.2 per cent from 13.7 per cent, while Ford's dropped to 23.9 per cent from 24.6 per cent. GM appeared to have halted a decadelong slide in market share, with its portion of the domestic market rising to 35.9 per cent from 35.4 per cent.

New small cars. The year 1990 was the year of the small car. Nissan introduced an all-new Sentra subcompact built at its Smyrna, Tenn., plant. Toyota redesigned its Tercel basic small car for introduction late in 1990 as a 1991 model and kept the lowest base price just under $7,000. Chrysler introduced low-priced "America" versions of its Plymouth Sundance and Dodge Shadow small cars.

The Ford Escort and Mercury Tracer family subcompacts were totally redesigned in partnership with Japan's Mazda Motor Corporation, which is partly owned by Ford. The new Escort and Tracer, built in Wayne, Mich., and Hermosillo, Mexico, relied heavily on Mazda engineering. The Japanese firm also helped Ford design production processes for the new line.

Saturn was the most eagerly awaited car of the year. It began as a design study in 1982, when GM found that Isuzu Motors, its Japanese affiliate, could build a small car for the U.S. market for $2,000 less than its own manufacturing operations could. GM decided its long-term health depended on erasing that productivity gap, and Saturn was the result.

The new subsidiary was given $3 billion to set up a manufacturing complex in Spring Hill, Tenn., on the most efficient basis possible, and it slowly swung into operation in the fourth quarter of 1990. The plant was set up to build 240,000 cars per year, along with engines and other automotive components.

Hourly workers at Saturn were given unprecedented authority to decide how to do their jobs most efficiently. In fact, all major decisions at Saturn require UAW approval. GM felt the combination of modern production equipment, a highly motivated work force, and a car line designed to match the plant's production process would make the plant fully competitive with foreign firms. Saturn cars were modestly priced at $7,995 to $11,775, but production began so slowly that the subsidiary did not have a true market test in 1990.   James V. Higgins

In **World Book,** see **Automobile.**

Automobile racing. In 1990, for the second time in three years, Ayrton Senna of Brazil won a two-man battle with his bitter rival, Alain Prost of France, for the World Drivers Championship. Arie Luyendyk of the Netherlands, who lived in the United States, won the Indianapolis 500, the world's richest race, earning $1,090,940 out of a total purse of $6,325,803.

Formula One. The 1990 World Drivers Championship was decided in 16 Grand Prix races for Formula One cars. There were 10 races in Europe and 1 each in Phoenix (won by Senna); Montreal, Canada (also won by Senna); Brazil; Mexico; Japan; and Australia.

In 1988, when Senna won, and in 1989, when Prost won, they were teammates on the McLaren-Honda team. But Prost disliked Senna so much that after the 1989 season he moved to the Ferrari team.

In 1990, with a Honda V-10 engine that generated more than 700 horsepower, Senna won six races. Prost won five. After the season, Senna re-signed with McLaren for 1991 for $12 million.

Indianapolis 500. In qualifying laps for the Indy 500, Emerson Fittipaldi of Brazil, in a 1990 Penske-Chevrolet, set records of 225.575 miles per hour (mph), or 363.028 kilometers per hour (kph), for one lap and 225.301 mph (362.587 kph) for four laps over the Indianapolis Motor Speedway's 2½-mile (4-kilometer) oval track. On May 27, 1990, in the 200-lap race, Fittipaldi led for most of the first 135 laps. But in the warm weather, he and Bobby Rahal of Dublin, Ohio, in a Lola-Chevrolet, were slowed by overheated tires that blistered.

Luyendyk, in a Lola-Chevrolet, won by 10.7 seconds over Rahal, with Fittipaldi third. Luyendyk averaged 185.984 mph (299.312 kph), the fastest speed ever for the Indy 500. The victory was Luyendyk's first in an Indy-car race.

The Indianapolis race was 1 of 16 in the Championship Auto Racing Teams (CART) series for Indy cars. Al Unser, Jr., became the series champion. He set a record average speed for Indy cars in a 500-mile (805-kilometer) race with an average of 189.727 mph (305.336 kph) at the Marlboro 500 in Brooklyn, Mich., in August.

Fatal accident. Bill Vukovich III, Rookie of the Year in the 1988 Indy 500, was killed on November 25 during a crash at the Mesa Marin Speedway in Bakersfield, Calif. He was the son of Bill Vukovich, Jr., runner-up at the Indy 500 in 1973, and the grandson of Bill Vukovich, who won the 1953 and the 1954 Indy 500 and was killed in the 1955 race.

NASCAR. The National Association for Stock Car Auto Racing (NASCAR) conducted the Winston Cup 29-race series for late-model sedans. Entering the final race on Nov. 18, 1990, in Atlanta, Ga., Dale Earnhardt of Doolie, N.C., in a Chevrolet, led Mark Martin of Greensboro, N.C., in a Ford, by six points.

Earnhardt finished third and Martin sixth in the race, and Earnhardt won the series. Earnhardt won nine races during the year and prize money of

Arie Luyendyk (in red car) closes in on A. J. Foyt and goes on to win the Indianapolis 500 in May with a record average speed for that race.

$3,083,056, including bonuses, the most ever by any driver in one year.

The richest NASCAR race was the $1,198,462 Daytona 500 on February 18 in Daytona Beach, Fla. Earnhardt led until a mile to go, when his right rear tire shredded. Derrike Cope of Spanaway, Wash., won in a Chevrolet and earned $188,150.

Other races. For the third consecutive year, Geoff Brabham of Australia won the International Motor Sports Association's 15-race series for grand touring production cars. Brabham won five races.

Jaguar XJR12's finished first and second in the two major 24-hour endurance races. On June 16 and 17 in Le Mans, France, the winning Jaguar was driven alternately by Price Cobb of Evergreen, Colo.; John Nielsen of Denmark; and Martin Brundle of Great Britain. On February 3 and 4 in Daytona Beach, those drivers finished second to a Jaguar driven by Davy Jones of Cortland, N.Y.; Jan Lammers of the Netherlands; and Andy Wallace of Great Britain.

In the National Hot Rod Association's 19-race series for dragsters, Joe Amato of Old Forge, Pa., won the featured top-fuel class for the third time in seven years. On September 29, in qualifying for a race in Topeka, Kans., Gary Ormsby of Roseville, Calif., recorded the fastest elapsed time for a quarter-mile at 4.881 seconds and the fastest speed at 296.05 mph (476.45 kph).　　Frank Litsky

In *World Book,* see **Automobile racing.**

Aviation. United States airlines hit hard financial times in 1990, as increases in jet fuel prices helped drive airline losses to record levels. Almost immediately after Iraq invaded Kuwait on August 2, fuel prices soared from 57 cents a gallon (3.8 liters) to more than $1.27 a gallon. By mid-October, the price was $1.39 a gallon. In response, U.S. airlines raised ticket prices almost 15 per cent over two months, but they were unable to recover their costs because high fares scared off passengers. As 1990 drew to a close, analysts predicted the industry would lose a record $1.5 billion to $2 billion for the year, and the survival of some carriers was in doubt.

Routes for sale. Pan American World Airways in October agreed to sell its routes between five U.S. cities and London and between Washington, D.C., and Paris to UAL Corporation, the parent company of United Airlines, for $400 million. The deal also included seven routes within Europe. In December, Trans World Airlines (TWA) agreed to sell its routes between London and six U.S. cities for $445 million to AMR Corporation, which owns American Airlines. The transactions required approval by the U.S. Department of Transportation and Great Britain, which had to consider the competitive effects on British Airways. Pan Am and TWA badly needed cash, and the sales were part of their efforts to concentrate on serving areas where they could make money. Sale approvals may, however, take months while transportation officials decide whether airlines can buy and sell routes, which they get free from the government.

More money woes. Financially troubled Eastern Airlines had an especially turbulent year. On April 18, U.S. Bankruptcy Court Judge Burton R. Lifland took the airline away from the control of Frank Lorenzo, chairman of Eastern's parent company, Texas Air Corporation. Lifland said that Texas Air's treatment of Eastern "is suggestive of parental neglect." Eastern had losses of $1.2 billion since filing for bankruptcy protection in March 1989. The judge appointed Martin Shugrue, a veteran of the airline business, as trustee to run the airline. But near the end of 1990, the carrier was still struggling, and some of its creditors wanted it put out of business.

On December 3, Continental Airlines, the fifth-largest air carrier in the United States, filed for protection from its creditors under bankruptcy laws. High fuel costs and debt payments were cited as the causes for its financial troubles. Company executives said service would continue as usual, and aviation analysts believed the company would stay in business.

Airline fatalities down. In 1990, there were 83 deaths in the United States involving major and commuter airlines, including charter and air taxi flights. The 83 fatalities compared with 397 deaths for 1989. Although this was a dramatic decrease, safety analysts said airline accidents occur too rarely, considering the millions of flights each year, to be used as a safety gauge.

Crashes. On February 14, an Indian Airlines airbus, en route from Bombay to Bangalore, India, crashed into an empty reservoir 50 yards (46 meters) short of the Bangalore runway, killing 93 of the 146 people aboard. On October 2, a hijacked Chinese passenger jet crashed into two other planes at an airport in the southern Chinese city of Guangzhou (formerly Canton) and exploded, killing 128 people.

In the United States, a major crash involved a South American airline. On January 25, an Avianca Airlines jet ran out of fuel while waiting to land at John F. Kennedy International Airport and crashed on Long Island, New York, killing 73. The crew told air-traffic controllers that their fuel was low, but they never officially declared an emergency. This would have given them immediate clearance for landing.

On December 3 in heavy fog, a Northwest Airlines Boeing 707 accelerating for take-off at Detroit Metropolitan Airport collided with a Northwest DC-9 taxiing on the same runway. The DC-9 caught fire, and eight people on board died.

Final accident reports. The National Transportation Safety Board issued final reports on three major accidents that occurred in 1989. In an April 10, 1990, report, it said that the Boeing Company, United Airlines, and the Federal Aviation Administration (FAA) shared responsibility for an accident on a United Airlines jet on Feb. 24, 1989. The airplane's cargo door had blown open while in flight over the Pacific Ocean,

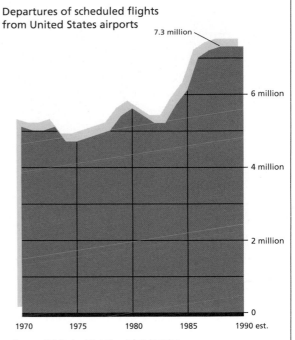

Heavier traffic, but generally safer flights

Departures of scheduled flights
from United States airports

7.3 million

6 million

4 million

2 million

0

1970   1975   1980   1985   1990 est.

Source: U.S. Federal Aviation Administration.

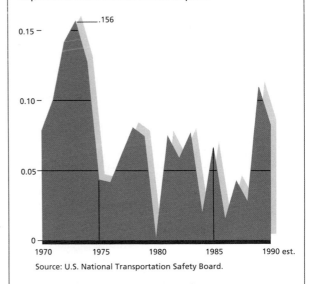

Fatal accidents per 100,000 scheduled
departures from United States airports

.156

0.15

0.10

0.05

0

1970   1975   1980   1985   1990 est.

Source: U.S. National Transportation Safety Board.

United States airports have grown steadily busier since the mid-1970's, *top,* but the rate of fatal crashes has fallen in most years, *above.*

Emergency crews arrive at the site on Long Island, New York, where an
Avianca jet crashed on January 25 after it ran out of gas, killing 73 people.

and the resulting outrush of air blew nine passengers
out of the plane. The report blamed United Airlines
for improper maintenance, Boeing for a flawed design, and the FAA for not acting forcefully enough
when a door opened on a similar Boeing 747 three
years earlier.

In a July 3, 1990, report, the safety board cited pilot
error as the probable cause of a Sept. 20, 1989, accident at La Guardia Airport in New York City. A USAir
jet skidded into the East River during an aborted take-
off, killing two passengers. The pilot had little experience flying the type of plane in the accident, a 737
jetliner.

On Nov. 1, 1990, the board concluded that United
Airlines had failed to detect a preexisting crack in an
engine fan disk of the DC-10 that crashed in Sioux
City, Iowa, on July 19, 1989. The crack led to an in-
flight engine explosion, which knocked out all three
systems for powering critical flight controls. The crash
killed 112 people. General Electric Company manufactured the faulty engine.

Pilots found guilty. The FAA on March 9, 1990,
revoked the licenses of three Northwest pilots who
tested positive for alcohol after landing their plane at
Minneapolis-St. Paul (Minn.) International Airport on
March 8. The flight, carrying 91 passengers, ended
safely, but an FAA inspector, acting on a tip, arrested
the three men at the airport. The pilots were tried on
August 20 in Minneapolis and found guilty of flying

while intoxicated. They were the first pilots to be convicted under a 1986 law that was aimed at deterring
drug and alcohol abuse in the transportation industry.
On Oct. 26, 1990, two of the pilots were sentenced to
one year in prison, and the third received a 16-month
term.

Legislation. The U.S. Congress in 1990 approved
what some observers called the most important aviation legislation in years by directing the phase-out of
most of the noisiest jetliners in the United States by
the end of the decade. The Transportation Department said the measure will cost airlines between $870-
million and $1.6 billion, depending upon whether air-
lines modify existing planes or purchase new ones.
The legislation was approved as part of the budget-
reconciliation bill and was signed into law by President George Bush on November 5. The legislation also
gave airports permission to impose "passenger facilities charges"—also known as boarding fees—on passengers to raise money for expansion and moderniza-
tion or to improve safety or security.

Historic purchase. United Airlines on October 15
agreed to purchase up to 128 wide-body jets from
Boeing, including the long-awaited 777 model, in a
$22-billion order, the largest ever placed by an airline.
Also in October, the Transportation Department
awarded United Airlines a prized new air route between Chicago and Tokyo.   Laurie McGinley

In *World Book,* see **Aviation.**

Awards and prizes presented in 1990 included the following:

Arts awards

Academy of Motion Picture Arts and Sciences. "Oscar" Awards: Best Picture, *Driving Miss Daisy.* **Best Actor,** Daniel Day-Lewis, *My Left Foot.* **Best Actress,** Jessica Tandy, *Driving Miss Daisy.* **Best Supporting Actor,** Denzel Washington, *Glory.* **Best Supporting Actress,** Brenda Fricker, *My Left Foot.* **Best Director,** Oliver Stone, *Born on the Fourth of July.* **Best Original Screenplay,** Tom Schulman, *Dead Poets Society.* **Best Screenplay Adaptation,** Alfred Uhry, *Driving Miss Daisy.* **Best Cinematography,** Freddie Francis, *Glory.* **Best Film Editing,** David Brenner, Joe Hutshing, *Born on the Fourth of July.* **Best Original Score,** Alan Menken, *The Little Mermaid.* **Best Original Song,** Alan Menken, Howard Ashman, "Under the Sea" from *The Little Mermaid.* **Best Foreign-Language Film,** *Cinema Paradiso* (Italy). See **Day-Lewis, Daniel; Tandy, Jessica.**

American Academy and Institute of Arts and Letters. Gold Medal for Architecture, Kevin Roche. **Gold Medal for History,** C. Vann Woodward. **Award for Distinguished Service to the Arts,** Paul Engle, cofounder of the University of Iowa Writer's Workshop.

American Dance Festival. Samuel H. Scripps-American Dance Festival Award, choreographer Twyla Tharp.

American Film Institute. Life Achievement Award, actor Kirk Douglas.

American Institute of Architects. Gold Medal, Fay Jones. **Honor Awards,** Perkins & Will, Chicago, for Capital High School in Santa Fe, N.Mex.; Michael Graves, Princeton, N.J., for the Clos Pegase Winery, Napa Valley, Calif.; Kallmann McKinnell & Wood Architects Incorporated, Boston, for the Becton Dickinson and Company Corporate Headquarters, Franklin Lakes, N.J.; John Hejduk, Riverdale, N.Y., for Wohnanlage mit Atelierturm, Berlin, Germany; Schwartz/Silver Architects, Boston, for a weekend residence in West Stockbridge, Mass.; Robert A. M. Stern Architects, New York City, for the International Headquarters of Mexx International, B.V., Voorschoten, the Netherlands; Frederick Bentz/Milo Thompson/Robert Rietow Incorporated for the Lake Harriet Band Shell, Minneapolis, Minn.; Hoover Berg Desmond, Denver, for Light of the World Catholic Church, Littleton, Colo.; Antoine Predock, Albuquerque, N.Mex., for the Nelson Fine Arts Center at Arizona State University in Tempe; Davids Killory, San Diego, for an addition to a residence in that city, Fay Jones + Maurice Jennings, Fayetteville, Ark., for Pinecote, a park pavilion near Picayune, Miss.; ELS/Elbasani & Logan Architects, Berkeley, Calif., for the Recreational Sports Facility at the University of California in that city; Frank O. Gehry & Associates, Santa Monica, Calif., for a residence in Los Angeles; Arne Bystrom, Seattle, for a ski residence in Sun Valley, Idaho; Lord, Aeck & Sargent, Atlanta, Ga., for Trinity School in that city; Richard Meier & Partners, New York City, for a residence in Westchester County, New York; Henry N. Cobb, Pei Cobb Freed & Partners, New York City, for the First Interstate Bank Tower at Fountain Place, Dallas; William Turnbull Associates, San Francisco, for Sea Ranch Employee Housing, Sea Ranch, Calif.; Bohlin Powell Larkin Cywinski, Pittsburgh, Pa., for the Software Engineering Institute at Carnegie-Mellon University in that city.

American Music Awards. Pop/Rock Awards: Female Vocalist, Paula Abdul. **Male Vocalist,** Bobby Brown. **Duo or Group,** New Kids on the Block. **Single,** "Girl You Know It's True," Milli Vanilli. **Album,** *Hangin' Tough,* New Kids on the Block. **Favorite New Artist,** Milli Vanilli.

Soul/Rhythm and Blues Awards: Female Vocalist, Anita Baker. **Male Vocalist,** Luther Vandross. **Duo or Group,** The O'Jays. **Single,** "Miss You Much," Janet Jackson. **Album,** *Don't Be Cruel,* Bobby Brown. **Favorite New Artist,** Milli Vanilli.

Country Music Awards: Female Vocalist, Reba McEntire. **Male Vocalist,** Randy Travis. **Duo or Group,** Alabama. **Single,**

Jessica Tandy flashes a radiant smile in March at winning the 1990 Academy Award as best actress for her performance in the motion picture *Driving Miss Daisy.*

"Deeper Than the Holler," Randy Travis. **Album,** *Old 8 x 10,* Randy Travis. **Favorite New Artist,** Clint Black.

Heavy Metal Awards: Favorite Artist, Guns N' Roses. **Favorite Album,** *Appetite for Destruction,* Guns N' Roses. **Favorite New Artist,** Skid Row.

Rap Music Awards: Favorite Artist, M. C. Hammer. **Favorite Album,** *Let's Get It Started,* M. C. Hammer. **Favorite New Artist,** Young MC.

Dance Music Awards: Favorite Artist, Paula Abdul. **Favorite Single,** "Miss You Much," Janet Jackson. **Favorite New Artist,** Tone-Lōc.

Cannes International Film Festival. Golden Palm, *Wild at Heart* (United States). **Grand Prize,** *The Sting of Death* (Japan) and *Tilai* (Burkina Faso). **First Jury Prize,** *Hidden Agenda* (Great Britain). **Second Jury Prize** (Best Artistic Contribution), Gleb Panfilov, *Mother.* **Best Actor,** Gérard Depardieu, *Cyrano de Bergerac.* **Best Actress,** Krystyna Janda, *The Interrogation.* **Best Director,** Pavel Lounguine, *Taxi Blues.* **Golden Camera,** Vitali Kanevski, *Don't Move, Die and Recover.*

Eastman School of Music, University of Rochester. George Eastman Medal, publisher and conductor Gilbert Kaplan.

Hyatt Foundation. Pritzker Architecture Prize, Aldo Rossi (Italy).

John F. Kennedy Center for the Performing Arts. Honors, jazz trumpeter Dizzy Gillespie, actress Katharine Hepburn, opera singer Risë Stevens, British-born composer Jule Styne, Austrian-born film director Billy Wilder.

National Academy of Recording Arts and Sciences. Grammy Awards: Record of the Year, "Wind Beneath My Wings," Bette Midler. **Album of the Year,** *Nick of Time,* Bonnie Raitt. **Song of the Year,** "Wind Beneath My Wings," Larry Henley and Jeff Silbar, songwriters.

Pop Awards: Pop Vocal Performance, Female, *Nick of Time,* Bonnie Raitt. **Pop Vocal Performance, Male,** "How Am I Supposed to Live Without You," Michael Bolton. **Pop Vocal**

Awards and prizes

Performance by a Duo or Group, "Don't Know Much," Linda Ronstadt and Aaron Neville. **Pop Instrumental Performance,** "Healing Chant," Neville Brothers.

Rock Awards: Rock Vocal Performance, Female, *Nick of Time,* Bonnie Raitt. **Rock Vocal Performance, Male,** *The End of the Innocence,* Don Henley. **Rock Vocal Performance by a Duo or Group,** *The Traveling Wilburys Volume One,* Traveling Wilburys. **Rock Instrumental Performance,** *Jeff Beck's Guitar Shop with Terry Bozzio and Tony Hymas,* Jeff Beck, Terry Bozzio, and Tony Hymas. **Hard Rock Performance, Vocal or Instrumental,** "Cult of Personality," Living Colour. **Metal Performance, Vocal or Instrumental,** "One," Metallica.

Rhythm and Blues Awards: Rhythm and Blues Vocal Performance, Female, *Giving You the Best That I Got,* Anita Baker. **Rhythm and Blues Vocal Performance, Male,** "Every Little Step," Bobby Brown. **Rhythm and Blues Vocal Performance by a Duo or Group,** "Back to Life," Soul II Soul. **Rhythm and Blues Instrumental Performance,** "African Dance," Soul II Soul. **Rhythm and Blues Song,** "If You Don't Know Me by Now," Kenny Gamble and Leon Huff, songwriters. **Rap Performance,** "Bust a Move," Young MC. **Traditional Blues,** "I'm in the Mood," John Lee Hooker and Bonnie Raitt.

Country Awards: Country Vocal Performance, Female, *Absolute Torch and Twang,* k. d. lang. **Country Vocal Performance, Male,** *Lyle Lovett and His Large Band,* Lyle Lovett. **Country Vocal Performance, Duo or Group,** *Will the Circle Be Unbroken, Vol. II,* The Nitty Gritty Dirt Band. **Country Vocal Collaboration,** "There's a Tear in My Beer," Hank Williams, Jr., and Hank Williams, Sr. **Country Instrumental Performance,** "Amazing Grace," Randy Scruggs. **Country Song,** "After All This Time," Rodney Crowell. **Bluegrass Recording,** *The Valley Road,* Bruce Hornsby and the Nitty Gritty Dirt Band.

Jazz Awards: Jazz Fusion Performance, *Letter from Home,* Pat Metheny Group. **Jazz Vocal Performance, Female,** *Blues on Broadway,* Ruth Brown. **Jazz Vocal Performance, Male,** *When Harry Met Sally,* Harry Connick, Jr. **Jazz Vocal Performance, Duo or Group,** "Makin' Whoopee," Dr. John and Rickie Lee Jones. **Jazz Instrumental Performance, Solo,** *Aura,* Miles Davis. **Jazz Instrumental Performance, Group,** *Chick Corea Akoustic Band,* Chick Corea Akoustic Band. **Jazz Instrumental Performance, Big Band,** *Aura,* Miles Davis.

Video Awards: Music Video, Short Form, "Leave Me Alone," Michael Jackson. **Music Video, Long Form,** *Rhythm Nation,* Janet Jackson.

Classical Awards: Album, *Bartok: Six String Quartets,* Emerson String Quartet. **Orchestra Recording,** *Mahler: Symphony No. 3 in D Minor,* Leonard Bernstein conducting the New York Philharmonic. **Opera Recording,** *Wagner: Die Walküre,* James Levine conducting.

National Academy of Television Arts and Sciences. Emmy Awards, Comedy: Best Series, "Murphy Brown." **Lead Actor,** Ted Danson, "Cheers." **Lead Actress,** Candice Bergen, "Murphy Brown." **Supporting Actor,** Alex Rocco, "The Famous Teddy Z." **Supporting Actress,** Bebe Neuwirth, "Cheers."

Drama Awards: Best Series, "L.A. Law." **Lead Actor,** Peter Falk, "Columbo." **Lead Actress,** Patricia Wettig, "thirtysomething." **Supporting Actor,** Jimmy Smits, "L.A. Law." **Supporting Actress,** Marg Helgenberger, "China Beach."

Other Awards: Drama or Comedy Special, *Caroline?* and *The Incident.* **Miniseries,** *Drug Wars: The Camarena Story.* **Variety, Music, or Comedy Series,** "In Living Color." **Variety, Music, or Comedy Special,** *Sammy Davis, Jr.'s 60th Anniversary Celebration.* **Lead Actor in a Miniseries or Special,** Hume Cronyn, *Age-Old Friends.* **Lead Actress in a Miniseries or Special,** Barbara Hershey, *A Killing in a Small Town.* **Supporting Actor in a Miniseries or Special,** Vincent Gardenia, *Age-Old Friends.* **Supporting Actress in a Miniseries or Special,** Eva Marie Saint, *People Like Us.*

New York Drama Critics Circle Awards. Best New Play, *The Piano Lesson,* August Wilson. **Best New Musical,** *City of*

Angels. **Best New Foreign Play,** *Privates on Parade,* Peter Nichols.

Antoinette Perry (Tony) Awards. Drama Awards: Best Play, *The Grapes of Wrath.* **Leading Actor,** Robert Morse, *Tru.* **Leading Actress,** Maggie Smith, *Lettice and Lovage.* **Featured Actor,** Charles Durning, *Cat on a Hot Tin Roof.* **Featured Actress,** Margaret Tyzack, *Lettice and Lovage.* **Direction,** Frank Galati, *The Grapes of Wrath.*

Musical Awards: Best Musical, *City of Angels.* **Leading Actor,** James Naughton, *City of Angels.* **Leading Actress,** Tyne Daly, *Gypsy.* **Featured Actor,** Michael Jeter, *Grand Hotel.* **Featured Actress,** Randy Graff, *City of Angels.* **Direction,** Tommy Tune, *Grand Hotel.* **Choreography,** Tommy Tune, *Grand Hotel.*

Best Revival of a Play or Musical, *Gypsy.* **Lighting Design,** Jules Fisher, *Grand Hotel.* **Costume Design,** Santo Loquasto, *Grand Hotel.* **Scenic Design,** Robin Wagner, *City of Angels.*

United States government. National Medal of Arts, theatrical director George Abbott, choreographer Merce Cunningham, actor Hume Cronyn, painter Jasper Johns, blues guitarist B. B. King, art patron David Lloyd Kreeger, painter Jacob Lawrence, art patron Harris Masterton, art patron Carroll Masterton, landscape architect Ian McHarg, opera singer Beverly Sills, actress Jessica Tandy, Southwestern Bell Corporation for corporate sponsorship of the arts.

Wolf Foundation. Wolf Prizes, Italian composer Luciano Berio, German painter Anselm Kiefer, and American violinist Yehudi Menuhin.

Journalism awards

American Society of Magazine Editors. National Magazine Awards. General Excellence, Circulation over 1 Million, *Sports Illustrated;* **Circulation of 400,000 to 1 Million,** *Metropolitan Home;* **Circulation of 100,000 to 400,000,** *Texas Monthly;* **Circulation Under 100,000,** *7 Days.* **Personal Service,** *Consumer Reports.* **Special Interests,** *Art & Antiques.* **Reporting,** *The New Yorker.* **Public Interest,** *Southern Exposure.* **Design,** *Esquire.* **Photography,** *Texas Monthly.* **Essays and Criticism,** *Vanity Fair.* **Fiction,** *The New Yorker.* **Feature Writing,** *The Washingtonian.* **Single-Topic Issue,** *National Geographic Magazine.*

Long Island University. George Polk Memorial Awards: National Reporting, Rick Atkinson, *The Washington* (D.C.) *Post,* for a series on the Stealth bomber. **Local Reporting,** *The Hartford* (Conn.) *Courant,* for articles on the recording of suspects' conversations with their lawyers by the police. **Foreign Reporting,** Nicholas D. Kristof and Sheryl WuDunn, *The New York Times,* for coverage of the 1989 Chinese student uprising. **International Reporting,** Stephen Engelberg and Michael R. Gordon, *The New York Times,* for stories on chemical-weapons technology in the Third World. **Political Reporting,** Andrew Melnykovych, Casper, Wyo. *Star-Tribune* for exposing collusion between the federal government and 12 oil companies to cut back royalty payments to Wyoming. **Regional Reporting,** Miranda Ewell and David Schrieberg, *San Jose Mercury News,* for a series on the inadequacies of California court interpreters. **Medical Reporting,** John M. Crewdson, *Chicago Tribune,* for his article on the response of the scientific and political communities to the AIDS crisis. **Local Television Reporting,** WCSC-TV, Charleston, S.C., for coverage of Hurricane Hugo. **Network Television Reporting,** CBS News for coverage of the Chinese student uprising. **Television Investigative Reporting,** Jonathan Kwitny for "The Kwitny Report" on WNYC-TV, a series of analyses of international and domestic events. **Radio Reporting,** Robert Knight, senior producer of "Undercurrents," for coverage of the U.S. invasion of Panama. **Career Award,** Fred M. Hechinger, *The New York Times,* for 45 years of reporting on education.

The Society of Professional Journalists, Sigma Delta Chi. Sigma Delta Chi Distinguished Service Awards, Newspaper Awards: Deadline Reporting, *San Francisco Examiner* for its coverage of the October 1989 earth-

"Peanuts" creator Charles Schulz, left, receives the ribbon of a Commander of Arts and Letters in January from French Culture Minister Jack Lang.

quake. **Non-Deadline Reporting,** Tom Hallman, Jr., Dave Hogan, Holley Gilbert, Julie Tripp, Fred Leeson, James Long, and Lauren Cown, *The* (Portland, Ore.) *Oregonian,* for a series on the impact of drug abuse in that city. **Investigative Reporting,** Bob Paynter, Keith McKnight, and Andrew Zajac, Akron, Ohio *Beacon-Journal,* for a series on Ohio Speaker of the House Vernal G. Riffe, Jr. **Editorial Writing,** Lawrence Levy, *Newsday,* for editorials on Long Island's economic problems. **Washington Correspondence,** Bill Lambrecht, *St. Louis* (Mo.) *Post-Dispatch,* for an article on shipment of toxic waste to developing nations. **Foreign Correspondence,** Nora Boustany, *The Washington Post,* for her continuing coverage of the civil war in Lebanon. **Photography,** Patrick Davison, *The Albuquerque* (N.Mex.) *Tribune,* for photographs exploring the threat to elk from the worldwide trade in elk-horn products. **Editorial Cartooning,** Don Wright, *The Palm Beach* (Fla.) *Post.* **Public Service in Newspaper Journalism, Circulation More than 100,000,** *Lexington* (Ky.) *Herald-Leader* for an investigation of the politics of education in Kentucky. **Public Service in Newspaper Journalism, Circulation Less than 100,000,** *Washington* (N.C.) *Daily News* for a story about carcinogens in the city's water supply, and *The* (Quincy, Mass.) *Patriot Ledger* for a series on the influx of Asian Americans into that city.

Magazine Awards: Magazine Reporting, Daniel Golden for an article in *The Boston Globe Magazine* on the plight of the Oglala Sioux of the Pine Ridge Reservation in South Dakota. **Public Service in Magazine Journalism,** *Common Cause Magazine* for a series examining the "corrupting influence of money on the political process" in Washington, D.C., and *The New Yorker* for a series on how utility interests blocked scientific investigations of the harmful potential of electromagnetic fields created by power lines.

Radio Awards: Radio Spot-News Reporting, KCBS, San Francisco, for reporting on the October 1989 earthquake. **Radio Investigative Reporting,** Phil Rogers, WBBM, Chicago, for an exposé of security lapses at O'Hare Airport. **Public Serv-**

ice in Radio Journalism, KGO Radio, San Francisco, for its retrospective on the earthquake. **Editorializing on Radio,** WBBM, Chicago, for editorials on the issue of access for disabled people.

Television Awards: Television Spot-News Reporting, KGO-TV, San Francisco, for its coverage of the earthquake. **Public Service in Television Journalism, Networks and Stations in the Top 40 Markets,** WITI-TV, Milwaukee, for an analysis of teen age sexual behavior. **Public Service in Television Journalism, All Other Markets,** KSAT-TV, San Antonio, Tex., for its exploration of the effects of uranium mining on a rural south Texas county. **Television Editorials,** Ed Quinn, Paul Sands, Don Lundy, Judy Vance, and John Beatty, KGTV, San Diego, for editorials on various issues. **Television Investigative Reporting,** Mark Feldstein and Diane Sperrazza, WUSA-TV, Washington, D.C., for their investigation of charges of drug abuse by Washington Mayor Marion S. Barry, Jr.

Research About Journalism: Gregory Gordon and Ronald E. Cohen, *Down to the Wire: UPI's Fight for Survival.*

University of Georgia. George Foster Peabody Broadcasting Awards, KCBS-AM, San Francisco, for "Earthquake '89"; CBS Radio, New York City, for "China in Crisis"; National Public Radio for Scott Simon's radio essays on "Weekend Edition Saturday"; Canadian Broadcasting Corporation for *Lost Innocence: The Children of World War II; Mei Mei: A Daughter's Song,* on American Public Radio's "Soundprint" series; Texaco Incorporated and the Metropolitan Opera Association for 50 years of broadcasts; WCSC-TV, Charleston, S.C., for services to viewers in the aftermath of Hurricane Hugo; KGO-TV, San Francisco, for public service after the 1989 earthquake; KING-TV, Seattle, for "Project Home Team," an examination of the problems of the working poor; KRON-TV, San Francisco, for a report on homeless children in that city; Cable News Network, Atlanta, Ga., for coverage of the student uprising in China; Central Independent Television London, for an examination of the plight of Cambodia; MTV for *Decade,* a look back at

Awards and prizes

the 1980's; CBS and Motown-Pangaea Productions, in association with Quintex Entertainment, for the miniseries *Lonesome Dove;* American Broadcasting Companies (ABC) and the Black-Marlens Company, in association with New World Television, for "The Wonder Years"; ABC and Secret, in association with Warner Brothers Television, for "China Beach"; ABC, Lou Rudolph Films, Motown Productions, and Allarcom and Fries Entertainment for the miniseries *Small Sacrifices;* Beyond International Group, Sydney, Australia, for an examination of the Chinese People's Liberation Army; Home Box Office for *Common Threads: Stories from the Quilt;* KCNC-TV, Denver, for *Yellowstone: Four Seasons After the Fire;* Public Affairs Television, New York City, for *The Public Mind,* Bill Moyers' look at public opinion formation; WLOX-TV, Biloxi, Miss., for an examination of Mississippi's progress in race relations during the last 25 years; Film News Now, New York City, for *Who Killed Vincent Chin?,* an examination of a murder in Detroit; Children's Television Workshop, New York City, for "Sesame Street"; National Broadcasting Company (NBC) News for *NBC News Special: To Be an American;* David Brinkley for "exceptional contributions" to broadcasting; J. Leonard Reinsch for "a lifetime of outstanding service to his chosen profession."

Literature awards

Academy of American Poets. Lamont Poetry Selection, *The City in Which I Love You,* Li-Young Lee. **Harold Morton Landon Translation Award,** *Variable Directions* by Dan Pagis, translated by Stephen Mitchell.

American Library Association. Newbery Medal, *Number the Stars,* Lois Lowry. **Caldecott Medal,** *Lon Po Po: A Red-Riding Hood Story from China,* Ed Young, illustrator.

Booker Prize, *Possession: A Romance,* A. S. Byatt.

Canada Council. Governor General's Literary Awards, English-Language: Fiction, *Whale Music,* Paul Quarrington. **Poetry,** *The Word for Sand,* Heather Spears. **Drama,** *The Other Side of the Dark,* Judith Thompson. **Nonfiction,** *Willie: The Life of W. Somerset Maugham,* Robert Calder. **Translation,** *The Eighth Day,* English translation by Wayne Grady of Antonin Maillet's *Le Huitième Jour.* **Children's Literature (Text),** *Bad Boy,* Diana J. Wieler. **Children's Literature (Illustration),** *The Magic Paintbrush,* illustrated by Robin Muller.

French-Language: Fiction, *La Rage,* Louis Hamelin. **Poetry,** *Monème,* Pierre Desruisseaux. **Drama,** *Mademoiselle Rouge,* Michel Garneau. **Nonfiction,** *L'Intolérance: une problématique générale,* Lise Noël. **Translation,** *Les Ages de l'amour,* French translation by Jean Antonin Billard of Dorothy Livesay's *The Phases of Love.* **Children's Literature (Text),** *Temps mort,* Charles Montpetit. **Children's Literature (Illustration),** *Benjamin et la saga des oreillers,* illustrated by Stéphane Poulin.

Canadian Library Association. Book of the Year for Children Award, *The Sky Is Falling,* Kit Pearson. **Amelia Frances Howard-Gibbon Illustrator's Award,** *Til All the Stars Have Fallen: Canadian Poems for Children,* illustrated by Kady MacDonald Denton.

Columbia University. Bancroft Prizes in American History, *Dark Journey: Black Mississippians in the Age of Jim Crow,* Neil R. McMillen; *The Indians' New World: Catawbas and Their Neighbors from European Contact Through the Era of Removal,* James H. Merrell.

Ingersoll Foundation. Ingersoll Prizes: T. S. Eliot Award for Creative Writing, British poet Charles Causley. **Richard M. Weaver Award for Scholarly Letters,** American historian Forrest McDonald.

Library of Congress. Rebekah Johnson Bobbitt National Prize for Poetry, *The Inner Room,* James Merrill.

National Book Critics Circle. National Book Critics Circle Awards, Fiction, *Billy Bathgate,* E. L. Doctorow. **General Nonfiction,** *The Broken Cord,* Michael Dorris. **Biography/Autobiography,** *A First-Class Temperament: The Emergence of Franklin Roosevelt,* Geoffrey C. Ward. **Poetry,** *Transparent Gestures,* Rodney Jones. **Criticism,** *Not by Fact Alone: Essays on the Writing and Reading of History,* John Clive. **Citation for**

Excellence in Book Reviewing, Carol Anshaw, free-lance critic. **Ivan Sandrof Award for Contributions to American Book Publishing,** James Laughlin, founder of New Directions Press.

National Book Foundation. National Book Awards: Fiction, *Middle Passage,* Charles Johnson. **Nonfiction,** *The House of Morgan: An American Banking Dynasty and the Rise of Modern Finance,* Ron Chernow. **Medal for Distinguished Contribution to American Letters,** novelist Saul Bellow.

PEN American Center. Faulkner Award, *Billy Bathgate,* E. L. Doctorow.

Royal Society of Canada. Jason A. Hannah Medal, A. A. Travill, Queen's University, Kingston, Ont. **Tyrrell Medal,** Hubert Charbonneau, University of Montreal; Jacques Legare, University of Montreal.

Whitbread Book of the Year Award, *Coleridge: Early Visions,* Richard Holmes.

Nobel Prizes. See **Nobel Prizes.**

Public service awards

Martin Luther King, Jr., Center for Nonviolent Social Change. Martin Luther King, Jr., Nonviolent Peace Prize, Soviet President Mikhail S. Gorbachev; Joseph Lowery, head of the Southern Christian Leadership Conference.

National Association for the Advancement of Colored People. Spingarn Medal, Governor L. Douglas Wilder of Virginia.

Alexander Onassis Foundation. Onassis Prize, former President Jimmy Carter.

City of Philadelphia. Philadelphia Liberty Medal, former President Jimmy Carter.

Templeton Foundation. John M. Templeton Prize for Progress in Religion, Australian biologist L. Charles Birch; and Indian lawyer Murlidhar Devidas Amte, who devoted his life to helping lepers and outcasts.

Harry S. Truman Award for Public Service, former Surgeon General of the United States C. Everett Koop.

Pulitzer Prizes

Journalism. Public Service, *The Philadelphia Inquirer* for a series revealing shortcomings in federal regulation of blood banks; and *Washington* (N.C.) *Daily News* for articles on cancer-causing chemicals in the municipal water supply. **General News Reporting,** *San Jose Mercury News* for its coverage of the October 1989 earthquake. **National Reporting,** Ross Anderson, Bill Dietrich, Mary Ann Gwinn, and Eric Naider, *Seattle Times,* for coverage of the *Exxon Valdez* oil spill. **Investigative Reporting,** Lou Kilzer and Chris Ison, Minneapolis and St. Paul, Minn. *Star Tribune,* for an exposé of citizens who had links with the St. Paul Fire Department and who profited from fires of suspicious origin. **Explanatory Journalism,** Steven Coll and David A. Vise, *The Washington Post,* for a series on the Securities and Exchange Commission. **Specialized Reporting,** Tamar Stieber, *Albuquerque* (N.Mex.) *Journal,* for articles linking the dietary supplement L-tryptophan and a rare blood disorder. **International Reporting,** Nicholas D. Kristof and Sheryl WuDunn, *The New York Times,* for their coverage of the student uprising in China. **Feature Writing,** Dave Curtin, *Colorado Springs* (Colo.) *Gazette Telegraph,* for a feature story about the rehabilitation of a family after a propane gas explosion disfigured three members. **Commentary,** Jim Murray, *Los Angeles Times,* for his sports columns. **Criticism,** Allan Temko, *San Francisco Chronicle,* for his architecture criticism. **Editorial Writing,** Thomas J. Hylton, Pottstown, Pa. *Mercury,* for editorials advocating preservation of farmland and open space in Chester County. **Editorial Cartooning,** Tom Toles, *The Buffalo* (N.Y.) *News.* **Spot News Photography,** The (Oakland, Calif.) *Tribune* for its photography of the 1989 earthquake. **Feature Photography,** David C. Turnley, *Detroit Free Press,* for photographs of events in China, East Germany, and Romania.

Bonnie Raitt and John Lee Hooker show off the Grammy Awards they won in February for their traditional blues recording "I'm in the Mood."

Letters. Biography, *Machiavelli in Hell,* Sebastian de Grazia. **Fiction,** *The Mambo Kings Play Songs of Love,* Oscar Hijuelos. **General Nonfiction,** *And Their Children After Them,* Dale Maharidge and Michael Williamson. **History,** *In Our Image: America's Empire in the Philippines,* Stanley Karnow. **Drama,** *The Piano Lesson,* August Wilson. **Poetry,** *The World Doesn't End,* Charles Simic.

Music. Music Award, *Duplicates,* a Concerto for Two Pianos and Orchestra, Mel Powell.

Science and technology awards

Fields Medals. Vladimir G. Drinfeld, Institute for Low Temperature Physics and Engineering, Kharkov, Soviet Union; Vaughan F. R. Jones, University of California at Berkeley; Shigefumi Mori, Research Institute of Mathematical Sciences, Kyoto University, Japan; Edward Wittem, Institute for Advanced Studies, Princeton, N.J.

Franklin Institute. Bower Award, Paul C. Lauterbur, University of Illinois, Urbana-Champaign.

Gairdner Foundation. Gairdner Foundation International Awards, Francis Collins, University of Michigan Medical Center, Ann Arbor; Victor Ling, Ontario Cancer Institute, Toronto; John R. Riordan, Hospital for Sick Children, Toronto; Oliver Smithies, University of North Carolina, Chapel Hill; Edwin M. Southern, Oxford University, England; E. Donnall Thomas, Fred Hutchinson Cancer Research Center, Seattle; Lap-Chee Tsui, Hospital for Sick Children.

Royal Society of Canada. Bancroft Award, Steven D. Scott, University of Toronto. **Thomas W. Eadie Medal,** Frank P. Ottensmeyer, Ontario Cancer Institute. **Flavelle Medal,** Peter W. Hochachka, University of British Columbia, Vancouver. **McLaughlin Award,** Tak W. Mak, Ontario Cancer Institute. **Rutherford Medal in Chemistry,** M. D. Fryzuk, University of British Columbia. **Rutherford Medal in Physics,** Scott D. Tremaine, University of Toronto.

United States government. National Medal of Science, Baruj Benacerraf, Dana-Farber Cancer Institute, Boston; Elkan R. Blout, Harvard School of Public Health, Boston; Herbert W. Buyer, University of California at San Francisco; George F. Carrier, Harvard University, Cambridge, Mass.; Allan M. Cormack, Tufts University, Medford, Mass.; Mildred S. Dresselhaus, Massachusetts Institute of Technology, Cambridge; Karl A. Folkers, Institute for Biomedical Research, University of Texas, Austin; Leonid Hurwicz, University of Minnesota, Minneapolis; Stephen C. Kleene, University of Wisconsin, Madison; Daniel E. Koshland, Jr., University of California at Berkeley; Edward B. Lewis, California Institute of Technology (Caltech), Pasadena; John McCarthy, Stanford University, California; Edwin M. McMillan, University of California at Berkeley; David G. Nathan, Children's Hospital, Boston; Robert V. Pound, Harvard University; Roger Revelle, Scripps Institution of Oceanography, University of California at San Diego; John D. Roberts, California Institute of Technology (Caltech); Patrick Suppes, Stanford University; E. Donnall Thomas, Fred Hutchinson Cancer Research Center.

United States government. National Medal of Technology, John V. Atanasoff, Iowa State University, Ames; Marvin Camras, Illinois Institute of Technology, Chicago; E. I. du Pont de Nemours & Company; Donald N. Frey, Northwestern University, Evanston, Ill.; Frederick W. Garry, General Electric Company, Fairfield, Conn.; Wilson Greatbatch Limited; Jack St. Clair Kilby, Texas Instruments Incorporated, Dallas; John S. Mayo, American Telephone and Telegraph Company's Bell Laboratories, Murray Hill, N.J.; Gordon E. Moore, Intel Corporation, Santa Clara, Calif.; David B. Pall, Pall Corporation, East Hills, N.Y.; Chauncey Starr, Electric Power Research Institute, Palo Alto, Calif.

University of Southern California. Tyler Prize for Environmental Achievement, Thomas Eisner and Jerrold Meinwald, Cornell University.   Sara Dreyfuss

In *World Book,* see **Pulitzer Prizes.**

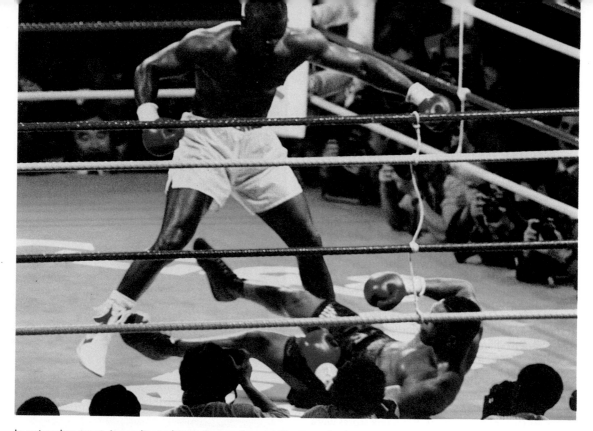

In a stunning upset, James (Buster) Douglas knocks out Mike Tyson in the 10th round to win the heavyweight championship in Tokyo in February.

recognized anyway, and he accepted a $24-million purse to fight Holyfield. The WBC, the WBA, and the IBF agreed that the Douglas-Holyfield winner should next fight Tyson.

Douglas and the 28-year-old Holyfield, of Atlanta, Ga., met on October 25 in Las Vegas, Nev. Douglas was overweight at 246 pounds (112 kilograms), and Holyfield knocked him out at 1 minute 10 seconds of the third round.

Holyfield decided to bypass Tyson and make his first defense against 42-year-old George Foreman on April 19, 1991, in Atlantic City, N.J. The WBC threatened to revoke Holyfield's title unless he fought Tyson first, and the dispute went to arbitration.

Foreman, a former heavyweight champion, retired in 1977 and started fighting again in 1987. He had won 24 consecutive bouts on his comeback.

Meanwhile, Tyson knocked out Henry Tillman after 47 seconds of the first round on June 16, 1990, in Las Vegas. Tyson knocked out Alex Stewart of Great Britain on December 8 in Atlantic City.

Other divisions. Pernell Whitaker, a lightweight from Norfolk, Va., was the only champion, aside from Holyfield, recognized by all three governing bodies. He achieved that distinction when he knocked out Juan Nazario of Puerto Rico in three rounds on August 11 at Lake Tahoe, Nev.   Frank Litsky

See also **Douglas, James (Buster).** In *World Book,* see **Boxing; Foreman, George; Tyson, Mike.**

Brazil. On March 15, 1990, Brazil entered a new political era with the inauguration of Fernando Collor de Mello to a five-year term as president. At 40 years of age, Collor was Brazil's youngest chief executive ever and the first popularly elected since 1960.

Collor pledged to make the free market dominant in the national economy by selling state-run enterprises that were dominant under previous military rule. On March 16, Collor introduced several goals for reforming the Brazilian economy. These included converting the nation's $31-billion deficit to a surplus and cutting inflation, which was 1,765 per cent in 1989, to less than 10 per cent.

Among the measures that Collor sought and that Congress approved in April 1990 were an 18-month freeze on all bank accounts of more than $1,200; a cutback in government subsidies to private industries; the elimination or consolidation of 24 government agencies; and new and higher taxes for corporations and wealthy individuals.

The austerity program proved popular among Brazil's creditors abroad. The Bank of Boston, in a reaction typical of many creditors, hailed it as "the most severe program of economic stabilization ever imposed in a Latin-American country, or perhaps in any country."

But in Brazil, the program quickly led to recession. By June, more than one-third of some 887,000 union workers in the manufacturing state of São Paulo had been laid off. According to the Industrial Federation of São Paulo, about 90 per cent of the state's industrial capacity was idle.

Automobile sales in Brazil dropped to nearly zero. Once-crowded cafes, hotels, and shops in Rio de Janeiro were practically empty. The city had already been suffering a 35 per cent drop in tourism going into the recession. In July, the United States Department of State warned Americans visiting the city to steer clear of once highly popular areas, including famed Copacabana beach, because of crime.

Rain forest Indians. In May, the Brazilian army began dynamiting 110 airstrips built by gold miners on Amazonian rain forest land reserved for the Yanomami Indians. The Yanomami are the Amazon's last major tribe still using Stone Age tools. Numbering about 10,000, many of them had never been in contact with the outside world until the 1980's. The army acted on instructions from Collor, who toured the area in March. Gold miners have caused extensive environmental damage in the Amazonian territory of Roraima and have brought diseases for which the Yanomami have no natural immunity. An estimated 900 Indians have died as a result.

Persian Gulf crisis. Of all Latin-American countries, Brazil was the hardest hit by the United Nations embargo on trade with Iraq, which followed Iraq's invasion of Kuwait in August. Prior to the embargo, which Brazil honored, Iraq and Brazil had developed a vigorous trade relationship.

Iraq had been supplying Brazil with more than half of its oil imports. In return, Brazilian companies had helped build hotels, highways, and a railroad in Iraq. Brazil had also supplied Iraq with a wide range of products, from cars and trucks to meat. By the time of the embargo, Brazil had become Iraq's second-largest source of industrial imports, which included weapons such as tanks, rockets, and armored cars.

Nuclear weapons project. In October, Brazil's top science official revealed a previously secret, though widely rumored, project to build an atomic bomb. The project had been started in 1975, when Brazil was under military rule. According to Brazilian physicists, before Collor closed down the project, Brazil was only two years away from producing a weapon comparable in explosive power to the one dropped on Hiroshima, Japan, during World War II (1939-1945).

One of the key figures in the bomb program, retired Air Force Brigadier Hugo de Oliveira Piva, had headed a group of 21 Brazilian rocketry scientists working in Iraq as employees of a private Brazilian company. Piva and the rest of the group returned to Brazil in October 1990. The group reportedly helped Iraq develop its ballistic missiles. Arms control experts also voiced fears that Piva might have passed on uranium enrichment technology needed for Iraq to develop its own atomic bomb.   Nathan A. Haverstock

See also **Collor de Mello, Fernando; Latin America** (Facts in brief table). In *World Book,* see **Brazil.**

British Columbia. Troubled by controversy and scandal, Premier William N. Vander Zalm addressed British Columbia residents by television on Jan. 17, 1990, blaming his lagging popularity on what he called "lies" by opponents inside and outside his party. Public opinion polls at the time showed Vander Zalm's Social Credit government 15 percentage points below the opposition New Democratic Party.

On July 12, Attorney General Stuart Smith resigned. He had been accused of interfering in a court case relating to alleged improprieties by another cabinet minister. Smith returned to the cabinet on December 13 as minister of regional and economic development. Also in December, Environment Minister John Reynolds resigned because, he said, Vander Zalm was preventing him from effectively tightening pollution-control standards.

Throughout the summer, discontent among the province's 77,000 Indians resulted in rail and road blockades. The discontent stemmed mostly from frustration with the long procedure of settling land claims. In August, the cabinet reversed a policy by which the province left negotiating Indian land claims to the federal government. On October 3, the province said it would begin to negotiate with the Nisga tribal council regarding the tribe's extensive claims in northwestern British Columbia.   David M. L. Farr

In *World Book,* see **British Columbia.**

Brunei. See Asia.

Building and construction. Economic stagnation, overbuilding, and the savings and loan crisis hit the United States construction industry like a sledge hammer in 1990. As a result of the savings and loan crisis, easily borrowed money became a thing of the past. By the end of August, new contract awards were down by 11 per cent from the same period in 1989, according to economists at McGraw-Hill Incorporated, a leading source of construction industry data.

In October 1990, the investment firm Bear, Stearns & Company, Incorporated, reported that some of the largest regional banks in the United States would write off billions of dollars in bad construction loans over the next 12 to 24 months. The cause of the bad debt: too many buildings and too few tenants. In 1990, the banks avoided lending money to developers and contractors except for commercial projects in which most space had been leased in advance.

Some markets took a nose dive. Of the $102.7 billion in new contracts awarded during the first eight months of 1990, only $4.4 billion went for manufacturing plants, a 34 per cent drop from the same period in 1989. New contracts for commercial buildings totaled $26.4 billion in that period, a 16 per cent decline. Single-family housing starts fell to 620,240, an 8 per cent decline, and multifamily housing tumbled to 188,924 new starts, a 28 per cent decline.

Spending on military construction took a roller coaster ride in 1990. As democratic reforms swept

Europe's tallest building, the 70-story Messeturm
—or Fair Tower—in Frankfurt am Main, Germany,
nears its October completion.

across eastern Europe and Germany moved toward unification, the United States Department of Defense in January put a freeze on construction projects worth $7 billion. For the first eight months of the year, new contracts totaled just $73.4 million, down 41 per cent from that period in 1989.

Then in August 1990, Iraq invaded Kuwait. The freeze was lifted on some U.S. military construction projects, and plans were announced for new hospitals, water supply systems, and housing for U.S. troops sent to Saudi Arabia.

The year's only bright spots in domestic construction came from public works. New contracts for airports rose by 28 per cent, for dams and waterway development by 13 per cent, and for highways by 2 per cent in the first eight months of 1990.

Notable achievements. Despite the weak markets, construction records were still set around the world. A long-awaited moment arrived on October 30 when British tunnelers beneath the English Channel made their first contact—by machine—with French tunnelers. The two teams met on December 1 and broke open the service tunnel, the smallest of the three tunnels that will connect Dover, England, and Calais, France. The two outer tunnels will carry electric trains. The 31-mile (50-kilometer) tunnel project, scheduled for completion in 1993, runs underwater for 23½ miles (37.8 kilometers), making it the longest underwater tunnel in the world.

On Sept. 19, 1990, the British tunnel boring machine, which had been boring toward the southeast for 16 months, broke into the *crossover chamber* 5 miles (8 kilometers) from the British coast. The crossover chamber will allow trains to switch tracks during tunnel maintenance. The machine boring northwest toward England had already cleared the 535-foot (160-meter) chamber.

In another tunneling first, contractors brought a hydroshield tunnel boring machine from West Germany to Edmonton, Canada, to complete a section of the Canadian city's light-rail system in January. The tunnel ran only 1,000 feet (300 meters), but through extremely soft soil. The hydroshield tunneling machine keeps the tunnel's soft face from collapsing by applying continuous pressure from a fluid. The technique had never before been used in North America.

In August, contractors in Milan, Italy, reached the halfway point in building an underground railroad station beneath the city's center. The difficult conditions posed by weak, sandy soil had sparked an original solution: The contractor built an arched subterranean structure before excavating the ground beneath it. The contractor had first injected *grout* (a thin cement or plaster) to stabilize the soil. Workers then pushed in 10 rows of pipes that ran the length of the station and created its arched crown. Construction crews excavated galleries next to the crown and built side supports. Arches were cast to spring from the supports and carry the pipes on the crown. The contractor could then excavate beneath the crown to create the station, which was scheduled to open in 1992.

In April 1990, the French firm Soletanche completed the world's deepest seepage cutoff wall at Mud Mountain Dam, an earth-and-rockfill embankment dam on the White River southeast of Seattle. To stop seepage through cracks in the dam, the firm installed a wall that penetrated about 400 feet (120 meters) from the dam's crest into bedrock.

Tall buildings. The tallest building in Europe, the Messeturm (Fair Tower) in Frankfurt am Main, Germany, was completed in October. The 70-story office building, which rises 841 feet 6 inches (256.5 meters), was designed by Chicago-based architect Helmut Jahn and built by a U.S. developer. The American developer spurred the German contractor to cut 5 months off the planned 42-month construction schedule. Instead of fire stairs just inside the outer walls, as German fire codes had required, the tower's core has stairwells that are pressurized with air to keep out smoke.

Construction started in May on Japan's tallest building. The Landmark Tower in Yokohama will rise 971 feet (296 meters) and will use semiactive dampers to control vibrations caused by wind. The dampers are concrete masses connected to the building by spring-like devices just below the roof. The $1.3-billion cost estimate for the building includes a 70-story office and hotel tower, a 5-story shopping mall, and parking for more than 1,400 cars.

The government of Hong Kong awarded its first contract in May for one of the world's largest projects. Bechtel Group Incorporated, a San Francisco-based engineering and construction company, will assist the colony in planning and executing a major transportation development program. The project includes a new international airport on Lantau Island, a major seaport expansion, and rail and highway connections. A planned suspension bridge between Lantau and Tsing Yi Island could have the world's longest main span.

A complex billed as the world's biggest, priciest, and glitziest casino opened in Atlantic City, N.J., in April. The $1.2-billion resort was designed in the style of the Taj Mahal, after which it was named. The foundering project had been rescued by entrepreneur Donald J. Trump after the death of its originator, millionaire recluse James Crosby, in 1986. The Trump Taj Mahal boasts a 44-story hotel, a casino measuring 120,000 square feet (11,100 square meters), a 5,200-seat exhibit hall and arena, and a rebuilt historic pier. It opened to mobs of tourists, but soon afterward Trump found himself overextended financially. In July 1990, he still owed subcontractors and suppliers for the Taj $70 million. In November, Trump agreed to turn over a 50 per cent share in the Taj Mahal to his creditors.   Janice Lyn Tuchman

In *World Book,* see **Building construction; Sky-scraper; Tunnel.**

French and British tunnel workers meet beneath the English Channel on December 1, three years after the digging of the "Chunnel" began.

Bulgaria

Bulgaria returned former Communists to power in free elections in June 1990. Despite the victory, the Communist Party—which renamed itself the Bulgarian Socialist Party in April—struggled for direction amid party infighting and an inability to persuade opposition parties to join a coalition government. Ongoing protests and widespread strikes finally brought down the Socialist government on November 29.

In November 1989, Communist reformers had ousted Todor Zhivkov, the hard-liner who had ruled since 1954. In February 1990, the party named Andrey K. Lukanov, an economist, to act as prime minister until the June elections. Petur T. Mladenov, who had replaced Zhivkov after helping to oust him, was named to the newly created post of president in April.

A heavy turnout in two rounds of voting on June 10 and June 17 gave the Socialists (formerly Communists) 211 seats in the 400-member Grand National Assembly, Bulgaria's single-chamber legislature. Lukanov stayed on as prime minister after his party's victory. The Union of Democratic Forces (UDF), an umbrella organization of 16 opposition parties, won 144 seats. A primarily Muslim party, the Movement for Rights and Freedom, picked up 23 seats despite limited access to the media and violent opposition from Bulgarian nationalists. Many of Bulgaria's Muslims, who are of Turkish ancestry, had fled to Turkey to escape attempts by the Zhivkov regime to force them to give up their religion and culture. Large numbers returned to Bulgaria after Zhivkov's ouster and the repeal of the discriminatory measures.

In July, Mladenov resigned amid charges that he had suggested calling in tanks to crush the protest that brought down Zhivkov. It was the Assembly's job to pick a new president by a two-thirds majority. After five rounds of balloting ended in deadlock, the Socialists withdrew their candidate and UDF leader Zhelyu Zhelev, a former philosophy professor, was elected on August 1. He became Bulgaria's first non-Communist head of state in 43 years. The Socialists had hoped to persuade the UDF to join a coalition government. "We prefer national consent," Lukanov told the Assembly, "to a monopoly of power." But the UDF refused to enter a coalition with the Socialists.

The Socialist Party depicted itself as a "modern party of democratic socialism." But the split between hard-liners and reformers made this depiction unconvincing to many Bulgarians. Public support for the party steadily declined during the year.

On September 22, the Socialist Party convened what it termed a Congress of Renewal. But bitter infighting produced just the reverse as the party dealt Lukanov's reform wing a double setback. The congress reelected Alexander Lilov, a conservative and top Zhivkov adviser until 1983, as party chairman. Lilov's supporters then pushed prominent reformers off the party's ruling Supreme Council.

The continued presence of Zhivkov officials in the Bulgarian government led to rising demands that the Socialists step down. On Aug. 26, 1990, demonstrators set fire to the Socialist Party headquarters in Sofia, Bulgaria's capital. President Zhelev denounced the rioters as extremists who "want dictatorship, not democracy."

The political deadlock virtually paralyzed any action on economic reform. The UDF opposition urged economic "shock therapy" to get reforms working. But the governing Socialists favored a gradual shift to a free-market economy. Food rationing and acute shortages of nearly all goods increased public anger at the government and fueled widespread demonstrations. The demonstrations developed into a nationwide strike on November 26, which persuaded Lukanov to resign three days later. On December 7, the Assembly elected Dimitar Popov, a politically independent judge, to succeed Lukanov. Popov was to head the government until elections were held in 1991.

Zhivkov, Bulgaria's former Communist leader, remained under house arrest. On Dec. 11, 1990, he was charged with embezzlement and abuse of power.

As winter approached, the outlook was bleak. Bulgaria, like other former Soviet allies, was hit hard by the Soviet Union's decision to accept only *hard* (internationally exchangeable) currency for its goods after Jan. 1, 1991.   Eric Bourne

See also **Europe** (Facts in brief table). In *World Book,* see **Bulgaria.**

Burkina Faso. See Africa.

Burma. The people of Burma (also called Myanmar) decisively rejected the nation's harsh military regime in parliamentary elections on May 27, 1990. But the ruling State Law and Order Restoration Council refused to hand over power, and its army troops crushed the resulting demonstrations.

The government, which ruled under martial law, had promised the elections in 1988. But the regime severely limited campaigning and oppressed the leaders of the main opposition party, the National League for Democracy (NLD). The head of the NLD, Aung San Suu Kyi, was kept under house arrest. Government troops also forced some 500,000 people to move from cities to rural areas in a "beautification" measure apparently designed to break up pockets of opposition.

Election results. Of the 485 parliamentary seats contested, the NLD won 392, 88 per cent of those for which it put up candidates, while the National Unity Party, which supported the military regime, won only 10 seats. Many of the NLD wins came among constituents in the military, suggesting that soldiers were becoming dissatisfied with their generals.

The regime reacted to defeat by stalling, ignoring calls for the release of Suu Kyi and other political prisoners. Officials said on July 27 that parliament's only job would be to write a constitution along guidelines provided by the regime and then submit it to a regime-appointed national convention.

In the fall, the regime arrested dozens of NLD mem-

An image of Burma's opposition leader Aung San Suu Kyi smiles in apparent approval of vote tallies showing her party's victory in May elections.

bers including Kyi Maung, who was leading the party in the absence of Suu Kyi. After some NLD members formed a rival government, the regime on December 20 outlawed the party.

Monks protest. On August 8, exactly two years after soldiers killed hundreds of demonstrators in Rangoon, the capital, some 300 Buddhist monks and students marched in Mandalay, the main religious center of the devoutly Buddhist country. Troops reportedly killed two monks and two students during the march, and this led to more demonstrations.

Monks then began refusing to accept soldiers' obligatory offerings of alms and declining to officiate at religious ceremonies for soldiers. Concerned that this would harm morale, the regime banned most Buddhist organizations, declared the monks' boycott illegal, and on October 22 began raiding monasteries in Mandalay and arresting monks.

Two Western human-rights organizations reported in May and August that the Burmese government used torture and was responsible for other "gross human-rights violations." The regime issued denials. On September 21, 17 Western nations protested that personnel in their embassies had suffered human-rights abuses and harassment.   Henry S. Bradsher

See also **Asia** (Facts in brief table). In *World Book,* see Burma.
Burundi. See Africa.
Bus. See Transit.

Bush, George Herbert Walker (1924-   ), 41st President of the United States, rode a popularity roller coaster in 1990 as he moved the nation close to war in the Middle East, became an outspoken supporter of Soviet President Mikhail S. Gorbachev, and reached a $492-million deficit-paring accord with congressional Democrats at the cost of splitting his own party.

Bush's approval rating in national opinion polls exceeded 70 per cent during much of the year but plunged to near 50 per cent in October. Part of that decline could be attributed to the success of Democratic efforts to remove some of the luster from the President's image. During congressional negotiations with the White House over tax hikes and spending cuts to reduce mounting budget deficits, Democrats pictured Bush as an indecisive champion of the rich. Bush rocked fellow Republicans in June by abandoning the "no new taxes" pledge he made during the 1988 presidential campaign, and he had to rely on Democrats to enact the budget agreement. A majority of Republicans in both the Senate and House of Representatives voted against him—a stunning defeat.

The Persian Gulf crisis. As 1990 drew to a close, Americans worried about prospects of war against Iraq and its strongman leader, Saddam Hussein. Earlier in the year—on August 2—the Iraqi army had invaded the tiny Persian Gulf oil kingdom of Kuwait. Many people wondered if Bush had boxed himself into a corner by insisting in the days following the in-

213

Bush, George Herbert Walker

vasion that he would accept nothing less than Iraq's unconditional withdrawal from Kuwait. Hussein vowed defiantly that Iraq would fight to keep Kuwait.

The spirit of cooperation between Bush and Gorbachev was dramatized 24 hours after the Iraqi invasion. In Moscow, Soviet Foreign Minister Eduard A. Shevardnadze and U.S. Secretary of State James A. Baker III jointly urged all nations to immediately halt arms shipments to Iraq. The Soviet Union had been a major supplier of weapons to Hussein's regime.

The prospect of an Iraqi stranglehold on the world economy, which is dependent on oil, prompted Bush on August 7 to send U.S. troops to Saudi Arabia to discourage Iraq from invading that nation as well. Saudi Arabia's King Fahd bin Abd al-Aziz Al-Saud approved the deployment of a multinational force to defend his country, a move agreed to by 11 other Arab nations. American forces soon were joined by soldiers from Egypt, Great Britain, France, Morocco, and other countries. The U.S. Navy was dispatched to blockade Iraq's seagoing trade.

Within three months, about 230,000 Americans and their planes, tanks, attack helicopters, and other weapons were in Saudi Arabia, or on ships in the Persian Gulf, as part of "Operation Desert Shield." In November, Bush ordered an additional 150,000 to 200,000 troops to the Middle East. That deployment included many reservists—the first mobilization of the military reserves in 20 years.

President George Bush chats with preschoolers at an antidrug rally in Philadelphia in July. "No crack [cocaine] in Philadelphia," he later urged.

Soviets stand with U.S. Bush was the driving force behind a succession of censure resolutions voted against Iraq by the United Nations (UN) Security Council. There were no dissenting votes (though two abstentions—Cuba and Yemen) on August 6 as the world body ordered an international embargo on trade with Iraq. And on November 29, the Council voted 12 to 2, with 1 abstention, to authorize the use of "all necessary means"—which was taken to mean military force—if Iraq did not withdraw from Kuwait by Jan. 15, 1991. Cuba and Yemen voted no, and China abstained. The Soviet Union voted in favor of both resolutions. Such unanimity against aggression would have been all but impossible during the Cold War, when the United States and the Soviet Union were frequent adversaries in Security Council votes.

The new era of U.S.-Soviet accord was underscored on Sept. 9, 1990, when Bush and Gorbachev met for a one-day summit conference in Helsinki, Finland. The two leaders threatened unspecified additional steps against Iraq if Hussein failed to heed UN demands to withdraw from Kuwait.

Growing concern in Congress. In a closed meeting with congressional leaders, Bush spoke of a possible "issue-forcing event" in the Middle East that would justify the start of war. Although most members of Congress praised Bush's handling of the Persian Gulf crisis, worries were expressed in both houses about the possibility of warfare and the effects it might have on U.S. society and the economy. Lawmakers cautioned Bush that the Constitution gives only Congress the authority to declare war. In November, Republican congressional leaders called for a special session to debate U.S. policy in the gulf, but Bush deflected them, promising that he would consult with Congress before launching any military action.

November tour. On November 16, Bush and his wife, Barbara, embarked on an eight-day tour of Europe and the Middle East. They visited Czechoslovakia and Germany, then went to Paris where the President joined Gorbachev at a 34-nation summit marking the end of the Cold War. Bush next met with leaders of Saudi Arabia, Egypt, and Syria and with the exiled emir of Kuwait. In Saudi Arabia, he and his wife spent Thanksgiving Day with American troops.

One of the President's principal objectives while traveling was to seek support for military action against Iraq should it continue to occupy Kuwait. Gorbachev said he would back Bush on the use of force.

U.S.-Soviet cooperation was not confined to the Persian Gulf crisis. In February, Gorbachev agreed to a Bush proposal to limit the number of Soviet and American troops stationed in central Europe. This promising development was threatened for a time by Soviet resistance to an independence movement in Lithuania, but the Lithuanians later agreed to postpone their demands to sever ties with Moscow. Lithuania was an independent nation from 1918 until 1940, when the Soviet Union annexed it.

At the start of a summit meeting in Washington, D.C., on May 30, President Bush and Soviet President Mikhail Gorbachev watch a 21-gun salute.

Gorbachev flew to Washington, D.C., on May 30 for a four-day summit. No electrifying accomplishments resulted, but Bush agreed to a trade pact that could lead to an eventual lowering of tariffs on Soviet goods. Bush had opposed the pact but changed his mind so Gorbachev, facing opposition at home, could return to Moscow with a symbolic victory. In December, in response to a growing economic crisis in the Soviet Union that was raising the specter of famine, Bush again came to Gorbachev's aid. He authorized up to $1 billion in federally guaranteed loans to enable the Soviet Union to buy food for its empty markets.

Relations with Israel. United States policy in the Middle East became more complicated on October 8, when Israeli police officers killed at least 17 Palestinian demonstrators in Jerusalem. The United States joined in two UN Security Council votes denouncing Israel for the killings and for its refusal to allow UN officials to investigate the incident. As a result of the United States stance on the issue, U.S.-Israeli relations suffered. In December, Israeli Prime Minister Yitzhak Shamir visited the White House to meet with Bush. On December 20, the United States voted for a Council resolution that called the occupied West Bank and the Gaza Strip "Palestinian territories" and criticized Israel for deporting Palestinians.

Economic summit. In July, Bush was host in Houston to an annual seven-nation economic summit. The major agreement involved a promise of lower subsidies for European farmers to make American agricultural products more competitive in Europe. But at year end, these subsidies continued to be a sticking point between the United States and Europe.

Visits to Latin America. Bush flew to Cartagena, Colombia, on February 15 for a brief meeting with the presidents of the world's three leading cocaine-producing countries: Colombia, Bolivia, and Peru. The four leaders signed an accord pledging to cooperate in fighting the illegal-drug trade. Bush visited Mexico after Thanksgiving and, in December, traveled to Brazil, Uruguay, Argentina, Chile, and Venezuela.

Health. On April 12, Bush had a routine physical examination that disclosed early glaucoma—fluid build-up in the eyeball—in his left eye that was treatable with eyedrops. In January, Barbara Bush underwent radiation treatments for Graves' disease, a thyroid disorder. And in February, a small skin cancer was removed from her upper lip.

Personal finances. The White House reported on May 2 that the Bushes made an error on their tax return and had filed an amended return reporting an additional $26,250 in 1989 income. They paid $108,879 in taxes on income of $483,030, plus $40.77 in interest.   Frank Cormier and Margot Cormier

See also **Congress of the United States; United States, Government of the.** In *World Book,* see Bush, George Herbert Walker.

Business. See Bank; Economics; Manufacturing.

215

Calderón Fournier, Rafael Angel (1949-), the son of a former president, was elected president of Costa Rica on Feb. 4, 1990. He was inaugurated on May 8, succeeding Oscar Arias Sánchez, winner of the 1987 Nobel Peace Prize. See **Costa Rica.**

Calderón was born on March 14, 1949, in Diriamba, Nicaragua. His family had fled to Nicaragua after his father was accused of trying to nullify the results of a 1948 presidential election. His father had been president from 1940 to 1944. The family soon moved to Mexico, where Calderón went to elementary and high school. After the family returned to Costa Rica, Calderón graduated with a law degree from the University of Costa Rica near San José.

Calderón was elected to the National Assembly in 1974. He was foreign minister from 1978 to 1980. He ran for president in 1982 and lost. In 1986, as the candidate of the Social Christian Unity Party, he ran again and lost to Arias with 46 per cent of the vote. Following his defeat, Calderón became executive director of a right wing group that campaigned against Arias' Central American peace plan—aimed at ending the civil war in Nicaragua. In 1990, Calderón ran again and won with 52 per cent of the vote, defeating the candidate of Arias' National Liberation Party.

Calderón is married to the former Gloria Bejarano Almada. They have four children.   Rod Such

California. See Los Angeles; San Diego; State government.

Cambodia. Intensive diplomacy during 1990 sought to end the warfare that has ravaged Cambodia (formerly Kampuchea) for two decades. But fighting continued between the Communist regime and an unstable coalition of three guerrilla groups. Two of the groups are anti-Communist, including one headed by Norodom Sihanouk, a former ruler of Cambodia. The third is the Communist Khmer Rouge, the rulers of Cambodia from 1975 through 1978.

UN peace plan. The five permanent members of the United Nations (UN) Security Council agreed on a Cambodian peace plan in Paris on Jan. 6, 1990. The plan called for a cease-fire, an end to outside military aid, and free elections. But follow-up talks in Indonesia broke down on March 1 over the coalition's demands that the present regime be dismantled and that the UN run the nation until elections.

After several other meetings failed, Vietnam and China held talks in Hanoi, Vietnam, in June. Vietnam, the main supporter of the Cambodian regime, and China, the key backer of the Khmer Rouge, agreed to get the two groups to work toward a settlement.

Fearing that the Khmer Rouge might return to power, U.S. officials announced on July 18 that the United States was withdrawing recognition of the coalition as the rightful government of Cambodia and would hold its first talks with Vietnam on the subject. These talks began on August 6 at the UN Headquarters. The five UN Council members agreed on August

After more than a decade of exile, Norodom Sihanouk, the leader of a Cambodian opposition guerrilla group, returns to Cambodia in February.

216

27 to put Cambodia under temporary UN control if the regime and the coalition agreed. The members also planned to set up a Supreme National Council (SNC) as an interim government until elections.

Deadlock. After China and Vietnam met again in September, the regime and the coalition agreed to accept the UN plan. But the SNC's first meeting broke down on September 20. UN Council members worked to overcome the deadlock. They hoped to convene a meeting in early 1991 to put the UN plan into action.

Savage war. While diplomats talked, ordinary people throughout much of Cambodia were caught between the regime and the Khmer Rouge guerrillas. Both sides forced civilians to help them and killed many. According to diplomats, Vietnam—which in 1989 officially withdrew its army from Cambodia—had thousands of advisers and even some artillery and tank units helping the regime. The regime denied the charge. China continued to supply the Khmer Rouge, but the U.S. Congress in October decided to halt aid to the anti-Communist guerrilla groups.

Power struggle. In June, the regime announced that foreign enemies had "set up a traitorous force" inside Cambodia to stage a coup, but the event later appeared to have been an internal power struggle that the regime's leaders won.   Henry S. Bradsher

See also **Asia** (Facts in brief table); **Vietnam.** In *World Book,* see **Cambodia.**

Cameroon. See Africa.

Canada experienced a troubled year in 1990. The federal government, led by Prime Minister Brian Mulroney, head of the Progressive Conservative Party, found itself frustrated in achieving its principal objectives. The goal of reconciling French-speaking Quebec to the federal system was thwarted when the Meech Lake constitutional accord was rejected. The accord's failure intensified demands in Quebec for independence (see **Close-Up**).

Dissatisfaction over the federal government's slowness in dealing with Indian and Inuit land claims led to unrest and armed stand-offs between law enforcement officers and members of several native groups. A broad new tax on goods and services aroused anger from coast to coast and brought the government into collision with the opposition Liberal Party, securely based in the appointive upper house of Parliament, the Senate.

As the year ended, the country faced an economic recession, a condition likely to accentuate tension among Canadians. Beset by these difficulties, the Mulroney government slumped to an unprecedented low point in public opinion polls. It had the support of 15 per cent of decided voters in October, compared with more than 30 per cent for each of two rival political parties, the Liberal Party and the New Democratic Party.

Indian unrest in the summer was triggered by the struggles of a band of Mohawk Indians living at Oka,

Que., 20 miles (30 kilometers) west of Montreal. To prevent the extension of a city-owned golf course onto what they considered ancestral lands, the Indians erected a barricade on a nearby road. On July 11, the Quebec provincial police stormed the barricade in an effort to enforce a court order to remove it. In the confusion, a police officer was killed by gunfire, and the police retreated.

An armed stand-off began. Other Mohawks living on the Kahnawake reserve on the St. Lawrence River across from Montreal expressed sympathy for the Oka Indians. The sympathizers blocked roads and a main bridge linking communities on the south shore of the St. Lawrence with the city. The action led to long detours for people driving to work in Montreal and to

Canada, provinces, and territories population estimates

	1990
Alberta	2,469,800
British Columbia	3,131,700
Manitoba	1,089,900
New Brunswick	723,900
Newfoundland	573,000
Northwest Territories	54,000
Nova Scotia	891,600
Ontario	9,731,200
Prince Edward Island	130,400
Quebec	6,762,200
Saskatchewan	1,000,300
Yukon Territory	26,000
Canada	**26,584,000**

City and metropolitan populations

	Metropolitan area 1990 estimate	City 1986 census
Toronto, Ont.	3,751,700	612,289
Montreal, Que.	3,068,100	1,015,420
Vancouver, B.C.	1,547,000	431,147
Ottawa-Hull	863,900	
Ottawa, Ont.		300,763
Hull, Ont.		58,722
Edmonton, Alta.	817,800	573,982
Calgary, Alta.	724,800	636,104
Winnipeg, Man.	647,100	594,551
Quebec, Que.	622,200	164,580
Hamilton, Ont.	594,600	306,728
London, Ont.	368,200	269,140
St. Catharines-Niagara	558,300	
St. Catharines, Ont.		123,455
Niagara Falls, Ont.		72,107
Kitchener, Ont.	346,000	150,604
Halifax, N.S.	312,000	113,577
Victoria, B.C.	278,700	66,303
Windsor, Ont.	260,700	193,111
Oshawa, Ont.	244,800	123,651
Saskatoon, Sask.	205,000	177,641
Regina, Sask.	190,600	175,064
St. John's, Nfld.	163,900	96,216
Chicoutimi-Jonquière	158,000	
Chicoutimi, Que.		61,083
Jonquière, Que.		58,467
Sudbury, Ont.	149,200	88,717
Sherbrooke, Ont.	134,300	74,438
Trois-Rivières, Que.	131,600	50,122
Saint John, N.B.	124,200	76,381
Thunder Bay, Ont.	123,600	112,272

Source: Statistics Canada.

Ramon J. Hnatyshyn reviews the troops at his swearing-in as Canada's 24th governor general in January 1990.

noisy confrontations between the residents, the police, and the Mohawks.

Faced with a growing threat to law and order, Quebec Premier Robert Bourassa asked the Canadian Armed Forces to intervene on August 8. Over the next two weeks, 3,300 soldiers, fully armed, took up positions at the south end of the Montreal bridge and at Oka, but the Mohawks maintained their positions.

Throughout the stalemate, the provincial government and the Mohawks conducted on-and-off negotiations monitored by both the federal government and a Paris-based human-rights organization. The Indians were allowed access to food and medical supplies, as well as spiritual and legal advisers. Discussion dragged on for weeks, with Mohawk negotiators frequently changing their demands. The talks reached a standstill when the Mohawks requested immunity from criminal prosecution. Quebec insisted that the barricades be dismantled before the Indians' pleas were considered.

On August 27, Bourassa ordered the army to remove the barricades. This was done peacefully in spite of threats made earlier by members of the militant Mohawk Warriors Society stationed at the barricades. At Oka, about 30 Mohawks made a last stand in a medical treatment center on the reserve. They surrendered to the army on September 26 after a stand-off of 11 weeks. The Indians were charged with rioting, obstruction of justice, and the possession of illegal weapons.

The Mohawk Warrior Society was a leading force in the Indian unrest in Quebec. Some members of the group were from the St. Regis-Akwesasne reserve on the St. Lawrence River above Montreal, a reserve that straddles the Canada-United States border. In May, armed clashes had occurred among the Mohawks over cigarette smuggling and the operation of bingo casinos on the U.S. section of the reserve. Two Indians had been killed in the skirmishes before Canadian and U.S. police moved in to occupy the reserve. Other Mohawks on the barricades were believed to have come from a Warriors' training center near Plattsburgh, N.Y.

Mohawk unrest drew attention to Indian complaints throughout Canada about the slow pace of the federal government's settling of land claims. The government had settled only 44 claims in 17 years, with another 275 awaiting adjudication. Currently, the federal and territorial governments spend approximately $4 billion Canadian ($3.4 billion U.S.) on Canadian native peoples. More money would be required to compensate Indians and Inuit in their land claims and to improve living conditions and economic opportunities on Canada's 2,283 Indian reserves. Most Indians earn only half the income of non-Indians.

In response to these complaints, the federal government promised to consider granting self-government

ate by filling 15 vacancies with individuals committed to support the GST. Still lacking a Progressive Conservative majority, the prime minister used—for the first time ever—a provision of the British North America Act of 1867 giving him power to appoint eight additional senators to break a deadlock between the two houses.

The eight new senators represent the four Senate districts: the Atlantic Provinces, Quebec, Ontario, and the West. As vacancies occur in the representation from these districts (senators must retire at age 75), they will be filled from the group of additional senators. The new appointments brought the Conservative standing to 54 in an expanded 112-seat chamber, which also held 52 Liberals, 4 independents, 1 Liberal-independent, and 1 Reform Party member.

The Liberal senators reacted furiously to Mulroney's appointments, holding up proceedings in the upper house for a week by engaging in demonstrations and long speeches. On October 18, an agreement was reached whereby Liberal senators promised not to block passage of other government measures, such as changes to the unemployment insurance plan, which had been stalled in the Senate since 1989. In return, the Conservatives agreed to allow eight proposed amendments to the GST to be considered when debate began after Oct. 29, 1990. The Conservative majority defeated all the Liberal amendments, leaving the possibility of amendments proposed by the independent senators.

The Senate gave final approval to the GST by a vote of 55 to 49 on December 13. The Senate's action cleared the way for the new tax to take effect on Jan. 1, 1991.

The political scene. The Conservatives, although frustrated by the setbacks to their legislative program, maintained a healthy majority in the Commons. At the opening of Parliament for the 1990 fall session, the party held 158 seats in the 295-seat chamber. The Liberals held 78 seats. The New Democratic Party had 44—having elected its first Quebec member in an election to fill a vacant seat on February 12—and the Reform Party, 1. There were also 9 members of the newly formed Bloc Québécois, intent on sovereignty for Quebec; 3 independents; and 2 vacancies.

The Liberal Party chose a new leader on June 23 at a convention in Calgary, Alta. Jean Chrétien, 56, had been a member of Parliament since 1963, holding many important cabinet posts under Prime Minister Trudeau. Defeated in a run for party leadership by John N. Turner in 1984, Chrétien had resigned from the Commons two years later to build support for another leadership bid. A federalist who had argued against the Meech Lake Accord despite the strong nationalist tide in Quebec, he faced a difficult task in reconciling the province to the idea of a unified Canada. Lacking confidence in his popularity with Quebec voters, Chrétien chose a seat in a French-speaking area of New Brunswick rather than one in Quebec from

on Indian reserves and to quicken the pace of land-claim settlements. There was also pressure for the provinces, owning their own lands, to become active participants in the process.

The GST. A challenge to the proposed tax on goods and services (GST) was the next issue to confront Mulroney. Set at a rate of 7 per cent, the suggested retail sales tax was given a thorough examination by the House of Commons in early 1990. It was approved and sent to the Senate for adoption. The Senate's constitutional authority is, in most respects, equal to that of the Commons. Over the years, the Senate has acted as a chamber of "sober second thought," examining legislation passed to it from the Commons and occasionally suggesting amendments. Many of these have been accepted by the lower house.

Taking up debate on the GST, the Liberal-dominated Senate—with many members who had been appointed by Liberal Pierre Elliott Trudeau during his 15 years as prime minister—sensed an opportunity to rebuild their party's fortunes. The Liberals made every effort to delay passage of the unpopular GST. When Parliament met on September 24, the Senate Banking and Finance Committee recommended that GST legislation be dropped.

An outraged Mulroney charged the Senate with opposing the will of the people as expressed through elected representatives in the Commons. He attempted to overcome the Liberal majority in the Sen-

The Meaning of Meech Lake

Throughout its history, Canada has struggled to define the terms upon which English- and French-speaking residents can live together in one country. In 1990, the dilemma came forward as Canadians considered a proposed constitutional agreement that was called the Meech Lake Accord after a site in the Quebec hills where it was negotiated.

In general, the 25 per cent of Canadians who are French-speaking view the country as a partnership between two groups of early settlers, the French and the English. As one of the main founding groups of modern Canada, they want to keep alive the unique features of their culture, such as the use of the French language, and also to have considerable power in governing their own province. English-speaking Canadians view Canada's federal system as a relationship among 10 equal provinces. Although most Canadians speak English, they are content to allow French as the language of the minority. They believe any power given to residents of Canada's mainly French province, Quebec, should be given to the other provinces as well. Members of other cultures, such as Indians, want their heritage and rights protected, too.

Quebec itself is a province that contains 6½ million of Canada's nearly 27 million people. Almost 83 per cent of Quebecers speak French. Thirty years ago, the province was a conservative society deeply influenced by the Roman Catholic Church. Now it has earned a reputation as progressive in both social and economic policies. As this change has occurred, Quebecers have won for themselves increased power over matters within the province, and some have demanded complete independence from Canada.

In 1976, René Lévesque of the Parti Québécois (PQ), a political party committed to Quebec becoming its own nation, took office as premier of the province. Four years later, the PQ sponsored a public vote on whether or not to try to negotiate independence. Independence was rejected by 60 per cent of the voters. Canada's Prime Minister Pierre Elliott Trudeau, himself a French-Canadian opposed to a separate Quebec, promised changes in the country's federal system to make the province more comfortable within it.

In 1981, Trudeau proposed the creation of a Canadian constitution with complete separation from Great Britain in legal matters. The document that had been serving as the constitution was the British North America Act of 1867. The act, defining the powers of the federal and provincial governments, could be amended only by Great Britain.

The Canadian Parliament passed the Constitution Act of 1982, which is now known as the constitution of Canada. The constitution included many clauses from the British North America Act, together with new provisions, such as one that allowed amendments to be approved in Canada itself and another that provided a charter of individual rights and freedoms.

The constitution angered many Quebec residents. They felt its provisions ignored Prime Minister Trudeau's promise of more security for Quebec and failed to protect the province's French heritage. The Quebec government refused to sign the new constitution.

An effort to reconcile Quebec to the constitution was taken up by Brian Mulroney, a Progressive Conservative Quebecer who became prime minister of Canada in 1984. In 1985, he was joined in the effort by the Liberal Party's Robert Bourassa, who became premier of Quebec. Bourassa put aside the question of independence and outlined five new powers that he believed would, if granted to Quebec, lead to the province accepting the constitution. These formed the basis of the Meech Lake Accord written by Mulroney and the 10 premiers of the provinces in meetings in April and June 1987. With one exception, the accord granted the powers requested by Quebec to all the provinces.

Specifically, the proposed amendments in the accord gave the provinces the right to nominate justices to the Supreme Court of Canada. The provinces could also screen applicants for immigration from outside the country into their provinces. (Quebec was interested in targeting French-speakers as new residents.) They could veto some future constitutional amendments, such as those affecting the position of the federal Senate. And, the provinces could collect federal funding even though they decided to opt out of new national shared-cost social programs. Quebec alone was the subject of a provision that called it a "distinct society" with a right to assert its identity.

For the accord to become law, it had to be approved by the Canadian Parliament and the legislatures of all 10 provinces. A time limit for approval was set at three years from the date of the first provincial ratification. Quebec approved the agreement on June 23, 1987, setting the clock ticking toward a final deadline of June 23, 1990.

Ratification proceeded smoothly at first, with Parliament and 8 of the 10 provinces voting to support the accord. Manitoba and New Brunswick, which had chosen new governments since

1987, held back. In April 1989, Newfoundland, under the leadership of a new premier, Clyde K. Wells, withdrew its ratification. Manitoba and New Brunswick embarked on public hearings before their legislatures voted.

Across the country, opposition to various provisions of the accord had been building. Some Canadians feared new powers given to the provinces would weaken the central government. One power—to veto future constitutional amendments—might make it difficult to pass amendments that a majority of Canadians favored. Other Canadians felt the wording in the accord was too ambiguous. The phrase "distinct society," for example, might result in Quebec promoting collective rights, such as the primacy of the French language, over individual rights claimed by minorities, women, or Indians. Finally, many Canadians objected to the way the provisions of the accord had been worked out—in closed-door negotiations without public debate.

Although the leaders of Canada's three major political parties endorsed the accord, there were notable exceptions, such as former Prime Minister Trudeau and Jean Chrétien, elected in June 1990 as leader of the federal Liberal Party.

Finally, Quebec had angered many Canadians by overriding a Supreme Court ruling and banning the use of English on exterior commercial signs. To many Canadians, the province appeared to be moving away from the policy that English and French have equal importance as Canada's official languages.

In June 1990, events moved swiftly. On June 3, Prime Minister Mulroney called a last-minute conference of all the premiers to discuss changes that might result in ratification by June 23. The 10 premiers bargained for seven days, adjourning at 1 a.m. on June 10. As a result, the premiers of the three provinces withholding approval agreed to present the accord to their legislatures.

During the next two weeks, New Brunswick accepted the accord. Passage was stalled in Manitoba by Cree Indian legislator Elijah Harper, who gave long speeches to delay ratification. He said he hoped to force the federal government to deal with claims of native peoples. A day before the deadline, Mulroney offered to give Manitoba, but not Newfoundland, additional time to consider the accord. The offer angered Newfoundland Premier Wells, who adjourned the provincial assembly without a vote. The deadline was not met, and the Meech Lake Accord died.

Shortly thereafter, Premier Bourassa said he would no longer take part in meetings of all the provinces on the constitution but would negotiate with the prime minister directly. Bourassa named a broadly representative committee to explore options for Quebec's future.

Political consequences of the failure of the accord were immediate. Support rose enormously for the forces favoring Quebec independence and fell for those who wanted Quebec to remain in the union, such as Chrétien. Six members of the Progressive Conservative caucus from Quebec left the party to form a separatist group—the Bloc Québécois—in Parliament. A Liberal member joined them. In a special election to fill an empty seat on August 13, the candidate of the Bloc Québécois won 68 per cent of the vote. He became the first Quebecer ever elected to the House of Commons by promising to separate Quebec from Canada.

Finally, the failure of the Meech Lake Accord was a devastating blow to the credibility of Prime Minister Mulroney, who had staked his political career on reconciling differences within Canada. Nearly six years after winning the largest number of seats in Parliament any party ever had won, the Progressive Conservatives found their popularity had been weakened in every part of the country.

The events of June 1990 left unresolved the differences of opinion between French- and English-speaking Canadians on Quebec's place in Canada. For the future, irrevocable changes seemed likely in Canada's federal-provincial relations.   David M. L. Farr

Canadian Prime Minister Brian Mulroney arrives in Ottawa to deliver a nationally televised address on the failure of the Meech Lake Accord.

Quebec residents protest the federal government's proposed new 7 per cent goods and services tax (GST), a form of sales tax.

which to run for Parliament. See **Chrétien, Jean Joseph-Jacques.**

In special elections on December 10 to fill two seats in Commons, Chrétien won the New Brunswick seat and a Liberal won in a Toronto district. This brought party standings in the 295-member Commons to Progressive Conservatives, 159; Liberals, 80; New Democrats, 44; Bloc Québécois, 9; independents, 2; and Reform Party, 1.

Few cabinet changes. Mulroney kept the senior positions in his cabinet largely unchanged in 1990. An exception was the post of minister of justice, which was given to Kim Campbell, a 42-year-old lawyer from Vancouver, B.C., on February 23. The first woman to hold the post, she guided a new abortion bill through the Commons to a successful outcome on May 29. If passed, the bill would make abortion legal if a doctor believes the physical, mental, or psychological health of a woman is threatened by pregnancy. In December, the abortion measure still awaited Senate approval.

Prime Minister Mulroney lost a close colleague on May 21 when Lucien Bouchard left the cabinet because of dissatisfaction over the government's handling of the Meech Lake Accord. Bouchard later became the leader of the Bloc Québécois in Parliament. His place as minister of the environment was taken over by Robert R. de Cotret, who moved from a financial management position as president of Treasury Board.

The economy. By the end of 1990, it was evident that Canada had slid into a recession, officially defined by the federal government as two quarters of declining output by the national economy. The recession began in the second quarter of the year, when the gross domestic product (GDP), the value of all goods and services produced within the nation's boundaries during the year, expressed in 1986 prices, fell by 0.4 per cent. The downturn was the first in seven years of uninterrupted growth in the Canadian economy. At midyear, on a seasonally adjusted annual basis, the GDP stood at $676.8 billion Canadian ($582 billion U.S.).

As economic growth stalled, weakness spread from one sector of the economy to another. All major components of domestic demand were affected, including housing starts and sales of passenger cars and other consumer goods. The policy pursued by the Bank of Canada to restrain inflation kept interest rates high, helping strengthen the Canadian dollar. The dollar reached a value of 88 cents U.S. by late August, then declined somewhat. The strong dollar hurt Canada's competitive position in world markets by making Canadian products more expensive in other countries. At the same time, slumps in the United States and Japan hurt Canadian export sales.

In November, the consumer price index stood at 5 per cent for the year. The projected impact of the GST in 1991 was expected to push up the rate of inflation still further. Unemployment rose in 1990, standing at 9.1 per cent of the labor force in November.

The federal budget. Finance Minister Michael Holcombe Wilson delivered his sixth budget on February 20. For the first time in 22 years, the budget contained no tax increases. Wilson, however, emphasized the government's determination to proceed with the GST in January 1991. Funding for major social programs was left intact, but federal grants to the provinces for health care and postsecondary education costs were frozen for two years. This ceiling on payments for health, welfare, and higher education was projected to save Ottawa $869 million ($747 million U.S.) in the fiscal year 1990-1991. The three wealthiest provinces, Ontario, British Columbia, and Alberta, would be hardest hit.

The 1990-1991 budget limited increases to 5 per cent—about the rate of inflation—in areas such as defense and foreign aid. Two large federal projects were scrapped: the massive *Polar 8* icebreaker ship and an ambitious operation in northern Alberta to produce petroleum from *oil sands*, sands soaked with a petroleumlike substance. The government announced that it planned to sell its oil company, Petro-Canada, founded in 1975, and its half interest in a satellite communications carrier, Telesat Canada.

Total federal spending was budgeted to increase 3.4 per cent to $147.8 billion ($127 billion U.S.) in 1990-1991. The deficit would decline to $28.5 billion ($24-billion U.S.) from $30.5 billion ($26 billion U.S.). Wilson stressed his concern over the interest costs on Canada's public debt—$1,500 a year as of 1990 for every Canadian and still increasing. This burden, he said, severely curtailed the ability of the government to initiate new programs.

Mulroney's diplomacy. Prime Minister Mulroney participated in the 16th economic summit of the world's richest industrial countries held in Houston in July 1990. Canadian efforts were directed toward achieving greater progress in the reduction of farm subsidies as part of multilateral trade negotiations in Belgium scheduled to end in December. The negotiations were aimed at reducing protectionism.

Mulroney also attended a London meeting of North Atlantic Treaty Organization (NATO) heads of government immediately preceding the economic summit. At both meetings, Mulroney took pains to convince world leaders that Canada, despite the worries brought on by the failure of the Meech Lake constitutional accord, was still a politically and economically stable nation.

Military operations. Canada participated in an international effort to persuade Iraq to withdraw from Kuwait after Iraq's invasion on August 2, first through diplomacy and then through economic sanctions. About 600 Canadians were believed to be working in Kuwait when the invasion occurred. Canada closed its embassy there on October 19 because of lack of food and water.

Federal spending in Canada

Estimated budget for fiscal 1990-1991*

Ministry (includes the department and all agencies for which a minister reports to Parliament):	Millions of dollars†
Agriculture	1,958
Atlantic Canada Opportunities Agency	340
Communications	
Canadian Broadcasting Corporation	1,018
Canadian Film Development Corporation	146
Other	748
Consumer and corporate affairs	190
Employment and immigration	5,237
Energy, mines, and resources	
Atomic Energy of Canada Limited	135
Other	1,028
Environment	973
External affairs	3,596
Finance	49,595
Fisheries and oceans	725
Forestry	159
Governor general	11
Indian affairs and northern development	3,522
Industry, science, and technology	
Canada Post Corporation	149
Other	2,388
Justice	606
Labour	259
National defence	12,024
National health and welfare	33,903
National revenue	1,639
Parliament	272
Privy Council	125
Public works	
Canada Mortgage and Housing Corporation	1,884
Other	1,307
Secretary of state	3,644
Solicitor general	
Royal Canadian Mounted Police	1,153
Other	1,160
Supply and services	628
Transport	2,984
Treasury Board	1,504
Veterans affairs	1,773
Western economic diversification	286
Total	**137,069**

* April 1, 1990, to March 31, 1991.
† Canadian dollars; $1 = U.S. 86 cents as of Dec. 1, 1990.

Spending since 1985

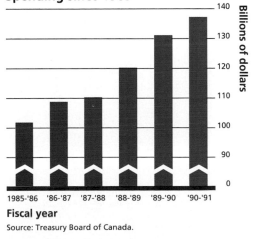

Source: Treasury Board of Canada.

The Ministry of Canada*

Brian Mulroney—prime minister
Charles Joseph Clark—secretary of state for external affairs
John Carnell Crosbie—minister for international trade
Donald Frank Mazankowski—deputy prime minister; president of the Queen's Privy Council for Canada; minister of agriculture
Elmer MacIntosh MacKay—minister of public works; minister for the purposes of the Atlantic Canada Opportunities Agency Act
Arthur Jacob Epp—minister of energy, mines, and resources
Robert R. de Cotret—minister of the environment
Henry Perrin Beatty—minister of national health and welfare
Michael Holcombe Wilson—minister of finance
Harvie Andre—minister of state; leader of the government in the House of Commons
Otto John Jelinek—minister of national revenue
Thomas Edward Siddon—minister of Indian affairs and Northern development
Charles James Mayer—minister of state (grains and oilseeds); minister of Western economic diversification
William Hunter McKnight—minister of national defence
Benoît Bouchard—minister of industry, science, and technology
Marcel Masse—minister of communications
Barbara Jean McDougall—minister of employment and immigration
Gerald Stairs Merrithew—minister of veterans affairs
Monique Vézina—minister of state (employment and immigration); minister of state (seniors)
Frank Oberle—minister of forestry
Lowell Murray—leader of the government in the Senate; minister of state (federal-provincial relations)
Paul Wyatt Dick—minister of supply and services
Pierre H. Cadieux—solicitor general of Canada
Thomas Hockin—minister of state (small businesses and tourism)
Monique Landry—minister for external relations
Bernard Valcourt—minister of fisheries and oceans
Gerry Weiner—minister of state (multiculturalism and citizenship); secretary of state of Canada
Douglas Grinslade Lewis—minister of transport
Pierre Blais—minister of state (agriculture); minister of consumer and corporate affairs
John Horton McDermid—minister of state (privatization and regulatory affairs)
Shirley Martin—minister of state (Indian affairs and Northern development)
Mary Collins—associate minister of national defence; minister responsible for the status of women
Alan Redway—minister of state (housing)
William Charles Winegard—minister for science
Kim Campbell—minister of justice and attorney general of Canada
Jean Corbeil—minister of labour; minister of state (transport)
Gilles Loiselle—minister of state (finance); president of the Treasury Board
Marcel Danis—minister of state (youth); minister of state (fitness and amateur sport); deputy leader of the government in the House of Commons

*As of Dec. 31, 1990.

Premiers of Canadian provinces

Province	Premier
Alberta	Donald R. Getty
British Columbia	William N. Vander Zalm
Manitoba	Gary A. Filmon
New Brunswick	Frank J. McKenna
Newfoundland	Clyde K. Wells
Nova Scotia	Roger S. Bacon
Ontario	Robert K. Rae
Prince Edward Island	Joseph A. Ghiz
Quebec	Robert Bourassa
Saskatchewan	Grant Devine

Government leaders of territories

Northwest Territories	Denis Paterson
Yukon Territory	Tony Penikett

On August 10, several days after he had held a short meeting with United States President George Bush, Prime Minister Mulroney announced that Canada would send two destroyers and a supply ship to the Persian Gulf. Their task would be to monitor the enforcement of sanctions imposed on Iraq by the United Nations Security Council. The vessels, with 934 sailors and soldiers aboard, left the naval base at Halifax, N.S., for the Middle East on August 24. In early October, a squadron consisting of 18 Canadian CF-18 jet fighters was sent to provide air cover for an international fleet blockading the Persian Gulf. The squadron was accompanied by 450 pilots and support personnel.

Canada announced a contribution toward the reduction of ground and air forces stationed in Germany under NATO sponsorship on September 21. In 1991, the 8,000 army and air force personnel stationed in Germany would be cut to 6,600, but the Canadian bases would remain in operation.

Facts in brief. Population: 26,729,000. Government: Governor General Ramon J. Hnatyshyn; Prime Minister Brian Mulroney. Monetary unit: dollar. Value of foreign trade: exports, $148 billion Canadian ($127-billion U.S.); imports, $135 billion Canadian ($116 billion U.S.).   David M. L. Farr

See also the Canadian provinces articles; **Canadian literature; Hnatyshyn, Ramon John; Lamer, Antonio; Montreal; Rae, Robert Keith; Toronto.** In *World Book,* see **Canada.**

Canadian literature. Short-story collections were prominent in 1990, with a new book by Alice Munro probably the strongest work of Canadian fiction of the year. *Friend of My Youth* demonstrated Munro's mastery, capturing ironic, frequently tragic patterns of life. Audrey Thomas' *The Wild Blue Yonder* viewed men's and women's struggles (often doomed) to complete each other. Joan Clark's *Swimming Towards the Light* followed a cast of characters from a summer in Nova Scotia during the 1940's to the present.

A number of young women writers also produced fine short fiction, including Janice Kulyk Keefer, whose collection *Travelling Ladies* depicted women in transit, displaced in both settings and sensibilities. Diane Schoemperlen experimented with form in *The Man of My Dreams*, which won praise for its concise, controlled prose. Poet Bronwen Wallace's fine, fresh story collection, *People You'd Trust Your Life To*, was published posthumously to wide praise. Wallace died of cancer in August 1989.

After a successful foray into the novel, Neil Bissoondath returned to stories of dislocation in *On the Eve of Uncertain Tomorrows*. W. D. Valgardson produced a mature collection in *What Can't Be Changed Shouldn't Be Mourned*. Brian Fawcett continued to document the take-over of private thought by public communications in *Public Eye*.

Novels. Among the year's significant novels was a first work of fiction from Al Purdy, the winner of two

Governor General's Awards for poetry. Purdy's *A Splinter in the Heart* told about a 16-year-old Ontario boy's summer in 1918. Brian Moore, a United States resident since 1959, retains Canadian citizenship and thus still qualifies as a Canadian writer. His *Lies of Silence*, a thriller set in Belfast, Northern Ireland, enmeshed his protagonist in a web of adultery and Irish Republican Army violence. Leslie Hall Pinder's *On Double Tracks* set a young woman lawyer and a 74-year-old judge against each other in a clash over native land claims. A first novel about four generations of the Wong family, *Disappearing Moon Cafe* by Sky Lee, told an insider's story of a British Columbia Chinese community. Another accomplished and lyric first novel, Nino Ricci's *Lives of the Saints*, was set in the 1960's in a mountain village in Italy before a mother and son depart for Canada. W. O. Mitchell released his third book in as many years, *Roses Are Difficult Here*, in which he returned to the topic of small-town life in Alberta. Other significant novels included *Evening Snow Will Bring Such Peace*, David Adams Richards' second installment in his New Brunswick family trilogy; Matt Cohen's *Emotional Arithmetic*; and Jack Hodgins' *Innocent Cities*.

Poetry. Notable poetry included Purdy's *The Woman on the Shore*, its probings of time and planetary space caught in solid images of finite human life. *She Tries Her Tongue, Her Silence Softly Breaks* by Caribbean-born Marlene Nourbese Philip was a virtuoso search for a temporal and historical mother. Other exceptional work included Patrick Lane's *Winter*, in which the prairie season served as metaphor for a state of mind; Margaret Avison's *No Time*; and Dionne Brand's *No Language Is Neutral*.

Biographies and memoirs. The year's best memoirs were Timothy Findley's eloquent *Inside Memory*, sharing his recollections on the writing process and the memorable individuals who have filled his life as an actor and writer. In a lively political memoir, *A Life on the Fringe*, former Senator Eugene A. Forsey, a constitutional expert and public affairs critic, defended his controversial, even paradoxical, views. In sports, *Gretzky: An Autobiography* told the life story of Canadian hockey hero Wayne Gretzky, now with the Los Angeles Kings.

History and politics. Prime Minister Pierre Elliott Trudeau left office in 1984, but his mystique was unfaded. In a year that saw many books about the former prime minister (and only one book about the present prime minister), Trudeau himself broke silence in *Towards a Just Society*, a summing-up of 16 years of government by the Trudeau administration. Coedited by Thomas S. Axworthy, the book disappointed some critics, who said Trudeau revealed little. *The Outsider*, a biography by journalist Michel Vastel, attempted to deflate Trudeau's mystique. *Pirouette*, by historians J. L. Granatstein and Robert Bothwell, looked at Trudeau and Canadian foreign policy. Best of the Trudeau books, bringing to light new facts, incidents,

Canadian Alice Munro examined the lives of ordinary people in her 1990 short-story collection, *Friend of My Youth.*

and slants, was *Trudeau and Our Times Vol. 1: The Magnificent Obsession*, which is the first volume of a projected two-volume work by Stephen Clarkson and Christina McCall.

In popular history, the prolific Pierre Berton looked at *The Great Depression, 1929-1939*. The third volume of the *Historical Atlas of Canada, Addressing the 20th Century*, from the University of Toronto Press, charted the transformation of Canada from a rural society to a culturally complex industrial nation.

Environmental and social issues. Canadians' increasing concern over the state of the natural world in 1990 was reflected in an escalating tide of "green" books. *Paradise Won: The Struggle for South Moresby*, by Elizabeth May, told the story of a prolonged and agonizing fight to save wilderness land. *A History of World Whaling* by historian Daniel Francis confirmed that conservation now must go beyond whaling moratoriums to saving the oceans. Farley Mowat's *Rescue the Earth!* brought together the feisty writer's interviews with leading environmentalists. *It's a Matter of Survival* by David Suzuki and Anita Gordon urged tough decisions to save the planet.

Through the year, a number of books appeared on the failures of Canadian social justice. Among them were *Criminal Neglect: Why Sex Offenders Go Free* by Sylvia Barrett and William Marshall and *A Rock and a Hard Place*, an insider's view of Canada's parole board by Lisa Hobbs Birnie.

Canseco, José, Jr.

Awards. The 1989 Governor General's Literary Awards for books in English went to Paul Quarrington for his comic novel *Whale Music* (fiction), Heather Spears for *The Word for Sand* (poetry), Robert Calder for *Willie: The Life of W. Somerset Maugham* (nonfiction), Judith Thompson for *The Other Side of the Dark* (drama), Diana J. Wieler for *Bad Boy* (children's literature: text), and Robin Muller for *The Magic Paintbrush* (children's literature: illustration). The awards for French-language books went to Louis Hamelin for *La Rage* (fiction), Pierre Desruisseaux for *Monème* (poetry), Lise Noël for *L'intolérance* (nonfiction), Michel Garneau for *Mademoiselle Rouge* (drama), Charles Montpetit for *Temps Mort* (children's literature: text), and Stéphane Poulin for *Benjamin et la saga des oreillers* (children's literature: illustration). Wayne Grady won the English translation prize for *On the Eighth Day*, his translation of Antonine Maillet's *Le huitième jour*; Jean Antonin Billard won the French translation prize for *Les Ages de l'amour*, a translation of Dorothy Livesay's *The Phases of Love*.

W. O. Mitchell received the Stephen Leacock Memorial Award for humor for *According to Jake and the Kid*. The Lionel Gelber Prize, established in 1989, went to Jonathan D. Spence for *The Search for Modern China*. Recipient of the 1989 Books in Canada/W. H. Smith First Novel Award was Sandra Birdsell for her much-praised *The Missing Child*.   Maureen Garvie

In *World Book,* see **Canadian literature.**

Canseco, José, Jr. (1964-   ), became baseball's highest-paid player on June 27, 1990, when he signed a five-year contract with the Oakland Athletics worth $23.5 million, an average of $4.7 million a year. Canseco ended the season ranking among the top five leaders in runs batted in, with 101, and in home runs, with 37.

Canseco and his twin brother, Osvaldo, were born on July 2, 1964, in Havana, Cuba, the sons of José and Barbara Canseco. His father had been an executive with the Esso Oil Company in Cuba. In 1965, the family moved to Opa-locka, Fla., near Miami.

Canseco did not play baseball until he was 12 years old. His professional baseball career began in 1982 when Oakland selected him in the 15th round of the free-agent draft. After a stint in the minor leagues, he was called up to the majors on Sept. 2, 1985, and struck out in his first plate appearance. Canseco's best year was 1988, when he became the first major league player to hit 40 home runs (he had 42) and steal 40 bases, a plateau no one else has achieved. He also batted .307, drove in 124 runs, and was voted the American League Most Valuable Player.

Canseco was married on Nov. 5, 1988, to Esther Haddad, the daughter of his junior high school baseball coach. The couple have homes in Miami and Oakland. Canseco's brother, known as Ozzie, plays baseball in the A's minor league system.   Rod Such

Cape Verde. See Africa.

Capriati, Jennifer (1976-   ), is the youngest United States tennis player and the second-youngest of any nationality (after Germany's Steffi Graf) to turn professional. Before turning pro at the age of 13 years 11 months, Capriati signed endorsement contracts worth an estimated $5 million.

Born on March 29, 1976, in New York City and raised mainly in Florida, Capriati learned tennis from her father. He is an Italian immigrant who played professional soccer and did movie stunts before turning tennis pro. Capriati's mother is an airline flight attendant. Jennifer was working out daily with a tennis ball machine by the time she was 4 years old. She still spends hundreds of hours a year practicing.

Capriati was only 12 when she won the U.S. Tennis Association's 18-and-under championships on both hard and clay courts in 1989. She was 13 when she took the U.S. and French Junior Opens and made the junior quarterfinals at Wimbledon. After turning pro, she became the youngest Grand Slam semifinalist ever but lost to Monica Seles of Yugoslavia in the French Open in June 1990. On October 28, she won her first regular women's pro tour event in the Puerto Rico Open in San Juan.

While on the tennis tour, Capriati maintains a straight-A standing in school (assignments are faxed to her). She is known for a lightning serve, a formidable backhand, and an unpredictable, aggressive style of playing.   Margaret Anne Schmidt

Carey, George Leonard (1935-   ), was chosen in 1990 to succeed Robert A. K. Runcie as archbishop of Canterbury, the spiritual head of the Church of England and of 70 million Anglicans worldwide. Queen Elizabeth II, temporal leader of the church, named the new archbishop on the recommendation of Margaret Thatcher, then Britain's prime minister, and a 16-member church commission. Carey, bishop of Bath and Wells in southwestern England since 1987, was scheduled to assume his new office soon after Runcie's retirement in January 1991.

Carey's relative youth and brief experience as a bishop made the appointment a surprise to many. But his selection was greeted with approval by a broad spectrum of church leaders. Carey belongs to the church's evangelical wing, which emphasizes the role of the Bible in religious faith. Although traditional in many matters, Carey strongly supports ordaining women, a policy the church has yet to adopt.

Carey was born on Nov. 13, 1935, in London's working-class East End. He left school at 15 but later earned a bachelor's degree and a doctorate in divinity, both from the University of London. Carey served in various positions in the Anglican clergy before being named principal of Trinity College in Bristol in 1982. He held that post until he became a bishop in 1987.

Carey and his wife, the former Eileen Harmsworth Hood, have four children.   Karin C. Rosenberg

Cat. In spring 1990, a veterinary researcher shed light on the cause of a fatal blood reaction referred to as "fading kitten syndrome." The syndrome may strike kittens with type A blood born in the first litter of a mother cat with type B blood. Urs Giger of the University of Pennsylvania in Philadelphia tested more than 3,000 cats, half of them purebred, and found that almost all domestic cats have type A blood but the frequency of type B blood varies widely among pure breeds. Thus, certain breeds are at increased risk of the syndrome as well as blood transfusion reactions.

The largest-ever United States show for pedigreed cats, the Third Annual Purina/Cat Fanciers Association Invitational, took place in November in St. Louis, Mo. More than 800 cats were entered.

The association's National Best Cat for 1990 was Grand Champion Katrina's Postmarque of Katra, a black Persian male bred by Kathy Schaub of Indianapolis and owned by Carolyn Henry of Springfield, Ill. The year's Best Kitten was Grand Champion South Paw Starlight, a white Persian female bred and owned by Judy and Greg Brocato of Rome, Ga. A dilute calico exotic shorthair spay, Grand Champion and Grand Premier Attraction's Amy Lou Retton was National Best Alter. Bred by Andrea Krupp of Newburgh, N.Y., and Linda Haley of Goffstown, N.H., the cat was owned by Dawn and Art Katser of Huntington Station, N.Y.   Thomas H. Dent

In *World Book,* see **Cat.**

Census. The United States Bureau of the Census undertook its 21st Decennial Census of Population and Housing in 1990. In doing so, the bureau compiled statistical evidence of the nation's changing social fabric.

According to figures released on December 26, the United States population was 249.6 million on April 1, 1990, the official census day. The figure represents a population growth of 23.1 million since the 1980 U.S. census.

Immigration in the 1980's accounted for the largest proportion of the population increase since the early 1900's, equivalent to about one-third of the total population increase. According to the Immigration and Naturalization Service, about 8 million people immigrated to the United States in the 1980's. The majority of the immigrants—some of whom arrived in the country illegally—came from Asia, Latin America, and Caribbean island nations. Most settled in coastal areas—many in California and Florida.

Southwestern expansion. Southern or Western states were home for at least 55 per cent of the population in 1990, according to the Census Bureau's state population figures. A decades-long boom in the South and West was enhanced by the recession of the early 1980's, which was especially severe in the industrial Northeast and Upper Midwest. Businesses and workers leaving the so-called rust belt joined retirees seeking mild climates.

Thus, the population growth in just four Southern or Western states—Arizona, California, Florida, and Texas—was equivalent to more than half the nation's total growth. Alaska and Nevada also had significant gains. Nevada's population grew by the largest percentage of any state—about 50 per cent, much of it in and around Las Vegas. Completion of the Trans-Alaska Pipeline created new jobs in Alaska and helped account for that state's population increase, the second-largest percentage at about 37.

Most Midwestern and Northeastern states, on the other hand, grew little. Only four states lost population during the 1980's: Iowa, North Dakota, West Virginia, and Wyoming. The population of the District of Columbia also declined.

An end to the "back to the land" movement may account for lower-than-expected growth rates in predominantly rural Southern states, such as Arkansas, Louisiana, Mississippi, and Tennessee. In the 1970's, many people left cities and towns for the promise of a simpler life in rural counties. But during the farm crisis of the 1980's, people began to leave depressed rural areas. Three of the states whose populations declined in the 1980's—Iowa, North Dakota, and Wyoming—seemed especially hurt by this trend.

Exodus to exurbia. While such Southwestern cities as El Paso, San Diego, and Phoenix made large population gains, some cities in the North and East lost residents. According to preliminary—and hotly contested—census figures released in August, New York City lost 0.5 per cent of its population during the 1980's; Chicago lost 9.3 per cent; Detroit, 19.4 per cent; and Philadelphia, 8.6 per cent.

As these cities apparently suffered losses, distant suburbs—what demographers call *exurbs*—made gains. Skyrocketing housing prices during the 1980's forced people to move farther and farther away from cities in a search for affordable homes. Quickly growing exurban areas include Massachusetts' Worcester County, west of Boston, and California's Riverside and San Bernardino counties, east of Los Angeles.

California illustrates the social forces driving population change in the 1980's. Hundreds of thousands of immigrants from Asia and Mexico took up residence in California during the 1980's. The boom in exurbia and the overall population shift to the South and West added to California's explosion of growth, particularly in the state's southern counties. With a population of 29.8 million—26 per cent above its 1980 total and more than the entire populations of Canada or Australia—California has become home to 1 in 8 Americans.

The politics of the census centered on reapportionment of the 435 seats in the U.S. House of Representatives. California gained 7 additional House seats, giving it the largest-ever total for a state: 52. Florida gained 4 seats; Texas, 3; and five states gained 1. New York appeared likely to lose 3 seats. Illinois, Michigan, Ohio, and Pennsylvania each lost 2 seats, and eight other states lost 1 each. Accompanying these changes

One Big Headache for the Head Counters

An army of census takers hit the streets in 1990 as the United States took a head count, just as it has done at 10-year intervals since 1790. But this decade's census created an uproar over charges that Americans had been woefully undercounted.

Since the Founding Fathers first called for a periodic population count, few if any censuses have come under such vocal attack. Officials from every one of the nation's 51 largest cities formally charged the U.S. Bureau of the Census—an agency of the Department of Commerce—with undercounting their populations. Experts called the mode of census taking obsolete, despite the bureau's attempts to make this the most accurate census ever. Innovations in 1990 included special efforts to count the nation's homeless and to conduct follow-up surveys.

High political and financial stakes were riding on the 1990 count because the results were to be used to reapportion the 435 seats in the U.S. House of Representatives and to distribute billions of dollars in federal and state funds. Cities and states had much to lose or gain: Lower-than-expected population figures could mean the loss of millions of dollars in aid for schools, roads, and other projects.

The effort got off to a rocky, but highly publicized, start on March 20. Throughout the night, the Census Bureau conducted its first effort to count every homeless person in the United States. Approximately 15,000 census takers across the

A census taker interviews a homeless man during the night of March 20, in the first-ever attempt to include the homeless in the U.S. census.

country fanned out to interview homeless people in bus stations, shelters, sidewalks, and all-night movie theaters. Critics said that poor planning caused many problems, but census officials insisted that most of the polling went smoothly and that the majority of the nation's homeless had been counted.

More criticism followed the distribution of census forms to about 100 million households for completion on or about the official census day, April 1. Because of delivery problems and apparent public confusion—or apathy—only 63 per cent of the forms were completed and returned to the bureau, considerably fewer than were returned in 1980 and 1970. In some large cities, response rates were less than 50 per cent.

Census Director Barbara E. Bryant on April 11 announced that the low response required the hiring of additional census workers to beef up a planned door-to-door follow-up survey. This boosted the bureau's 10-year budget of $2.5 billion by about $100 million.

For weeks, more than 300,000 census takers attempted to contact households that had not returned their census forms. The results were then tabulated, and preliminary figures were released in September. They were met with a chorus of boos.

"Statistical grand larceny," cried New York City Mayor David N. Dinkins. Saying that minorities and other population groups had been undercounted, New York City—along with Boston; Chicago; Atlanta, Ga.; and more than 6,000 other communities—challenged the figures. Los Angeles officials said that entire city blocks had been missed, and the 39 residents of tiny Jacksonburg, Ohio, protested that only 14 of their number had been counted. In response to the uproar, Bryant promised that the figures would be significantly adjusted before the bureau released its final population counts.

The failings of a person-by-person head count had never seemed so apparent. Statisticians said that more advanced survey techniques had rendered the old-fashioned method obsolete. Some experts suggested that the nation should establish an ongoing weekly census of small samples of the population, from which national data could be drawn. Skeptics said that such a survey could provide accurate state and national figures, but that only a head count would be reliable for polling smaller populations.

Of course, census taking has never been an exact science—and, if nothing else, the 1990 census was at least speedy. The survey was the fastest ever conducted, with the occupants of 99 per cent of U.S. dwellings counted and tabulated weeks ahead of the 1980 timetable, according to the Census Bureau.   William R. Cormier

will be shifts in the amount of federal funding for government programs based on population.

But thousands of communities insisted that the 1990 census totals for their populations were too low (see **Close-Up**). Supporting such claims was evidence that certain types of people are likely to be missed by the census and follow-up recounts. For example, people who have difficulty reading or writing English may not be able to complete census questionnaires or understand the importance of answering questions accurately. According to the Census Bureau, about 1 per cent of the population was missed during the 1990 census, and most of those not counted were poor people in isolated rural areas or in urban slums.

During the 1980's, the Census Bureau developed mathematical formulas to account for this underreporting. But officials in the Department of Commerce, of which the Census Bureau is a part, said that statistically adjusting the census would undermine public faith in the bureau's figures. Some of the department's critics accused it of blocking the adjustment plan to avoid increasing population counts in areas that traditionally vote Democratic. By law, Commerce Secretary Robert A. Mosbacher had until July 15, 1991, to decide whether to adjust the 1990 census results or leave the figures unchanged.   Jinger Hoop

See also **City; Population; State government.** In *World Book,* see **Census; Population.**

Central African Republic. See **Africa.**

Chad. In one of the swiftest political turnabouts in Africa in recent memory, Chad's President Hissein Habré was driven from power in December 1990 by an invading rebel force. The conquering army was led by General Idriss Deby, Habré's former military commander in chief, who fled the country in 1989 after a failed coup. Deby's troops struck with a sudden blow from neighboring Sudan in early November. They pushed relentlessly westward against feeble resistance, nearing Chad's capital, N'Djamena, by the end of the month. On December 1, Habré fled to Cameroon. The rebels entered the city on December 2, and Deby proclaimed himself president two days later.

A false sense of security. Just a month earlier, Habré had seemed securely in control of the country. His long-standing dispute with Libya's leader, Colonel Muammar Muhammad al-Qadhafi, over ownership of the Aozou Strip—a mineral-rich area in northern Chad that Libya has also claimed—appeared to be over. In the 1980's, Libya supported a military force led by former Chadian President Goukouni Oueddei, whom Habré had ousted in a 1982 coup. When Habré, with the help of troops from France, defeated Oueddei's troops and their Libyan allies in 1987, Qadhafi agreed to a cease-fire. He and Habré continued to dispute the ownership of the Aozou Strip, however.

Then, in May 1990, Qadhafi gave an unexpected speech in which he apparently accepted Chad's right to the Aozou Strip. It looked as though Chad, which

had been disrupted by warfare or the threat of warfare for some 25 years, might finally be at peace. Then came General Deby's invasion.

The new president. Habré and Western observers charged that Deby was backed by Libya, though Deby and Libya denied it. If Deby did receive Libyan support, he and Qadhafi may have worked out an agreement concerning the Aozou Strip. But Deby declared that he would fight if necessary to keep that area part of Chad, so the future relationship of Chad and Libya was a question mark at year-end.

After taking power in Chad, Deby dissolved the parliament, suspended the Constitution, and named a 33-member Council of State to help him govern the country. Despite such antidemocratic actions, Deby proclaimed that the years of strongman rule in Chad would be coming to an end. Although nominally a republic, Chad has long been under the control of the military. Deby promised that the Patriotic Salvation Movement—the name of his rebel group—would establish a multiparty democracy.

The economy. Chad desperately needs peace to build its shattered economy. The landlocked nation is one of the poorest countries in Africa, and the years of costly and destructive civil war prevented economic development. Deby—assuming he stays in power—will have his hands full.   David L. Dreier

See also **Africa** (Facts in brief table). In *World Book,* see **Chad.**

Chamorro, Violeta Barrios de (1929-   ), was elected president of Nicaragua on Feb. 25, 1990. Her upset victory over incumbent President Daniel Ortega ended more than a decade of rule by the leftist Sandinista National Liberation Front. After taking office in April, Chamorro faced the daunting task of unifying a country that had been torn apart by a civil war between Sandinistas and American-backed *contra* rebels since the early 1980's. See **Nicaragua.**

Chamorro became active in politics after the 1978 assassination of her husband, Pedro Joaquín Chamorro, a newspaper editor and publisher who had crusaded against Nicaragua's military dictator Anastasio Somoza Debayle. The assassination fueled the revolution that ousted Somoza in 1979 and brought the Sandinista Front to power. The new leaders invited Chamorro's widow to join their junta. But she stepped down within a year, unhappy with the Sandinistas' military build-up and Communist ties. Returning to the family-owned newspaper, *La Prensa*, she began to criticize the Sandinista regime headed by Ortega. In 1989, Ortega agreed to hold an election. His chief opposition came from the National Opposition Union, a 14-party coalition that chose Chamorro as its candidate.

Violeta Barrios was born in Rivas on Oct. 18, 1929. She married Pedro Chamorro in 1950. Reflecting Nicaragua's division, two of the four Chamorro children supported her campaign and two remained committed to the Sandinista Front.   Karin C. Rosenberg

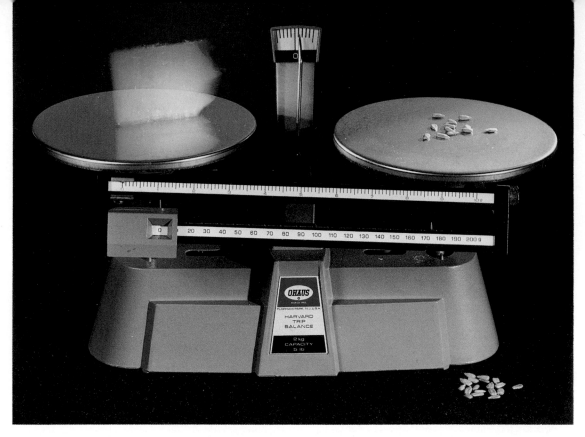

A sample of "frozen smoke" weighs less than 13 sunflower seeds, about 0.0025 ounce. A silica aerogel, the material was developed at a California lab.

Chemistry. Chemists in the United States identified the essence of body odor in 1990. George Preti of the Monell Chemical Senses Center in Philadelphia made the announcement at a meeting of the American Chemical Society in August. Preti and his colleagues collected perspiration on absorbent pads that male volunteers had worn in their armpits. The scientists then isolated a number of compounds from the perspiration using a method of analysis known as *gas chromatography*.

Researchers sniffed each compound to rate its odor. The results came as a surprise. The prime culprit was neither of the compounds previously named as the main causes of body odor. Instead, another organic compound called *3-methyl-2-hexanoic acid* was by far the nastiest of several dozen odor-causing substances that occur in perspiration directly or as a result of the action of bacteria on it. The makers of deodorants can now target their efforts at this compound. The result should be more effective and longer-lasting products.

"Smart" fluids. In March, researchers at the University of Michigan in Ann Arbor reported that a new class of fluids could improve the mechanical controls for automobiles, airplanes, and submarines. In response to intense electric fields, the fluids change from the consistency of water to the consistency of peanut butter in a fraction of a second.

The substances, called *electro-rheological fluids* (ERF's), are the brainchild of materials engineer Frank

E. Filisko. Two of his colleagues, Robert D. Ervin and Zheng Lou, have used ERF's in developing *actuators*—devices that control the in-flight vibrations of aircraft —for the United States Air Force. Their goal is to create actuators that can harden and soften 200 times per second.

Because of this quick response, ERF-driven devices could damp vibrations far more effectively than hydraulic systems can. And because the fluids respond to electric charges, they could be controlled by a computer programmed to send the right charge at the right time.

ERF's have other advantages besides quick response. The fluids require no moving parts, precise grinding, or special fitting. They also are inexpensive enough for use in consumer products. The first commercial applications of ERF's are likely to come from the automotive industry. For example, computer-controlled "smart" shock absorbers might provide a more even ride than today's shocks do.

New form of carbon. Pure, crystalline carbon has occurred naturally in two forms—graphite and diamond. In 1990, scientists produced a third form: *fullerite*. It was named after engineer Buckminster Fuller because its molecular structure resembles the geodesic domes he popularized.

Fullerite is made of soccer-ball-shaped molecules, nicknamed *buckyballs* (from *Buckminster*), that consist of 60 or 70 carbon atoms. In September, physicists

Donald R. Huffman and Lowell D. Lamb of the University of Arizona in Tucson—together with co-workers from the Max Planck Institute for Nuclear Physics in Heidelberg, Germany—reported that they had created pure fullerite crystals.

The crystals were made by vaporizing graphite. In graphite, hexagon-shaped atoms of carbon are arranged in sheets, which are stacked. During vaporization, the sheets presumably peel off and curl back upon themselves, much as wood shavings curl when planed from a plank. But unlike the shavings, the carbon atoms form new bonds and rearrange themselves. The result is soot, which the scientists collected with the solvent benzene. The soot solution was then gently heated to evaporate it, leaving the fullerite crystals behind.

Molecules of the newly found carbon were first observed in vapor in 1985. Now that scientists can produce solid fullerite crystals in large quantities, they expect to gain a better understanding of their properties and to find practical uses for them. For instance, the fullerite crystals might make a superior lubricant because they are stable and slow to react. Or they might be used in materials that take advantage of the empty interiors of the molecules to, for example, isolate radioactive isotopes.

Lifelike molecules. In January 1990, chemists at the Massachusetts Institute of Technology in Cambridge reported they had created a chemical system that could be considered a primitive form of life. By imitating natural processes, the scientists induced molecules to copy themselves in a laboratory solution. The ability to reproduce is at the heart of most definitions of life.

Chemist Julius Rebek, Jr., and his colleagues started with a U-shaped molecular framework. To one end of the U, they chemically bonded a molecule that resembles an *amino acid*, a building block of proteins. To the other end, they attached a molecule that has the characteristics of both proteins and DNA (*deoxyribonucleic acid*, the material that makes up genes).

The two molecules then spontaneously reacted, linking in the kind of bond that proteins form. Next, the newly formed molecule snapped loose from the U and became a model for replication, much as DNA serves as a model for its replication in living systems. The molecular model successfully matched up the constituent molecules— amino-acidlike and protein/DNA-like— to create a copy of itself. Essentially, it stored, and then used, chemical information.

This chemical synthesis brings scientists a step closer to reproducing a fundamental process of nature: the way in which molecules in living things carry information to make copies of themselves. The understanding gained from this achievement could lead to a better grasp of how life began and to a means of building machines that can maintain and reproduce themselves.   Peter J. Andrews

In *World Book,* see **Chemistry.**

Chess. World champion Gary Kasparov of the Soviet Union defended his title against former world champion and fellow countryman Anatoly Karpov in a 24-game match in 1990. The first 12 games were held in New York City from October 8 to November 7. After battling to a 6-6 tie, the contestants moved to Lyon, France, resuming play on November 24.

Under the rules of international chess, 1 point is given for a win and ½ point for a draw. The first player to win six games or amass 12½ points wins.

On December 31, Kasparov played Karpov to a draw in the 24th game to win the match 12½ to 11½ and keep his title. He won $1.7 million in prize money.

Olympiad. A Soviet team won the gold medal for men at the biennial Chess Olympiad held in Novi Sad, Yugoslavia, from November 17 to December 3. The United States took the silver medal. England won the bronze. In women's competition, Hungary won the gold medal. The Soviet women won the silver medal, and the Chinese women took the bronze.

U.S. Championship. Lev Alburt of New York City won the 1990 U.S. Championship by prevailing in a series of one-on-one elimination matches among the nation's top 16 players in August in Jacksonville, Fla. In July, Elena Donaldson of Seattle won the 1990 U.S. Women's Championship in Spartanburg, S.C.

Other tournaments. The Chess Summit Match was held in March in Reykjavík, Iceland. The match was a showdown between the Soviet Union, the United States, England, and a team from the five Nordic countries—Denmark, Finland, Iceland, Norway, and Sweden. The Soviet team won, edging out the English.

In April, Alexander Khalifman of the Soviet Union won the New York City International, which pitted 63 of the best players in the world against one another. In June, Dmitry Gurevich of Chicago won the National Open in Las Vegas, Nev., topping 1,116 competitors. Igor Gleck of the Soviet Union led a field of 1,158 players to win the 1990 World Open in July in Philadelphia. In August, Yasser Seirawan of Seattle won the U.S. Open in Jacksonville.

Younger chess players. Ilya Gurevich, 18, of Worcester, Mass., won the 1990 World Junior Championship held in Santiago, Chile, in August. Nawrose Nur of New York City won the world chess championship for boys under the age of 14.

More than 2,240 young U.S. players competed in national school team chess championships in 1990. In Kansas City, Mo., in April, Stuyvesant High School of New York City won the national high school championship. In Salt Lake City, Utah, in May, the Dalton School of New York City captured the national championship for ninth grade and under. Samm Fees Junior High School of Arizona won the eighth grade and under team championship. The Dalton School also won the elementary school team chess championship in competition held in Hollywood, Fla., in May.   Al Lawrence

In *World Book,* see **Chess.**

Electrical workers examine wires damaged in a Commonwealth Edison fire in July that knocked out power to 40,000 Chicago customers.

Chicago. Richard M. Daley, elected mayor in a special election in April 1989, spent much of 1990 solidifying his control over the city government. In nearly every move he made during his first full year in office, Daley seemed to be preparing for his expected reelection bid in the April 1991 regular election. He announced his candidacy on Dec. 10, 1990.

By year's end, it appeared that Daley, a Democrat, would face at least two serious opponents in the 1991 election. In early November, former Mayor Jane M. Byrne, also a Democrat, announced that she would seek to regain the office she held from 1979 to 1983. Later in the month, Danny K. Davis, a City Council member from Chicago's West Side, announced his candidacy. And R. Eugene Pincham, a former judge and a leader of the Harold Washington Party—named for the city's first black mayor, who died in 1987—was also considering a mayoral bid. The Harold Washington Party scored a success on October 25 when the Supreme Court of the United States ruled that its candidates must be placed on the ballot for the Nov. 6, 1990, general election for state and county offices.

Budget. In November, the City Council approved a $3.17-billion "hold-the-line" budget for 1991 that avoided new taxes but contained funds for the hiring of 600 additional police officers. Critics said the budget was overly optimistic in that it relied on the robust growth of revenue from several sources and the continuation of a state income tax surcharge.

Officials indicted. On December 19, federal prosecutors in Chicago announced the indictments of five local figures on racketeering and extortion charges. The indictments resulted from a long-running United States government probe, code-named Operation Gambat, of Chicago's First Ward, a political subdivision encompassing much of the downtown area. For years, the ward has allegedly been under the influence of a group of politicians, lawyers, and business leaders with ties to organized crime.

The indictments were a shocking testimony to the extent of that influence. City Council member Fred B. Roti was accused of taking bribes to fix court cases and obtain zoning changes from the council. State Senator John A. D'Arco, Jr., was charged with extorting cash in return for sponsoring bills in the state legislature. And former Cook County Circuit Court Judge David J. Shields was accused of accepting bribes to fix the outcome of cases over which he presided.

Even more serious charges were leveled against Ward Democratic Party Secretary Pat Marcy. He was accused of bribing judges to obtain acquittals in two separate murder trials, in 1977 and 1981. (Roti was accused of also taking part in the second of those bribery incidents.) The fifth person indicted was Pasquale F. De Leo, D'Arco's law partner, for allegedly extorting money and bribing judges.

Much of the evidence against the defendants was obtained with video and audio tape recorders hidden in a restaurant frequented by First Ward figures. Federal prosecutors indicated that more Gambat indictments would be forthcoming.

Third airport. On February 15, Mayor Daley unveiled plans for a third municipal airport for the Chicago area. The airport, which would be larger than O'Hare International, would be located on the city's far South Side. The plan was criticized by many of the 3,400 homeowners whose property would have to be condemned to make way for the huge facility and by Republican officials who favored other sites in the far south suburbs or across the state line in Indiana. A commission with representatives from both Illinois and Indiana will make the final site selection.

Census dispute. On August 29, the U.S. Census Bureau released preliminary 1990 census figures showing that Chicago's population dropped by 9.3 per cent during the 1980's to 2,725,979. Shortly thereafter, city officials charged that census takers had missed 79,648 dwelling units—a claim census officials promised to check before issuing final totals sometime in 1991.

Crime. The Chicago Police Department blamed drug-dealing street gangs for a 14 per cent surge in the homicide rate in 1990. During the year, an average of 2.2 murders a day were committed in the city.

School plan struck down. On November 30, the Illinois Supreme Court ruled that a 1988 state law decentralizing the Chicago school system was unconstitutional. The court did not find fault with the purpose of the law—giving parents greater control over the schools their children attend. But the justices said a new system must be devised for the election of the councils that now control the schools. Under the law, community residents without school-age children elect 2 nonparent members of a school's 10-member council. Parents elect 6 council members who are parents, and teachers elect 2 teachers to the council.

Power failures. Several electrical outages in July, August, and September angered Chicagoans and had the city government thinking about taking over power-generating operations within city limits from the Commonwealth Edison Company. The first of the blackouts, on July 28, was caused by a fire at a generating plant and knocked out power for up to three days to some 40,000 customers. The other outages were blamed by the utility on damage to cables and on animals chewing on power lines.

Stadiums. On September 30, the Chicago White Sox played—and won—their last game in Comiskey Park, in use since 1910 and the nation's oldest major league baseball stadium. The Sox were to open the 1991 season in a new ball park being built just across the street from Comiskey. On June 4, the Chicago Bears signed a tentative agreement to play football in a new domed stadium to be built on the lakefront. But the state legislature delayed consideration of funding for the project until 1991.   John F. McCarron

In *World Book,* see **Chicago.**

Children's books. See Literature for children.

Chile. More than 16 years of military rule ended on March 11, 1990, when Patricio Aylwin Azócar, 72, was sworn in as Chile's president for a five-year term. A Christian Democrat, Aylwin was Chile's first popularly elected leader since a 1973 military coup.

Aylwin sought during 1990 to consolidate a fragile democracy's hold on power. His every move was scrutinized and second-guessed by the former dictator, General Augusto Pinochet Ugarte, who remained commander in chief of the armed forces.

On May 28, 1990, Aylwin reprimanded Pinochet for attempting to undermine the authority of his new civilian government. The military had issued a statement critical of Aylwin for establishing a commission to investigate human-rights abuses under military rule. Aylwin had asked Pinochet to release files of the National Information Center, a secret police force widely accused of such abuses. But Pinochet refused, denying that any such files existed.

In June, the head of the civil police called for Pinochet's resignation after a mass grave was uncovered near a 1973 military prison camp. The grave held bodies of people executed by troops after the coup that put Pinochet in power. On Sept. 28, 1990, Chile's Supreme Court upheld a law passed under military rule that gave amnesty for human-rights abuses committed from 1973 to 1978.   Nathan A. Haverstock

See also **Aylwin Azócar, Patricio; Latin America** (Facts in brief table). In *World Book,* see **Chile.**

China drifted through 1990 without a clear sense of direction. While most other Communist countries were rejecting centralized economic controls and seeking to establish new economic systems, China's leaders, almost all of whom were men in their mid-80's, fought indecisively over what policies to follow. The next generation waited passively for orders—or for the old men to die.

China's elderly leaders faced two options. In simple terms, one choice was to resume the economic liberalization begun in 1978, which had stimulated production and raised living standards. But liberalization had led to inflation and increased corruption. It had also sparked public questioning of the Communist Party's monopoly on power.

The other choice was to continue the policies of economic centralization begun in late 1988 to combat inflation. But these policies were accompanied by an economic slump and increased unemployment. They also brought a government crackdown on people seeking a loosening of political controls. Thus, the decision was not only a matter of economics but also a question of how closely the Communist Party should control decision-making and public expression.

The party emphasized stability —that is, little or no change. On March 12, the Central Committee, the Communist Party's main policy forum, called for stronger ties to the people, thus admitting that popular confidence in its leadership was weak. The leaders seemed more concerned about preventing social unrest and maintaining the party's control than stimulating the economy. But formerly loyal and unquestioning citizens—particularly students and other urban, educated people   exhibited a growing tendency to think independently about policy questions and, in doing so, challenged the leaders' authority.

Dynasty in decline. Austerity measures and the "worst economic slump in a decade" were threatening China's social stability, according to a United States Central Intelligence Agency study made public by the U.S. Congress on June 28. Many foreign observers believed that the public had lost faith in its leaders—that, in traditional Chinese terms, the Communists were a dynasty in decline because they had lost "the mandate of heaven."

The man regarded as the emperor of this dynasty was Deng Xiaoping. At age 86, Deng no longer held any official positions, but he was the key figure among the generation that established Communist power in China in the 1940's. Although unwilling to let the party relinquish its power, Deng was relatively liberal. He supported economic reform and opening up political discussion.

His opposition centered on 85-year-old Chen Yun, an important party leader. Worried about the effects of change, Chen wanted to maintain rigid controls on the economy and on public expression.

The competition between their approaches had reached a critical point in 1989 when demonstrators in

Hong Kong students protest the February 1990 passage of a Chinese law to govern the island in 1997, when Hong Kong becomes part of China.

Beijing, the capital, demanded a more democratic system. On June 4, 1989, the government used force to crush the demonstration, and 700 or more people were killed in and around the city's center, Tiananmen Square. That event, seen as a defeat for Deng's policies, reverberated through Chinese politics in 1990. The conservatives who had led the crackdown seemed to have the upper hand over the reformers in the continuing policy struggle.

Premier Li Peng set a conservative tone for the first session of China's legislature since the crackdown—and since anti-Communist upheavals began in Eastern Europe in late 1989. Li told the National People's Congress on March 20, 1990, that Communism "will stand rock-firm in the East." He charged that "hostile forces at home and abroad" were trying to overthrow China's Communist system "under the banners of freedom, democracy, and human rights."

Li promised some relaxation of economic controls to stimulate the depressed economy. But he said that the government would keep tight controls on production, supplies of raw materials, and prices. Li also indicated that inefficient industries would continue to be subsidized, an activity that fueled inflation and kept the national deficit high.

Although Li remained premier, he was replaced on September 7 as minister of the State Commission for

Restructuring the Economy, a liaison job more than a policymaking one. Succeeding him was Chen Jinhua, whose ties to Chen Yun were even closer than Li's.

Economy. In a speech published on October 9, Li indicated that China's five-year economic development plan for 1991-1995 would reinforce central controls. He said there would be fewer big development projects. "We do not want to seek overly rapid growth," Li said, but the economy grew slower than the goal of 6 per cent in 1990.

A quotation attributed to Deng on October 22 reflected the continuing policy debate. Deng apparently said that more rapid economic reforms were needed. Jiang Zemin, the general secretary of the Communist Party, also called for faster reforms. The state statistical bureau announced on October 24 that debt was rising rapidly and revenues were falling.

Li promised to continue the reformers' policy of increasing foreign trade. In 1990, China exported goods worth $52.5 billion, 16 per cent of the value of its production of goods and services, or *gross national product*. But by late in the year, China had accumulated a foreign debt of $51.5 billion. The nation tried to join the General Agreement on Tariffs and Trade, the group of nations that regulates world trade, but China's subsidy system and other distortions of free-trade principles blocked its bid for membership. Efforts to lure more foreign investors also had limited results.

Population growth. Significant economic growth was needed just to keep up with the expanding population. A census showed that on July 1 China's population was 1.134 billion—about 20 million people above the goal set by the government in hopes of limiting the burden on China's crowded land and limited resources. With the population growing by about 17 million people per year, new efforts were made to limit family size.

Police and military. After failing to prevent the 1989 Tiananmen Square demonstrations, China's internal security police force was reorganized in early 1990. Major General Zhou Yushu was put in charge, and some regular army units were transferred to the Beijing police command.

As an apparent reward for having crushed the Tiananmen challenge, the People's Liberation Army received a budget increase in March. After adjustments for inflation, it was the first increase after a decade of cuts. But the extra funds were not expected to fully counteract the army's problems of aging weaponry, declining morale, and falling standards.

The most extensive reshuffle of top military commanders since 1987 occurred during the spring. Several officers who played key roles in the Tiananmen crackdown were promoted. Sensitive assignments in the Beijing military region went to officers who were considered close to General Yang Baibing, the general secretary of the Central Military Commission. Yang, the younger brother of China's president, 83-year-old Yang Shangkun, was a hard-line opponent of reforms.

Protesters and exiles. On January 11, China lifted the martial law imposed in Beijing during the crackdown. A few days later, some 570 jailed protesters were released. The release of 211 people was announced on May 10, while 431 jailed protesters were said still to be under investigation. On June 6, another 97 dissidents were released. According to some foreign estimates, many thousands of others were still held, but this could not be confirmed. A Chinese diplomat who defected in Washington, D.C., in May carried a document saying that China regarded the release of prisoners as a means to influence the United States to grant trade concessions.

On June 25, Chinese officials allowed the nation's best-known dissident, astrophysicist Fang Lizhi, to leave the U.S. Embassy in Beijing, where he and his wife had taken sanctuary from arrest after the Tiananmen Square crackdown. By agreement with U.S. officials, a U.S. Air Force plane flew the couple to exile in Great Britain. Another prominent dissident, writer Wang Ruowang, was released from 16 months in detention on October 29.

Some Chinese who fled abroad after the crackdown tried to keep the democracy movement alive. But during 1990 they fell into disagreements and lost influence at home. An effort to post a ship off China's coast to broadcast democratic messages failed when the exiles could not get adequate support.

For years, Chinese dissidents have tried to hijack airliners to escape the country. One hijacker on October 2 was resisted by the pilot of a Xiamen Airlines Boeing 737. They struggled as the plane landed at Guangzhou (formerly Canton), and it crashed into a loaded plane about to take off. In the resulting fire, at least 128 people were killed, the worst aviation disaster ever reported in China.

Ethnic unrest occurred in Tibet and Xinjiang provinces. China lifted martial law in Lhasa, the capital of Tibet, on April 30. It had been imposed in March 1989, after the government suppressed nationalist demonstrations. But Tibetans continued to smolder with resentment of Chinese control and with the desire for the return of the land's exiled spiritual leader, the Dalai Lama. In July, Jiang—making the first visit to Tibet by a top party official since 1980—promised flexibility in government policies but warned that separatism would not be permitted.

The U.S. human-rights group Asia Watch said on May 28 that political repression and the torture of protesters had greatly increased in Tibet since 1987. Another American human-rights organization said on September 21 that persecution of religion threatened to wipe out Tibet's unique form of Buddhism.

In the western province of Xinjiang, a separatist movement among Muslims erupted for at least the third time in a decade. On April 5 and 6, fighting occurred at Baren, a town near the Soviet and Afghan borders. Chinese officials said 22 people died, including 6 policemen who were mutilated, in an "armed counterrevolutionary rebellion." Diplomatic reports said the toll was far higher, perhaps 50 or more, with dozens injured.

Hostility toward ethnic Chinese, a minority who dominate the province politically and economically, was reported from other parts of Xinjiang. Authorities arrested thousands of people, tightened controls on mosques, and closed some Muslim schools accused of promoting separatism.

The 11th Asian Games opened in Beijing on September 22. China made intensive preparations for the arrival of athletes and spectators from throughout Asia, taking care to prevent demonstrations against the government. But visiting athletes were outraged by what they considered unfair arrangements that enhanced China's chances of winning events. China won more than half the gold medals.

Foreign relations. After criticizing the Soviet Union early in 1990 for deviating from true Marxism, Premier Li played down reports of such a rift during an April visit to Moscow. The two countries signed agreements for further reductions of troops along their border and for increased trade. China also held the highest-level talks with Vietnam since 1979. Chinese officials expanded contacts with South Korea, despite objections from North Korea, and obtained new aid from Japan.   Henry S. Bradsher

See also **Asia** (Facts in brief table); **Taiwan.** In *World Book,* see **China.**

Chrétien, Jean Joseph-Jacques (1934-   ), be-
came leader of the Liberal Party in Canada at a convention in Calgary, Alta., on June 23, 1990. Chrétien's landslide victory over former Prime Minister John N. Turner came at a time when party members were divided over the Meech Lake accord (see **Canada [Close-Up]**). Chrétien calls himself an advocate of strong central government, opposed to Quebec separating from the nation.

Chrétien was born on Jan. 11, 1934, in Shawinigan, Que., the 18th of 19 children. Bell's palsy left the right side of his face paralyzed and made him deaf in one ear. Friends say the disabilities have made him strong and determined.

Chrétien studied law at Laval University in Quebec City and practiced in Shawinigan before winning his first federal election in 1963. Thereafter, he served 23 years in the House of Commons, 16 of them as a cabinet minister in several posts. In 1984, Chrétien lost a bid for party leadership to Turner and, following a dispute with Turner in 1986, resigned the cabinet to work as a lawyer in Ottawa, Ont.

Chrétien married the former Aline Chainé of Shawinigan in 1957. She is a classical pianist. They have three grown children, including an adopted Indian son.   Margaret Anne Schmidt

Churches. See **Eastern Orthodox Churches; Jews and Judaism; Protestantism; Religion; Roman Catholic Church.**

City. Cities in the United States faced much the same problems in 1990 that have been troubling them for years: illegal drug use and trade, violent crime, inadequate affordable housing, floundering school systems—and lack of money to do anything about these problems. Worse, a new concern was added to the list during the year: the results of the 1990 census, which threatened to have broad social and economic effects in many cities.

The census problem began even before the Bureau of the Census started to count heads in 1990. New York City, Chicago, the U.S. Conference of Mayors, and the National League of Cities were among the plaintiffs who in November 1988 filed suit against the Department of Commerce. The Census Bureau is an agency of the Commerce Department.

Census population figures are used to determine how some federal funds are distributed. They also determine how many seats a state has in the U.S. House of Representatives, and they are used in the reapportionment of seats in state legislatures. The plaintiffs in the lawsuit contended that their shares of money and their congressional seats would be reduced unless the 1990 census count was adjusted to compensate for the expected undercounting of minority groups.

In July 1989, in agreeing to a settlement of the lawsuit, the Census Bureau said it would take a special survey of 150,000 homes to develop a way to compensate for the undercount. Such an undercount results historically from the many people in major cities and inner-city neighborhoods—especially illegal immigrants and the homeless—not filling out census questionnaires.

The official census day was April 1, 1990. On August 29, the Census Bureau announced preliminary population figures for the 50 states. They came as a shock to cities throughout the nation. They showed that half of the country's 20 largest cities had declined in population since the 1980 census. Detroit displayed the biggest drop—19.4 per cent—and fell below 1 million population to 970,156. Michigan gives special taxing powers to cities of more than 1 million, so the census figures meant that Detroit might lose, at least temporarily, its authority to tax utilities and might have to lower its city income tax rate.

One out of every seven cities and counties—including the 51 largest cities—challenged the Census Bureau's statistics. They hoped that their population totals would show increases when the head counts became final. See **Census (Close-Up).**

The drug problem. The illegal use of drugs is the top concern of urban officials, according to a survey by the National League of Cities released in early January. The league surveyed elected officials in 314 cities of more than 10,000 population in November and December 1989. Fifty-eight per cent of those surveyed said the drug problem was worsening in their cities. Fewer than 10 per cent said they had made progress in the war on drugs.

Drugs were also at the top of the list when the United States Conference of Mayors met later in January 1990 in Washington, D.C. The problem was the main topic during the mayors' annual three-day winter meeting.

The crime problem. *The New York Times* in July surveyed 22 major U.S. cities, and all but 5 reported increases in homicides during the first six months of 1990, compared with the same period of 1989. The largest increase was in Seattle, where homicides soared 75 per cent. Then came Boston, up 56 per cent; New York City, 45 per cent (for the first three months only, if 87 arson deaths in one fire are included); San Francisco, 41 per cent; Memphis, 31 per cent; and Milwaukee, 25 per cent.

Some police officials attributed the increase in homicides to, in large part, the increasingly violent drug trade and the growing availability of firearms to teenagers. "It's kids, guns, and dope. That's the crux of it," Detective James Rock of the Denver Police Department's homicide bureau told the *Chicago Tribune*.

Of the five cities that reported decreases in homicides, Tucson, Ariz., led with a 44 per cent drop. It was followed by Portland, Ore., down 33 per cent; Miami, Fla., 16 per cent; and Cleveland, 10 per cent.

Providing housing. Cities were taking a variety of steps in 1990 to provide additional affordable housing for their citizens. In New Orleans, for example, elderly poor people began moving into a 93-unit apartment complex in March. The $5.2-million project was a converted hospital that had been vacant for several years.

In San Jose, city officials rezoned land that had been reserved for industry. This reversed a policy established 25 years earlier to attract business to California's high-technology "Silicon Valley." After the rezoning, work began on 2,000 units of moderately priced housing, located on an 80-acre (32-hectare) site and scheduled for completion by mid-1991.

Seattle's stagnating Chinatown district got a boost when the city's landmark review board in September approved plans for a $40-million hotel and condominium project. The city required the developer to designate 10 per cent of the units for moderate-income families.

School integration financing. The Supreme Court of the United States on April 18 ruled that federal judges may order local officials to increase taxes to pay for public school integration plans. At issue was a case involving the Kansas City, Mo., public schools, which once were segregated by law but had since become about 70 per cent black after many white families moved to the suburbs.

The city was unable to finance its share of costs for integrating the schools, including the creation of *magnet schools* to attract whites back to the city. Magnet schools offer innovative courses and sometimes specialized training to attract students from a broad urban area, rather than from a neighborhood. They are often used in desegregation efforts.

50 largest cities in the world

Rank	City	Population
1.	Mexico City	10,263,275
2.	Seoul, South Korea	9,645,932
3.	Tokyo	8,353,674
4.	Moscow	8,275,000
5.	Bombay, India	8,227,332
6.	New York City	7,071,639
7.	São Paulo, Brazil	7,033,529
8.	Shanghai	6,880,000
9.	London	6,767,500
10.	Jakarta, Indonesia	6,761,886
11.	Cairo, Egypt	6,052,836
12.	Beijing	5,760,000
13.	Hong Kong	5,756,000
14.	Teheran, Iran	5,734,199
15.	Lima, Peru	5,493,900
16.	Istanbul, Turkey	5,475,982
17.	Tianjin, China	5,300,000
18.	Karachi, Pakistan	5,208,170
19.	Bangkok, Thailand	5,153,902
20.	Rio de Janeiro, Brazil	5,093,232
21.	Delhi, India	4,884,234
22.	Leningrad, Soviet Union	4,295,000
23.	Santiago, Chile	4,225,299
24.	Shenyang, China	4,130,000
25.	Bogota, Colombia	3,982,941
26.	Pusan, South Korea	3,516,807
27.	Ho Chi Minh City, Vietnam	3,460,500
28.	Wuhan, China	3,340,000
29.	Calcutta, India	3,305,006
30.	Madras, India	3,276,622
31.	Guangzhou, China	3,220,000
32.	Madrid, Spain	3,123,713
33.	Berlin, Germany	3,062,979
34.	Chicago	3,005,072
35.	Yokohama, Japan	2,992,644
36.	Sydney, Australia	2,989,070
37.	Baghdad, Iraq	2,969,000
38.	Los Angeles	2,968,579
39.	Lahore, Pakistan	2,952,689
40.	Alexandria, Egypt	2,917,327
41.	Buenos Aires, Argentina	2,908,001
42.	Rome	2,830,569
43.	Chongqing, China	2,730,000
44.	Melbourne, Australia	2,645,484
45.	Pyongyang, North Korea	2,639,448
46.	Taipei, Taiwan	2,637,100
47.	Osaka, Japan	2,636,260
48.	Harbin, China	2,590,000
49.	Hanoi, Vietnam	2,570,905
50.	Chengdu, China	2,540,000

Sources: 1980 census for cities in the United States; 1976-1990 censuses and estimates for cities in other countries.

Mayors march against drugs in Chicago in June during the United
States Conference of Mayors hosted by Mayor Richard M. Daley, center.

Kansas City voters had since 1969 refused to raise taxes for the school district, which had 34,000 pupils in 1990. A U.S. District Court judge had ordered the local property tax to be nearly doubled. The Supreme Court ruled that the judge's increase was an "abuse of discretion," but it said that the "court order directing a local government body to levy its own taxes is plainly a judicial act within the power of a federal court."

Parental choice in schools. The Wisconsin state legislature in March passed a bill allowing the use of public funds to send 970 low-income students from Milwaukee's public schools to private, nonsectarian schools. The bill had been proposed by Wisconsin Governor Tommy G. Thompson. He and other backers of the bill said it will give more educational choice to students from poor families.

Milwaukee's superintendent of schools, Robert Perkins, said the bill posed a threat to public education because it would leave city schools with fewer financial resources and students who are the hardest to educate. Other critics of the bill worried about taxpayers' money going to schools that do not have to comply with all the regulations the state imposes on public schools. The 970 students represent 1 per cent of the 97,000 in the city's public school system.

Bouncing back. Some cities were bouncing back in 1990 from economic woes. Houston, for example, in July hosted the annual economic summit of the leaders of seven industrialized nations and used the occa-

sion to celebrate the city's two years of steady employment growth. The unemployment rate in Houston—a center of the U.S. oil industry—had bottomed out in 1987, following a five-year decline in oil prices that resulted in the loss of 225,000 jobs. By 1990, 80 per cent of those jobs had been recovered.

In Pittsburgh, officials of Carnegie-Mellon University recommended on February 23 that the city use its idled steel mills to build high-speed trains and tracks. The first project recommended was for a 19-mile (31-kilometer) line from downtown Pittsburgh to the Greater Pittsburgh International Airport, using *magnetic levitation*, or *maglev*. This technology uses electromagnets to raise a train's cars above a guideway and propel them at high speeds.

Many American cities are considering maglev trains to carry many of the travelers who now crowd the nation's airports and roads. After the university's recommendation, several Pittsburgh businesses, universities, and unions joined with state and county agencies to form Maglev, Incorporated, a company that is to conduct a two-year, $1½-million study of how to make the city the nation's center for manufacturing maglev railroad lines.

Earthquake aftermath. Oakland, San Francisco, and Santa Cruz—the cities hardest hit in the Oct. 17, 1989, earthquake that rocked northern California— were following different paths to reconstruction in 1990. Oakland took advantage of decreased inner-city property values to attract new businesses. Its 12-block redevelopment, Oakland City Center, also helped draw new firms to the city. But some 1,500 residents still were without permanent shelter, and 13 of 78 buildings damaged by the quake were still closed in 1990.

In San Francisco, city officials decided to tear down the quake-damaged Embarcadero Freeway, and sections of two other highways were not scheduled to reopen until 1991. Detours caused tremendous traffic jams. In the city's Marina district, 7 of 115 damaged buildings remained closed by city inspectors.

Santa Cruz, a city of 41,000 population, had only one building under construction by October 1990, with five more approved for its downtown mall, which lost 25 buildings in the quake.

Other development. Construction of a 50-story office tower in downtown Detroit began in the spring of 1990 as a joint venture of Houston and Tokyo investors. The $250-million project is scheduled for completion in the fall of 1991, but several Michigan utilities and a large law firm already had leased space in 1990.

Private and public cooperation was critical in planning for a 12-acre (4.9-hectare) project in Newark, N.J. It is to be funded by Newark's business community, state bonds, and federal aid and is expected to cost $200 million when all phases are completed by the mid-1990's. Newark Mayor Sharpe James called the $70-million performing arts building in the project "a keystone for Newark's renewal over the next three decades." Los Angeles architect Barton Myers was named on Nov. 7, 1990, to design the project, which will also include shops and restaurants.

Kapolei, a new community near Honolulu, Hawaii, began to take form in November with the construction of a shopping center. The new community will spread over 32,000 acres (13,000 hectares) and will include 40,000 houses, a resort, a harbor, and a 900-acre (360-hectare) park for light industry. Kapolei is being built by the estate of James Campbell, a sugar cane magnate who bought the land on Oahu in 1877.

Olympic city. Atlanta, Ga., on Sept. 18, 1990, was chosen over Athens, Greece, as the site of the 1996 Summer Olympic Games. Atlanta persuaded Olympic officials that the city had the resources to construct $418 million worth of facilities and to raise $1.2 billion to stage the games.

Top cities for business. A Harris poll of 400 business executives, released on Oct. 2, 1990, ranked Seattle as the number-one city in the United States in which to locate a business. Sacramento, Calif., finished second, followed by Portland; Norfolk, Va.; and San Diego. The poll rated 31 U.S. cities on such factors as taxes and regulation, as well as cost and availability of skilled workers.　Donna Rosene Leff

See also **Chicago; Detroit; Elections; Los Angeles; New York City; Philadelphia; San Diego.** In *World Book,* see **City.**

A new baseball stadium, right, rises next to Chicago's Comiskey Park, built in 1910 and scheduled for demolition at the end of the 1990 season.

Four civil rights pioneers meet in February at the Greensboro, N.C., lunch counter where they were refused service in 1960, triggering sit-ins.

Civil rights

The Congress of the United States passed three important civil rights bills in 1990, but only two became law. In October, Congress gave its final approval to the Civil Rights Act of 1990, which was designed to overturn five rulings by the Supreme Court of the United States in 1989. The rulings made it more difficult for workers to win discrimination lawsuits against their employers. One controversial provision of the bill shifted back to businesses the burden of proof in demonstrating that hiring and promotion standards challenged in court as discriminatory to women and racial minorities were a business necessity.

President George Bush vetoed the bill on Oct. 22, 1990, contending that it would have led to employers adopting quotas for hiring women and minorities. Supporters of the bill disagreed. Opponents of the bill also objected to a provision allowing workers to sue for punitive damages up to $150,000. On October 24, the Senate failed by one vote to override the veto.

Handicapped rights. On July 26, Bush signed the Americans with Disabilities Act, which gave an estimated 43 million handicapped Americans the same protections against discrimination provided to women and racial minorities under the Civil Rights Act of 1964. See **Handicapped.**

Protection for older workers. A third civil rights law, the Older Workers Benefit Protection Act, was approved with little debate and signed in October 1990. The law, which prohibits employers from denying benefits to workers based on their age, overturned a 1989 Supreme Court ruling that such actions did not violate federal bans on age discrimination.

The Supreme Court in 1990 issued several major rulings on minority rights. In *Metro Broadcasting, Inc., v. Federal Communications Commission*, the court on June 27 upheld two affirmative-action policies of the commission that give minority-owned companies advantages in getting broadcast licenses. The majority opinion was the last written by Justice William J. Brennan, Jr., considered the court's most liberal member, before he retired on July 20.

On April 18, the Supreme Court ruled in *Missouri v. Jenkins* that federal judges may order school districts to increase taxes to pay for desegregation. The court said, however, that it is unconstitutional for judges themselves to increase taxes. The case arose when a federal judge in Kansas City, Mo., ordered the city to nearly double local property taxes to finance a school desegregation plan despite a Missouri law that bars such increases unless approved by voters.

The justices on January 10 overturned fines levied by a federal judge against four City Council members in Yonkers, N.Y., who had refused to vote for legislation needed to racially integrate local housing. The four men voted in August 1988 against implementing a court-ordered housing desegregation plan that city officials had agreed to earlier in the year. In *Spallone v. United States*, the Supreme Court said that the judge first should have waited to see if heavy fines imposed on the city at the same time were sufficient to compel the council to adopt the plan.

On June 11, 1990, the high court ruled for the second time in two years that the First Amendment to the Constitution bans laws aimed at stopping political protesters from burning or defacing the American flag. The ruling in *United States v. Eichman* struck down a 1989 federal law making it illegal to mutilate or destroy a United States flag or to keep one on the ground.

International report. Amnesty International, a London-based human-rights organization, reported in July that human-rights violations had occurred in 142 countries in 1989. The group said that thousands of people were imprisoned, tortured, or killed by their government. Among the countries cited for large-scale killings were China, where at least 1,000 unarmed, prodemocracy protesters were shot, and Romania, where hundreds died during the overthrow of President Nicolae Ceaușescu.

Civil rights chiefs. President Bush named John R. Dunne, a former New York state legislator, to be the Justice Department's assistant attorney general for civil rights, the nation's top civil rights post. The Senate confirmed Dunne's appointment on March 9, 1990. In 1989, the Senate had rejected Bush's first choice for the job, Detroit lawyer and former sheriff William Lucas, citing his lack of civil rights experience.

In February 1990, Bush selected Arthur A. Fletcher, a moderate Republican and former federal labor and urban affairs official, to head the U.S. Commission on Civil Rights. He replaced William Barclay Allen, who resigned in 1989 after generating widespread criticism for a number of controversial actions.

Japanese American reparations. The Justice Department in October 1990 made the first reparation payments to Japanese Americans forcibly sent to detention camps from 1942 to 1945, while the United States was involved in World War II against Japan, Germany, and Italy. Under a 1988 law, the federal government agreed to pay about $20,000 each to the approximately 125,000 Japanese Americans who were interned because officials believed—with little evidence—that they posed a threat to U.S. security.

Voting rights. The Los Angeles County Board of Supervisors must redraw election district boundaries to create one district with a Hispanic majority, a federal appeals court ruled on Nov. 3, 1990. In June, a federal judge found that a 1981 redistricting plan made it difficult for Hispanics to win election to the board. Several civil rights groups and the Justice Department sued the county in 1988, claiming that the 1981 plan was created to protect the seats of the five supervisors, who were all non-Hispanic whites, by diluting the Hispanic vote.

Texas judges. Hispanics in Texas lost a ruling on the legality of that state's system of electing judges by countywide vote. A federal appeals court said in September 1990 that provisions of the Voting Rights Act of 1965 did not apply to judicial elections because judges are not public servants under the law. The League of United Latin American Citizens had charged that countywide voting hampered the election of Hispanic judges.

Partnership award. A woman who charged sex discrimination when she was rejected for a partnership at a major accounting firm became in May 1990 the first person to win a partnership as part of her award. A federal judge ruled that Price Waterhouse had allowed negative sexual stereotypes to influence the partnership selection process when considering Ann B. Hopkins for the position. Partners at the firm had told Hopkins that she could improve her chances of being named a partner if she behaved and dressed in a more feminine manner.

Racial violence. The Justice Department in 1990 began collecting statistics about *hate crimes*—crimes motivated by racial, ethnic, or sexual prejudice—under a law signed by President Bush on April 23. The

Classical music

new law requires the department to collect statistics on such crimes for five years to determine whether changes are needed in federal antibias laws.

Bensonhurst trials. One man was convicted of murder, three defendants were found guilty of lesser charges, and one man was acquitted of all charges in 1990 in one of New York City's most widely publicized racially motivated crimes. The five were among eight men charged in the 1989 fatal shooting of Yusuf K. Hawkins, a 16-year-old black student. Hawkins was attacked by a white mob when he went to see a used car in the Bensonhurst neighborhood of Brooklyn. See **Courts.**

Selma march reenactment. In early March 1990, about 150 people walked 50 miles (95 kilometers) from Selma to Montgomery, Ala., to mark the 25th anniversary of a historic march held to win equal voting rights for blacks. Thousands of people gathered in Selma before the march and in Montgomery afterward to commemorate the 1965 protest and hear civil rights leaders call for a renewed emphasis on civil rights.

The original march from Selma to Montgomery, headed by civil rights leader Martin Luther King, Jr., began with bloodshed as police officers beat, clubbed, and gassed marchers. The attack on the marchers helped spur Congress to pass the Voting Rights Act of 1965.　　Linda P. Campbell and Geoffrey A. Campbell

In *World Book,* see **Civil rights.**

Classical music. The death of conductor Leonard Bernstein and the 100th anniversary season of New York City's Carnegie Hall were two of the most notable events in the world of music in 1990. Bernstein had experienced some of his greatest successes at Carnegie Hall. His transformation from young unknown to young celebrity occurred there in 1943, when he was called in as a last-minute substitute to conduct, with stunning success, the New York Philharmonic (see **Close-Up**).

.Over the years, the phrase "to play at Carnegie Hall" has come to indicate reaching the pinnacle of success. The concert hall was the place where Russian composer Peter Ilich Tchaikovsky conducted his own Concerto for Piano and Orchestra No. 1 in B flat minor and Czech composer Antonín Dvořák heard the world premiere of his Symphony No. 9, *From the New World.* Such performing legends as violinist Jascha Heifetz and pianist Vladimir Horowitz also made their United States debuts there.

To mark the anniversary, the directors of Carnegie Hall commissioned 14 new compositions. These included Steven Stucky's *Angelus,* which the Los Angeles Philharmonic performed in late September as the gala season got underway.

Anniversaries. Many ensembles in the United States in 1990 paid special attention to American composer Aaron Copland, who turned 90 in November. Among them was the St. Paul (Minn.) Chamber Or-

chestra, whose all-Copland program that month was broadcast by National Public Radio. But some concerts became memorial programs after the Pulitzer Prize-winning composer died on December 2.

The Chicago Symphony Orchestra celebrated the beginning of its 100th season—and marked its last under music director Sir Georg Solti—with a gala in October. Solti, who was to retire in April 1991, will become director emeritus. In March 1990, the orchestra had introduced John Corigliano's Symphony No. 1 as the first of nine works commissioned for its centennial. The composer said he wrote it to honor friends who died of AIDS. In November, the symphony premiered Ned Rorem's "Goodbye My Fancy," a powerful oratorio that set poetry and prose by American poet Walt Whitman to an elegant, rhapsodic score.

The Baltimore Symphony Orchestra turned 75 in 1990. The San Antonio Symphony was 50. New York City's Metropolitan Opera held a gala concert in March to celebrate the 50th anniversary of opera on the radio. The Met's Saturday afternoon broadcasts, sponsored by Texaco, Incorporated, helped create an audience for opera in the United States. Also passing the 50-year mark was the Tanglewood Music Festival in Massachusetts.

Opera events. Lyric Opera of Chicago kicked off its program "Toward the 21st Century" with a production of Dominick Argento's *The Voyage of Edgar Allan Poe* in October 1990. Over the next 10 years, the company plans to present 17 operas from this century as well as 3 newly commissioned works by United States composers.

The Stuttgart Opera in Germany made headlines by producing in June three biographical operas by composer Philip Glass: *Satyagraha* (about Indian leader Mohandas K. Gandhi), *Akhnaten* (about the ancient Egyptian king and religious reformer), and *Einstein on the Beach* (about the great German physicist). Another special event during the year was a 17-hour telecast of Richard Wagner's *The Ring of the Nibelung* on the Public Broadcasting Service. The performance by the Met was presented on four consecutive nights.

A full slate of artistic events accompanied the Goodwill Games, an international sports competition held in August in Seattle. The most discussed program was a multimillion-dollar staging of Sergei Prokofiev's rarely performed epic opera, *War and Peace,* based on the classic 1869 Russian novel by Leo Tolstoy.

Another acclaimed production in 1990 was the New York City Opera's presentation of Arnold Schoenberg's *Moses and Aron* in July. The first U.S. performances of *Judith* by German composer Siegfried Matthus made a strong impression when introduced by the Santa Fe (N. Mex.) Opera in August.

Premieres. Opera companies had their share of new works in 1990. In April, Chamber Opera Chicago offered Lawrence Rapchak's *The Lifework of Juan Diaz,* based on a story by science-fiction writer Ray Bradbury, and Philadelphia's American Music Theater

Festival staged William Bolcom's *Casino Paradise*. Libby Larsen's *Frankenstein, the Modern Prometheus* was premiered by the Minnesota Opera Company in May. That month also saw the debuts of Glass's *Hydrogen Jukebox* at the Spoleto Festival USA in Charleston, S.C., and Einojuhani Rautavaara's *Vincent*, about Dutch painter Vincent van Gogh, in Helsinki, Finland.

Jean Genet's play *The Balcony* became an opera, courtesy of composer Robert DiDomenica. It was produced by the Opera Company of Boston in June. In July, New York City's Lincoln Center for the Performing Arts debuted John Moran's *The Manson Family*, an operatic treatment of the murderous career of Charles Manson. The Norwegian National Opera premiered Antonio Bibalo's *Macbeth*, based on William Shakespeare's play, in September.

Orchestral premieres. The most significant of the year's orchestral premieres probably was Mel Powell's concerto *Duplicates*, commissioned by the Los Angeles Philharmonic. The work, which won the Pulitzer Prize for music, features two pianos and orchestra.

Some new works included unusual combinations. Among them were Mario Davidovsky's Concerto for String Quartet and Orchestra presented by the Philadelphia Orchestra, and Timpani Concerto No. 1 by James Oliverio, offered by the Cleveland Orchestra.

Other premieres included Gian Carlo Menotti's *For the Death of Orpheus* (Atlanta, Ga.); Stephen Albert's Cello Concerto (Baltimore); Symphony No. 4 by Lou Harrison (New York City); Ezra Laderman's Cello Concerto (Chicago); Henry Brant's *Prison of the Mind* (Dallas); *Jagannath* by Christopher Rouse (Houston); Michael Runyan's *The Age of the Offered Hand* (Indianapolis); David Del Tredici's *Steps* (New York City); Shulamit Ran's Symphony No. 1 and Bolcom's Symphony No. 5 (Philadelphia); *Sasima* by Roberto Sierra (San Antonio); Elliott Carter's Violin Concerto (San Francisco); and Daniel Asia's Symphony No. 1 (Seattle).

Labor dispute. The most prominent labor-management crisis of 1990 in the music world occurred in San Francisco. A breakdown in contract negotiations between the management of the San Francisco Opera and members of the orchestra delayed the opening of the fall season by a week.

Openings. The Opéra de la Bastille, a new opera house in Paris built on the site of the historic prison, had its first opera production in March 1990—Hector Berlioz' *The Trojans*. The new Hong Kong Cultural Center played host in January to a series of performances by such artists as soprano Jessye Norman, cellist Yo-Yo Ma, violinist Isaac Stern, and the Boston Symphony Orchestra.

Notes on people. The New York Philharmonic chose German conductor Kurt Masur of the Gewandhaus Orchestra in Leipzig to succeed Zubin Mehta as music director, beginning in 1991. When conductor Riccardo Muti announced in March 1990 that he would leave the Philadelphia Orchestra after his con-

---

Classical music: A Year Book Close-Up

Bernstein Lays Down His Baton

When Leonard Bernstein died of a heart attack on Oct. 14, 1990, the United States lost its foremost classical music celebrity. Best known as a talented conductor, Bernstein was also a respected composer, pianist, and teacher.

For 11 years the musical director of the New York Philharmonic, Bernstein had a conducting style that was larger than life, full of grand, emotional gestures, startling leaps into the air, and—during at least two concerts—accidental falls from the podium. His theatrical manner unsettled some audiences, but most praised Bernstein's ability to embody the music he brought to life.

As a composer, Bernstein was equally energetic, writing film scores, musicals, ballets, song cycles, operas, and symphonies. Among his most acclaimed works were both serious and popular compositions: the ballet *Fancy Free* (1944), the symphony *Jeremiah* (1944), and the musicals *Candide* (1956) and *West Side Story* (1957).

An outgoing and affectionate man, Bernstein devoted considerable time to teaching music students and conducting student orchestras. He helped introduce classical music to a wide audience through his television appearances and books such as *The Joy of Music* (1959).

Bernstein had announced his retirement only five days before his death. Until then, the 72-year-old had been busy teaching, composing, making concert tours, and living a life as richly textured as a symphony.   Jinger Hoop

Leonard Bernstein (1918-1990)

Cellist-conductor Mstislav Rostropovich conducts the National Symphony in a February concert in the Soviet Union, which he left in 1974.

tract expired in 1992, management scrambled to find a successor. German conductor Wolfgang Sawallisch of the Bavarian State Opera in Munich was chosen. Riccardo Chailly, an Italian, took over as chief conductor of the Royal Concertgebauw Orchestra of Amsterdam, the Netherlands. Resignations in 1990 included Menotti as artistic director of the Spoleto Festival in Italy and Nicola Rescigno as artistic director of the Dallas Opera.

Soprano Joan Sutherland gave a number of farewell performances in 1990, including one in October at the Sydney Opera House in her native Australia. Three of the world's great tenors—José Carreras, Placido Domingo, and Luciano Pavarotti—shared a stage in Rome, along with an orchestra of 200, for a July concert. Soprano Leontyne Price wrote a book for children about one of her most famous roles, the heroine of Giuseppe Verdi's *Aida*.

Political changes in eastern Europe affected the music world in 1990. Czechoslovak-born composer Karel Husa finally saw his *Music for Prague*, performed more than 7,000 times throughout the world, played in Prague, his native city, 22 years after its premiere. Cellist-conductor Mstislav Rostropovich, who left the Soviet Union in 1974, returned to his homeland in February to conduct the National Symphony and give a cello recital.   Peter P. Jacobi

In *World Book,* see **Classical music; Opera.**

Clothing. See **Fashion.**

Coal should be the cornerstone of the United States long-range energy plan, the National Coal Council concluded on June 8, 1990. The council, a nonprofit committee that advises the Department of Energy, said that domestic coal reserves contain 43 per cent more energy than the world's reserves of oil and natural gas combined. Greater use of coal would assure the nation of adequate energy supplies at reasonable prices with less reliance on imported oil. But the council cited a variety of obstacles, including environmental problems, that must be overcome before coal can fulfill its potential.

Production. The National Coal Association (NCA) on June 21 predicted that U.S. coal production would set a record in 1990 for the fourth consecutive year. The NCA, an industry group based in Washington, D.C., estimated that 1.002 billion short tons (909 million metric tons) of coal would be produced, about 2 per cent more than in 1989. Coal exports were expected to total about 101 million short tons (92 million metric tons), about the same as in 1989.

Labor settlement. The United Mine Workers of America on Feb. 20, 1990, announced that its members had approved an agreement to end a bitter 10-month strike against the Pittston Company. The strike involved mines in Virginia, West Virginia, and Kentucky. Pittston agreed to drop a plan opposed by the union that would have required miners and pensioners to shoulder more of the cost of health care cover-

Miners far below the surface watch the operation of a robot miner, which can dig 6 short tons (5.4 metric tons) of coal per minute.

age. The four-year contract also provided for pay increases and job security. The company won a number of concessions, including more flexibility in scheduling workers so mining operations could continue seven days a week.

Hanson, P.L.C., a large international mining firm based in London, took control of Peabody Coal Company, the largest U.S. coal producer, in 1990. In February, Hanson announced it would buy 45 per cent of Peabody's stock for $504 million. In March, Hanson agreed to buy the rest of Peabody for $715 million.

Research. Avco Research Laboratory in Everett, Wash., in February announced the development of a new coal-fired home-heating system. The system is smaller, cleaner, and more efficient than the huge coal boilers of the past. The furnace burns pulverized coal in pulses—the way an automobile engine burns gasoline. Ash is collected in a vacuum bag that must be emptied only twice each heating season.

Researchers at the University of Arkansas in Little Rock said in August that they had developed new coal-conversion technology that could permit increased use of the huge U.S. coal reserves. The process uses bacteria to ferment coal to produce alcohol in much the same way that bacterial cultures produce beer or wine. The coal-derived alcohol can substitute for gasoline, scientists said.   Michael Woods

See also **Energy supply; Mining.** In *World Book,* see **Coal.**

Coin collecting. A commemorative silver dollar honoring the late President Dwight D. Eisenhower was introduced on Jan. 16, 1990, in ceremonies at his Gettysburg, Pa., farm. The coin depicts "Ike" as supreme commander of Allied forces in Europe during World War II, a post he held from 1942 to 1945, and as President of the United States (1953-1961). Proofs struck by the Philadelphia mint sold for $29, and uncirculated coins minted at West Point, N.Y., were priced at $26. In addition, a six-coin proof set, including the Eisenhower dollar, was priced at $46.

Other commemoratives. Canada in 1990 issued a commemorative silver dollar marking the 300th anniversary of British explorer Henry Kelsey's travels in Canada's western prairies. The United Nations minted a gold $100 coin to commemorate its International Literacy Year. The coin shows an Eskimo mother teaching her child the Inuktitute language.

Proof cents without mint marks. The U.S. Mint announced in August that 3,700 of the 1990 proof sets struck at the San Francisco mint included one-cent coins without the "S" mint mark. Most of the sets had been shipped to buyers before the mistake was detected. Because the sets will likely become valuable, they generated much excitement among collectors.

FTC investigates coin-grading company. The coin-grading industry was dealt a blow in August when the Federal Trade Commission (FTC) acted against the largest grading concern in the United

245

Collor de Mello, Fernando

States, Professional Coin Grading Service (PCGS) of Irvine, Calif. Coin-grading companies evaluate coins and assign each one a quality grade. A graded coin is then *slabbed*—sealed in a tamper-proof plastic case. The supposed purpose of this service is to protect buyers against purchasing coins at inflated prices.

The FTC disputed PCGS's claims that its grading was totally objective, that investing in coins evaluated by the company was risk-free, and that PCGS-graded coins were an absolutely reliable liquid investment—one that could be sold at any time for a known amount of cash. PCGS signed an agreement pledging not to make such claims in the future. Meanwhile, collectors had become disillusioned with the coin-grading business, and the market for slabbed coins tumbled.

Record sale prices. World price records for ancient coins were set in June when Sotheby's galleries in New York City auctioned the collection of Texas multimillionaire Nelson Bunker Hunt for $12.7 million. Among the coins sold was a Roman bronze sestertius minted in A.D. 135 during the reign of Emperor Hadrian, which brought $214,500, and a silver Greek decadrachm minted in 410 B.C., which sold for $572,000.

Gold and silver prices rose in 1990. The U.S. Eagle coin, containing 1 troy ounce (31.1 grams) of gold, sold for $399 on January 2 and for $406.50 at year-end. The 1-ounce silver Eagle rose from $5.21 to $5.45 at year's end.　　David T. Alexander

In *World Book*, see **Coin collecting.**

Collor de Mello, Fernando (1949-　　), was inaugurated on March 15, 1990, as Brazil's youngest president at the age of 40 and the first to be elected directly by the people since 1960. The next day, Collor introduced drastic economic measures to curb inflation. See **Brazil.**

Collor was born Aug. 12, 1949, in Rio de Janeiro, the son of a wealthy sugar plantation owner and senator. At the age of 14, Collor was on the floor of the Senate when his father and a political rival exchanged pistol shots, accidentally killing another senator. After both men were acquitted following a trial, Collor's father moved the family to Brasília, retired from politics, and used his sugar cane fortune to buy a newspaper and several radio and television stations.

After studying economics and journalism at the University of Brasília, Collor became president of his father's media group in 1978. Collor's political career began in 1979 when the military government appointed him mayor of Maceió. In 1982, he was elected to Congress, and in 1986 he was elected governor of Alagoas.

In the course of his political career, Collor has joined five different political parties. He founded the National Reconstruction Party in 1989 to campaign for the presidency and won a runoff election for president that December.

In 1984, Collor married Rosane Malta. He has two sons by a previous marriage.　　Rod Such

Colombia. César Gaviria Trujillo took the oath of office for a four-year term as Colombia's president on Aug. 7, 1990, following a campaign marred by drug-related killings. "Narco-terrorism today is the principal threat to our democracy, and we will face it without making concessions," Gaviria declared.

Gaviria had stepped in to replace the Liberal Party's initial candidate, who was assassinated in 1989, reputedly by drug traffickers. The new president had gained national prominence in 1988 by negotiating the release of one of his rivals for the presidency, Álvaro Gómez Hurtado, who had been kidnapped by political rebels. Another of Gaviria's rivals for the post, Antonio Navarro Wolff, had been among the kidnappers as leader of a rebel group known as M-19. The M-19 laid down its arms in April in exchange for pardons and the right to establish a political party. As president, Gaviria named Wolff minister of health.

Wolff resigned the cabinet post, however, to lead his followers to an electoral triumph on December 9 when Colombians elected members of an assembly to write a new constitution for the country. Surprisingly, Wolff and the former M-19 rebels won the largest block of the 70 seats in the assembly—19.

The war on drugs. But even while such ironies emerged, the country's war on drug trafficking was unrelenting. Four days after Gaviria's inauguration, police fatally wounded Gustavo de Jesús Gaviria (no relation to the president), removing from the scene one of the Medellín drug cartel's top operatives, a man whose responsibility included bombings and assassination. Despite such successes, the human cost of the drug war continued to mount in 1990. In the two years through September, 22 Colombian journalists were killed for covering drug-related stories.

Extradition. Colombia continued to balk at extraditing apprehended drug traffickers to the United States, where they have been indicted. As of August 26, 14 Colombians awaited extradition in Colombian jails, and President Gaviria had extradited none since assuming office. One reason for the Colombian resistance was anger over the verdict in the drug trial of Mayor Marion S. Barry of Washington, D.C., who was acquitted on all except a single misdemeanor count. Reports said that Colombians regarded the Barry trial as a symbol of the United States lack of seriousness about fighting illegal drugs at home.

Rebel attack. By year's end, authorities were fighting a renewal of armed insurrection. In November, 40 people were killed near Taraza, 250 miles (400 kilometers) north of Bogotá, when rebels attacked an army base and police station. Government troops retaliated in December by bombing and raiding a main rebel base in the eastern Andes.　　Nathan A. Haverstock

See also **Latin America** (Facts in brief table). In *World Book,* see **Colombia.**

Colorado. See **State government.**

Common Market. See **Europe.**

Comoros. See **Africa.**

Computer.

Computer. The worldwide sales growth of computers continued to slow in 1990. According to one market research company, the International Data Corporation of Framingham, Mass., computer sales during the year rose approximately 9.7 per cent to nearly $151 billion. Although that figure was down only slightly from 1989, it was considerably less than the 17 per cent sales increase posted in 1988. Over the next four years, experts said, the annual sales growth rate is likely to drop even further, to about 9.0 per cent. In the United States in 1990, computer sales were even weaker than they were in the international market, rising just 6.3 per cent to $52.9 billion.

International and U.S. sales were strongest for the largest, highest-powered computers, known as *mainframes*, and for low-priced home computers. But the year was a particularly bad one for producers of minicomputers, midsized machines with intermediate data-handling capabilities. Several large minicomputer manufacturers, including Digital Equipment Corporation of Maynard, Mass., announced massive workforce reductions in 1990.

Mainframe computers. In the first week of September, the International Business Machines Corporation (IBM) and Fujitsu Limited of Japan debuted their next generation of technology.

Fujitsu—Japan's largest computer manufacturer and the world's second-biggest maker of mainframe computers—unveiled what it claimed was the world's fastest mainframe. Although company officials did not offer specific performance figures on their new machine, they asserted that it was 10 per cent faster than mainframes introduced in June by two other Japanese manufacturers, Hitachi Limited and the NEC Corporation. According to most computer-industry analysts, those units have peak speeds of 100 million to 200 million instructions per second. Fujitsu expects to attract about 300 customers for its new computer over the next three years.

In what some experts called the most important development in the computer industry in 25 years, IBM, the largest computer company in the world, introduced a new generation of mainframes that will work in tandem with smaller computers. In this approach, the central computer serves as the storehouse and processing center for data, which can then be retrieved and further processed by desktop computers.

Home computers. IBM, with its competitors at its heels, also launched an aggressive assault in 1990 on the home-computer market. Marketing researchers predict that home computers will be one of the industry's most robust growth areas in coming years, expanding by 16 per cent annually through 1995.

In June, IBM introduced the PS/1 family of computers, designed specifically for home users. The PS/1 units, which have list prices between $999 and $1,999, do not use any new technology. In fact, they are based on the same 80286 Intel Corporation microprocessor used in the AT computers that IBM introduced in

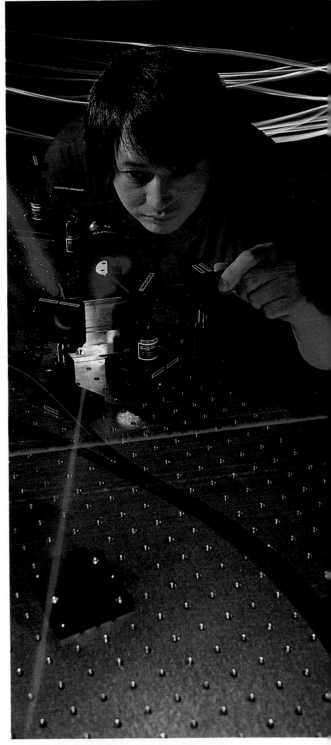

An AT&T Bell Laboratories engineer adjusts an experimental laser system that may lead to a computer using light rather than electricity.

the mid-1980's. The main difference in the PS/1 is its lower price and IBM's efforts to market the new line through large department stores such as Sears, Roebuck and Company.

Other companies reacted quickly to the PS/1. In July, the Tandy Corporation of Fort Worth, Tex., introduced a home computer, the RL 1000, with 24 software programs for people who want a computer for nonbusiness applications. Such buyers may represent as much as 75 per cent of the potential home-computer market. The RL 1000 is priced at $759 to $1,299.

Another entrant in the field was Apple Computer, Incorporated. In October, responding to criticism that its machines were overpriced, Apple introduced three new Macintosh models, costing as little as $999. The moderately priced units reflected Apple's intention to move from selling a relatively small volume of expensive computers to selling a greater number of lower-priced machines.

Multimedia computing. In addition to the new hardware, new applications for computers began to emerge in 1990. Perhaps the most promising was *multimedia computing*, a system in which text, audio, graphics, still images, and full-motion video are combined by a desktop computer. Multimedia can be used for a variety of purposes, such as to create training videos and sales presentations.

The most technically difficult aspect of multimedia is converting full-motion video images into digital information that can be manipulated by the computer and then played back with the same quality as the original image. IBM and Intel have been working jointly on that problem for several years in a project called *digital video interactive* (DVI). In June, IBM demonstrated DVI images using a *local area network* (LAN), several personal computers linked together.

The demonstration indicated that the technology is much closer to commercial application than had been thought. IBM announced that Delta Airlines would be its first customer for DVI, using the LAN approach. Company officials said the technology would be made available to other buyers on a limited basis in early 1991.

Copyright victory for Lotus. A federal judge ruled in July 1990 that Paperback Software International of Berkeley, Calif., had infringed on Lotus Development Corporation's copyright of its premier product, the spreadsheet program Lotus 1-2-3. In an effort to spark the sales of its own spreadsheet program, Paperback Software had employed a similar *user interface*—the way in which the program is presented on the computer screen—and a system of computer commands resembling those given in 1-2-3.

Following the ruling, Lotus sued two other California-based competitors—Borland International of Scotts Valley and the Santa Cruz Operation of Santa Cruz—on similar grounds. Elliot W. King

See also **Electronics.** In *World Book,* see **Computer. Congo.** See **Africa.**

Congress of the United States. The second and final session of the 101st Congress, in 1990, triggered a mounting public outcry about the way in which lawmakers go about their business. Yet the election-year session produced landmark legislation and made a start on significant revisions of national priorities.

Achievements. Much public criticism focused on the year's halting negotiations between Congress and the Administration of President George Bush as the two sides struggled toward a budget accord. Bush and congressional leaders announced with great fanfare on September 30 that they had reached agreement on a massive deficit-reduction package, only to have the House of Representatives reject the deal on October 5. As a result, the spending authority of the United States government ended at midnight on Friday, October 5, and all but essential government services shut down for the weekend. On October 27, Congress finally passed a deficit-reduction bill that included major tax increases and spending cuts.

Ironically, considering the stop-and-go negotiations, the deficit-cutting bill may prove to be the major accomplishment of the 1990 session. It not only provided a blueprint for a five-year, $492-billion reduction in deficit spending but also, in a little-noted provision, authorized a $20-billion "peace dividend" shift of spending from military to domestic programs. Bush and the lawmakers seemed to think that greater outlays at home in the 1990's, when recession threatened, would be smart economics as well as smart politics.

Congress voted for other far-reaching measures—to clean the air, increase immigration, subsidize child care, expand opportunities for the disabled, and overhaul the farm and housing programs. Altogether, Congress provided for the largest spending increases in 10 years for public works, housing, environmental protection, and education.

Congress also dealt with the problems of the savings and loan industry, providing a new $22-billion installment toward the staggering cost of cleaning up the mess (see **Bank [Close-Up]**). Lawmakers voted for stronger measures to investigate, prosecute, and punish savings officials suspected of fraud.

Measures rejected. Congress rejected three proposals advocated by conservatives: constitutional amendments to require a balanced budget and to permit a ban on flag burning, and strict restrictions on providing federal subsidies for art that might be considered indecent or pornographic. Another proposed constitutional amendment, long sought by Republicans, would have banned federal budget deficits. The House of Representatives rejected the proposal on July 17 by a 279-150 vote, only 7 votes fewer than needed. Five Republicans voted against the amendment, and 110 Democrats, most of them Southern conservatives, voted for it.

Congressional failures in 1990 came mostly in areas close to Congress's own political interests. Lawmakers were unable to agree on how to change the much-criticized system of financing their own campaigns through heavy reliance on donations from special interests. Senators balked at depriving themselves of speaking fees for appearances before interest groups. And lobbying power as well as differences of opinion led to a deadlock on such anticrime proposals as curbing assault weapons and reimposing the death penalty for some federal crimes.

In other instances, Congress acted and Bush vetoed. On October 22, near the end of the session, the President vetoed a major civil rights bill. It was the 15th successive Bush veto to be sustained by Congress. Other vetoed measures included a bill to provide workers with unpaid leave to care for sick children and relatives and a bill to revise the Hatch Act restricting the political activities of federal employees.

Environmental protection. To enact the Clean Air Act of 1990, a Senate-House conference committee labored 15 weeks to fashion a compromise aimed at substantially reducing acid rain, urban smog, airborne toxins, and ozone-depleting chemicals by the year 2000. The House passed the measure 401 to 25 on Oct. 26, 1990. The next day's Senate vote was 89 to 10.

On August 4, in a rush toward a summer recess, the House gave final approval to a bill inspired by a rash of oil spills from Alaska to New York. The bill sets tougher standards for ship construction, increases eightfold the pollution liability of tanker owners, allows the federal government to oversee cleanup of oil spills, and authorizes a $1-billion cleanup fund.

Immigration reform. The first comprehensive overhaul of immigration laws in 66 years emerged as the session ended. When it goes into effect in 1992, the new law will increase annual legal immigration by nearly 40 per cent, from 500,000 to between 675,000 and 700,000. The number admitted on the basis of job skills will be more than doubled, and tens of thousands will be admitted from Ireland and other countries whose citizens had been largely excluded in recent years. No longer could immigrants be barred because of ideology or sexual preference. The House voted for the bill 264 to 118 after dropping Senate-approved language that Hispanic members complained could lead to the creation of a national identity card. The Senate, which first voted for the bill 89 to 8, passed the amended version by voice vote on Oct. 27, 1990.

Child care. In another 11th-hour action, Congress on the same day passed the first-ever peacetime child-care legislation, voting $22 billion in tax credits and grants for working parents. Most of the money was earmarked for low-income families.

One of Bush's earliest battles with Congress reached a climax on June 29 when he vetoed legislation that would have required employers to provide up to 12 weeks of unpaid job leave to workers caring for a newborn or adopted child or for a seriously ill family member. Bush contended that such matters should be "crafted at the workplace by employers and employ-

South African antiapartheid leader Nelson Mandela is applauded at a joint session of Congress on June 26, one of his stops on a North American tour.

ees, not through government." On July 25, the House voted 232 to 195 to override the veto—falling 53 votes short of a needed two-thirds.

Civil rights measures. On July 13, the Senate gave final approval, 91 to 6, to a landmark Americans with Disabilities Act barring discrimination against the estimated 43 million U.S. citizens who are physically or mentally impaired. The "emancipation proclamation" for the disabled would give them the same civil rights protections in jobs, accommodations, and services that apply to members of minority groups. The House approved the bill 377 to 28.

In another action, the House voted 406 to 17 on October 3 for a measure aimed at reversing the effects of a 1989 Supreme Court decision that allowed employers to limit the benefits of older workers. The bill states that such benefits are protected under the 1967 Age Discrimination in Employment Act.

A sweeping civil rights bill aimed at making it easier for minorities and women to win suits alleging job discrimination was vetoed by Bush on October 22. Bush said his veto was prompted by a conviction that the bill would encourage employers to adopt hiring and promotion quotas to protect themselves against job-bias suits. The Senate sustained Bush's veto two days later by a single vote, 66 to 34. To override the veto, 67 votes were needed. Passage of the measure had been a top legislative priority of several civil rights organizations, which denounced Bush's action.

249

Members of the United States House of Representatives

The House of Representatives of the first session of the 102nd Congress consisted of 267 Democrats, 167 Republicans, and 1 independent (not including representatives from American Samoa, the District of Columbia, Guam, Puerto Rico, and the Virgin Islands), when it convened on Jan. 3, 1991, compared with 257 Democrats and 176 Republicans with two vacancies when the second session of the 101st Congress convened. This table shows congressional district, legislator, and party affiliation. Asterisk (*) denotes those who served in the 101st Congress; dagger (†) denotes "at large."

Alabama
1. H. L. Callahan, R.*
2. William L. Dickinson, R.*
3. Glen Browder, D.*
4. Tom Bevill, D.*
5. Bud Cramer, D.
6. Ben Erdreich, D.*
7. Claude Harris, D.*

Alaska
†Donald E. Young, R.*

Arizona
1. John J. Rhodes III, R.*
2. Morris K. Udall, D.*
3. Bob Stump, R.*
4. Jon L. Kyl, R.*
5. Jim Kolbe, R.*

Arkansas
1. Bill Alexander, D.*
2. Ray Thornton, D.
3. John P. Hammerschmidt, R.*
4. Beryl F. Anthony, Jr., D.*

California
1. Frank Riggs, R.
2. Wally Herger, R.*
3. Robert T. Matsui, D.*
4. Vic Fazio, D.*
5. Nancy Pelosi, D.*
6. Barbara Boxer, D.*
7. George E. Miller, D.*
8. Ronald V. Dellums, D.*
9. Fortney H. (Pete) Stark, D.*
10. Don Edwards, D.*
11. Tom Lantos, D.*
12. Tom J. Campbell, R.*
13. Norman Y. Mineta, D.*
14. John T. Doolittle, R.
15. Gary A. Condit, D.*
16. Leon E. Panetta, D.*
17. Calvin Dooley, D.
18. Richard H. Lehman, D.*
19. Robert J. Lagomarsino, R.*
20. William M. Thomas, R.*
21. Elton Gallegly, R.*
22. Carlos J. Moorhead, R.*
23. Anthony C. Beilenson, D.*
24. Henry A. Waxman, D.*
25. Edward R. Roybal, D.*
26. Howard L. Berman, D.*
27. Mel Levine, D.*
28. Julian C. Dixon, D.*
29. Maxine Waters, D.
30. Matthew G. Martínez, D.*
31. Mervyn M. Dymally, D.*
32. Glenn M. Anderson, D.*
33. David Dreier, R.*
34. Esteban E. Torres, D.*
35. Jerry Lewis, R.*
36. George E. Brown, Jr., D.*
37. Alfred A. McCandless, R.*
38. Robert K. Dornan, R.*
39. William E. Dannemeyer, R.*
40. C. Christopher Cox, R.*
41. William D. Lowery, R.*
42. Dana Rohrabacher, R.*
43. Ronald C. Packard, R.*
44. Randy (Duke) Cunningham, R.
45. Duncan L. Hunter, R.*

Colorado
1. Patricia Schroeder, D.*
2. David E. Skaggs, D.*
3. Ben Nighthorse Campbell, D.*
4. Wayne Allard, R.
5. Joel Hefley, R.*
6. Daniel Schaefer, R.*

Connecticut
1. Barbara B. Kennelly, D.*
2. Samuel Gejdenson, D.*
3. Rosa DeLauro, D.
4. Christopher Shays, R.*
5. Gary Franks, R.
6. Nancy L. Johnson, R.*

Delaware
†Thomas R. Carper, D.*

Florida
1. Earl Hutto, D.*
2. Pete Peterson, D.
3. Charles E. Bennett, D.*
4. Craig T. James, R.*
5. Bill McCollum, R.*
6. Cifford B. Stearns, R.*
7. Sam M. Gibbons, D.*
8. C. W. Bill Young, R.*
9. Michael Bilirakis, R.*
10. Andy Ireland, R.*
11. Jim Bacchus, D.
12. Thomas F. Lewis, R.*
13. Porter J. Goss, R.*
14. Harry A. Johnston II, D.*
15. E. Clay Shaw, Jr., R.*
16. Lawrence J. Smith, D.*
17. William Lehman, D.*
18. Ileana Ros-Lehtinen, R.*
19. Dante B. Fascell, D.*

Georgia
1. Lindsay Thomas, D.*
2. Charles F. Hatcher, D.*
3. Richard B. Ray, D.*
4. Ben Jones, D.*
5. John Lewis, D.*
6. Newt Gingrich, R.*
7. George Darden, D.*
8. J. Roy Rowland, D.*
9. Edgar L. Jenkins, D.*
10. Doug Barnard, Jr., D.*

Hawaii
1. Neil Abercrombie, D.
2. Patsy T. Mink, D.*

Idaho
1. Larry LaRocco, D.
2. Richard H. Stallings, D.*

Illinois
1. Charles A. Hayes, D.*
2. Gus Savage, D.*
3. Marty Russo, D.*
4. George Sangmeister, D.*
5. William O. Lipinski, D.*
6. Henry J. Hyde, R.*
7. Cardiss Collins, D.*
8. Dan Rostenkowski, D.*
9. Sidney R. Yates, D.*
10. John Edward Porter, R.*
11. Frank Annunzio, D.*
12. Philip M. Crane, R.*
13. Harris W. Fawell, R.*
14. J. Dennis Hastert, R.*
15. Edward R. Madigan, R.*
16. John W. Cox, Jr., D.
17. Lane A. Evans, D.*
18. Robert H. Michel, R.*
19. Terry L. Bruce, D.*
20. Richard J. Durbin, D.*
21. Jerry F. Costello, D.*
22. Glenn Poshard, D.*

Indiana
1. Peter J. Visclosky, D.*
2. Philip R. Sharp, D.*
3. Tim Roemer, D.
4. Jill Long, D.*
5. James Jontz, D.*
6. Danny L. Burton, R.*
7. John T. Myers, R.*
8. Frank McCloskey, D.*
9. Lee H. Hamilton, D.*
10. Andrew Jacobs, Jr., D.*

Iowa
1. Jim Leach, R.*
2. Jim Nussle, R.
3. David R. Nagle, D.*
4. Neal Smith, D.*
5. Jim Ross Lightfoot, R.*
6. Fred Grandy, R.*

Kansas
1. Pat Roberts, R.*
2. James C. Slattery, D.*
3. Jan Meyers, R.*
4. Dan Glickman, D.*
5. Dick Nichols, R.

Kentucky
1. Carroll Hubbard, Jr., D.*
2. William H. Natcher, D.*
3. Romano L. Mazzoli, D.*
4. Jim Bunning, R.*
5. Harold (Hal) Rogers, R.*
6. Larry J. Hopkins, R.*
7. Carl C. (Chris) Perkins, D.*

Louisiana
1. Robert L. Livingston, Jr., R.*
2. William J. Jefferson, D.
3. W. J. (Billy) Tauzin, D.*
4. Jim McCrery, R.*
5. Thomas J. (Jerry) Huckaby, D.*
6. Richard Hugh Baker, R.*
7. James A. (Jimmy) Hayes, D.*
8. Clyde C. Holloway, R.*

Maine
1. Thomas H. Andrews, D.
2. Olympia J. Snowe, R.*

Maryland
1. Wayne T. Gilchrest, R.
2. Helen Delich Bentley, R.*
3. Benjamin L. Cardin, D.*
4. Thomas McMillen, D.*
5. Steny H. Hoyer, D.*
6. Beverly B. Byron, D.*
7. Kweisi Mfume, D.*
8. Constance A. Morella, R.*

Massachusetts
1. Silvio O. Conte, R.*
2. Richard E. Neal, D.*
3. Joseph D. Early, D.*
4. Barney Frank, D.*
5. Chester G. Atkins, D.*
6. Nicholas Mavroules, D.*
7. Edward J. Markey, D.*
8. Joseph P. Kennedy II, D.*
9. John Joseph Moakley, D.*
10. Gerry E. Studds, D.*
11. Brian J. Donnelly, D.*

Michigan
1. John Conyers, Jr., D.*
2. Carl D. Pursell, R.*
3. Howard E. Wolpe, D.*
4. Frederick S. Upton, R.*
5. Paul B. Henry, R.*
6. Bob Carr, D.*
7. Dale E. Kildee, D.*
8. Bob Traxler, D.*
9. Guy Vander Jagt, R.*
10. Dave Camp, R.
11. Robert W. Davis, R.*
12. David E. Bonior, D.*
13. Barbara-Rose Collins, D.
14. Dennis M. Hertel, D.*
15. William D. Ford, D.*
16. John D. Dingell, D.*
17. Sander M. Levin, D.*
18. William S. Broomfield, R.*

Minnesota
1. Timothy J. Penny, D.*
2. Vin Weber, R.*
3. Jim Ramstad, R.
4. Bruce F. Vento, D.*
5. Martin O. Sabo, D.*
6. Gerry Sikorski, D.*
7. Collin C. Peterson, D.
8. James L. Oberstar, D.*

Mississippi
1. Jamie L. Whitten, D.*
2. Mike Espy, D.*
3. G. V. (Sonny) Montgomery, D.*
4. Mike Parker, D.*
5. Gene Taylor, D.*

Missouri
1. William L. (Bill) Clay, D.*
2. Joan Kelly Horn, D.
3. Richard A. Gephardt, D.*
4. Ike Skelton, D.*
5. Alan D. Wheat, D.*
6. E. Thomas Coleman, R.*
7. Mel Hancock, R.*
8. Bill Emerson, R.*
9. Harold L. Volkmer, D.*

Montana
1. Pat Williams, D.*
2. Ron Marlenee, R.*

Nebraska
1. Doug Bereuter, R.*
2. Peter Hoagland, D.*
3. Bill Barrett, R.

Nevada
1. James H. Bilbray, D.*
2. Barbara F. Vucanovich, R.*

New Hampshire
1. Bill Zeliff, R.
2. Dick Swett, D.

New Jersey
1. Robert E. Andrews, D.
2. William J. Hughes, D.*
3. Frank Pallone, Jr., D.*
4. Christopher H. Smith, R.*
5. Marge Roukema, R.*
6. Bernard J. Dwyer, D.*
7. Matthew J. Rinaldo, R.*
8. Robert A. Roe, D.*
9. Robert G. Torricelli, D.*
10. Donald M. Payne, D.*
11. Dean A. Gallo, R.*
12. Richard A. Zimmer, R.
13. H. James Saxton, R.*
14. Frank J. Guarini, D.*

New Mexico
1. Steven H. Schiff, R.*
2. Joe Skeen, R.*
3. William B. Richardson, D.*

New York
1. George J. Hochbrueckner, D.*
2. Thomas J. Downey, D.*
3. Robert J. Mrazek, D.*
4. Norman F. Lent, R.*
5. Raymond J. McGrath, R.*
6. Floyd H. Flake, D.*
7. Gary L. Ackerman, D.*
8. James H. Scheuer, D.*
9. Thomas J. Manton, D.*
10. Charles E. Schumer, D.*
11. Edolphus Towns, D.*
12. Major R. Owens, D.*
13. Stephen J. Solarz, D.*
14. Susan Molinari, R.*
15. Bill Green, R.*
16. Charles B. Rangel, D.*
17. Ted Weiss, D.*
18. Jose E. Serrano, D.*
19. Eliot L. Engel, D.*
20. Nita M. Lowey, D.*
21. Hamilton Fish, Jr., R.*
22. Benjamin A. Gilman, R.*
23. Michael R. McNulty, D.*
24. Gerald B. Solomon, R.*
25. Sherwood L. Boehlert, R.*
26. David O'B. Martin, R.*
27. James T. Walsh, R.*
28. Matthew F. McHugh, D.*
29. Frank Horton, R.*
30. Louise M. Slaughter, D.*
31. William Paxon, R.*
32. John J. LaFalce, D.*
33. Henry J. Nowak, D.*
34. Amory Houghton, Jr., R.*

North Carolina
1. Walter B. Jones, D.*
2. Tim Valentine, D.*
3. H. Martin Lancaster, D.*
4. David E. Price, D.*
5. Stephen L. Neal, D.*
6. Howard Coble, R.*
7. Charlie Rose, D.*
8. W. G. (Bill) Hefner, D.*
9. J. Alex McMillan III, R.*
10. Cass Ballenger, R.*
11. Charles H. Taylor, R.

North Dakota
†Byron L. Dorgan, D.*

Ohio
1. Charles Luken, D.
2. Willis D. Gradison, Jr., R.*
3. Tony P. Hall, D.*
4. Michael G. Oxley, R.*
5. Paul E. Gillmor, R.*
6. Bob McEwen, R.*
7. David L. Hobson, R.
8. John A. Boehner, R.
9. Marcy Kaptur, D.*
10. Clarence E. Miller, R.*
11. Dennis E. Eckart, D.*
12. John R. Kasich, R.*
13. Donald J. Pease, D.*
14. Thomas C. Sawyer, D.*
15. Chalmers P. Wylie, R.*
16. Ralph Regula, R.*
17. James A. Traficant, Jr., D.*
18. Douglas Applegate, D.*
19. Edward F. Feighan, D.*
20. Mary Rose Oakar, D.*
21. Louis Stokes, D.*

Oklahoma
1. James M. Inhofe, R.*
2. Mike Synar, D.*
3. Bill Brewster, D.
4. Dave McCurdy, D.*
5. Mickey Edwards, R.*
6. Glenn English, D.*

Oregon
1. Les AuCoin, D.*
2. Robert F. Smith, R.*
3. Ron Wyden, D.*
4. Peter A. DeFazio, D.*
5. Mike Kopetski, D.

Pennsylvania
1. Thomas M. Foglietta, D.*
2. William H. (Bill) Gray III, D.*
3. Robert A. Borski, Jr., D.*
4. Joseph P. Kolter, D.*
5. Richard T. Schulze, R.*
6. Gus Yatron, D.*
7. W. Curtis Weldon, R.*
8. Peter H. Kostmayer, D.*
9. E. G. (Bud) Shuster, R.*
10. Joseph M. McDade, R.*
11. Paul E. Kanjorski, D.*
12. John P. Murtha, D.*
13. Lawrence Coughlin, R.*
14. William J. Coyne, D.*
15. Don Ritter, R.*
16. Robert S. Walker, R.*
17. George W. Gekas, R.*
18. Rick Santorum, R.
19. Wiliam F. Goodling, R.*
20. Joseph M. Gaydos, D.*
21. Thomas J. Ridge, R.*
22. Austin J. Murphy, D.*
23. William F. Clinger, Jr., R.*

Rhode Island
1. Ronald K. Machtley, R.*
2. John F. Reed, D.

South Carolina
1. Arthur Ravenel, Jr., R.*
2. Floyd Spence, R.*
3. Butler Derrick, D.*
4. Elizabeth J. Patterson, D.*
5. John M. Spratt, Jr., D.*
6. Robert M. (Robin) Tallon, D.*

South Dakota
†Tim Johnson, D.*

Tennessee
1. James H. Quillen, R.*
2. John J. Duncan, Jr., R.*
3. Marilyn Lloyd, D.*
4. James H. Cooper, D.*
5. Bob Clement, D.*
6. Bart Gordon, D.*
7. Donald K. Sundquist, R.*
8. John S. Tanner, D.*
9. Harold E. Ford, D.*

Texas
1. Jim Chapman, D.*
2. Charles Wilson, D.*
3. Steve Bartlett, R.*
4. Ralph M. Hall, D.*
5. John W. Bryant, D.*
6. Joe Barton, R.*
7. Bill Archer, R.*
8. Jack Fields, R.*
9. Jack Brooks, D.*
10. J. J. (Jake) Pickle, D.*
11. Chet Edwards, D.
12. Preston P. (Pete) Geren, D.*
13. Bill Sarpalius, D.*
14. Greg Laughlin, D.*
15. Eligio (Kika) de la Garza, D.*
16. Ronald D. Coleman, D.*
17. Charles W. Stenholm, D.*
18. Craig A. Washington, D.*
19. Larry Combest, R.*
20. Henry B. Gonzalez, D.*
21. Lamar S. Smith, R.*
22. Tom DeLay, R.*
23. Albert G. Bustamante, D.*
24. Martin Frost, D.*
25. Michael A. Andrews, D.*
26. Richard K. Armey, R.*
27. Solomon P. Ortiz, D.*

Utah
1. James V. Hansen, R.*
2. Wayne Owens, D.*
3. William Orton, D.

Vermont
†Bernard Sanders, ind.

Virginia
1. Herbert H. Bateman, R.*
2. Owen B. Pickett, D.*
3. Thomas J. (Tom) Bliley, Jr., R.*
4. Norman Sisisky, D.*
5. Lewis F. Payne, Jr., D.*
6. James R. Olin, D.*
7. D. French Slaughter, Jr., R.*
8. James P. Moran, Jr., D.
9. Frederick C. Boucher, D.*
10. Frank R. Wolf, R.*

Washington
1. John R. Miller, R.*
2. Al Swift, D.*
3. Jolene Unsoeld, D.*
4. Sid Morrison, R.*
5. Thomas S. Foley, D.*
6. Norman D. Dicks, D.*
7. Jim McDermott, D.*
8. Rod Chandler, R.*

West Virginia
1. Alan B. Mollohan, D.*
2. Harley O. Staggers, Jr., D.*
3. Robert E. Wise, Jr., D.*
4. Nick J. Rahall II, D.*

Wisconsin
1. Les Aspin, D.*
2. Scott Klug, R.
3. Steven Gunderson, R.*
4. Gerald D. Kleczka, D.*
5. Jim Moody, D.*
6. Thomas E. Petri, R.*
7. David R. Obey, D.*
8. Toby Roth, R.*
9. F. James Sensenbrenner, Jr., R.*

Wyoming
†Craig Thomas, R.*

Nonvoting representatives
American Samoa
Eni F. H. Faleomavaega, D.*

District of Columbia
Eleanor Holmes Norton, D.

Guam
Ben Blaz, R.*

Puerto Rico
Jaime B. Fuster, D.*

Virgin Islands
Ron de Lugo, D.*

Members of the United States Senate

The Senate of the first session of the 102nd Congress consisted of 56 Democrats and 44 Republicans when it convened on Jan. 3, 1991. Senators shown starting their term in 1991 were elected for the first time in the Nov. 6, 1990, elections, except for John F. Seymour (R., Calif.), who was appointed on Jan. 2, 1991, by Governor-elect Pete Wilson to fill Wilson's Senate seat. Others shown ending their current terms in 1997 were reelected to the Senate in the 1990 balloting. The second date in each listing shows when the senator's term expires.

State	Term	State	Term	State	Term
Alabama		**Louisiana**		**Ohio**	
Howell T. Heflin, D.	1979-1997	J. Bennett Johnston, Jr., D.	1972-1997	John H. Glenn, Jr., D.	1974-1993
Richard C. Shelby, D.	1987-1993	John B. Breaux, D.	1987-1993	Howard M. Metzenbaum, D.	1976-1995
Alaska		**Maine**		**Oklahoma**	
Theodore F. Stevens, R.	1968-1997	William S. Cohen, R.	1979-1997	David L. Boren, D.	1979-1997
Frank H. Murkowski, R.	1981-1993	George J. Mitchell, D.	1980-1995	Don Nickles, R.	1981-1993
Arizona		**Maryland**		**Oregon**	
Dennis DeConcini, D.	1977-1995	Paul S. Sarbanes, D.	1977-1995	Mark O. Hatfield, R.	1967-1997
John McCain III, R.	1987-1993	Barbara A. Mikulski, D.	1987-1993	Bob Packwood, R.	1969-1993
Arkansas		**Massachusetts**		**Pennsylvania**	
Dale Bumpers, D.	1975-1993	Edward M. Kennedy, D.	1962-1995	John Heinz, D.	1977-1995
David H. Pryor, D.	1979-1997	John F. Kerry, D.	1985-1997	Arlen Specter, R.	1981-1993
California		**Michigan**		**Rhode Island**	
Alan Cranston, D.	1969-1993	Donald W. Riegle, Jr., D.	1976-1995	Claiborne Pell, D.	1961-1997
John F. Seymour, R.	1991-1993	Carl Levin, D.	1979-1997	John H. Chafee, R.	1976-1995
Colorado		**Minnesota**		**South Carolina**	
Timothy E. Wirth, D.	1987-1993	David F. Durenberger, R.	1978-1995	Strom Thurmond, R.	1956-1997
Hank Brown, R.	1991-1997	Paul D. Wellstone, D.	1991-1997	Ernest F. Hollings, D.	1966-1993
Connecticut		**Mississippi**		**South Dakota**	
Christopher J. Dodd, D.	1981-1993	Thad Cochran, R.	1978-1997	Larry Pressler, R.	1979-1997
Joseph Lieberman, D.	1989-1995	Trent Lott, R.	1989-1995	Thomas A. Daschle, D.	1987-1993
Delaware		**Missouri**		**Tennessee**	
William V. Roth, Jr., R.	1971-1995	John C. Danforth, R.	1976-1995	James Sasser, D.	1977-1995
Joseph R. Biden, Jr., D.	1973-1997	Christopher S. (Kit) Bond, R.	1987-1993	Albert A. Gore, Jr., D.	1985-1997
Florida		**Montana**		**Texas**	
Bob Graham, D.	1987-1993	Max Baucus, D.	1978-1997	Lloyd M. Bentsen, Jr., D.	1971-1995
Connie Mack III, R.	1989-1995	Conrad Burns, R.	1989-1995	Phil Gramm, R.	1985-1997
Georgia		**Nebraska**		**Utah**	
Sam Nunn, D.	1972-1997	J. James Exon, D.	1979-1997	Edwin Jacob Garn, R.	1974-1993
Wyche Fowler, Jr., D.	1987-1993	Robert Kerrey, D.	1989-1995	Orrin G. Hatch, R.	1977-1995
Hawaii		**Nevada**		**Vermont**	
Daniel K. Inouye, D.	1963-1993	Harry M. Reid, D.	1987-1993	Patrick J. Leahy, D.	1975-1993
Daniel K. Akaka, D.	1990-1995	Richard H. Bryan, D.	1989-1995	James M. Jeffords, R.	1989-1995
Idaho		**New Hampshire**		**Virginia**	
Steven D. Symms, R.	1981-1993	Warren B. Rudman, R.	1980-1993	John W. Warner, R.	1979-1997
Larry E. Craig, R.	1991-1997	Robert C. Smith, R.	1991-1997	Charles S. Robb, D.	1989-1995
Illinois		**New Jersey**		**Washington**	
Alan J. Dixon, D.	1981-1993	Bill Bradley, D.	1979-1997	Brock Adams, D.	1987-1993
Paul Simon, D.	1985-1997	Frank R. Lautenberg, D.	1982-1995	Slade Gorton, R.	1989-1995
Indiana		**New Mexico**		**West Virginia**	
Richard G. Lugar, R.	1977-1995	Pete V. Domenici, R.	1973-1997	Robert C. Byrd, D.	1959-1995
Dan R. Coats, R.	1989-1997	Jeff Bingaman, D.	1983-1995	John D. Rockefeller IV, D.	1985-1997
Iowa		**New York**		**Wisconsin**	
Charles E. Grassley, R.	1981-1993	Daniel P. Moynihan, D.	1977-1995	Robert W. Kasten, Jr., R.	1981-1993
Tom Harkin, D.	1985-1997	Alfonse M. D'Amato, R.	1981-1993	Herbert Kohl, D.	1989-1995
Kansas		**North Carolina**		**Wyoming**	
Robert J. Dole, R.	1969-1993	Jesse A. Helms, R.	1973-1997	Malcolm Wallop, R.	1977-1995
Nancy Landon Kassebaum, R.	1978-1997	Terry Sanford, D.	1986-1993	Alan K. Simpson, R.	1979-1997
Kentucky		**North Dakota**			
Wendell H. Ford, D.	1974-1993	Quentin N. Burdick, D.	1960-1995		
Mitch McConnell, R.	1985-1997	Kent Conrad, D.	1987-1993		

A June 11 Supreme Court ruling triggered another congressional battle, this one over desecration of the American flag. In a 5 to 4 ruling, the court overturned a 1989 federal law prohibiting flag desecration.

On June 21, 1990, the House decisively rejected a proposed constitutional amendment that would have enabled Congress and the states to enact flag-desecration laws. The 254 to 177 vote in favor of the amendment fell 34 votes shy of the two-thirds needed for passage of a proposed amendment. The Senate followed suit on June 26, voting 58 to 42 in favor of the amendment, or 9 votes short of the total needed.

Farm bill. On October 25, the Senate voted 60 to 36 for a new farm bill that would trim 25 per cent from projected five-year spending, mostly by reducing the acreage on which farmers can receive crop subsidies. The bill marked a sharp departure from a long-term trend toward ever-higher agricultural subsidies. The measure also created a 1-million-acre (400,000-hectare) wetlands reserve and established national standards for food labeled as "organically grown." The House vote was 318 to 100.

Housing. Also passed in the final hours was the National Affordable Housing Act, the first major new housing bill in a decade. It expanded old housing programs and created some new ones, including incentives for renters to buy their housing units. The act also authorized $2 billion in *block grants*—funds given to state and local governments to use as they see fit, instead of separate grants for specific projects—which the Administration had opposed.

AIDS. In response to the AIDS epidemic, Congress on August 4 approved by voice vote legislation authorizing five-year spending of $4.4 billion. The money will help the cities and states hit hardest by the epidemic provide health care and support services for the afflicted. Bush initially opposed the bill because it creates a separate, costly program for a single disease, but he signed it without comment.

Ethics investigations. The spectacle of members of Congress under investigation for suspected ethical lapses continued in 1990, though not on the scale that led to the resignation of Speaker of the House James C. Wright, Jr. (D., Tex.), in 1989.

Two members of Congress were reprimanded for their conduct by their colleagues in 1990. Senator David F. Durenberger (R., Minn.), accused of financial improprieties, was "denounced" by his colleagues on July 25 for "unequivocally unethical" conduct in his financial dealings. The vote, without dissent, also ordered Durenberger to pay $120,000 in restitution to various charities and to the Senate.

In the House, Representative Barney Frank (D., Mass.) was reprimanded on July 26 for bringing discredit upon Congress through an 11-month involvement with a male prostitute. Frank apologized.

Representative Gus Savage (D., Ill.) was formally criticized in January by the House ethics committee, called the Committee on Standards of Official Conduct, for making what it termed improper "sexual advances" to a female Peace Corps volunteer during a 1989 official trip to Zaire. The full House took no action, but the committee said it was putting members "on notice" that leniency might not be shown in the future. Savage apologized to the woman involved.

Representative Donald E. (Buz) Lukens (R., Ohio) resigned on October 24 after being accused of fondling a female elevator operator in the Capitol. Lukens lost a May primary race for renomination. On Jan. 3, 1991, he began serving a 30-day jail term for having sex with an underage girl in 1988.

In November 1990, the Senate ethics committee began televised hearings in an investigation of five senators who intervened with federal regulators on behalf of financier Charles H. Keating, Jr., whose Lincoln Savings & Loan Association collapsed at an estimated cost to the taxpayers of $2 billion. The "Keating Five," who had received $1.3 million in contributions from Keating, were Alan Cranston of California, Dennis DeConcini of Arizona, John H. Glenn, Jr., of Ohio, Donald W. Riegle, Jr., of Michigan, all Democrats, and Republican John McCain III of Arizona. The hearings recessed in mid-December with the outcome still uncertain and resumed on Jan. 2, 1991.

Representative Floyd H. Flake (D., N.Y.), pastor of the 5,000-member Allen African Methodist Episcopal Church in the New York City borough of Queens, was indicted on Aug. 2, 1990, on federal charges of embezzlement. Flake and his wife, Elaine, were accused of stealing $75,000 between 1983 and 1987 from a federally sponsored senior citizens housing project built by his church. The couple pleaded not guilty, and Flake won reelection in November.

Conviction overturned. On June 29, 1990, a federal appeals court in New York overturned the October 1989 conviction of former Representative Robert Garcia (D., N.Y.) on extortion charges. The court found that his acceptance of $170,000 in payoffs from a manufacturer did not meet the legal definition of extortion. Garcia, who resigned from Congress on Jan. 2, 1990, was freed from a federal prison where he had been serving a three-year term. His wife's conviction on the same charge also was reversed.

Pay hikes. On Jan. 1, 1991, House members got a pay increase of 29.5 per cent, raising their salaries from $96,600 to $125,100 a year, but they were no longer allowed to keep speaking fees. Senators received a smaller increase, from $98,400 to $101,900, but could accept up to $26,568 in speaking fees.

Leadership change. Cranston resigned as Senate Democratic whip after announcing on November 8 he had cancer and would not run for reelection in 1992. Senate Democrats on November 13 chose Senator Wendell H. Ford of Kentucky to succeed Cranston as majority whip.   Frank Cormier and Margot Cormier

See also **United States, Government of the.** In *World Book*, see **Congress of the United States.**
Connecticut. See State government.

Conservation

Conservation. A bitter conflict between the timber industry and the environmental community came to a head on June 22, 1990, when the United States Fish and Wildlife Service (FWS) declared the northern spotted owl a *threatened species* (a species not yet endangered but likely to become so). Only 2,000 pairs of spotted owls are known to exist, and they live only in the old-growth forests of Oregon, Washington, northern California, and the southern part of Canada's British Columbia. The federal government must, under the provisions of the Endangered Species Act, protect the spotted owl's habitat to ensure its survival.

But this land of giant fir, cedar, redwood, and spruce is also the home of a thriving timber industry, one of the Pacific Northwest's economic mainstays. Protecting the owl would require a sharp cutback in the amount of logging permitted in the region's national forests.

Timber industry representatives claimed that 28,000 jobs would disappear by the year 2000 as a result of this. Environmentalists countered that once the forests are cut down, there will be no timber industry at all. Already 90 per cent of the region's old-growth forests have been cut down. Four days after the FWS announcement, the Administration of President George Bush declared that it was delaying broad action and would assemble a group of officials to study ways of protecting both the spotted owl and logging jobs. Bush also stated that he would ask Congress to change the Endangered Species Act so that, in cases of "severe economic disruption," a species' population would be allowed to decline unprotected.

Frogs, toads, and salamanders, including many once-abundant species, were vanishing from all parts of the globe at a rapid rate during 1990. This awesome—and mystifying—wildlife crisis was first identified at a scientific conference in 1989. When field researchers compared notes, they found that golden toads, for example, normally numbered in the thousands around Costa Rica's Monteverde *cloud forest* (a dense tropical forest almost constantly covered by clouds). In 1989, however, only one male was spotted, and, as of late 1990, none was seen.

Scientists with a particular interest in these creatures convened conferences in Irvine, Calif., in February 1990 and in New Orleans in August to try to clarify the situation. The scientists concluded that there appear to be multiple reasons for the amphibian disappearance, one of the foremost being destruction of wetlands and rain forest habitat in both the tropics and temperate regions. Amphibians are also vulnerable to water pollution, acid rain, and the introduction of alien fish species that prey on them. But the mystery is compounded by the fact that amphibians have also disappeared from unpolluted habitats undisturbed by human beings. The scientific community is in the process of expanding its research on frogs and their relatives and more closely monitoring their populations around the world.

Other wildlife under siege. The number of animals and plants listed by the United States as endangered or threatened grew to 1,116 by October. Aside from the northern spotted owl, the year's additions included the golden-cheeked warbler, a tiny bird that nests in central Texas and winters in Central America, and five plants that grow only in the San Joaquin Valley of California.

A number of bird species were declining rapidly. A group of conservation experts met in March to devise an emergency plan to aid the red cockaded woodpecker, which lives exclusively in old-growth forests of the Southeast. About 60 per cent of the birds live on federal lands. A 1989 United States Forest Service directive that prohibited *clear-cutting* (cutting down all the trees) within ¾ mile (1.2 kilometers) of any colony of red cockaded woodpeckers failed to stop the birds' decline.

Even mallard ducks were in trouble. Wildlife experts estimated that the number of these ducks migrating to U.S. and Canadian breeding grounds in the spring of 1990 was 50 per cent less than in 1955. Wildlife biologists also estimated that the breeding population of scaup, blue-winged teal, and other ducks was 22 per cent below the 1955 to 1989 average. Destruction of wetlands was blamed as the primary cause, aggravated by prolonged drought along the waterfowl flyways.

Good and bad news for dolphins. In April 1990, the three largest brands of canned tuna in the United States—Star-Kist, Chicken of the Sea, and Bumblebee—announced that they would no longer use tuna caught by nets that also trap and kill dolphins. Dolphins often swim on the ocean's surface above schools of tuna. Their presence guides fishing crews seeking large schools of the commercially valuable fish. But when fleets cast their nets for tuna, they also snare dolphins. Thousands of dolphins are captured and drowned every year. For several years, American conservationists and concerned consumers have boycotted companies marketing tuna, demanding that the netting of dolphins be stopped. And, by November, conservationists were protesting that the owners of Bumblebee had reneged on their pledge and were still using tuna that was not caught using "dolphin safe" methods.

Another menace to dolphins lay in the enormous drift nets that are used by Japan, Taiwan, and South Korea to catch squid in the North Pacific Ocean. The nets are used in a large area of the ocean, and their "incidental" kill includes not only dolphins but also sea turtles, seabirds, and all sorts of fishes.

In late summer, Taiwanese fishing vessels equipped with drift nets were spotted in Trinidad, indicating that the deadly nets were about to invade the Atlantic Ocean. A United Nations (UN) resolution passed in December 1989 calls for a moratorium on drift netting, beginning after June 1992. But there is no international mechanism for policing the ban.

A diver frees a bird from a huge drift net in the Pacific Ocean. These nets drift for miles, trapping birds and sea mammals as well as fish.

The United States Congress in October banned the use of drift nets within 200 nautical miles (370 kilometers) of the U.S. coast. It also prohibited U.S. fishing fleets from using drift nets anywhere.

From August through October, hundreds of dead and dying dolphins washed ashore on the Mediterranean coasts of Spain, France, and Italy. The bodies of many others were sighted floating farther out at sea. Scientists examining the carcasses concluded that the dolphins were victims of a virus that causes pneumonia and attacks the liver. They also theorized that the animals were weakened by chemical pollutants that undermined their natural defense against disease. During the first four months of 1990, 400 dead dolphins washed ashore along the Gulf of Mexico from Texas to Florida. They, too, were thought to be victims of polluted water.

Habitat conservation. One of the greatest causes of habitat loss is human development, which either eliminates the habitat of a species or fragments it so that the animals are separated and prevented from breeding. A study released in June 1990 by the World Resources Institute, an international research group, in collaboration with the UN revealed that 40 million to 50 million acres (16 million to 20 million hectares) of one type of habitat—tropical rain forest—are being destroyed every year. The area being lost annually—roughly equal to the state of Washington—is far greater than presumed from the last estimate made in 1980.

Conservation

The international conservation community in 1990 managed to protect thousands of additional square miles of rain forest and other wilderness. The World Parks Endowment purchased 11,250 acres (4,550 hectares) in Guatemala to create a new reserve in Central America. Another Central American country, Belize, established its first national park in June. The 80,000-acre (32,400-hectare) virgin tropical forest provides habitat for jaguars, tapirs, river otters, crocodiles, and toucans.

The world's largest tropical flooded-forest conservation area was created in mid-1990 in the Brazilian state of Amazonas. It covers nearly 3,200 square miles (8,300 square kilometers) and provides shelter for rare primates and birds.

In early 1990, China began forming what may be the world's largest wildlife sanctuary, the Qian Tang Reserve in Tibet. Covering 100,000 square miles (259,000 square kilometers), it is 10 times larger than the entire Serengeti ecosystem in Africa. The new sanctuary will protect such rare species as Tibetan antelope, wild yak, snow leopards, and Tibetan brown bears. Other protected rain forest areas were established in the Central African Republic, Thailand, Venezuela, and Vietnam.   Eugene J. Walter, Jr.

See also **Environmental pollution; Ocean.** In the Special Reports section, see **The African Elephant: Saved from Extinction?** In *World Book,* see **Conservation.**

Consumerism. Living costs in the United States rose rapidly in the summer and fall of 1990, after Iraq's August 2 invasion of Kuwait sent oil prices skyrocketing. Energy prices rose 5.6 per cent in September alone, the largest monthly increase since the government started tracking energy costs in 1957. Rising oil prices were expected to hike the cost of many other consumer products and services as well. Airfares, for example, soon soared to much higher levels because of rising fuel prices.

The U.S. government's Consumer Price Index (CPI) grew 0.8 per cent in both August and September and 0.6 per cent in October, pushing the index 6.3 per cent higher than in October 1989. The CPI, compiled by the Bureau of Labor Statistics of the Department of Labor, is the standard measure of living costs. The CPI increase for 1990 was expected to exceed 6 per cent by year-end, the largest in nine years.

Recipients of federal benefits linked to the CPI—such as social security and Supplemental Security Income—were assured of a 5.4 per cent increase on Jan. 1, 1991. The increase compared with a 4.7 per cent rise the previous year.

Legislation. After a lengthy battle with the White House over proposals to reduce the federal budget deficit, Congress in October imposed higher taxes on numerous consumer items, including alcoholic drinks, cigarettes, and gasoline. Legislators also created a federal surcharge on airline tickets.

Cartoon by Dick Locher © 1990 *Chicago Tribune.* Reprinted by permission of Tribune Media Services.

"Prices are down this year; however, we have deleted some standard equipment!"

A bill limiting the amount of television advertising targeted to children became law in October without President George Bush's signature. The measure restricts the amount of such advertising to 10½ minutes per hour on weekends and 12 minutes per hour on weekdays.

A measure to put some restrictions on the rates and practices of cable television companies was passed in the House of Representatives in September 1990. President Bush threatened to veto the bill, and its passage was blocked in the Senate.

On September 1, bank customers began getting faster clearance of the checks they deposit. Under provisions of a law passed in 1987, U.S. banks can hold checks written on a local bank only two days, rather than three, and hold out-of-town checks five days, instead of seven.

In September, the Senate voted to reject a bill that would have required car manufacturers to increase automobile fuel efficiency by 20 per cent by 1995. The auto industry and the Bush Administration had opposed the measure.

Food labeling. In July, the U.S. Food and Drug Administration proposed sweeping regulations designed to make food labels more uniform and informative. The action was bolstered by a food-labeling bill passed by Congress in October and signed by Bush in November. The rules, replacing a 17-year-old voluntary system, will regulate the use of such claims as "low cholesterol" and "high fiber." Food makers will also be required to disclose how much total fat, saturated fat, cholesterol, and fiber are in their products. See **Food.**

Legal actions. During the year, the U.S. Federal Trade Commission (FTC) launched a campaign against "infomercials," half-hour television programs billed as talk shows and investigative reports that are actually paid advertisements. Most of the programs are aired on cable and independent TV stations.

In one case, the FTC charged Twin Star Productions, Incorporated, a Scottsdale, Ariz., production company, with making false claims for products sold to promote weight loss or to cure baldness or impotence. In a consent order, the company and its officers agreed to make refunds of $1.5 million.

In January, prosecutors concluded a celebrated case of money laundering, bankruptcy fraud, and mail fraud when a federal court in Alexandria, Va., sentenced David DeFusco to 60 months in prison and sentenced his wife, Annette DeFusco, to 35 months. The couple, operators of a time-share vacation scheme, had pleaded guilty to the charges in 1989.

In August, a federal appeals court in Washington, D.C., overturned a Federal Trade Commission ruling to encourage competition among optometrists. The agency had hoped to negate restrictions by more than 40 states on the sale of corrective lenses in shopping centers.   Arthur E. Rowse

In *World Book,* see **Consumerism.**

Costa Rica. A self-described "great friend of the United States," Rafael Angel Calderón Fournier of the conservative Social Christian Unity party, was sworn in for a four-year term as Costa Rica's president on May 8, 1990. Calderón is a lawyer and the son of a former president who had fled into exile in 1948.

Prior to running for office, Calderón had served as the executive director of the Costa Rican Association for the Defense of Democracy and Liberty, a right wing group that criticized the Central American peace plan of outgoing President Oscar Arias Sánchez. The association reportedly had close ties to top Republican Party officials in the United States. According to U.S. congressional documents, it was largely financed by the National Republican Institute for International Affairs, which receives federal funds through the U.S. Information Agency. Controversy arose when Democrats in the U.S. Congress charged that funds for the association were used illegally for Calderón's presidential campaign, but Calderón denied the charges.

Calderón inherited what he called "the worst fiscal crisis" in Costa Rica's history. The deficit stood at $163.8-million at the end of 1989. This was twice the level that Costa Rica had agreed to maintain when it received aid from the International Monetary Fund, an agency of the United Nations.   Nathan A. Haverstock

See also **Calderón Fournier, Rafael Angel; Latin America** (Facts in brief table). In *World Book,* see **Costa Rica.**

Courts. A highly charged drama in a New York City courtroom ended in 1990 with the conviction of five youths for an attack on a woman jogger in the city's Central Park in April 1989. The defendants —Anton McCray, 16; Yusef Salaam, 16; Raymond Santana, 15; Kevin Richardson, 16; and Kharey Wise, 18—were found guilty of raping and severely beating the woman, a 28-year-old investment banker. Richardson also was convicted on a charge of attempted murder. On Sept. 12, 1990, McCray, Salaam, and Santana were sentenced to 5 to 10 years in prison, the maximum terms they could receive as juvenile offenders. Richardson and Wise awaited sentencing at year-end.

The convictions were based largely on confessions the defendants made to police officers. The officers were investigating a "wilding" spree by 30 or more youths through Central Park on April 19, 1989. That rampage included attacks on other individuals as well as the assault on the investment banker.

Throughout the trial, friends and family of the youths, who are black, contended that the boys were innocent victims of white society. A sixth youth was scheduled to be tried in early 1991.

Bensonhurst defendants found guilty. Two other trials that aggravated racial tensions in New York City culminated in guilty verdicts against two white youths accused in the killing of a black teenager. On May 17, 1990, Joseph Fama, 19, was convicted of fatally shooting 16-year-old Yusef K. Hawkins on Aug. 23, 1989, in Bensonhurst, a section of the borough of Brooklyn. Keith Mondello, also 19, was found guilty just one day later of organizing a bat-wielding mob—which included Fama—that confronted Hawkins and three other black youths who had come to Bensonhurst to look at a used car. On June 11, Fama and Mondello received the maximum sentences for their crimes: Fama was sentenced to 32 years to life in prison, and Mondello to 5 to 16 years.

On July 3, another defendant in the case, John S. Vento, was acquitted of intentional murder but convicted on several lesser charges. The jury deadlocked on a second murder charge. Vento was retried on that charge in the fall. On December 6, he was acquitted.

On December 4, two other defendants in the case, James Patino and Joseph Serrano, were acquitted of murder, though Serrano was convicted of a misdemeanor weapons-possession charge. Three other defendants were also being prosecuted at year-end.

Child molestation case ends—finally. The longest criminal trial in United States history ground to its conclusion on January 18, when a jury in Los Angeles acquitted two defendants on 52 counts of child sexual abuse at their family-owned day-care center. The trial of Peggy McMartin Buckey, 63, and her son, Raymond Buckey, 31, had taken 28 months and was followed by nine weeks of jury deliberations. But the ordeal was not over. The jury deadlocked on 12 other molestation charges against Raymond Buckey, making it necessary

to try him again later in the year. On July 27, another Los Angeles jury reached an impasse over those charges, and the judge declared a mistrial. The prosecutor said the case would not be pursued further.

The case began in 1983, when McMartin, Buckey, and five other relatives and day-care workers were arrested on charges of sexually abusing children at the McMartin Pre-School in Manhattan Beach, Calif. Charges against the other five were later dropped.

Murderer convicted after 19 years. John E. List, a fugitive from the law for almost two decades, was convicted in Elizabeth, N.J., on April 12 of murdering his entire family in 1971. On May 1, the judge in the case sentenced the 64-year-old List to life in prison.

In 1971, List shot his wife, mother, daughter, and two sons at their Westfield, N.J., home and then fled into hiding. He was spotted in Richmond, Va., in June 1989 after his picture appeared on the television program "America's Most Wanted."

Guilty plea for "junk bond" king. On April 24, 1990, Michael R. Milken, the former "junk bond" chief of the investment banking firm of Drexel Burnham Lambert Incorporated, pleaded guilty to six counts of securities fraud and conspiracy. He agreed to pay $600-million in fines and penalties, the largest criminal settlement in U.S. history. On November 21, Milken was also sentenced to 10 years in prison.

Imelda Marcos acquitted. On July 2, a federal jury in New York City acquitted Imelda Marcos, the

Mark and Crispina Calvert hold their son, Christopher, in October after a judge denied parenthood rights to a surrogate mother who bore the child.

widow of former Philippine President Ferdinand E. Marcos, of racketeering and fraud charges. Mrs. Marcos had been accused—along with her husband, who died in September 1989—of stealing more than $200-million from the Philippines. A codefendant, Saudi businessman Adnan M. Khashoggi, was also acquitted.

Exxon Valdez verdict. On March 22, 1990, a jury in Anchorage, Alaska, found Joseph J. Hazelwood, captain of the Exxon Valdez, not guilty of being drunk and reckless while directing the movements of the huge oil tanker. The jury did, however, convict Hazelwood of a lesser charge, the negligent discharge of oil. The Exxon Valdez ran aground off the coast of Alaska in March 1989, causing the worst oil spill ever to occur in U.S. waters. Hazelwood was sentenced on March 23, 1990, to pay $50,000 in restitution and to spend 1,000 hours assisting in the oil cleanup.

Surrogate mother denied parenthood role. A California woman who had served as a surrogate mother, carrying a fetus to full development in her womb for another couple, lost a court battle on October 22 to share parental rights with the genetic parents. A superior court judge in Santa Ana, Calif., told the surrogate mother, Anna L. Johnson, that she had simply served as a "home" for the baby during its development and had no further claims on it. Johnson received $10,000 from the genetic parents, Crispina and Mark Calvert, to carry the fetus, which had been conceived in a laboratory.

Frozen-embryo ruling reversed. Overturning a 1989 decision, the Tennessee Court of Appeals on Sept. 13, 1990, granted joint custody of seven frozen embryos to a divorced couple, Junior L. Davis and Mary Sue Davis Stowe. A Tennessee judge had granted custody to Stowe in 1989, treating the embryos as unborn children rather than part of the property settlement in the divorce. Stowe wanted to use the embryos to achieve pregnancy, but Davis said he did not want to be forced to become a father.

Gotti acquitted again. On Feb. 9, 1990, at the State Supreme Court in New York City, John Gotti, reputedly the nation's top Mafia boss, was acquitted on charges that he ordered the shooting of a union official who was wounded in 1986. The not-guilty verdict marked the third time since 1986 that law-enforcement authorities had failed to convict the 49-year-old Gotti for alleged mob related crimes. On Dec. 12, 1990, Gotti was indicted a fourth time, on 11 counts of loan sharking, conspiring to commit murder, and other crimes.

Miami cop gets seven years. William Lozano, a Miami, Fla., police officer convicted of manslaughter in 1989 for the death of two motorcycle riders, was sentenced on Jan. 24, 1990, to seven years in prison. In January 1989, Lozano shot and killed the driver of a motorcycle who was fleeing a police car. A rider on the motorcycle died of crash injuries.   David L. Dreier

See also **Crime; Supreme Court of the United States.** In **World Book,** see **Courts.**

Crime. A grisly series of murders shocked the residents of Gainesville, Fla., in August 1990. Five college students, all but one of them women, were found stabbed to death near the campus of the University of Florida. All had suffered multiple stab wounds. Three of the women were mutilated by the killer, and one was also decapitated.

The terror began on the afternoon of Sunday, August 25, when the bodies of Sonya Larson, 18, and Christina Powell, 17, both University of Florida freshmen, were discovered at their apartment. Later the same day, Alachua County sheriff's deputies found the body of Christa Hoyt, 18, a student at Santa Fe Community College in Gainesville. On Tuesday morning, two more victims were discovered: Tracy Paules, 23, a senior at the university, and her apartment-mate, Santa Fe student Manuel Tobada, 23.

Detectives theorized that all the crimes were committed by the same person because of the similar nature of the murders and because the female victims were all petite brunettes. The investigators speculated that Tobada was an unintended victim whom the killer was surprised to find in Paules' apartment.

Gunman goes on rampage. Just two months before the Gainesville slayings, another Florida city—Jacksonville—made crime headlines. On June 18, James E. Pough, a 42-year-old construction worker, walked into an automobile loan office and opened fire with a semiautomatic assault rifle. After killing nine people and wounding four others, Pough turned the gun on himself and shot himself fatally.

Investigators could not determine the reason for Pough's attack. Although he was at first reported to have been angry about the repossession of a car, that motive was ruled out. Moreover, ballistics tests with Pough's rifle identified him as the killer of two people who had been found shot to death in Jacksonville the preceding weekend.

Cultists charged in murder of family. In early January, police investigators unearthed the bodies of five family members buried at a farm near Kirtland, Ohio. The discovery led to the filing of murder or conspiracy charges against the former leader of a religious cult and 12 of his followers.

The murder victims—Dennis Avery; his wife, Cheryl; and their three children, aged 7, 13, and 15—had been members of a religious commune with paramilitary overtones headed by Jeffrey Lundgren, 39. The Averys and several other families had followed Lundgren, a self-styled prophet, from Kansas City, Mo., to Kirtland in the mid-1980's. Authorities who reconstructed the crime said the Averys were killed in April 1989 and buried in the barn at the farm. They said the murders may have been part of a religious ritual. After the killings, the commune broke up.

Besides Lundgren, the 13 people charged in the case included Lundgren's wife, Alice, and son, Damon.

Murder, other violent crimes on rise. Homicide rates in large United States cities are soaring, and vio-

An arson fire at the Happy Land Social Club in New York City on March 25 killed 87 people. A Bronx man was charged with the crime just hours later.

lent crime in general is increasing throughout the nation, law enforcement officials reported in 1990.

A study published in July by *The New York Times*, based on information released by the police departments of major U.S. cities, showed that murder was up significantly in almost every large urban area, compared with 1989. Some of the greatest increases occurred in New York City, up 18 per cent; Chicago, up 14 per cent; and Philadelphia, up 19 per cent. Boston posted an astounding 56 per cent increase in its homicide rate, though the actual number of killings for the first half of the year—78—was far fewer than the 200 or more that occurred in several other, larger cities. In New York, the homicide leader in terms of sheer numbers, 990 people had been killed by July 1990, and the total was about 2,000 by year's end.

Figures released in April by the Federal Bureau of Investigation (FBI) revealed that all types of violent crime in the United States rose an average of 5 per cent from 1988 to 1989. The statistics—from small cities, rural areas, and suburbs as well as large metropolitan areas—showed the following increases: murder, 4 per cent; robbery, 7 per cent; rape, 1 per cent; and aggravated assault, 5 per cent.

New York City arson fire kills 87. The homicide figures for New York City did not include 87 people who were burned to death in an arson fire at a social club. The Happy Land Social Club, an unlicensed drinking and dancing establishment in the borough of the Bronx, was gutted by fire in the early hours of March 25. Most of the victims were trapped on the second floor of the small, windowless building.

Just hours later, Julio Gonzalez, 36, a Bronx resident who emigrated from Cuba in 1980, was arrested for the crime. He was later charged with arson, 174 counts of murder (two different counts for each victim), and other offenses. The police said Gonzalez had argued with his former girlfriend, an employee at the club, and was ejected by a bouncer. As an act of revenge, he allegedly returned to the club with a container of gasoline and started the blaze.

Stick-up of armored car nets $11 million. In one of the biggest heists in U.S. history, robbers in Rochester, N.Y., stole an estimated $10.8 million from an armored car on June 26. The robbery occurred while the vehicle, owned by the Armored Motor Service of America, Incorporated, was on its way to the Federal Reserve Bank in Buffalo, N.Y. When the driver stopped at a store for sandwiches, he and the guard were surprised by a man with a shotgun, who ordered them to drive to a nearby wooded area. There, the gunman and at least one accomplice bound and gagged the two crew members and transferred the money sacks from the armored car to another vehicle.

"Suicide doctor." Jack Kevorkian, a retired Detroit-area pathologist who helped a woman kill herself, was charged with first-degree murder on December 3 in Clarkston, Mich. Kevorkian had developed a device to enable people to commit suicide by injecting themselves with a lethal dose of drugs. In June, Janet Adkins, a Portland, Ore., woman with Alzheimer's disease used the device to commit suicide. Reclining in the back of the physician's specially equipped van, Adkins pressed a button that started the flow of drugs into her veins. Immediately afterward, Kevorkian contacted the police and described what had occurred. On December 13, an Oakland County District Court dismissed the murder charge, saying that Adkins, not Kevorkian, caused her death.

Leading S&L official charged. Charles H. Keating, Jr., who has become a symbol of the troubled U.S. savings-and-loan industry, was indicted on charges of criminal fraud on September 18 in Los Angeles. Keating, the former chairman of the now bankrupt American Continental Corporation, and three of his associates were charged with using false statements to sell high-risk bonds. The bonds were sold at branches of Lincoln Savings & Loan Association of Irvine, Calif., which Keating controlled through American Continental. Keating denied any wrongdoing, and a trial was pending at year-end. See **Bank (Close-Up).**

Alleged Mafia figures indicted. Twenty-one men described by U.S. Attorney General Richard L. Thornburgh as leaders or important members of organized crime in New England were indicted in Boston and Hartford, Conn., on March 26. The 21 are members of a reputed crime family headed by Raymond J. Patriarca, Jr. The defendants, who included Patriarca, were charged with a variety of criminal activities, including murder, drug trafficking, extortion, and mail fraud.

The indictments came after a five-year FBI probe of the Patriarca family. Among the evidence obtained by the FBI agents was a secret recording of an alleged Mafia induction ceremony. Thornburgh said the tape provided the first direct proof — as opposed to the testimony of witnesses — that the Mafia exists.

Man suspected in wife's death kills himself. Charles Stuart, a 29-year-old Boston man who had claimed that a robber shot and killed his wife, apparently committed suicide by jumping from a bridge into Boston Harbor on January 4 after becoming the prime suspect in the case. Stuart had told the police that as he and his pregnant wife, Carol, sat in their car on Oct. 23, 1989, they were robbed and shot by a black assailant. Carol Stuart was shot in the head and killed, and Stuart was himself seriously wounded in the stomach. The police later concluded, however, that Stuart shot his wife and then himself. They theorized that Stuart gave himself a wound to make his story convincing to detectives.

Before the police suspected that Stuart was the killer, they conducted an intensive search for the alleged black assailant. When the evidence against Stuart was disclosed, the black community of Boston expressed outrage that his account of the murder had been so readily believed.   David L. Dreier

In *World Book,* see **Crime.**

Cuba. Tension between Cuba and the Soviet Union grew worse in 1990. As aid from the Soviet Union was either delayed or cut back, rationing and shortages in Cuba became widespread. Even newsprint was scarce.

In June, a high-ranking Cuban defector confirmed that the Soviet Union had sharply trimmed its economic assistance, vital to the Cuban economy. Ramón González Vergara, who was vice secretary of the Soviet-Cuban Council for Mutual Economic Assistance, based in Moscow, defected while in East Germany on June 18. He flew to the United States on July 3.

Vergara reported that in early 1990 the Soviets had announced the termination of oil supplies to Cuba in excess of the island's domestic needs. Cuba earned $500 million in *hard* (internationally exchangeable) currency in 1988 from the resale of excess oil, more than it did from sugar exports that year. Vergara also described tense discussions at which the Soviets had informed Cuban representatives of drastic cuts in low-interest debt financing. He said the Soviet Union also announced that it would begin trading in hard currency in 1991, eliminating barter trade deals at subsidized prices. Cuba is low on hard currency and would be harshly affected by this decision.

According to Vergara, the Soviets also demanded that Cuba begin making repayments on its debt to the Soviet Union in 1995. Cuba's total debt to the Soviets in 1990 was estimated at $24 billion.

Delays. Soviet supplies on which the Cuban economy depended were often delayed in 1990. In February, President Fidel Castro ordered bread rationing due to late shipments of flour and grain. In October, the official newspaper of the Cuban Communist Party reported that reductions in the amount of newsprint imported from the Soviet Union would require publications to cut back on the frequency of publication and the size of each issue. Two paper plants on the island were reported idled by a lack of pulp and bleaching agents, which also come from the Soviet Union.

Dissidents. The year 1990 saw further crackdowns on Cuban dissidents. On July 18, 11 members of the Pro-Human Rights Youth Association were sentenced to terms varying from 3 years' house arrest to 15 years in prison. They were convicted on charges of terrorism and inciting rebellion.

Political reforms. On October 5, Cuba's Communist Party announced that it would take steps to streamline a bloated bureaucracy and cut the number of national and provincial party posts in half. The party also announced that, though it refused to embrace the multiparty politics and market economies being adopted in eastern Europe, it would introduce direct, secret voting and allow more than a single candidate in coming elections for municipal and provincial party committees.   Nathan A. Haverstock

See also **Latin America** (Facts in brief table). In *World Book,* see **Cuba.**

Cyprus. See **Middle East.**

Czechoslovakia

Czechoslovakia. The "velvet revolution," which quickly and peacefully toppled Czechoslovakia's Communist government in 1989, found the road to reform difficult in 1990. Sharp conflict arose between those who wished to dismantle the old ruling structures by the wholesale removal of Communists and those anxious to avoid political witch hunts. The latter camp, which included President Václav Havel, warned against hunting down qualified people simply because they had served under the Communist regime.

The deadlock continued through the summer, despite victories by Havel's supporters in June parliamentary elections. After the elections, another issue arose to divide the country and further slow the political process: Slovak nationalism. With the end of Communist rule, ethnic Slovaks began to demand a greater say in running the Slovak republic, one of the two republics that make up the nation. The other is the Czech republic. Some Slovak nationalists called for the creation of an independent Slovak state. In December, the Federal Assembly passed legislation under which the two republics will rotate the presidency of the central bank. The central government will retain responsibility for such matters as national defense, foreign policy, and economic strategy.

The pace of economic reform also provoked clashes. Some advocated the rapid and radical dismantling of an economy run almost entirely by the central government. Others favored a gradual transition to a

Czechoslovak President Václav Havel joins his party's victory celebration in Prague after June elections for parliament.

market economy in the hope of sparing the country high unemployment and high inflation.

On September 3, Prime Minister Marián Calfa presented a plan for economic reform to the Federal Assembly. It proposed selling off small state-owned businesses first. This was to be followed by the introduction of market mechanisms to set prices and by the distribution of stock in large state enterprises to turn them over to the private sector.

The economy, meantime, was at a standstill. A government decision in October to auction off 100,000 shops, restaurants, and small businesses prompted fears of unemployment and led to widespread strikes.

Promoting close relations with the West dominated Havel's activities during the first half of 1990. Through a number of state visits, he pursued goals of stable relations with the Soviet Union and Czechoslovakia's integration into a new security organization that would embrace eastern and western Europe.

Havel told a joint session of the U.S. Congress in February that the United States could best help Czechoslovakia by assisting the Soviet Union on its road to democracy. The United States later agreed to lower tariffs on Czechoslovak imports, as did the European Community (EC or Common Market).

Relations with the Soviet Union were affected by Soviet economic difficulties. Tough negotiations over the summer led to a trade accord in September that required payment in *hard* (internationally exchangeable) currency for most goods traded between the two countries after Jan. 1, 1991. Czechoslovakia has relied on inexpensive Soviet petroleum and raw materials for its manufacturing industries. In turn, the Soviet Union has purchased two-fifths of Czechoslovakia's exports. The Soviet Union spoke of reducing deliveries of raw materials. But in October 1990, it agreed to step up oil supplies to Czechoslovakia in return for oil drilling equipment and other products. The Soviet Union also agreed that Czechoslovakia could offset oil payments in 1991 with Soviet trade debts to Czechoslovakia.

The withdrawal of nearly 75,000 Soviet troops from Czechoslovakia continued during the year and was scheduled to be completed by mid-1991.

Elections on June 8 and 9, 1990, for the 300-member Federal Assembly gave 168 seats to the movements that brought down the Communists—the Czech Civic Forum and its Slovak counterpart, Public Against Violence. The two groups fell short, however, of the three-fifths majority needed to enact a new constitution, an item on the agenda for 1991. The Christian Democrats won only 40 seats in the Assembly and were beaten even by the Communists, who took 47 seats. The Assembly reelected Alexander Dubček, leader of a reform movement in 1968, as its chairman. It reelected Havel to a two-year term as president on July 5, 1990.   Eric Bourne

See also **Europe** (Facts in brief table); **Havel, Václav.** In *World Book,* see **Czechoslovakia.**

Members of the Erick Hawkins Dance Company perform in the premiere of *New Moon,* a poetic work about renewal, in New York City in February.

Dancing. The largest ballet companies in the United States underwent important transitions in 1990. The most dramatic events swirled around the Joffrey Ballet and Gerald Arpino, who founded the Joffrey in 1956 with Robert Joffrey. Arpino, who became artistic director of the company on Joffrey's death in 1988, resigned on May 1, 1990. He bowed out because the company's board voted to set up a managing committee that would have stripped him of such powers as the right to hire and fire personnel. Among the reasons the board cited for its action was the company's $2-million deficit.

The Joffrey Ballet was performing in Los Angeles when Arpino quit. Its programs quickly became a shambles when Arpino denied the company permission to perform the ballets he or Joffrey had choreographed. The company's long-range prospects became just as uncertain when several financial supporters said they would no longer fund the troupe.

By mid-May, however, several of Arpino's key opponents on the board, including board cochairman Anthony A. Bliss, had resigned. On May 25, Arpino and the board reached a new agreement that confirmed his position as artistic director.

Although the Joffrey had to cancel some of its summer programs because of Arpino's resignation, it had managed to raise more than $1 million by June to offset part of its deficit. The company performed in Europe in September.

Dance Theatre woes. Facing a projected $1.7-million deficit, Arthur Mitchell, artistic director of the Dance Theatre of Harlem, temporarily disbanded his company in March. In November, the troupe announced that it would continue to have a home base in Los Angeles.

American Ballet Theatre (ABT) celebrated its 50th anniversary in January without an artistic director. In September 1989, Mikhail Baryshnikov, artistic director of the ABT since 1980, had suddenly resigned in a dispute with the company's board of trustees.

Some observers believed the ABT would seek a new director whose reputation matched Baryshnikov's star status. But on March 9, 1990, the board announced that Jane Hermann, the company's executive director, and Oliver Smith, the company's scenic designer and a director of the troupe from 1945 to 1980, would serve as codirectors. The decision aroused some controversy because Hermann's previous experience lay with the administrative, rather than creative, side of dance. In June 1990, the company announced that Natalia Makarova, a former ABT ballerina, would act as artistic adviser.

Although the ABT's repertory for 1990 had already been planned—the major event being the world premiere of Twyla Tharp's *Brief Fling* in March in San Francisco—the impact of the new regime was soon felt in other areas. Tharp and fellow choreographer Kenneth MacMillan, who had been named as artistic

Dancing

associates by Baryshnikov, were dropped. Hermann said the ABT would not commission as many experimental ballets as it had done under Baryshnikov, and she reinstituted the guest-star policy Baryshnikov had abolished. The ABT's season at New York City's Metropolitan Opera House in May and June featured such guests as Vladimir Vasiliev and Yekaterina Maximova, stars of Moscow's Bolshoi Ballet, and ABT alumni Fernando Bujones and Carla Fracci.

Released from the ABT, Tharp found a home for her works with the Hubbard Street Dance Company of Chicago. In June, this jazz-based troupe won sole rights to perform Tharp's dances for three years.

New York City Ballet. The mood at the New York City Ballet was relatively calm but significantly different in the absence of Jerome Robbins, who had been with the troupe since 1949. In 1989, Robbins had resigned as coartistic director, effective Jan. 1, 1990.

Robbins was on hand, however, to supervise a retrospective of his ballets at the New York State Theater in New York City in June. The two-week festival presented 27 of his works, spanning 45 years. The major event was a revival of *Watermill*, a meditative piece inspired by Asian theater techniques. Edward Villella, who starred in the original performance of the piece in 1972, returned for the revival and gave, at age 53, an even more sensitive portrayal of the protagonist than he had done in his youth.

Alvin Ailey. Also in transition was the Alvin Ailey American Dance Theater. In January 1990, the company's board permanently named long-time Ailey dancer Judith Jamison to succeed Ailey, who died in 1989, as artistic director. Jamison announced a new policy in which the Ailey group would be in residence at various cities where it would rehearse, schedule educational programs and perform. Baltimore was named as the first resident city, effective in 1991.

Soviet presence. The Soviet Union's policy of *glasnost* (openness) was increasingly felt in the United States in 1990. More Soviet troupes than ever performed at U.S. theaters. More significantly, many Soviet dancers and choreographers worked with U.S. companies. Elena Vinogradova, wife of the director of Leningrad's Kirov Ballet, staged *Paquita* for the Pacific Northwest Ballet in Seattle in May. Also that month, the Boston Ballet produced what it called a "glasnost *Swan Lake*." Alternating as the Swan Queen and prince were six U.S.-Soviet couples.

In September, the Universal Ballet Academy opened in Washington, D.C. This ballet school, staffed by teachers from various schools in the Soviet Union, is directed by Oleg Vinogradov, director of the Kirov, who plans to spend about four months a year in Washington. The school was funded by the Unification Church, whose leader, Sun Myung Moon, has a long-standing interest in dance.

Canadian dance received unusual prominence in the United States when the Brooklyn Academy of Music's Next Wave Festival presented Next Wave/Next Door, a four-part series featuring Canadian companies, in November. Another highlight of the festival was performances by the Monnaie Dance Group/Mark Morris in October. Morris is a young but increasingly well-regarded American modern-dance choreographer whose company has been in residence at the Théâtre de la Monnaie in Brussels, Belgium, since 1988.

In 1989, Morris had choreographed a dance for Baryshnikov, and in 1990, the two assembled a troupe of dancers, named the White Oak Dance Project, from various ballet and modern dance groups. Beginning on October 24, the troupe embarked on an 18-city U.S. tour. Morris created several new dances for the tour, including *Pas de Poisson*.

Premieres. Two of the year's more unusual modern-dance premieres were created by two of the most famous American choreographers. On April 25 at the City Center Theater in New York City, Paul Taylor unveiled what was only his second full-evening work, *Of Bright & Blue Birds & the Gala Sun*. The dance, whose title is taken from a poem by U.S. poet Wallace Stevens, is a morality tale about the breakdown of society.

Martha Graham premiered her first dance to popular music—her 180th work—on October 2, also at City Center. *Maple Leaf Rag*, a light-hearted dance with bits of self-parody, is set to four pieces by American composer Scott Joplin.   Nancy Goldner

In *World Book*, see **Ballet; Dancing.**

Day-Lewis, Daniel (1958-   ), received the Academy of Motion Picture Arts and Sciences Award for best actor in 1990. He won the Oscar for his stunning performance in *My Left Foot*, the story of Irish writer and painter Christy Brown, who was born with cerebral palsy. To prepare for the role of the severely disabled Brown, Day-Lewis spent two months at a cerebral palsy clinic near Dublin, Ireland. He learned to type and paint with his left foot, the only part of the body that Brown could control. During filming, Day-Lewis stayed in character even off camera, moving about in a wheelchair, having others feed him, and speaking in a thick, slurred voice.

Day-Lewis was born in London, the son of British poet laureate Cecil Day-Lewis. He began acting at school. His first screen appearance was a nonspeaking part in *Sunday, Bloody Sunday* (1971) at age 12. Fourteen years later, he came to the notice of film critics for his portrayal of a street punk in *My Beautiful Laundrette* (1985). Soon afterward, he played the prissy aristocrat Cecil Vyse in *A Room with a View* (1985). The role of a womanizing brain surgeon in *The Unbearable Lightness of Being* (1988) gave an additional boost to Day-Lewis' growing reputation for chameleonlike versatility. His stage appearances include the title role in *Hamlet* with London's National Theatre Company in 1989.

Day-Lewis guards his privacy, not officially giving out even his birth date.   Karin C. Rosenberg

Deaths in 1990 included those listed below, who were Americans unless otherwise indicated.

Abdul Rahman Putra, Tengku (1903-Dec. 6), Malaysian prince who led his country in winning independence from Great Britain in 1957 and served as Malaysia's first prime minister from 1963 to 1970.

Abernathy, Ralph David (1926-April 17), civil rights leader.

Allen, George H. (1922-Dec. 31), former head coach of football's Los Angeles Rams and Washington Redskins.

Anderson, Sigurd (1904-Dec. 21), Norwegian-born Republican governor of South Dakota from 1951 to 1955.

Arden, Eve (Eunice Quedens) (1912?-Nov. 12), actress who played the wise-cracking "Our Miss Brooks" on television in the 1950's.

Bailey, Pearl (1918-Aug. 17), singer and actress known for her warm, throaty voice.

Balin, Ina (Ina Rosenberg) (1937-June 20), motion-picture and stage actress who made her film debut in *The Black Orchid* (1959).

Ballard, Harold (1903-April 11), Canadian owner of the Toronto Maple Leafs hockey team; member of the Hockey Hall of Fame.

Bennett, Joan (1910-Dec. 7), star of 1930's and 1940's films and of the TV soap opera "Dark Shadows" (1966-1971).

Bernstein, Leonard (1918-Oct. 14), renowned composer and conductor. See **Classical music (Close-Up).**

Bettelheim, Bruno (1903-March 13), Austrian-born psychiatrist famous for working with emotionally disturbed children.

Binns, Edward (1916-Dec. 4), star of the TV police series "Brenner" (1959-1964).

Blakey, Art (1919-Oct. 16), legendary jazz drummer whose band, the Jazz Messengers, nurtured many top jazz stars.

Bridges, Harry (Alfred Renton Bridges) (1901-March 30), Australian-born president of the International Longshoremen's and Warehousemen's Union from 1938 to 1977.

Broyard, Anatole (1920-Oct. 11), book critic.

Buehrig, Gordon M. (1904?-Jan. 22), automobile designer who created such classic cars as the Auburn and the Cord.

Bunshaft, Gordon (1909-Aug. 6), modernist architect who designed Lever House (1952) and other major skyscrapers.

Caccia of Abernant, Lord (Harold A. Caccia) (1905-Oct. 31), British ambassador to the United States from 1956 to 1961; made a life peer in 1965.

Callaghan, Morley (1903-Aug. 25), Canadian novelist.

Capucine (Germaine Lefebvre) (1933-March 17), French actress and former model who co-starred with Peter Sellers in the *The Pink Panther* (1964).

Caradon, Lord (Hugh Mackintosh Foot) (1907-Sept. 5), British ambassador to the United Nations from 1964 to 1970; made a life peer in 1964.

Carlson, Edward E. (1911-April 3), former chief executive of UAL Corporation, a hotel and airline chain.

Carney, James F. (1915-Sept. 16), Roman Catholic archbishop of Vancouver, Canada, since 1969.

Carreras, Sir James (1909-June 9), British motion-picture producer who headed Hammer Film Productions, a studio famous for its horror films; knighted in 1970.

Carvel, Thomas (Thomas A. Carvelas) (1906-found dead Oct. 21), inventor who patented the first machine to make soft ice cream; founder and first chairman of the Carvel Corporation ice cream chain.

Casiraghi, Stefano (1960?-Oct. 3), Italian financier; husband of Princess Caroline of Monaco.

Chandler, Spud (Spurgeon Ferdinand Chandler) (1907-Jan. 9), pitcher for the New York Yankees from 1937 to 1947; the American League's Most Valuable Player in 1943.

Charleson, Ian (1949-Jan. 6), British actor who portrayed an Olympic runner in *Chariots of Fire* (1981).

Childs, Marquis W. (1903-June 30), columnist for the *St. Louis* (Mo.) *Post-Dispatch* who won the 1970 Pulitzer Prize for commentary.

Mary Martin,
star of *Peter Pan*

José Napoleón Duarte,
Salvadoran president

Arthur J. Goldberg,
Supreme Court justice

Greta Garbo, reclusive
Swedish-born actress

Christy, June (Shirley Luter) (1925-June 21), jazz singer who gained fame as "the misty Miss Christy" with the Stan Kenton Orchestra in the 1940's.

Church, Marguerite Stitt (1892-May 26), Republican representative from Illinois from 1951 to 1963.

Clancy, Tom (1923?-Nov. 7), Irish singer and actor; a founder of the Clancy Brothers folk-singing group.

Clark, Joseph S. (1901-Jan. 12), mayor of Philadelphia from 1952 to 1956 and Democratic U.S. senator representing Pennsylvania from 1957 to 1969.

Clifton, Sweetwater (Nathaniel Clifton) (1922-Aug. 31), former Harlem Globetrotter; one of the first black players in the National Basketball Association (NBA).

Collins, Allen (1952?-Jan. 23), rock guitarist who was a cofounder of the group Lynyrd Skynyrd.

Condos, Steve (1919?-Sept. 16), tap-dancer.

Conigliaro, Tony (1945-Feb. 24), outfielder for the Boston Red Sox from 1964 to 1970 and again in 1975.

Copland, Aaron (1900-Dec. 2), composer who won the 1945 Pulitzer Prize for his ballet *Appalachian Spring*.

Cousins, Norman (1915-Nov. 30), editor of *Saturday Review* from 1940 to 1971 and 1973 to 1977.

Cramer, Doc (Roger Maxwell Cramer) (1905-Sept. 9), outfielder who played for four major league teams between 1929 and 1948 and was chosen for five All-Star games.

Cremin, Lawrence A. (1925-Sept. 4), professor of education and former president of Teachers College of Columbia University in New York City; winner of the Pulitzer Prize for history in 1981; member of the Year Book Board of Editors from 1962 to 1982.

Deaths

Patriarch Pimen,
Russian Orthodox leader

Rex Harrison,
veteran British actor

Pearl Bailey,
singer and actress

Stevie Ray Vaughan,
blues guitarist

Crown, Henry (Henry Krinsky) (1896-Aug. 14), co-founder and former chairman of Material Service Corporation, a conglomerate with holdings in many industries.

Cruzan, Nancy Beth (1957-Dec. 26), comatose victim of a 1983 automobile accident whose parents finally obtained a judge's permission to remove her feeding tube after a landmark legal fight over the right to die.

Cugat, Xavier (Francisco de Asis Javier Cugat Mingall de Brue y Deulofeo) (1900-Oct. 27), Spanish-born bandleader who introduced the rumba to the United States.

Cullen, Bill (1920-July 7), veteran TV game show host.

Cummings, Bob (Charles Clarence Robert Orville Cummings) (1908-Dec. 2), debonair actor who turned from a successful film career to star in "The Bob Cummings Show" on TV from 1955 to 1959.

Dahl, Roald (1916-Nov. 23), British author known for his children's books, including *James and the Giant Peach* (1962) and *Charlie and the Chocolate Factory* (1964).

Danaher, John A. (1899-Sept. 22), Republican senator from Connecticut from 1939 to 1945 and judge on the U.S. Court of Appeals from 1953 to 1969.

Dauphinee, John (1913-May 11), former general manager and chief executive of the Canadian Press news agency.

Davies, Bob (1920-April 22), guard who led the Rochester (N.Y.) Royals to an NBA championship in 1951; member of the Naismith Memorial Basketball Hall of Fame.

Davis, Deane C. (1900-Dec. 8), Republican governor of Vermont from 1969 to 1973.

Davis, John E. (1913?-May 12), Republican governor of North Dakota from 1957 to 1961.

Davis, Sammy, Jr. (1925-May 16), multitalented entertainer. See **Close-Up.**

Dawidowicz, Lucy S. (1915-Dec. 5), historian whose book *The War Against the Jews* (1975) was a pioneering study of the Holocaust.

Day, Bobby (Robert J. Byrd) (1934-July 27), rock 'n' roll singer and bandleader whose hits included "Little Bitty Pretty One" (1957) and "Rockin' Robin" (1958).

Day, Hap (Clarence Henry Day) (1901-Feb. 17), Canadian hockey star; defenseman for the Toronto Maple Leafs from 1924 to 1937; member of the Hockey Hall of Fame.

De Mestral, Georges (1908?-Feb. 8), Swiss engineer who in 1948 patented the Velcro fastener.

Dexter, John (1925-March 23), British theatrical and opera director who won Tony Awards for directing *Equus* (1974) and *M. Butterfly* (1988).

Diaz, Bo (Baudilio José Diaz) (1953-Nov. 23), Venezuelan catcher who played with the Boston Red Sox, Cleveland Indians, Philadelphia Phillies, and Cincinnati Reds in the 1970's and 1980's.

Dixon, George (1933-Aug. 6), U.S.-born Canadian football star who was a leading ball carrier for the Montreal (Que.) Alouettes in the 1960's; member of the Canadian Football Hall of Fame.

Doe, Samuel K. (1952-Sept. 10), president of Liberia since he seized power in a 1980 coup.

Donovan, Hedley W. (1914-Aug. 13), editor in chief of Time Incorporated from 1964 to 1979.

Drake, John Gibbs St. Clair (1911-June 15), social anthropologist and pioneer in black studies.

Duarte, José Napoleón (1926-Feb. 23), president of El Salvador from 1984 to 1989.

Duff, Howard (1917-July 8), actor who played detective Sam Spade on radio and Sheriff Titus Semple on TV's "Flamingo Road."

Dunne, Irene (1901?-Sept. 4), actress known for the ladylike beauty she displayed in such films as *Cimarron* (1930) and *I Remember Mama* (1948).

Durrell, Lawrence (1912-Nov. 7), British author best known for his series of four novels set in Egypt called *The Alexandria Quartet* (1957-1960); brother of the naturalist Gerald Durrell.

Dürrenmatt, Friedrich (1921-Dec. 14), Swiss dramatist whose best-known plays include *The Visit* (1956) and *The Physicists* (1962).

Edgerton, Harold E. (1903-Jan. 4), electrical engineer who pioneered in high-speed photography.

Edmondson, Edmond A. (1919-Dec. 8), Democratic representative from Oklahoma from 1953 to 1973.

Edwards, Douglas (1917-Oct. 13), first network TV news anchor, with CBS.

Ekern, Carl (1954?-Aug. 1), linebacker for the Los Angeles Rams from 1976 to 1978 and from 1980 to 1988.

Enriquez, Rene (1933-March 23), actor who played Lieutenant Ray Calletano on TV's "Hill Street Blues" in the 1980's.

Erté (Romain de Tirtoff) (1892-April 21), Russian-born artist known for his art deco painting, sculpture, and theatrical design.

Evans, Ronald E. (1933-April 7), Apollo 17 astronaut.

Farnsley, Charles R. P. (1907-June 19), mayor of Louisville, Ky., from 1948 to 1953; Democratic U.S. representative from Kentucky from 1965 to 1967.

Farrell, Charles (1901-May 6), former silent-film actor who played Margie's father on the 1950's TV series "My Little Margie."

Faulk, John Henry (1913-April 9), radio humorist whose court battle against blacklisting in the entertainment industry effectively ended the practice in 1962.

Figueres Ferrer, José (1906-June 8), president of Costa Rica in 1948 and 1949, from 1953 to 1958, and from 1970 to 1974.

Fogerty, Tom (1941-Sept. 6), guitarist with the rock band Creedence Clearwater Revival.

Forbes, Malcolm S. (1919-Feb. 24), publisher and editor in chief of *Forbes* magazine.

Franchi, Sergio (1933?-May 1), Italian-born singer whose hits include ''O Sole Mio'' and ''Memory.''

Frank, Ilya M. (1908-June 22), Soviet physicist who shared the 1958 Nobel Prize in physics.

Frederick, Pauline (1906?-May 9), veteran TV and radio news broadcaster.

Frid, Armando (1866-July 28), retired Argentine cowboy who lived 124 years, the greatest authenticated age reached by any human being.

Garbo, Greta (Greta Lovisa Gustafsson) (1905-April 15), legendary Swedish-born movie actress known for her passion for privacy.

Gardner, Ava (1922-Jan. 25), screen beauty whose best-known films include *Mogambo* (1953) and *The Barefoot Contessa* (1954).

Gardiner of Kittisford, Lord (Gerald A. Gardiner) (1900-Jan. 7), Lord Chancellor of Great Britain, the nation's highest judicial official, from 1964 to 1970; made a life peer in 1963.

Garnworthy, Lewis S. (1922-Jan. 26), former Anglican archbishop of Toronto, Canada.

Gathers, Hank (1966?-March 4), Loyola Marymount University basketball star.

Gavin, James M. (1907-Feb. 23), U.S. Army lieutenant general who led airborne troops during World War II (1939-1945).

Gilford, Jack (Jacob Gellman) (1907-June 4), veteran actor known for his pliable face.

Goddard, Paulette (Marion Levy) (1905?-April 23), actress who starred with her then-husband Charlie Chaplin in the films *Modern Times* (1936) and *The Great Dictator* (1940).

Gold, Arthur (1917-Jan. 3), Canadian pianist who performed for nearly 40 years in a piano duo with Robert Fizdale.

Goldberg, Arthur Joseph (1908-Jan. 19), former U.S. secretary of labor, Supreme Court justice, and ambassador to the United Nations.

Gordon, Dexter (1923-April 25), jazz saxophonist who starred in the 1986 film *'Round Midnight*.

Goulding, Raymond W. (1922-March 24), humorist who, with Bob Elliott, made up the Bob and Ray comedy team.

Graham, Nan Wood (1899-Dec. 14), stenographer who posed as the tight-lipped farm wife in the painting *American Gothic* (1930) by her brother, Grant Wood.

Graziano, Rocky (Thomas Rocco Barbella) (1921-May 22), middleweight boxing champion of the world in 1947 and 1948 whose 1955 autobiography, *Somebody Up There Likes Me*, became a best seller.

Gucci, Aldo (1905?-Jan. 19), head of the Italian leather goods company bearing his name.

Guinier, Ewart (1910-Feb. 4), first chairman of Harvard University's Department of Afro-American Studies.

Gunter, Cornell (Cornelius Gunter) (1936?-Feb. 26), lead vocalist for The Coasters, who recorded such hits as ''Yakety Yak'' (1957) and ''Charlie Brown'' (1959).

Hale, Alan, Jr. (1918-Jan. 2), actor who played the skipper on the 1960's TV series ''Gilligan's Island.''

Halston (Roy Halston Frowick) (1932-March 26), fashion designer.

Hammer, Armand (1898-Dec. 10), chairman and chief executive officer of Occidental Petroleum Corporation.

Harmon, Tom (1919-March 15), sportscaster who won the Heisman Trophy in 1940 as the nation's outstanding college football player when he played for the University of Michigan.

Harrison, Rex (Reginald Carey Harrison) (1908-June 2), British actor who won both a Tony Award and an Oscar for his performance as Professor Henry Higgins in *My Fair Lady*; knighted in 1989 as Sir Reginald Harrison.

Harrison, William Henry (1896-Oct. 8), Republican representative from Wyoming from 1951 to 1955, 1961 to 1965, and 1967 to 1969; grandson of President Benjamin Harrison.

Harwood, Elizabeth J. (1938-June 22), British operatic soprano.

Barbara Stanwyck, movie and TV actress

Aaron Copland, revered composer

Ralph David Abernathy, civil rights leader

Ryan White, advocate for AIDS patients

Henson, Jim (1936-May 16), creator of Kermit the Frog and the other Muppets. See **Close-Up.**

Herschler, Edgar J. (1918-Feb. 5), Democratic governor of Wyoming from 1975 to 1987.

Hofstadter, Robert (1915-Nov. 17), physicist who won the Nobel Prize in physics in 1961.

Holmes à Court, Robert (1937-Sept. 2), Australian oil company executive, born in South Africa, who was once Australia's richest man.

Hussein Onn (1922-May 28), prime minister of Malaysia from 1976 to 1981.

Ireland, Jill (1936-May 18), British actress who wrote the best seller *Life Wish* (1987) about her battle with breast cancer.

Izac, Edouard V. M. (1891-Jan. 18), Democratic representative from California from 1937 to 1947.

Jackson, Gordon (1923-Jan. 14), British actor who played Hudson the butler on the TV series ''Upstairs, Downstairs'' from 1970 to 1975.

Jeanneret, Marsh (1917-Aug. 10), Canadian publisher who headed the University of Toronto Press from 1953 to 1977.

Johnson, Kripp (Corinthian Johnson) (1923?-June 22), founder of the 1950's rock 'n' roll group the Del Vikings.

Jones, Stormie (1977-Nov. 11), world's first recipient of a heart-liver transplant, in 1984.

Kahane, Meir (Martin David Kahane) (1932-Nov. 5), American-born Israeli militant; founder of the Jewish Defense League in the United States and the Kach party in Israel.

Keller, Charlie (1916-May 23), New York Yankees outfielder whose power hitting earned him the nickname King Kong Keller in the 1940's.

Two Bright Stars Gone

The entertainment world lost two of its brightest stars on May 16, 1990, when singer-dancer-actor Sammy Davis, Jr., died of throat cancer and puppeteer Jim Henson died of pneumonia. The two were vastly different both professionally and personally. Davis was best known as a nightclub entertainer and a recording star, while Henson achieved fame through the "Sesame Street" television show for children. Davis' private life was well publicized and often controversial, while the public knew virtually nothing about Henson, the man behind the Muppets.

Yet Davis and Henson shared a major asset for an entertainer—a tremendous versatility. Comedian Joey Bishop, a close friend of Davis', said, "He could dance as well as anyone, he could sing as well as anyone, he had the timing and delivery of the best comedians." Joan Ganz Cooney, head of the company that produces "Sesame Street," said of Henson, "He was our era's Charlie Chaplin, Mae West, W. C. Fields, and the Marx Brothers, and, indeed, he drew from all of them to create a new art form. . . ."

Sammy Davis, Jr., was born on Dec. 8, 1925, in the Harlem section of New York City. His father was a dancer in a vaudeville troupe led by an uncle, Will Mastin, and his mother was a chorus girl in the troupe. Sammy broke into show business at the age of 3 with Mastin's troupe. Within a few years, the troupe evolved into The Will Mastin Trio, starring Sammy Davis, Jr. Davis never attended school, but his father and uncle often found someone around the theaters where they worked to tutor the boy.

Sammy Davis, Jr.
(1925-1990)

When Davis turned 18, he was drafted into the United States Army. There, he encountered racial prejudice, and frequently responded with his fists. Fortunately, he met a black sergeant who gave him reading lessons. Davis spent most of his Army time in a special services unit, entertaining other members of the armed forces.

After the end of World War II in 1945, Davis was discharged from the Army, and the Mastin Trio began entertaining in nightclubs. Eventually, the group landed a spot as the summer replacement for a network television show. By the mid-1950's, Davis had become a star.

In November 1954, Davis lost his left eye in an automobile accident. After his recuperation, he converted to Judaism, having found what he called "an affinity" between blacks and Jews as oppressed peoples.

Davis' professional life became a whirlwind of recording dates, nightclub and theater appearances, TV guest shots, and movie performances. He spent much of his private life with a group of fellow entertainers known as the Rat Pack, who included Frank Sinatra, Dean Martin, Joey Bishop, and Peter Lawford. As the only black in the group, Davis drew criticism from some of the black press for "living white." And he drew further criticism—and hate mail—in 1960 when he married Swedish actress Mai Britt. The marriage, Davis' second, ended in divorce. He later married Altovise Gore, a black dancer.

By his own admission, Davis lived a hard life that included late hours, heavy drinking, chain-smoking, chronic gambling, and drug abuse. In 1974, he developed liver and kidney problems and as a result moderated his life style.

Professionally, however, he remained the same Sammy Davis, Jr. His pace eventually slowed, but he remained active even a year before his death. In 1989, he completed a world tour with Sinatra and Liza Minnelli, and he promoted *Why Me?*, an autobiography. "I think in his 64 years he lived 100 years," said comedian Milton Berle.

James Maury Henson was born on Sept. 24, 1936, in Greenville, Miss., where his father was a soil and crop specialist for the United States Department of Agriculture. The family later moved to Maryland, and Henson enrolled at the University of Maryland. While a freshman there, Henson and classmate June Nebel—whom he later married—created a show for a television station in Washington, D.C. The show starred his Muppet creations. A Muppet is a combination of a foam-rubber hand puppet and a marionette. In most cases, a Muppet's head is a hand puppet, and the hands and the rest of the body may be controlled by rods or wires.

During the 1960's, the Muppets performed in television commercials and were regulars on TV variety shows. They vaulted to stardom in 1969 with the debut of "Sesame Street," a TV program for preschoolers. The show was intended to help children learn numbers, letters, and so on—and it did—but the Muppets seemed so human and their dialogue was so witty that the show also had a strong appeal to parents.

A prime-time television program, "The Muppet Show," starring Miss Piggy and Kermit the Frog, elevated Henson to superstardom in 1976. The show, which ran until 1981, may have been the most popular program in television history. It reached about 235 million viewers in more than 100 countries.

In 1983, Henson launched another Muppet show, "Fraggle Rock," which ran until 1987. In 1985, a Saturday morning cartoon series, "The Muppet Babies," went on the air.

In 1979, Henson made his first motion picture, *The Muppet Movie*. He followed this with *The Great Muppet Caper* in 1981 and *The Muppets Take Manhattan* in 1984. And one of his businesses, the Creature Shop, made costumes and created special effects for the 1990 hit *Teenage Mutant Ninja Turtles*. At the time of his death, Henson was putting finishing touches on a deal announced in August 1989 in which the Walt Disney Company would buy Henson Associates, Incorporated, owner of the Muppets, for a price estimated at $100 million to $150 million. The deal fell through in December 1990 when Disney and Henson's heirs could not agree on final terms.

After Henson's death, his "Sesame Street" associate Cooney said, "Jim was dedicated to children's education and for all his commercial success he never left his idealism. Fortunately, for the children of the world, Henson's work will live on." And, fortunately, for the adults of the world as well. Jay Myers

Jim Henson
(1936-1990)

Kelly, Patrick (1954?-Jan. 1), fashion designer known for witty clothes covered with buttons, bows, and sequins.

Kennedy, Arthur (1914-Jan. 5), actor nominated five times for an Academy Award.

Klassen, Elmer T. (1908-March 6), postmaster general of the United States from 1972 to 1975.

Kliban, Bernard (1935-Aug. 12), artist known for his cartoons of portly striped cats.

Kreisky, Bruno (1911-July 29), chancellor of Austria from 1970 to 1983.

Kushner, Rose (1929-Jan. 7), medical writer who wrote *Why Me?* (1975) about her battle with breast cancer.

Landrum, Phillip M. (1907-Nov. 19), Democratic representative from Georgia from 1953 to 1977.

Lanson, Snooky (Roy Landman) (1914?-July 2), singer on TV's "Your Hit Parade" in the 1950's.

Lausche, Frank J. (1895-April 21), Democratic governor of Ohio from 1945 to 1947 and from 1949 to 1957; U.S. senator from that state from 1957 to 1969.

Lavagetto, Cookie (Harry A. Lavagetto) (1912-Aug. 10), infielder for the Brooklyn Dodgers from 1937 to 1947; later managed the Washington Senators and Minnesota Twins.

Le Duc Tho (1911-Oct. 13), Vietnamese leader who declined the 1973 Nobel Peace Prize he was awarded for negotiating a cease-fire agreement in the Vietnam War.

LeMay, Curtis E. (1906-Oct. 1), U.S. Air Force general and former Air Force chief of staff.

Lockwood, Margaret (Margaret Day) (1916-July 15), British actress who starred in *The Lady Vanishes* (1938).

Mack, Walter S., Jr. (1895-March 18), president of the Pepsi-Cola Company from 1938 to 1951.

MacLennan, Hugh (1907-Nov. 7), Canadian author whose best-known novel is *Two Solitudes* (1945), about tensions between English Canadians and French Canadians.

Mannes, Marya (1904-Sept. 13), author and social critic.

Marble, Alice (1913-Dec. 13), tennis player who won four U.S. women's singles titles—1936, 1938, 1939, and 1940—and the women's singles at Wimbledon in 1939.

Martin, Kiel (1945-Dec. 28), actor who played J. D. LaRue on TV's "Hill Street Blues" (1981-1987).

Martin, Mary (1913-Nov. 3), actress best remembered for playing Peter Pan on the Broadway stage and on TV.

Maserati, Ettore (1894?-Aug. 4), Italian race car builder.

Matheson, Scott M. (1929-Oct. 7), Democratic governor of Utah from 1977 to 1985.

Matsunaga, Spark M. (1916-April 15), Democratic representative from Hawaii from 1963 to 1977 and senator from that state from 1977 until his death.

Maw, Herbert B. (1893-Nov. 17), Democratic governor of Utah from 1941 to 1949.

Mayes, Rufus (1947?-Jan. 9), offensive lineman for the Cincinnati Bengals from 1970 to 1976.

McConnell, James V. (1925-April 9), psychology professor at the University of Michigan from 1956 to 1988; author of *Understanding Human Behavior*, a leading college psychology textbook; former member of the editorial advisory boards of *Science Year* and *The World Book Health & Medical Annual*.

McCrea, Joel (1905-Oct. 20), actor who starred in such Westerns as *Wells Fargo* (1937) and *The Virginian* (1946).

Medina, Harold R. (1888-March 14), judge known for his fair conduct of a trial of American Communists in 1949.

Mellinger, Frederick (1915?-June 2), founder of the Frederick's of Hollywood lingerie chain.

Menninger, Karl A. (1893-July 18), psychiatrist who helped found the Menninger Clinic in Topeka, Kans.

Merivale, John (1917?-Feb. 6), Canadian-born British actor who played a brave family man on the ocean liner *Titanic* in the film *A Night to Remember* (1958).

Merrill, Gary (1915-March 5), bushy-browed actor whose best-known films include two 1950 classics, *Twelve O'Clock High* and *All About Eve*.

Meyner, Robert B. (1908-May 27), Democratic governor of New Jersey from 1954 to 1962.

Deaths

Malcolm S. Forbes, magazine publisher

Bronko Nagurski, Hall of Fame fullback

An Wang, Chinese-born computer genius

Morley Callaghan, Canadian novelist

Middleton, Drew (1913-Jan. 10), journalist who covered military and international affairs for *The New York Times*.

Minshall, William E., Jr. (1911-Oct. 15), Republican representative from Ohio from 1955 to 1975.

Moravia, Alberto (Alberto Pincherle) (1907-Sept. 26), Italian novelist.

Muggeridge, Malcolm (1903-Nov. 14), British journalist and TV commentator known for his biting wit.

Mumford, Lewis (1895-Jan. 26), philosopher, historian, city planner, and architecture critic.

Munro, Ross (1913-June 21), Canadian journalist; president of the Canadian Press news agency.

Mydland, Brent (1952-found dead July 26), keyboard player for the rock group the Grateful Dead.

Nagurski, Bronko (Bronislaw Nagurski) (1908-Jan. 7), star fullback for the Chicago Bears in the 1930's; member of the Pro Football Hall of Fame.

Nakashima, George (1905-June 15), furniture designer.

Natwick, Grim (Myron Natwick) (1890-Oct. 7), animator who created the cartoon cutie Betty Boop in 1930.

Nelson, Louis (1902-April 5), jazz trombonist; last surviving member of the original Preservation Hall Band.

Noyce, Robert N. (1927-June 3), physicist who in 1959 patented *integrated circuitry* (a method of putting an entire electronic circuit on a single semiconductor chip) and who helped found Fairchild Semiconductor and Intel Corporation, two leading manufacturers of semiconductors.

O'Brien, Lawrence F. (1917-Sept. 27), chairman of the Democratic National Committee in 1968 and 1969 and from 1970 to 1972; commissioner of the NBA from 1975 to 1984.

O Fiaich, Tomás Cardinal (1923-May 8), head of the Roman Catholic Church in Ireland and Northern Ireland.

Oliver, Susan (Charlotte Gercke) (1937-May 10), a star of the 1960's TV series *Peyton Place*.

Olsen, Arnold (1916-Oct. 9), Democratic representative from Montana from 1961 to 1971.

O'Neal, Maston E., Jr. (1907-Jan. 9), Democratic representative from Georgia from 1965 to 1971.

O'Neill of the Maine, Lord (Terence Marne O'Neill) (1914-June 13), prime minister of Northern Ireland from 1963 to 1969; made a life peer in 1970.

Paley, William S. (1901-Oct. 26), founder and first president of CBS Inc.

Pattison, Edward W. (1932-Aug. 22), Democratic representative from New York from 1975 to 1979.

Percy, Walker (1916-May 10), author who wrote about the Southern United States in such novels as *The Moviegoer* (1961).

Perls, Laura (1905-July 13), German-born psychoanalyst who, with her husband, Frederick S. (Fritz) Perls, founded the Gestalt school of psychotherapy.

Pertini, Sandro (1896-Feb. 24), president of Italy from 1978 to 1985.

Peter, Laurence J. (1919-Jan. 12), Canadian-born educator and psychologist who co-wrote the 1969 best seller *The Peter Principle*, which states, "In a hierarchy, every employee tends to rise to his level of incompetence."

Pimen, Patriarch (Sergei Mikhailovich Izvekov) (1910-May 3), head of the Russian Orthodox Church since 1971.

Powell, Michael L. (1905-Feb. 19), British film director, screenwriter, and producer who made *The Red Shoes* (1948).

Puig, Manuel (1932-July 22), Argentine novelist who wrote *The Kiss of the Spider Woman* (1979).

Rajneesh, Bhagwan Shree (1931-Jan. 19), Indian religious leader who in 1981 established a commune known as Rajneeshpuram near Antelope, Ore.

Ray, Johnnie (1927-Feb. 24), singer known for his sobbing, emotional rendering of such 1950's hits as "Cry" and "Just Walkin' in the Rain."

Reifel, Benjamin (1906-Jan. 2), Republican representative from South Dakota from 1961 to 1971; first Sioux Indian elected to the U.S. House of Representatives.

Reischauer, Edwin O. (1910-Sept. 1), U.S. ambassador to Japan from 1961 to 1966; professor of East Asian studies at Harvard University in Cambridge, Mass., from 1939 to 1942 and from 1946 to 1981.

Revere, Anne (1903-Dec. 18), actress who won a 1945 Academy Award for her supporting role as Elizabeth Taylor's mother in *National Velvet*.

Ritt, Martin (1914-Dec. 8), director of *Sounder* (1972), *Norma Rae* (1979), and other films.

Robbie, Joe (1916-Jan. 7), lawyer and owner of football's Miami Dolphins.

Robinson, J. Kenneth (1916-April 8), Republican representative from Virginia from 1971 to 1985.

Rodale, Robert D. (1930-Sept. 20), chief executive officer of Rodale Press Incorporated, a magazine and book publisher.

Rolvaag, Karl F. (1912-Dec. 20), Democratic-Farmer-Labor governor of Minnesota from 1963 to 1967; later U.S. ambassador to Iceland.

Roosevelt, Elliott (1910-Oct. 27), author and son of President Franklin D. Roosevelt.

Rose, David. (1910-Aug. 23), British-born Hollywood composer whose greatest hit was "The Stripper" (1962).

Rothschild, Lord (Nathaniel Mayer Victor Rothschild) (1910-March 20), British millionaire banker and decorated World War II intelligence agent.

Rowe, Paul (1917?-Aug. 26), U.S.-born Canadian fullback for the Calgary (Alta.) Stampeders in the 1940's; member of the Canadian Football Hall of Fame.

Rule, Elton H. (1917-May 5), former president of the American Broadcasting Companies (ABC) TV network.

Rumor, Mariano (1915-Jan. 22), five-time prime minister of Italy in the 1960's and 1970's.

St. Jacques, Raymond (James Arthur Johnson) (1930-Aug. 27), actor whose film debut was in *Black Like Me* (1964).

Schriner, Sweeney (David Schriner) (1911-July 5), Canadian hockey star; member of the Hockey Hall of Fame.

Seibert, Earl (1911-May 20), Canadian hockey star; member of the Hockey Hall of Fame.

Selznick, Irene Mayer (1907-Oct. 10), theatrical producer.

Seton, Anya (Ann Seton) (1904-Nov. 8), author of popular historical novels, including *Dragonwyck* (1944) and *Foxfire* (1951); daughter of Canadian naturalist Ernest Thompson Seton and American travel writer Grace Gallatin Seton.

Sewell, Joe (1898-March 6), batter who struck out only 114 times in a major league career that spanned 11 seasons; member of the National Baseball Hall of Fame.

Shannon, Del (Charles Westover) (1939-Feb. 8), rock singer and guitarist whose biggest hit was "Runaway" (1961).

Shepherd, Lemuel C., Jr. (1896-Aug. 6), commandant of the U.S. Marine Corps from 1952 to 1955.

Shero, Fred A. (1925-Nov. 24), Canadian-born hockey player; head coach of the Philadelphia Flyers from 1971 to 1978 and of the New York Rangers from 1978 to 1981.

Sieminski, Alfred D. (1911-Dec. 13), Democratic representative from New Jersey from 1951 to 1959.

Sinkwich, Frank (1920-Oct. 22), halfback at the University of Georgia in Athens who won the 1942 Heisman Trophy as the outstanding U.S. college football player and later played as a professional for the Detroit Lions.

Skinner, B. F. (Burrhus Frederic Skinner) (1904-Aug. 17), psychologist famous for his research into the learning process and behavior modification.

Smith, C. R. (Cyrus Rowlett Smith) (1899-April 4), aviation pioneer who helped found American Airlines; U.S. secretary of commerce in 1968.

Smith, William French (1917-Oct. 29), attorney general of the United States from 1981 to 1985.

Snyder, Mitch (Mitchell Darryl Snyder) (1943-July 5), advocate for homeless people.

Stanwyck, Barbara (Ruby Stevens) (1907-Jan. 20), actress who starred in such film classics as *Double Indemnity* (1944) and in the TV Western "The Big Valley" (1965-1969).

Stewart of Fulham, Lord (Robert Michael Maitland Stewart) (1906-March 10), Britain's foreign secretary in the 1960's; made a life peer in 1979.

Stratton, Samuel S. (1916-Sept. 13), Democratic representative from New York from 1959 to 1989.

Swann, Lord (Michael Meredith Swann) (1920-Sept. 22), chairman of the British Broadcasting Corporation from 1973 to 1980; made a life peer in 1981.

Tayback, Vic (Victor Tabback) (1930-May 25), actor who played the diner owner on TV's "Alice" from 1976 till 1985.

Taylor, Billy (1919-June 12), Canadian hockey center who played for four National Hockey League teams in the 1940's.

Terry-Thomas (Thomas Terry Hoar Stevens) (1911-Jan. 8), gap-toothed British comedian who starred in *I'm All Right Jack* (1959) and *It's a Mad Mad Mad Mad World* (1963).

Tognazzi, Ugo (1922-Oct. 27), Italian actor who played the nightclub owner in the film *La Cage aux Folles* (1978).

Torgeson, Earl (1924-Nov. 8), first baseman who played with five major league clubs from 1947 to 1961.

Turner, Dame Eva (1892-June 16), British opera star regarded as one of her country's greatest sopranos.

Turner, Joe (1907-July 21), jazz pianist.

Van Heusen, Jimmy (Edward Chester Babcock) (1913-Feb. 7), songwriter who won four Oscars for such tunes as "Swingin'" on a Star" (1944) and "High Hopes" (1959).

Vaughan, Sarah (1924-April 3), jazz singer known for her wide vocal range.

Vaughan, Stevie Ray (1954-Aug. 27), blues guitarist.

Vishniac, Roman (1897-Jan. 22), Russian-born photographer who captured a wide range of subjects, from microscopic life forms to Jews in Eastern Europe.

Wagner, Earl T. (1908-March 6), Democratic representative from Ohio from 1949 to 1951.

Rocky Graziano, champion boxer

B. F. Skinner, pioneer in behavior modification

Sarah Vaughan, jazz singer

Irving Wallace, author of best sellers

Wallace, Irving (1916-June 29), author of such best sellers as *The Chapman Report* (1960) and *The Prize* (1962).

Wang, An (1920-March 24), Chinese-born electrical engineer, physicist, and inventor who founded Wang Laboratories, a leading manufacturer of word processors.

Washington, Fred (1967?-Dec. 21), rookie defensive tackle for the Chicago Bears.

Wayne, Johnny (John Louis Weingarten) (1918-July 18), Canadian comedian who, with Frank Shuster, formed the comedy team of Wayne and Shuster.

Wearin, Otha D. (1903-April 3), Democratic congressman from Iowa from 1933 to 1939 who later became a writer of Western history and a member of the Cowboy Hall of Fame.

Wharton, J. Ernest (1899-Jan. 19), Republican representative from New York from 1951 to 1965.

White, Patrick (1912-Sept. 30), British-born Australian novelist who won the 1973 Nobel Prize for literature.

White, Ryan (1971-April 8), AIDS patient who won a court battle to attend public school and who fought for greater understanding for victims of the deadly disease.

Wilson, Earl (1906-April 27), Republican representative from Indiana from 1941 to 1959 and from 1961 to 1965.

Wyeth, Nathaniel C. (1912?-July 4), inventor of the PET (polyethylene terephthalate) plastic soda bottle; brother of painter Andrew Wyeth.

Wynne, Paul (1943?-July 5), TV reporter who chronicled his life with AIDS on "Paul Wynne's Journal."

Zwach, John M. (1907-Nov. 11), Republican representative from Minnesota from 1967 to 1975.   Sara Dreyfuss

Delaware. See **State government.**

De Maizière, Lothar (1940-   ), was elected prime minister of East Germany on April 12, 1990. He was the country's first freely elected leader since its founding in 1949—and also its last. De Maizière's primary task was to speed the monetary, economic, and social union with West Germany. The two Germanys merged on Oct. 3, 1990, and de Maizière joined Chancellor Helmut Kohl's interim government as minister without portfolio (see **Germany**). On December 17, however, de Maizière resigned from his cabinet post after failing to disprove charges that he had been an informer for the Stasi, the East German secret police. He denied the charges and pledged to work toward clearing his name.

De Maizière (pronounced *duh mayz YAIR*) was born March 2, 1940, in Nordhausen, in the state of Thuringia. His ancestors were Huguenots, French Protestants, who fled to Germany to escape religious persecution. He attended the Hans Eisler College of Music in East Berlin from 1959 to 1965. For nearly 10 years, he played the viola in theater and other orchestras, including the Berlin Radio Symphony Orchestra. An arm ailment forced him to stop playing professionally in 1976. De Maizière then studied law through correspondence courses from Humboldt University in East Berlin. After receiving his degree, he concentrated on defending anti-Communist dissidents.

De Maizière is married. He and his wife have three daughters.   Carol L. Hanson

Democratic Party. Dispirited after losing three straight presidential elections, the Democratic Party found an energizing rallying cry in 1990: unfair taxation. Democrats painted Republican President George Bush as a friend of the rich who wanted to place the heaviest tax burden on the middle class.

Bush's approval rating in public-opinion polls in early 1990 exceeded 70 per cent. In the face of such popularity, no prominent Democrats seemed eager to challenge the President's expected reelection bid in 1992. By year-end, however, congressional Republicans had revolted against Bush on tax policy, Democrats had scored gains in Congress in the November elections, and Bush's approval rating had plunged to near 50 per cent. Those developments prompted speculation that Bush might be vulnerable in 1992.

The Moynihan plan. Democratic Senator Daniel P. Moynihan of New York launched the 1990 tax debate in December 1989 by proposing a $62-billion rollback in social security payroll taxes. Reducing social security deductions, Moynihan argued, would help low- and middle-income Americans, whose tax burden had increased in the past decade. He said the rollback would also expose the fact that surpluses in the social security trust fund, which are intended to finance benefits for future retirees, are being used to mask the full extent of federal deficit spending.

Talk of taxes dominated a March 1990 issues conference in New Orleans, sponsored by the Democratic Leadership Council (DLC), an organization of moderate-to-conservative Democrats. A procession of speakers blasted Bush's most memorable 1988 campaign pledge: "Read my lips. No new taxes." Senator Lloyd M. Bentsen, Jr., of Texas, the 1988 Democratic vice presidential nominee, termed the promise "pure Bushlips." Citing the President's proposed budget for the 1991 fiscal year, which ends on Sept. 30, 1991, Bentsen said it was hypocritical of the President to say "No new taxes" while at the same time proposing programs "requiring . . . $20 billion in new revenues." Ronald H. Brown, chairman of the Democratic National Committee (DNC), added, "For 10 years the Republicans talked about tax cuts, but for all the while taxes kept going up for everybody but the rich."

The DNC endorsed the Moynihan plan at an Indianapolis meeting in March 1990. Bentsen and other prominent congressional Democrats opposed the plan, however, because it would enlarge the federal deficit.

Image quest. Democrats continued to maneuver on the tax question during the year as they sought a winning issue that would distinguish them from the Republicans in voters' minds. Their efforts to reestablish the perception of the Democratic Party as the party of the people took a fresh turn in May when more than three dozen liberal Democrats in Congress announced that they were forming a Coalition for Democratic Values. Led by Senator Howard M. Metzenbaum of Ohio, who had never been a leader in party affairs, the group issued a manifesto declaring, "The nation does not need two Republican parties."

In a midyear reversal that did more than any manifesto to energize Democrats, Bush abandoned his no-new-taxes pledge. The President's turnabout was the price for fashioning an agreement with congressional Democrats on a five-year plan to pare $492 billion from the deficit through tax hikes and spending cuts. Many Republicans opposed the accord, but Bush bowed to Democrats' insistence that the tax system be made fairer by imposing most of the new income taxes on the wealthiest Americans. The Republican split on taxes provided Democrats with the unifying issue they had been seeking for almost a decade.

Speaking at a June meeting of Democratic leaders in Portland, Ore., DNC Chairman Brown noted with satisfaction that it now appeared to be the Republicans' turn to have an identity crisis. "We have got a Republican Party that is coming unraveled," he said. "When you take the Cold War and taxes away from them, they don't have much to run on."

New York City to host next convention. The 1992 Democratic National Convention will be held at New York City's Madison Square Garden, Brown announced on July 11, 1990. New York, scene of the 1976 and 1980 conventions, offered the Democrats $22 million in cash and services to attract the meeting. New Orleans, the runner-up, had offered just $12 million. Another factor in the decision may have been that Governor Mario M. Cuomo of New York was considered a possible candidate for the 1992 Democratic nomination.

A cool reception for Jackson. Black civil rights activist Jesse L. Jackson, a presidential candidate in 1984 and 1988, remained active in Democratic affairs in 1990, though closer than usual to the sidelines. Appearing at the DLC meeting in New Orleans, Jackson delivered a speech that many of the participants found puzzling and that angered more than a few. Jackson said he welcomed the organization to the "new mainstream," claiming that the DLC had embraced his positions on taxation, military spending cuts, education, and economic development. There was no applause during the address, and DLC Director Alvin From said, "It is foolish for anyone to think the party has moved in Jesse Jackson's direction."

At its Indianapolis meeting, the DNC approved nominating rules for 1992 that may help Jackson should he make a third bid for the presidency. Delegates to the national convention will be allocated to candidates strictly on the basis of the proportion of votes each receives in primaries and caucuses. Under the previous rules, the winning candidate in a state's primary or caucus was awarded extra delegates from that state. Another new rule denies delegates from a state to candidates who fail to win at least 15 per cent of the vote.　　Frank Cormier and Margot Cormier

See also **Elections.** In *World Book,* see **Democratic Party.**

Denmark. Danish Prime Minister Poul Schlüter called for parliamentary elections in 1990 following disagreements with the opposition Social Democrats on how to boost Denmark's slumping economy. His Conservative People's Party lost 5 seats in the December 12 elections, giving them only 30 seats in the 179-member Folketing (parliament). The Social Democrats gained 14 seats, bringing their total to 69. Schlüter, who favors cutting taxes, again formed a government with the six non-Socialist parties.

Denmark and the Common Market. Denmark found itself next to a potential superpower following the October unification of East and West Germany. As a way of offsetting German power, many Danes began to see the advantages of forging closer bonds within the European Community (EC or Common Market). Even though Denmark had belonged to the EC for 17 years, numerous Danes were lukewarm about it. In part, they felt EC membership conflicted with their traditional ties to Norway and Sweden, neither of which was an EC member. Danish public opinion polls, however, showed a rise in the number of people who expected the EC to play a growing, constructive role in Denmark's future.

The change in Danish attitudes was reflected in the government's evolving stand at EC meetings. At an April summit of the leaders of EC nations in Dublin, Ireland, only Denmark and Great Britain declined to endorse a plan for greater political unity, arguing that it was too vague. But at a September meeting of EC finance ministers, Denmark urged speed in moving toward economic union and a single EC currency.

A blaze at sea claimed at least 166 lives when the Danish ferry *Scandinavian Star* caught fire off the coast of Norway on April 7. Most of the victims died from smoke inhalation. About 360 people, however, escaped the burning ship in lifeboats. Norwegian police linked the blaze to several recent unsolved cases in which fires aboard Danish ferries in the North Sea were thought to have been deliberately set.

Human-rights meeting. Copenhagen, Denmark's capital, hosted a four-week meeting on human rights held by the Conference on Security and Cooperation in Europe (CSCE). A concluding statement on June 27 pledged CSCE members to promote democratic systems, including free multiparty elections. It was the first time that the Soviet Union, a CSCE member, had opposed the idea of a single-party state.

The Persian Gulf crisis disclosed a more assertive Denmark, in contrast to Danish neutrality of recent years. Iraq's invasion of Kuwait in August involved "a clear threat to European security," Minister of Foreign Affairs Uffe Ellemann-Jensen said. The Danish parliament agreed by a large majority to dispatch one of the country's destroyers to join other European warships in the Persian Gulf.　　Joseph Fitchett

See also **Europe** (Facts in brief table). In *World Book,* see **Denmark.**

Detroit. The population of Detroit in 1990 was given, tentatively, as 970,156, a 19.4 per cent drop from its 1980 population of 1.2 million. The latest figure was the preliminary total from the 1990 United States census released in August by the U.S. Bureau of the Census. Detroit Mayor Coleman A. Young immediately charged that census takers had missed many of the city's residents when making their count.

Much more than pride was at stake. Detroit needed 1 million people to continue collecting hundreds of millions of dollars in federal and state assistance and city taxes. Under state law, Detroit can levy higher taxes than other Michigan cities as long as it has 1 million or more residents.

With so much riding on the outcome, Young sent an army of volunteers and city employees on a door-to-door canvass to find at least 30,000 city residents who had been overlooked in the census. On October 25, the mayor announced that the canvassers had located 121,350 people who had not been counted. The Census Bureau upgraded its original estimate of Detroit's population after reviewing its records, putting the city over the 1-million mark.

A city on the ropes? City leaders wondered how much longer Detroit's population would stay above that magic number of 1 million. Detroit has been losing population since about 1950, when it had more than 1.8 million people. Today, many sections of Detroit consist of empty lots overgrown with weeds.

Dinosaur

The city's problems extend to its economy, which has been declining for years. In February 1990, the Chrysler Corporation closed an outmoded assembly plant in downtown Detroit, putting about 3,500 employees out of work. Still, there were some bright spots in the economy. Construction progressed on a new Chrysler plant nearby, and most of the laid-off workers may be hired there when the plant opens in 1992.

City deficit leads to layoffs. Detroit ended the 1989-1990 fiscal year with an estimated $33.8-million deficit. To save money during the year, Mayor Young laid off 222 city employees and ordered others to cut back on travel and overtime. To save even more in the 1990-1991 budget year, Young proposed massive cuts in the city's payroll and in city services.

Police probe. The city was rocked in 1990 by a Federal Bureau of Investigation (FBI) probe of corruption in the police department. The scandal centered on former Deputy Police Chief Kenneth Weiner, who allegedly embezzled more than $1 million from an account used to fund undercover police operations. According to federal authorities, Weiner used the money to set up dummy corporations in California. Some of the taxpayer money allegedly went to pay rent on a Beverly Hills, Calif., house owned by Police Chief William Hart's daughter.

Devil's Night. Mayor Young mobilized more than 35,000 neighborhood residents and municipal workers to patrol the city on the night of October 30, known locally as Devil's Night. On that night each year, arsonists light hundreds of fires. Despite Young's effort to hold down the damage in 1990, 281 fires were reported in the city on Devil's Night and over the next two days of the Halloween period.

Planes collide. Two jet airliners collided on a runway in heavy fog at Detroit Metropolitan Airport on December 3. One of the planes caught fire, killing eight people. See **Aviation.**

Mandela visits. Detroiters in 1990 raised more than $1¼ million for South African antiapartheid leader Nelson R. Mandela. Mandela visited the city on June 28, during an 11-day North American tour. While in Detroit, Mandela visited a Ford Motor Company assembly plant and was honored at a huge rally at Tiger Stadium.

Lady of the House. Michigan got its first black congresswoman on November 6 with the election of Democrat Barbara-Rose Collins to the U.S. House of Representatives. Collins is a three-term member of the Detroit City Council and a former state representative.

New archbishop. In May, Bishop Adam Maida, a church legal expert from Green Bay, Wis., was appointed the new archbishop of the Roman Catholic Archdiocese in Detroit. Bishop Maida succeeded Edmund Cardinal Szoka, who left to take a position at the Vatican in Rome.   Constance C. Prater

In *World Book,* see **Detroit.**

Dinosaur. See Paleontology.

Disasters. The worst natural disaster of 1990 was a deadly earthquake that rocked northern Iran on June 21. The quake destroyed or severely damaged more than 100 towns and villages, burying many of the estimated 40,000 victims under rubble.

Disasters that resulted in 25 or more deaths in 1990 include the following:

Aircraft crashes

Jan. 25—Cove Neck, N.Y. A Colombian jetliner crashed in fog and rain, killing 73 of the 158 people aboard.

Feb. 14—Bangalore, India. An Indian Airlines jetliner crashed and burned while attempting to land, killing 93 of the 146 people aboard.

Oct. 2—Guangzhou, China. A hijacked Chinese jetliner crashed into two parked jets at Guangzhou airport, setting off an explosion that caused at least 128 deaths.

Nov. 14—Near Zurich, Switzerland. All 45 people aboard an Italian airliner died after it crashed into a hillside during a rainstorm.

Nov. 21—Samui Island, Thailand. A plane carrying 38 people crashed in a heavy rainstorm, killing all aboard.

Earthquakes

April 26—Qinghai province, China. At least 126 people died in an earthquake.

May 29—Northern Peru. A powerful quake claimed at least 101 lives and perhaps as many as 200.

June 21—Northern Iran. An earthquake killed an estimated 40,000 people.

July 16—Luzon island, Philippines. A quake left at least 1,650 people dead.

Explosions and fires

Jan. 14—Saragossa, Spain. An electrical fire in a discothèque produced poisonous smoke that killed 43 people.

April 16—Bihar state, India. A leaking gas cylinder exploded on a commuter train, starting a fire that caused at least 80 deaths.

Sept. 24—Bangkok, Thailand. A truck carrying liquefied natural gas crashed and exploded in a busy intersection, causing at least 54 fatalities.

Mine disasters

Feb. 7—Near Merzifon, Turkey. A methane gas explosion ripped through a coal mine, killing 67 miners.

Aug. 26—Dobrnja, Yugoslavia, near Sarajevo. More than 170 coal miners died in a mine explosion, Yugoslavia's worst mining disaster ever.

Oct. 18—Near Karviná, Czechoslovakia. A methane gas explosion and fire tore through a coal mine, killing 22 miners and leaving 8 missing.

Shipwrecks

Jan. 14—Near Mushiganj, Bangladesh. A ferry collided with another vessel and sank in the Dhaleswari River, leaving about 100 people missing and feared drowned.

Jan. 24—Anqing, China. A ferry sank after being struck by an oil tanker on the Yangtze River, killing 70 people.

Jan. 28—Near Patuakhali, Bangladesh. About 130 people were feared drowned after a ferry collided with another vessel and sank in the Lohalia River.

March 6—Near Iquitos, Peru. A riverboat sank in the Amazon River, drowning about 135 people, most of them children.

April 6—Near Moulmein, Burma (also called Myanmar). A double-decker ferry overturned in gale-force winds and sank in the Gyaing River, drowning up to 210 people.

May 20—Off Borneo, Indonesia. A passenger ship sank in the Java Sea, killing at least 68.

July 10—Off the Bahamas. Thirty-nine Haitians drowned after their sailboat capsized in choppy seas while being towed by Bahamian authorities.

Aug. 27—Nantou, Taiwan. A tourist boat overturned in Sun Moon Lake, drowning at least 21 people and leaving another 34 missing and feared drowned.

Sept. 2—Off Nigeria. Some 70 vacationers died after their boat capsized in the Atlantic Ocean.

Sept. 11—Uttar Pradesh state, India. An overloaded boat capsized in the Mahava River, causing at least 150 deaths.

Dec. 6—Off Nigeria's Cross River state. A boat capsized and sank in the Atlantic Ocean, drowning about 60 people.

Dec. 30—Near Calcutta, India. A boat capsized in the Jalangi River, drowning at least 42 passengers.

Storms and floods

Jan. 21-24—Central and southern Tunisia. At least 30 people died in torrential rains and floods.

Jan. 25—Northern Europe. A fierce storm with torrential rains and hurricane-force winds killed at least 95 people, including 45 in Great Britain and 19 in the Netherlands.

May 9-11—Andhra Pradesh state, India. A cyclone caused more than 400 deaths.

June 14—Central and eastern Ohio. Heavy thunderstorms caused flash floods that left at least 26 people dead.

Mid-June—Southern China. Severe flooding killed at least 108 people in Yunnan province and 254 in Hunan province.

June 23-25—Philippines, Taiwan, and China. Typhoon Ofelia caused an estimated 80 fatalities.

Late August—Gujarat state, India. Heavy rains caused five rivers to burst their banks, drowning at least 48 people.

August 28—Northern Illinois. A tornado killed at least 29 people in Plainfield, Crest Hill, and Joliet.

Early September—China and Taiwan. Typhoon Abe caused 108 deaths.

Sept. 11-12—South Korea. South Korea's heaviest single-day downpour in 70 years flooded the Seoul area and caused the Han River to overflow its banks, leaving more than 200 people dead or missing.

Sept. 16—Southeastern Honduras. A flash flood overturned a school bus on the road between El Naranjal and Cantarranas, drowning 25 children and 7 adults.

Sept. 19—Japan. Typhoon Flo caused at least 29 fatalities.

Sept. 22-24—Chihuahua, Mexico. Flash floods swept at least 45 people to their deaths and left another 30 missing.

Oct. 8—Bangladesh. Up to 5,000 members of fishing crews lost their lives after a cyclone swept more than 350 boats and trawlers out to sea.

Nov. 13—Philippines. Typhoon Mike left at least 188 people dead and 178 missing in the Philippines.

Other disasters

Jan. 4—Near Sukkur, Pakistan. A passenger train, accidentally switched onto a track where an empty freight train stood, rammed the freight, killing at least 307 people in the worst rail accident in Pakistani history.

April 14—Near Huinco, Peru. A truck carrying about 70 people fell down a cliff into a river, killing at least 40.

June 15—Port Harcourt, Nigeria. A school building collapsed, killing at least 100 schoolchildren.

July 2—Mecca, Saudi Arabia. About 1,420 Muslim pilgrims suffocated or were trampled to death in a stampede in a pedestrian tunnel.

July 13—The Pamirs mountains, Soviet Union. An avalanche killed 40 mountain climbers.

Dec. 21—San José Iturbide, Mexico. A bus went off a corner on a mountain road and plunged over a cliff, killing at least 48 people.   Sara Dreyfuss

An Iranian woman mourns amid the wreckage left by a devastating earthquake that rocked Iran in June, killing an estimated 40,000 people.

Dixon, Sharon Pratt (1944-   ), was elected mayor of Washington, D.C., on Nov. 6, 1990, the first black woman mayor of a large United States city. Seeking government office for the first time, she was the least-known candidate and had not been expected to win in the September 11 primary election. She also had the smallest campaign staff and campaign fund and the lowest standing in the polls of any of the five candidates for the Democratic nomination. See **Washington, D.C.**

A lawyer and former vice president of Potomac Electric and Power Company, Dixon was the only candidate to call for the resignation of then-Mayor Marion S. Barry, Jr. Barry was convicted on a misdemeanor cocaine possession charge in August and was not running for reelection.

Sharon Pratt was born Jan. 30, 1944, in Washington, D.C. She is the daughter of retired Superior Court Judge Carlisle E. Pratt. Her mother died of cancer when the little girl was 4 years old. She attended Howard University in Washington, D.C., receiving a bachelor's degree in 1965 and a law degree in 1968.

Dixon served four terms as Washington, D.C.'s Democratic national committeewoman from 1977 to 1990. From 1985 to 1989, she was treasurer of the Democratic National Committee.

Dixon is divorced and the mother of two college-age daughters.   Carol L. Hanson

Djibouti. See **Africa.**

Dog. The Westminster Kennel Club held its 114th annual show on Feb. 12 and 13, 1990, at Madison Square Garden in New York City. More than 2,900 dogs representing more than 140 breeds and varieties were in competition.

Judge Frank T. Sabella of Santa Fe, N.Mex., selected a 3-year-old male Pekingese, Champion Wendessa Crown Prince, as Best-in-Show. Edward B. Jenner of Burlington, Wis., was the champion's owner.

Favorite breeds. In 1990, the American Kennel Club (AKC) reported that it had registered 1,257,700 dogs in 1989, nearly 40,000 more than were registered in 1988. For the sixth consecutive year, cocker spaniels led the list of registered breeds. Labrador retrievers were the second most popular breed, followed by poodles, golden retrievers, German shepherd dogs, Rottweilers, chow chows, dachshunds, beagles, and miniature schnauzers.

Legislation concerning vicious dogs continued to be a hot topic in 1990. Since the mid-1980's, a rash of killings by dogs, many of them of the variety known as "pit bulls," have sparked state laws regulating dog ownership. The AKC and other interest groups fought laws that targeted specific breeds, instead promoting "generic" vicious-dog laws concerning fierce or uncontrollable dogs of any breed.

In 1990, state legislatures in Florida, New Jersey, North Carolina, and Pennsylvania enacted generic vicious-dog laws. All but the North Carolina statute include clauses that prevent local communities from enacting breed-specific laws.

America's "first dog," Millie, an English springer spaniel owned by United States President George Bush and first lady Barbara Bush, achieved a degree of literary fame in 1990. *Millie's Book, As Dictated to Barbara Bush* topped *The New York Times* best-seller list for hard-cover nonfiction on September 30 and remained a best seller for several weeks. The book, whose author is listed as Mildred Kerr Bush, was purported to be a memoir.

Crufts. In February 1990, the Crufts dog show—England's most prestigious dog event—was held in London for the last time. The Crufts show was scheduled to move to Birmingham, England, in January 1991, its 100th year. About 22,000 dogs were expected to compete in the Birmingham show.

AKC news. The AKC announced that it had sponsored 10,345 events involving more than 1.6 million dogs in 1989. In October 1990, the club began moving its registration functions and support systems to Raleigh, N.C., with the move to be completed by March 1991. The AKC executive offices, event operations, and library will remain in New York City. At its November 1990 meeting, the AKC Board of Directors named Robert Maxwell of Hauppauge, N.Y., as chief executive officer.   Roberta Vesley

In *World Book,* see **Dog.**

Dominican Republic. See **Latin America.**

Douglas, James (Buster) (1960-   ), won—and lost—the heavyweight boxing crown during 1990. On February 11, Douglas stunned the boxing world with a 10th-round knockout of undefeated champion Mike Tyson in Tokyo. Douglas had gone into the fight a heavy underdog, with a record of 29 wins, 4 losses, and 1 draw. But at 6 feet 4 inches (193 centimeters), he had a 5-inch (13-centimeter) advantage in height over Tyson, and a 12-inch (30-centimeter) advantage in reach. Sportswriters heralded the KO as one of the greatest upsets in boxing history. And they contrasted the unassuming manner of the new champ, who is known as "Buster," with the brash style of Tyson. See **Boxing.**

Douglas lost the heavyweight title in his next fight—against Evander Holyfield in Las Vegas, Nev., on October 25. Rumors abounded that Douglas had not prepared for the match, especially when he weighed in at 246 pounds (112 kilograms), a 14½-pound (6.6-kilogram) gain since the Tyson fight. A third-round KO ended Douglas' brief reign as champion and seemed to confirm the rumors.

Douglas was born on April 7, 1960, in Columbus, Ohio, the son of a middleweight boxing contender. In high school, however, young Douglas chose basketball over boxing. After a year at Mercyhurst College in Erie, Pa., Douglas returned to Columbus and began training under his father.   Karin C. Rosenberg

Drought. See **Water; Weather.**

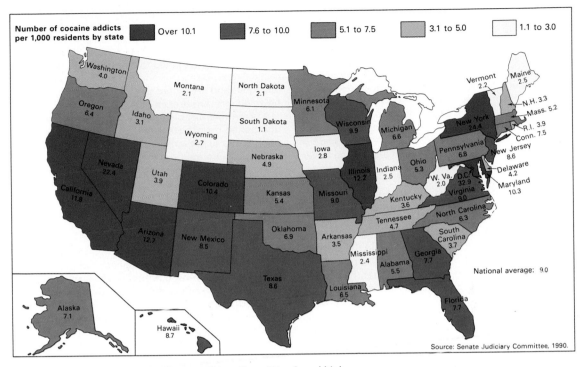

Number of cocaine addicts per 1,000 residents by state

Over 10.1 | 7.6 to 10.0 | 5.1 to 7.5 | 3.1 to 5.0 | 1.1 to 3.0

Washington 4.0
Montana 2.1
North Dakota 2.1
Minnesota 6.1
Vermont 2.2
Maine 2.5
Oregon 6.4
Idaho 3.1
South Dakota 1.1
Wisconsin 9.9
Michigan 6.6
N.H. 3.3
Mass. 5.2
Wyoming 2.7
Iowa 2.8
New York 24.4
R.I. 3.9
Conn. 7.5
Nevada 22.4
Utah 3.9
Nebraska 4.9
Pennsylvania 6.8
New Jersey 8.6
California 11.8
Colorado 10.4
Illinois 12.2
Indiana 2.5
Ohio 5.3
W. Va. 2.0
D.C. 32.9
Delaware 4.2
Maryland 10.3
Kansas 5.4
Missouri 9.0
Kentucky 3.6
Virginia 9.0
Arizona 12.7
New Mexico 8.5
Oklahoma 6.9
Arkansas 3.5
Tennessee 4.7
North Carolina 6.3
South Carolina 3.7
Mississippi 2.4
Alabama 5.5
Georgia 7.7
National average: 9.0
Texas 8.6
Louisiana 6.5
Florida 7.7
Alaska 7.1
Hawaii 8.7

Source: Senate Judiciary Committee, 1990.

A study released in May by the Senate Judiciary Committee found high rates of cocaine addiction in such states as California and New York.

Drug abuse. Concerns about cocaine, including the much-publicized conviction of Washington, D.C., Mayor Marion S. Barry, Jr., for cocaine possession, dominated the news about drug abuse in 1990 (see **Washington, D.C.**). The connection between drug abuse and crime remained a major national problem. A Senate committee report in May cited Justice Department statistics based on tests given to a random sample of suspects arrested for a wide range of crimes in major cities. The report said that almost half of the suspects tested positive for cocaine use in 1989.

Nevertheless, there were signs that cocaine use was declining. A survey of high school seniors, released by the University of Michigan in February 1990, showed that the percentage of seniors nationwide who said they used cocaine in the previous month dropped to 2.8 per cent in 1989, down from a peak of 6.7 per cent in 1985. The annual survey is considered the most reliable index available of drug abuse by teen-agers.

There was indication, too, that the almost-epidemic use of cocaine may have slowed in some cities. *The Miami (Fla.) Herald* reported that half as many people died of cocaine overdoses in the Miami area in July 1990 as in July 1989.

Declines in drug use also showed up in studies involving marijuana, alcohol, and nicotine. The Michigan survey showed marijuana use continued a downward trend begun in 1978, when users peaked at 37.1 per cent of those surveyed. In 1989, the rate of use was 16.7 per cent. The study showed a less pronounced drop in the number who said they had consumed alcohol within the previous month, which dropped from 72.1 per cent in 1978 to 60 per cent.

Cigarette smoking by high school students dropped from 36.7 per cent in 1978 to 28.6 per cent in 1989, according to the Michigan survey. But cigarettes remained a major health problem. The U.S. surgeon general's annual report on smoking and health, issued in September 1990, said smoking causes more than 390,000 deaths per year.

Intravenous drug abuse accounted for more than 30 per cent of the more than 157,000 AIDS cases reported in the United States since 1981. As a result of the AIDS crisis, many communities offered programs to help addicts kick their habit. In August 1990, the U.S. Centers for Disease Control in Atlanta, Ga., announced that these programs had success rates varying from 16 per cent in Chicago to 47 per cent in Miami.

Crack babies. Babies exposed before birth to crack—a cheap, smokable form of cocaine—by absorbing it from their mother's blood are four times more likely than other babies to be born premature and have low birth weights, birth defects, and neurological problems. The U.S. Department of Health and Human Services in 1990 estimated that, if the present trend continued for a decade, there could be 4 million cocaine-exposed babies.　　David C. Lewis

In *World Book,* see **Drug abuse.**

Drugs

Drugs. Organ rejection is a major problem in the 30,000 transplants performed worldwide each year. In August 1990, however, physicians from the University of Pittsburgh in Pennsylvania reported that an experimental drug, FK506, could revolutionize organ transplantation by helping prevent the body's rejection of transplanted organs. Rejection sometimes forces surgeons to perform two or three transplants on the same person. In studies on about 800 patients, FK506 reversed even advanced stages of rejection in kidney, heart, liver, lung, and pancreas transplants. It made patients less vulnerable to infection and caused fewer side effects than cyclosporine, the best antirejection drug in widespread use in 1990.

Ingredient ban. As part of a review begun in 1972 of 300,000 nonprescription drug products, the United States Food and Drug Administration (FDA) on Nov. 7, 1990, banned 223 ingredients used to treat conditions ranging from acne to warts. The FDA said the ingredients were not proved effective. Manufacturers, however, can submit evidence to the FDA that the banned ingredients in their products are effective and should be reapproved. In October, under the same 18-year review, the FDA banned 111 unproven ingredients used in nonprescription diet or appetite suppression products.

Respiratory drug for infants. The FDA on August 6 approved the use of Exosurf Neonatal, a drug to treat respiratory distress syndrome (RDS). RDS is a breathing disorder that affects about 50,000 premature infants each year. It kills about 5,000, making RDS one of the leading causes of death among premature infants. Infants born with RDS lack natural *surfactant*, a material that coats the inside of the lungs, keeping them from collapsing when the infant exhales. The drug is a substitute for the natural surfactant.

Enzyme replacement therapy. A new drug, approved by the FDA in March, replaces an enzyme that is missing or deficient in children with *severe combined immunodeficiency disease* (SCID). An enzyme is a protein substance that influences a chemical reaction. About 40 children worldwide have SCID, a genetic disease that is usually fatal. SCID patients are unable to fight off chicken pox, pneumonia, and other infections. The condition also is known as "bubble boy" disease, because some patients must be placed in sterile, bubblelike enclosures to survive.

Osteoporosis studies. Drugs used in the treatment of *osteoporosis*, a bone disorder that affects at least 24 million Americans, were the focus of several major studies during 1990. Osteoporosis occurs mainly in elderly women and involves a gradual loss of bone mass that makes bones brittle and vulnerable to fractures. Fractures occur most frequently in the wrist, spine, or hip. Complications from hip fractures are a major cause of death in older women.

Researchers from seven medical centers reported in July that a new osteoporosis drug, etidronate, is highly effective in preventing spinal bone fractures in elderly women. The study involved 429 women with osteoporosis. They were given etidronate for 14 days every three months for two years to slow bone loss; they also were given calcium to rebuild bone. Etidronate, already marketed to treat a rare bone disorder called Paget's disease, dramatically strengthened spinal bones and prevented spinal fractures. It did not, however, prevent broken hips.

A government-sponsored study, reported in March, questioned the effectiveness of sodium fluoride, widely used to prevent spinal fractures. It found that patients taking the drug experienced nausea and back pain and had a higher risk of hip fractures than patients not taking the drug.

Proper storage. The FDA on February 28 cautioned epilepsy patients taking carbamazepine, sold under the brand name Tegretol, to store the drug tightly closed in a dry place. New studies indicated that carbamazepine could lose up to one-third of its effectiveness if stored under humid conditions, such as those existing in most bathrooms. Chewable tablet and liquid forms of the drug were not studied.

The FDA said the studies may explain why epilepsy patients complain that the drug varies unpredictably in its effectiveness. The FDA asked manufacturers to change the drug's packaging to keep out moisture.

New warning labels. All nonprescription aspirin products must carry a warning label for pregnant women, the FDA ordered on July 2. The label must caution them not to take aspirin during the last three months of pregnancy unless directed to do so by a physician. The FDA said aspirin can affect fetal circulation and contraction of the uterus, causing problems during delivery. Manufacturers have one year to comply with the new labeling requirement.

Alzheimer's drug study. A study published on August 16 in *The New England Journal of Medicine* concluded that the only government-approved drug for Alzheimer's disease, Hydergine, may make the condition worse. An estimated 2 million Americans have Alzheimer's disease, which causes progressive loss of memory and other symptoms. Researchers compared patients given the drug for 24 weeks with those given a *placebo* (inactive substance). Hydergine patients deteriorated more quickly than those given no medication. Although the study involved only 80 patients, scientists said it was the most extensive evaluation of Hydergine ever conducted in the United States.

Colon cancer drug approved. A drug that could help the more than 21,000 Americans diagnosed each year with advanced colon cancer was approved by the FDA on June 20. The FDA said the drug, levamisole, is used in veterinary medicine to treat animals with intestinal worms. Levamisole is intended for use after surgery in patients whose cancer has spread to nearby lymph nodes. Administered in combination with an established anticancer drug, fluorouracil, it can reduce the death rate by about 33 per cent.　　Michael Woods

See also **Medicine.** In *World Book,* see **Drug.**

Eastern Orthodox Churches. A spiritual leader of the world's more than 250 million Eastern Orthodox Christians visited the Western Hemisphere for the first time in history in 1990. Dimitrios I, the ecumenical patriarch of Constantinople (Istanbul, Turkey), made pastoral visits in July to eight United States cities.

In Washington, D.C., Dimitrios met with President George Bush and on July 12 presided over the 30th Biennial Clergy-Laity Congress of the Greek Orthodox Archdiocese. There, he heard members endorse a proposal that the church allow married priests to become bishops, a recommendation requiring agreement among self-governing Orthodox churches worldwide. Also in Washington, he visited St. Nicholas Cathedral of the Orthodox Church in America, despite the fact that the Constantinople patriarchate has never recognized the Orthodox Church in America's claim to be the country's official Orthodox body.

United States Orthodox leaders regarded Dimitrios' visit as a gesture of his determination to encourage an end to church fragmentation in the United States, arising from immigrant groups that set up many ethnic churches. The patriarch also was awarded an honorary doctor's degree by Holy Cross Seminary in Brookline, Mass., and met with Orthodox delegations from the Ukrainian and Albanian churches.

Moscow patriarchate. Aleksei II was elected patriarch of Moscow on June 7, succeeding Patriarch Pimen, who died on May 3. It was the first contested election of a Russian Orthodox patriarch in Soviet history. Aleksei II, an Estonian, is the first non-Russian ever elected leader of the 50-million-member church, the largest Orthodox church in the world. On Sunday, September 23, he led the first full divine liturgy since 1918 in Moscow's Uspensky Cathedral, the most important Orthodox house of worship in the Soviet Union. It marked another significant event in the growing revival of the Orthodox Church under President Mikhail S. Gorbachev's *glasnost* (openness) policy. On October 1, the Soviet government passed a law restoring religious freedom to Soviet citizens.

Other news. Israeli settlers occupied a hospice owned by the Greek Orthodox Church in Jerusalem's Christian Quarter, claiming they had a valid sublease. On April 27, in a rare display of religious unity in the city, 150 clergy representing nine major Christian groups protested the occupation by overseeing the first closing in 800 years of the Church of the Holy Sepulcher.

The Ukrainian Orthodox Church in Canada, long considered uncanonical, was received into the ecumenical patriarchate.

An Indiana art dealer, who in 1989 was ordered to return four mosaics to the Greek Orthodox Church of Cyprus, appealed in January 1990 to the U.S. Court of Appeals in Chicago to overturn the ruling. The court on October 24 upheld the order to return the mosaics to the church.   Stanley Samuel Harakas

In *World Book,* see **Eastern Orthodox Churches.**

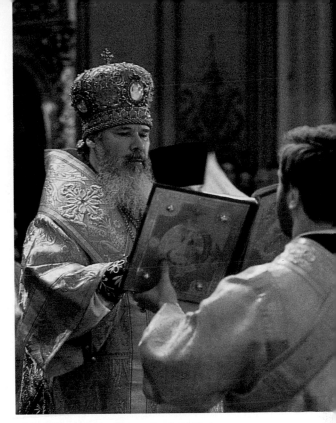

Aleksei II is enthroned as patriarch of Moscow, head of the Russian Orthodox Church, in June. He succeeded Patriarch Pimen, who died on May 3.

Economics. The world economy continued to grow in 1990, though at a slower rate than in 1989. In the United States, the economic growth rate was only about 1 per cent after adjusting for inflation. By year-end, most U.S. economists were predicting a recession, which is usually defined as six or more months of economic stagnation.

U.S. statistics. Nevertheless, the American economy experienced its eighth consecutive year of growth in 1990, a peacetime record. The nation's *gross national product (GNP)*—its goods and services output—reached an annual rate of $5.5 trillion.

The inflation rate increased in 1990, continuing an upward trend begun in 1986. The rate was expected to reach almost 5 per cent annually, as measured by the *GNP Implicit Price Deflator*, a reflection of prices throughout the economy. A narrower measure of inflation, the *Consumer Price Index*, increased more sharply—exceeding 6 per cent.

In June, 118.4 million U.S. civilians were employed, but the figure soon began to decline. By the end of December, the civilian unemployment rate had increased to 6.1 per cent. The rise in the overall unemployment rate would have been greater were it not for a slowdown in the growth of the U.S. labor force. Unemployment most severely hit workers in construction and in manufacturing. See **Labor.**

Iraq's invasion of Kuwait in August and the subsequent jump in oil prices heightened economic wor-

Economics

ries, though by December oil supplies were ample and oil prices were falling. But autumn's higher oil prices raised the operating costs of many industries and dimmed their earnings prospects.

Fears of recession. The uncertainties created by the crisis in the Persian Gulf appeared to shake both business and consumer confidence in the economy—which, economists warned, would further slow economic growth. In such a climate, businesses tend to delay investments and consumers postpone purchases. In October, the Conference Board, a business research group based in New York City, reported that consumer confidence in the economy was at its lowest level since the 1982 recession. By year-end, stock prices in the Dow Jones Industrial Average had fallen about 12 per cent from a peak in July.

Financial experts agreed that the economy was heading for trouble even before the Persian Gulf crisis began. The government budget deficit was ballooning; consumer debt, as a proportion of after-tax income, was at the highest percentage since the mid-1940's; the number of businesses going bankrupt was on the rise; and productivity—measured as output per hour—was falling. As the year wore on, housing starts declined, plant and equipment spending slowed, retail sales flattened, and after-tax corporate profits, on average, stagnated.

Many of the nation's banks, hurt by a soft real estate market and bad debts to developing countries,

sought to retrench. The banking industry's problems were dwarfed, however, by those in the savings and loan industry. By 1990, about 500 failed savings and loan institutions had been taken over by the federal government. See **Bank (Close-Up).**

Budget deficit. Confidence in the economy was apparently also weakened by the government's difficulty in deciding on a plan to reduce the federal budget deficit, which for fiscal 1990 soared to a near-record $220 billion. Only after months of negotiation did President George Bush and Congress agree on October 27 to a plan to cut $492 billion from the deficit by fiscal 1995. Economists questioned whether the five-year debt-reduction plan could bring the federal budget into balance. The plan's estimated impact, they said, was based on unusually optimistic economic assumptions.

The budget deficit was expected to reach a record high of $253 billion for fiscal 1991, which began on Oct. 1, 1990. Economists said that several factors would cause the increase, including the stagnating economy, which would decrease tax revenue; the rising costs of the savings and loan bailout; and the government's increasing interest payments on the federal debt. In October alone, interest payments on the deficit were $18.08 billion.

The Federal Reserve Board (the Fed), which sets U.S. monetary policy, had a muted reaction to the deficit-reduction package, though the Fed had long indicated

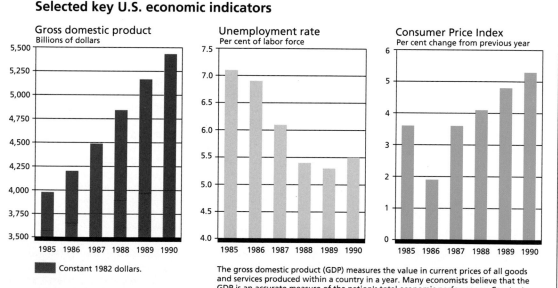

Selected key U.S. economic indicators

Gross domestic product
Billions of dollars

Constant 1982 dollars.

All 1990 figures are estimates from The Conference Board. Figures for other years are from the U.S. Departments of Commerce and Labor.

Unemployment rate
Per cent of labor force

Consumer Price Index
Per cent change from previous year

The gross domestic product (GDP) measures the value in current prices of all goods and services produced within a country in a year. Many economists believe that the GDP is an accurate measure of the nation's total economic performance. Constant dollars show the amount adjusted for inflation. The unemployment rate is the percentage of the total labor force that is unemployed and actively seeking work. The Consumer Price Index (CPI) measures inflation by showing the change in prices of selected goods and services consumed by urban families and individuals.

it would lower interest rates if the government tightened its fiscal policy. After the budget accord passed, the Fed let the *federal funds rate* (the interest banks pay each other for overnight loans) fall—but only by 0.25 of a percentage point. Later, the weakening economy prompted more rate cuts, including a cut of 0.5 percentage point in the *discount rate* (the rate banks pay to borrow from the Fed) in December.

Interest rates, both short and long term, were relatively stable through most of 1990. Short-term rates inched downward, reflecting the economic slowdown. Long-term rates rose moderately in early 1990, then flattened and declined.

The Department of the Treasury in early November had its largest bond sale ever—at the lowest rates in almost a year—despite a decline in purchases by investors in other countries. The sale appeared to ease concerns over flagging foreign interest in U.S. stocks and bonds. But foreign investment in U.S. industry and real estate declined in 1990 as investor confidence in the American economy seemed to wane.

The world economy, in general, grew at a rate of about 2 per cent, the lowest rate since 1982. Asia, led by Japan, again posted the highest growth rates, estimated at an average of 5 per cent. But many developing nations had little if any economic growth. The Latin-American economy, as a whole, contracted. In Africa, economic growth barely kept up with population growth.

Inflation in the major industrial nations—the United States, Canada, Japan, and most of the countries of western Europe—averaged about the same as in 1989, roughly 4 per cent. Inflation in developing nations, particularly Latin America, continued at much higher rates. But several countries in which inflation had been exceptionally severe in 1989—Argentina, Poland, and Yugoslavia—implemented austerity programs that pared inflation substantially.

Less developed nations, especially in Latin America and Africa, continued to grapple with foreign debt problems. By year-end, the developing nations' total foreign debt was expected to exceed $1.3 trillion, with slightly more than $500 billion owed to commercial banks and the rest to government agencies.

The Brady Plan to help developing nations reduce their commercial bank debt produced only modest results. Under the plan, named after U.S. Secretary of the Treasury Nicholas F. Brady, Mexico, the Philippines, Venezuela, and Costa Rica implemented debt-reduction accords with the banks. Uruguay negotiated a debt-reduction agreement, but by year's end it had not been put into force. Brazil began debt-reduction negotiations but made little progress. Meanwhile, the interest developing nations owed to banks kept mounting.   Richard Lawrence

See also **Bank; International trade; Manufacturing; Stocks and bonds;** and individual country articles. In *World Book,* see **Economics.**

Ecuador. See **Latin America.**

Education. A new United States secretary of education, Lamar Alexander, was named by President George Bush on Dec. 17, 1990. Alexander, a former governor of Tennessee, replaced Lauro F. Cavazos, who resigned—reportedly under White House pressure—on December 12.

New goals set. Anxiety about the quality of education provided by public elementary and high schools in the United States remained high throughout 1990. Bush, in his State of the Union address in January, announced six ambitious national educational goals. The nation's governors in February formally approved the goals, which urged that by the year 2000:

■ All children start school "ready to learn."

■ The high school graduation rate rise to at least 90 per cent of all high school students.

■ All students master challenging academic subject matter.

■ The nation's students rank first in the world in science and mathematics achievement.

■ Adult illiteracy be eliminated.

■ All schools be drug free and violence free.

The state governors and the President also approved 21 specific objectives, ranging from universally available preschools to sharply increased numbers of college students majoring in mathematics, science, and engineering. The goals and objectives grew out of an educational summit meeting between the President and the governors in 1989.

Educational reform. Deep-seated bureaucratic practices are undermining the nation's efforts at educational reform, according to a report released by the National Endowment for the Humanities on Nov. 13, 1990. The report said that education suffered from an overuse of flawed standardized tests, poor textbook selection procedures, inadequate teacher education, and an emphasis on research, rather than on teaching undergraduates, at colleges and universities.

Several revisions to the Scholastic Aptitude Test (SAT) and Achievement Tests were announced by the College Entrance Examination Board on October 31. The names were also changed to SAT I, for the verbal and mathematics skills test, and SAT II, for testing in specific subjects. The changes place more emphasis on reading skills, allow the use of calculators, and provide for an optional written essay.

These standardized tests had been widely criticized for alleged bias against women and minorities. Some critics maintained that the reforms did not go far enough and were more cosmetic than substantive. The new tests were scheduled to be administered beginning in 1994.

Educating teachers. The quality of teachers and teaching was the topic of a book entitled *Teachers for the Nation's Schools,* published in November 1990. The author, John I. Goodlad, a former dean of education at the University of California at Los Angeles, criticized the training of new teachers. Among other things, Goodlad charged that the training in

Education

education schools turned many elementary and secondary teachers into "technocrats."

The first recruits in a new project called Teach for America, a kind of "Peace Corps for teachers," went into the field in September. Teach for America was founded by 22-year-old Princeton graduate Wendy Kopp, and corporations and foundations contributed more than $2 million to the program in 1990. Teach for America was designed to attract top-ranking graduates of the nation's leading liberal arts and sciences colleges. In September, 505 recent graduates—including 85 from Yale, Princeton, Harvard, Stanford, Brown, and Cornell universities—began two-year teaching commitments in urban and rural public schools in five states.

Research or teaching? In a hard-hitting speech in April, Stanford University President Donald Kennedy charged that the reward system for professors was encouraging them to place greater emphasis on doing research than on their performance in the classroom. Kennedy said that undergraduate students were suffering as a result. He declared bluntly, "Junior faculty who show outstanding teaching ability fail at the tenure line too often, to the dismay of students who understandably wonder about Stanford's values. It is time to reaffirm that education—that is, teaching in all its forms—is the primary task."

The creation of a new reward system in higher education that would redress the balance between research and teaching on the nation's campuses was recommended in November in a report by the Carnegie Foundation for the Advancement of Teaching. Such a system would reward professors equally for focusing on different tasks during different phases of their careers. Junior professors, for example, might make publishing their top priority, while senior faculty members concentrate on the classroom.

Parent involvement. The campaign to spur reforms in public education by granting parents a greater say in selecting their children's school gained momentum in 1990. Lawmakers in Idaho and Utah passed bills permitting public-school students to attend schools outside of their regular school system, joining five other states that had already done so.

The Wisconsin legislature in March approved a bill allowing almost 1,000 low-income students in Milwaukee to enroll in private, nonreligious schools annually at state expense. The first 391 students to take part in the controversial voucher plan enrolled in eight nonpublic schools in September. The plan was challenged in the courts. A state circuit court upheld its legality in August, but the Milwaukee chapter of the National Association for the Advancement of Colored People and a coalition of education organizations petitioned a higher Wisconsin court to overturn the ruling.

A major program in support of a radical educational experiment in another troubled urban school system —Chicago—was announced in October by the John D. and Catherine T. MacArthur Foundation. Since the

beginning of the 1989-1990 school year, councils of six elected parents, two community representatives, two teachers, and a principal have been running each of Chicago's public schools, making budget, staffing, curriculum, and other decisions. The MacArthur Foundation pledged $40 million over the next 10 years to train parents and community members, upgrade teachers' skills, and draft new curriculums in the Chicago schools. In November, the Illinois Supreme Court ruled that a new system must be devised for the election of the school councils.

Cultural immersion versus segregation was an issue at the center of another educational storm in September. Milwaukee's school board, seeking new solutions to the severe academic troubles of many black male students, voted to open two African-American Immersion Schools in 1991. The schools are intended to help black boys by providing them with a special curriculum emphasizing black culture and with programs designed to foster self-esteem and responsibility. The move by Milwaukee, however, helped kindle a national debate over the appropriateness of segregating black students in such "immersion" schools and of curriculums based largely on African-American history and culture.

Educating a work force. The education of students bound directly for the nation's work force after high school graduation emerged as a major issue among policymakers in 1990. In May, the U.S. Department of Labor and the Department of Education sponsored a three-day conference on this issue in Washington, D.C. The aim of the conference was finding ways to provide the nation's 20 million young people not bound for college with the skills they need to join the nation's work force. Among the solutions proposed at the meeting were apprenticeship programs enabling students to receive both regular school instruction and on-the-job training in a trade.

A report calling for sweeping changes in the transition from school to work was published in June by a national commission of leading business, education, labor, and civic leaders. Entitled *America's Choice: High Skills or Low Wages*, its recommendations included requiring all teen-agers to earn a national certificate of educational achievement by age 16 in order to qualify for employment or further education and training. It also proposed linking the last two years of high school with a new system of technical training for students not planning on attending college.

College costs. The College Entrance Examination Board reported in September that tuition and fees at the nation's top private colleges increased 8 per cent during the 1990-1991 school year to an average of $9,391. It was the 10th consecutive year that tuition increases had outpaced inflation.

Ironically, the federal student-aid system—designed to help students pay the rising cost of a college education—itself came under attack in 1990. Between February and October, the Senate Permanent Subcommittee on Investigations, chaired by Senator Sam Nunn (D., Ga.), held eight hearings into abuses of the federal student loan system. The hearings focused on the failure of students to repay loans, a problem that cost the federal government nearly $2 billion in 1989. The bulk of the bad loans were made to students attending trade and technical schools.

The student loan problem was heightened in July 1990 when the U.S. Department of Education announced that delinquent loans had forced the Kansas-based Higher Education Assistance Foundation, the largest of 55 government-chartered agencies that guarantee federal loans, to the brink of bankruptcy. The Education Department took several steps to tighten the federal loan program, including placing sanctions on institutions with high proportions of student loans in default.

The total 1990 cost of educating all the nation's students was $359 billion, an increase of 6.9 per cent over the 1989 level. Spending for elementary and secondary education rose to an estimated $231 billion. This represented an inflation-adjusted hike of 34 per cent over education costs of the early 1980's. Higher education's budget increased to an estimated $153 billion in 1990, or 6.5 per cent above 1989.

Unfair financing. Courts struck down all or part of the system of financing public education in several states during 1990. The courts ruled that students in poor communities unable to spend much money on schooling were denied educational opportunities.

The New Jersey Supreme Court in June declared unconstitutional the state's heavy reliance on the local property tax in its education-funding formula. It ordered New Jersey to provide equal funding for poor school districts and rich ones. Before the ruling, New Jersey's poorest school systems spent an average of $4,841 per student; its richest school systems, $7,079.

In September, a district judge in Texas overturned school-finance legislation passed in June by the Texas state legislature. The bill had been designed to reduce the spending disparities between rich and poor school districts. But, in his ruling, the judge declared that the law did not go far enough and gave the Texas lawmakers a year to produce a new plan.

Kentucky's governor in April signed an ambitious school-reform law passed in response to a 1989 court ruling that went far beyond blaming spending disparities. The court had ruled that the state's entire system of public education—from the state bureaucracy to the local school boards—was responsible for Kentucky's educational inequities.

Enrollments. An estimated 59.8 million students were enrolled in U.S. schools and colleges in autumn 1990, an increase of nearly 400,000 over 1989. About 46.2 million students were enrolled in elementary and secondary schools and a record 13.6 million in colleges and universities.   Thomas Toch

See also **City; State government.** In *World Book,* see **Education.**

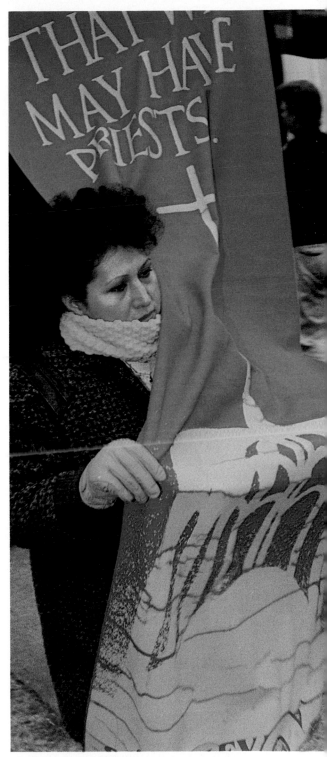

Chicago Roman Catholics protest the closing of a seminary, one of a number of Catholic schools scheduled to close because of funding problems.

Egypt

Egypt began 1990 in serious financial straits amid political discontent and persistent civil violence. President Hosni Mubarak seemed unwilling or unable to reverse the economic slide.

Although money sent home by Egyptians working abroad, earnings from tourism, and Suez Canal fees increased slightly, government revenues from petroleum, cotton, and textile exports fell sharply. Unable to either increase exports or decrease imports, the government watched its trade deficit climb to $7.5-billion and its foreign debt rise to $50 billion in 1990. The situation further endangered Egypt's ability to win new loans from international lending agencies.

Persian Gulf crisis. Egypt took the lead among Arab countries in organizing opposition to Iraq for its invasion of Kuwait in August. Egypt was a major Arab contributor to the multinational force stationed in Saudi Arabia.

Many political observers suggested that Mubarak acted to demonstrate his reliability as an ally of the United States, which provides Egypt with $2.3 billion in aid annually. He also hoped to win monetary and political concessions from the United States. In fact, in the fall, the United States canceled Egypt's $7.1-billion military debt.

Little reform. Despite Egypt's severe economic problems and intense pressure from international financial institutions, Mubarak failed to institute reforms, claiming that austerity measures would cause riots. Even without austerity measures, however, the impact of the economic situation on ordinary Egyptians grew increasingly harsh.

Inflation, which increased by 25 to 30 per cent in 1990, was especially apparent in the rising cost of food, 60 per cent of which is imported. The price of bread doubled in 1990, creating severe hardships for the poor. Meanwhile, the population—which at nearly 55 million makes Egypt the most populous Arab country—increased by 1 million people every nine months.

Unrest and civil violence. The political violence that plagued Egypt in 1989 continued in 1990. Hoping to ease unrest, Mubarak in January fired Interior Minister Zaki Badr, criticized by Egyptians for his heavy-handed measures to suppress dissent. Thousands of Islamic fundamentalists had been arrested since his appointment in 1986.

Badr's departure did not end the violence, however. Police killed 16 fundamentalists during disturbances on May 2, 1990, in the Al Fayyum region south of Cairo, Egypt's capital. During the spring, clashes between Christian Copts and Islamic fundamentalists in southern Egypt resulted in the destruction of homes and businesses. On October 12, Rifaat Mahgoub, the speaker of Egypt's parliament and the country's second-ranking official, was assassinated by unidentified gunmen.

Elections. Mubarak's National Democratic Party retained control of the People's Assembly, Egypt's parliament, in elections held on November 30. Mubarak's supporters won 348 of 437 seats, with independents capturing 83 seats and leftists, 6 seats. In May, Egypt's Supreme Constitutional Court had ruled that the parliament elected in 1987 was unconstitutional because electoral rules had limited the number of independents on the ballot. Notably, Egypt's major opposition parties boycotted the November 1990 vote, contending it was undemocratic.

Foreign affairs. The decision by the Arab League to return its headquarters to Cairo provided further evidence in 1990 of Egypt's return to the Arab fold. The league had moved to Tunis, Tunisia, in 1979, after Egypt signed a peace treaty with Israel. Egypt had been readmitted to the league in 1989.

Attempts by Egypt and the United States to negotiate a peaceful solution to the Israeli-Palestinian problem collapsed in June 1990 when Israel rejected the latest initiative. This failure created more difficulties for Mubarak.

The insistence by Iraq's President Saddam Hussein on a link between any solution to the Persian Gulf crisis and the Palestinian problem won enormous popular approval in the Arab world. As a result, Egyptian officials announced that Egyptian forces in Saudi Arabia would act only in a defensive role and would not join in an attack on Iraq.   Christine Helms

See also **Middle East** (Facts in brief table). In **World Book,** see **Egypt.**

Elections. The midterm elections of 1990 produced modest Democratic gains in the United States Congress. Democrats won a 56 to 44 edge in the Senate, picking up 1 seat in 36 contests. Two-term Republican Rudy Boschwitz of Minnesota was upset by liberal Democrat Paul D. Wellstone, a college professor.

Democratic strength in the House of Representatives increased from 258 to 267 seats. Newly elected Representative Bernard Sanders of Vermont, a Socialist who ran as an independent, caucused with the Democrats, bringing their number effectively to 268. The Republicans dropped from 175 to 167 seats. (There were two vacancies at the time of the election.)

The longest-serving House member to lose was Democrat Robert W. Kastenmeier of Wisconsin, who had served in Congress for 32 years. Kastenmeier was beaten by Republican newcomer Scott Klug, a television newsman.

Governorships. In the governors' races, Democrats emerged from the election with a 28 to 19 edge over Republicans. Two other governorships went to independents, and one race was undecided. The Democrats' preelection margin had been 29 to 21. Overall, Democratic gains in the Southeast and Southwest coupled with Republican successes in the Northeast and Midwest strengthened the moderate wing of the Republican Party (GOP), long eclipsed by conservatives.

Control of the governor's mansion shifted from one party to another in 14 states. Six incumbents were defeated—many because they raised taxes or presided over slumping state economies—and eight other governorships also shifted from one party to another. Two governorships held by retiring Democrats went to maverick Republicans who ran as independents: Lowell P. Weicker, Jr., of Connecticut and Walter J. Hickel of Alaska.

In showcase races, Democratic state Treasurer Ann W. Richards upset Republican businessman Clayton Williams in Texas, and Republican Senator Pete Wilson edged out Democrat Dianne Feinstein, former mayor of San Francisco, in California. Democrats who unseated incumbent Republicans were former Senator Lawton Chiles, who won over Bob Martinez in Florida; state Treasurer Joan M. Finney, over Mike Hayden in Kansas; lawyer Ben Nelson, over Kay A. Orr in Nebraska; and millionaire media executive Bruce G. Sundlun, over Edward D. DiPrete in Rhode Island. Democrats replaced retiring Republicans in New Mexico and Oklahoma.

Republicans who toppled sitting Democrats were state Senator John Engler, defeating James J. Blanchard in Michigan, and state Auditor Arne Carlson, defeating Rudolph G. Perpich in Minnesota. Carlson entered the race just nine days before the election after GOP candidate Jon Grunseth withdrew following accusations of sexual misconduct. Republicans also claimed formerly Democratic governorships in Massachusetts and Ohio. In Arizona, because of votes for write-in candidates, neither of the major candidates received one vote more than 50 per cent, the majority required to win. The legislature was expected to meet early in 1991 to set the date for a runoff election.

Issues. Taxes were a major issue in most states where the governorship shifted from one party to another. Tax revolt measures were defeated in California, Colorado, Massachusetts, Montana, Nebraska, and Utah, but approved in Oregon and in Dade County (Miami), Florida.

Californians rejected a sweeping "Big Green" environmental initiative, and voters in other states turned down antipollution proposals. New Yorkers spurned an environmental bond issue, and bond issues generally fared poorly. Voters, however, approved restrictions on the length of terms of public officials in Oklahoma, Colorado, California, and Kansas City, Mo.

Because polls showed widespread discontent with officeholders, many analysts had predicted widespread losses for incumbents. Only one member of the Senate (a Republican) lost a bid for reelection; and in the House, 391 of the 406 incumbents who sought new terms won. Three Democrats often mentioned as possible 1992 presidential candidates, however, had close calls—New York Governor Mario M. Cuomo, New Jersey Senator Bill Bradley, and Missouri Representative Richard A. Gephardt. House Republican Whip Newt Gingrich of Georgia, leader of an intraparty tax revolt against President George Bush, was reelected by only 1,000 votes.

Democrat Ann W. Richards waves the Texas state flag after her November 6 victory over Republican Clayton Williams in the governor's race.

Many analysts regarded President Bush as the big loser on November 6. He campaigned long and hard at a time when rumors of war and recession worked against the GOP. Bush's tax policy split his party on the eve of the elections—a factor that many saw as the main reason Republicans did not fare better in congressional races.

Mayoral races in 1990 resulted in Sidney J. Barthelemy winning a second term in New Orleans and City Councilman Jim Whelan defeating James L. Usry, indicted on corruption charges, in Atlantic City, N.J. Sharon Pratt Dixon won election as mayor of Washington, D.C., becoming the first black woman to head a major U.S. city.

1992 elections. Analysts predicted affirmative action would be an issue in 1992, after Republican candidates in North Carolina—Senator Jesse A. Helms—and California—Governor-elect Wilson—won close races hinging on white discontent over racial hiring quotas. Before the 1992 elections take place, boundaries of congressional districts will be redrawn to reflect the results of the 1990 census. Analysts say new Democratic control of governorships and state legislatures gave the Democratic Party an advantage in the redistricting.   Frank Cormier and Margot Cormier

See also **City; Congress of the United States; Democratic Party; Republican Party; State government.** In *World Book,* see **Election; Election campaign.**
Electric power. See **Energy supply.**

Electronics. The hottest consumer electronics product in 1990 was the palm-sized video camcorder. Sony Corporation was first with the TR-5, a miniature camcorder that offered most of the features found on older, larger models. The camcorder's small size was due in part to the use of an 8-millimeter videocassette, a tape format much smaller than the VHS type.

The TR-5 proved so popular that by year's end most video manufacturers offered a down-sized camcorder of their own. Companies supporting VHS, the rival video format, responded by introducing a small camcorder using a VHS-Compact cassette. Leading the VHS-C camp was Panasonic with a product called the Palmcorder. The 8-millimeter format offered longer playback time—one hour, compared with only 30 minutes for VHS in the standard playback (SP) mode.

Technical innovations. Electronics companies in 1990 offered a glimpse of products to come. The Eastman Kodak Company, working jointly with Philips of the Netherlands, developed a way to store 35-millimeter photographs on compact discs (CD's). The discs are played on a compact disc player capable of reading digitized images and displaying them on a video screen. The special Philips-made machines can also play audio discs. If the disc player is connected to a standard television set, photographs can be enlarged, reduced, or manipulated in other ways using a remote control. Officials said Kodak did not expect to market the photo CD product until 1992.

A consumer tries an electronic still camera equipped with a graphic printer, a product that went on sale in Japan in April 1990.

Matsushita Electric Industrial Company—known for its Panasonic and Technics brands—developed a voice recognition circuit for use in videocassette recorders (VCR's) in 1990. The hope is that voice recognition will make VCR's easier to program.

DAT (digital audio tape) decks were put on sale in limited quantities by Sony in 1990. With a DAT deck, music can be both played and recorded with almost no distortion. The format's future turned cloudy, though, when an agreement between machine makers and the record industry—aimed at preventing DAT owners from making large numbers of duplicate tapes—broke down. The principal cause of the breakdown was the development of a digital compact cassette (DCC) tape recorder by Philips that plays back both *analog* (conventionally recorded) tapes and digital tapes. The recording industry in general endorsed the DCC system.

Electronics firms acquire studios. MCA Incorporated, a major producer of entertainment programs, was purchased by Matsushita in December. In 1989, likewise, Sony had acquired Columbia Pictures Entertainment, Incorporated. Officials at both Sony and Matsushita believe they must control a source of video programming if future video hardware systems are to be successful.   Frank Vizard

See also **Computer.** In *World Book,* see **Electronics.**
Ellis Island. In the Special Reports section, see **Ellis Island, Museum of Memories.**

El Salvador. Peace talks between leftist guerrillas and the El Salvador government, sponsored by the United Nations, stalled once again in 1990. And the United States Congress seemed to grow weary of funding the longest U.S.-backed campaign against an internal rebellion since the Vietnam War (1957-1975).

From 1980 to 1990, the U.S. Congress approved $4-billion in aid to El Salvador's armed forces. In 1990, Congress voted to cut military aid to El Salvador in half, to $42.5 million. Many members of Congress thought that El Salvador's armed forces had not done enough to improve their record on human rights. The military's reported involvement in the murders of six Jesuit priests, their housekeeper, and her daughter on Nov. 16, 1989, was a source of particular concern.

Salvador's President Alfredo Cristiani Burkard announced on Jan. 13, 1990, that a colonel, two lieutenants, and five enlisted men had been arrested in the slayings. But a September 14 U.S. congressional report said "that a concerted effort has been made by the armed forces of El Salvador . . . to contain the investigation" and "prevent the conviction of Colonel [Guillermo Alfredo] Benavides."   Nathan A. Haverstock

See also **Latin America** (Facts in brief table). In *World Book,* see **El Salvador.**
Employment. See Economics; Labor.
Endangered species. See Conservation. In the Special Reports section, see **The African Elephant: Saved from Extinction?**

Endara, Guillermo (1936-   ), worked during 1990 to consolidate his authority as president of Panama and to speed the nation's recovery from the violent events of 1989. Endara had been installed as president on Dec. 20, 1989, while United States military forces were preparing their invasion. He staged a hunger strike in March 1990 to protest delays in receiving U.S. aid. See **Panama.**

Endara was born in Panama in May 1936. He attended Tulane University of Louisiana in New Orleans, then studied law and political science at the University of Panama in Panama City. After postgraduate work at New York University School of Law in New York City, Endara began to practice law in Panama in 1963.

Endara was a protégé of Arnulfo Arias Madrid, who was elected president of Panama three times and was ousted each time by Panama's military. In 1968, after winning the presidential election, Arias appointed Endara minister of planning and political economy. But the new government was only 11 days old when it was overthrown. Endara was forced into hiding. In 1971, he was imprisoned and then sent into exile.

In 1989, Endara ran for the presidency as the head of a coalition of forces opposed to the rule of General Manuel Antonio Noriega. Endara was the apparent winner of the voting, but Noriega ruled the elections null and void.

On June 10, 1990, Endara married Ana Mae Diaz Chen. He has a daughter from a prior marriage.   Rod Such

Energy supply. The United States Department of Energy (DOE) on Aug. 15, 1990, urged Americans to adopt a series of energy conservation measures and outlined a strategy for increasing U.S. oil production to help compensate for a cutoff of oil supplies from Iraq and Kuwait. On August 6, the United Nations imposed an economic boycott on Iraq in an attempt to force that country's withdrawal from Kuwait, which it had invaded on August 2 (see **Middle East; United Nations**). Before the invasion, the United States imported an average of 730,000 barrels of petroleum per day from Iraq and Kuwait, about 9 per cent of annual U.S. oil imports.

Conservation measures. Energy Secretary James D. Watkins said the conservation program could save about 280,000 barrels of crude oil per day. He said that U.S. motorists could save about 100,000 barrels of oil per day by properly inflating their tires. Studies indicate that about 50 per cent of all cars and light trucks have underinflated tires, which reduce gasoline mileage.

The DOE estimated that a 20 per cent increase in carpooling could save another 90,000 barrels per day. Driving at or below posted speed limits could conserve 50,000 barrels per day. And another 40,000 barrels could be saved daily if 20 per cent of U.S. households with two cars drove the more energy-efficient vehicle.

Increased output. Along with conservation measures, Watkins announced a plan to increase U.S. oil

output by 270,000 barrels per day, mainly by boosting production from Alaska's North Slope oil fields.

Watkins also urged the state of California to resolve a dispute involving a large offshore oil reserve near Santa Barbara. The reserve, which has an estimated production capacity of 80,000 barrels per day, was developed by Chevron Corporation and 17 partners. Production at the field had been stalled for nearly three years, however, because local governments and environmentalists, fearing spills, objected to Chevron's plans to use tankers to transport the oil. On November 27, Chevron announced it would begin production at the reserve and transport the oil by pipeline.

Multifuel car. As part of its energy conservation program, the government on September 13 awarded contracts to General Motors Corporation and the Ford Motor Company for the purchase of 65 "flexible fuel vehicles" for use by federal agencies. The vehicles can run on *ethanol* (an alcohol fuel made from grain), *methanol* (made from natural gas and other materials), gasoline, or any combination of the three. Computerized sensors in the vehicles monitor the fuel mixture and automatically adjust the engine for proper performance. Government officials said that many more of the vehicles would be purchased in the future to encourage the development and use of alternative fuels.

United States energy production during the first half of 1990 rose to 34 quadrillion British thermal units (Btu's), up 3 per cent from the first 6 months of 1989, the DOE reported on September 26. (A Btu is the amount of energy needed to raise the temperature of 1 pound [0.45 kilogram] of water by 1 Fahrenheit degree [0.56 Celsius degree]). Energy consumption declined by about 1 per cent to 40 quadrillion Btu's. The DOE attributed the decline to warmer-than-normal winter weather and slower-than-normal economic conditions. Imports of energy rose by about 7.6 per cent during the first six months of 1990.

Coal accounted for about 34 per cent of all U.S. energy production; natural gas, 27 per cent; and petroleum, about 26 per cent. The remaining 13 per cent was produced by nuclear power or hydroelectric plants and other sources.

Plant conversion. The world's first conversion of a nuclear power station into a power plant that burns natural gas was completed in March in Midland, Mich. The $650-million Midland Cogeneration Venture (MCV) transformed the idle Midland Nuclear Power Station into the biggest gas-fired cogeneration plant in the United States.

Unlike conventional electric generating stations, cogeneration plants produce and sell two energy products—electric power and steam. MCV generates electricity that is sold to Consumers Power Company and steam that is sold to a nearby chemical plant.

Consumers Power began building MCV as a nuclear power plant in 1973 and spent $4.2 billion on the project. But financial problems forced the abandonment of the plant in 1984, when it was 85 per cent completed. MCV officials said that there are 15 to 20 other nuclear power plants in the United States, abandoned at various stages of construction, that also could be converted to burn natural gas or coal.

Seabrook operational. After two decades of protests and huge cost overruns, the Seabrook Nuclear Power Station in New Hampshire began regular commercial operation on Aug. 19, 1990. The plant had become a symbol of the national debate over the safety of nuclear power. When utility officials applied for a construction permit for Seabrook in 1973, they planned to build two nuclear reactors for less than $1-billion, with the first starting commercial operation in 1979. But opponents of nuclear energy and long construction delays forced them to scale back the project to a single unit that cost $6.6 billion.

Nuclear power plants supplied about 20.5 per cent of U.S. electricity during the first half of 1990, up from 17.9 per cent during the first six months of 1989, according to the DOE. As of June 30, 1990, there were 112 operable nuclear generating units in the country.

Nuclear power worldwide. The International Atomic Energy Agency, an agency based in Vienna, Austria, that promotes the safe and peaceful use of nuclear energy, reported in February that the number of operating nuclear power plants in the world reached 435 in 1989. During that year, 10 new plants started regular operation. By early 1990, nuclear power plants produced about 17 per cent of the world's electricity.

Wind power has tremendous untapped potential for meeting U.S. energy needs, a new study of wind resources concluded on September 25. The study, conducted for the DOE, found that only four states—Alabama, Florida, Louisiana, and Mississippi—do not have usable winds for operating wind turbines. (Usable wind is wind blowing at an average of 16 miles [26 kilometers] per hour at 165 feet [50 meters] above ground level.) All other states have usable winds.

The study found, however, that none of the states has seriously tapped this energy source. Even California, which has 15,000 wind turbines, has developed only 20 per cent of the areas with usable winds. More than a dozen other states have a wind energy potential equal to or greater than California's. Theoretically, harnessing the winds could meet all U.S. energy needs, the study concluded. But energy storage, transmission, and other problems associated with wind turbines still limit their practical application.

Using what we have. The application of existing knowledge about energy efficiency could sharply reduce future U.S. demand for electricity, according to studies reported in August by the Electric Power Research Institute. The institute, based in Palo Alto, Calif., conducts research and development for the electric utility industry.

The institute concluded that adoption of the most efficient electric technologies by consumers, busi-nesses, and industry could reduce estimated energy consumption by 24 to 44 per cent by the year 2000. But the savings would be difficult and expensive to achieve, requiring a firm nationwide commitment to energy efficiency.

Consumers, for instance, would have to equip their homes with advanced heat pumps for heating and cooling and advanced water heating systems. Stores and other commercial buildings would have to be designed specifically for energy efficiency, using high-efficiency cooling and lighting systems. Industrial plants would have to switch to new variable-speed electric motors and a variety of newer technologies for heating and melting metals and other materials.

Modular nuclear plant. The DOE on February 27 awarded the Westinghouse Electric Corporation a $50-million contract for the development of a simpler, safer nuclear power plant. Westinghouse and other electric utilities will contribute $50 million to the effort to develop AP600, a 600-megawatt nuclear power plant that would be assembled on-site from factory-built modules. Unlike conventional nuclear power stations, which are designed individually, AP600 would be built according to a standardized design, reducing both costs and the time needed for government safety reviews.   Michael Woods

In *World Book,* see **Energy supply.**

Engineering. See **Building and construction.**

England. See **Great Britain.**

Environmental pollution. The year 1990 marked the 20th anniversaries of three events of particular importance to environmentalists in the United States. In 1970, Americans celebrated the first Earth Day; the U.S. Environmental Protection Agency (EPA) was created; and important amendments to the federal Clean Air Act were enacted. Twenty years later, environmentalists reflected on their past accomplishments and renewed their commitment to tackle important unresolved environmental problems.

Earth Day. On Sunday, April 22, 1990, millions of Americans gathered in parks and other public places to commemorate the anniversary of Earth Day with balloons, bands, and banners. As part of a national environmental movement, people planted trees, launched recycling campaigns, and shared information on strategies to reduce pollution.

Clean Air Act of 1990. President George Bush had hoped to kick off the Earth Day festivities by signing into law sweeping new changes to the Clean Air Act, a cornerstone of the government's attempts to combat pollution. But congressional debate over this bill—which promised to strengthen and expand controls on air polluters for the first time in 13 years—dragged on for six months past Earth Day.

Bush signed the bill into law on November 15. The new law, the Clean Air Act of 1990, was a blueprint for reducing pollution that causes acid rain, smog, and damage to the earth's protective layer of ozone in the

Workers clean up an oil spill on southern California's Huntington Beach after a tanker accident a few miles off the coast on February 7.

upper atmosphere. For example, the act lowered allowable emissions of sulfur dioxide to the level released in 1980. The 1990 law also reduced permissible emissions of nitrogen oxides. Both pollutants contribute to the formation of acid rain and smog, an eye and lung irritant

Areas where smog levels routinely exceed legal standards will be required to institute additional controls. Communities may be required to use new types of gasoline that produce less pollution when burned, to place stricter controls on car and truck tail-pipe emissions, and to extend strict limits on emissions to small industrial sources of pollution, such as bakeries and dry cleaners.

The new law also limits the release of cancer-causing air pollutants. Only benzene and six other chemicals known to cause cancer were regulated under the previous Clean Air Act. The revised law will regulate emissions of at least 182 more chemicals. About 90 per cent of the emissions from the 30 most severe regional polluters are to be controlled. The law also mandates that by 1995 the EPA propose a strategy to reduce the urban cancer risk from air pollutants by 75 per cent.

In addition to dozens of other new provisions, the act establishes a Chemical Safety Hazard Investigation Board to look into chemical accidents. The law also creates a research program to evaluate the hazards posed by the accidental release of toxic chemicals.

Widening ozone hole. In early October, researchers at the National Aeronautics and Space Administration's Goddard Space Flight Center in Greenbelt, Md., announced that for the second year in a row seasonal thinning in the layer of ozone in the upper atmosphere above Antarctica was as severe as during the worst year on record. Chlorine-containing air pollutants, such as chlorofluorocarbons (CFC's), contribute to the destruction of this layer of ozone, which protects life on earth by absorbing almost all of the sun's damaging ultraviolet radiation. In some areas above Antarctica, nearly all the ozone at the base of the upper atmosphere has been depleted, according to a Goddard scientist's report. The findings surprised researchers, who had previously observed a yearly variation between mild and severe ozone depletions.

In September, U.S. government-funded scientists announced that chlorinated pollutants had destroyed up to 35 per cent of the ozone layer above the Arctic. The level of destruction is up to three times greater than previously detected. Because of differences in the circulation of the atmosphere above the Arctic and Antarctica, an ozone "hole" has not formed above the Arctic.

Ozone-protection treaty. Representatives of 59 nations meeting in London agreed on June 29 to stop producing CFC's and halons—chemicals believed most responsible for the ozone layer depletion. Most nations will halt production by the year 2000; develop-

289

Environmental activists depict the garbage problem as a "trash monster" during Earth Day celebrations in New York City on April 22.

ing nations have until 2010. The agreement exceeds the provisions called for in an earlier treaty known as the Montreal Protocol.

To comply with the new timetable for a CFC and halons phase-out, the revised Clean Air Act requires the EPA to ban U.S. production of the five most destructive CFC's by 2000, along with three types of halons and carbon tetrachloride, a solvent. The new Clean Air Act also schedules a slowdown in the production of hydrochlorofluorocarbons (HCFC's), a related group of chemicals, by 2015 and their total phase-out by 2030. Until then, HCFC's are expected to replace CFC's as refrigerants.

Acid rain. The U.S. government's $535-million National Acid Precipitation Assessment Program (NAPAP) in 1990 concluded its 10-year study of the impact of acid rain on air and water quality in the United States. Although NAPAP officially ceased operations on October 1, the new Clean Air Act requires that the EPA revive it to continue its assessment.

Throughout the year, NAPAP released several dozen documents describing research into the effects of acid rain. According to the program, the overall impact of acid rain has been limited. The research suggests that only 10.5 per cent of the lakes in the Adirondack Mountains and 6 to 7 per cent of the streams in mid-Atlantic states owe their acidity to sulfur-containing compounds, which make up a portion of acid rain. These areas are considered the most harmed by acid

rain in the United States. NAPAP also concluded that acid rain has not reduced crop yields or visibly harmed "the vast majority" of U.S. forests.

The organization also said that it had understated acid rain's effects and that in some regions acid rain appears to have caused severe problems. According to a study presented at a February NAPAP conference, for example, acid rain has led to the death of all fish in roughly 8 per cent of the lakes in New York's Adirondack Mountains.

Haze remains the most visible effect of the air pollutants that cause acid rain. These pollutants account for 60 per cent of the haze in the Eastern United States and 30 per cent of the haze in the West, according to a NAPAP document.

The revised Clean Air Act is expected to dramatically reduce emissions of the pollutants that cause acid rain. Nevertheless, a NAPAP assessment issued in mid-September noted that reductions in acid rain will be proportionately less than emission reductions over most of the East. This is because pollution emissions are not evenly distributed. About 50 per cent tend to settle fairly close to their source; the rest stay aloft and travel farther. Also, mountains, prevailing winds, and rainfall patterns can dramatically affect the proportional fallout of pollutants.

Oil-spill cleanup. In August, Congress established a new oil-spill cleanup fund, paid for by a tax on crude oil. The fund provides up to $1 billion in federal funds per oil spill—up to $500 million of that for the restoration or replacement of natural resources. The March 1989 *Exxon Valdez* oil spill in Alaska's Prince William Sound—the largest tanker spill ever in U.S. waters—galvanized support for a federal law creating the fund, which had been stymied in Congress for 15 years.

The law requires most tankers and barges to have by the year 2015 double hulls, which limit the risk of spillage after collisions. The law also mandates that all shippers and all ports develop improved contingency plans for dealing with spills. Shippers' liability for spills also increased dramatically. Before the law took effect, tanker owners were liable for damages up to $14 million, depending on the size of the ship. Now, shippers are responsible for damages of up to $500 million per spill. In cases of gross negligence or cover-up, there would be no limit on the shipper's financial responsibility.

The *Exxon Valdez* spill also highlighted the oil industry's inability to cope with large spills. In September 1990, the industry established a network for containing and cleaning up such spills in U.S. waters. Expected to be fully operational by March 1993, the Marine Spill Response Corporation will clean up catastrophic spills and conduct research to improve cleanup technology.   Janet Raloff

See also **Conservation.** In *World Book,* see **Environmental pollution.**

Equatorial Guinea. See **Africa.**

Scavengers in the Ethiopian port of Massawa, captured by rebel forces in February, collect grain that has survived a government bombing raid.

Ethiopia. Events during 1990 severely weakened the regime of President Mengistu Haile-Mariam. After peace talks stalled, government forces resumed civil wars with the Eritrean People's Liberation Front (EPLF)—which sought a separate state in Eritrea in the far north—and with the Tigre People's Liberation Front—a separatist group in the Tigre region just south of Eritrea.

Mengistu's army is the largest in sub-Saharan Africa, and more than 70 per cent of Ethiopia's budget is allocated to the military. The civil wars did not go well for the Marxist regime. As relations between the United States and the Soviet Union warmed, the Soviets agreed to remove their military advisers from Ethiopia. All Cuban troops had left, and Ethiopia's ties to eastern European nations were being broken.

To fill the gap left by departing allies, Mengistu reopened diplomatic ties with Israel. In exchange for Israeli advisers and military equipment, some of the estimated 17,000 Ethiopian Jews were allowed to immigrate to Israel. With Libya, Syria, and other Islamic states supporting the EPLF, Israel hoped to avoid Eritrea's becoming an Islamic nation. Ironically, many EPLF leaders are Christian, and Mengistu has also received aid from Islamic countries.

The vulnerability of the Mengistu army was evident in the EPLF seizure of the key port city of Massawa (also spelled Mitsiwa) in February. About 30,000 government soldiers were killed, wounded, or captured in a two-month struggle for the city. The EPLF rebels, using abandoned or confiscated Soviet equipment, reduced the presence of the Mengistu army in Eritrea to the regional capital, Asmara, where some 120,000 government troops were stranded.

The shift toward capitalism in eastern Europe and the Soviet Union forced Mengistu to adopt new policies in 1990. In a five-hour speech on March 5, Mengistu stunned Ethiopians by announcing that the government would sell state-held land to private owners, encourage private enterprise, and allow farmers to own land and sell crops in private markets. Mengistu said that state-owned businesses were to become profitable or they would be sold or shut down. The name of the ruling Workers' Party was to be changed to the Democratic Unity Party. Thus ended Ethiopia's 17-year experiment with Marxism.

Inadequate rainfall in Eritrea, parts of Tigre, and other northern areas put more than 4 million people at risk of famine. Both the government and the rebels interfered with relief efforts, though in November the EPLF agreed to open Massawa to food shipments on vessels flying the United Nations flag.

Ethiopia in 1990 was one of the six poorest nations in the world. A 50 per cent drop in the price of coffee—the nation's major export crop—worsened the poverty.   J. Gus Liebenow and Beverly B. Liebenow

See also **Africa** (Facts in brief table). In *World Book,* see **Ethiopia.**

Europe

As the Cold War came to an end in 1990, Europe faced a dramatic restructuring. For more than four decades, the Cold War had split Europe into two blocs: one in western Europe allied with the United States and the other in eastern Europe backed by the Soviet Union. Only a handful of European countries were neutral. A parade of diplomatic events during 1990 marked stages in Europe's adjustment to the collapse of Communist governments in the eastern bloc.

Along with the unexpected political upheaval in eastern Europe, western Europe confronted a restructuring of its own making. During 1990, the European Community (EC or Common Market) accelerated the movement toward the full economic integration of its member states: Belgium, Denmark, France, Great Britain, Greece, Ireland, Italy, Luxembourg, the Netherlands, Portugal, Spain, and a newly unified Germany. By Jan. 1, 1993, all economic barriers among the 12 EC nations are to be removed, allowing the free movement of goods, people, and money.

With the easing of east-west tensions, EC members engaged in a first round of talks about closer cooperation on security. Such talks could eventually lead to a cooperative defense establishment for European nations. At the same time, western European governments saw the need to help newly liberated nations in eastern Europe in their efforts to achieve political and economic stability.

One Germany came into being on Oct. 3, 1990, when West Germany, Europe's leading economic power, was reunited with East Germany. Following its defeat in World War II (1939-1945), Germany had been divided into zones that later became West Germany and East Germany. German unification had become a possibility after the opening of the Berlin Wall on Nov. 9, 1989.

France and Britain at first sought to slow Germany's rush toward unification, fearing that an even more powerful Germany might stand apart from European economic unity and collective security arrangements. In an effort to calm these fears, West German leaders called for more rapid and tighter EC integration. After East Germans voted for unification in large numbers on March 18, 1990, western European leaders accepted the inevitable, hoping that a unified Germany would actually strengthen the EC.

But the final decision on German unification rested with the four Allied powers that had defeated Germany in World War II: France, Great Britain, the Soviet Union, and the United States. In June, one of the last barriers to Allied approval fell when Soviet President Mikhail S. Gorbachev gave permission for a united Germany to remain in the North Atlantic Treaty Organization (NATO), the security alliance of 16 nations in North America and western Europe. Under a treaty that was signed on September 12, the four Allies gave up their remaining rights as occupying powers, freeing the two Germanys to reunite on October 3. See **Germany.**

Toward 1992. As the Germanys moved toward union, so did the European Community. At an EC summit meeting in Dublin, Ireland, in June 1990, the leaders of EC nations agreed to hold two intergovernmental conferences in December: one on monetary union and the other on political union.

To further monetary union, the EC leaders agreed in October to form a European central bank, which would operate independently of member governments—somewhat along the lines of the U.S. Federal Reserve System. The bank's role would be to manage the money supplies of EC nations. The creation of the bank, scheduled to begin operation in 1994, paves the way for replacing national currencies with a single European currency. The agreement, known as Economic and Monetary Union (EMU), was reached despite opposition from Margaret Thatcher, then Britain's prime minister. Thatcher objected to giving up control over Britain's monetary policy and to adopting a European currency in place of the British pound. Meetings began in December 1990 to draw up an EMU treaty.

Nine of the 12 EC members had already aligned their exchange rates under the European Monetary System. In October, Britain became the 10th member to do so. Greece and Portugal have not joined.

Some progress was made on the trade front as well. The European Commission, the EC's executive body, proved surprisingly vigorous in promoting free trade in Europe—for U.S. companies too. The commission also tried to prevent state-owned companies from receiving privileged treatment from their governments. But the commission was less successful in negotiating away trade barriers between the EC and Japan. And EC farm subsidies and farm price supports proved a major obstacle to success in four years' negotiations on reducing world trade barriers.

EC political union came under discussion in 1990 at the urging of French President François Mitterrand and German Chancellor Helmut Kohl. What form political union might take was to be debated by the foreign ministers of EC countries, beginning in December. France and Britain preferred that the national governments and parliaments of EC members play the leading role in a future political structure. Germany and most of the smaller countries hoped to see more authority given to the European Parliament, the legislative arm of the EC. But the issue dominating debate on political cooperation during 1990 was the nature of post-Cold War European security arrangements.

What role for NATO? During the Cold War, NATO provided for the collective defense of western Europe

Fireworks light up the sky over the Reichstag in Berlin, the past home of the German parliament, as East and West Germany unite on October 3.

against possible Soviet aggression. NATO's 16 members are Canada, Iceland, Norway, Turkey, and the United States, plus all the EC nations except Ireland. The disintegration of the Warsaw Pact, NATO's counterpart in the Soviet bloc, called into question NATO's future role. The threat of a ground invasion from the east dimmed as the Soviet Union withdrew its forces from eastern Europe and lost its influence over armed forces in the region.

At a NATO summit meeting in London on July 5 and 6, U.S. President George Bush won acceptance of a U.S. plan to maintain NATO as the backbone of defense cooperation in Europe. Under the U.S. plan, NATO would, however, cut its troop strength and nuclear weaponry and tone down its anti-Soviet rhetoric. European leaders approved the U.S. approach because it was aimed at getting Gorbachev to agree that a united Germany could remain in NATO.

Iraq's invasion of Kuwait on August 2 intensified the European debate on security. The United States quickly organized a military force to defend Western interests in the Persian Gulf region, especially the petroleum that both Europeans and Americans rely upon. Although grateful to the United States, many Europeans—who expected an era of international cooperation to follow the collapse of the Cold War—were alarmed at finding the defense of their interests again dependent on U.S. military force.

Britain and France both provided military assistance to the U.S.-led gulf effort. They acted in part to show that they still were world powers and thus to fend off suggestions that their permanent seats in the United Nations (UN) Security Council should be given to Germany and Japan. Although Kohl was eager to help his allies, he said that the German Constitution prohibited him from sending troops outside Europe. All the European leaders—except for Thatcher, who was more hawkish than Bush—pressed the Bush Administration to seek backing from the UN Security Council before acting against Iraq, so that any U.S. action would have international political legitimacy.

Many Europeans, however, felt uneasy at having to follow U.S. policy, possibly even in attacking Iraq. Their unease was increased by the scale of the U.S. build-up in the gulf, which speeded the withdrawal of U.S. forces from Europe. (By Christmas, nearly half the 230,000 U.S. troops in Europe had been transferred to the gulf, and there seemed little likelihood that they would return.) During the Cold War, U.S. domination of NATO had been seen as a valuable safeguard against the threat of Soviet aggression. But few Europeans wished to see a U.S.-led NATO become the vehicle for intervention in crises around the world.

European security alternatives. European leaders felt, however, that the moment was not ripe for the EC, which includes neutral Ireland, to assume a military role itself. And many European leaders were eager to see the United States maintain some military presence in Europe, where the Soviet Union remained

the strongest military power. Some Europeans foresaw a larger role for the Western European Union (WEU), a defense organization of nine EC members that also belong to NATO. Officials of the WEU viewed their organization as a bridge between the EC and NATO. In addition, they felt the WEU could promote a collective European defense effort and perhaps even develop a multinational European peacekeeping force. Such a force might be needed in the event of turmoil in eastern Europe.

A number of Europeans held hopes that the Conference on Security and Cooperation in Europe (CSCE) could lay the groundwork for a new, peaceful order in Europe, both eastern and western. This body—which was created at Helsinki, Finland, in 1975—has provided a forum for improving relations among the European nations, the Soviet Union, the United States, and Canada. It reassured the Soviets by recognizing post-World War II boundaries in eastern Europe that had never been settled by a peace treaty. The CSCE also provided a framework for discussing disarmament in Europe, and it helped advance human rights in the Soviet bloc.

By the time a CSCE summit took place in Paris on Nov. 19-20, 1990, however, most government leaders recognized that the organization could not serve as a substitute for NATO in safeguarding European security. Because the CSCE worked by consensus, any member could paralyze action by a veto in a crisis. Although the CSCE would remain a consultative body for defusing conflicts, it was not an alliance to deter aggression.

The key event at the CSCE summit was the signing of a treaty that reduced conventional forces—including tanks, artillery, and combat aircraft—in Europe. The treaty covered the main armaments from the Atlantic Ocean to the Ural Mountains in the Soviet Union. It affected 22 nations: the United States and its 15 NATO allies as well as the Soviet Union and its 5 former allies in eastern Europe. The effect of the treaty's sweeping cuts was to eliminate the threat of a surprise attack on western Europe by Soviet conventional forces. Political changes in eastern Europe had greatly reduced that threat already. See **Armed forces.**

Threats to security. Many unresolved questions remained to imperil European security. They arose from the political changes in eastern Europe. As the former Soviet satellites struggled to develop democracies and free-market economies after four decades of Soviet domination, the Soviet Union itself slid into political disunity and economic disintegration.

In an effort to prevent chaos, the EC—led by Germany—sought ways to help stabilize its eastern neighbors. The EC coordinated economic aid to eastern Europe from the wealthier nations, and in December it authorized $1 billion in emergency food aid for the Soviet Union. West Germany poured money into East Germany prior to unification and provided financial help to other countries in the region.

Facts in brief on European countries

Country	Population	Government	Monetary unit*	Foreign trade (million U.S.$)	
				Exports†	Imports†
Albania	3,298,000	Communist Party First Secretary and People's Assembly Presidium Chairman Ramiz Alia; Council of Ministers Chairman Adil Çarçani	lek (5.19 = $1)	378	255
Andorra	52,000	The bishop of Urgel, Spain, and the president of France	French franc & Spanish peseta	1	531
Austria	7,490,000	President Kurt Waldheim; Chancellor Franz Vranitzky	schilling (10.44 = $1)	31,200	37,900
Belgium	9,946,000	King Baudouin I; Prime Minister Wilfried Martens	franc (30.72 = $1)	100,300	100,100 (includes Luxembourg)
Bulgaria	9,015,000	President Zhelyu Zhelev; Prime Minister Dimitar Popov	lev (2.85 = $1)	20,300	21,000
Czechoslovakia	15,700,000	President Václav Havel; Premier Marián Čalfa	koruna (23.83 = $1)	24,500	23,500
Denmark	5,122,000	Queen Margrethe II; Prime Minister Poul Schlüter	krone (5.71 = $1)	27,700	26,400
Finland	4,976,000	President Mauno Koivisto; Prime Minister Harri Holkeri	markka (3.58 = $1)	22,200	22,000
France	56,375,000	President François Mitterrand; Prime Minister Michel Rocard	franc (5.03 = $1)	183,100	194,500
Germany	77,454,000	President Richard von Weizsäcker; Chancellor Helmut Kohl	mark (1.48 = $1)	354,100	561,600
Great Britain	57,537,000	Queen Elizabeth II; Prime Minister John Major	pound (0.51 = $1)	151,000	189,200
Greece	10,062,000	President Constantine Karamanlis; Prime Minister Constantine Mitsotakis	drachma (153.84 = $1)	5,900	13,500
Hungary	10,544,000	President Arpad Goncz; Prime Minister Jozsef Antall	forint (60.96 = $1)	19,100	18,300
Iceland	255,000	President Vigdis Finnbogadóttir; Prime Minister Steingrímur Hermannsson	krona (54.7 = $1)	1,400	1,600
Ireland	3,755,000	President Mary Robinson; Prime Minister Charles Haughey	pound (punt) (0.56 = $1)	20,300	17,300
Italy	57,838,000	President Francesco Cossiga; Prime Minister Giulio Andreotti	lira (1,118 = $1)	141,600	143,100 (includes San Marino)
Liechtenstein	28,000	Prince Hans Adam I; Prime Minister Hans Brunhart	Swiss franc	no statistics available	
Luxembourg	367,000	Grand Duke Jean; Prime Minister Jacques Santer	franc (30.72 = $1)	100,300	100,100 (includes Belgium)
Malta	350,000	President Vincent Tabone; Prime Minister Eddie Fenech Adami	lira (0.30 = $1)	710	1,360
Monaco	30,000	Prince Rainier III	French franc	no statistics available	
Netherlands	14,803,000	Queen Beatrix; Prime Minister Ruud Lubbers	guilder (1.67 – $1)	110,300	100,900
Norway	4,224,000	King Olav V†; Prime Minister Gro Harlem Brundtland	krone (5.81 = $1)	22,200	18,700
Poland	38,611,000	President Lech Walesa	zloty (9,500 = $1)	24,700	22,800
Portugal	10,314,000	President Mário Alberto Soares; Prime Minister Aníbal Cavaço Silva	escudo (131.2 = $1)	11,000	17,700
Romania	23,379,000	President Ion Iliescu; Prime Minister Petre Roman	leu (34.93 = $1)	11,500	8,750
San Marino	23,000	2 captains regent appointed by Grand Council every 6 months	Italian lira	(included in Italy)	
Spain	39,479,000	King Juan Carlos I; Prime Minister Felipe González Márquez	peseta (94.74 = $1)	40,200	60,400
Sweden	8,336,000	King Carl XVI Gustaf; Prime Minister Ingvar Carlsson	krona (5.58 = $1)	52,200	48,500
Switzerland	6,528,000	President Arnold Koller§	franc (1.27 = $1)	51,200	57,200
Turkey	57,301,000	President Turgut Özal; Prime Minister Yildirim Akbulut	lira (2,867.39 = $1)	11,700	14,300
Union of Soviet Socialist Republics	289,588,000	Communist Party General Secretary & President Mikhail S. Gorbachev	ruble (0.56 = $1)	110,700	107,300
Yugoslavia	23,971,000	President Borisav Jović; Federal Executive Council President Ante Marković	dinar (10.39 = $1)	13,100	13,800

*Exchange rates as of Dec. 7, 1990, or latest available data. †Latest available data.

‡Crown Prince Harald acted as head of state in 1990 while his father, King Olav V, recovered from a stroke.

§Koller was succeeded on Jan. 1, 1991, by Flavio Cotti.

Romanians stream into the U.S.S.R. to be reunited with relatives in Moldavia after the border, closed for 50 years, opened for six hours on May 6.

Germany also took the lead in sending food and other economic assistance to the Soviet Union. This effort aimed not only at helping the Soviet people get through the winter but also at keeping alive their hopes that conditions could improve under Gorbachev. European leaders were alarmed that the Soviet Union might collapse into civil war, perhaps as rival groups clashed within the armed forces. Short of that, western European governments braced for a flood of refugees from the Soviet Union that could swamp social services in western Europe and even destabilize eastern European countries.

Anxious to protect their own economies, EC nations tightened their laws on immigration in 1990 and also gave up any thoughts of admitting new members to the EC before 1993. As the nations of the EC closed ranks, the neutral countries became increasingly alarmed at the prospect of finding themselves left out of the new Europe. Four neutral countries—Austria, Finland, Sweden, and Switzerland—belong to the European Free Trade Association (EFTA), along with NATO members Iceland and Norway. EFTA had hoped at the start of the year to create an enlarged tariff-free trading zone with the EC. But EFTA was rebuffed after it pressed for a say in certain significant areas of EC policymaking.

The growing EC unity was powerfully symbolized by the building of a tunnel beneath the English Channel to connect Britain and the Continent. The first link-up of French and British sections of the tunnel occurred on Dec. 1, 1990. The surprise ouster of Thatcher as Britain's prime minister only days before was widely viewed as a sign that she had misjudged British public opinion on European unity. Thatcher had been outspoken in her resistance to tighter EC integration and in her preference for maintaining Britain's special relationship with the United States.

In these critical times, many long-time European leaders seemed to be losing popularity and authority, perhaps because they had been in power so long. This trend affected not only Thatcher, who had been in office for 11 years, but other heads of government as well: France's Mitterrand after 9 years in office; Wilfried Martens in Belgium after 10 years; and Felipe González Márquez in Spain and Ruud Lubbers in the Netherlands, both in office 8 years.

Only the German team of Kohl and his long-serving foreign minister, Hans-Dietrich Genscher, appeared to be gaining strength. Their vision, however, had been shaped during the years in which the West German government had avoided a major international role. It seemed likely to be tested as the German people grew accustomed to being a unified nation at the heart of Europe.   Joseph Fitchett

See also the various European country articles. In the World Book Supplement section, see **Germany.** In *World Book,* see **Europe.**

Explosion. See **Disasters.**

Farm and farming. The Congress of the United States passed a five-year farm law in 1990 that set new limits on eligibility for some government subsidies, gave grain and cotton farmers more flexibility to grow crops in response to market demand, and launched major environmental initiatives. The new farm law, officially named the Food, Agriculture, Conservation and Trade Act of 1990, was passed by Congress in October and signed into law on November 28 by President George Bush, who praised its environmental provisions.

Farm bill. Under the farm subsidy program in effect since the 1930's, farmers who agreed to leave a certain percentage of their land fallow received above-market payments from the government for the crops they produced. Most farmers, lawmakers, and agriculture officials agreed that the 1990 farm bill should loosen government restrictions that had forced farmers to plant for government subsidies rather than to meet market demand. For example, the previous farm bill, passed in 1985, had increased subsidies for corn, wheat, and cotton and made soybeans and other oilseed crops less profitable. As a result, U.S. farmers were unable to take advantage of the growing world market for soybeans, used in an increasing number of consumer products and in livestock feed. But there was disagreement over how to increase flexibility in the farm program.

Congress quickly rejected a proposal by Secretary of Agriculture Clayton K. Yeutter to let farmers plant any mix of crops while receiving subsidies based on previous harvests. Finally, after months of debate, Congress adopted an alternative farm flexibility plan as part of an agreement between Bush and Congress to reduce the federal budget deficit by $492 billion over five years. More than $13 billion of that amount was to come from cuts in federal spending for agriculture.

Congress agreed to reduce by 15 per cent the amount of a farmer's grain and cotton acreage eligible for subsidies. Beginning with 1991 crops—crops planted in the fall of 1990—farmers were able to plant any crop on that 15 per cent of their land, except fruits, vegetables, and dry beans. They could graze livestock on those acres.

The new flexibility in planting was one of several changes made to encourage soybean production. Congress also approved a new soybean program that allows farmers to repay price support loans for less than their value if market prices plummet. The 1990 law gave a boost to other oilseed crops, such as sunflowers and canola. Farmers could grow those crops on acreage previously allotted to grain and still receive grain subsidies. That provision was the closest Congress came to the original Yeutter proposal. Price supports for dairy products, wool, sugar, tobacco, honey, and peanuts were trimmed by 1 per cent to contribute to the budget reduction effort.

Some farmers feared that income lost because of lower subsidies would not be recaptured in increased

A farmer injects a cow with an experimental genetically engineered hormone, banned by several states, that boosts milk production.

sales. Prospects for higher farm income were weakened further by Iraq's invasion of Kuwait on August 2, which raised the prices of oil and petroleum-based pesticides and fertilizers.

Environmental provisions. The 1985 farm law was the first farm legislation to intertwine farm policy with environmental protection. The 1990 law went further by requiring all farmers to maintain records on hazardous pesticide use.

Under the new law, farmers may receive $3,500 to $5,000 a year for adopting measures to prevent contamination of water. Congress also acted to increase the efficiency of the Conservation Reserve Program (CRP), which pays farmers to take easily eroded cropland out of production. The law changes the focus of the program from land likely to be eroded by wind to land where erosion is likely to cause pollution in streams and ground water. Also under the law, farmers may receive subsidies while rotating crops to reduce chemical use. The law also established the first national standards for organic foods.

Although the law reduced penalties for growing crops on wetlands, environmentalists predicted that the new sanctions would be more strictly enforced. The previous penalties were so severe many agriculture officials were reluctant to impose them. Also, farmers would be paid to remove as many as 1 million acres (405,000 hectares) of wetlands from agricultural production for 30 years or longer.

Farm and farming

Before the farm law was passed, the Bush Administration agreed to exempt from environmental regulation millions of acres of wetlands permanently converted to cropland before 1985. Farmers had complained bitterly about a 1989 government decision that would have required farmers to secure permits for changes on land drained long ago.

Clean Air Act. Another major piece of legislation enacted in 1990, the Clean Air Act, could have major implications for U.S. farmers. The measure, signed into law by President Bush on November 15, required ethanol—usually made from corn—and other clean fuels to be used in vehicles in 44 cities with the worst carbon monoxide pollution beginning in 1992 and in 9 cities with the worst ozone pollution beginning in 1995. Congress gave a further boost to ethanol by extending tax breaks that encourage its production until the year 2000.

"Big Green" shot down. Voters in California on Nov. 6, 1990, rejected a sweeping environmental measure that included a controversial provision on agricultural pesticides. The provision would have required farmers to phase out the use of pesticides that cause cancer or birth defects in laboratory animals, no matter how little the amount of pesticide residue on the food. Farmers and chemical firms opposed the proposal because it specified that no food carrying the residue of a pesticide that was banned in California could be shipped into the state. Analysts said that economic uncertainty contributed to the defeat of the proposition, known as "Big Green," by 64 per cent of the voters.

Banner year. Although farmers faced 1991 with new uncertainties about weakening income and exports, 1990 was a profitable year. With help from government subsidies and rising exports, U.S. farmers earned record income for the fourth consecutive year. In 1990, farm income reached $49 billion. In fiscal 1990—Oct. 1, 1989, to Sept. 30, 1990—farm exports reached $40.1 billion, the fourth consecutive annual increase. It was the first time that U.S. farm exports had exceeded $40 billion since 1981.

U.S. production. Farm income in 1990 was bolstered by bountiful crops. United States corn production rose to 7.93 billion bushels (201.6 million metric tons), up 5 per cent from 1989. Wheat production rebounded from a 1989 drought that hit the Upper Midwest "wheat belt" the hardest. Overall wheat production rose to 2.7 billion bushels (74.7 million metric tons), up 35 per cent. Winter wheat, which accounts for three-fourths of the U.S. wheat crop, rose by 40 per cent. The spring wheat crop rose by 20 per cent to set a record. Durum wheat, which is manufactured into pasta, rose by 32 per cent. Cotton rose by 22 per cent.

Soybeans declined by 1 per cent; grain sorghum, 9 per cent; oats, 4 per cent; peanuts, 13 per cent; and rice, less than 1 per cent.

Beef production declined by 1 per cent, and pork fell by 3 per cent. Poultry rose by more than 6 per cent.

Global production. From 1987 to 1989, the world consumed more grain than the world's farmers produced. But world grain production set a record in 1990 as it shot ahead of consumption. Record global wheat production rose by 11 per cent as countries throughout the world harvested record crops. Rice production rose by 1 per cent, also setting a record. Global corn production rose by 2 per cent, while the soybean harvest worldwide was unchanged. Cotton production rose nearly 9 per cent.

World beef production changed little for the fourth consecutive year. Pork production declined slightly, broiler chicken production rose by 5 per cent, and world turkey output rose by 6 per cent.

The Soviet Union produced its second-largest grain crop ever. A collapse in the food distribution system and a breakdown in political and economic links within the nation, however, led to food rationing. Many countries responded by sending emergency food supplies and offering financial aid for food purchases. On December 12, Bush approved up to $1 billion in U.S.-backed commercial loans for Soviet purchases of U.S. farm products.

Researchers in 1990 made progress in field-testing ways to reduce the use of chemicals in agriculture. Using genetic engineering techniques, scientists from the Monsanto Company inserted a gene from a common bacterium into cotton plants to make the cotton toxic to caterpillars. In the first field tests of the genetically altered cotton plants, Agriculture Department scientists found that caterpillars of the tobacco budworm, the cotton bollworm, the pink bollworm, and the beet army worm died within a few days after eating a bite or two of the cotton plants.

To learn more about the genetic makeup of plants, the Agriculture Department launched a major research project to locate plant genes that determine such traits as yield; tolerance to heat, cold, and drought; and resistance to disease. The department hopes that knowledge gained through the project will reduce the need for pesticides and other agricultural chemicals and enable scientists to design crops to meet specific needs in the marketplace.

Agriculture Department scientists in 1990 also developed a faster and cheaper way to insert genes into insects and plant material. They mixed insect genes and microscopically thin strands of silicon carbide into a saline solution. When the solution and insect eggs were placed in a $180 laboratory blender called a vortex mixer, the strands punched tiny holes in the insect eggs through which the genes entered. Previously, scientists, using equipment that cost $15,000, inserted the genes into the eggs using a miniature hypodermic needle while watching the process under a microscope.   Sonja Hillgren

See also **Environmental pollution; Food.** In *World Book,* see **Agriculture; Farm and farming.**

For his fall 1990 Paris showing, designer Emanuel Ungaro showed coats with vibrant colors, printed floral skirts, and wide-brimmed hats.

Fashion simmered down considerably in 1990. The shaky economic situation in Europe and North America played a major role in the avoidance of wild shapes. Fashion analysts felt that women were reluctant to spend money on clothes that would go out of style quickly.

As in 1989, the jacket remained the key to daytime dressing. The newest versions were hip length, usually accompanied by slender skirts that stopped above the knees. A pacesetter in the jacket trend was Karl Lagerfeld for Chanel in Paris, who introduced loose versions of the famous Chanel jacket slit vertically at the hem and also more precise versions with black borders outlining hot pink, tangerine, or white. Other trendsetters were Giorgio Armani in Milan, Italy, and Calvin Klein in New York City. At all levels of fashion around the world, their ideas were copied and reinterpreted.

The chief fashion innovation in 1990 was an explosion of color, with astonishing displays of bright yellow, orange, red, purple, and green illuminating the runways of the world. Customers remained unconvinced, however. They accepted the bright shades only tentatively. The bulk of their purchases focused as usual on black, beige, and navy. With the rising cost of clothing, buyers were afraid they would tire of a bright color or that it would be unflattering.

Evening shapes remained simple in 1990, but fabrics became elaborate. Brocades, embroidered satins, and laces were important, but the most popular style was the slender black dress, worn extremely short, with black stockings and high-heeled shoes.

In the winter of 1990, the short, swingy coat—which had been the runner-up the year before—moved into first place, perhaps because it looked racy over short skirts. The lower-calf to ankle-length coat continued to sell, particularly in cold climates. Casual styles, such as anoraks and parkas, were prominent in fabrics ranging from water-repellent poplin for daytime wear to satin and velvet for evening.

All roads lead to Paris. In 1990, more designers from other countries introduced their ready-to-wear collections in Paris, as the Japanese have done since the early 1980's. John Galliano and Katharine Hamnett moved over from London in 1990. Oscar de la Renta said he would bring his fall collection there in March 1991, making him among the first Americans showing in Paris. Gianni Versace and Valentino settled in Paris for the couture, or made-to-order, openings.

Couture revival. One of the surprising developments of 1990 was a revival of interest in couture clothing. In Paris, the revival took the form of lavish shows by couture houses, intended mostly to call attention to accessories and perfumes. The House of Lanvin, for instance, hired ready-to-wear designer Claude Montana to revamp its image. Montana's first couture collection, for the fall 1990 season, was considered a disaster when he presented throwaway clothes reminiscent of the 1960's. He redeemed himself with an exhilarating ready-to-wear collection for spring 1991. These designs were sleekly tailored, described as the streamlined futurism of mostly white clothes with silver accents.

Inexplicably, the trend toward buying couture rose in New York City as well. For more than 25 years, Arnold Scaasi had been practically the only well-known couturier in the city. Interest in him began skyrocketing when he designed the inaugural ballgown for first lady Barbara Bush in 1989.

In general, though, fashion analysts believed buyers were finding that the cost of made-to-order clothing was not much higher than top-priced ready-to-wear by such leaders as Geoffrey Beene, Oscar de la Renta, Bill Blass, and James Galanos. When clothes were made specially for the buyer, she could change the color, the fabric, or the neckline. And, she could come back for adjustments until the fit was perfect.

The size of the market was sufficient to draw other practitioners to the New York scene. John Anthony, who specialized in coats and suits on Seventh Avenue; Gene Meyer, who apprenticed with Geoffrey Beene; and Vera Wang, formerly a fashion editor at *Vogue*, opened couture businesses that did well in 1990.

In London, the House of Hartnell hired Marc Bohan, formerly of Christian Dior, to revive that company's couture business. It was part of a move to call attention to couture designers in Britain.   Bernadine Morris

In *World Book,* see **Clothing; Fashion.**

Finland felt the impact of changes in the Soviet Union in 1990. After World War II (1939-1945), Finland had developed a strategy, often dubbed *Finlandization,* for accommodating the Communist superpower politically and economically. This strategy combined political neutrality, which was intended to reassure its Soviet neighbor on security issues, with commercial practices tailored to the centrally planned Soviet economy. The objective was to prevent Soviet interference in Finland's internal affairs.

Finnish-Soviet relations. During the 1980's, Finns had debated the wisdom of seeking compromise with the Soviet Union. In 1990, Finns faced a new challenge: how to deal with the collapse of Soviet power. The dimension of the change in the international political climate became clear at a summit held in Helsinki, the Finnish capital, in September. At the meeting, Soviet President Mikhail S. Gorbachev joined United States President George Bush in condemning Iraq's August invasion of Kuwait. For Finland, the collapse of east-west antagonism brought into question the continued value of Finnish neutrality.

Under a trade arrangement that went into effect in 1948, Finland had provided the Soviet Union with a variety of industrial goods and some consumer goods in exchange for Soviet petroleum and natural gas. But by 1990, the Soviet Union was absorbing less than 10 per cent of Finland's exports, compared with 22 per cent as recently as 1985. Moscow could not afford to pay for even this reduced amount with its quota of energy exports. And the confusion in the Soviet Union made it impossible to set up a new system of payments. The loss of a long-time, reliable customer contributed to Finnish fears of a recession.

Finland and western Europe. To preserve its neutral status—and its relationship with the Soviet Union—Finland had not sought membership in the European Community (EC or Common Market). Instead, it belonged to the six-nation European Free Trade Association (EFTA) and pushed for deals between the EC and EFTA. But hopes for special EC-EFTA ties were undermined in 1990 as members of the former Soviet bloc began seeking closer EC links, too.

As Finnish leaders cautiously questioned the nation's traditional ties, industrialists copied the example of Nokia, a computer manufacturer and Finland's largest privately owned firm, and concentrated their efforts on developing markets in western Europe.

As winter began, Finland feared the arrival of hungry Soviet refugees. In hopes of persuading Soviet citizens to stay put, Finnish farmers sent surplus food to Karelia, a Soviet border region taken from Finland in World War II.   Joseph Fitchett

See also **Europe** (Facts in brief table). In *World Book,* see **Finland.**

Fire. See **Disasters.**

Flood. See **Disasters.**

Florida. See **State government.**

Food. A health-conscious public in the United States continued to seek out more nutritious foods in 1990. According to a survey conducted during the year by the Food Marketing Institute, a food-industry group in Washington, D.C., 90 per cent of shoppers said they were paying at least some attention to the nutritional content of the foods they eat. And, confirming the continuation of another healthful trend, the survey found that Americans ate more fruits and vegetables in 1990. They reduced their consumption of red meat in favor of fish and chicken. The institute also found a significant increase in the percentage of people who said they were limiting their intake of fat and oils.

Food manufacturers capitalized on this interest in nutrition by introducing new product lines offering less fat, cholesterol, sugar, and calories. Such lines, particularly in dairy and bakery products, quickly won popularity and were expanded.

In February, the U.S. Food and Drug Administration (FDA) approved the first low-calorie substitute for fat. The new product, Simplesse—a blend of proteins derived from egg whites and milk—was developed by the NutraSweet Company of Deerfield, Ill. Although Simplesse was approved for use only in a frozen dessert similar to ice cream, the company said it could be used in a number of foods that ordinarily have a high fat content, such as mayonnaise and sour cream. The product cannot withstand heat, however, and so it cannot be used in cooking. Several other fat substitutes, including the Procter & Gamble Company's Olestra, which *can* be used in cooked foods, were still awaiting FDA approval at year-end.

Food labeling. Consumer groups in 1990 stepped up their pressure on the federal government to improve food labeling. In response, Congress in October passed a food labeling bill that requires the food industry to supply a variety of uniform nutritional information on nearly all packaged food. For the most part, food-industry groups supported the enactment of a nutrition-labeling law.

On July 12, the FDA issued its own proposed regulations for food labeling. The rules, scheduled to take effect after a public-comment period of 30 to 120 days, contained many of the same provisions as the bill passed by Congress. The agency also restricted the health claims that a manufacturer can make to several nutrient-health linkages supported by scientific evidence. These links include calcium with the maintenance of strong bones, reduced salt with the possible prevention of high blood pressure, and high fiber content and less fat with the possibility of avoiding heart disease and some forms of cancer.

Food safety remained a concern for many Americans in 1990, though consumer confidence in the nation's food supply had rebounded somewhat from the scares of the year before. There were no major controversies to match 1989's twin furors over Alar on apples and the feared contamination of Chilean grapes with cyanide. But consumers were still concerned about the spraying of pesticides on crops and the administration of antibiotics and hormones to livestock. Such worries contributed to a growing popularity for "organic" fruits, vegetables, and meats—those produced without the use of drugs or synthetic chemicals.

In an effort to combat the possible contamination of food with bacteria or other microorganisms, the FDA and the U.S. Department of Agriculture in 1990 expanded their use of the Hazard Analysis Critical Control Points system in food inspections. In that system, inspectors concentrate their efforts on the points in the food-processing and food-handling network where contamination is most likely to occur.

Seafood inspection. On September 12, the Senate passed a bill requiring federal inspection of seafood sold in the United States. Under the provisions of the bill, the Agriculture Department would run the inspection program, the FDA would set tolerances for contaminants in seafood, and the National Oceanic and Atmospheric Administration (NOAA) would monitor water quality and restrict fishing in polluted areas. A seafood inspection bill in the House of Representatives failed to pass before Congress adjourned on October 28. The Administration of President George Bush favored a voluntary inspection program run by the FDA and NOAA and paid for with user fees rather than tax dollars.

Total food sales reached an estimated $614.8 billion in 1990, a 4.8 per cent rise over 1989. In real

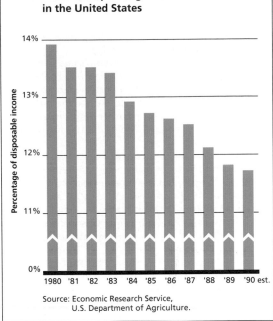

Consumer spending on food in the United States

Percentage of disposable income

1980 '81 '82 '83 '84 '85 '86 '87 '88 '89 '90 est.

Source: Economic Research Service,
U.S. Department of Agriculture.

The proportion of *disposable income* (money left after taxes) that Americans spend for food declined steadily during the 1980's.

terms—adjusted for inflation—sales declined by 1 per cent. Weekly grocery expenditures per household remained constant at $74.

Eating out remained a popular choice for Americans. Some 42 per cent of the food dollars spent in 1990 went for restaurant meals, a 1.8 per cent increase over 1989 in real terms. Menu prices rose 4.4 per cent, which was slightly less than the 4.6 per cent rise in 1989.

Reflecting Americans' heightened interest in nutrition and health, menus offered more light entrees, especially salads. Restaurant patrons, for their part, seemed increasingly to prefer simply prepared foods served in a casual atmosphere. That was a marked departure from the 1980's, when elaborate dishes and posh surroundings were all the rage.

Fast-food eateries once again outpaced other segments of the industry in growth, but their rate of growth continued to slow. Fast-food sales totaled $70.4 billion, a 3 per cent rise in real terms. Table-service restaurants posted $77.2 billion in sales, a 1 per cent increase after inflation.

World crop production rose in 1990, with many nations, including the United States and Canada, reporting near-record grain harvests. World grain reserves, which in 1989 had fallen to their lowest level since 1975, rose 1 per cent in 1990.　　Bob Gatty

See also **Farm and farming.** In *World Book,* see **Food; Food supply.**

301

Football

Football. The New York Giants became champions of the National Football League's (NFL) 1990 season, defeating the Buffalo Bills in Super Bowl XXV by a score of 20 to 19, the closest Super Bowl ever. The University of Colorado and Georgia Tech shared the unofficial national college championship.

NFL season. Professional football's image was marred in 1990. Two teams experienced problems over the presence of female reporters in locker rooms. After Arizona voters refused to declare the birthday of civil rights leader Martin Luther King, Jr., a legal holiday, the NFL canceled Phoenix as the site of the 1993 Super Bowl.

The league also had successes. To start with, it found ways to increase its income from television.

The NFL lengthened the regular season to 17 weeks for 1990 and 1991 and 18 weeks for 1992 and 1993. Each team would continue to play 16 games and have one or two weeks off. The longer season created extra games for TV, and the 10-team play-offs were expanded to 12 teams.

With those added attractions, Paul Tagliabue, who became the NFL commissioner in October 1989, helped negotiate the most lucrative contracts in entertainment history. The three major over-the-air networks—CBS Inc.; the National Broadcasting Company (NBC); and the American Broadcasting Companies (ABC)—and two cable networks—ESPN and Turner Network Television (TNT)—agreed to pay NFL

teams $3.643 billion from 1990 to 1993. Each team averaged $17 million annually in the previous contract, $32 million in the new one.

Television ratings held up, helped by the success of the popular San Francisco 49ers. On Jan. 28, 1990, in Super Bowl XXIV in New Orleans, they overwhelmed the Denver Broncos, 55-10. In the 1990 season, the 49ers won their first 10 games, then lost to the Los Angeles Rams, 28-17. They finished with a 14-2 record, the best in the 28-team league, and won their third consecutive division title.

The 49ers rewarded quarterback Joe Montana, 34, with a four-year contract worth $15 million. His 1990 salary of $4 million was the highest in professional football history.

Play-offs. In the National Conference, the division champions were the 49ers, the Giants (13-3), and the Chicago Bears (11-5). The three wild-card teams were the Philadelphia Eagles (10-6), the Washington Redskins (10-6), and the New Orleans Saints (8-8).

In the American Conference, the division champions were the Bills (13-3), the Los Angeles Raiders (12-4), and the Cincinnati Bengals (9-7). The wild-card teams were the Miami Dolphins (12-4), the Kansas City Chiefs (11-5), and the Houston Oilers (9-7). The Broncos fell to 5-11 and last place in their division.

In the first round of the play-offs, the Bears defeated the Saints, 16-6, and the Redskins smothered the Eagles, 20-6, in the National Conference. That set up contests between the 49ers and the Redskins on January 12 and between the Bears and the Giants on January 13. The Giants won, 31-3, and the 49ers defeated the Redskins, 28-10. In the conference finals, the Giants beat the 49ers, 15-13, behind the play of place-kicker Matt Bahr, who scored all of the Giants' points with five field goals.

In the American Conference, the first-round winners were the Dolphins, 17-16, over the Chiefs, and the Bengals, who routed Houston, 41-14. The Bengals lost to the Raiders, 20-10, and the Dolphins were eliminated by the Bills, 44-34. In the conference finals, the Bills overwhelmed the Raiders, 51-3, with an outstanding defense that made six interceptions and held running back Marcus Allen to only 26 yards rushing.

In Super Bowl XXV, on Jan. 27, 1991, in Tampa, Fla., the Giants won, keeping possession of the football for 40 minutes 33 seconds, a Super Bowl record. Giants running back Ottis Anderson was voted the Most Valuable Player. He gained 102 yards on 21 carries, including a 24-yard run in a third-quarter scoring drive that lasted 9 minutes 29 seconds.

Locker-room incidents. The New England Patriots and the Bengals were involved in locker-room incidents involving female reporters. A league investigator determined that three Patriots players were guilty of sexual harassment of Lisa Olson of the *Boston Herald*. Tagliabue fined the players a total of $22,500, fined the Patriots $25,000 for failing to take quick action, and ordered the Patriots to pay $25,000 more for

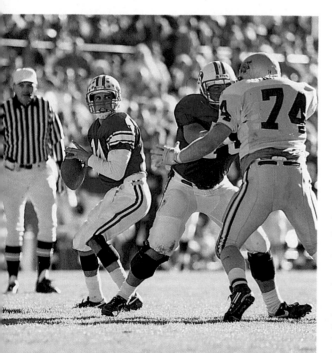

Quarterback Ty Detmer of Brigham Young, who won the Heisman Trophy in December, drops back for a pass. He set a season record for passing yardage.

instructional material for all NFL teams on how to deal with the media. After coach Sam Wyche of the Bengals barred Denise Tom of *USA Today* from his locker room, Tagliabue fined him $27,941, a fraction of his salary.

Other news. Many Arizona residents were angry when the NFL stripped the 1993 Super Bowl from Phoenix. They said that an initiative to adopt King's birthday as a legal holiday was narrowly defeated by about 15,000 votes, though only 3 per cent of the state's population is black. They also said many voters had opposed a legal holiday not because of racial bias but because it would have meant higher pay for state employees and thus higher taxes.

The World League of American Football, a springtime satellite league created by the NFL, planned to start playing in March 1991. It had six teams in the United States (New York City; Raleigh-Durham, N.C.; Orlando, Fla.; Sacramento, Calif.; San Antonio; and Birmingham, Ala.), one in Canada (Montreal), and three in Europe (London; Barcelona, Spain; and Frankfurt, Germany).

The Oilers, the Detroit Lions, and the Atlanta Falcons used a wide-open run-and-shoot offense in 1990 that utilized four wide receivers. Warren Moon, the Oilers' quarterback, became the first player to pass for 20,000 yards in the NFL and 20,000 in the Canadian Football League (CFL).

The Winnipeg Blue Bombers won the CFL's Grey Cup championship game by routing the Edmonton Eskimos, 50-11, on Nov. 25, 1990, in Vancouver, B.C.

NFL stars. Derrick Thomas, the Chiefs' outside linebacker, set an NFL record with seven quarterback sacks in one game. The Pro Football Hall of Fame elected coach Tom Landry, quarterback Bob Griese, running back Franco Harris, offensive tackle Bob St. Clair, defensive tackle Buck Buchanan, and linebackers Jack Lambert and Ted Hendricks.

College. The weekly polls of the Associated Press (AP) panel of writers and broadcasters and the United Press International (UPI) board of coaches produced new leaders all season.

On September 8, Brigham Young upset Miami of Florida, the early-season number one, 28-21, and Notre Dame became number one. On October 6, Stanford upset Notre Dame, 36-31, and Michigan became number one. On October 13, Michigan State upset Michigan, 28-27, and Virginia became number one. On November 3, Georgia Tech upset Virginia, 41-38, and Notre Dame regained the top ranking. On November 17, Penn State upset Notre Dame, 24-21, and Colorado became number one.

When the regular season ended, the best records belonged to Georgia Tech (10-0-1), Texas (10-1), Houston (10-1), Colorado (10-1-1), and Louisville (9-1-1). Colorado's record was tainted by a 33-31 victory over Missouri on October 6 because the winning touchdown as time ran out was scored on a fifth down, a result of miscounting by the seven game officials.

The 1990 college football season
College conference champions

Conference	School
Atlantic Coast	Georgia Tech
Big Eight	Colorado
Big Sky	Nevada
Big Ten	Illinois—Iowa—Michigan—Michigan State (tie)
Big West	San Jose State
Gateway	Northern Iowa—Southwest Missouri State (tie)
Ivy League	Cornell—Dartmouth (tie)
Mid-American	Central Michigan—Toledo (tie)
Mid-Eastern	Florida A&M
Ohio Valley	Eastern Kentucky—Middle Tennessee (tie)
Pacific Ten	Washington
Patriot	Holy Cross
Southeastern	Tennessee
Southern	Furman
Southland	Northeast Louisiana
Southwest	Texas
Southwestern	Jackson State
Western Athletic	Brigham Young
Yankee	Massachusetts

Major bowl games

Bowl	Winner	Loser
All American	North Carolina State 31	Southern Mississippi 27
Aloha	Syracuse 28	Arizona 0
Amos Alonzo Stagg (Div. III)	Allegheny (Pa.) 21	Lycoming (Pa.) 14
Blockbuster	Florida State 24	Penn State 17
Blue-Gray	Blue 17	Gray 14
California	San Jose State 48	Central Michigan 24
Copper	California 17	Wyoming 15
Cotton	Miami (Fla.) 46	Texas 3
East-West Shrine	West 24	East 21
Fiesta	Louisville 34	Alabama 7
Florida Citrus	Georgia Tech 45	Nebraska 21
Freedom	Colorado State 32	Oregon 31
Gator	Michigan 35	Mississippi 3
Hall of Fame	Clemson 30	Illinois 0
Holiday	Texas A&M 65	Brigham Young 14
Hula	East 23	West 10
Independence	Louisiana Tech 34 (tie)	Maryland 34 (tie)
John Hancock	Michigan State 17	Southern California 16
Liberty	Air Force 23	Ohio State 11
Orange	Colorado 10	Notre Dame 9
Peach	Auburn 27	Indiana 23
Rose	Washington 46	Iowa 34
Senior	AFC 38	NFC 28
Sugar	Tennessee 23	Virginia 22
NCAA Div. I-AA	Georgia Southern 36	Nevada, Reno 13
NCAA Div. II	North Dakota State 51	Indiana (Pa.) 11
NAIA Div. I	Central State (Ohio) 38	Mesa State (Colo.) 16
NAIA Div. II	Peru State (Nebr.) 17	Westminster (Pa.) 7

All-America team (as picked by AP)
Offense
Quarterback—Ty Detmer, Brigham Young
Running backs—Eric Bieniemy, Colorado; Darren Lewis, Texas A&M
Wide receivers—Herman Moore, Virginia; Lawrence Dawsey, Florida State
Tight end—Chris Smith, Brigham Young
Center—John Flannery, Syracuse
Guards—Joe Garten, Colorado; Ed King, Auburn
Tackles—Antone Davis, Tennessee; Stacy Long, Clemson
Return specialist—Raghib (Rocket) Ismail, Notre Dame
Place-kicker—Philip Doyle, Alabama

Defense
Linemen—Chris Zorich, Notre Dame; Russell Maryland, Miami (Fla.); Huey Richardson, Florida; Kenny Walker, Nebraska
Linebackers—Alfred Williams, Colorado; Maurice Crum, Miami (Fla.); Michael Stonebreaker, Notre Dame
Backs—Darryl Lewis, Arizona; Tripp Welborne, Michigan; Ken Swilling, Georgia Tech; Stanley Richard, Texas
Punter—Cris Shale, Bowling Green

Player awards
Heisman Trophy (best player)—Ty Detmer, Brigham Young
Lombardi Award (best lineman)—Chris Zorich, Notre Dame
Outland Award (best interior lineman)—Russell Maryland, Miami (Fla.)

National Football League final standings

American Conference

Eastern Division

	W.	L.	T.	Pct.
*Buffalo Bills	13	3	0	.813
*Miami Dolphins	12	4	0	.750
Indianapolis Colts	7	9	0	.438
New York Jets	6	10	0	.375
New England Patriots	1	15	0	.063

Central Division

	W.	L.	T.	Pct.
*Cincinnati Bengals	9	7	0	.563
*Houston Oilers	9	7	0	.563
Pittsburgh Steelers	9	7	0	.563
Cleveland Browns	3	13	0	.188

Western Division

	W.	L.	T.	Pct.
*Los Angeles Raiders	12	4	0	.750
*Kansas City Chiefs	11	5	0	.688
Seattle Seahawks	9	7	0	.563
San Diego Chargers	6	10	0	.375
Denver Broncos	5	11	0	.313

National Conference

Eastern Division

	W.	L.	T.	Pct.
*New York Giants	13	3	0	.813
*Philadelphia Eagles	10	6	0	.625
*Washington Redskins	10	6	0	.625
Dallas Cowboys	7	9	0	.438
Phoenix Cardinals	5	11	0	.313

Central Division

	W.	L.	T.	Pct.
*Chicago Bears	11	5	0	.688
Tampa Bay Buccaneers	6	10	0	.375
Green Bay Packers	6	10	0	.375
Detroit Lions	6	10	0	.375
Minnesota Vikings	6	10	0	.375

Western Division

	W.	L.	T.	Pct.
*San Francisco 49ers	14	2	0	.875
*New Orleans Saints	8	8	0	.500
Los Angeles Rams	5	11	0	.313
Atlanta Falcons	5	11	0	.313

*Made play-off.

Super Bowl champion—New York Giants (defeated Buffalo Bills, 20-19)

Individual statistics

Leading scorers, touchdowns

	TD's	Rush	Rec.	Ret.	Pts.
Derrick Fenner, Seattle	15	14	1	0	90
Marcus Allen, L.A. Raiders	13	12	1	0	78
Thurman Thomas, Buffalo	13	11	2	0	78
Lorenzo White, Houston	12	8	4	0	72
Merril Hoge, Pittsburgh	10	7	3	0	60
James Brooks, Cincinnati	9	5	4	0	54
Eddie Brown, Cincinnati	9	0	9	0	54
Ernest Givins, Houston	9	0	9	0	54
Sammie Smith, Miami	9	8	1	0	54

Leading scorers, kicking

	PAT	FG	Longest	Pts.
Nick Lowery, Kansas City	37-37	34-37	48	139
Scott Norwood, Buffalo	50-52	20-29	48	110
David Treadwell, Denver	34-36	25-34	49	109
Norm Johnson, Seattle	33-34	23-32	51	102
Pat Leahy, New York Jets	32-32	23-26	47	101
Pete Stoyanovich, Miami	37-37	21-25	53	100
Gary Anderson, Pittsburgh	32-32	20-25	48	92
Jim Breech, Cincinnati	41-44	17-21	46	92
Jeff Jaeger, L.A. Raiders	40-42	15-20	50	85

Leading quarterbacks

	Att.	Comp.	Yds.	TD's	Int.
Jim Kelly, Buffalo	346	219	2,829	24	9
Warren Moon, Houston	584	362	4,689	33	13
Steve DeBerg, Kansas City	444	258	3,444	23	4
Jay Schroeder, L.A. Raiders	334	182	2,849	19	9
Dan Marino, Miami	531	306	3,563	21	11
Bubby Brister, Pittsburgh	387	223	2,725	20	14
John Elway, Denver	502	294	3,526	15	14
Ken O'Brien, N.Y. Jets	411	226	2,855	13	10
Boomer Esiason, Cincinnati	402	224	3,031	24	22
Jeff George, Indianapolis	334	181	2,152	16	13

Leading receivers

	Number caught	Total yards	Avg. gain	TD's
Haywood Jeffires, Houston	74	1,048	14.2	8
Drew Hill, Houston	74	1,019	13.8	5
John L. Williams, Seattle	73	699	9.6	0
Ernest Givins, Houston	72	979	13.6	9
Andre Reed, Buffalo	71	945	13.3	8
Albert Bentley, Indianapolis	71	664	9.4	2
Curtis Duncan, Houston	66	785	11.9	1
Stephone Paige, Kansas City	65	1,021	15.7	5
Anthony Miller, San Diego	63	933	14.8	7
Bill Brooks, Indianapolis	62	823	13.3	5
Webster Slaughter, Cleveland	59	847	14.4	4

Leading rushers

	No.	Yards	Avg.	TD's
Thurman Thomas, Buffalo	271	1,297	4.8	11
Marion Butts, San Diego	265	1,225	4.6	8
Bobby Humphrey, Denver	288	1,202	4.2	7
Barry Word, Kansas City	204	1,015	5.0	4
James Brooks, Cincinnati	195	1,004	5.1	5
Derrick Fenner, Seattle	215	859	4.0	14
Sammie Smith, Miami	226	831	3.7	8
John Stephens, New England	212	808	3.8	2
Christian Okoye, Kansas City	245	805	3.3	7

Leading punters

	No.	Yards	Avg.	Longest
Mike Horan, Denver	58	2,575	44.4	67
Rohn Stark, Indianapolis	71	3,084	43.4	61
Lee Johnson, Cincinnati	64	2,705	42.3	70
Reggie Roby, Miami	72	3,022	42.0	62

Individual statistics

Leading scorers, touchdowns

	TD's	Rush	Rec.	Ret.	Pts.
Barry Sanders, Detroit	16	13	3	0	96
Cleveland Gary, L.A. Rams	15	14	1	0	90
Neal Anderson, Chicago	13	10	3	0	78
Jerry Rice, San Francisco	13	0	13	0	78
Ottis Anderson, N.Y. Giants	11	11	0	0	66
Emmitt Smith, Dallas	11	11	0	0	66
Andre Rison, Atlanta	10	0	10	0	60
Herschel Walker, Minnesota	9	5	4	0	54
Calvin Williams, Philadelphia	9	0	9	0	54

Leading scorers, kicking

	PAT	FG	Longest	Pts.
Chip Lohmiller, Washington	41-41	30-40	56	131
Kevin Butler, Chicago	36-37	26-37	52	114
Mike Cofer, San Francisco	39-39	24-36	56	111
Roger Ruzek, Philadelphia	45-48	21-29	53	108
Greg Davis, Atlanta	40-40	22-33	53	106
Chris Jacke, Green Bay	28-29	23-30	53	97
Steve Christie, Tampa Bay	27-27	23-27	54	96
Morten Andersen, New Orleans	29-29	21-27	52	92
Mike Lansford, L.A. Rams	42-43	15-24	46	87

Leading quarterbacks

	Att.	Comp.	Yards	TD's	Int.
Phil Simms, N.Y. Giants	311	184	2,284	15	4
Randall Cunningham, Philadelphia	465	271	3,466	30	13
Joe Montana, San Francisco	520	321	3,944	26	16
Jim Harbaugh, Chicago	312	180	2,178	10	6
Rodney Peete, Detroit	271	142	1,974	13	8
Jim Everett, L.A. Rams	554	307	3,989	23	17
Chris Miller, Atlanta	388	222	2,735	17	14
Mark Rypien, Washington	304	166	2,070	16	11
Vinny Testaverde, Tampa Bay	365	203	2,818	17	18

Leading receivers

	Number caught	Total yards	Avg. gain	TD's
Jerry Rice, San Francisco	100	1,502	15.0	13
Andre Rison, Atlanta	82	1,208	14.7	10
Keith Byars, Philadelphia	81	819	10.1	3
Henry Ellard, L.A. Rams	76	1,294	17.0	4
Gary Clark, Washington	75	1,112	14.8	8
Anthony Carter, Minnesota	70	1,008	14.4	8
Art Monk, Washington	68	770	11.3	5
Sterling Sharpe, Green Bay	67	1,105	16.5	6
Kelvin Martin, Dallas	64	732	11.4	0
Richard Johnson, Detroit	64	727	11.4	6

Leading rushers

	No.	Yards	Avg.	TD's
Barry Sanders, Detroit	255	1,304	5.1	13
Earnest Byner, Washington	297	1,219	4.1	6
Neal Anderson, Chicago	260	1,078	4.1	10
Randall Cunningham, Philadelphia	118	942	8.0	5
Emmitt Smith, Dallas	241	937	3.9	11
Johnny Johnson, Phoenix	234	926	4.0	5
Cleveland Gary, L.A. Rams	204	808	4.0	14
Ottis Anderson, N.Y. Giants	225	784	3.5	11
Herschel Walker, Minnesota	184	770	4.2	5
Mike Rozier, Houston—Atlanta	163	717	4.4	3

Leading punters

	No.	Yards	Avg.	Longest
Sean Landeta, N.Y. Giants	75	3,306	44.1	67
Mike Saxon, Dallas	79	3,413	43.2	62
Rich Camarillo, Phoenix	67	2,865	42.8	63
Tommy Barnhardt, New Orleans	70	2,990	42.7	65

The final regular-season polls from AP and UPI ranked Colorado first, Georgia Tech second, Texas third, and Miami fourth. The unofficial national championship would be decided in the bowl games on New Year's Day 1991.

On January 1, Georgia Tech routed Nebraska, 45-21, in the Florida Citrus Bowl in Orlando, and Miami whipped Texas, 46-3, in the Cotton Bowl in Dallas. Colorado defeated Notre Dame, 10-9, in the Orange Bowl in Miami. With 43 seconds left, Raghib (Rocket) Ismail of Notre Dame returned a punt 91 yards for the apparent winning touchdown, only to have the play wiped out by a clipping penalty.

The next day, in the final AP poll, Colorado was ranked first with 1,475 points and Georgia Tech second with 1,441. In the final UPI poll, Georgia Tech won by 1 point with 847 to Colorado's 846. In each poll, Miami finished third, Florida State fourth, Washington fifth, and Notre Dame sixth.

College stars. Ty Detmer, Brigham Young's junior quarterback, was voted the Heisman Trophy as the outstanding college player. Ismail, a wide receiver and running back, finished second. Ismail won the Walter Camp Foundation's vote as the player of the year. Defensive tackle Russell Maryland of Miami won the Outland Award as the best interior lineman, and nose tackle Chris Zorich of Notre Dame won the Lombardi Award as the best lineman.   Frank Litsky

In *World Book,* see **Football.**

France. A number of events during 1990 called into question France's future role on the international scene. Among them were German unification, changed east-west relations, and an erosion of French prestige in Africa. French President François Mitterrand seemed to play for time, postponing a debate on fundamental French policies while the public adjusted to the idea that change was unavoidable.

France and Europe. Although French leaders publicly supported German unification, they worried that a newly unified, more powerful Germany would mean a loss of French influence in Europe. Concern focused on Germany's future economic dominance. France felt the best chance for maintaining its own position came from anchoring Germany firmly within the European Community (EC or Common Market)—a group in which France plays a leading role. A partnership between France and Germany had for years been the driving force behind European economic union. That partnership continued in 1990. In April, France joined Germany in proposing that the community consider political union as well.

The plan for political union called for a common EC policy on defense in the post-Cold War era. In November, France backed a stonger defense role for the Conference on Security and Cooperation in Europe (CSCE). This body, which includes European nations, the Soviet Union, and the United States, has been a major forum for east-west discussions.

France's plans for cooperative European defense attempted to minimize the future role of the North Atlantic Treaty Organization (NATO) in guaranteeing European security. In 1966, France had withdrawn militarily from the western security alliance. Although France remained a member of NATO politically, it did not wish to see European security after the Cold War dependent on an organization dominated by the United States. At a NATO summit in London on July 5 and 6, 1990, France rejected U.S. proposals for a new approach to nuclear deterrence. France has its own nuclear arsenal and declined to endorse a NATO policy declaring nuclear arms "weapons of last resort."

France and the Persian Gulf. After Iraq invaded Kuwait on August 2, Mitterrand supported the U.S. decision to confront Iraq with a trade embargo and the threat of military action. French cooperation in the Persian Gulf received public support in France. But it was attacked by Mitterrand's fellow Socialists, who disliked his combative posture; by French industrialists, who were reluctant to break ties with a major customer—Iraq; and by French conservatives. The conservatives were angered when Syria took advantage of the preoccupation with Kuwait to act in Lebanon, crushing Christian forces that France backed.

Mitterrand sought to distance himself diplomatically from U.S. policy in the gulf region. In a speech at the United Nations on September 24, he stated that an Iraqi declaration of intent to withdraw from Kuwait would make "everything possible," including discussions on the Arab-Israeli conflict.

France in Africa. Mitterrand also sought to silence criticism at home that France was supporting undemocratic regimes in Africa. Thus, he ordered French forces in Chad, a former French colony, not to intervene when Chad's president, Hissein Habré, was overthrown in early December, even though Chad's new leader, Idriss Deby, was reportedly backed by Libya. The French had helped Habré fight off attacks by Libya through the 1980's.

France at home. Mitterrand's prestige helped the minority Socialist government of Prime Minister Michel Rocard survive no-confidence votes in May and November. The May vote came about after the government offered an amnesty for elected officials who had received illegal campaign contributions. Even Mitterrand had been linked to such funds. Rocard survived a second no-confidence vote in November over an unpopular new tax to pay for social benefits.

The parliament responded in May to increasing violence against Arab immigrants by passing a law that would bar anyone found guilty of inciting racial hatred from holding elected office or government jobs. The law was aimed chiefly at followers of Jean-Marie Le Pen, leader of the far-right National Front. Le Pen supports evicting the 3.4 million North African Muslims who live in France.   Joseph Fitchett

See also **Europe** (Facts in brief table). In *World Book,* see **France.**

Fujimori, Alberto (1938-   ), the son of Japanese immigrants, was elected president of Peru in a runoff election on June 10, 1990, against novelist Mario Vargas Llosa. See **Peru.**

Fujimori was born in Lima, the Peruvian capital, on July 28, 1938, to Naochi and Matsue Fujimori, who had immigrated to Peru in 1934 from Japan. He graduated from Lima's La Molina National University of Agriculture in 1961 as an *agronomist* (a person trained in farm management). Fujimori pursued postgraduate studies in France and the United States, where he received a master's degree in mathematics in 1969 from the University of Wisconsin at Madison.

After serving on the faculty at La Molina, Fujimori was named dean of the faculty of sciences in 1984 and later that year was elected rector of the university.

Fujimori entered politics in 1985 as a consultant on rural issues for the successful presidential campaign of Alan García Pérez. Fujimori helped found the Cambio 90 (Change 90) party in 1988 and ran for the presidency on its ticket.

Although his parents were Buddhists, Fujimori is Roman Catholic. In 1974, he married Susana Higuchi, a civil engineer. They have four children.   Rod Such

Gabon. See **Africa.**

Gambia. See **Africa.**

Gas and gasoline. See **Energy supply; Petroleum and gas.**

Genetic engineering. See **Biology.**

Geology. The discovery of a sample of what is believed to be the oldest known ocean floor was reported in January 1990 by a team of geologists working on the drillship *JOIDES Resolution.* The team found the 175-million-year-old rock in the far western Pacific Ocean about 1,500 miles (2,400 kilometers) south of Japan.

To obtain the sample, the scientists penetrated 3½ miles (5.6 kilometers) of seawater and ½ mile (0.8 kilometer) of overlying volcanic rock. Fossils of *radiolaria* (a type of microscopic sea creature) of a known age found in the overlying rock indicated that the sample dated from the middle Jurassic Period, about 175 million years ago.

This ancient oceanic crust was formed much more recently than the oldest known continental rocks, which are about 4 billion years old. Oceanic crust is younger because of the movement of the tectonic plates that make up the earth's outer surface. Geologists estimate it takes about 200 million years for oceanic crust and the plates on which it rides to travel from the midocean ridges, where it forms, to *subduction zones,* where the plates and crust descend beneath other plates.

Caribbean meteorite impact? Since the early 1980's, geologists have debated whether widespread extinctions, including that of the dinosaurs, 65 million years ago at the end of the Cretaceous Period, were caused by a series of environmental disasters triggered

A flaming river of lava from Hawaii's Kilauea Volcano, the world's most active volcano, buries a road near the town of Kalapana in May.

by a meteorite hitting the earth. One of the major problems with this theory is that scientists have not found an impact crater of the right age and size. Several studies reported in 1990 suggested that the crater may be in the western Caribbean region.

In May, geologists Alan R. Hildebrand and William V. Boynton of the University of Arizona in Tucson reported finding evidence of unusually thick deposits of sedimentary rock in the western Caribbean Sea, Haiti, and Cuba. According to the scientists, the Cuban deposit, which is up to 1,640 feet (500 meters) thick, contains 120 cubic miles (500 cubic kilometers) of rock. They reported that all the rock was deposited at the same time—at the end of the Cretaceous Period and the beginning of the Tertiary Period that followed. The deposit in Haiti, which was also found at the Cretaceous-Tertiary (K-T) boundary, is thinner, but it contains tiny grains of rock often found at impact sites.

In December, Hildebrand and G. T. Penfield of Houston reported finding evidence of a buried impact crater on the Yucatán Peninsula, at the northwestern edge of the Caribbean Sea. According to the scientists, the crater is at or near the K-T boundary.

In April, a report based on geologic records argued that huge boulders found at the K-T boundary in a limestone formation in Cuba were blasted off the sea floor by a meteorite impact just south of Cuba. Researchers who visited the site in June, however, disputed this conclusion. Geologists Robert S. Dietz and John McHone of Arizona State University in Tempe argued that natural weathering of the limestone had created the boulders.

Huge landslides. A symposium on giant landslides on oceanic volcanoes, held in December, produced a number of research reports expanding on a discovery made in December 1989. At that time, a team of geologists headed by James G. Moore of the United States Geological Survey (USGS) in Menlo Park, Calif., reported finding enormous underwater landslides off the Hawaiian Islands. These landslides cover an area extending for 38,600 square miles (100,000 square kilometers) around the islands. Some individual landslides contain as much as 1,200 cubic miles (5,000 cubic kilometers) of rock.

At the symposium, P. Labazuy and J-F. Lenat of the Center for Volcanic Research in Clermont-Ferrand, France, reported finding deposits created by submarine landslides off the island of Reunion, near Madagascar in the Indian Ocean. In addition, geologists Robin T. Holcomb of the USGS in Seattle and Roger C. Searle of the University of Durham in Great Britain suggested that the giant slopes of rocky debris that seem to surround all oceanic islands were formed by landslides. If so, volcanic slides may cover as much as 10 per cent of the ocean floor, an area about 4½ times the size of the United States.   Eldridge M. Moores

In *World Book,* see **Geology.**

Georgia. See **State government.**

Germany was reunited on Oct. 3, 1990, ending 45 years of division that had followed World War II. For Germans, the year revolved around events that merged the Federal Republic of Germany (West Germany) and the German Democratic Republic (East Germany) into one fully sovereign German state. For Europeans, German unification signaled the end of the Cold War that had divided postwar Europe into an eastern bloc backed by the Soviet Union and a western bloc allied with the United States. The front between the two blocs had run right through Germany.

All-German elections. Both Germanys had set their sights on unification within weeks of the opening of the Berlin Wall on Nov. 9, 1989. But not even optimists predicted that union would be achieved in time to hold all-German elections—the first since 1932—by the end of 1990. On Dec. 2, 1990, however, voters in both Germanys elected a single national parliament. The elections were a triumph for the West German architects of unification: Chancellor Helmut Kohl and Foreign Minister Hans-Dietrich Genscher. Kohl's Christian Democrats won 44 per cent of the vote; Genscher's Free Democrats, the other party in the center-right coalition, scored 11 per cent. Their new coalition held a strong majority in the 662-seat Bundestag (lower house of parliament).

The main opposition party, the Social Democrats, won about 34 per cent of the vote, their worst showing in three decades. The leader of the Social Democrats, Oskar Lafontaine, had appeared lukewarm about rapid unification. The Greens, an environmental party, opposed union and drew less than the 5 per cent of the vote needed to secure seats in parliament.

The drive for unification had shifted into high gear after East Germans elected their first non-Communist government on March 18. Eager to end uncertainty about their future and to gain economic and political aid from West Germany, East Germans voted in large numbers for the local counterpart of Kohl's Christian Democrats. That party had campaigned on a platform of speedy unification.

The unexpectedly swift achievement of unification depended thereafter on leaders in the two Germanys and in the four Allied powers that defeated Germany in World War II (1939-1945): France, Great Britain, the Soviet Union, and the United States. After the war, the Allies had divided Germany into occupation zones that later became East Germany and West Germany, and they still held some occupation rights in Germany. From the outset of the "two-plus-four talks" (two Germanys plus four Allies) in 1990, the United States and the Germanys took the position that unification should take months, not years. In addition, Kohl and the U.S. government wanted a united Germany to remain in the North Atlantic Treaty Organization (NATO), the western security alliance.

Britain and France at first opposed the rush toward unification. To ease their fears that a united Germany might decide to go its own way, Kohl sought to

Chancellor Helmut Kohl addresses the combined parliaments of East and West Germany, which met in the Reichstag in Berlin on October 4.

strengthen German ties to the European Community (EC or Common Market).

Soviet opposition. The greatest opposition to rapid unification came from the Soviet Union, which had suffered the heaviest losses from German armies during the war. In addition, the Soviet people chafed at the thought of East Germany, a strong Soviet ally, in NATO. But Soviet President Mikhail S. Gorbachev yielded to the western powers after obtaining promises of German economic assistance and of U.S. political support for his domestic reforms. In addition, the western powers tried to reassure the Soviet Union by stressing that a united Germany would strengthen European stability and not threaten Soviet security.

Kohl overcame the last Soviet objections to the western plan for unification at a meeting with Gorbachev in the Soviet Union on July 16. Gorbachev approved NATO membership for a unified Germany. Kohl, in return, pledged to limit the size of Germany's armed forces to about 370,000 troops. The two leaders agreed on the gradual withdrawal of the nearly 400,000 Soviet troops stationed in East Germany, probably over a four-year period. During this time, Germany would help build housing in the Soviet Union for the troops.

The economic union of the Germanys occurred on July 1. East Germans could exchange up to 4,000 East German marks at a 1-to-1 rate for West German Deutsche marks. Wages and pensions also were converted at that rate, and other East German marks could be exchanged at 2 to 1. Some West German officials argued that the generous exchange rate would fuel inflation by putting so many Deutsche marks into circulation. Kohl, however, claimed it was needed to stem the flight of East Germans into West Germany. As East Germans feared, unemployment soared when inefficient businesses shut down after economic union.

Prior to political unification, East Germany was reorganized administratively along West German lines. Five states abolished by the Communists were reestablished: Brandenburg, Mecklenburg-Western Pomerania, Saxony, Saxony-Anhalt, and Thuringia. It seemed likely that Berlin would eventually become the German capital again.

On August 31, the two Germanys signed a treaty in East Berlin covering all legal aspects of their merger. Another treaty approving unity was signed by the World War II Allies on September 12 in Moscow. That treaty gave up the last Allied occupation rights, restoring to Germany the full freedom from outside control it had lost after the war. Under the treaty, Germany reaffirmed its intention to keep its existing borders and not seek to recover territory it had lost as a result of the war. A separate treaty guaranteeing the border between Germany and Poland was signed on November 14.

Toward the future. At year's end, the new German state faced three major questions:

■ Could it cope with the economic burden resulting

from the collapse of Communism? Industry in East Germany turned out to be in far worse shape than suspected. With the dismantling of East Germany's state-run system, unemployment was expected to soar to as high as 4 million, nearly half the East German work force.

■ Would the German public remain committed to a strong western military alliance? The threat of invasion from the east had greatly diminished with the collapse of Soviet power in eastern Europe. After the pullout of Soviet troops, the former East Germany was to remain largely demilitarized. Eventually, NATO troops might be asked to leave the western German area. By Christmas, about half the U.S. troops in Germany had been sent to the Persian Gulf.

■ Would Germany work toward making the European Community a pillar of stability in a new Europe? Or would it turn away from the EC and concentrate on expanding its economic influence in eastern Europe? Throughout the year, German leaders stressed their determination to remain firmly anchored in the west. Debate began on German proposals for closer EC economic and political integration in Rome in December. Such steps indicated that the newly united Germany would stand alongside its EC partners in shaping post-Cold War Europe.   Joseph Fitchett

See also **Europe** (Facts in brief table). In the World Book Supplement section, see **Germany**.

Ghana. See **Africa**.

Golf. The leading golfers of 1990 were Nick Faldo of England and Wayne Levi, Lee Trevino, and Beth Daniel of the United States. The year's leading golf story, however, was not their exploits but the uproar caused by the membership policies of certain private clubs that discriminated on the basis of race, religion, or sex.

Through the years, important tournaments had often been held at clubs whose only members were white and male. The Professional Golfers' Association (PGA) 1990 championship, one of the four major tournaments for men, was held from August 9 to 12 at the Shoal Creek Country Club in Birmingham, Ala., which had no black members.

Civil rights groups protested this exclusion. They encouraged television sponsors to withdraw commercials and threatened to picket the tournament. After four major corporations announced their decision to withhold sponsorship, the club finally accepted one black man as an honorary member and said it would add one as a regular member.

In the aftermath, the PGA tour said it would not hold future men's or senior men's tournaments at clubs that discriminated. Similar standards were set for tournaments on the Ladies Professional Golf Association (LPGA) tour and those held by the United States Golf Association.

Tom Watson, a leading professional golfer, resigned from the Kansas City (Mo.) Country Club after it rejected the membership application of Henry Block, a Jew and the chairman of H & R Block, a tax-preparation company. Subsequently, the country club accepted Block as a member.

The yearlong tours were lucrative. The PGA tour consisted of 45 tournaments with prize money of $45 million, the PGA senior tour had 41 tournaments worth $20 million, and the LPGA tour had 38 tournaments worth $16 million. The PGA also inaugurated the Ben Hogan tour for younger professionals, with 30 tournaments worth $100,000 each.

Men. Faldo became the first non-American to win the point race for PGA Player of the Year since the award was begun in 1947. He won his second consecutive Masters title and then the British Open.

Levi finished first on the tour with four victories and second in earnings with $1,024,647. Greg Norman of Australia led in earnings with $1,165,477 and scoring average with 69.10. Jodie Mudd won the two richest tournaments, the Tournament Players Championship ($270,000) and the Nabisco Championship ($450,000).

In the four major tournaments, Faldo won the Masters, held from April 5 to 8 in Augusta, Ga., by defeating Raymond Floyd in a play-off. Hale Irwin, at the age of 45, became the oldest man to win the United States Open, held from June 14 to 18 in Medinah, Ill., defeating Mike Donald in a play-off. Faldo then won the British Open, held from July 19 to 22 in St. Andrews, Scotland, by five strokes, and Wayne Grady of Australia won the PGA championship by three strokes.

Senior. Trevino and Jack Nicklaus turned 50 years old and became eligible for the senior tour. Nicklaus won his first tournament, the Tradition, and later the Tournament Players Championship.

Trevino became the first senior to reach $1 million in earnings in one year, totaling $1,190,518. He had seven victories, including the senior U.S. Open, and six second places. Mike Hill, George Archer, and Juan (Chi Chi) Rodriguez won four tournaments each. Gary Player of South Africa won the PGA senior championship and the British Open for seniors.

LPGA. Daniel easily became the LPGA Player of the Year. She led the tour with seven victories to five for Patty Sheehan. Daniel led in earnings with $863,578, an LPGA record.

Betsy King won two of the four major tournaments—the Nabisco Dinah Shore, held from March 29 to April 1 in Rancho Mirage, Calif., by two strokes, and the U.S. Women's Open, held from July 12 to 15 in Duluth, Ga., by one stroke. Because the Open was delayed by rain, 36 holes were played on the final day. In that span, King, the defending champion, overcame Sheehan's 11-stroke lead.

In the other major tournaments, Cathy Johnston won the du Maurier Limited Classic, held from June 28 to July 1 in Kitchener, Canada, and Daniel won the Mazda LPGA championship, held from July 26 to 29 in Bethesda, Md.   Frank Litsky

In *World Book,* see **Golf**.

An antipoll-tax demonstration in March in London turned into a street war involving thousands and injuring more than 430 police and civilians.

Great Britain. Prime Minister Margaret Thatcher stunned Great Britain and the world when she resigned on Nov. 22, 1990, after failing to win the Conservative Party's leadership election on November 21. She had been expected to run in a second round of balloting among the Conservative members of Parliament the following week but resigned instead. Michael Heseltine, former defense minister who resigned from Thatcher's government in 1986, challenged her in the election. Although she beat him 204 to 152 votes, she was short of the required majority of votes plus 15 per cent to win reelection.

On November 28, John Major, chancellor of the exchequer in Thatcher's government, became prime minister, inheriting such problems as an inflation rate nearing 11 per cent, unemployment at 6 per cent, a huge trade deficit, and the flat-rate poll tax that most of the country wanted changed. He was expected to take a softer stand on European economic unity than Thatcher, who opposed Britain's losing its independent currency in a single system for the European Community (EC or Common Market). See **Major, John.**

Poll tax anger. The focal point of resentment against the Thatcher government was the "community charge," generally known as the "poll tax." It replaced the local property tax for funding local government services, and hostility against it began even before it went into effect in England and Wales on April 1. It had gone into effect in Scotland in 1989.

Antagonism centered on the fact that everybody between age 18 and 65 had to pay the same amount, regardless of their income. Taxes on individuals were set by local governments. The central government set and collected a uniform rate on businesses and redistributed the money to local governments.

The Labour Party declared war on the new tax, and a number of Labour members of Parliament said they would refuse to pay. So did large numbers of ordinary citizens, who faced being taken to court. Conservative loyalties were severely strained too, as senior members normally loyal to Thatcher warned of impending political disaster.

In early March 1990, protesters disrupted local councils as the councils prepared to implement the tax. In London, the worst rioting in recent times broke out on March 31, when an antitax rally, attended by 40,000 people, became a street war. A battle between police and demonstrators broke out in Trafalgar Square, and thousands of protesters then went on the rampage in London's fashionable West End, looting shops and burning cars. More than 350 police and 86 civilians were injured. Government and police blamed a minority of young militants for the riots. Rally organizers likewise blamed small groups of troublemakers but also accused the police of losing control.

On April 3, the government announced that the 20 councils that spend the most would have their budgets capped in an effort to reduce the bills of more than 4 million taxpayers. Councils controlled by Labour set the highest rates. Conservative and Labour officials alike said that the government miscalculated what the councils would spend and consequently what their rates would be. They said that millions of households would be worse off than before the poll tax and that the tax would double the number of taxpayers. On July 19, Environment Secretary Christopher Patten announced a package of reforms and government subsidies, totaling 3.26 billion pounds (about U.S. $6 billion), to help keep poll tax bills down.

Spring election test. The annual local elections on May 3 were a severe test for the government but not the total disaster the Conservatives had feared. Although Labour made widespread gains, the Conservatives held on to a number of key seats and increased their majorities in the London boroughs of Wandsworth and Westminster, where the poll tax rates were the lowest in Britain.

Thatcher favorite resigns. Relations with the countries of western Europe continued to create difficulties for the government during 1990. On July 14, Thatcher accepted the resignation of her closest Cabinet ally, Trade and Industry Secretary Nicholas Ridley, over an interview in *The Spectator*. Ridley had described European monetary union, a proposed merger of the EC's banking systems and currencies, as "a German racket designed to take over the whole of Europe." He asserted that handing over British political sovereignty to the EC would be like surrendering to Nazi dictator Adolf Hitler. Thatcher shared Ridley's general distrust of Europe, but the political uproar in Britain and West Germany over the interview left her no option.

Currency integration. Thatcher had long resisted bringing the pound into the exchange rate mechanism (ERM) of the EC's European Monetary System. But finally, on October 5, she announced that Britain would join, effective October 8. The ERM imposes strict controls over the fluctuations in the exchange rates of the currencies of its members, numbering 10 with Britain's entry. The British pound became, in effect, linked to the German mark, the dominant currency in the ERM.

Recession threat. The Confederation of British Industry warned that the country was heading for a recession unless interest rates were brought down. The number of people unable to pay the mortgage on their homes was rising alarmingly. In October, then-Chancellor of the Exchequer Major surprised most people by announcing that interest rates were being cut from 15 to 14 per cent. Immediately stocks and the pound rose sharply, and Major was the hero of the hour at the Conservative Party's annual conference.

Privatization proceeds. The government continued its privatization programs by selling off the water industry and preparing to sell the electricity industry to private investors. The electricity industry was to be sold in three stages, beginning in November with the

Great Britain's Duke and Duchess of York and Princess Eugenie, born March 22, leave London's Portland Hospital on March 30.

sale of 12 distribution companies in England and Wales. The sale, for 10 billion pounds (about U.S. $20-billion), was one of the world's largest public offerings, and the government was making the stock attractive to small investors by offering free shares or discounts on their electric bills.

Labour's new image. Labour continued to abandon the left wing policies that had brought it electoral disaster. It adopted a platform eliminating the word *socialist*. In May, the party released a 20,000-word policy document called *Looking to the Future*. It was the culmination of a three-year effort by party leader Neil G. Kinnock to win back middle-ground voters. The document called for income tax cuts for the poor and tax increases for the wealthy but insisted that most middle-class earners would not pay more. Labour also pledged to repeal the poll tax and replace it with a property tax linked to income. The document called for a new partnership between government and industry.

The party's over. The Labour Party's revival during 1990 drew voters away from the center parties, and on June 3, one of them, the Social Democratic Party, folded. It had been formed nine years earlier to "break the mould" of British two-party politics.

Rushdie affair. On February 4, Salman Rushdie, British author of the novel *The Satanic Verses* (1988), issued a 7,000-word essay maintaining the right of unlimited freedom of expression for the artist. Rushdie went into hiding in February 1989 after Iranian leader Ayatollah Ruhollah Khomeini called for his death, claiming the book blasphemed Islam. On April 9, 1990, the High Court refused permission to a group of British Muslims to bring a lawsuit charging blasphemous libel against Rushdie and his publisher. The court said Britain's blasphemy laws applied only to Christianity. In December, Rushdie issued a statement supporting Islam. He said he would not authorize a paperback version of his novel and would not allow its translation into any more foreign languages. Iran's spiritual leader, Ayatollah Ali Hoseini Khamenei, said that the death decree was irreversible.

"Mad cow disease." Fears that a deadly disease popularly known as *mad cow disease* could spread to human beings arose after a cat was found to have died from it. The fears led to a widespread British boycott of beef products in 1990. The disease, *bovine spongiform encephalopathy*, had been identified in 1989 as coming from a high-protein cattle food containing sheep remains. Sheep were known to have been infected with this disease for hundreds of years. Professor Richard Lacey, a Leeds University microbiologist, said that 6 million cows might have to be slaughtered. Government scientists accused Lacey of being an alarmist, but more than 2,000 schools responded in May 1990 by removing beef from their menus.

A food war with Europe loomed when Austria, France, West Germany, Italy, and Switzerland announced either a ban or restrictions on British beef. Thatcher claimed that the European actions were illegal and motivated by commercial reasons. The turmoil died down when the European Commission—the EC's executive branch—backed Great Britain and ordered the ban to be lifted.

Prison siege. The longest-running prison siege in the recent history of the British penal system started on April 1 at Strangeways prison, Manchester, after prisoners went on the rampage and took over the jail. The authorities sealed off the prison but decided not to storm it, fearing heavy loss of life. One prisoner was killed in his cell, and a prison officer died of a heart attack. Police tactics included playing loud music and aiming water jets at prisoners on the roof. On April 25, the last small group of prisoners gave up. Penal reformers blamed overcrowding, violence, and drugs.

Lords revolt. The House of Lords on June 4 rejected by 133 votes a government bill to allow prosecution of suspected World War II (1939-1945) criminals living in Britain. It was the biggest revolt in the Lords since Thatcher came to power. Members of the Lords objected to the principle of legislation allowing prosecutions for crimes committed more than 40 years ago outside Britain by people who had not been British citizens. There were said to be three such suspects living in Britain, all aging immigrants from eastern Europe.   Ian J. Mather

See also **Ireland; Northern Ireland.** In *World Book,* see **Great Britain.**

Greece. Prospects brightened in 1990 for a stable, effective government in Greece. Constantine Mitsotakis was sworn in as prime minister on April 11 after April 8 elections gave his conservative New Democracy party 150 seats in the 300-member Parliament. Mitsotakis also won the support of one independent deputy, just enough for a majority. The main opposition groups were the Panhellenic Socialist Movement (PASOK), which took 123 seats, and a Communist-led alliance that won 19.

It had taken three elections in less than one year to form a workable parliamentary majority, chiefly because of new election laws. The Socialist government, alarmed by its declining popularity, had in 1989 pushed through laws designed to prevent any single party from winning a majority. Resulting stalemates left Parliament unable to form a government and elect the country's president.

On May 4, 1990, the newly formed Parliament finally elected a president: Constantine Karamanlis (also spelled Caramanlis), aged 83, who had held the office from 1981 to 1985. Despite austerity measures taken by the government, New Democracy gained ground in local elections in October. In the race for mayor of Athens, the Greek capital, a conservative candidate defeated Melina Mercouri, a movie star and former Socialist cabinet minister.

A long-running dispute over the future of United States military bases in Greece was settled on July 8. Under an eight-year agreement, two bases in the Athens region were closed. But large installations on the island of Crete—including a base at Souda Bay that can accommodate the U.S. Navy's Sixth Fleet—were again leased to the United States in exchange for $1.5 billion in military aid.

Corruption trials. Officials of the former Socialist government began coming to trial on various corruption charges in 1990. The first trial ended on August 11 in the conviction of Nikos Athanassopoulos, a former deputy finance minister, for fraud in connection with government grain sales in 1986 to the European Community (EC or Common Market). Athanassopoulos admitted that he had approved a swindle designed to avoid paying EC duties. But he claimed he had acted in Greece's interest by authorizing practices that were widespread among EC nations. He was sentenced to 3½ years in jail.

On October 2, Agamemnon Koutsogeorgas, a former minister of justice, was jailed in connection with a $200-million banking scandal. Andreas Papandreou awaited trial on charges of wiretapping opponents while he was prime minister, from 1981 to 1989.

After Iraq's August invasion of Kuwait, Greece at first hesitated to let U.S. forces use Greek soil and airspace. But it later offered support, including the use of ships to transport troops.   Joseph Fitchett

See also **Europe** (Facts in brief table). In *World Book,* see **Greece.**

Grenada. See **Latin America.**

Groening, Matt (1955-   ), the creator of "The Simpsons," won an Emmy in 1990 for that animated television series. Originally created as a series of cartoon shorts on "The Tracey Ullman Show," "The Simpsons" quickly became a hit. Fans of the bickering blue-collar family also snapped up a flood of Simpsons paraphernalia, especially T-shirts featuring the wise-guy sayings of Bart Simpson, the obnoxious, underachieving son of the family.

Matthew Groening (pronounced *GRAY ning*) was born and raised in Portland, Ore. His father, Homer, worked as a cartoonist in the 1950's. While a high school student, Groening contributed cartoons to the student newspaper and yearbook. In 1977, he received a bachelor's degree from Evergreen State College in Olympia, Wash., where he ran the campus newspaper.

After graduation, Groening moved to Los Angeles to become a writer. While working at a series of odd jobs, he began producing and mailing to friends a newsletter in the form of a comic strip starring a satirical, buck-toothed rabbit named Binky. In 1980, the weekly *L.A. Reader* newspaper, for which Groening was working as a delivery man, began publishing his cartoon strip, called "Life in Hell." More than 100 newspapers carry the cartoon.

Groening is married to Deborah Caplan, his business manager. They have a son, Homer.   Barbara A. Mayes

In the Special Reports section, see **Once Again, "Toons" Are Tops.**

Guatemala. As 1990 ended, Guatemalans faced a runoff election on Jan. 6, 1991, to pick a new civilian president. The two front-runners who emerged from the balloting on Nov. 11, 1990, were Jorge Carpio Nicolle, head of the National Centrist Union, and Jorge Serrano Elías of the Solidarity Action Movement.

Serrano swept the runoff, defeating Carpio by a 2-to-1 margin. Serrano, a born-again Christian, had the support of many evangelical Christians. Many evangelicals switched their loyalty to Serrano after their favorite, Efraín Ríos Montt, was barred by the Supreme Court of Justice from seeking election to the office he had seized in 1982.

The 1990 campaign was marred by violence. Nine candidates or party leaders, three journalists, and two political activists were assassinated. Several of the killings were attributed to Guatemala's armed forces. Responding to human-rights abuses, the United States Congress cut military aid to Guatemala by 50 per cent and economic aid by 25 per cent. On December 2, Guatemalan troops opened fire on 2,000 protesters, killing at least 11 people. In June, the murder of an American innkeeper, Michael DeVine, strained U.S. relations after evidence linked his death to the military.   Nathan A. Haverstock

See also **Latin America** (Facts in brief table). In *World Book,* see **Guatemala.**

Guinea. See **Africa.**

Guyana. See **Latin America.**

Haiti. In a landslide victory, Jean-Bertrand Aristide, a Roman Catholic priest and advocate for the poor, was elected president of Haiti on Dec. 16, 1990. Early official results gave Aristide 70.6 per cent of the vote, compared with 12.6 per cent for his closest rival, Marc Bazin, an economist.

The 1990 elections—Haiti's first democratic elections since gaining independence from France in 1804—were peaceful for the most part. The voting was monitored by nearly 1,000 foreigners, including former United States President Jimmy Carter and official observers from the United Nations and the Organization of American States. An attempt to hold presidential elections in 1987 was disrupted by thugs who killed 34 voters as army troops stood by.

Aristide entered the field of 11 presidential candidates late. As a result, the movement he headed—the National Front for Democracy and Change—did not run enough candidates to win a majority in parliament, and he moved to form a coalition government.

Aristide advocates *liberation theology,* which holds that the church's chief mission is to fight poverty and social injustice. His victory reportedly alarmed Haiti's traditional centers of power, including the army. But the army remained loyal on Jan. 7, 1991, crushing a coup attempt by an associate of former dictator Jean-Claude Duvalier.   Nathan A. Haverstock

See also **Latin America** (Facts in brief table). In *World Book,* see **Haiti.**

Jean-Bertrand Aristide, winner of Haiti's December presidential elections, waves to supporters during his campaign, which focused on concerns of the poor.

Handicapped. An estimated 43 million people in the United States with physical or mental disabilities gained sweeping protection against discrimination in private employment with the passage in July 1990 of the Americans with Disabilities Act. Provisions of the measure, which are to be phased in over a period of two to seven years, also are intended to ensure people with disabilities access to a wide range of services and public facilities. The new disabled-rights act was hailed as the most comprehensive civil rights legislation since the Civil Rights Act of 1964.

The new law extends to most private businesses the antibias provisions of the Rehabilitation Act of 1973, which had applied only to the federal government and employers receiving federal funds. The new law bans job discrimination against people with disabilities and requires employers to make "reasonable accommodations" in the workplace for such employees. It also expands the definition of "disabled" to include people with AIDS, those who are carriers of the AIDS virus, and drug and alcohol addicts in treatment programs.

The law requires all retail businesses to be accessible to people with disabilities unless the changes needed to accomplish this would result in undue hardship. All new or renovated buildings and new buses, railcars, and key transit stations also must be accessible. In addition, telecommunications companies are required to provide service that enables people with speech and hearing impairments to communicate by telephone.

New books on deafness published in 1990 included *In Silence: Growing Up Hearing in a Deaf World* by Ruth Sidransky and *What's That Pig Outdoors?: A Memoir of Deafness* by Henry Kisor.

Air travel rules. New regulations requiring airlines to improve services for people with disabilities were issued by the U.S. Department of Transportation on March 2, 1990. Under the rules, all new or refurbished aircraft with at least 30 seats must have movable armrests on half the aisle seats so that physically handicapped people can be seated more easily. In addition, all new wide-body aircraft must have at least one accessible lavatory and must carry special wheelchairs for use by handicapped people wishing to move up and down the aisles.

Closed-caption law. People who are hearing impaired may be able to view captions summarizing the conversation in television programs on their TV screen at the push of a button beginning in 1993. Under a law passed by Congress in October 1990, all new television sets sold in the United States after July 1993 must be equipped with a computer chip that provides caption service without the use of a special decoder. Like a decoder, the chip converts coded signals broadcast by a television station into subtitles that appear at the bottom of a TV screen.   Barbara A. Mayes

In *World Book*, see **Handicapped**.
Harness racing. See **Horse racing**.

Children at the Rehabilitation Institute of Chicago celebrate the signing into law of the Americans with Disabilities Act on July 26.

Havel, Václav (1936-   ), was reelected president of Czechoslovakia on July 5, 1990. He was initially elected president, the first non-Communist since 1948, on Dec. 29, 1989, but he accepted on the condition that free parliamentary elections take place in 1990 and that the newly elected parliament choose a president. The lawmakers voted Havel to a two-year term, a transition period for the country to establish a free-market economy and adopt a new constitution. Many Czechoslovaks trusted him and considered his election essential to guarantee that the changes in government would be permanent. See **Czechoslovakia**.

Havel was born on Oct. 5, 1936, in Prague. His father was a famous restaurant owner and had extensive real estate in the commercial center of the city until it was seized after the Communist take-over in 1948. Because of his upper-class birth, Havel was denied regular admission to a university. Instead, he worked days as a laborer while studying nights at a technical college and the Prague Academy of the Arts. At 19, he began publishing critical essays but soon turned to writing plays. He has received numerous literary prizes from many different countries.

Beginning in the 1970's, Havel was arrested and jailed repeatedly for his human-rights activities, most recently from January to May 1989.

Havel and his wife, Olga, were married in 1965 and have no children.   Carol L. Hanson

Hawaii. See State government.

Health and disease. Researchers in 1990 identified a number of genes believed to cause some inherited diseases or to make an individual likely to develop a certain disease. Genes are segments of DNA (*deoxyribonucleic acid*) that contain coded hereditary information. Thousands of genes are carried by chromosomes, tiny threadlike structures in the nucleus of cells. Human beings have 23 pairs of chromosomes.

Neurofibromatosis gene. Scientists on July 12 announced their identification of the gene responsible for *neurofibromatosis* (NF). NF is one of the most common inherited diseases, second only to cystic fibrosis, occurring in about 1 in 4,000 live births. About 100,000 people in the United States and 1½ million people worldwide have NF.

Using sophisticated laboratory techniques, researchers found the NF gene on one section of chromosome 17. Part of the reason for the difficulty in finding the exact location of the gene, the researchers said, was that there were three smaller genes embedded in the huge NF gene. Its impressive length could explain why the disease is so common; it offers many opportunities for *mutation*, or change. The researchers suspect that the gene's function in the body is to suppress the growth of tumors. Thus, if the gene were deactivated through mutation, the result would be abnormal growth of many tumors.

NF symptoms range from skin discolorations to disfiguring and painful tumors that grow on nerves along the face and other parts of the body. These tumors become cancerous and life-threatening in about 5 per cent of the patients. Mistakenly known as *elephant man's disease*, NF gained wide public attention in recent years in the popular motion picture and play about Joseph Merrick, a grossly deformed man who lived in London in the 1800's. Experts now believe that Merrick suffered not from NF but from another disfiguring disease, *Proteus syndrome*.

Scientists predicted that the identification of the NF gene could lead to relatively rapid development of a test to diagnose NF. They emphasized, however, that it could take years of additional research to develop treatments to control, or possibly even cure, NF.

Lung cancer gene. An August 1990 study reported the existence of a lung cancer gene. Researchers tested tissue from lung cancer patients and concluded that the gene was "turned on" in them, producing a protein that turned the chemicals in cigarette smoke into cancer-causing substances. Researchers speculated that the gene is activated more easily in some people than in others, making them likely to get cancer if they smoke. Some people may be born with such a high likelihood of the gene becoming activated that they are in danger of developing lung cancer without smoking. In other people, the gene may remain inactive, explaining why some long-term cigarette smokers do not get lung cancer.

Gene for alcoholism? Researchers in April reported the identification of a gene that may play an important role in causing alcoholism. During autopsies, they studied the brains of 35 alcoholics and 35 nonalcoholics and located the gene on chromosome 11. This gene is a *receptor*, or molecular doorway, for dopamine, a chemical that plays an important role in helping brain cells communicate with one another and also appears to be involved in pleasure-seeking behavior. This receptor gene was found in 24 of the alcoholics and 7 of the nonalcoholics.

In December, however, researchers at the National Institute on Alcohol Abuse and Alcoholism, an agency of the U.S. Department of Health and Human Services, reported they had been unable to confirm the results of the April study. This did not disprove the idea that alcoholism is partly hereditary, but the researchers suggested more work is needed to identify the gene or genes that might play a role.

Gene for arthritis. The discovery of a gene that causes a form of osteoarthritis, the most common kind of arthritis, was reported in September. Scientists identified the gene in all 9 arthritic members of a 19-member family with an unusually high incidence of the disease. The gene causes the body to produce a defective form of *collagen*, a major component of the protective cartilage on joint surfaces. As a result, the cartilage breaks down more quickly than is normal, causing pain, inflammation, and stiffness of elbows, knees, hips, and fingers. An estimated 16 million Americans suffer from osteoarthritis. Early detection of this gene in people would enable them to plan career and leisure activities that would avoid speeding up the arthritic degeneration of their joints.

Healthy babies for older moms. Women who delay starting a family until they are in their 30's face only a slightly higher risk than do younger women of producing low-birth-weight babies and no increased risk of having stillborn or premature babies. This was the result of a study concluded in March of 3,917 women, who were mainly white, well educated, and nonsmokers. The study did not check for Down syndrome and other hereditary diseases, because almost all the mothers were tested during pregnancy.

Piggyback herpesvirus. The herpes simplex type 1 virus enters a cell piggyback fashion, through a site intended for a protein that stimulates cell division, researchers announced in June. Cells have receptor or docking sites for the protein, which circulates in the blood. Once docked to the site, the protein slips easily inside the cell, carrying herpes type 1 with it. Type 1 is one of the most prevalent viruses in the United States, with about 8 out of 10 people showing signs of previous infection. It causes cold sores and has been implicated in other disorders. Scientists say new drugs could be developed to mimic the protein enough to bind with herpesviruses, removing them from the blood without entering the cell.   Michael Woods

See also **Biology.** In *World Book,* see **Cell; Disease; Health; Neurofibromatosis.**

Hnatyshyn, Ramon John (1934-   ), was sworn in as Canada's 24th governor general on Jan. 29, 1990, succeeding Jeanne M. Sauvé. As governor general, Hnatyshyn (pronounced *na TIHSH ehn*) represents Canada's head of state, Queen Elizabeth II. He is Canada's first governor general of Ukrainian heritage.

Hnatyshyn was born on March 16, 1934, in Saskatoon, Sask., where his father practiced law. His mother, Helen Constance Pitts, was active in international women's groups.

Hnatyshyn started practicing law in 1957, after earning a law degree at the University of Saskatchewan. His practice has included business and corporate law, public and trade law, civil suits, and mediation.

A Progressive Conservative, Hnatyshyn was elected to Parliament in 1974 and served for 14 years in the House of Commons. During that time, he held a number of posts, including minister of justice and attorney general of Canada. In that post, he reformed the system by which federally appointed judges are named, replacing party patronage with selection based on wide consultation among legal groups. In 1988, he was appointed queen's counsel for Canada.

Hnatyshyn is known for an ability to inspire good will among Canadians who differ politically. He and his wife, the former Karen Gerda Nygaard Andreasen, have two sons.   Margaret Anne Schmidt

Hobbies. See **Coin collecting; Stamp collecting; Toys and games.**

Hockey. The Edmonton Oilers, in their 11th season in the National Hockey League (NHL), won the Stanley Cup for the fifth time. They did it without some key figures from their previous championship teams—center Wayne Gretzky (traded), defenseman Paul Coffey (traded), goalie Grant Fuhr (injured), and coach Glen Sather (now general manager).

Regular 1989-1990 season. The Calgary Flames, the Stanley Cup defending champions, won the Smythe Division with 99 points, second in the league only to the 101 of the Boston Bruins, who took the Adams Division. Edmonton finished second in the Smythe Division with 90 points, better than the Norris division-winning Chicago Black Hawks (88) and the New York Rangers (85), tops in the Patrick Division.

Gretzky, playing for the Los Angeles Kings, won his eighth Ross Trophy as scoring leader with 142 points, and he led in assists with 102. On Oct. 15, 1989, he broke Gordie Howe's career scoring record of 1,850 points and finished the season with 1,979. Brett Hull of the St. Louis Blues led in goals (72).

Play-offs. Because 16 of the 21 teams qualified for the Stanley Cup play-offs, Los Angeles staggered in despite a 34-39-7 record. In the first round, Los Angeles upset Calgary, 4 games to 2, and Edmonton just got by the Winnipeg Jets, 4 games to 3.

In the conference finals, Edmonton eliminated Chicago, 4 games to 2, and Boston overran the Washington Capitals, 4 games to 0. Edmonton defeated Boston in the cup finals, 4 games to 1. The first game was the longest in the history of the Stanley Cup finals, lasting 5 hours 32 minutes before Edmonton won, 3-2, in the third sudden-death overtime.

An unexpected hero for Edmonton was Bill Ranford, traded from Boston in 1988 as a prospective backup goalie. In the play-offs, he replaced the injured Fuhr, held Boston to eight goals in the finals, and was voted the Conn Smythe Trophy as the play-offs' Most Valuable Player (MVP). The regular-season MVP award went to center Mark Messier of Edmonton.

Other news . The all-star team comprised Messier at center, Hull and Luc Robitaille of Los Angeles at wing, Ray Bourque of Boston and Al MacInnis of Calgary on defense, and Patrick Roy of the Montreal Canadiens in goal.

The NHL agreed to expand the league by adding seven teams by the year 2000. The first new team was planned for the San Francisco Bay area for the 1991-1992 season, with Tampa Bay and Ottawa joining in 1992-1993. Brothers George and Gordon Gund sold the Minnesota North Stars for $31.5 million and agreed to pay $50 million for the bay area franchise. They named the team the San Jose Sharks.

In May 1990, the Soviet Union won its 22nd world championship since 1954. In the medal round of the competition from April 16 to May 2 in Switzerland, Sweden finished second, Czechoslovakia third, Canada fourth, and the United States fifth.   Frank Litsky

In *World Book,* see **Hockey.**

National Hockey League standings

Clarence Campbell Conference

James Norris Division

	W.	L.	T.	Pts.
Chicago Black Hawks*	41	33	6	88
St. Louis Blues*	37	34	9	83
Toronto Maple Leafs*	38	38	4	80
Minnesota North Stars*	36	40	4	76
Detroit Red Wings	28	38	14	70

Conn Smythe Division

	W.	L.	T.	Pts.
Calgary Flames*	42	23	15	99
Edmonton Oilers*	38	28	14	90
Winnipeg Jets*	37	32	11	85
Los Angeles Kings*	34	39	7	75
Vancouver Canucks	25	41	14	64

Prince of Wales Conference

Charles F. Adams Division

Boston Bruins*	46	25	9	101
Buffalo Sabres*	45	27	8	98
Montreal Canadiens*	41	28	11	93
Hartford Whalers*	38	33	9	85
Quebec Nordiques	12	61	7	31

Lester Patrick Division

New York Rangers*	36	31	13	85
New Jersey Devils*	37	34	9	83
Washington Capitals*	36	38	6	78
New York Islanders*	31	38	11	73
Pittsburgh Penguins	32	40	8	72
Philadelphia Flyers	30	39	11	71

*Made play-off.

Stanley Cup winner—
Edmonton Oilers (defeated
Boston Bruins, 4 games to 1)

Scoring leaders	Games	Goals	Assists	Pts.
Wayne Gretzky, Los Angeles	73	40	102	142
Mark Messier, Edmonton	79	45	84	129
Steve Yzerman, Detroit	79	62	65	127
Mario Lemieux, Pittsburgh	59	45	78	123
Brett Hull, St. Louis	80	72	41	113
Bernie Nicholls, N.Y. Rangers	79	39	73	112
Pierre Turgeon, Buffalo	80	40	66	106
Pat LaFontaine, N.Y. Islanders	74	54	51	105
Paul Coffey, Pittsburgh	80	29	74	103
Joe Sakic, Quebec	80	39	63	102
Luc Robitaille, Los Angeles	80	52	49	101
Ron Francis, Hartford	80	32	69	101

Leading goalies (25 or more games)	Games	Goals against	Avg.
Patrick Roy, Montreal	54	134	2.53
Mike Liut, Hartford/Washington	37	91	2.53
Reggie Lemelin, Boston	43	108	2.81
Daren Puppa, Buffalo	56	156	2.89
Andy Moog, Boston	46	122	2.89

Awards

Calder Trophy (best rookie)— Sergei Makarov, Calgary
Hart Trophy (most valuable player)— Mark Messier, Edmonton
Lady Byng Trophy (sportsmanship)— Brett Hull, St. Louis
Masterton Trophy (perseverance, dedication to hockey)—
   Gord Kluzak, Boston
Norris Trophy (best defenseman)— Ray Bourque, Boston
Ross Trophy (leading scorer)— Wayne Gretzky, Los Angeles
Selke Trophy (best defensive forward)— Rick Meagher, St. Louis
Smythe Trophy (most valuable player in Stanley Cup)—
   Bill Ranford, Edmonton
Vezina Trophy (most valuable goalie)— Patrick Roy, Montreal

Honduras. On Jan. 27, 1990, Rafael Leonardo Callejas of the center-right National Party was sworn in for a four-year term as Honduran president. An expert in farm management, Callejas pledged to reduce Honduras' 30 per cent unemployment rate. He also promised to cultivate closer ties with Europe to lessen Honduras' dependency on the United States.

Hondurans were cheered by the end of the civil war in neighboring Nicaragua and the demobilization of *contra* rebels whose camps had been in Honduran territory. The demobilization was carried out from April through June under United Nations supervision.

On March 2, the Callejas administration introduced an austerity program that included a 100 per cent devaluation of the nation's currency and a 20 per cent hike in fuel costs. The unpopular measures led to labor troubles. On August 7, some 10,000 banana workers ended a two-week strike only after receiving assurances of a 25 per cent pay raise. Hospital employees and workers at Honduras' only oil refinery, who struck in solidarity with banana workers, received similar raises.

In September, President Callejas told representatives of the Organization of American States that the crisis in the Persian Gulf was having a "terrible" impact on Honduras, the result of higher oil prices that fed inflation.   Nathan A. Haverstock

See also **Latin America** (Facts in brief table). In *World Book,* see **Honduras.**

Horse racing. Thoroughbred racing in the United States in 1990 will be remembered not for triumphs but for tragedy. During the sport's showcase—the Breeders' Cup races on October 27 at Belmont Park near New York City—three horses died after breakdowns during two races an hour apart.

In July, the 4-year-old Sunday Silence, the 1989 Horse of the Year, tore a leg ligament. That same month, Sunday Silence's main rival, the 4-year-old Easy Goer, chipped an anklebone. The 5-year-old Criminal Type then became the leading older horse, only to injure an ankle. All three horses were retired.

On Breeders' Cup day, during the $1-million Sprint, the highly regarded Mr. Nickerson suffered an acute pulmonary hemorrhage, fell, and died minutes later on the track. Shaker Knit tripped over the fallen horse, leaving Shaker Knit's rear legs paralyzed, and a day later he was humanely destroyed.

Two races after the Breeders' Cup Sprint came the $1-million Breeders' Cup Distaff, matching the 5-year-old mare Bayakoa and the already legendary 3-year-old filly Go for Wand. Ninety yards (82 meters) from the finish, with Go for Wand inches in front of Bayakoa, she took a bad stride. She crumbled to the track, got up, tried to keep racing, then fell in a heap from a shattered front ankle. She was given a lethal injection.

Later that day, the 3-year-old Unbridled, the Kentucky Derby winner, rallied from last to win the $3-million Breeders' Cup Classic. Unbridled became the

Major horse races of 1990

Race	Winner	Value to winner
Arlington Million	Golden Pheasant	$600,000
Belmont Stakes	Go and Go	$411,600
Breeders' Cup Classic	Unbridled	$1,350,000
Breeders' Cup Distaff	Bayakoa	$450,000
Breeders' Cup Juvenile	Fly So Free	$450,000
Breeders' Cup Juvenile Fillies	Meadow Star	$450,000
Breeders' Cup Mile	Royal Academy	$450,000
Breeders' Cup Sprint	Safely Kept	$450,000
Breeders' Cup Turf	In the Wings	$900,000
Budweiser International	Fly Till Dawn	$450,000
Cartier Million (Ireland)	Rinka Das	$793,976
Champion Stakes (England)	In the Grove	$409,436
Derby Stakes (England)	Quest for Fame	$569,775
Hollywood Futurity	Best Pal	$495,000
Hollywood Gold Cup	Criminal Type	$550,000
Irish Derby (Ireland)	Salsabil	$477,156
Jockey Club Gold Cup	Flying Continental	$503,100
Kentucky Derby	Unbridled	$581,000
King George VI and Queen Elizabeth Diamond Stakes (England)	Belmez	$456,068
Molson Export Million	Izvestia	$600,000
Pimlico Special	Criminal Type	$600,000
Preakness Stakes	Summer Squall	$445,900
Prix de l'Arc de Triomphe (France)	Saumarez	$853,500
Rothmans International (Canada)	French Glory	$619,650
Santa Anita Handicap	Ruhlmann	$550,000
Super Derby	Home at Last	$600,000
Travers Stakes	Rhythm	$707,000

Major U.S. harness races of 1990

Race	Winner	Value to winner
Cane Pace	Jake and Elwood	$108,987
Hambletonian	Harmonious	$673,000
Little Brown Jug	Beach Towel	$186,037
Meadowlands Pace	Beach Towel	$576,750
Messenger Stakes	Jake and Elwood	$163,527
Woodrow Wilson	Die Laughing	$521,750

Sources: *The Blood-Horse* magazine and U.S. Trotting Association.

year's leading money winner with 1990 earnings of $3,718,149.

On November 15, the 15-year-old Alydar, a leading sire, broke a bone in his right hind leg kicking his stall door. After surgery, he fell, broke his thighbone, and was destroyed. The next day, Northern Dancer, the dominant sire of the last 25 years, suffered a serious case of colic and was put to death at the age of 29.

Harness. Among pacers and trotters, the horse of the year was Beach Towel, a 3-year-old pacer. He won 18 of 23 races and earned $2,091,860, the first time a harness horse had won $2 million in one year. His victories included the Breeders' Crown, Little Brown Jug, Adios, Meadowlands Pace, and Canada's leading harness race, the Prix d'Été.

The 12 Breeders' Crown races, held on November 2 and 30 at Pompano Beach, Fla., were harness racing's equivalent of the Breeders' Cup series for thoroughbreds. Among the Breeders' Crown winners was Miss Easy, a 2-year-old filly.

Miss Easy, with 15 victories in 17 races, earned $1,128,956, the first filly to exceed $1 million in a year. On September 25 in Lexington, Ky., her mile in 1 minute 51⅖ seconds set a record for 2-year-olds and equaled the fastest ever by a female horse of any age. On November 30, in a Breeders' Cup race for colts, Artsplace won in 1 minute 51⅕ seconds, breaking Miss Easy's record for 2-year-old pacers. Frank Litsky

In *World Book,* see **Harness racing; Horse racing.**

Hospital. Policy and funding uncertainties in 1990 left hospitals in the United States wondering about their future solvency—and even their very survival. The American Hospital Association (AHA), based in Chicago, reported in 1990 that 80 hospitals had closed in 1989, including 65 community hospitals (general acute-care facilities) and 15 noncommunity hospitals (specialty and other nonacute-care facilities). The closings brought the total for the 1980's to 698—508 community and 190 noncommunity hospitals.

Rural hospitals were especially hard hit; 44 rural facilities closed in 1989, compared with 21 urban hospitals. This led to concern among policymakers about the future of rural hospitals. In 1989, Congress had authorized seven state demonstration projects to restructure rural facilities and enhance their prospects; $9.8 million was appropriated for the program, which was expected to begin in late 1991.

Funding uncertainty. The budget negotiations also left hospitals unsure about Medicare funding. The budget bill that finally passed in October 1990 included a five-year reduction of about $33 billion in provider payments, with hospitals absorbing half that amount in the form of rates set at slightly less than hospitals' own cost increases.

The AHA complained in October that 51.7 per cent of hospitals reported that Medicare payments did not cover their costs as it was, which they found especially troubling because Medicare beneficiaries are a majority of their patients.

Staffing shortages. Hospitals continued to face shortages of workers, and a United States Department of Health and Human Services report in April 1990 predicted more of the same for years to come.

The AHA reported that the average hospital vacancy rate for registered nurses was 12.7 per cent at the end of 1989. And the Association of American Medical Colleges reported in July 1990 that graduate physicians were starting to avoid taking residencies in some hospitals, notably those in New York City. The association theorized that they might be deterred by high numbers of AIDS patients in such facilities, though several factors were thought to be involved. Hospitals in many cities reported overcrowding of emergency rooms and significant economic losses on treating trauma patients as these institutions became the health-care providers "of last resort" for more and more low-income people.

Reform hopes dim. The Pepper Commission, named after its first chairman, the late Representative Claude D. Pepper of Florida, in September became the latest health-care panel to recommend universal coverage for the 33 million Americans lacking insurance for hospital and medical care. The report was criticized by some members of Congress because its plan for funding such coverage was vague and based on tax increases. Emily Friedman

In *World Book,* see **Hospital.**

Housing. See **Building and construction.**

Houston. Continuing an upturn that began in 1988, Houston's economy showed further signs of improvement in 1990, despite uncertainties about the national economy. Sales of existing homes, which had been in a severe slump during much of the 1980's, were at a record pace through September 1990 and were up 10.5 per cent from the first nine months of 1989. The construction of new homes also increased.

The sharp rise in oil prices after Iraq's invasion of Kuwait on Aug. 2, 1990, was welcome news in Houston, where the oil industry has long been a major segment of the economy. The Federal Reserve Bank of Dallas estimated that every $1 increase in the price of a barrel of crude oil would mean 17,000 additional jobs in Texas, a significant proportion of them in Houston. The city's unemployment rate fell to 5.3 per cent in August, the lowest it had been since 1982.

Economic summit. One of the high points of the year in Houston came in July when the city hosted the 1990 economic summit of industrialized nations. The annual meeting brought together the leaders of Canada, France, Great Britain, Italy, Japan, the United States, and West Germany to discuss the state of the world economy. Houston, President George Bush's adopted hometown, rolled out the red carpet for the three-day summit. Civic leaders hoped the international attention would help dispel the city's down-at-the-heels image, making the effort worthwhile.

Law enforcement. Houston became the nation's largest city with a woman police chief when Elizabeth M. Watson was named to that post in January. She replaced Lee P. Brown, who was appointed New York City's police commissioner after being widely credited with improving Houston's police-community relations.

Watson was greeted by an alarming increase in the city's homicide rate, which she blamed primarily on a worsening drug problem. The number of killings during the year jumped by almost 20 per cent; by late December, the city had recorded 600 homicides, compared with 512 for all of 1989. Seemingly senseless incidents, exemplified by the gunning down of a young woman who was driving home from work in an ordinarily safe neighborhood, stunned the community. The killer, the teen-aged son of a police officer, had wanted the woman's car because his own had run out of gas.

Public apprehension about crime was heightened in September when, to comply with a federal judge's order to relieve overcrowding at the Harris County Jail, officials released more than 250 inmates. The freed prisoners, some of them felons, cheered and waved defiantly at television cameras.

Education. The Houston Independent School District battled a widespread perception in 1990 that the city's schools were nearly out of control. Rising concern over drug abuse, assaults, and gang activities prompted district Superintendent Joan Raymond to call for a summit with the Houston Police Department to address the problems. Raymond proposed that school security guards be given uniforms and guns. And, in an experiment aimed at preventing drug dealers and other outsiders from roaming freely on school campuses, she announced that students at 10 high schools must wear identification badges.

The level of academic achievement at Houston's schools during the year gave district officials more cause for worry. A major concern was the high-school dropout rate. One study estimated that 40 per cent of the students who were ninth graders in 1990 would quit school before earning a diploma.

The University of Houston (UH), meanwhile, welcomed a new president, Marguerite Ross Barnett. Barnett, who assumed her new post on September 1, had been president of the University of Missouri at St. Louis. UH thus became the nation's largest university to be headed by a black woman.

Transit. Debate continued during the year over whether the Metropolitan Transit Authority should build a $1-billion light rail system, which would use electrically powered cars that run on a street-level track. Although voters in 1988 endorsed the construction of a rail system, opponents gathered support in 1990 for another ballot on the question. Rail supporters, led by Mayor Kathryn J. Whitmire, argued that further delay could jeopardize federal funding for the project. Neither side expected the matter to be resolved soon.   Timothy J. Graham

In *World Book*, see **Houston.**

Elizabeth M. Watson, right, is sworn in as Houston's chief of police in January, becoming the first woman police chief of a major U.S. city.

Hungarians dismantle a red star before a crowd of onlookers in Budapest in March as one more symbol of Communist Party authority is scrapped.

Hungary faced a tough winter as 1990 drew to a close and the government battled the social problems that resulted from economic reform. Mounting inflation—30 per cent by October—and rising unemployment seriously aggravated the political problems faced by the emerging democracy.

Expectations that the transition to a market economy would yield quicker results with less pain left many Hungarians disillusioned with the government. Local elections in September and October of 1990 mirrored the disillusion. Voter turnout was low, and the ruling coalition trailed its chief opposition. The apathy reflected growing anxiety over factory closings, price hikes, and fresh hardships for an estimated 2 million of Hungary's 10½ million people living at or below the official poverty line.

The poor get poorer. Hungary had first enacted economic reforms under a 1968 plan, the New Economic Mechanism (NEM), giving it a head start over other eastern European countries in their later transition to a market economy. The reforms facilitated foreign investment. With the advent of a democratic government in 1990, more western companies formed joint ventures with Hungarian firms. Yet living standards had declined from the mid-1980's, and they further declined in 1990. Hungary's foreign debt had also grown—to nearly $22 billion, giving it the largest per capita foreign debt in eastern Europe.

To curb the debt, the International Monetary Fund

(IMF) made a five-year, $5-billion loan to Hungary dependent upon further economic reform. For consumers, this meant price increases on August 1, including a 30 per cent hike in heating and electricity costs for the average household. On October 26, a plan to raise gasoline prices 65 per cent brought Hungary to a virtual standstill as taxi and truck drivers blockaded the main routes for three days. The government then halved the price hike.

Adding to Hungary's economic woes was the collapse of COMECON, the Soviet-bloc trade organization, and a decision by the Soviet Union to accept only *hard* (internationally exchangeable) currency for its exports after Jan. 1, 1991. The result was layoffs at Hungary's big engineering firms, which had depended on the Soviet market. Trade losses were estimated at $1 billion for 1991. Hungary held a trade surplus in Soviet rubles, however, of $720 million.

Other economic reforms introduced in 1990 gave priority to privatization, with the aim of reducing state ownership of businesses from 92 per cent to 40 per cent over five years. A follow-up measure approved the sale of 10,000 state-owned firms.

Two parties dominated elections for Hungary's 386-seat National Assembly in late March and early April. The conservative Hungarian Democratic Forum won 164 seats. Its chief rival, the liberal Alliance of Free Democrats, won 92. The Socialist (formerly Communist) Party took 33 seats.

When the Assembly convened in May, it named an interim president: Arpad Goncz, a playwright who had spent six years in jail for his involvement in Hungary's 1956 anti-Communist uprising. Goncz, a member of the Alliance of Free Democrats, was elected to a five-year term as president in August 1990.

In May, Goncz named historian Jozsef Antall, leader of the Democratic Forum, prime minister. To gain a parliamentary majority, Antall formed a coalition with two smaller parties: the Independent Smallholders, a farmers' party with 44 seats, and the Christian Democrats with 21. In October, Hungary was admitted to the 23-nation Council of Europe, becoming the first member of the former Soviet bloc to join this western political organization.

Violence against ethnic Hungarians continued in Romania's Transylvania region. Under Romania's Communist regime, Hungarian villages there had been threatened with destruction. The election of a new Romanian government in 1990 stirred hope for an end to discrimination against the Hungarian minority. Instead, the situation worsened in March when Romanian nationalists staged violent anti-Hungarian demonstrations in Tirgu Mures. Under these pressures, the government backed away from a promise to restore the region's Hungarian-language education.　　　Eric Bourne

See also **Europe** (Facts in brief table). In *World Book*, see **Hungary.**

Hussein, Saddam (1937-　　　), president of Iraq, triggered an international crisis in August 1990 by ordering his nation's military forces to invade the neighboring country of Kuwait (see **Middle East**). Hussein, who has maintained power by ruthlessly suppressing opposition, has been condemned for serious human-rights violations, including using chemical weapons against Iraqi civilians accused of supporting a rebel movement. Before the invasion, however, his opposition to Iran and his diplomatic skills had won Iraq trade concessions and military support from many nations, including the United States.

Hussein was born in 1937 near the town of Tikrit, north of Baghdad, Iraq's capital. In 1956, while a student in Baghdad, he joined the Arab Baath Socialist Party. In 1959, after participating in a failed attempt to kill Iraqi dictator Abdul Karim Kassem, Hussein fled to Syria. He then moved to Egypt and entered the University of Cairo law school.

Hussein returned to Iraq in 1963 after Kassem was killed in a revolt led by members of the Baath Party. Later that year, one faction of the party took control of the government, and Hussein was jailed for two years. In 1968, he helped organize a coup that returned the party's other faction to power. He was elected acting deputy chairman of the ruling Revolutionary Command Council, the first of several important posts he held during his rise to power. Hussein became president of Iraq in 1979.　　　Barbara A. Mayes

Ice skating. Jill Trenary of Colorado Springs, Colo., the United States champion, won the world women's figure-skating championship in 1990. But in August, at a time when figure-skaters normally forego competition to work on their coming year's routines, she lost in the Goodwill Games to Kristi Yamaguchi of Fremont, Calif.

Kurt Browning of Edmonton, Canada, won the world men's title for the second straight year and also won in the Goodwill Games. Christopher Bowman of Van Nuys, Calif., the main U.S. contender, adlibbed routines in the world championships and the Goodwill Games, an unheard-of breach in this sport.

Figure skating. The world championships, held from March 6 to 11 in Halifax, Canada, were the last to include compulsory figures. The margin Trenary gained in those figures, in which she finished 1st and Midori Ito of Japan 10th, was just enough to let her win overall. Although Ito, the defending champion, won the subsequent original and long programs, she placed 2nd in the final standings.

In the U.S. championships, held in February in Salt Lake City, Utah, Yamaguchi finished second to Trenary in singles and won the pairs title with Rudi Galindo of San Jose. Todd Eldredge of South Chatham, Mass., won the men's singles title.

In the world championships, Yamaguchi took fourth in singles and fifth in pairs with Galindo. In the skating portion of the Goodwill Games, which ended on

Jill Trenary of Colorado Springs, Colo., arches back during the world figure-skating championships in Halifax, Canada, which she won in March.

August 4 in Tacoma, Wash., Yamaguchi defeated Trenary for the first time, then retired from pairs competition to concentrate on singles.

Although Browning skated erratically in the Canadian championships, he kept his title. In the world championships, he overtook the Soviet Union's Viktor Petrenko by outskating the European and Soviet champion in the free program.

In the world championships, Bowman stood fifth going into the free skating. Thirty seconds into his program, he abandoned his choreographed routine, did what came to him, and moved up to third place. In the Goodwill Games, he finished sixth after experimenting in competition with his original program.

As usual, Soviet couples were dominant. Ekaterina Gordeyeva and Sergei Grinkov won their fourth world championship in pairs, and Marina Klimova and Sergei Ponomarenko won their second in ice dancing.

Speed skating. The four major world championships were held in February in Austria, Norway, and Canada. The winners were Johann Olav Koss of Norway in men's all-around, Ki Tae Bae of South Korea in men's sprint, Jacqueline Börner of East Germany in women's all-around, and Angela Hauck of East Germany in women's sprint.   Frank Litsky

In *World Book*, see **Ice skating.**

Iceland. See **Europe.**

Idaho. See **State government.**

Illinois. See **Chicago; State government.**

Immigration. Congress adopted the first big overhaul of United States immigration laws in a quarter century on Oct. 27, 1990, to take effect in 1992. The Immigration Act of 1990, signed into law on November 29, dramatically expands immigration to the United States, at the same time uniting families and attracting skilled workers. The main provision of the legislation raises the cap on the number of visas granted to U.S.-bound foreigners from 500,000 a year in 1990 to 700,000 in the year 1994. The legislation also more than doubles the number of visas granted specifically on the basis of work skills, increasing that number from 54,000 a year to 140,000.

Supporters praised the overhaul as confirmation of the nation's historic "open-door" policy. A 1924 immigration law, on the other hand, set quotas country by country. In 1965, quotas were ended in favor of the current system, making family ties with U.S. residents the main determinant for entry.

Illegal immigration. The U.S. Immigration and Naturalization Service (INS) announced new guidelines on Feb. 2, 1990, that may prevent as many as 100,000 illegal aliens from being deported. These aliens are children and spouses of immigrants legalized in 1986, when Congress granted amnesty to 1.7 million undocumented aliens. INS Commissioner Gene McNary said the new "family fairness" guidelines would apply only to illegal immigrants residing in the country since the amnesty took effect.

The INS reported on March 21, 1990, that illegal immigration across the Mexican border to the United States had surged in recent months, reversing a three-year downturn. Arrests of illegal aliens were up nearly 30 per cent, totaling 801,937 from May 1988 through February 1989—compared with 617,317 for the same period a year earlier.

A government task force reported on Sept. 30, 1990, that it found evidence "many employers" were discriminating in hiring—rejecting legal immigrants with proper work documents in favor of undocumented workers, whom they can usually hire for lower wages. Congress had warned employers they could risk penalties for hiring undocumented workers in a 1986 revision of laws concerning illegal immigration. Congress took no immediate action on a task force recommendation that the top fine for hiring discrimination be raised from $2,000 to $4,000.

Ellis Island revisited. In 1990, thousands of people poured through New York City's Ellis Island, gateway for millions of immigrants who reached U.S. shores between 1892 and 1954. The people who came this time were tourists, many of them descendants of immigrants. A $156-million restoration project reopened the island on September 9 as a museum of immigration.   William R. Cormier

In the Special Reports section, see **Ellis Island, Museum of Memories.** In *World Book,* see **Immigration.**

Income tax. See **Taxation.**

India. The coalition government of Prime Minister Vishwanath Pratap Singh lost a confidence vote in the lower house of Parliament on Nov. 7, 1990, by 346 votes to 142. On November 10, Chandra Shekhar became prime minister at the head of a minority government. But Shekhar, a socialist, could count on only 56 parliamentary votes. He came to power with the agreement of the largest single bloc in Parliament, the Congress Party members led by former Prime Minister Rajiv Gandhi. Gandhi declined to seek the post, hoping to force new elections that might give his party a majority in the lower house.

Singh's coalition had governed since the Congress Party lost its parliamentary majority in elections in November 1989. But the small coalition was dependent upon support from Communists and the Bharatiya Janata Party (BJP). The BJP seeks to make India a Hindu state, abolishing special rights for minorities—especially Muslims, who make up about 11 per cent of the population. In political maneuvering for the votes of the nation's Hindu majority, the BJP withdrew its support for Singh, causing his fall from power.

A controversial jobs plan had caused grave problems for Singh. In the 1989 elections, Singh's Janata Dal party sought votes by supporting an old recommendation that 27 per cent of all civil service jobs in the national government be set aside for backward castes—disadvantaged members of India's Hindu class system. For decades, some of these jobs had been reserved for people in lower Hindu castes or those of some ethnic groups outside the caste system. By 1990, 22.5 per cent of government jobs were reserved for these Indians. Singh announced on August 7 that he would add 27 per cent more reservations, thus blocking almost half the civil service jobs from competition on merit.

Singh's decision touched off violent protests among students worried about their limited job prospects. According to press reports, more than a dozen people committed suicide in protest. Street battles erupted between opponents of the decision and its supporters, who were backed by the police.

The BJP then sparked a dispute over a religious site in the northern state of Uttar Pradesh. On October 30, the BJP launched an effort to tear down a 460-year-old Muslim mosque to build a Hindu temple on the site, which many Hindus believed was the birthplace of the Hindu deity Rama. Trying to prevent religious conflicts, Singh ordered the army to protect the building, but many Hindu soldiers failed to prevent Hindus from damaging the mosque. Violence spread across north India, with hundreds killed and more than 100,000 arrested.

The Congress Party lost control of six states in elections for state assemblies in February. After Singh applied pressure on weak state governments, Congress lost control of several more, eventually governing only Andhra Pradesh, Karnataka, and Maharashtra. Gandhi was widely accused of ineffective party leadership.

Separatist tensions. Terrorism increased in Punjab state, where militants from the Sikh religious community have long fought for independence. On April 3, terrorists bombed a Hindu religious procession, killing 32 people. In the month of August, a record 600 deaths were attributed to terrorist-related violence, more than double the August 1989 figure. The death toll for the year neared 2,000. But the police insisted that the total was lower, saying that much of the killing was the result of ordinary crime.

Singh won praise for boldly visiting Punjab shortly after becoming prime minister. But he conceded that he had missed a chance for peace in early 1990 by not holding the first state elections since 1985. With the state gripped in fear, Singh won Parliament's approval on Oct. 4, 1990, to continue to rule the state from New Delhi, the national capital, and postponed elections again.

Clashes in Kashmir. In mountainous Jammu and Kashmir, the only Indian state with a Muslim majority, conflict worsened as militants sought independence or union with neighboring Pakistan, a Muslim nation. Opposition to Indian control of the valley around Srinagar, Kashmir's summer capital, turned into a popular uprising after police there opened fire on a demonstration on January 20, killing about 50 people. Throughout the year, Indian police and soldiers replied to harassment or ambushes with attacks on by-

Indians gather at the grave of Kashmir's most senior Muslim religious leader, Mohammad Farooq, who was assassinated on May 21.

standers, arson, and other actions that hardened opposition. Pakistan blamed the Indian government for the May 21 assassination of Kashmir's senior Muslim cleric, Mohammad Farooq, and the killing of at least 47 supporters in his funeral procession.

India accused Pakistan of training guerrilla fighters and sending them to Kashmir. Although India produced captured guerrillas who supported the story, Pakistan denied it. During the spring, tensions mounted as both countries made military preparations and engaged in border fights.

In northeastern India, rebel forces in the states of Assam, Nagaland, and Manipur agreed in August to coordinate their fights for independence. An Assam liberation front, which complained that Assam had been deprived of its share of economic development funds, briefly stopped the state's oil exports. The Indian government lost control of much of the region.

Economic worries. While politicians argued whether the government should loosen its tight control of economic development—policies adapted from the now-abandoned Soviet model—a vibrant private business sector helped India achieve an economic growth rate of some 5 per cent in 1990. But agricultural productivity stagnated, and government spending pushed the federal budget deeply into deficit.   Henry S. Bradsher

See also **Asia** (Facts in brief table). In *World Book,* see **India.**

Chippewa Indians in northern Wisconsin rally in April in support of treaty rights allowing them to spearfish walleye pike in public lakes.

Indian, American. An 11-week stand-off between armed Mohawk Indians and the Canadian Army in Oka, Que., near Montreal, ended on Sept. 26, 1990, after the Indians laid down their weapons. The confrontation erupted over plans by Oka officials to expand a golf course using land regarded as sacred by the Mohawks. See **Canada; Montreal.**

Resource settlement. Chippewa Indians in Wisconsin are entitled to 50 per cent of that state's "harvestable natural resources," a federal judge ruled on May 9. The decision covers fish, deer, and small game. State and tribal officials hoped the ruling would end a bitter dispute over the Indians' treaty rights.

The dispute arose in the mid-1980's after a series of court rulings upheld treaties signed by the Chippewa and the U.S. government in the 1800's. Those treaties gave the Chippewa the right to hunt, fish, and gather forever on land in northern Wisconsin the Chippewas gave to the government. But the Chippewa's exercise of those rights, particularly their spearfishing of spawning walleye pike, had triggered angry, sometimes violent, protests. Non-Indian anglers argued that the spearfishing limited their own catch, depleted the walleye population, and harmed tourism.

On Oct. 11, 1990, the judge ruled that the Chippewa could not sue the state of Wisconsin for monetary damages for having prevented them from exercising their treaty rights for more than 100 years. The Chippewa had asked for $273 million in damages.

MacDonald conviction. Suspended Navajo tribal leader Peter MacDonald was convicted of 41 counts of bribery, extortion, conspiracy, and ethics violations on October 17 in Navajo District Court in Window Rock, Ariz. MacDonald had been accused of soliciting and accepting thousands of dollars in cash, loans, and other favors from people doing or seeking to do business with the tribe. On October 23, MacDonald was sentenced to nearly six years in prison and fined $11,000. The conviction barred him from holding tribal office for four years. In November, the Navajo elected former tribal Chairman Peterson Zah to the newly created post of president.

Land settlement. The Puyallup Indians of Washington state on March 24 abandoned their claims to 20,000 acres (8,100 hectares) of land along Tacoma's waterfront in return for a settlement worth $162 million. Under the terms of the agreement, the Puyallup will receive land, cash payments, and trusts promising education and jobs.

Reconciliation. South Dakota celebrated its first Native Americans Day on October 8, a day observed as Columbus Day in the rest of the United States. The establishment of the new holiday on the second Monday in October was one of several steps taken by South Dakota officials during 1990 to promote understanding between Indians and non-Indians.

On February 1, the representatives of eight Sioux tribes and South Dakota Governor George S. Mickelson signed a proclamation declaring 1990—the 100th anniversary of the Battle of Wounded Knee—as a year of reconciliation. In 1890, U.S. troops massacred more than 200 Sioux at an army camp on Wounded Knee Creek in southwestern South Dakota.

Peyote ban. An Oregon law prohibiting the use of the hallucinogenic drug peyote in religious ceremonies does not infringe on Native Americans' freedom of worship, the Supreme Court of the United States ruled on April 17, 1990. About half the states ban the religious use of the drug. Native Americans attacked the ruling, pointing out that Indians have been using peyote in religious rituals for at least 500 years.

Gambling dispute. A bitter dispute over the presence of gambling casinos on the St. Regis Indian Reservation, a Mohawk reservation along the United States-Canada border, claimed the lives of two Mohawks in May. The reservation straddles the St. Lawrence River in northern New York and southern Canada. The men died during a night of gun battles that forced thousands of Mohawks to flee the reservation or to barricade themselves in their homes.

Gambling advocates argue that the highly profitable casinos provide much-needed jobs for the reservation. Opponents, however, argue that the casinos spread corruption and undermine the traditional Indian way of life.　　Barbara A. Mayes

In *World Book,* see **Indian, American.**

Indiana. See **State government.**

Indonesia had steady economic growth during 1990, spurred by soaring oil and natural gas export earnings after events in the Middle East hiked international fuel prices (see **Middle East**). Domestic and foreign investment surged, and the government encouraged more investment by cutting tariffs and other trade barriers through reforms introduced on May 28.

The chairman of an international organization that provides aid for some 90 per cent of Indonesia's economic development said in April that Indonesia had "taken off on the path of sustainable economic growth." Nonetheless, the group urged more efforts to alleviate poverty. Government data showed that between 1984 and 1987, the percentage of the population living in poverty dropped from 22 per cent to 17 per cent.

On August 14, three former Indonesian leaders called for limits to presidential powers, a more fairly elected legislature, and legal reform. A few days later, 58 other former leaders suggested that Suharto should step down when his fifth presidential term ends in 1993. That same month, government officials said they would stop censoring imported foreign publications and telling Indonesian newspaper editors what they could or could not publish.

A leading government protester was released on Sept. 16, 1990, after five years in jail. The dissident, Hartono R. Dharsono, had helped bring Suharto to power in the mid-1960's. He was imprisoned after charging that under Suharto special interests had throttled democracy, leading to rampant corruption.

While supporters hailed Dharsono as a possible future president, Suharto kept silent about his own plans and maneuvered to keep men loyal to him in charge of the armed forces. Meanwhile, his children used their connections to expand their already-extensive business holdings—often angering other business people.

Revolt smoldered in several parts of the large nation. At the western tip of Sumatra, Muslim extremists killed more than 70 security force members between April and August during a flare-up of independence demands. In East Timor—where independence demonstrations had greeted visiting Pope John Paul II in October 1989—some 150 students demonstrated for freedom during a Jan. 17, 1990, visit by United States Ambassador John C. Monjo. A separatist movement also continued in Irian Jaya, the Indonesian part of New Guinea Island.

Diplomatic relations with China were restored on August 8, during Chinese Premier Li Peng's visit to Indonesia. While in Jakarta, the capital, Li said his country would not act to influence ethnic Chinese Indonesians, who make up 3 per cent of the population.　　Henry S. Bradsher

See also **Asia** (Facts in brief table). In the Special Reports section, see **Riding a Wave of Prosperity on the Pacific Rim.** In *World Book,* see **Indonesia.**

International trade grew by roughly 5 per cent in 1990, a markedly lower rate of increase than in 1988 or 1989, when the rates were 9 per cent and 7 per cent. The more moderate expansion reflected a global economic slowdown. In the last six months of the year, as oil prices soared in the wake of a crisis in the Middle East, oil-exporting nations reaped much higher trade revenues, but higher fuel costs for importers tended to depress overall trade. Total world trade in 1990 was estimated at $3.2 trillion.

The United States made scant progress in trying to reduce its *trade deficit*—the amount of imports not offset by exports—despite a weaker dollar and slowing domestic economic growth. In 1990, the U.S. trade deficit once again exceeded $100 billion. Exports increased at a slower rate than in 1988 or 1989. Non-oil imports increased only modestly, but sharply higher oil prices greatly inflated the nation's oil-import bill.

Nonetheless, the worrisome trade imbalances among the world's three largest economies—those of the United States, Japan, and Germany—eased. The trade surpluses of both Japan and Germany declined. The declines were especially large in terms of each country's *gross national product*—the total value of the goods and services it produced. The smaller surpluses reflected stronger currency and higher domestic demand in each country. But the continuing U.S. trade deficit further increased the U.S. foreign debt, which approached $800 billion.

Soviet citizens line up to purchase Big Macs and French fries at Moscow's first McDonald's, which opened on January 30.

GATT talks fail. Dominating the international trade scene in 1990 were negotiations at the General Agreement on Tariffs and Trade (GATT) in Geneva, Switzerland, where more than 100 nations sought to reduce tariffs and other trade barriers and draft new rules governing investment policy, intellectual property rights, and international trade in services. But the negotiations, known as the Uruguay Round, stalled over an agricultural trade dispute between the 12-nation European Community (EC or Common Market) and the United States and other agricultural exporters. The EC refused to reduce its farm export subsidies to the extent demanded by the United States and other nations. Trade ministers met in Brussels, Belgium, in early December to try to break the impasse but failed.

U.S.-Japan pacts. Despite the GATT discord, the United States in 1990 appeared to settle a number of trade problems with other countries, particularly Japan. Japan agreed to modify various government regulations to help United States firms and those of other countries sell some products to Japanese customers, including telecommunications equipment and certain electronic services.

Broader policy commitments were covered in an accord known as the Structural Impediments Initiative. The agreement, signed in June, was intended to help cut the large imbalance in trade and payments between the United States and Japan. Japan promised to expand its public works spending, tighten its antitrust policies, modernize its retail distribution system, and encourage more efficient use of its land. The United States pledged to reduce its federal budget deficit, promote increased private savings, and improve its educational system. Even before these measures were announced, the U.S. trade deficit with Japan had begun to decline. The 1990 deficit was estimated at slightly above $40 billion, the lowest since 1985.

Enterprise for the Americas. United States President George Bush gave Latin America increased attention in 1990. On June 27, he announced the Enterprise for the Americas Initiative, proposing an eventual free-trade zone stretching from "Anchorage [Alaska] to Tierra del Fuego [Argentina]." He also proposed creating a $1.5-billion fund over five years to help promote more open investment policies in Latin America. In a radical policy shift, Bush asked Congress to forgive Caribbean and Latin-American debts owed to the U.S. government. Congress approved part of the proposal to write off the debts. In a quick follow-up to Bush's proposals, the United States signed agreements with Bolivia, Chile, Colombia, Costa Rica, Ecuador, and Honduras for the creation of bilateral commissions to study ways to promote mutual trade and investment.

On June 11, Bush and Mexican President Carlos Salinas de Gortari announced that they planned to negotiate a free-trade pact. In September, Bush took a first step toward the negotiation, which was expected to start in 1991, by formally notifying Congress of his plan. Canada, which in 1988 concluded a free-trade pact with the United States, said it wanted to participate in the U.S.-Mexico talks, raising the prospect of a free-trade zone covering all of North America.

Two other actions strengthened trade ties in the hemisphere. The U.S. Congress approved legislation making permanent the duty-free benefits accorded to about 20 Caribbean Basin countries and expanded those benefits. Bush in October proposed extending the benefits to Bolivia, Colombia, Ecuador, and Peru.

Eastern Europe. The United States also forged closer relations with the countries of eastern Europe in 1990, as the formerly Communist nations adopted Western economic and trade policies. Bush and Soviet President Mikhail S. Gorbachev on June 1 signed a trade agreement to lower U.S. tariffs on Soviet goods, to assure U.S. business access to Soviet facilities, and to protect U.S. patents, copyrights, and trademarks in the Soviet Union. Bush said he would not ask Congress to approve the plan until the Soviets eased emigration restrictions. On December 12, Bush cleared the way for up to $1 billion in government credit guarantees for food shipments to the Soviet Union.

In November, the United States and Czechoslovakia implemented a trade agreement including provisions similar to those in the Soviet accord. Bulgarian and U.S. officials drafted a trade agreement in October with the expectation that the pact would be implemented in 1991.

The United States meanwhile launched a series of investment-treaty negotiations with eastern European governments. The treaties were to provide U.S. investors in those countries with nondiscriminatory treatment, the right to return profits to the United States, and protection against government take-overs. Treaties with Poland and Czechoslovakia were signed in March and April. Negotiations proceeded with Bulgaria, Hungary, Yugoslavia, and the Soviet Union.

In another move to expand trade relations with eastern Europe, the United States and 16 allied nations agreed in June to relax controls on certain products and technologies exported to that area. The trade group relaxed export controls on computers, machine tools, and telecommunications equipment.

Aid for economic reform. In May, 40 nations, including the United States and the Soviet Union, agreed to create the European Bank for Reconstruction and Development to further aid eastern European economic reforms. The agency, to be based in London, was due to begin operating in 1991 with starting capital of $12 billion.

Also in May, members of the United Nations International Monetary Fund agreed to enlarge the fund's resources by 50 per cent, or roughly $60 billion, in 1991. The fund will increase lending to developing nations undertaking economic reform.   Richard Lawrence

See also **Economics.** In **World Book,** see **International trade.**

Iowa. See **State government.**

Iran in 1990 remained largely isolated from the international community two years after agreeing to a cease-fire in the war with Iraq and a year after the death of the country's founder and supreme spiritual leader, Ayatollah Ruhollah Khomeini. Ayatollah Ali Hoseini Khamenei, Iran's supreme religious leader, and President Ali Akbar Hashemi Rafsanjani continued to strengthen their power bases. But Iran's internal political situation remained unstable.

Khamenei and his hard-line supporters continued to oppose openings to the West, especially to the United States. In February, Khamenei reaffirmed the death penalty imposed on British author Salman Rushdie by Khomeini in 1989 for writing a book some Muslims denounced as blasphemous to Islam. Rafsanjani, who appeared more concerned with practical results, continued to advocate increased foreign contacts. But he moved slowly, and *komitehs,* secret committees that enforce Islamic law, remained a powerful force in Iranian daily life.

Earthquake. A major earthquake devastated two provinces in northwestern Iran on June 21, 1990. The quake, the worst to hit the country since 1978, left 40,000 people dead, 60,000 people injured, and 105,000 families homeless. Some observers thought the disaster might lead to better relations with the West. Iran accepted all offers of aid, except those from Israel and South Africa, including about $300,000 in relief supplies from the United States. But the presence of foreign rescue workers distressed government officials, who asked them to leave after only a week.

Economy. Iran made little progress in solving its enormous economic problems in 1990. The country lacked the huge sums needed to repair the devastation caused by the war with Iraq and rebuild areas damaged by the earthquake. The inflation rate in 1990 was an estimated 25 per cent; the unemployment rate was 30 per cent.

The economic situation was expected to worsen because of the country's high population growth rate, estimated at from 3.2 to 4.0 per cent. At these rates, Iran's population of 58 million will double by 2007.

Iran stood to benefit from the international economic blockade imposed on Iraq for invading Kuwait in August 1990, however. Higher world oil prices boosted Iran's oil revenues.

Terrorism. Investigators probing the bombing of a Pan American World Airways jet over Scotland in 1988 reported in October 1990 that Iran had probably commissioned the bombing. They contended that Iran paid other groups to plant the bomb in revenge for the accidental downing of an Iranian commercial jetliner by a U.S. Navy cruiser in 1988.

Human rights. Iranian exiles in 1990 condemned Rafsanjani's government for continuing human-rights abuses, including mistreating prisoners and holding public executions. The government was also accused of ordering the assassinations of two Iranian political opponents living abroad.

Iranian women carrying a picture of Ayatollah Khomeini demonstrate against the United States in June, one year after the supreme leader's death.

Relations with Iraq. Two years after fighting stopped in the Iran-Iraq war, the two countries continued to argue over negotiations for a peace treaty, an exchange of prisoners, troop withdrawal, and territorial rights. In August, however, after the United Nations imposed an embargo on Iraq, that country took steps to stabilize its relations with Iran. Iraq agreed to abandon Iranian territory captured during the war and also began returning Iranian prisoners of war.

Rafsanjani's position in the Persian Gulf crisis was unclear. He criticized Iraq's invasion of Kuwait. But he also denounced the presence of foreign forces in the Middle East.

U.S. relations. Robert Polhill and Frank H. Reed, two Americans held hostage in Lebanon by groups reportedly linked to Iran, were freed in April. United States President George Bush praised Iran for unspecified assistance in winning the hostages' freedom. Their release was believed to have been orchestrated in part by Rafsanjani.

Although Rafsanjani cautiously worked to expand foreign contacts in 1990, he continued to criticize the United States for, among other things, failing to produce a goodwill gesture after the release of the American hostages. Periodic statements by the government about renewing U.S. ties were quickly condemned by hard-liners.   Christine Helms

See also **Middle East** (Facts in brief table). In *World Book,* see **Iran.**

Iran-contra affair prosecutions continued in 1990 with the trial of retired Navy Rear Admiral John M. Poindexter, a former national security adviser to President Ronald Reagan. On April 7, Poindexter was convicted in federal court in Washington, D.C., on five felony counts of conspiracy, lying to Congress, and obstructing a congressional inquiry into the affair. The 1985-1986 undercover operation involved the sale of arms to Iran and the diversion of profits from those sales to finance *contra* rebels fighting the Marxist Sandinista government of Nicaragua. That government lost power in a 1990 election. See **Nicaragua.**

The jury found that Poindexter had deceived Congress about the White House's role in an arms shipment to Iran in November 1985 and about White House support of the contras in violation of a congressional ban on military aid to the rebels. The jurors rejected a claim by Reagan, made in videotaped testimony, that no crimes were committed.

On June 11, 1990, Poindexter was sentenced to six months in prison. He remained free pending an appeal that was to be heard on Feb. 28, 1991.

Poindexter was the highest-ranking official of the Reagan Administration to be brought to trial in the Iran-contra investigation and the first to be given a prison term. His predecessor in the national security post, Robert C. McFarlane, pleaded guilty in 1988 to four misdemeanor counts of misleading Congress about the affair. McFarlane was fined $20,000 in

March 1989 and placed on two years' probation. Former Marine Lieutenant Colonel Oliver L. North, a National Security Council aide, was convicted in May 1989 of three felonies: obstructing Congress, destroying government documents, and accepting an illegal gift—a home security system—from an associate.

New hearings for North. On July 20, 1990, an appeals court in Washington, D.C., overturned one of North's convictions and ordered new hearings on the other two. North had been fined $150,000 and ordered to perform 1,200 hours of community service. Over the dissent of the chief judge, a three-judge panel ruled that testimony North gave Congress under a limited grant of immunity from prosecution may have been improperly used against him at his trial.

Other outcomes. Retired Air Force Major General Richard V. Secord, North's top nongovernment contact in the Iran-contra operation, was sentenced on Jan. 24, 1990, to two years' probation. Secord had pleaded guilty in November 1989 of lying to congressional investigators. On Sept. 18, 1990, Thomas G. Clines, a former agent of the Central Intelligence Agency and Secord associate, was convicted of four tax fraud charges stemming from the diversion of arms-sales profits. And on February 1, another former partner of Secord's, Albert A. Hakim, was fined $5,000 and placed on two years' probation. Hakim pleaded guilty in 1989 to helping North buy a home security fence and covering up the deal.   William R. Cormier

Iraq. Iraq's President Saddam Hussein ordered his forces into neighboring Kuwait on Aug. 2, 1990, after negotiations failed to resolve differences between the two countries. Within weeks, United States President George Bush forged an international consensus that led to an economic boycott of Iraq and the deployment of a multinational force in Saudi Arabia.

Hussein annexed Kuwait and forbade foreigners in Iraq and Kuwait to leave. He also moved foreign hostages to key military and industrial sites in Iraq and Kuwait to deter attacks by U.S. forces. Most of the hostages were held until December 6, when Hussein announced that they were free to go. On Jan. 17, 1991, the multinational force launched an air strike against military targets in Iraq and Kuwait.

Iraqi grievances. Iraq's invasion of Kuwait followed months of hostile complaints by Iraq that some members of the Organization of Petroleum Exporting Countries (OPEC), namely Kuwait and the United Arab Emirates, were exceeding production quotas. Since the late 1980's, despite objections, the two countries had not abided by their quotas.

In July 1990, Iraq's Foreign Minister Tariq Aziz released a letter listing Iraq's charges against Kuwait. Iraq said Kuwait and the United Arab Emirates had flooded world oil markets, driving down prices. Reduced oil revenues had made it difficult for Iraq to pay the interest on its $50-billion international debt and had increased that debt.

President Saddam Hussein talks to a British boy during a videotaped meeting with British hostages in Iraq broadcast by Iraqi TV in August.

Iraq also alleged that Kuwait had built oil and military installations on Iraqi territory. In addition, Iraq accused Kuwait of pumping more than its allotment of oil from the Rumaila oil field—which the two countries share—on the Iraq-Kuwait border.

Finally, Aziz complained that Kuwait had not canceled its loans made to Iraq during the Iran-Iraq war. Iraq had said it deserved compensation for its losses in the war because it had acted as a buffer between Iran and the rest of the Arab world. The letter concluded by threatening military action "if words fail to protect Iraqis." Shortly afterward, Kuwait and the United Arab Emirates agreed to abide by their OPEC oil production quotas.

The governments of Iraq have long expressed a desire to absorb Kuwait. Iraq also has sought control of the Kuwaiti islands of Bubiyan and Warba in the northern Persian Gulf, just off Iraq's southern border. To reach Iraq's only major port, Al Basrah, ships must travel far up the Shatt al Arab waterway, which is difficult to navigate and defend.

Military technology. In March, U.S. and British officials arrested six people, reportedly for attempting to smuggle detonators for nuclear weapons to Iraq. In April, British customs officials seized eight large steel tubes bound for Iraq that they said could have been used to form the barrel of a gun capable of firing shells hundreds of miles. Iraq insisted that the tubes were intended for industrial purposes. Some political observers suggested these purchases represented attempts by Hussein to increase his regional status.

Embargo. After the invasion of Kuwait, the United Nations passed 12 resolutions aimed at forcing Iraq to withdraw. The resolutions imposed an economic embargo on Iraqi trade, authorized military action to enforce that embargo, rejected Iraq's annexation of Kuwait, and authorized the use of "all necessary means" to eject Iraq from Kuwait if sanctions failed.

Embargo effects. The sanctions imposed on Iraq effectively halted from 90 to 95 per cent of Iraq's oil exports. Oil earnings normally provide more than 95 per cent of Iraq's revenues. Analysts noted that, ironically, the loss of oil income might not be a major factor in Iraq's ability to withstand the embargo. They said that because the country had abundant water and land suitable for farming, it would be able to feed its population for some time. By year-end, however, Iraq was experiencing a shortage of spare parts for computers and other machinery.

Journalist hanged. An Iranian-born correspondent for a London newspaper who was accused of spying for Israel was hanged by Iraq on March 14, despite pleas for clemency from world leaders. Farzad Bazoft had been arrested in September 1989 after making an unauthorized visit to a secret Iraqi military installation where 700 people had reportedly died in August 1989 in an explosion.   Christine Helms

See also **Middle East** (Facts in brief table); **United Nations.** In *World Book,* see **Iraq.**

Ireland. The coalition government headed by Prime Minister Charles Haughey enjoyed a relatively calm 1990 until late in the year. Political excitement stirred on November 7, when the presidential election was won for the first time by a woman, Mary Robinson. She was a left wing Dublin lawyer and—in a predominantly Roman Catholic country—a supporter of contraception and homosexual rights.

Robinson, an independent backed by the Labour Party, defeated former Northern Ireland civil rights activist Austin Currie of the Fine Gael (Gaelic People) party and Brian Lenihan, the Fianna Fáil (Soldiers of Destiny) candidate. Lenihan had been deputy prime minister and defense minister until Haughey ousted him on October 31, just one week before the election, for lying about his role in a 1982 government crisis. Until this scandal, Lenihan was expected to win the election easily. Although the office of president is largely symbolic, experts speculated that Lenihan's defeat could signal trouble for Haughey's coalition government, even topple it. Robinson took office on Dec. 3, 1990.

Talks on Ireland's future. On May 28, the Irish and British governments thought they had cleared the way for the most fundamental talks about the future of Ireland since 1920, when the British government divided Ireland into two separate countries—Ireland and Northern Ireland. Dublin and London agreed to conduct political dialogues to redefine the relationship between people in both parts of Ireland and between Ireland and Britain. The British government's aim was to return a large degree of self-rule to Northern Ireland.

The Unionist parties of Northern Ireland, which represent most of the Protestant majority, opposed Dublin's having any voice in Northern Ireland's government, as provided in the 1985 Anglo-Irish Agreement. They wanted Northern Ireland to remain part of the United Kingdom. But just as it appeared that Dublin and London had found a way for the Unionists to accept negotiations, Peter Brooke, secretary of state for Northern Ireland, told the House of Commons no definite date could be set for talks to begin. Squabbling had erupted over when the Dublin government should come into the talks.

Dublin meeting. Ireland, which served as president of the European Community (EC or Common Market) for six months in 1990, hosted a meeting in Dublin on May 16 between EC members and Iran. No progress was made on the issues of hostages or Iran's death edict against British author Salman Rushdie. On August 24, however, the Irish government secured the release of hostage Brian Keenan, a Belfast teacher who held dual Irish and British citizenship. Keenan was a lecturer at the American University in Beirut and was captured in April 1986 by pro-Iranian forces.   Ian J. Mather

See also **Northern Ireland.** In *World Book,* see **Ireland.**

Iron and steel. See Steel industry.

Israeli police guard Palestinians detained after a confrontation on Jerusalem's Temple Mount in October that left at least 17 Palestinians dead.

Israel. Israel's coalition government collapsed on March 15, 1990, in a bitter debate over a United States-sponsored plan for holding Israeli-Palestinian peace talks. The right wing Likud bloc, headed by Prime Minister Yitzhak Shamir, rejected the plan, which called for negotiations on limited self-government for the Israeli-occupied West Bank and Gaza Strip.

Attempts to form a new government dragged on for nearly three months, to the anger of many Israelis. Shamir finally formed a majority coalition that was approved by the Knesset, Israel's parliament, on June 11. It was the most conservative governing coalition in the country's history.

Palestinian uprising. At least 17 Palestinians died and more than 300 were injured on October 8 during a violent confrontation between Palestinians and Israeli police in an area of Jerusalem known to Jews as the Temple Mount, one of Islam's holiest sites. It was the single most violent incident in the three-year-old Palestinian *intifada* (uprising), in which about 777 Palestinians and 54 Israelis have been killed.

The incident began when a Jewish group called the Temple Mount Faithful announced plans to lay a symbolic foundation stone for a new Jewish Temple on the Temple Mount. During Biblical times, several Jewish temples stood on the site, now occupied by two Islamic mosques. Thousands of Palestinians gathered on the Temple Mount to protect the mosques.

The Israelis contended that the Palestinians provoked the incident by attacking the police and by throwing stones at Jewish worshipers at the Wailing Wall, Judaism's most sacred site, which abuts the Temple Mount. The government also insisted that the attack was organized by the Palestine Liberation Organization to refocus world attention on the Palestinian problem during the Persian Gulf crisis.

The Palestinians contended that the attack on the police was spontaneous and had been provoked by the police. They also insisted that the police had continued firing on the Palestinians long after Jewish worshipers had fled to safety.

The Israeli government released an official report on the incident on October 26. While criticizing Israeli police for not anticipating violence, it generally backed the government version of events. The Temple Mount killings triggered widespread violence, including numerous attacks on Israelis by Palestinians.

Immigration. An estimated 200,000 Jewish immigrants, most from the Soviet Union, arrived in Israel in 1990, more than the total number of immigrants that arrived during the 1980's. Government subsidies for the immigrants put new strains on Israel's already sluggish economy. Most of the newcomers were unable to find work, which boosted the country's unemployment rate to 9.3 per cent. Many were scientists or engineers who found few opportunities in Israel's already tight academic and technological job market.

Israel

The flood of immigrants wreaked havoc on Israel's tight housing market. Many poor Israelis were forced out of their apartments by soaring rents, aggravated by generous government housing subsidies paid to immigrants. Tent cities popped up across the country.

Many Israelis protested angrily when the government announced in April 1990 that it had already spent the $500 million allocated for the resettlement program in 1990 and that an additional $250 million would be diverted from other government projects. Israelis were also angered by cuts in government food subsidies that boosted the cost of milk and other staples by 33 per cent. In December, the country was hit by a series of strikes by workers protesting stiff tax increases imposed to raise more funds for resettlement.

U.S. relations. The influx of immigrants contributed to a deterioration in relations between Israel and the United States in 1990. In March, U.S. Secretary of State James A. Baker III said that the United States should not grant Israel a $400-million emergency loan for the resettlement program unless Israel agreed to halt the growth of Jewish settlements in the occupied territories. The United States approved the loan in October after Shamir pledged that there would be no new Jewish settlements in the territories.

Shamir also promised not to settle Soviet immigrants in Israeli-annexed East Jerusalem. On Oct. 15, 1990, however, a Cabinet committee voted to encourage Jewish settlement in the city. The move reflected Israeli anger at the United States for supporting the formation of a United Nations delegation to investigate the Temple Mount killings. Shamir visited the United States in December to discuss Israeli concerns related to Iraq's invasion of Kuwait. The United States and its allies began an air attack against Iraq on Jan. 17, 1991. Fears that Israel might be drawn into the war increased after Iraqi missiles hit Tel Aviv and Haifa on January 18 (see **Middle East**).

Relations between the United States and Israel had reached a low ebb in April 1990 when the Israeli government admitted that it had secretly channeled nearly $2 million in U.S. aid to 150 Jewish settlers who occupied four buildings in the Christian Quarter of East Jerusalem on April 11. Israel's attempt to establish a Jewish presence in the Christian Quarter triggered a storm of international protest, including unusual criticism from Jewish groups in the United States. In May, Israel's Supreme Court ordered most of the settlers to vacate the buildings. At year-end, a few settlers remained, pending a final court decision.

Human rights. Israel came under increasing criticism from human-rights groups in 1990. In a May report, the Swedish branch of the Save the Children organization documented the deaths of 159 Palestinian children under the age of 16 between December 1987 and December 1989. The deaths resulted from injuries inflicted by the Israeli army.   Christine Helms

See also **Jews and Judaism; Middle East** (Facts in brief table). In *World Book,* see **Israel.**

Italy. Voicing concern about the spread of organized crime in Italy, President Francesco Cossiga said in an open letter to Parliament on Sept. 26, 1990, that the Mafia controlled whole sectors of the nation. Gang wars became increasingly violent, with 775 murders reported in southern Italy during the first half of the year—a 10 per cent increase over the first six months of 1989.

The Mafia and similar Italian crime syndicates had gained enormous illegal profits through alliances with drug smuggling operations, including Colombia's Medellín cartel, a major cocaine ring, according to a report presented by Prime Minister Giulio Andreotti on Oct. 17, 1990. The report said that these profits had enabled the syndicates to spread northward to Milan and other cities from their strongholds in Sicily and regions elsewhere in southern Italy. In the north, they reportedly bought businesses for *laundering* (hiding the illegal origins of) drug money and bribed government officials. Andreotti's interior minister and fellow Christian Democrat, Antonio Gava, had resigned the day before the report, on October 16, amid accusations that he had protected Mafia leaders from prosecution.

EC presidency. In July, Italy assumed the presidency of the European Community (EC or Common Market), a job that rotates every six months among the 12 EC members. The role was filled largely by Gianni De Michelis, Italy's Socialist foreign minister. De Michelis enjoyed upsetting his more traditional colleagues by his devotion to discothèques and by unexpected diplomatic initiatives.

Looking eastward. De Michelis was instrumental in setting up the so-called "Adriatic-Danube" group, made up of nations located on the Adriatic Sea or Danube River. The group met on April 9 to discuss projects such as building a new highway network, which had become possible with the easing of east-west tensions.

De Michelis also pressed for the founding of a similar group by nations that had once belonged, at least in part, to Austria-Hungary: Italy, Austria, Czechoslovakia, Hungary, and Yugoslavia. The five-nation group, called the Pentagonal, met in Venice, Italy, on July 31 and August 1 to discuss improving transportation in the region.

In the Persian Gulf crisis, following Iraq's August invasion of Kuwait, De Michelis helped coordinate European support for United States actions. The EC as a group declined to fund troop movements. It pledged aid, however, to states that had suffered economically from an embargo on trade with Iraq, such as Jordan and Turkey. Italy sent warships and warplanes to join a task force in the Persian Gulf.

EC unity. The EC launched two intergovernmental conferences at a summit in Rome on December 14 and 15. The conferences were expected to last through much of 1991. One conference was to negotiate the establishment of a European central bank and the creation of a single currency. The other was to pursue EC political union, including a cooperative policy on foreign affairs and defense. De Michelis advanced the process, in part by helping the other members outmaneuver Margaret Thatcher, then Britain's prime minister, who opposed a single currency. See **Europe**.

Despite Italy's high diplomatic profile, leadership was lacking at home. By failing to reform a huge government bureaucracy and improve public services, Italy continued to lag behind its EC partners as they moved toward a single market by the end of 1992.

Cold War guerrillas. Italy was shaken in November 1990 when Andreotti disclosed the existence of underground organizations that had been set up in western European countries during the 1950's. Their mission was to train resistance groups that could fight in the event of an invasion by the Soviet Union and its allies. Such groups had existed in all the countries that belong to the North Atlantic Treaty Organization (NATO), the western security alliance.

The group in Italy was named Gladio after the short sword wielded by gladiators in ancient Rome. Gladio was accused of working with intelligence organizations in the United States and Italy to discredit left wing groups. It was even suspected of committing such acts as the 1980 bombing of the Bologna railway station, in which 80 people died.   Joseph Fitchett

See also **Europe** (Facts in brief table). In *World Book*, see **Italy**.

Ivory Coast. In the nation's first multiparty elections, held in October 1990, President Félix Houphouët-Boigny, 85, was elected to a seventh five-year term. Although 20 opposition parties were allowed to participate in the elections, Houphouët-Boigny's Ivory Coast Democratic Party claimed 80 per cent of the vote. Opposition leaders said the victory had been won with fraud and intimidation.

Economic problems had led to public demands earlier in the year for political reform. In February, students rioted in Abidjan, the capital, and in March government workers demonstrated against a proposed pay cut. The army took to the streets in May, demanding higher pay and better living conditions.

The government tried to quell the civil unrest by reducing controlled prices on food and other commodities. But that action only led to further economic problems, and the regime finally had little choice but to allow competitive elections.

Despite his nation's problems, Houphouët-Boigny constructed Africa's largest Christian church and one of the largest in the world, the Roman Catholic Basilica of Our Lady of Peace, in the town of Yamoussoukro. The basilica, estimated to have cost $400 million to build, was dedicated in September by Pope John Paul II.   J. Gus Liebenow and Beverly B. Liebenow

See also **Africa** (Facts in brief table). In *World Book*, see **Ivory Coast**.

Jamaica. See **Latin America**.

Japan. Japan's ruling Liberal-Democratic Party (LDP), which was rocked by scandals and a tax dispute in 1989, made a comeback in 1990. After decades of prominence, the LDP had lost control of the upper house of parliament in July 1989 elections. But on Feb. 18, 1990, Japanese voters gave the LDP a majority of seats in the more powerful lower house, the House of Representatives.

National elections. The LDP began the election campaign afraid of losing its majority. Charged with being controlled by financial interests, LDP politicians talked of reform. But the party, which is supported by Japanese big businesses, spent $1.4 billion during the short, intense campaign—almost four times the cost of the entire 1988 United States presidential election campaign. Much of the money was used for gifts to constituents; in Japan, a vote is said to be worth a refrigerator. The Japan Socialist Party, whose gains in 1989 had cost the LDP its majority in the upper house, spent only about 1 per cent as much as the LDP, though it benefited from much volunteer help.

The LDP won 275 seats in the 512-member house, including victories for several politicians implicated in a 1989 influence-peddling scandal. Despite an overall loss of 20 seats, the LDP still retained a majority. Eleven independent candidates quickly joined forces with the party, assuring it of 286 votes.

The Japan Socialist Party improved its position from 83 seats to 136. But much of the Socialists' gains came at the expense of parties other than the LDP. The Komeito, Democratic Socialist, and Japanese Communist parties all suffered losses. As a result, the Socialists, who once appeared capable of putting together a coalition to replace the LDP in power—remained alone as the opposition leader.

Kaifu's stock rises. The LDP's 1989 loss had led bosses of the party's many feuding factions to choose as prime minister a relatively young but untainted politician with little power—Toshiki Kaifu. The bosses regarded Kaifu as a caretaker in the job while the party lived down its scandals. But by leading the LDP to its February victory and by other moves, Kaifu temporarily consolidated his hold on national leadership. In the summer, opinion polls showed that about 60 per cent of the population approved of Kaifu's performance—equaling the highest rating for a Japanese prime minister since polling began. Nevertheless, Kaifu angered party leaders by refusing to give Cabinet posts to LDP members tainted by scandal.

Much of Kaifu's popularity came from his handling of foreign relations, particularly the heated trade relations with the United States. United States companies had complained of obstacles to their sales in Japan, while Japan had criticized the United States for its deficit spending and its companies' failure to adapt products to the Japanese market.

When talks on trade impediments bogged down, U.S. President George Bush and Kaifu met in Palm Springs, Calif., on March 2 and 3. Kaifu was later per-

One year after Emperor Hirohito's death, burial rituals are completed as a shrine believed to contain his spirit is taken to a mausoleum on January 7.

sonally credited with working with reluctant Japanese officials to map out a preliminary agreement in April to open some Japanese markets to foreign trade. According to the agreement, Japan would spend more money on developing airports, parks, and other public projects that could provide work for American companies. Japan also planned to modernize its retail store system to reduce the costs of imported goods and stimulate consumer spending among its savings-oriented population. Although later trade talks ran into snags, Kaifu's work helped take much of the friction out of the issue, and an agreement was struck in June.

Kaifu's reputation was also strengthened at the July economic summit in Houston, an annual meeting of leaders from the world's seven major industrial powers. Taking an unusually assertive role for a Japanese prime minister, Kaifu staked out an independent position—reluctant to provide money to the Soviet Union but willing to help China.

Defense issues. Iraq's August 2 invasion of Kuwait caused problems in Japan's economy and intensified the debate over Japan's proper role in world affairs. Of all the industrialized nations, Japan is the most dependent on oil from the Persian Gulf. When the United States and some Arab and European countries sent military forces into the region, Japan reacted slowly to requests for help. Finally, Japanese officials offered $1 billion.

Angry at such a meager offer from the wealthy country, the U.S. House of Representatives voted to reduce the American military presence in Japan unless the Japanese government did more to pay for it. Faced with worldwide criticism, Japan on September 14 agreed to provide $2 billion toward maintaining military forces against Iraq and another $2 billion in economic aid for Egypt, Jordan, and Turkey.

The situation reopened an old debate over whether Japan's Constitution—written under United States guidance after World War II (1939-1945)—permits the deployment of Japan's self-defense forces outside home waters. Kaifu proposed a bill creating a "United Nations Peace Cooperation Corps" to support troops against Iraq. The force would include Japanese civilians and some defense personnel—and would be unarmed.

Some military officers objected to being sent unarmed and argued for a more meaningful role in the crisis. But many politicians, including some LDP leaders, attacked the proposal for possibly opening the way to a revival of Japanese militarism. Others argued that it was time for Japan to discard its policies of pacifism and isolationism and stand alongside its allies as a military force.

The proposal threatened to split the LDP, and Kaifu temporarily put off any decision by allowing the bill to die in a parliamentary committee. He was widely criticized as ineffective, and his popularity declined.

Other foreign affairs. The Japanese government's annual defense-policy report issued on September 18 dropped the usual description of the Soviet Union as a potential threat. The change followed a visit by Soviet Foreign Minister Eduard A. Shevardnadze. In Tokyo on September 7, Shevardnadze said that Soviet officials might discuss ownership of four islands in the Kuril Islands chain that the Soviet Union seized from Japan at the end of World War II. For more than 40 years, a dispute over the islands had blocked normal diplomatic and trade relations, depriving the Soviet Union of much-desired Japanese investment.

Speaking at a May banquet in Tokyo for South Korean President Roh Tae Woo, Japanese Emperor Akihito formally apologized for the suffering caused by Japan's rule in the Korean peninsula from 1910 until the end of World War II. Kaifu also expressed his "sincere remorse and honest apologies." The apologies, following years of evasion about the brutality of Japanese rule, improved relations with South Korea. On April 30, Japanese officials had also agreed to drop some restrictions on the hundreds of thousands of Koreans living in Japan, most of whom are the descendants of forced laborers brought to Japan during World War II. On September 28, a Japanese delegation signed a pact with Communist North Korea to open discussions on establishing diplomatic ties.

Kaifu visited Eastern Europe in January and promised $2 billion in aid to help rebuild the nations' devastated economies. In April and May, he visited several Asian countries where Japan had major investments and reassured officials that Japan intended to respect their interests.

Economy. Japan's stock market had an unsettled year. From a peak on Dec. 29, 1989—when stock prices were three times the 1985 level—the market dropped 27 per cent in a few months. After a brief resurgence, prices fell again, and by late September 1990 stock prices were 40 per cent below the peak. The decline caused widespread problems and raised fears that real estate would also lose its recent gains in value.

The Persian Gulf crisis compounded financial worries in Japan and boosted interest rates. Japanese banks then began to restrict loans, including those overseas. Observers feared that declining Japanese foreign investment could slow economies worldwide.

Emperor Akihito, who became emperor when his father, Hirohito, died on Jan. 7, 1989, was publicly enthroned on November 12. Another part of the traditional succession rites, a private religious ceremony in which the new emperor was believed to become a deity, sparked heated debate. The belief in the divinity of Japan's emperor has been officially discouraged since the late 1940's, when Japan ceased being a monarchy and became a democracy.   Henry S. Bradsher

See also **Asia** (Facts in brief table). In *World Book,* see **Japan.**

Emperor Akihito—Japan's figurehead monarch since the death of Hirohito—formally proclaims his enthronement on November 12.

Jews and Judaism. The Palestinian crisis in Israel, rising anti-Semitism in Europe and the Soviet Union, and massive emigration and resettlement of Soviet Jews were major issues of concern for the Jewish community in the United States during 1990.

Relations with Israel. Criticism of the Israeli government's military actions against Palestinians living in Israel and in areas occupied after the 1967 Six-Day War grew among American Jewish religious leaders, particularly of the Reform and Conservative branches of Judaism. The often violent clashes between Israeli forces and Arab demonstrators caused many Jews both in Israel and in the United States to demand greater accountability and restraint by the Israeli government. Similarly, large-scale arrests and detentions of suspected terrorists and rioters raised human-rights concerns among American Jews. John Ruskay, of the Jewish Theological Seminary of America, observed that there is great sadness toward Israel shared by growing numbers of American Jews, that after 40 years and a Holocaust, Israel has ended up holding thousands of Palestinians against their will.

There was also concern among many Jews in the United States about the apparent rise of political and religious extremism in Israel. The violence in Israel by followers of right wing leader Meir Kahane after his assassination in New York City in November indicated that such extremism, while representative of a small minority of Israelis, was a problem.

Thousands of Parisians on May 14 protest anti-Semitism after vandals desecrated an ancient Jewish cemetery in Carpentras, France.

Anti-Semitism. In the predawn hours of May 10, an ancient Jewish cemetery was desecrated in Carpentras in the south of France. Vandals uprooted or shattered 34 tombstones and violated the graves of recently buried people. People of many religions throughout the world were shocked. The desecration prompted 80,000 people, including French President François Mitterrand, to march in Paris on May 14 in a silent protest against anti-Semitism. But during the following week, in copycat crimes, graves were vandalized in at least six other Jewish cemeteries in France.

A Vatican statement following the French cemetery attacks asserted that the Roman Catholic Church "stands united with all those around the world who have expressed their strong condemnation of these acts so radically opposed to fundamental human values." The Protestant World Council of Churches issued a message "reaffirming our commitment to stand with our Jewish brothers and sisters in our continued denunciation of anti-Semitism."

In the Soviet Union, right wing nationalist groups were increasingly active in spreading anti-Semitic propaganda. They reflected old prejudices that blamed social and economic problems on Jews, and even called for their expulsion. The Russian extremist group Pamyat (Memory) was particularly violent in its public harassment of Jews and its threats of *pogroms* (organized attacks) against the Jewish community of Moscow. On October 12, however, a Moscow court acting under a new law sentenced a Pamyat leader to two years in jail for fanning ethnic enmity. He had disrupted a writers' meeting in January by shouting ethnic slurs at the Jews present.

A March survey conducted in the Moscow area found that 48 per cent of the 500 adults who responded believed that anti-Jewish feelings in the Soviet Union were on the rise.

Emigration of Soviet Jews. The *glasnost* (openness) policies of Soviet President Mikhail S. Gorbachev allowed greater numbers of Jews to leave in 1990 than at any other period in the previous 60 years. It was estimated that as many as 200,000 Soviet Jews would emigrate in 1990. Growing anti-Semitism, continuing limits on religious freedom, and economic and social discrimination were all factors in the decisions of Soviet Jews to leave. Although most of them settled in Israel, a record-breaking 20,000 in October alone, many immigrated to the United States and other western countries.

American Jews organized "Operation Exodus" and raised $540 million to help resettle Soviet Jews in the United States. After 70 years of Communist repression, many Soviet Jews had to learn about their heritage for the first time, prompting Jewish organizations worldwide to sponsor educational programs. It has been called "the reclamation of an entire Jewish generation."　Howard A. Berman

See also **Israel.** In *World Book,* see **Jews; Judaism.**

Protesters in Jordan burn United States flags in August to demonstrate their support of Iraq's President Saddam Hussein.

Jordan. An international economic blockade imposed on Iraq in August 1990 after that country invaded Kuwait seriously damaged Jordan's already ailing economy. During the 1980's, Jordan had developed deep economic ties to Iraq.

King Hussein I attempted to take a middle position in the Persian Gulf conflict. He condemned the invasion and agreed to observe sanctions against Iraq. At the same time, however, he criticized the presence of foreign troops in Saudi Arabia. His attempts to act as a neutral broker between Iraq and the United States earned him rare and united support among his subjects, most of whom supported Iraq's President Saddam Hussein. But Western governments and those of Saudi Arabia and Egypt severely criticized him for being pro-Iraq (see **Middle East**).

Economic effects. Before the blockade, about 70 per cent of Jordan's exports were sold to Iraq, its neighbor to the east, which supplied Jordan with enough oil to meet about 80 per cent of its energy needs. Trade with Iraq accounted for 50 per cent of Jordan's *gross national product* (the value of all goods and services produced).

The loss of jobs resulting from the blockade increased Jordan's unemployment rate from 20 per cent to an estimated 33 per cent. Compounding the problem was the return of some 220,000 Jordanians who had been working in Kuwait. Financial aid for these workers as well as for the thousands of refugees from Iraq and Kuwait who crowded into camps in Jordan severely strained the government's resources. Tourism, an important source of revenue, plummeted, with losses for the year expected to reach $500 million. In October, the government cut the workweek and imposed other austerity measures to reduce fuel consumption by 20 per cent.

Political reforms. Before the Persian Gulf conflict developed, King Hussein had begun an ambitious program to liberalize Jordan's political system. In 1990, the government suspended martial law, in effect since the 1967 Arab-Israeli war. It also lessened its influence over the country's three major newspapers.

The economy. Before the blockade, the government had also begun to grapple seriously with Jordan's economic problems. In early 1990, it instituted economic reforms mandated by international lending agencies as a condition for obtaining additional loans. King Hussein also replaced many government officials and mounted a campaign to clamp down on official corruption. In addition, the government cut capital spending and increased exports of phosphates and other commodities.   Christine Helms

See also **Middle East** (Facts in brief table). In *World Book,* see **Jordan.**

Judaism. See Jews and Judaism.

Kampuchea. See Cambodia.

Kansas. See State government.

Kentucky. See State government.

Kenya. President Daniel T. arap Moi continued in 1990 to reject demands for democratic reform. The Kenya African National Union refused to give up its monopoly on power, and the Moi regime harshly limited press freedom and the independence of the courts. Moi accused the Kikuyu and Luo ethnic groups of causing unrest in order to seize power.

Some of the worst abuses occurred in July with the arrest of four opposition leaders and the suppression of prodemocracy rallies in Nairobi and other cities with gunfire and tear gas. At least eight people were killed. Underscoring the conflict during the year were the deaths under mysterious circumstances of two influential critics of the government. Foreign Minister Robert Ouko was found dead in February, and an Anglican clergyman, Bishop Alexander Muge, died in an August car crash that may have been deliberately caused.

Kenya's problems were compounded by rising unemployment and Africa's highest population growth rate—3.6 per cent. Kenya faced a $1-billion trade deficit and a possible loss of foreign aid, which accounts for one-third of the nation's operating revenue each year. In July, the United States and other nations warned Moi that his government's human-rights violations might result in a reduction or cutoff of economic aid.   J. Gus Liebenow and Beverly B. Liebenow

See also **Africa** (Facts in brief table). In *World Book,* see **Kenya.**

Korea, North. Relations between Communist North Korea and its only traditional supporters, the Soviet Union and China, cooled in 1990. Neither neighbor sent the amount of economic aid that President Kim Il-sŏng had long depended upon. In addition, the Soviet Union on September 30 established diplomatic relations with South Korea, and China said it planned to set up a trade office in Seoul, South Korea.

Soviet experts said North Korea's economy was in bad shape, with only 50 per cent of industry operating and food in short supply. Other reports said North Korea's failure to pay its debts blocked new borrowing, and the country had to appeal to Japan for metals to keep some factories open.

Apparently because of his country's economic problems and loss of foreign support, Kim eased his isolationist policy in 1990. A visit to Pyongyang, the capital, by leading Japanese politicians concluded with the September 28 signing of an agreement to take steps toward establishing normal diplomatic relations between the two countries. Japan agreed to pay reparations for its occupation of the Korean Peninsula from 1910 to 1945. On Oct. 11, 1990, North Korea released two Japanese sailors whom it had held since 1983. Kim also moved cautiously in September 1990 to improve relations with South Korea after four decades of armed hostility (see **Korea, South**).   Henry S. Bradsher

See also **Asia** (Facts in brief table). In *World Book,* see **Korea.**

Korea, South. South Korea's international ties changed dramatically during 1990, as the nation broadened its foreign contacts and held the highest-level talks with North Korea since the Korean War (1950-1953).

New party. President Roh Tae Woo announced on Jan. 22, 1990, that his Democratic Justice Party was joining with two conservative opposition parties: the Reunification Democratic Party led by Kim Young Sam and the New Democratic Republican Party headed by Kim Jong Pil. The merger, which formed a new group, the Democratic Liberal Party (DLP), gave Roh (pronounced *Noh*) majority support in the National Assembly for the first time.

Many South Koreans saw the move as Kim Young Sam's attempt to position himself as Roh's eventual successor. But Roh gave no indication that the arrangement meant Kim was the favorite. Some members of Kim's party refused to join the DLP and formed a new Democratic Party, which defeated the DLP in a special election to fill two vacant National Assembly seats on April 3.

Kim Dae Jung, South Korea's most prominent opposition leader fighting for increased democracy, angrily denounced the merger as a betrayal of voters who supported the opposition. In July, members of his large opposition party fought with DLP members in the Assembly after the government violated Assembly rules to force passage of new laws.

Delegates from North and South Korea meet in Seoul in September to prepare for the first meeting of the nations' prime ministers.

In Seoul, the capital, South Korean police break up a sit-in by students demonstrating for political and economic reforms in May.

Charges dropped. The government in February dropped charges against Kim Dae Jung for failing to report a colleague's illegal trip to North Korea. In October, the government also released from jail an elderly Presbyterian minister, Moon Ik Hwan, who had been sentenced in 1989 to 10 years' imprisonment for his unauthorized meeting with North Korean President Kim Il-sŏng.

Unrest flared in April and May 1990 as unions charged that labor rights were being suppressed. Students also rioted in nationwide protests over such economic matters as high inflation rates, rising housing costs, and a stock market slump that wiped out many small investors' savings. Facing the largest antigovernment protests since he came to power in 1988, Roh postponed a trip to the United States and Canada. He told South Koreans on May 7, 1990, that some aspects of creating the DLP "have disappointed the public." He promised to "lead the affairs of the state with an extraordinary determination."

Scandal. An army private who deserted the Defense Security Command disclosed on October 4 that the command kept secret files on 1,300 Korean politicians, religious leaders, journalists, labor leaders, and student activists. The resulting scandal forced Roh to fire the head of the security command and Defense Minister Lee Sang Hoon.

On December 27, Roh shuffled his Cabinet, apparently in an effort to improve the DLP's image before 1991 local elections. Prime Minister Kang Young Hoon was replaced with Ro Jai Bong.

Relations with North Korea thawed a little. Prime ministers of the two Koreas met for the first time in history in Seoul, South Korea's capital, in September 1990. They also met in North Korea's capital in mid-October and again in Seoul in December.

The Soviet Union and China, two long-time supporters of North Korean hostility toward South Korea, improved their own ties with Seoul in 1990. They hoped to benefit from South Korea's booming economy through foreign trade and investment. Soviet President Mikhail S. Gorbachev met Roh in San Francisco on June 4 in the first such high-level contact between the countries. On September 30, the Soviet Union established full diplomatic relations with South Korea. China agreed on October 20 to exchange unofficial trade offices with South Korea—considered a first step toward establishing full relations.

The United States announced on January 30 a reduction of more than 2,000 of its 45,000 troops stationed in South Korea as protection against North Korea. Some South Korean students continued to protest against U.S. support for the government.

Economy. After 1989's 6.7 per cent economic growth rate—slow for South Korea—the economy in 1990 grew by almost 9 per cent.   Henry S. Bradsher

See also **Asia** (Facts in brief table); **Korea, North.** In *World Book,* see **Korea.**

Kuwait

Kuwait was invaded by Iraqi forces on Aug. 2, 1990. On August 8, Iraq annexed Kuwait, declaring it a province of Iraq.

The invasion triggered an exodus of Kuwaiti citizens as well as thousands of foreign workers. Amir Jabir al-Ahmad al-Jabir Al-Sabah, the ruler of Kuwait, fled to Saudi Arabia and set up a government in exile. By December, only half of Kuwait's 700,000 native-born citizens remained in the country.

Kuwaiti refugees reported that Iraqi forces were looting the country, confiscating computers, construction material, medical supplies, and other goods for shipment to Iraq. The refugees also reported numerous human-rights abuses by Iraqi troops.

The invasion initially united Kuwaiti supporters of the ruling Al-Sabah family and opponents who have pressed for a more democratic government. Government critics had condemned the ruling family's policies, including censoring the press and dissolving parliament in 1986. Some felt that producing more oil than allotted to the country by the Organization of Petroleum Exporting Countries may have provoked Iraq's attack. At a meeting of Kuwaiti exiles in Saudi Arabia in October 1990, Kuwait's crown prince pledged to establish a more democratic form of government if Kuwait is liberated. Critics of the government remained skeptical.   Christine Helms

See also **Iraq; Middle East** (Facts in brief table); **United Nations.** In *World Book,* see **Kuwait.**

Labor. United States unemployment slowly began to increase in the last six months of 1990, as fears of a recession grew. The economy continued to show modest expansion, however, dodging the official definition of a recession—six or more months of economic stagnation.

Civilian unemployment increased from about 5.3 per cent in midyear to 6.1 per cent in December, as many companies laid off employees. Construction workers were hard-hit by the layoffs, as were workers in manufacturing industries. Led by a boom in health-care services, the service sector of the economy showed an overall hiring increase. But retailers, banking firms, and other service providers laid off thousands of employees.

Faced with stiff competition from overseas companies and domestic rivals, U.S. employers continued to seek to hold down labor costs. They used contract, temporary, and part-time workers instead of permanent full-timers; provided employees with bonuses and lump-sum payments instead of wage increases; gave existing employees bonuses and overtime instead of hiring new workers; and shifted part of the cost of health insurance to employees. Unions, which accepted some of the changes, continued to seek increased income and job security for workers.

Wages, salaries, and benefits for all workers rose about 5.2 per cent in 1990, up one-tenth of a percentage point from 1989, according to the Bureau of Labor Statistics (BLS) Employment Cost Index, the nation's most comprehensive measure of such changes. But wages adjusted for inflation—or *real wages*—did not increase. According to a January BLS announcement, the real wages of U.S. workers fell 1 per cent in 1989, in part because of the year's rising inflation rate. The decline in real wages, which began in 1987, accelerated in the first 10 months of 1990, with workers squeezed by a 3.5 per cent fall in real pay. Most of the decline could be attributed to rising energy costs due to tensions in the Middle East.

According to the BLS Employment Cost Index, the wages of blue-collar workers represented by organized labor rose more slowly than those of nonunion blue-collar workers—3.9 per cent versus 4.9 per cent. The difference in the rates, noted since 1984, appeared to be narrowing. Other BLS data showed that in 1989 the median weekly earnings of union workers remained higher than those of nonunion workers—$497 compared with $372.

Union membership in 1989 held steady at 17 million workers, but the overall U.S. labor force continued to grow in 1989. Thus, the ratio of union workers to all workers fell from about 1 in 4 in the early 1980's to about 1 in 6 in 1989, the BLS reported in February 1990. Approximately 2 in 5 government workers were represented by organized labor. In the private sector, union membership ranged from 1 in 3 workers in transportation and public utilities to fewer than 1 in 40 in finance, insurance, and real estate.

Labor-management agreements. A 10-month strike by the United Mine Workers of America against the Pittston Company ended in February 1990 as union members ratified an agreement struck on New Year's Day. The union had permitted the membership vote to proceed after fruitlessly attempting to persuade state and federal courts to dismiss $64 million in strike-related fines.

The 54-month contract provided Pittston workers with annual increases of 40 cents per hour for three years and a $1,000 ratification bonus. To promote prudent use of health care, the company agreed to give employees $500 every six months to offset health insurance deductibles or to keep if no medical claims were made. In a theme sounded in several other 1990 settlements, the union traded modifications in work rules—in this case, to support more coal production—in exchange for greater job security.

After rejecting a January 30 Amoco Corporation wage offer, the Oil, Chemical and Atomic Workers International Union in February accepted an accord providing a higher wage increase. The new agreement gave workers an 80-cent-per-hour raise in the contract's first year and wage increases in the second and third years totaling 9.5 per cent. Company contributions to health insurance costs increased by $55 per month for family coverage in the first year, and by $45 and $50 per month in the next two years. The contract set a pattern for oil industry settlements later in 1990.

Major league baseball owners and players reached a contract compromise on March 19, one month after the owners locked players out of spring training. The dispute involved salary arbitration, benefits contributions, minimum salaries, and *free agency*—in which some players can offer their services to the highest bidder. The new contract included a raise in the minimum player salary from $68,000 to $100,000.

In March, the United Automobile Workers (UAW) ended their four-year strike against Colt Firearms. Colt management agreed to sell the firearms division to Colt's Manufacturing Company, which is partially owned by the employees; to reinstate the 1,000 strikers; and to give employees a $13-million settlement. The U.S. National Labor Relations Board (NLRB), charged with supervising distribution of the payment, called it the largest settlement of its kind.

The International Brotherhood of Teamsters voted on August 13 to accept a United Parcel Service contract despite union leaders' July recommendation to reject it. The three-year pact, covering 141,000 workers, provided yearly pay increases of 50 cents per hour for most full-time workers but froze until 1993 the wages of part-timers and air operations workers. The contract also lowered the pay scale for new drivers. The company provided lump-sum bonuses of $1,000 for full-time workers and $500 for part-timers.

General Motors Corporation, a UAW strike target since late August, on September 17 agreed to a three-year contract covering more than 300,000 workers. The pact provided a pay increase of 3 per cent in the first year and lump-sum bonuses of 3 per cent in the second and third years.

Analysts said the contract benefited both labor and management because the union obtained far-reaching job guarantees and income security, while the company retained the right to trim staffing as needed to meet domestic and international competition. Similar pacts were concluded with Ford Motor Company—covering almost 100,000 workers—on October 7, and with Chrysler Corporation—covering 63,000 workers—on October 30.

Ongoing strikes. On March 2, some 9,000 Amalgamated Transit Union workers went on strike against Greyhound Bus Lines Incorporated over wage issues. The strike was prolonged in part by Greyhound's refusal to replace nonunion drivers hired during the strike with strikers willing to return to work. The stalemate, which left some small towns without bus service, led to violence. Gunshots were fired into buses driven by replacement workers, and a bus crushed one picketer. The union's complaints of unfair labor practices by the company were substantiated by NLRB rulings against Greyhound in the spring and fall. Greyhound sued the union for civil damages, and on June 5 the company filed for protection from its creditors under Chapter 11 of the bankruptcy code.

Violence also accompanied a strike at the *Daily News*, New York City's largest-circulation daily news-

The Communications Workers of America in April begin a campaign against phone companies' plans to use computers to replace human operators.

Labor

paper. After 10 months of fruitless contract negotiations, 9 of the paper's 10 unions went on strike in late October. Well prepared for a walkout, the paper's management quickly assembled a nonunion replacement staff. Although the paper continued publication, circulation and advertising dropped drastically. Delivery services were hampered as more than 40 delivery trucks were firebombed or vandalized.

Negotiations. Employees' quest to purchase United Airlines Incorporated ended abruptly on October 9, when UAL Corporation, United's parent company, ended buy-out talks. The United Employee Acquisition Corporation had been unable to obtain the necessary $4.4-billion financing. With the buy-out plan a failure, contract bargaining between the company and union members resumed.

The U.S. Postal Service and four of its major unions failed to reach a new contract agreement before their existing contracts expired in mid-November. The disputed issues—including benefits, wage increases, and the use of automation and contract workers—were referred to binding arbitration.

Legal issues. In June, the Supreme Court of the United States upheld the right of federal legislators to create affirmative action programs. The case dealt with a congressionally mandated Federal Communications Commission policy to give minorities an advantage in obtaining broadcast licenses. Also in June, the Supreme Court ruled that state governments cannot

use a job candidate's political-party affiliation as the basis for employment decisions.

The government's Equal Employment Opportunity Commission in January declined to accept a federal district court ruling upholding *United Automobile Workers v. Johnson Controls.* The suit pitted workers against a manufacturer of automobile batteries. At issue were company policies barring the employment of fertile women in jobs that would put them in contact with lead, which can cause birth defects. In March, the U.S. Supreme Court agreed to review the potentially far-reaching labor issue during its 1990-1991 term.

In mid-March, about 500 compliance officers from the Department of Labor conducted a three-day investigative sweep at businesses across the United States, looking for violations of U.S. child-labor laws. The investigators discovered violations involving about 7,000 minors at 1,460 businesses. Some involved illegal employment of children under 13; others concerned teen-agers operating dangerous equipment or working longer or later hours than the law allowed.

Labor legislation. President George Bush vetoed the Family and Medical Leave Act on June 29. The bill would have required businesses with 50 or more employees to provide up to 12 weeks of unpaid leave each year for the birth or adoption of a child or for the serious illness of the employee or close relatives. Bush said he opposed the bill because he favored "innovative" individual labor-management agreements. The House of Representatives failed to override the veto, but in August, replacement bills were introduced in the House and Senate. In a related matter, Congress in October voted to provide $22 billion in child-care tax credits and grants for working parents.

Bush also vetoed the Civil Rights Bill of 1990, saying the measure was a "hiring quotas" bill, a charge its congressional supporters denied. Among other issues, the bill sought to counteract Supreme Court decisions narrowing the rights of employee plaintiffs in suits against their employers. The Senate failed by one vote to overturn the veto, and the bill's supporters vowed to revive it in 1991. Another veto in October killed a civil rights bill designed to help minorities and women win job-discrimination lawsuits. See **Civil rights.**

On July 26, Bush signed into law the Americans with Disabilities Act, which had passed overwhelmingly in both houses of Congress. The law prohibits several forms of discrimination, including discrimination against disabled workers by private firms or by state and local governments. See **Handicapped.**

Labor Secretary Elizabeth H. Dole resigned in late November to become head of the American Red Cross. Experts praised her efforts to improve the training of American workers. Bush named Representative Lynn M. Martin (R., Ill.) to replace her.   Robert W. Fisher

See also **Economics; Manufacturing.** In *World Book,* see **Labor force; Labor movement.**

Lamer, Antonio (1933-   ), was appointed chief justice of Canada on July 1, 1990. He replaced retiring Chief Justice Brian Dickson.

Lamer (pronounced *lah MAIR*) was born on July 8, 1933, in what he describes as a tough, working-class neighborhood of Montreal, Que. He served in the Royal Canadian Army before receiving a law degree from the University of Montreal. He lectured there for many years in law and criminology. He also earned a doctor of laws degree from the University of Moncton and another doctor's degree from the University of Ottawa. Lamer entered law practice in Quebec City in 1957. He founded the Association of Defence Attorneys of the Province of Quebec. From 1969 to 1978, he served as justice of the Superior Court of Quebec.

Lamer was justice of the Quebec Court of Appeal from 1978 to 1980. After his appointment to the Supreme Court in 1980, he became known as one of the court's most liberal judges. His decisions placed limits on the police and curbed the use of evidence gathered through wiretaps and entrapment. Lamer served as chairman of the Law Reform Commission of Canada, national chairman of the Criminal Law Section of the Canadian Bar Association, and special counsel to the Quebec minister of justice.

Lamer's favorite vacation is taking his wife, two children, and some books aboard his 1938 cabin cruiser, which he keeps at a lake on the Quebec-New England border.   Margaret Anne Schmidt

Laos. Guerrilla resistance to the Communist government flared up in early 1990. The United Lao National Liberation Front had announced in December 1989 that it had established a revolutionary provisional government, but it seemed to have only a small force of guerrillas, who harassed government troops.

A radio station claimed on Sept. 1, 1990, that Laotian students in the Soviet Union and eastern Europe had demonstrated for democracy in their homeland. A Thai newspaper reported on October 20 that more than 40 senior Laotian officials had established a group to work for democracy. Press reports a few days later said the Laos government had arrested former officials for such work.

Council of Ministers Chairman Kaysone Phomvihan was reported to be incapacitated by illness when he failed to appear at celebrations on the country's national day, September 2. On October 18, he made his first public appearance in four months.

Minister of Foreign Affairs Phoune Sipaseuth met with United States Secretary of State James A. Baker III in New York City on October 3. The officials discussed limiting narcotics trafficking from Laos and continuing efforts to account for the 545 U.S. servicemen missing in Laos since the Vietnam War (1957-1975). The remains of two Americans had been recovered in January.   Henry S. Bradsher

See also **Asia** (Facts in brief table). In *World Book,* see **Laos.**

Latin America. Obtaining credit to put people to work topped the political agenda of Latin-American leaders during 1990. Country after country sought to reach terms with foreign banks and lenders and restore their credit ratings. There was a special urgency about the quest for credit. Latin Americans were fearful that unless they put their economic houses in order, and quickly, available world investment funds would go elsewhere, to the newly democratized nations of eastern Europe and to the Soviet Union.

At the start of 1990, 27 Latin-American countries owed foreign banks and governments a record $435-billion, with $18 billion in repayments overdue. Since the debt crisis reached serious proportions in 1982, the countries owing these debts had paid out $250 billion in principal and interest and had received only $50-billion in new loans. Foreign banks, whose earnings were hurt by Latin-American defaults, were wary about sending good money after bad.

The impact of the credit crunch was reflected in the results of several presidential elections in late 1989 and in 1990. Latin-American voters tended to choose candidates who appeared to be business-oriented and likely to be acceptable in foreign credit and financial communities. Thus, in a runoff election on June 10, 1990, voters in Peru favored Alberto Fujimori, an expert in farm management, over novelist Mario Vargas Llosa. During his campaign, Fujimori, the son of Japanese immigrants, hinted that his ancestry put him in a favorable position to win increased trade and credit from Japan.

New leaders. Rulers of the extreme left and right peacefully yielded power to democratically elected civilians in Nicaragua and Chile. Nicaraguans inaugurated their first woman head of state, Violeta Barrios de Chamorro, replacing the leftist Sandinista regime that came to power in a 1979 revolution. In Chile, right wing military officers, who came to power in a 1973 coup, yielded to President Patricio Aylwin Azócar, a Christian Democrat.

Elsewhere in Latin America in 1990, the accent was on youth. Five countries inaugurated presidents still in their 40's, including Colombia, Costa Rica, Honduras, and Uruguay. Fernando Collor de Mello, 40, became Brazil's youngest chief of state.

Suriname coup. On December 24, Suriname's former dictator Désiré D. Bouterse led a military coup that ousted civilian President Ramsewak Shankar. Bouterse designated Johan Kraag to head an interim government that he said would hold elections within 100 days. Shankar had been in a bitter dispute with Bouterse, who ruled Suriname from 1980 to 1988. The Organization of American States denounced the coup.

Austerity. Once in power, all of the new leaders imposed austerity programs that exacted a fearful toll in human hardship. Currencies were devalued as much as 100 per cent. There were huge price increases on products ranging from gasoline to food staples and an end to government subsidies on transportation and

A United Nations officer uses a welding torch to destroy weapons collected in June from *contra* rebels in Nicaragua as the eight-year civil war ended.

utility bills that had benefited the urban poor. Pressured by financial lenders abroad and by the United States government, most of the new leaders promised to sell unprofitable, state-run enterprises that had become employers of last resort, despite already staggering rates of unemployment.

The results of austerity were soon apparent. Brazil, which implemented perhaps the harshest program in Latin-American history, plunged into a severe recession. In Peru, where the previous government had refused to pay its debts, austerity worked hardship on the estimated 80 per cent of the labor force without permanent employment. Inflation, which had exceeded 3,000 per cent in the 12 months preceding the June 1990 election, had also eroded living standards. Appearing on national television in August 1990, Peru's finance minister held in his hand the currency required to buy a $40,000 house in 1985 and said, "Now, it can buy only a tube of toothpaste."

Brady plan. A plan worked out by U.S. Secretary of the Treasury Nicholas F. Brady sought to assist those countries that had imposed hardship programs with the aim of restoring credit. For example, Venezuela, the scene of bloody riots and violence that killed 300 people when austerity was imposed in 1989, reached agreement with foreign creditor banks on March 20, 1990, with the help of the U.S. government.

Under terms of the Venezuelan accord, about 25 per cent of the country's $20.5-billion debt to banks

was written off. With guarantees of future debt repayments from the U.S. government and international financial agencies, the banks agreed to boost the flow of capital to Venezuela. Much of the new credit was to be used to expand the country's oil production.

The restructuring of Venezuela's debts under the Brady plan was partly modeled on a similar agreement reached with Mexico in 1989. During 1990, negotiations on half a dozen other restructuring plans went forward with nations willing to pay the price of austerity to regain access to international credit markets.

Relations with Japan. Within Latin America, there was heightened interest in promoting good relations with Japan. The world's foremost exporter of capital, Japan appeared to be positioning itself for a greater role in Latin America, challenging the United States, which has become the world's largest debtor nation. On June 18, during an official visit to Japan by Mexican President Carlos Salinas de Gortari, Japanese officials announced an $850-million loan to help Mexico City battle air pollution.

From 1984 through March 1989, Japan had invested $32 billion in Latin America, as much as it did in Asia or Europe—and nearly half as much as it invested in the United States. Of Japan's investment in Latin America, only 17 per cent was in manufacturing.

But there were signs in 1990 that the percentage invested in manufacturing would rise dramatically. Japan was scheduled to double its annual investment

Facts in brief on Latin-American political units

Country	Population	Government	Monetary unit*	Foreign trade (million U.S.$) Exports†	Imports†
Antigua and Barbuda	82,000	Governor General Sir Wilfred Jacobs; Prime Minister Vere C. Bird	dollar (2.7 = $1)	30	302
Argentina	32,700,000	President Carlos Saúl Menem	austral (4,965 = $1)	9,600	4,300
Bahamas	256,000	Governor General Sir Henry Taylor; Prime Minister Lynden O. Pindling	dollar (1.00 = $1)	733	1,700
Barbados	263,000	Governor General Dame Nita Barrow; Prime Minister Lloyd Erskine Sandiford	dollar (2.01 = $1)	173	582
Belize	184,000	Governor General Dame Minita E. Gordon; Prime Minister George Price	dollar (2 = $1)	120	176
Bolivia	7,520,000	President Jaime Paz Zamora	boliviano (3.35 = $1)	634	786
Brazil	153,180,000	President Fernando Collor de Mello	cruzeiro (148.75 = $1)	34,200	18,000
Chile	13,377,000	President Patricio Aylwin Azócar	peso (350.74 = $1)	7,000	4,700
Colombia	32,414,000	President César Gaviria Trujillo	peso (559.05 = $1)	5,760	5,020
Costa Rica	3,083,000	President Rafael Angel Calderón Fournier	colón (103.5 = $1)	1,300	1,400
Cuba	10,415,000	President Fidel Castro	peso (0.80 = $1)	5,500	7,600
Dominica	86,000	President Clarence Augustus Seignoret; Prime Minister Eugenia Charles	dollar (2.7 = $1)	46	66
Dominican Republic	7,312,000	President Joaquín Balaguer Ricardo	peso (11.2 = $1)	711	1,800
Ecuador	11,069,000	President Rodrigo Borja Cevallos	sucre (885.5 = $1)	2,200	1,600
El Salvador	5,381,000	President Alfredo Cristiani Burkard	colón (5.0 = $1)	497	1,100
Grenada	92,000	Governor General Sir Paul Scoon; Prime Minister Nicholas Brathwaite	dollar (2.7 = $1)	32	93
Guatemala	9,462,000	President Vinicio Cerezo Arévalo	quetzal (5.22 = $1)	1,020	1,500
Guyana	881,000	President Hugh Desmond Hoyte; Prime Minister Hamilton Green	dollar (45 = $1)	215	216
Haiti	6,427,000	President Ertha Pascal Trouillot	gourde (5 = $1)	200	344
Honduras	5,292,000	President Rafael Leonardo Callejas	lempira (5.67 = $1)	1,000	1,400
Jamaica	2,557,000	Governor General Florizel Glasspole; Prime Minister Michael Manley	dollar (7.8 = $1)	948	1,600
Mexico	90,379,000	President Carlos Salinas de Gortari	peso (2,935.6 = $1)	23,100	23,300
Nicaragua	3,994,000	President Violeta Barrios de Chamorro	córdoba (1,850,000 = $1)	250	550
Panama	2,464,000	President Guillermo Endara	balboa (1 = $1)	220	830
Paraguay	4,392,000	President Andrés Rodríguez Pedotti	guaraní (1,243 = $1)	1,020	1,010
Peru	22,857,000	President Alberto Fujimori	inti (493,720.5 = $1)	3,550	2,500
Puerto Rico	3,282,000	Governor Rafael Hernández Colón	U.S. dollar	13,200	11,800
St. Christopher and Nevis	48,000	Governor General Clement Athelston Arrindell; Prime Minister Kennedy Alphonse Simmonds	dollar (2.7 = $1)	30	95
St. Lucia	157,000	Governor General Sir Stanislaus James; Prime Minister John Compton	dollar (2.7 = $1)	77	178
St. Vincent and the Grenadines	115,000	Acting Governor General David Jack; Prime Minister James F. Mitchell	dollar (2.7 = $1)	64	87
Suriname	409,000	Acting Commander of the National Army Ivan Graanoogst; President Johan Kraag	guilder (1.79 = $1)	425	365
Trinidad and Tobago	1,303,000	President Noor Hassanali; Prime Minister Arthur Napoleon Raymond Robinson	dollar (4.25 = $1)	1,400	1,200
Uruguay	3,151,000	President Luis Alberto Lacalle	peso (1,514 = $1)	1,500	1,100
Venezuela	20,202,000	President Carlos Andrés Pérez	bolívar (50.59 = $1)	10,400	10,900

*Exchange rates as of Dec. 7, 1990, or latest available data. †Latest available data.

in Mexico to $1.5 billion in 1990. A substantial proportion of this was earmarked for assembly plants on the U.S.-Mexican border, where duty-free components are assembled by low-wage Mexican labor for export to the U.S. market. Perhaps with an eye to the future, Mexico's president was reportedly sending his own children to a bilingual school in Mexico City that gave instruction in the Japanese language.

Brazil also sought to increase Japanese investment. Brazil has 1.2 million immigrants of Japanese descent—one of the largest such communities outside Japan. Boasting a support pool of executives, secretaries, and translators familiar with the Japanese language and customs, Brazil tried to encourage Japanese companies to locate there.

Economic integration. On June 27, the Administration of U.S. President George Bush unveiled a new "Enterprise for the Americas" program designed to encourage the growth of free-market economies. Bush offered to forgive some $7 billion in debt owed by Latin-American nations to the U.S. Agency for International Development, which administers the U.S. foreign-aid program. Bush also agreed to contribute $100 million to a new fund at the Inter-American Development Bank, which is financed mainly by the U.S. government, to encourage private investment in Latin America. The Bush Administration encouraged European nations and Japan to make similar contributions.

But what particularly caught the attention of Latin-American leaders was Bush's expression of support for regional economic integration—long a Latin-American dream—and the creation of a free trade zone encompassing North, Central, and South America. To promote this integration, Bush visited Argentina, Brazil, Chile, Uruguay, and Venezuela in December.

In June, five Central American countries agreed to revitalize their own Central American Common Market, which had been torn by conflicts, and to eliminate regional protectionist barriers to trade by 1992. In July, the presidents of Brazil and Argentina set Jan. 1, 1995, as the target date for launching their own common market. In September 1990, Paraguay and Uruguay announced that they, too, would like to join, and Chile reportedly was not far behind.

In August, the 13 members of the Caribbean Community and Common Market, an economic union that encourages trade among its members, approved an agreement to eliminate regional trade barriers by July 1991. Also in August 1990, the 11 members of the Latin American Integration Association, which includes 10 South American nations and Mexico, announced an immediate 50 per cent reduction in tariffs.

Another step toward economic integration came on August 20, when President Bush signed a law to make the 1983 Caribbean Basin Initiative permanent. The initiative provides duty-free entry to the United States of an increasing range of products from nations in the Caribbean Sea and Central America, leading to greater Caribbean exports.

Finally, and perhaps more important to future economic integration, the United States and Mexico, with Canada pledging to join, agreed in September 1990 to begin talks on trade liberalization and the eventual creation of a common market between the three nations. The talks were scheduled to begin in 1991.

Persian Gulf crisis. The economies of more than a dozen Latin-American countries reeled from the higher oil prices brought on by the crisis in the Persian Gulf. Worst affected was Brazil, which imported much of its oil from Iraq. The trade embargo imposed by the United Nations (UN) on Iraq and Iraqi-occupied Kuwait also meant a sharp loss in trade for Brazil, which had become Iraq's second most important source of industrial imports, including armaments.

Venezuela again rose to the occasion, as it had during the 1973 Arab oil embargo, by pumping more oil to make up for shortages. Venezuela sought to lessen the effects of the crisis on some of its neighbors by offering its oil on favored terms.

All Latin-American countries, including Cuba, honored the embargo. 0n Sept. 25, 1990, Argentina became the first Latin-American nation to send armed forces to the Persian Gulf—two ships crewed by 350 sailors. The move was viewed as particularly significant because Argentina had maintained neutrality during World War II (1939-1945) until shortly before the Allied victory.

Amazon rain forests. Concern continued over the destruction of the Amazon rain forests. On June 7, 1990, the World Resources Institute, an environmental research center in Washington, D.C., released a report produced with the UN that said the forests were being destroyed faster than previously believed. Tropical rain forests play a vital role in maintaining earth's environmental balance, especially by removing carbon dioxide from the atmosphere. Carbon dioxide is known as a *greenhouse gas*, because, like the glass in a greenhouse, it traps heat radiated from the earth's surface and prevents it from escaping into space.

Drawing upon data from satellites, the report found that Brazil is losing between 12½ million and 22½ million acres (5 million and 9 million hectares) of rain forest a year, or from 25 per cent to nearly 50 per cent of the total global loss. The report said Brazil ranks third among the world's nations as a producer of greenhouse gases, which in Brazil are released mainly by burning forests. Many scientists believe the planet's climate is warming due to the release of these gases.

Reactions to the destruction of the rain forest have been many and varied. Biologists have rushed to learn more about plant and animal species in the Amazon that are being driven to extinction. Brazilian and Venezuelan anthropologists have also made contact with the last of the Stone Age Indians in remote areas of the Amazon, to study their way of life before that life is disrupted forever by the destruction of the forests.

Chico Mendes murder. The son of a Brazilian rancher confessed on the opening day of his trial that he had killed Amazonian environmental activist and labor leader Francisco (Chico) Mendes in 1988. The unexpected admission came on Dec. 12, 1990, when Darci Alves da Silva took the witness stand and declared, "I killed Chico Mendes." A rubber tapper, Mendes had fought to preserve the Amazon from development by ranchers and others. Da Silva and his father were both convicted of the murder and were each sentenced to 19 years in prison.

High prices for art. Paintings by Latin-American artists fetched record prices at international auctions. A self-portrait by Mexico's Frida Kahlo sold for $1,430,000 at the New York City auction house of Sotheby's on May 2. The sale doubled the previous Latin-American record, set by a painting by Colombia's Fernando Botero at an auction in 1989.

A growing number of exhibitions and shows of Latin-American art in 1990 culminated in New York City in a four-month-long celebration of Mexico's rich culture. The crowning event was "Mexico: Splendors of 30 Centuries," an exhibit that opened at the Metropolitan Museum of Art on October 10 for a three-month period.   Nathan A. Haverstock

See also **Nobel Prizes;** articles on the various Latin-American nations. In the Special Reports section, see **Puerto Rico—The 51st State?** In *World Book,* see Latin America and articles on the individual countries.

Law. See **Civil rights; Courts; Crime; Supreme Court of the United States.**

Lebanon. Syria, which has 40,000 troops in Lebanon and controls about two-thirds of the country, forced the surrender of Lebanese General Michel Awn (also spelled Aoun) in October 1990, ending his 11-month rebellion against the government. On October 13, Syrian forces and Lebanese army troops stormed the presidential palace outside Beirut where Awn, the leader of a largely Christian army, had established his headquarters. Awn fled to the French Embassy.

Awn had considered himself the only legitimate head of government since September 1988, when civil conflict prevented Lebanon's parliament from electing a successor to outgoing President Amin Gemayel. Gemayel named Awn, a Maronite Christian, as the head of an interim military government.

Awn refused to surrender power or leave the presidential palace after parliament elected Ilyas Harawi as president in November 1989. During 1990, Awn's forces frequently clashed with Syrian troops, Muslim forces, and a rival Christian militia.

Awn's ouster paved the way for an agreement later in October calling for the removal of all militias from Beirut. But it was unclear to what extent Syria would dominate Lebanese politics in the future.

Syria moved against Awn 10 months after Harawi had asked for help in putting down Awn's revolt. Political observers suggested that Syria agreed to Harawi's request for several reasons. Syria may have felt that international preoccupation with Iraq, which

Tanks attack the Beirut headquarters of General Michel Awn, whose 11-month revolt against the Lebanese government ended with his surrender in October.

347

Lesotho

invaded Kuwait in August 1990, would dampen any negative reaction. Iraq, which had backed Awn, was also diverted. Awn had previously lost United States and French support in 1989 by launching offensives against his opponents and by seeking assistance from the Iranian-backed Hezbollah (Party of God) militia.

National reconciliation. On Sept. 21, 1990, Harawi signed into law constitutional amendments to a "charter of national reconciliation" adopted by parliament in 1989. The amendments overturn an outdated system for sharing power between Christians and Muslims established in 1943. Under that system, Christians dominated national politics, even after Muslims became the more populous group.

Under the new system, a Christian will continue to hold the presidency, but the prime minister, who must be a Muslim, will countersign all official documents. Parliament, which gained some powers, will have its seats equally divided between Christians and Muslims.

Prime Minister Salim al-Huss and his Cabinet resigned on December 19 to allow formation of a more broadly based government. Education Minister Omar Karami, appointed to succeed al-Huss, named a new Cabinet on December 24. But the leaders of several Christian militias opposed the new government.   Christine Helms

See also **Middle East** (Facts in brief table). In *World Book,* see Lebanon.

Lesotho. See **Africa.**

Liberia. President Samuel K. Doe, who took power in Liberia in a 1980 coup, was executed by rebel forces on Sept. 10, 1990. Despite Doe's death, violence continued as two competing rebel factions and the remnants of Doe's army fought for control of the country. But in November, a peacekeeping force from five neighboring nations that had arrived three months earlier arranged a cease-fire and began to restore order in Liberia.

The civil war started in December 1989 when about 150 guerrillas of the National Patriotic Front of Liberia (NPFL) crossed over the border from Ivory Coast. The rebels were members of the Gio and Mano ethnic groups, which had suffered atrocities at the hands of Doe and had opposed the monopoly on power held by Doe and his Krahn kinsfolk. The leader of the NPFL, Charles Taylor, was a former official of the Doe regime.

The NPFL's ranks expanded as Taylor recruited new members from other ethnic groups who also opposed Doe's oppressive rule. During a six-month advance toward the capital city of Monrovia, the rebels dealt brutally with Krahn villages and with others they accused of aiding Doe. Doe's forces were equally savage in punishing suspected rebel sympathizers.

By June, the NPFL had occupied most of the country. Isolated in the fortified executive mansion in Monrovia with 5,600 guards, Doe ignored pleas to resign.

As the rebel force closed in on Monrovia in July, it

Rebels opposed to Liberia's President Samuel K. Doe march toward the capital city of Monrovia. In September, Doe was overthrown and executed.

Liberia

★ National capital

• Other town

Liberia lies on the west coast of Africa, bordering the Atlantic Ocean. The country has a tropical climate because it is near the equator.

split into two competing groups. The leader of the new faction, Prince Y. Johnson, accused Taylor of seeking to stay in power after the war.

Johnson's troops dominated in the siege of Monrovia. They captured Doe when he ventured outside his mansion under a flag of truce to visit the headquarters of the peacekeeping force.

Foreign intervention. Although the United States had been Doe's primary military and economic supporter through most of the 1980's, it declined to interfere militarily in the civil war. In August, however, U.S. marines from an offshore task force evacuated more than 1,000 Americans and other foreigners.

The force that did intervene was sent by the Economic Commission of West African States (ECOWAS), which had declared the Liberian civil war a threat to peace in the region. The 6,000 troops from Gambia, Ghana, Guinea, Nigeria, and Sierra Leone began arriving in Monrovia on August 21 and gradually extended their control down the coast. On November 28, the peacekeeping force arranged a cease-fire among the warring groups. ECOWAS rejected the presidential claims of Taylor, Johnson, and Doe's successor, David Nimley. On November 21, they installed as interim president Amos Sawyer, a popular Liberian scholar who had been the choice of exiled Liberian civilian leaders.   J. Gus Liebenow and Beverly B. Liebenow

See also **Africa** (Facts in brief table). In *World Book*, see **Africa; Liberia.**

Library. Public libraries in the United States reported varying success in their battle to maintain adequate funding during 1990. Voters in Portland, Ore., approved a three-year tax aimed at raising $30.9 million for the city's libraries. Michigan's state legislature came to the rescue of Detroit's public library system with a $1.2-million grant to save five branch libraries just 26 hours before they were to shut permanently.

But for the third year in a row, the New York City Public Library received a smaller share of that city's annual budget. The latest reduction, a $2.35-million drop for fiscal year 1991, was expected to result in cutbacks in the hours of service at branch libraries, the purchase of books and other materials, and the maintenance of buildings. The library's literacy program was also cut back.

Spotlight on literacy. The United Nations designated 1990 as International Literacy Year, and U.S. librarians participated in a growing national and international campaign to solve the problem of illiteracy. On April 25, during National Library Week, thousands of libraries joined in "A Night of a Thousand Stars," an event designed to promote family reading. As part of the program, libraries recruited celebrities to read to children.

At the Columbus (Ohio) Metropolitan Library, then-world heavyweight boxing champion James (Buster) Douglas had some 300 children in the palm of his sizable hand. In Los Angeles, 62 stars turned out—one for each library branch. Singer Aretha Franklin read at the Bloomfield Township (Mich.) Public Library. In the Brooklyn section of New York City, rapper KRS-One told a packed house, "The library is the heart and brain of civilization. You should be here picking this brain."

Romanian support. In January, the American Library Association (ALA) established an emergency fund to aid in the rehabilitation of Romania's libraries and their collections. In late December 1989, forces loyal to deposed dictator Nicolae Ceaușescu had ravaged the Central University Library in Bucharest, Romania's capital. Some 500,000 rare books, manuscripts, documents, photographs, and other irreplaceable items were destroyed. Efforts by the ALA committee resulted in the shipment to Romania of about 240,000 books and journals worth more than $4 million.

School closing. Many librarians were angered and dismayed by the decision of Columbia University in New York City to close its School of Library Service, the oldest graduate library education program in the United States. The university cited weaknesses in the library program's enrollment, finances, and faculty research in explaining its decision.

ALA news. ALA President Patricia Wilson Berger, director of information resources and services at the National Institute of Standards and Technology, presided over the association's 109th annual conference. Held in Chicago from June 23 to 28, 1990, the meeting

Libya

was attended by 20,000 participants. At the end of the conference, Richard M. Dougherty, professor in the School of Information and Library Studies at the University of Michigan in Ann Arbor, was installed as the ALA's new president.

South Africa boycott. After a vigorous debate, ALA members voted at the conference to continue supporting an economic boycott against companies doing business in South Africa, which has officially eased many forms of racial discrimination but still maintains a system of *apartheid* (segregation). Since 1986, U.S. librarians have refused to buy books from publishers who also sell their material in South Africa. A 1989 report by a fact-finding team sent to South Africa by the Association of American Publishers and the Fund for Free Expression had recommended an end to the boycott. The report had argued that U.S. publications are needed in the struggle to develop a progressive society in South Africa.

In June 1990, on a visit to the United States, however, South African black nationalist leader Nelson R. Mandela argued that economic sanctions were needed "now more than ever." Librarians thus were asked to choose between demonstrating their opposition to apartheid and maintaining their commitment to universal access to information. In the end, ALA members voted to reaffirm their support for the boycott.   Peggy Barber

In *World Book,* see **Library.**

Libya. Leader of the Revolution Muammar Muhammad al-Qadhafi kept a low profile in 1990 after suffering a number of political reverses during the late 1980's.

His goals, however, remained puzzling. On one hand, Qadhafi continued to build up his military forces. On the other hand, he sought to improve relations with the West through economic ties and conciliatory political gestures. In mid-1990, for example, he expelled from Libya 145 members of the Palestine Liberation Front, a terrorist group responsible for a foiled raid on an Israeli beach in May.

Persian Gulf crisis. Qadhafi initially condemned Iraq for invading Kuwait in August and taking foreign hostages. Following the build-up of United States-led forces in Saudi Arabia, however, he stated that these troops were a greater threat than Iraq to Middle Eastern stability.

Fire hoax? Libya reported on March 14 that fire had destroyed a chemical plant in Rabta, about 40 miles (65 kilometers) south of Tripoli, Libya's capital. In 1988, U.S. officials had accused Libya of manufacturing poison gas at the plant. Qadhafi, however, insisted that the plant was a pharmaceutical factory. United States intelligence officials later concluded that reports of the fire were probably a ruse devised by Qadhafi to mislead the United States and other countries into believing that the plant was no longer in operation.

Refueling test. American military intelligence reported in March 1990 that Libya had successfully tested an in-flight refueling system for fighter-bombers. Aerial refueling allows aircraft to fly farther, fly at lower altitudes—making radar detection more difficult—and carry a heavier payload. According to military experts, this refueling capability, combined with Libya's acquisition of chemical weapons, poses a threat to a range of Middle Eastern targets.

Terrorism. United States intelligence officials in October revealed evidence linking Libya to the bomb that destroyed a Pan American World Airways jetliner over Lockerbie, Scotland, on Dec. 21, 1988, killing 270 people.

The evidence, still circumstantial, focused on a detonator recovered at the crash site. The detonator is similar to 10 timer-activated detonators seized from two Libyan intelligence agents arrested in the African country of Senegal in 1988. The agents were also carrying Semex, the explosive used in the Pan Am bomb.

Regional relations. In early summer 1990, Libya restored diplomatic ties with Jordan, broken in 1984 after rioters burned the Jordanian Embassy in Tripoli. In March 1990, Qadhafi offered Egypt monetary compensation for some 100,000 Egyptian workers expelled from Libya in 1985.   Christine Helms

See also **Middle East** (Facts in brief table). In *World Book,* see **Libya.**

Liechtenstein. See Europe.

Literature. As the United States in 1990 stood on the brink of the last decade of the century, some of its major novelists seemed to pause for an emotional and intellectual inventory of the times.

One stunning example was *Rabbit at Rest,* the fourth and final novel in John Updike's distinguished series exploring the life and times of Rabbit Angstrom, basketball star turned American Everyman. Rabbit's decline and approaching death at almost the same time the Cold War ended symbolized the spiritual fatigue of a generation brought up to regard Communism as its most dangerous enemy.

Similarly, *Vineland,* the reclusive Thomas Pynchon's first novel since 1973, was a brilliantly comic tale, set in California, that explored a massive shift in American radical politics from activism to self-absorption in the 1980's. And *The Tongues of Angels,* Reynolds Price's eighth novel, was a visionary tale that echoes a trend toward mysticism that seemed to have overtaken certain parts of the country during the same period.

The year was an unusually fruitful one in terms of high-quality novels with themes other than social commentary. Among them was *Because It Is Bitter, and Because It Is My Heart,* the prolific Joyce Carol Oates's powerful tale of a young woman's climb out of a tawdry life. Ann Beattie's fourth novel, *Picturing Will,* touchingly explored new senses of family as the traditional nuclear clan disintegrated. Richard Ford's *Wildlife* amply clothed the skeleton of minimalist fiction in a novel—Ford's fourth—about a young man's observations of the collapse of his parents' marriage. Peter Matthiessen's *Killing Mister Watson* was a microscopic examination of the criminality that has often accompanied the pursuit of wealth in America.

Other important novels of 1990 were Gore Vidal's *Hollywood: A Novel of America in the 1920's*, Valerie Martin's *Mary Reilly*, David Carkeet's *The Full Catastrophe*, Philip Roth's *Deceptions*, Frederick Busch's *Harry and Catherine*, Jessica Hagedorn's *Dogeaters*, David Thomson's *Silver Light*, Sue Miller's *Family Pictures*, Judith Rossner's *His Little Women*, Jay Parini's *The Last Station: A Novel of Tolstoy's Last Year*, Scott Spencer's *Secret Anniversaries*, Christine Bell's *The Perez Family*, Alice Hoffman's *Seventh Heaven*, Frederick Barthelme's *Natural Selection*, Brian Moore's *Lies of Silence*, Barbara Kingsolver's *Animal Dreams*, T. Coraghessan Boyle's *East Is East*, George Garrett's *Entered from the Sun*, Kurt Vonnegut's *Hocus Pocus*, Larry McMurtry's *Buffalo Girls*, Jamaica Kincaid's *Lucy*, Paul Auster's *The Music of Chance*, and Leslie Epstein's *Pinto and Sons*. Making impressive debuts as first-time novelists were Seth Morgan, author of *Homeboy;* James Hynes, *The Wild Colonial Boy;* and Dennis McFarland, *The Music Room.*

Short stories. A distinguished novelist of the American West showed that his genius extended to short fiction in *Collected Stories of Wallace Stegner.* Lee Smith also contributed a collection of significant short stories in *Me and My Baby View the Eclipse*, as did John L'Heureux, *Comedians;* Eileen Drew, *Blue Taxis: Stories About Africa;* John Metcalf, *Adult Entertainment*; Tim O'Brien, *The Things They Carried;* Amy Hempel, *At the Gates of the Animal Kingdom;* Madison Smartt Bell, *Barking Man;* John Hersey, *Fling;* Christopher Tilghman, *In a Father's Place;* Lorrie Moore, *Like Life;* Richard Bausch, *The Fireman's Wife;* David Leavitt, *A Place I've Never Been;* and Jim Harrison, *The Woman Lit by Fireflies.*

Fiction from other countries. Among the best fiction from Great Britain and Ireland were P. D. James's fine 11th mystery, *Devices and Desires;* Iris Murdoch's *The Message to the Planet;* Martin Amis' *London Fields;* Charles Palliser's *The Quincunx;* Anita Brookner's *Lewis Percy;* Fay Weldon's *The Cloning of Joanna;* John Mortimer's *Titmuss Regained;* Ian McEwan's *The Innocent;* William Trevor's *Family Sins and Other Stories;* Edna O'Brien's story collection *Lantern Slides;* Kingsley Amis' *The Folks That Live on the Hill;* D. M. Thomas' *Lying Together;* and A. S. Byatt's *Possession*, which won the Booker Prize.

Salman Rushdie's *Haroun and the Sea of Stories*, a book for children, was the Indian-born British novelist's first book to be issued from hiding. Rushdie was ordered killed in 1989 by Ayatollah Ruhollah Khomeini, leader of Iran, for writing *The Satanic Verses*, which Khomeini called blasphemous.

The fine Canadian writer Alice Munro contributed

Novelist John Updike concluded the story of his popular character Rabbit Angstrom—who represents the American Everyman—in *Rabbit at Rest.*

Literature

Friend of My Youth, and her countryman Mordecai Richler, *Solomon Gursky Was Here*. From South Africa came J. M. Coetzee's *Age of Iron* and Nadine Gordimer's *My Son's Story*.

Translations. Many good novels and short-story collections appeared in translation. Among them were *Palace Walk*, a novel by the Egyptian Nobel laureate Naguib Mahfouz; *Constancia and Other Stories for Virgins*, by Mexico's Carlos Fuentes; *Bohin Manor*, by Poland's Tadeusz Konwicki; and *The General in His Labyrinth*, by Colombia's Gabriel García Márquez.

Biography and autobiography. Robert A. Caro's *Means of Ascent* was the second installment of a planned four-volume life of Lyndon B. Johnson, controversial for its emphasis on the late American President's character flaws.

In *Captain Sir Richard Francis Burton*, Edward Rice explored the astonishing life of (in the book's apt subtitle) "The Secret Agent Who Made the Pilgrimage to Mecca, Discovered the Kama Sutra, and Brought the Arabian Nights to the West."

Among 1990's leading literary biographies were Paul Mariani's *Dream Song*, a life of the poet John Berryman; Deirdre Bair's *Simone de Beauvoir*, an examination of the career of the French feminist intellectual; William H. Pritchard's *Randall Jarrell: A Literary Life*, an account of the life of the fine critic who wanted to be a great poet; Richard Holmes's *Coleridge*, an outline of the life of the English poet; Peter

Kurth's *American Cassandra*, an exploration of the contradictions in the career of journalist Dorothy Thompson; Richard Lingeman's *Theodore Dreiser*, the concluding volume in an inventory of the troubled later years of the novelist; and Brian Boyd's *Vladimir Nabokov*, a look at the early years of the Russian-American writer in the land of his birth.

Two important books with the same title—*Jackson Pollock*—studied the life of a major American abstract expressionist painter. One was by Steven Naifeh and Gregory White Smith, the other by Ellen G. Landau. *Van Gogh*, by David Sweetman, exploded some of the long-held myths about the Dutch painter.

Other significant biographies of the year were Stanley A. Blumberg and Louis G. Panos' *Edward Teller: Giant of the Golden Age of Physics;* Laurie Lisle's *Louise Nevelson: A Passionate Life;* Jeremy Wilson's *Lawrence of Arabia;* Laurence Bergreen's *As Thousands Cheer: The Life of Irving Berlin;* Sally Bedell Smith's *In All His Glory: The Life of William S. Paley;* and Jean Lacouture's *De Gaulle: The Rebel, 1890-1944.*

The year's notable autobiographies were led by the late Soviet dissident-physicist Andrei D. Sakharov's monumental *Memoirs;* Liu Binyan's *A Higher Kind of Loyalty*, the Chinese journalist's affecting memoir of dissidence in his homeland; Kate Millett's *The Loony-Bin Trip*, the story of the feminist's descent into and return from mental illness; Dean Rusk's *As I Saw It*, the former U.S. secretary of state's memoir, told to his son Richard; *Darkness Visible*, novelist William Styron's story of his struggle with clinical depression; *Etchings in an Hourglass*, the third of the late travel writer Kate Simon's extraordinary autobiographies; and *A Hole in the World*, journalist Richard Rhodes's painful memoir of an abused childhood.

Letters. Among the year's foremost collections of correspondence were *Loving Letters from Ogden Nash*, edited by the poet's daughter Linell Nash Smith; *Five O'Clock Angel*, the letters of playwright Tennessee Williams to his friend Maria St. Just, which she edited; and *Letters of Katherine Anne Porter*, edited by Isabel Bayley.

History. Of the many books dealing with the Civil War (1861-1865), one of the best was *Forged in Battle: The Civil War Alliance of Black Soldiers and White Officers*, by Joseph T. Glatthaar. *The Civil War*, by Geoffrey C. Ward with Ric Burns and Ken Burns, was the costly but best-selling print version of the Public Broadcasting Service television series of the same title.

Jonathan D. Spence's *The Search for Modern China* authoritatively examined four centuries of Chinese history. Edward Seidensticker's *Tokyo Rising* was a lively chronicle of the Japanese capital since the great earthquake of 1923. Richard Pipes's *The Russian Revolution* was a comprehensive view of the birth of Marxism-Leninism in the Soviet Union.

Three excellent books analyzed the role of Soviet dictator Joseph Stalin in the years of terror that followed his rise to power. These were Robert C. Tucker's

Nobel Prize winner Gabriel García Márquez wrote about the final days of Venezuelan leader Simón Bolívar in *The General in His Labyrinth.*

Stalin in Power: The Revolution from Above, 1928-1941; Walter Laqueur's *Stalin: The Glasnost Revelations;* and Louis Rapoport's *Stalin's War Against the Jews: The Doctors' Plot and the Soviet Solution.*

Contemporary affairs. A number of nonfiction works in 1990 explored the ethics and dynamics of money. Among the muckraking books that looked at the world of Wall Street financial plundering were Bryan Burrough and John Helyar's best-selling *Barbarians at the Gate: The Fall of RJR Nabisco* and Hope Lampert's *True Greed: What Really Happened in the Battle for RJR Nabisco.* David Burnham's *A Law unto Itself* dealt with the accountability of the sometimes arrogant Internal Revenue Service. Kevin Phillips' *The Politics of Rich and Poor* argued that the wealthy became wealthier and the poor became poorer under the policies of President Ronald Reagan. *The Prize* by Daniel Yergin detailed the rise of our oil-based society and its consequences for the world.

Two controversial books by black authors explored racial politics. In *Preferential Policies*, Thomas Sowell attacked affirmative action. In *The Content of Our Character*, Shelby Steele argued that blacks too often tend to see themselves as victims of racism.

Two notable books dealt with education. Roger Kimball's *Tenured Radicals* argued convincingly that leftist political activities often have disturbing impact on university humanities curriculums. Samuel G. Freedman's *Small Victories* was a touching scrutiny of a year in the life of a teacher and her impoverished students at a high school in New York City.

Two books revealed many embarrassing secrets about the U.S. government's once-intimate relationship with former Panamanian dictator Manuel Antonio Noriega. Frederick Kempe's *Divorcing the Dictator* and John Dinges' *Our Man in Panama.*

Saddam Hussein and the Crisis in the Gulf, by Judith Miller and Laurie Mylroie, was hastily written—after Iraq's invasion of Kuwait—by a *New York Times* editor and a Middle Eastern expert at Harvard University, respectively. The book turned out to be a remarkably informative and even compelling account of the rise of a ruthless dictator with grandiose ambitions.

Janet Malcolm's *The Journalist and the Murderer*, which explored the way in which author Joe McGinniss obtained information from a convicted murderer for a book, stirred a controversy over the ethics of the relationship between journalist and subject. Morley Safer's *Flashbacks* chronicled the CBS correspondent's return to his professional roots in Vietnam.

Women and children. *Soviet Women*, by Francine du Plessix Gray, was an admirable examination of gender differences in the Soviet Union since the Russian Revolution of 1917. *The Spiritual Life of Children* was Robert Coles's third distinguished oral history of the concerns of American youngsters. *What Lisa Knew*, by Joyce Johnson, examined with sensitivity the child-abuse death of a young girl and the celebrated trial of Joel Steinberg, who had unofficially adopted her.

Best-selling books of the 1980's

Fiction	Hard-cover copies sold
1. *Clear and Present Danger,* Tom Clancy	1,607,715
2. *The Dark Half,* Stephen King	1,550,000
3. *The Tommyknockers,* Stephen King	1,429,929
4. *The Mammoth Hunters,* Jean M. Auel	1,350,000
5. *Daddy,* Danielle Steel	1,321,235
6. *Lake Wobegon Days,* Garrison Keillor	1,300,000
7. *The Cardinal of the Kremlin,* Tom Clancy	1,287,067
8. *Texas,* James A. Michener	1,176,758
9. *Red Storm Rising,* Tom Clancy	1,126,782
10. *It,* Stephen King	1,115,000

Nonfiction	
1. *Iacocca,* Lee Iacocca with William Novak	2,572,000
2. *Fatherhood,* Bill Cosby	2,335,000
3. *The 8-Week Cholesterol Cure,* Robert E. Kowalski	2,250,000
4. *Fit for Life,* Harvey Diamond and Marilyn Diamond	2,023,000
5. *In Search of Excellence,* Thomas J. Peters and Robert H. Waterman, Jr.	1,375,000
6. *All I Really Need to Know I Learned in Kindergarten,* Robert Fulghum	1,280,000
7. *Jane Fonda's Workout Book,* Jane Fonda	*
8. *The Frugal Gourmet,* Jeff Smith	*
9. *A Brief History of Time,* Stephen W. Hawking	1,130,000
10. *Yeager,* Chuck Yeager and Leo Janos	*

*Sales figures submitted to *Publishers Weekly* in confidence, for use only in determining position on the list.

Source: Reprinted from the Jan. 5, 1990, issue of *Publishers Weekly*, published by Cahners Publishing Company, a division of Reed Publishing USA; © 1990 by Reed Publishing USA.

Science. Two important books provided evidence that increasing global warming will result in profound environmental changes: David E. Fisher's *Fire & Ice: The Greenhouse Effect, Ozone Depletion, and Nuclear Winter*, and Jonathan Weiner's *The Next One Hundred Years: Shaping the Fate of Our Living Earth.* *The Ants*, by Bert Hoelldobler and Edward O. Wilson, was an authoritative and lyrically written insect study. *Piltdown: A Scientific Forgery*, by Frank Spencer, examined the famous 1912 forgery of a "missing link" in human history called Piltdown Man. It suggested that the person most likely responsible was Charles Dawson, "discoverer" of the fraudulent skull.

Best sellers. The most interesting best-selling nonfiction book of the year was George F. Will's *Men at Work*, the political columnist's close-up look at four craftsmen of professional baseball. Leading the best-selling novels was Scott Turow's *The Burden of Proof.* Other top-sellers were Dr. Seuss's *Oh, The Places You'll Go!*, Deborah Tannen's *You Just Don't Understand: Talk Between the Sexes*, Martin Handford's *The Great Waldo Search*, Charles J. Givens' *Wealth Without Risk*, John Bradshaw's *Homecoming*, Tom Clancy's *Clear and Present Danger*, John Naisbitt and Patricia Aburdene's *Megatrends 2000*, and Burrough and Helyar's *Barbarians at the Gate.*   Henry Kisor

See also **Awards and prizes** (Literature awards); **Canadian literature; Literature for children; Poetry.** In *World Book,* see **Literature.**

353

Literature for children

Number the Stars, Lois Lowry's novel about a Danish girl who protects Jews from the Nazis, won the Newbery Medal for best children's book of 1990.

Literature for children. Children's books published in 1990 featured many multicultural and environmental subjects in stories and illustrations. Picture books for preschoolers continued to be plentiful along with a variety of poetry books. For older children, books about friendship and the problems of growing up were popular topics.

Outstanding books of 1990 included the following:

Picture books. *Black and White* by David Macaulay (Houghton Mifflin). Several tales merge in a cleverly designed, challenging book. All ages.

Box and Cox by Grace Chetwin, illustrated by David Small (Bradbury). Two men rent the same room and do not know it (one works days, the other nights). Humorous illustrations add to the fun. Ages 5 to 8.

Come a Tide by George Ella Lyon, illustrated by Stephen Gammell (Orchard Bks.). Bright, detailed illustrations capture a story of rescue from floodwaters after a torrential rain. Ages 4 to 7.

Dirty Dave by Nette Hilton, illustrated by Roland Harvey (Orchard Bks.). Comical tale and paintings of three outlaws and Dad, who loves to sew. Ages 3 to 6.

Dinosaur Garden by Liza Donnelly (Scholastic). A boy plants a dinosaur garden, with surprising results. Humorous color illustrations, glossary. Ages 4 to 8.

The Dragon's Robe by Deborah Nourse Lattimore (Harper & Row). In a Chinese tale, Kwan Yin follows an old man's advice. Beautiful paintings in the Chinese style. Ages 6 to 9.

The Empty Pot by Demi (Henry Holt). Ping loves flowers and can make anything grow, until the emperor gives each child a seed to see who will inherit his kingdom. Paintings aid this clever tale. Ages 4 to 8.

Fish Eyes: A Book You Can Count On by Lois Ehlert (Harcourt Brace Jovanovich). Vivid illustrations help a child learn to count and add. Ages 4 to 8.

Frida the Wondercat by Betsy Everitt (Harcourt Brace Jovanovich). A mysterious present arrives that changes Frida, but Louise solves the problem. Bright, exaggerated paintings. Ages 3 to 8.

Hail to Mail by Samuel Marshak, illustrated by Vladimir Radunsky (Henry Holt). A letter follows John Peck all over the world. Wonderful, funny paintings. Ages 4 to 8.

Hansel and Gretel, retold and illustrated by James Marshall (Dial). Comical characters make this retelling a delight. Ages 4 to 8.

How Two-Feather Was Saved from Loneliness by C. J. Taylor (Tundra). An Indian legend tells how Two-Feather fell in love with a vision and what she taught it. Rich paintings. Ages 6 and up.

The Lady with a Ship on Her Head by Deborah Nourse Lattimore (Harcourt Brace Jovanovich). With much humor and extravagant illustrations, Madame Pompenstance wins a prize. Ages 4 to 8.

Little Tricker the Squirrel Meets Big Double the Bear by Ken Kesey, illustrated by Barry Moser (Viking). The bear meets his match in Tricker in a rollicking tale. All ages.

The Magic Paintbrush by Robin Muller (Viking Kestrel). A magic paintbrush causes more problems than it is worth. All ages.

Oh, the Places You'll Go! by Dr. Seuss (Random House). A child is encouraged to go out and face what life has to offer. All ages.

On Christmas Eve by Peter Collington (Knopf). For children in homes without chimneys, this magical wordless story will have special appeal. All ages.

A Piece of Luck by Simon Henwood (Farrar, Straus & Giroux). When a man finds a piece of luck, greed begins to take over. Unusual paintings. All ages.

Possum Magic by Mem Fox, illustrated by Julie Vivas (Gulliver Bks.). Grandma Poss has made Hush invisible, but now Hush wants the spell removed. Wonderful paintings for this Australian tale. Ages 4 to 7.

Tam Lin by Jane Yolen, illustrated by Charles Mikolaycak (Harcourt Brace Jovanovich). Jennet braves the fairy folk to save Tam Lin. Ages 6 to 12.

The Wild Christmas Reindeer by Jan Brett (Putnam). Teeka learns that a soft voice is better than a loud one. Luminous, detailed paintings. Ages 4 to 7.

Fantasy. *Herb Seasoning* by Julian Thompson (Scholastic). Herb tries to find out where his life should go, and a spinning wheel at Castles in the Air offers him several choices. Ages 12 and up.

Jason and the Golden Fleece by Leonard Everett Fisher (Holiday House). Stunning paintings accompany Jason's adventures. Ages 7 to 11.

The Kitchen Knight, retold by Margaret Hodges, illustrated by Trina Schart Hyman (Holiday House). The adventures of Sir Gareth, a knight from the King Arthur legends, are captured perfectly in dramatic paintings. Ages 8 to 12.

Land of the Long White Cloud: Maori Myths, Tales and Legends by Kiri Te Kanawa, illustrated by Michael Foreman (Arcade). A fine, varied collection of adventures, recalled by the New Zealand opera star from her childhood, has beautiful paintings. Ages 6 and up.

Mattimeo by Brian Jacques (Philomel Bks.). In this sequel to *Redwall*, some of the children are kidnapped, and Matthias and others seek them. Ages 12 and up.

On Fortune's Wheel by Cynthia Voigt (Atheneum Pubs.). A young innkeeper's daughter and a lord encounter desperate circumstances when they leave the kingdom. Ages 12 and up.

The Philadelphia Adventure by Lloyd Alexander (Dutton). Vesper Holly is enmeshed in a kidnapping and international intrigue when President Ulysses S. Grant asks her for help. Ages 10 to 14.

The Pit by Ann Cheetham (Henry Holt). Chilling, graphic ghost tale is set in plague-ridden London. Ages 9 to 12.

R-T, Margaret, and the Rats of NIMH by Jane Leslie Conly, illustrated by Leonard Lubin (Harper & Row). When Artie (R-T) and Margaret become lost while camping, they are helped and, in turn, help the rats of the National Institute of Mental Health. Ages 9 to 12.

Stonewords: A Ghost Story by Pam Conrad (Harper & Row). Zoe's best friend is a ghost, and Zoe uncovers the reason for her appearances. Ages 10 and up.

Tehanu: The Last Book of Earthsea by Ursula K. Le Guin (Atheneum Pubs.). Ged and Tenar are reunited with the abused and maimed child Therru, who was introduced in the beginning of another cycle of tales. Ages 12 and up.

Poetry. *Bird Watch* by Jane Yolen, illustrated by Ted Lewin (Philomel Bks.). All kinds of birds are strikingly presented with dramatic paintings. All ages.

Fresh Brats by X. J. Kennedy, illustrated by James Watts (Margaret K. McElderry Bks.). More nonsense about an assortment of brats. Ages 8 and up.

Johnny Appleseed by Reeve Lindbergh, illustrated by Kathy Jakobsen (Joy St.). Pioneer planter John Chapman (Johnny Appleseed) and his gifts are revealed, with bright folk-art paintings. Ages 4 to 9.

Mummy Took Cooking Lessons by John Ciardi, illustrated by Merle Nacht (Houghton Mifflin). Humorous poems should tickle the funny bone. Ages 7 to 12.

Paul Revere's Ride by Henry Wadsworth Longfellow, illustrated by Ted Rand (Dutton). Fine paintings show the spirit and drama of the poem. Map, other information. All ages.

Ragged Robin: Poems from A to Z by James Reeves, illustrated by Emma Chichester Clark (Little, Brown). A fresh variety of poems, with attractive illustrations. Ages 4 to 8.

Ed Young's illustrations for *Lon Po Po*, a Chinese folk tale that Young also translated, won the 1990 Caldecott Medal for best picture book for children.

Soda Jerk by Cynthia Rylant, illustrated by Peter Catalanotto (Orchard Bks.). A town's occupants and a soda jerk's feelings are revealed in his poems. Ages 12 and up.

Trail of Stones by Gwen Strauss, illustrated by Anthony Browne (Knopf). Poems created from familiar fairy tales but with unusual speakers. Tantalizing. Ages 12 and up.

Fiction. *The Boy in the Moon* by Ron Koertge (Joy St.). Frieda, Kevin, and Nick have always been best friends until Kevin spends the summer in California. Ages 12 and up.

Chain of Fire by Beverly Naidoo, illustrated by Eric Velasquez (Lippincott). Naledi and her friends try to prevent the moving of a black village to a new site chosen by whites. Ages 12 and up.

Face to Face: A Collection of Stories by Celebrated Soviet and American Writers, edited by Thomas Pettepiece and Anatoly Aleksin (Philomel Bks.). American and Soviet tales about some children's memorable experiences. Ages 12 and up.

The Journey Home by Isabelle Holland (Scholastic). Maggie and Annie try to adjust to their adopted home in the West after they leave New York. Ages 8 to 12.

Newfound by Jim Wayne Miller (Orchard Bks.). Robert must learn to cope with his parents' divorce and his move to his grandparents' farm in Tennessee. Ages 12 and up.

Literature for children

Rachel Chance by Jean Thesman (Houghton Mifflin). Rachel, 15, is determined to find her brother, who was stolen from the family. Ages 10 to 14.

Saturnalia by Paul Fleischman (Harper & Row). William, an Indian apprentice, finds friends and enemies among the whites in 1681 in Boston, as he secretly searches for his brother. Ages 12 and up.

Send No Blessings by Phyllis Reynolds Naylor (Atheneum Pubs.). Beth, the oldest of eight children, wants an education, but when Harless Prather offers her love and marriage, she must choose. Ages 12 and up.

The Shining Company by Rosemary Sutcliff (Farrar, Straus & Giroux). Prosper follows Prince Gorthyn when he goes to fight the Saxons, unaware of the treachery to come. Ages 12 and up.

Tales from Gold Mountain: Stories of the Chinese in the New World by Paul Yee, illustrated by Simon Ng (Macmillan). Unusual tales of Chinese experiences in the United States. Ages 8 and up.

Tug of War by Joan Lingard (Lodestar Bks.). Hugo is separated from his family when they flee Latvia during World War II (1939-1945), and each fears that the others may be dead. Ages 12 and up.

White Peak Farm by Berlie Doherty (Orchard Bks.). Members of the Tanner family have hopes and dreams that do not always conform to family expectations. Ages 10 and up.

Your Move, J. P.! by Lois Lowry (Houghton Mifflin). J. P. falls in love, lies to impress Angela, and gets a surprise. Ages 8 to 12.

Animals, people, places, and things. *Antarctica* by Helen Cowcher (Farrar, Straus & Giroux). Penguins, Weddell seals, and the human threat to their environment. Stunning paintings. Ages 4 to 8.

Dinosaurs Alive and Well: A Guide to Good Health by Laura Krasny Brown and Marc Brown (Joy St.). Cartoon-style illustrations and a cheerful text teach a child about health. Ages 4 to 8.

Ellis Island: New Hope in a New Land by William J. Jacobs (Scribners). A brief history of the island and the immigrants who landed there. Fine photographs. Ages 7 to 10.

Exploring Spring: A Season of Science Activities, Puzzlers, and Games by Sandra Markle (Atheneum Pubs.). A unique blend of riddles, information, activities, and experiments. Well illustrated. Ages 8 to 12.

Great Northern Diver: The Loon by Barbara Juster Esbensen, illustrated by Mary Barrett Brown (Little, Brown). Fascinating loon lore is well told, with lovely, clear paintings. Ages 6 to 10.

Hidden Stories in Plants by Anne Pellowski, illustrated by Lynn Sweat (Macmillan). Myths and tales precede clear instructions for a variety of creative play with plants. Ages 8 to 12.

Insect Metamorphosis from Egg to Adult by Ron and Nancy Goor (Atheneum Pubs.). Fine color photographs show how insects change in form as they develop into adults, while the simple text explains the process. Ages 6 to 10.

Look! The Ultimate Spot-the-Difference Book by April Wilson (Dial). Fascinating scenes challenge the reader's powers of observation. The key at the end of the book provides information as well as answers. All ages.

Orchestranimals by Vlasta van Kampen and Irene C. Eugen, illustrated by Vlasta van Kampen (Scholastic). As the animals appear for the concert, the reader learns about their instruments from the text and the realistic illustrations. Ages 5 to 8.

The Riddle of the Rosetta Stone by James Cross Giblin (Crowell). The puzzle of hieroglyphics is slowly solved. Photographs, prints, drawings, index, bibliography. Ages 9 to 12.

Totem Pole by Diane Hoyt-Goldsmith, photographs by Lawrence Migdale (Holiday House). David of the Tsimshian Indian clan describes his life and his pride in his father's woodcarving. Color photographs. Ages 8 to 12.

Awards in 1990. The Newbery Medal for the best American children's book was awarded to Lois Lowry for *Number the Stars*. The Caldecott Medal for "the most distinguished American picture book for children" went to Ed Young, the illustrator of *Lon Po Po*, a Chinese folk tale. The Mildred L. Batchelder Award cited Dutton Children's Books for its publication of *Buster's World* by Bjarne Reuter.   Marilyn Fain Apseloff

In *World Book,* see **Caldecott Medal; Literature for children; Newbery Medal.**

Los Angeles. In a landmark decision that could dramatically alter Los Angeles County's political landscape, a federal judge ruled on June 4, 1990, that the county Board of Supervisors intentionally discriminated against Hispanics in 1981 when it drew new electoral district boundaries. United States District Judge David V. Kenyon found that the board had violated the federal Voting Rights Act of 1965 by mapping districts so as to exclude Hispanics from representation in the county government. Some 35 per cent of the county's 8.7 million residents are Hispanic. Judge Kenyon ordered the board to draft a new redistricting plan designed to help Hispanics win their first seat on the powerful five-member board.

On August 4, Judge Kenyon approved a reapportionment plan establishing new political boundaries for the county, including the creation of a district with a Hispanic majority. The revised map was drawn up by two civil rights groups that had filed a lawsuit against the county board in 1988. A U.S. appeals court affirmed Kenyon's ruling on Nov. 3, 1990.

New rail line. After a 29-year absence, rail transit returned to Los Angeles County on July 14, when the Metro Blue Line began service from Long Beach to downtown Los Angeles. The 22-mile (35-kilometer) street-level rail line is the first segment of a planned 150-mile (240-kilometer) rail system, which will also include a subway. The system, with a projected cost of at least $10 billion, is expected to be completed about the year 2020. Officials of the Los Angeles County Transportation Commission, which is constructing the huge rail network, expressed hope that the system will ease congestion and air pollution in the automobile-choked Los Angeles area.

Sheriff's deputies accused of corruption. A federal grand jury indicted 10 Los Angeles County sheriff's deputies on Feb. 22, 1990, for allegedly skimming $1.4 million from individuals involved in the drug trade. The officers were all members of elite teams that investigated major narcotics cases. Sheriff Sherman Block called the case the worst corruption scandal in the history of the department.

One of the 10 suspects, a sergeant, pleaded guilty on March 7 to conspiracy and tax evasion charges. On December 10, six deputies were convicted of conspiring to steal money during drug raids; a seventh was convicted of a lesser charge involving the *laundering* (hiding the illegal origin of) drug money. Block suspended another 16 deputies and dismantled the special narcotics investigation team.

Water rationing. On July 24, the Los Angeles City Council approved a water-rationing plan for city residents and businesses. Although the plan was largely voluntary, it included—for the first time in the city's history—fines for excessive water use. The ordinance, signed into law the same day by Mayor Thomas Bradley, banned lawn and garden watering during certain hours and set fines of $50 to $150 for repeated violations. Fines also were provided for the hosing of sidewalks and parking lots and for failing to repair leaks or allowing water to flow into gutters.

Medfly victory. State agriculture officials lifted a quarantine on home grown fruit on November 9 after declaring victory in their 16-month battle against the Mediterranean fruit fly, or Medfly, in southern California. Medflies destroy fruits, nuts, and vegetables. The $52-million eradication campaign began after the discovery of a single Medfly on the east side of Los Angeles in July 1989. At its height, the effort aroused angry protests, as pesticides were sprayed over several hundred square miles of residential areas.

Budgets. Bradley signed a record $3.68-billion budget for the city on June 4, 1990, that included Los Angeles' first parking tax—a 10 per cent levy added onto the cost of parking in a pay lot. The budget also included a 10 per cent increase in the city's business tax and a doubling of the fee for garbage removal. The Los Angeles County board approved a $10.2-billion budget on August 7 that restored threatened cuts in funding for county hospitals and clinics.

Sales tax hike. Los Angeles County voters on November 6 approved a half-cent increase in the local sales tax to raise $400 million a year to speed development of the Metro rail system and for other transit and expressway improvements.   Victor Merina

In *World Book,* see **Los Angeles.**
Louisiana. See **State government.**
Luxembourg. See **Europe.**

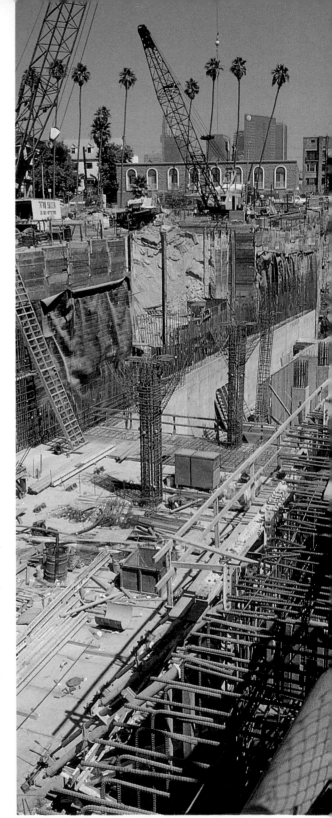

Work proceeded in 1990 on the first leg of a Los Angeles subway system. The 4.4-mile (7-kilometer) segment is slated to begin operation in late 1993.

Lynch, David

Lynch, David (1946-   ), a film director known for his arresting, often grotesque, images, reached a wide audience in 1990. His television series, "Twin Peaks," premiered on the American Broadcasting Companies (ABC) network. Produced and directed by Lynch and a collaborator, the mystery series featured a tangled plot and bizarre characters that intrigued audiences and TV critics. His motion picture *Wild at Heart*, a violent love story, won the Golden Palm Grand Prize at the 1990 Cannes International Film Festival. Lynch also created and produced a TV documentary series, "American Chronicles"; directed television commercials and a rock video; and continued to draw "The Angriest Dog in the World," a weekly cartoon strip.

Lynch was born in Missoula, Mont., on Jan. 20, 1946. He studied painting at various art schools and created his first film as an attempt "to see a painting move." In 1970, Lynch enrolled in the American Film Institute in Los Angeles. There, he began work on *Eraserhead* (1977), a gruesome comedy that had a successful run as a cult film. Lynch received an Academy Award nomination for the direction of his next movie, *The Elephant Man* (1980), but flopped with *Dune* (1984), a $45-million science-fiction epic. His career rebounded with *Blue Velvet* (1986), though the film portrayed sadistic acts that offended some moviegoers.

Twice married and divorced, Lynch has one daughter and one son.   Jinger Hoop

Madagascar. See **Africa.**

Entertainment Weekly, one of 1990's new magazines, provides a consumer's guide to movies, television, videos, and other media.

Magazine. Several magazines changed hands in the United States in 1990. Time Warner Incorporated bought the Lane Publishing Company for about $225-million in March—its first major acquisition since Time and Warner Communications merged in 1989. Lane publishes *Sunset*, a West Coast magazine about gardening, food, home design, and recreation. With the purchase, Time Warner became the largest U.S. publisher of regional magazines, and it gained a West Coast base from which to launch new publications.

Publisher Owen J. Lipstein sold *American Health*, the magazine he founded in 1982, to the Reader's Digest Association for $29.1 million in early 1990. In August, Lipstein's New American Magazine Company sold a 50 per cent share in *Mother Earth News, Psychology Today*, and *Smart* to the Japanese Independent Communications Company for just under $15 million. This was the first significant Japanese investment in a U.S. magazine publishing company.

Magazines for men. *Men*, a magazine that had yet to appear, merged with *Smart* in September. Starting in 1991, the new general-interest publication was to carry the title *Smart: For Men*. In June 1990, *Manhattan, inc.*, which profiled the rich and successful, merged with the men's fashion magazine *M* to form *M inc.* The new monthly, owned by Fairchild Publications Incorporated, was targeted at affluent male readers.

Another addition to the men's special interest category was *Details*, a style magazine revamped by Advance Publications Incorporated in September. The new *Details*, which was aimed at men from the ages of 18 to 34, covered a variety of topics from music to fashion. Murdoch Magazines launched the quarterly *Men's Life* in September, hoping to attract "regular guys." Murdoch Magazines is a division of media magnate Rupert Murdoch's News Corporation. *Men's Life* folded after one issue, though News Corporation said it planned to relaunch the magazine when the economy improved.

Other new magazines. *Entertainment Weekly* was launched by Time Warner in February. This guide to motion pictures, videos, records, television programs, and books was aimed at two-income couples who lack the time to shop around for entertainment. *Egg* magazine, a life-style magazine published by Forbes Incorporated, also debuted in February. Hearst Magazines test-marketed *Countryside*, a quarterly with articles on the home, gardening, and nature aimed at young professionals.

Awards. The Magazine Publishers of America (MPA) named Richard F. McLoughlin, the retired president and chief operating officer of the Reader's Digest Association, to receive the 1990 Henry Johnson Fisher Award, the magazine industry's most prestigious honor. The MPA's Stephen E. Kelly Award, granted for outstanding advertising in magazines, went to Wieden & Kennedy Incorporated, an advertising agency in Portland, Ore., for its Nike footwear campaign.

The American Society of Magazine Editors presented its National Magazine Awards for editorial excellence in April. Winners were *Consumer Reports* for personal service; *Art & Antiques* for special interests; *The New Yorker* for reporting and for fiction; *The Washingtonian* for feature writing; *Southern Exposure* for public-interest journalism; *Esquire* for design; *National Geographic Magazine* for a single-topic issue; *Texas Monthly* for photography; and *Vanity Fair* for essays and criticism. For general excellence, presented by circulation size, the winners were *7 Days* (less than 100,000); *Texas Monthly* (100,000 to 400,000); *Metropolitan Home* (400,000 to 1,000,000); and *Sports Illustrated* (more than 1 million).

The number of advertising pages in magazines in the United States totaled 156,500 for the first 11 months of 1990. This was a drop of 4 per cent from the same period in 1989.

The combined circulation per issue of all consumer magazines surveyed by the Audit Bureau of Circulations (ABC) in the United States climbed to 367.6 million during the first six months of 1990, up 1.2 per cent over the same period in 1989. (The ABC is an independent company that issues circulation figures, verified by auditors.) Sharon Roccaforte

In *World Book,* see **Magazine.**

Maine. See **State government.**

Major, John (1943-), a Conservative, became prime minister of Great Britain on Nov. 28, 1990, after Margaret Thatcher's surprising resignation. On November 21, she had failed to receive the required number of votes from the Conservative members of Parliament to be reelected leader of the Conservative Party. She was expected to run in the second round of balloting the following week but resigned instead on November 22. See **Great Britain.**

The leader of the majority party in Parliament—in this case, the Conservative Party—becomes prime minister. The 47-year-old Major won 185 votes out of 372, falling 2 votes short of the required majority. Two other contenders quickly conceded defeat, however, and declared their support for Major. He had been chancellor of the exchequer since October 1989.

Major was born on March 29, 1943, in southwest London. After a business loss, the family moved to Brixton, a poor section of south London. Major attended Rutlish Grammar School, a state school in Wimbledon, but at 16 he quit. At 18, he began working in a London bank, passing his banker's examinations 2½ years later. First elected to Parliament in 1979, he soon became a favorite of Thatcher's and held a number of posts in her government, including a three-month term as foreign secretary in 1989.

Major and his wife, Norma, were married in 1970 and have a daughter and a son. Carol L. Hanson

Malawi. See **Africa.**

Malaysia. Mahathir bin Mohamad won a third term as prime minister by leading his political party, the New United Malays National Organization (UMNO), to victory in parliamentary elections on Oct. 20 and 21, 1990. For months, observers had speculated that the prime minister would take advantage of Malaysia's past three years of prosperity by trying to win a new mandate. On October 4, Mahathir announced the dissolution of Parliament. The short, intense election campaign that followed was one of the nation's dirtiest and most bitter.

The campaign focused on Mahathir's claims of "peace, stability, and prosperity" and on his opposition's charges of official corruption. The ruling party faced the most serious challenge in its 33 years of dominance. UMNO, the majority party of Malaysia's ethnic Malays, had long headed the National Front coalition, which also represented some ethnic Chinese and Indian Malaysians. For the first time, UMNO's main opponent was another multiracial political group. The opposition was led by Prince Razaleigh Hamzah, a former finance minister who founded a new political party, named Spirit of '46. The new party made election alliances with the leading Chinese and Indian opposition parties and with an Islamic group.

UMNO's National Front won 127 out of 180 parliamentary seats, thus keeping a two-thirds majority. Despite Razaleigh's poor showing, his Spirit of '46 party won every seat from his home state, Kelantan. The opposition also won control of Sabah, a state whose oil and timber resources earn much of the nation's export revenue.

The worst rioting since Malays and ethnic Chinese clashed in 1969 occurred on September 7 over the imposition of tolls on a highway through a predominantly Chinese suburb of Kuala Lumpur, the capital. Mahathir's government had turned over the operation of roads to private companies as part of plans to boost economic growth. But the rioting forced the government on September 13 to halt toll collections indefinitely.

Foreign investment poured into Malaysia as international companies took advantage of the nation's inexpensive resources and dependable work force. The gross national product grew at an annual rate of 9.5 per cent in the first half of 1990, up from 8 per cent in 1989. An oil exporter, Malaysia benefited from rising oil prices after the Iraqi invasion of Kuwait in August. But the environment suffered from the boom. While supplying two-thirds of the world's hardwoods, Malaysia had begun to deplete its forests, and industrial haze sometimes blanketed the Kuala Lumpur area. Henry S. Bradsher

See also **Asia** (Facts in brief table). In the Special Reports section, see **Riding a Wave of Prosperity on the Pacific Rim.** In *World Book,* see **Malaysia.**

Maldives. See **Asia.**

Mali. See **Africa.**

Malta. See **Europe.**

Mandela, Nelson

Mandela, Nelson (1918-   ), a long-time opponent of South Africa's white-dominated government, was released from prison near Cape Town on Feb. 11, 1990. Mandela was convicted in 1964 of sabotage and conspiracy and was sentenced to life imprisonment. He spent more than 27 years behind bars. Upon gaining his freedom, Mandela struck a conciliatory note, saying that blacks and whites must work together to create a new South Africa.

Nelson Rolihlahla Mandela was born on July 18, 1918, in a village in the Transkei territory of South Africa. His father was a chief of the Madiba clan.

After attending schools in the Transkei, Mandela enrolled at Fort Hare University in the Cape Province. While at the university, Mandela became involved in politics, leading a protest against the school's authorities that resulted in his suspension. He completed his undergraduate studies by correspondence and then earned a law degree in Johannesburg.

In 1944, Mandela and two other activists formed the Youth League of the African National Congress (ANC), the main black group opposing the South African government. In the 1950's, he helped organize many ANC protests and gained prominence in the organization.

Mandela was charged with treason in 1956. He was acquitted in 1961, but a year later he was once more in custody. Not until 1990 was he again free.

Mandela married his second wife, Winnie Mandela, in 1958. They have two daughters.   David L. Dreier

Manitoba. Premier Gary A. Filmon's two-year minority government won a narrow majority in elections on Sept. 11, 1990. The Progressive Conservative (PC) administration increased its standing from 25 to 30 members in the 57-seat Legislative Assembly. Political analysts said that Filmon's popularity increased after his determined opposition to the controversial Meech Lake constitutional accord (see **Canada [Close-Up]**). Filmon was also helped by having distanced his administration and his party from the unpopular federal PC government. After the election, Filmon promised to hold public hearings to develop the province's post-Meech stand on such issues as Senate reform and immigration policies.

The election reduced the Liberal Party's seats from 20 to 7. The Liberals lost the official opposition role, which passed to the New Democratic Party (NDP), led by Gary Doer. Despite predictions of failing popularity, NDP seats rose from 12 to 20.

The Manitoba government granted the province's 2,000 physicians the right to binding arbitration in disputes over fee levels for a period of four years. Arbitration panels deciding the disputes are to be guided by such factors as overall provincial revenues and doctors' overhead costs. Arbitration was granted as the result of a 47-hour physicians' strike on the weekend of August 25 and 26. Physicians gave up the right to strike in return.   David M. L. Farr

In *World Book,* see **Manitoba.**

Manufacturing. The eight-year-old economic expansion in the United States chugged along in 1990 but coughed and sputtered in the fourth quarter due to the effects of rising oil prices, the threat of war, and federal budget confusion. At the end of 1990, after two years of slow growth, the U.S. economy seemed to be entering a recession, the first since 1982.

But American manufacturers were in better shape in 1990 to weather a potential recession than they were in the 1981-1982 recession. After years of modernizing plants, streamlining work forces, and keeping inventories lean, manufacturers' costs were in line with lower expectations.

One indicator of a coming recession was the monthly index of the National Association of Purchasing Management (NAPM). Each month, more than 300 purchasing executives from a wide range of industries are surveyed on the state of their orders, production, and other indications of economic health. An index level of more than 50 per cent usually signifies an expanding manufacturing economy.

The level stood at 50.2 per cent in April 1990. It was 47.4 per cent in July and 44.4 per cent in September. October's 43.4 per cent marked the fourth consecutive monthly decline. Normally, a level below 44 indicates a slumping industrial sector on the way to recession. In November, the index slipped to 41.3 per cent, the lowest since November 1982, in the last recession.

Production. For the first six months of the year, the chemical, pharmaceutical, oil refining, primary metal, metal fabrication, and wood and lumber industries led the way to continued growth. Computers and communications equipment sales and production were also strong. Orders for aircraft were still robust after a strong performance in 1989.

But paper production, especially for paper used in printing, softened in 1990 because magazines and newspapers were carrying fewer advertisements and using less paper as a result. Production of linerboard and corrugated paper packaging, used in construction, was also soft. Construction supply manufacturers were hurt as fewer new homes were built.

Other manufacturers that saw production declines included defense suppliers, harmed by cuts in federal defense spending. Reduced investment by businesses in new plants and machinery began to affect makers of computers and industrial equipment. Consumers, who fueled expansion with their spending through most of the 1980's, cut back on their purchases in 1990, bringing losses to automobile, apparel, and appliance makers, among others.

Factory output. From November 1989 to November 1990, the economy grew at a rate of barely 1 per cent, the weakest nonrecession rate since World War II (1939-1945). Output rose at an annual rate of 2.5 per cent in the first half and was up 3.7 per cent in the third quarter. Most of the first-half strength came from a brief rebound in car production. But overall output began to slump in October, when the level was

Using an innovative "team" concept to build cars, General Motors workers
in Spring Hill, Tenn., assemble the new Saturn, unveiled in October.

off 0.9 per cent, and fell a precipitous 1.7 per cent in
November, the largest one-month drop since January
1982, according to the Federal Reserve System, the
agency that regulates U.S. banking.

Factory orders. Orders for *durable goods* (machinery and home appliances designed to last three or
more years) and *nondurable goods* (goods expected
to last for less than three years) were flat for most of
1990. New durable-goods orders started the year off
with a 10.5 per cent decline in January to $118.2 bil-
lion, the sharpest drop in 32 years. November saw the
same percentage decline.

In June, durable-goods orders fell 3.2 per cent to
$124.7 billion, with cutbacks in defense spending and
a decline in consumer spending the leading causes. In
the second quarter, sales of durable goods nose-dived
by 8.7 per cent. Nondurables dropped 4.4 per cent,
the third consecutive quarterly decline. Together, total new factory orders fell 1.5 per cent in June.

In August, orders for durable and nondurable goods
rose 1.8 per cent in value to $244.5 billion, mainly due
to price increases for petroleum products in the wake
of Iraq's invasion of Kuwait on August 2. Durable-
goods orders in August were down 0.8 per cent.

September saw the second monthly drop in a row
for durable-goods orders, down 1.4 per cent from August levels. Defense equipment orders were lower, but
spending on computers and office automation equipment was up 6.3 per cent.

Total September factory orders were $244.5 billion,
a 0.1 per cent gain following a 1.7 per cent rise in August. Durable-goods orders were up 3.6 per cent in
October at $129.4 billion after declines in August and
September. This was the sharpest rise in five months,
and it baffled those who said a recession was imminent. Orders for transportation equipment were up
14.8 per cent. The Boeing Company in October received a $22-billion order for 128 jets from United Air-
lines, the largest order ever placed by a single airline.

Operating rates. United States factories operated
at 82.6 per cent of capacity in February and 82.7 per
cent in March. The level rebounded to 83.5 per cent in
July but dropped to 80.9 per cent in November, the
lowest level since May 1987.

Exports. In 1990, the growth of exports was the
only real strength in the economy. Growth was led by
exports of *capital goods* (machinery, tools, and other
equipment for use in production), aircraft, computers,
scientific instruments, and chemical and paper products. According to *Business Week*, exports were expected to grow 8 per cent in 1990 to $310 billion. Ac-
cording to the NAPM, export orders increased in
October for the 34th consecutive month.

United States factories had increased sales to overseas markets and in 1990 exported 20 per cent of their
output—a record. The NAPM reported that more
than 75 per cent of the companies it surveyed shipped
goods overseas. But foreign demand slowed in 1990.

Maryland

The United States biggest trading partner, Canada, was already in its own recession, and other foreign countries were more cautious. In July, exports dropped 6.4 per cent from June to $32 billion. But exports were still growing at a 7.1 per cent annual rate.

Productivity — measured in output per worker-hour — fell at a 2.7 per cent annual rate in the first quarter but was up 1.6 per cent in the second quarter. Improved productivity is one way to keep prices down despite rising employee wages and benefits.

Factory productivity was up 2.1 per cent in 1990 because more goods were being produced by fewer workers. In the first half of 1990, factory output advanced at an annual rate of 4.9 per cent in the first quarter and 3.0 per cent in the second quarter. Total nonfarm productivity rose at an annual rate of 1.6 per cent in the third quarter, but manufacturing productivity jumped at an annual rate of 5.6 per cent.

Capital spending — that is, spending on new plants and equipment — was affected by lower plant operating rates, lower corporate profits, higher interest rates, and government defense cutbacks. All combined to blunt capital spending plans. Early in 1990, the Department of Commerce estimated capital spending would increase in 1990 to $513 billion, from 1989's $476 billion. This estimated increase of 7.6 per cent would be down slightly from 1989's 8.6 per cent gain. But as 1990 wore on, capital spending was expected to grow by only 5.4 per cent, according to a September report from the Commerce Department. With weak new orders, manufacturers were in no position to spend money on new plants and equipment.

Machine tool orders. Machine tools are power-driven tools — such as lathes, milling machines, grinders, and metal-forming presses — used to cut or shape metal parts. These metal parts, in turn, are used in the manufacture of products ranging from cars to appliances. Machine tools are complex, precision machines that are often tied into computer systems. Orders of these tools are seen as an indicator of the strength of overall industrial production and of manufacturers' capital spending plans. Aircraft, automotive, and steel producers are big buyers of machine tools.

For the first 10 months of 1990, machine tool orders were up 2.1 per cent from the same period in 1989, according to the Association for Manufacturing Technology. Orders increased nearly 1.9 per cent in October 1990 from September levels, despite the economic slowdown. New orders totaled $269.3 million in October, compared with $264.3 million in September.

Machine tool builders have done well in exporting their products abroad. In 1990, they increased their exports by 24 per cent, reaching the highest level since 1981.   Ronald Kolgraf

In *World Book,* see **Manufacturing.**

Maryland. See **State government.**

Massachusetts. See **State government.**

Mauritania. See **Africa.**

Mauritius. See **Africa.**

Medicine. A long-awaited era in medicine began in the United States on Sept. 14, 1990, when a 4-year-old girl became the first human being to undergo a federally approved attempt at *gene therapy.* Gene therapy involves inserting new genes into a patient's cells in an effort to treat or cure certain diseases.

The girl, whose name was not disclosed for reasons of privacy, was born with a rare disorder of the immune system called *adenosine deaminase* (ADA) *deficiency.* The cause of the ailment is a lack of the ADA gene, which directs the body's cells to make the enzyme ADA, critical for normal functioning of the immune system. Only about 10 children are born worldwide each year with the hereditary condition. Until recently, most died of infections in childhood.

The researchers treated the girl at the National Institutes of Health (NIH) in Bethesda, Md. A government advisory panel on July 31 granted the first federal approval for using gene therapy to treat human disease. The procedure occurred just a few hours after the United States Food and Drug Administration (FDA), whose approval was also required for the new therapy, granted permission.

A revolutionary approach? Physicians believe gene therapy can be used to replace missing or defective genes that cause many hereditary diseases. It also may be used to implant genes that direct a patient's cells to make anticancer substances or proteins useful in treating other diseases. Experts have predicted that gene therapy eventually will revolutionize medicine, permitting physicians to cure a wide range of diseases that cannot be treated effectively today.

About two weeks before the experimental procedure, physicians had removed some of the child's own white blood cells and genetically altered them so that each contained a normal copy of the ADA gene. The cells were then transfused back into the girl's body.

Doctors hoped the genetically altered cells would begin producing the needed enzyme. But they said it could take 6 to 12 months to determine whether the treatment was successful. In mid-December, the researchers reported that the early results of the therapy looked promising.

The government panel, organized by the NIH, also approved the use of gene therapy on small groups of patients with advanced *melanoma,* a skin cancer. In advanced cases of melanoma, the cancer has spread to other organs and is regarded as incurable. Physicians will attempt to treat the disease by giving patients a gene that orders blood cells to make *tumor necrosis factor* (TNF), an antitumor substance produced naturally in the body. The gene used in the tests, however, can produce up to 100 times the quantity of TNF normally found in the body.

Surgery before birth. In a major advance in fetal medicine, doctors in 1990 reported the first successful major surgical operations on unborn infants. The operations were performed, several weeks prior to birth, to correct a common and usually fatal birth defect called *hernia of the diaphragm*. This defect occurs when the stomach and other abdominal organs slip through a hole in the diaphragm, the sheet of muscle that separates the chest and abdomen. The displaced organs take up so much space that the lungs cannot develop normally. About 1 out of every 2,500 fetuses develops the defect. Most affected die in infancy because their lungs are too small to function.

A team of physicians at the University of California at San Francisco reported the first two successful surgeries for the condition in the May 31 issue of *The New England Journal of Medicine*. In both cases, the defect was diagnosed through ultrasound examination performed on the mother during pregnancy.

Working through a small incision in the mother's uterus, surgeons lifted out the fetus's left arm, cut into its chest, and pushed the stomach and other organs back into its abdomen. They closed the hole in the diaphragm with a patch of surgical fabric and used another piece of fabric to enlarge the abdomen to hold the organs. Experts predicted that the operations would lead to attempts to treat a variety of other serious congenital disorders prior to birth.

Women and heart surgery. Doctors tend to delay coronary bypass surgery on women until they are much sicker than male heart patients, a study of 2,300 bypass operations concluded in April. Researchers at Cedars-Sinai Medical Center in Los Angeles said the finding helps explain why women are twice as likely as men to die during or soon after bypass surgery.

The study revealed that about 66 per cent of women were in the advanced stages of heart disease at the time of surgery, compared with only about 45 per cent of the men. In the past, physicians blamed women's higher mortality rate on anatomical differences; women tend to have hearts and coronary arteries that are smaller than men's, making bypass surgery technically more difficult. The operation usually involves removing a blood vessel from the leg and using it to route blood around clogged portions of the coronary arteries on the surface of the heart.

Artificial heart sidelined. The FDA on January 11 withdrew its approval of the Jarvik-7 artificial heart, ending all use of the device on human beings. The FDA cited deficiencies in manufacturing the artificial heart, in servicing the equipment used to operate it, and in conducting clinical trials. Cardiac surgeon William C. DeVries of the Humana Medical Center in Louisville, Ky., pioneered use of the device as a permanent artificial heart in 1982. After disappointing results, surgeons used it only as a temporary replacement in patients awaiting a heart transplant.

Hepatitis B treatment. Scientists from 12 U.S. medical centers and two drug companies on Aug. 2, 1990, reported that a synthetic version of *interferon*, a disease-fighting protein produced naturally in the body, may be the first effective treatment for hepatitis B, a viral disease that can damage the liver. Hepatitis B is the world's ninth-leading cause of death and

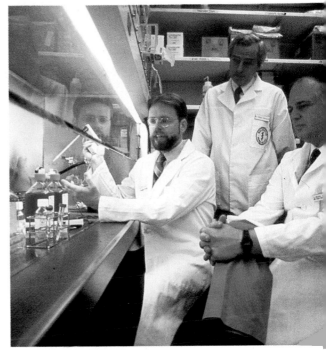

National Institutes of Health researchers in September began the first federally approved attempt at gene therapy in human beings.

the chief cause of liver cancer and cirrhosis. About 300 million people worldwide have chronic hepatitis B infections, including about 1.5 million Americans.

The researchers found that interferon caused a remission of the infection in nearly 40 per cent of patients. They also discovered that the drug actually cures about 10 per cent of infected patients, eliminating the hepatitis virus from the body. Interferon works by strengthening the human immune system and preventing the hepatitis virus from reproducing.

Human growth hormone and aging. Injections of human growth hormone (HGH) can reverse muscle wasting and certain other body changes associated with aging, scientists from the Medical College of Wisconsin in Milwaukee reported on July 5. HGH is a growth-promoting substance normally produced in small amounts by the pituitary gland.

The researchers gave growth hormone to 21 men, aged 61 to 81. After six months of treatment, the men had regained some of the physical characteristics of people 20 years younger. The men lost an average of 15 per cent of the body fat that gradually replaces muscle tissue during aging. Patients gained almost 10 per cent in muscle and other lean tissue, apparently reversing age-related shrinkage of the heart and other organs. The men also developed thicker, more youthful skin and stronger bones in the spine.

Researchers cautioned that HGH should not be widely used until more is known about possible side effects. But they said growth hormone treatment may help frail elderly people whose muscles are wasting or who need more strength to recover from surgery.

Pregnancy and weight gain. A panel of medical specialists on June 6 recommended that healthy women should gain more weight during pregnancy than previously thought advisable. The panel, organized by the Institute of Medicine, said the average pregnant woman should gain 25 to 35 pounds (11 to 16 kilograms) rather than the 20 to 25 pounds (9 to 11 kilograms) recommended previously. The institute is an agency of the Washington, D.C.-based National Academy of Sciences, which advises the federal government on scientific matters.

Gaining additional weight should have no adverse effect on the mother's health and may reduce the risk of delivering a low-birth-weight infant. The panel also said that pregnant women eating a healthy diet need not take vitamin or mineral supplements—with the possible exception of a small daily dose of iron. Most pregnant women in the United States get adequate amounts of all other nutrients in an ordinary, well-balanced diet.   Michael Woods

See also **AIDS; Biology; Health and disease; Public health.** In the World Book Supplement section, see **Blood.** In *World Book,* see **Cancer; Childbirth; Genetics; Medicine.**
Memory. In the Special Reports section, see **Why Do We Forget? What Can We Do About It?**

Mental illness. A major advance in the treatment of obsessive compulsive disorder (OCD) occurred in 1990. In January, the United States Food and Drug Administration approved the use of the drug clomipramine to treat the disorder. OCD is a mental condition that affects about 5 million Americans. It causes a person to be obsessed with the same thought or to compulsively repeat certain actions, such as hand washing. Cleanliness is the most common obsession. OCD can seriously disrupt a patient's life, making it impossible to hold a job or even leave home.

Clomipramine, marketed by Ciba-Geigy Pharmaceuticals under the brand name Anafranil, is an antidepressant. Experts said it relieves the symptoms of OCD by affecting cells in a certain part of the brain that take up a chemical messenger called *serotonin.* One theory on the cause of OCD links the disorder to deficiencies of serotonin, and clomipramine blocks the brain from dissipating serotonin.

Court ruling. The Supreme Court of the United States ruled on February 17 that prison officials can force mentally ill inmates to take antipsychotic drugs. In a 6 to 3 decision, the court found that prisoners with severe forms of mental illness who pose a danger can be medicated without a court hearing.

The ruling came on an issue that had sharply divided mental health professionals, judges, and attorneys. The case pitted two professional associations against each other, the American Psychological Associ-

ation and the American Psychiatric Association. In a friend-of-the-court brief, the American Psychological Association argued that antipsychotic medications have serious side effects and that prison officials should use alternatives such as physical restraints or seclusion. Psychologists, unlike psychiatrists, cannot prescribe drugs. The court sided with the American Psychiatric Association, whose brief argued that drugs are the most effective method for treating severe mental illness.

Phobias begin early. Phobias and certain other common mental health problems occur earlier in life than previously believed, a study conducted by the National Institute of Mental Health (NIMH) in Rockville, Md., concluded in June. NIMH researchers said that experts previously believed such disorders occurred in a fairly even distribution throughout adult life. But in the study group, which included more than 2,000 subjects, half of all the phobia cases in males occurred by age 14 and half of all the phobia cases in females developed by age 13. Half of all cases of panic disorder occurred by age 24.

Chronic fatigue syndrome. New evidence was reported on July 3 linking chronic fatigue syndrome (CFS) with clinical depression, not Epstein-Barr virus. Researchers studied a group of patients with persistent fatigue, frequent respiratory infections, and other symptoms of CFS. They found no link between viral infection and symptoms. CFS patients, however, had higher rates of previous and current depression, compared with a control group of healthy people.

In November, however, the Centers for Disease Control in Atlanta, Ga., launched a study to examine evidence that immune-system irregularities cause CFS. A growing body of research indicates that the immune systems of CFS patients are fighting intruders, perhaps long after the intruders have been destroyed.

Testing intelligence. A poor score on a mental ability test may result more from inability to focus attention than on poor mental abilities, Canadian psychologists reported in June. Students took mental ability tests in a quiet room free of distractions and again in a noisy room. Students able to focus their attention and resist distraction scored better than students easily distracted.

Schizophrenia's two forms. British psychiatrists in August reported evidence for the existence of two distinct forms of schizophrenia, a serious mental disorder characterized by delusions, hallucinations, and disorientation. One form begins in adolescence and involves severe symptoms. The other first appears in adulthood and usually is less serious. The researchers found that the form beginning in adolescence was associated with physical abnormalities in the brain that could have resulted from genetic or environmental factors. The brains of people with late-onset disease appeared normal.   Michael Woods

See also **Psychology.** In *World Book,* see **Mental illness.**

Mexico. President Carlos Salinas de Gortari continued to display exceptional skill in 1990 in managing Mexico's economic revival. Salinas also managed to maintain an approval rating of 70 per cent among the country's diverse voters.

In September, Mexico regained access to global credit markets when a state-owned enterprise—for the first time in nearly 10 years—floated a $1-billion bond issue in overseas commercial markets. That same month, the Mexican government issued new and much liberalized regulations to encourage development of the nation's vast mineral resources. The amount of bureaucratic red tape required of foreign companies seeking exploration rights was sharply reduced. Although Mexico retained absolute control over its petroleum industry, the new rules resulted in a search for a mechanism that would allow foreign companies to participate in expanding oil production.

Common market. Following an agreement in principle reached in June between Salinas and United States President George Bush, Bush in September asked the U.S. Congress for authority to negotiate a comprehensive free-trade agreement with Mexico. Soon after, Canada expressed a desire to participate in the talks, which could lead to the adoption of a North American common market by the year 2000.

Going private. Drawing on his domestic popularity, Salinas encountered little opposition from organized labor in moving ahead with plans to privatize money-losing, government-run enterprises. In May 1990, Mexico's Chamber of Deputies approved a constitutional amendment that returned Mexico's banks—nationalized in 1982—to private hands. In December, Mexico sold a 20.4 per cent stake in Teléfonos de México, the government telephone company, to three foreign companies, including the Southwestern Bell Corporation of the United States, for $1.76 billion.

Stock market. Mexico's stock market chalked up one of the best performances of any in the world, increasing in value by more than 50 per cent by mid-1990, according to the *Financial Times* of London. On Wall Street in New York City, a mutual fund was created that traded shares on the Mexican exchange exclusively. The fund sought to reward investors by buying up shares of state-run Mexican companies before they were privatized.

On the negative side of the ledger, Petróleos Mexicanos, Mexico's oil monopoly, proved unready to increase production and thereby profit from the higher oil prices brought on by the Persian Gulf crisis. Mexican oil officials adopted measures intended to counter declining production, which was down from a high of 3 million barrels a day in 1982 to 2½ million in 1990.

Foreign investment. Liberalized rules led to huge new foreign investments in Mexico in 1990. PepsiCo, the U.S. soft drink giant, announced plans to buy a controlling interest in Mexico's largest cookie maker for $300 million on October 2. Also, previous foreign

Asking compassion for the poor, Pope John Paul II offers a Mass at a vast, sprawling slum outside Mexico City during an eight-day visit to Mexico in May.

investments in Mexico began to pay big dividends. The Ford Motor Company, which had started building a plant in Chihuahua in 1983, reported that it was turning out 1,000 new car engines a day in 1990—produced by a highly skilled Mexican work force.

A high-technology industrial zone has materialized within a California-sized area of northern Mexico. Among the goods manufactured there are automobiles by Volkswagen and Nissan, cameras by Eastman Kodak Company, computers by International Business Machines Corporation, appliances by Whirlpool Corporation, and forklift trucks by Caterpillar Incorporated—all sold widely in the U.S. market.

Papal visit. Pope John Paul II arrived in Mexico on May 6 for an eight-day visit and was greeted at the airport by President Salinas despite the long-standing absence of official relations between Mexico and the Vatican. The pope preached against the use of birth control devices. Mexico's population growth rate has shrunk from 3.5 per cent in the mid-1970's to slightly less than 2 per cent in 1990. Although Mexico is a predominantly Roman Catholic country, more than half of its married women reportedly use some form of contraception. And the government has adopted the goal of reducing the birth rate to 1 per cent by the end of the century.   Nathan A. Haverstock

See also **Latin America** (Facts in brief table). In *World Book,* see **Mexico.**

Michigan. See **Detroit; State government.**

Middle East

The Middle East once again became the focus of an international crisis when Iraqi forces invaded Kuwait on Aug. 2, 1990. Iraq's President Saddam Hussein ordered the attack on Kuwait after negotiations between the two countries over oil production quotas and other issues broke down (see **Iraq**). United States President George Bush quickly forged an American-led international coalition that condemned Iraq and sent a military force to Saudi Arabia to deter an Iraqi attack on that country. On Jan. 17, 1991, the multinational force launched an air strike against military targets in Iraq and Kuwait.

The United Nations (UN) Security Council had passed 12 resolutions, each intended to increase pressure on Iraq to withdraw from Kuwait. The second resolution, passed on Aug. 6, 1990, imposed an economic blockade on Iraq that effectively halted oil shipments from that country and Kuwait (see **United Nations**).

By November, Bush had sent some 230,000 U.S. troops to Saudi Arabia. European countries contributed from 20,000 to 30,000 ground troops, as well as air and naval forces. A similar number of troops was sent by Arab states, chiefly Egypt and Syria.

Hussein responded to the blockade and threat of force by increasing his forces in Kuwait and making hostages of the estimated 9,000 North Americans, Europeans, and Australians in Iraq and Kuwait. Many were moved to strategic military or industrial sites to serve as "human shields" to discourage U.S. attacks.

The crisis escalated in early November when Bush announced that the United States would significantly boost its troop strength in Saudi Arabia. By January 1991, U.S. forces numbered about 430,000. The build-up changed the multinational military coalition from a defensive force to a force capable of offensive action. On Nov. 29, 1990, the Security Council passed a resolution authorizing the use of military force to eject Iraqi troops from Kuwait if they failed to withdraw by Jan. 15, 1991.

On Nov. 30, 1990, Bush acknowledged domestic and foreign anxieties about the possibility of war in the Persian Gulf by unexpectedly offering to send Secretary of State James A. Baker III to Iraq and to receive Iraq's Foreign Minister Tariq Aziz. Bush said he wanted to make sure Hussein understood that the U.S.-led coalition would resort to military force, if necessary, to eject Iraqi troops from Kuwait. Although Hussein accepted Bush's offer, the diplomatic exchange did not take place because of a dispute over dates. A meeting between Baker and Aziz on Jan. 9, 1991, in Geneva, Switzerland, failed to produce a peaceful solution to the crisis.

By December 1990, nearly all Arab countries favored an Arab solution to the crisis. Only Saudi Arabia rejected a peace initiative proposed by Algeria's Presi-

Iraqi tanks roll through the city of Kuwait on August 2 in an invasion that triggered an international military response against Iraq.

dent Chadli Bendjedid. Syria and Egypt further stated that they would not participate in any offensive actions against Iraq.

Hostages freed. On December 6, Hussein announced that all hostages in Iraq and Kuwait were free to leave. Some analysts speculated that Hussein may have hoped this gesture would weaken the coalition's resolve to use force and deepen the American public's concern that the United States would be drawn into a lengthy war. The last of the foreigners wishing to leave Iraq departed on December 11.

Economic effects. The Persian Gulf crisis widened the gap between rich and poor states in the Middle East. The economic blockade against Iraq, a major energy exporter, dealt a severe blow to a number of countries in the region already reeling from rising foreign debt, inflation, and unemployment. Jordan, for example, had derived more than 50 per cent of its *gross national product* (the value of all goods and services produced) from trade with Iraq, which had supplied 80 per cent of Jordan's energy needs. Turkey lost 60 per cent of its energy supplies and the $5 million per day it had earned transshipping Iraqi crude oil across its territory.

Countries that had depended heavily on Iraqi oil were forced to buy oil on the world market at higher prices. Some countries, such as the Philippines, India, and Pakistan, also lost an important source of income—money sent home by citizens working in Iraq and Kuwait, who fled after the invasion. Before Iraq invaded Kuwait, about 1½ million foreign citizens had been working in those two countries.

Oil-rich Arab countries, meanwhile, reaped a bonanza from increased petroleum production to help meet world energy demands and soaring energy prices. Saudi Arabia, for example, was expected to earn from $80 billion to $100 billion in oil revenues in 1990, nearly double its oil income in 1989.

Political effects. The Persian Gulf crisis exposed growing political tensions within the Arab world that Arab leaders had downplayed publicly. Before the in-

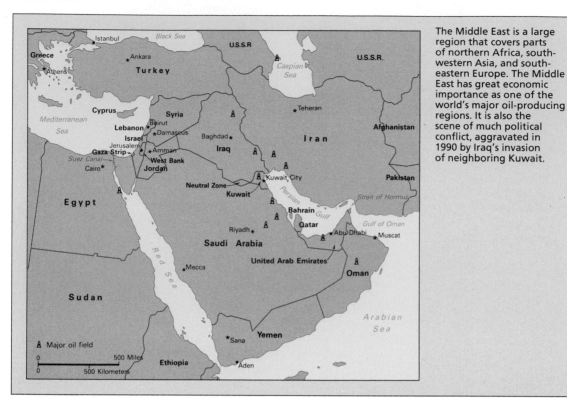

The Middle East is a large region that covers parts of northern Africa, south-western Asia, and south-eastern Europe. The Middle East has great economic importance as one of the world's major oil-producing regions. It is also the scene of much political conflict, aggravated in 1990 by Iraq's invasion of neighboring Kuwait.

vasion, Arab leaders had privately expressed concerns that differences in political systems, population, wealth, and resources were threatening Arab unity. Arab leaders feared that these differences could hinder regional economic development, reduce the diplomatic effectiveness of the Arab bloc, and even lead to increased conflict among Arab countries.

Although a majority of states in the Arab League backed a resolution condemning Iraq for the invasion, the voting pattern highlighted the members' differences. Libya and the Palestine Liberation Organization (PLO) voted against the resolution. Jordan, Sudan, and Mauritania voted against Iraq, but with reservations. Algeria and Yemen abstained. Tunisia refused to even attend the meeting at which the vote was held.

Although most Arabs initially disapproved of the invasion, many became increasingly resentful of the presence of the American-led military forces in the Middle East. The deployment of foreign troops in Saudi Arabia—which controls Mecca and Medina, Islam's most sacred sites—offended many Muslims. The presence of the multinational force was also an unpleasant reminder of the period in the early 1900's when Great Britain and France had controlled much of the Middle East.

In addition, Saddam Hussein won popular Arab support by demanding that any sanctions imposed on him because of his move into Kuwait also be applied to Israel for having occupied the West Bank and Gaza Strip after the 1967 Six-Day War. He also insisted on a link between any solution to the Persian Gulf crisis and the Palestinian problem.

Israeli dilemmas. Israel faced serious challenges in 1990 in both domestic and foreign relations. Government policies encouraging large-scale Jewish immigration to Israel and the growth of Jewish settlements in the Israeli-occupied West Bank and Gaza Strip led to a heated debate within Israel, to strained relations with the U.S. government, and to increasing Arab violence. After Israeli police killed at least 17 Palestinians on October 8 in a confrontation in Jerusalem on what is known to Jews as the Temple Mount, Israel found itself in the middle of a UN debate over its treatment of the Palestinians.

The rift between Israel and the United States widened when the United States backed three UN resolutions critical of Israel. The United States voted on October 12 to censure Israel for using excessive force against the Palestinians on the Temple Mount. On October 24, the United States supported a resolution that deplored Israel's refusal to cooperate with a UN commission assigned to investigate the incident. On December 20, the United States voted for a resolution that called the West Bank and the Gaza Strip "Palestinian territories" and criticized Israel for planning to deport four Palestinians.

The United States also declined Israel's offer of military support for the multinational force in Saudi Arabia. Israeli officials complained bitterly that although Israel was the most reliable U.S. ally in the Middle East, the United States was ignoring its concerns in an attempt to maintain Arab support for the action against Iraq.

Violence of the intifada. The Palestinian *intifada* (uprising) in the occupied territories marked its third anniversary on December 9. In early 1990, the conflict continued at a simmer, chiefly because of hopes that ongoing talks between the United States and the PLO would produce a plan for Israeli-Palestinian negotiations. The violence escalated significantly after the United States broke off the talks on June 20 because the PLO had failed to condemn a foiled speedboat attack on Israel in May by a radical faction of the PLO.

The upsurge in violence was also fueled by Palestinian opposition to Jewish immigration and by increasing acts of violence against Palestinians by Jewish extremists. In addition, the uprising gained increased momentum from Saddam Hussein's demand that the Palestinian problem be addressed in any diplomatic negotiations on the Persian Gulf crisis.

By year-end, at least 777 Palestinians and 54 Israelis had been killed in the intifada. At least 155 Palestinians were killed by other Palestinians for allegedly collaborating with the Israelis.

After the Temple Mount killings, intifada leaders called on Palestinians to "escalate the struggle by any means possible." In response, Palestinians acting alone or in twos began attacking civilians in Israel and the occupied territories. By year-end, at least 8 Israelis had been stabbed to death and about 12 more wounded in knife attacks.

In an attempt to control the violence, Israeli authorities sealed off the West Bank and Gaza Strip for several days in late October, preventing many Palestinians from traveling to their jobs in Israel. Thousands of Palestinians lost their jobs because of new government restrictions on Arab workers and a campaign by some Jewish groups to pressure Israeli employers to replace Palestinian workers with Soviet immigrants.

Human rights. The human-rights record in the Middle East in 1990 remained bad. Many abuses resulted from strife between ethnic or religious groups and from government repression of groups demanding either more rights or independence.

The government of Sudan, which is dominated by Muslims from the northern part of the country, continued to wage a costly war against southern Sudanese, mainly blacks who practice Christianity or local religions. In Egypt, Muslim fundamentalists launched increasingly violent attacks on members of the Coptic Orthodox Church. In addition, the governments of Iraq and Turkey instituted harsh measures against their Kurdish minorities in response to stepped-up activity by Kurdish guerrilla groups. Human-rights advocates also condemned beheadings in Saudi Arabia and public hangings in Iran.

In several notable incidents in 1990, women in the

Foreign workers who fled from Kuwait and Iraq after Iraq invaded Kuwait in August crowd a makeshift refugee camp in Jordan.

Middle East demanded more rights and greater legal protection. In November, about 50 Saudi women drove automobiles through Riyadh, Saudi Arabia's capital, to protest a traditional ban on driving by women. In Iran, amid growing dissatisfaction with Islamic restrictions, there were increased reports of women being publicly beaten for failing to wear a veil that covered all but the face.

Israel was cited by numerous human-rights groups in 1990 for abuses against Palestinian detainees, the harassment of political activists, and the use of excessive force against demonstrators. The Swedish branch of the Save the Children organization reported in May that many Palestinian children had been killed or injured by Israeli forces.

Calls for democracy. During 1990, there were growing demands for democracy in Arab countries. Some of the loudest demands came from Kuwaitis, who criticized the government's censorship of the press and demanded the reestablishment of parliament, which had been dissolved in 1986. Kuwait's prodemocracy movement was dealt a serious blow in mid-May when 12 leaders of the movement were arrested.

Most Arab leaders ignored demands for more representative government. Some leaders argued that liberalization would not result in multiparty systems but in a victory for Islamic conservatives, who have become increasingly powerful since the 1970's. Indeed, in elections held in Jordan in 1989 and in Algeria in 1990,

Facts in brief on Middle Eastern countries

Country	Population	Government	Monetary unit*	Foreign trade (million U.S.$) Exports†	Imports†
Bahrain	531,000	Amir Isa bin Salman Al-Khalifa; Prime Minister Khalifa bin Salman Al-Khalifa	dinar (0.38 = $1)	2,400	2,500
Cyprus	708,000	President George Vassiliou (Turkish Republic of Northern Cyprus: Acting President Rauf R. Denktaş)	pound (0.43 = $1)	767	1,900
Egypt	54,673,000	President Hosni Mubarak; Prime Minister Atef Sedky	pound (2 = $1)	2,550	10,100
Iran	58,073,000	Leader of the Islamic Revolution Ali Hoseini Khamenei; President Ali Akbar Hashemi Rafsanjani	rial (64.21 = $1)	12,300	12,000
Iraq	18,600,000	President Saddam Hussein	dinar (0.32 = $1)	12,500	10,200
Israel	4,647,000	President Chaim Herzog; Prime Minister Yitzhak Shamir	shekel (2.03 = $1)	10,400	12,400
Jordan	3,172,000	King Hussein I; Prime Minister Mudar Badran	dinar (0.66 = $1)	910	1,700
Kuwait	2,154,000	Amir Jabir al-Ahmad al-Jabir al-Sabah; Prime Minister & Crown Prince Sad al-Abdallah al-Salim al-Sabah‡	dinar (N/A)	7,100	5,200
Lebanon	3,026,000	Prime Minister Omar Karami; President Ilyas Harawi	pound (705 = $1)	1,000	1,500
Oman	1,517,000	Sultan Qaboos bin Said Al-Said	rial (0.39 = $1)	3,600	1,900
Qatar	380,000	Amir and Prime Minister Khalifa bin Hamad Al-Thani	riyal (3.64 = $1)	2,200	1,000
Saudi Arabia	13,366,000	King & Prime Minister Fahd bin Abd al-Aziz Al-Saud	riyal (3.75 = $1)	24,500	21,800
Sudan	25,923,000	Prime Minister Umar Hasan Ahmad al-Bashir	pound (4.5 = $1)	550	1,200
Syria	12,941,000	President Hafez al-Assad; Prime Minister Mahmud Zubi	pound (21 = $1)	1,300	1,900
Turkey	57,301,000	President Turgut Özal; Prime Minister Yildirim Akbulut	lira (2,867.39 = $1)	11,700	14,300
United Arab Emirates	1,624,000	President Zayid bin Sultan Al-Nuhayyan; Prime Minister Rashid bin Said Al-Maktum	dirham (3.67 = $1)	10,600	8,500
Yemen	10,848,000	President Ali Abdallah Salih; Prime Minister Haydar Abu Bakr al-Attas	rial (12.05 = $1)	935	1,898

*Exchange rates as of Dec. 7, 1990, or latest available data. †Latest available data.

‡Iraq invaded Kuwait on Aug. 2, 1990, deposed its government, and on August 8 declared Kuwait part of Iraq.

Islamic fundamentalist candidates won a large number of parliamentary seats.

The Persian Gulf crisis, however, spurred democratic trends in some countries. In early November, King Fahd bin Abd al-Aziz Al-Saud of Saudi Arabia announced his intention to establish a consultative assembly. Sultan Qaboos bin Said of Oman also announced in November his aim of widening representation in that country's Consultative Assembly, whose appointed members act in an advisory role.

Population bomb. Explosive birth rates outstripped economic gains in many Middle Eastern countries in 1990. This increase, with the growing influx of people to urban areas, intensified the already serious problems plaguing the region's large cities.

Hard-pressed Middle Eastern governments were increasingly unable to supply their people with such basic services as housing, education, and medical care. Many governments were also forced to increase spending on food imports.

Water problems. The Middle East possesses two-thirds of the world's proven oil reserves, but water is scarce. In many countries, chronic water shortages became increasingly severe in 1990. Negotiations to resolve disputes over water resources—such as the Euphrates River, on which Turkey, Syria, and Iraq depend—made little progress.   Christine Helms

See also articles on the various Middle Eastern countries. In *World Book,* see **Middle East** and individual Middle Eastern country articles.

Mining. The Aluminum Company of America (Alcoa) on June 1, 1990, closed the last bauxite mine in the United States. Near Little Rock, Ark., the mine and an associated refinery had been in operation for more than 90 years. Bauxite is a claylike ore that is refined into alumina, the raw material used to make aluminum. Alcoa said the bauxite deposits were so depleted that it was no longer economical to mine them.

Strip-mining rules. Coal-mining companies will find it harder to evade a U.S. law requiring them to restore strip-mined land under a new law enforcement plan announced by the Department of the Interior in January. The department said it planned to set up a computer system holding the names of all coal companies and their owners as well as past violators of the Surface Mining Control and Reclamation Act of 1977. Companies or owners found to have past violations may have their mining permits revoked or may be refused new permits.

Amazon mining. Brazil on Jan. 9, 1990, reversed a 1989 decision, hailed by environmentalists around the world, to eject thousands of gold miners from land belonging to the Yanomami Indians in Roraima territory in the northern Amazon region. Critics had charged that mining operations threatened the survival of the Yanomami, a local Indian group. They said the miners killed too much game and polluted local rivers that once were an important source of fish for the tribe. Miners and prospectors also were blamed for outbreaks of influenza, measles, and other infectious diseases among the Indians.

But the miners and non-Indian people in the area urged that the miners, who had discovered $1 billion worth of gold in recent years, be allowed to stay. The miners also threatened to wage a guerrilla war to protect their operations.

In January 1990, the government announced a plan to allow the miners to continue working in about 5 per cent of the Yanomami's 35,000-square-mile (91,000-square-kilometer) territory. In May, the government bombed 110 illegal airfields in Yanomami territory used by the miners. But miners continued to reenter the restricted area. More airfields were bombed in November.

Mexican mining boost. In an effort to revitalize its mining industry, Mexico on September 27 announced new regulations to encourage foreign investment in the exploration and mining of new mineral deposits. The regulations make it easier for foreign investors to obtain government permits to explore for new mineral deposits. They also ease limitations on foreign financial control of mining firms. Mexican officials said that due to restrictive laws, mining firms had explored only about 20 per cent of the land believed to hold rich mineral deposits.   Michael Woods

In *World Book,* see **Mining.**

Minnesota. See **State government.**
Mississippi. See **State government.**
Missouri. See **State government.**

Mitsotakis, Constantine (1918-   ), was sworn in as prime minister of Greece on April 11, 1990, and became the leader of the nation's first conservative government in nine years. Mitsotakis' party, New Democracy, won 150 of the 300 seats of Parliament in the April 8, 1990, elections. To obtain the necessary majority of 151 seats to form a government, he gained the support of the sole independent deputy. See **Greece.**

Mitsotakis defeated his principal rival, former Prime Minister Andreas Papandreou of the Panhellenic Socialist Movement, who had held office from 1981 until 1989, when his scandal-ridden government fell. Mitsotakis has been a member of the New Democracy party since 1978 and its leader since September 1984.

Mitsotakis was born on Oct. 18, 1918, in Khania on the island of Crete. In 1940 and 1941, during World War II, he fought against the Nazi forces on the Greek-Bulgarian border and escaped Nazi death sentences twice.

Mitsotakis is a graduate of the University of Athens, where he studied law and economics. He began his long political career with his election to the Greek Parliament in 1946 at age 28. After a military junta took over in Greece, in 1967, Mitsotakis fled abroad, living in exile for 5½ years and returning after the junta fell in 1974.

Mitsotakis and his wife, Marika, have three daughters and one son.   Carol L. Hanson

Mongolia. In 1990, Mongolia moved from a Communist dictatorship that followed the Soviet Union's orders toward a multiparty democracy with an independent position in the world. Mongolia had been under Soviet control since the early 1920's, when Russian Communists installed a government headed by the Mongol People's Revolutionary Party (MPRP). By 1990, as the Soviet Union grappled with internal reform and became less willing to subsidize its client states, non-Communists were speaking out in Ulan Bator, Mongolia's capital.

Defying official bans, the opposition Mongolian Democratic Union began holding outdoor rallies in January 1990. In subzero temperatures, protesters blamed the MPRP for shortages of food and consumer goods and demanded an end to the party's privileges. In an effort to control reform pressures, the MPRP replaced General Secretary Jambyn Batmonh with Gombojavyn Ochirbat on March 14.

The parliament, the Great People's Hural (also spelled Khural), on March 21 relieved Batmonh of his other job as its powerful chairman. They named Punsalmaagiyn Ochirbat (no relation to MPRP leader Ochirbat) to the post. The Great Hural replaced Dumaagiyn Sodnom with Sharabyn Gungaadorj as prime minister and on March 23 amended the Constitution to end the MPRP's position as the only legal party.

The Democratic Union and other groups renewed their demonstrations in April and May, seeking fur-

A Mongolian on horseback collects a voter's ballot in Mongolia's first-ever multiparty local and parliamentary elections in July.

ther reform and a completely new political structure. The government agreed in early May to begin consulting the opposition and to hold local and parliamentary elections in July.

The MPRP —running against poorly organized opposition groups—won 357 of the 430 seats in the Great Hural. Four opposition parties won 39 seats, and nonparty candidates won the rest. Perhaps more significantly, on a ballot question asking voters' party preference, the MPRP won only 61.7 per cent. As a result, it got 31 of 53 seats in the Little Hural, a legislative body created to handle daily business.

When the new Great Hural met on September 3, it elected Punsalmaagiyn Ochirbat to the new post of national president. After a three-day debate, a non-Communist, Radnaasurengiyn Gonchigdorj, was elected vice president. Gungaadorj was replaced as prime minister by Dashiyn Byambasuren, who was expected to introduce and extend free-market reforms.

Foreign relations. On May 4, Punsalmaagiyn Ochirbat became the first Mongolian head of state to visit China in 28 years. China agreed to help Mongolia "find a sea outlet" and develop its industries. Ochirbat and MPRP leader Gombojavyn Ochirbat visited Moscow in mid-May, seeking economic aid. The United States promised trade assistance.   Henry S. Bradsher

See also **Asia** (Facts in brief table). In *World Book,* see **Mongolia.**

Montana. See **State government.**

Montreal. Indian unrest, a mayoral election, and economic problems dominated the news in Montreal in 1990.

An armed stand-off between Mohawk Indians and the Canadian Armed Forces cut off access to much of the city for most of the summer. The confrontation began on July 11, when police from the province of Quebec stormed a barricade set up on a country road in the resort town of Oka. The Indians put up the barricade to protest the proposed expansion of a municipal golf course onto ancestral burial grounds. By the time the struggle ended later that day, the police had retreated in confusion, leaving behind cars and bulldozers and taking with them one dead officer.

Almost immediately, the Mohawk Warriors Society blocked one of the major bridges over the St. Lawrence River into Montreal. The Quebec government asked the federal Armed Forces to intervene. The resulting stalemate lasted 78 days, cost taxpayers $22 million Canadian ($19 million U.S.) in military expenditures, and caused concern that law and order might break down completely in the city. In one particularly ugly incident, white residents stoned a convoy of cars attempting to take women and children away from the barricades to safety. Bystanders accused police of doing little to intervene.

The crisis gradually wound down as the Armed Forces took control from the police. The warriors surrendered from their last outpost, in a medical treatment center, on September 26. At least 21 Mohawks were charged with criminal acts. Later, authorities found that many of them were not Canadian but U.S. citizens and had arrest warrants outstanding.

An armed robbery —one of Canada's largest ever—meant the loss of nearly $15.6 million Canadian ($13 million U.S.) in December. A predawn ambush took place at Montreal International Airport (Dorval), where a private airplane chartered by Brink's Canada taxied down a runway shortly after landing. Armed with Soviet-made AK-47 assault rifles, thieves stopped the plane and drove off with the loot in stolen vans.

Mayoral election. A municipal election swept the ruling Montreal Citizens' Movement (MCM) and Mayor Jean Doré back into power on November 4. It was a contest in which only 30 per cent of the electorate voted, the lowest turnout in 20 years. Doré garnered 67.7 per cent of the vote, and his party obtained 41 of the 50 seats in the City Council.

Economy. A combination of economic recession and constitutional uncertainty about the future status of Quebec in Canada caused businesses to cut back and cost thousands of Montrealers their jobs in 1990. At year's end, unemployment in Montreal soared well past the 10 per cent mark to its highest level since the recession of the early 1980's. Unlike during the 1980 recession, many of the thousands who lost their jobs in 1990 came from executive, professional, or white-collar backgrounds.

Scarcely an industry was left untouched by the recession. Air Canada laid off 3,000 employees, as did aerospace manufacturer Pratt & Whitney. The state-owned railway, Canadian National, cut 1,500 white-collar jobs and warned of more cuts to come.

A decline in housing prices and increased vacancy rates in the apartment sector drove down condominium prices. Housing experts reported declines of more than 25 per cent in the prices of luxury condominiums.

The general economic downturn and political turmoil over the Meech Lake constitutional accord, which would have clarified Quebec's status within Canada, led to the indefinite postponement of a high-speed railroad link. The high-speed system, capable of carrying passengers at speeds up to 300 kilometers (190 miles) per hour, would have served Montreal, Toronto, and several other major Canadian metropolitan areas. At year-end, the system was still being studied by officials at various levels of government.

In November, local investors succeeded in keeping the city's baseball team, the Montreal Expos, from moving. Owner Charles M. Bronfman had threatened to sell the team for $100 million Canadian ($86 million U.S.). Local investors, led by Claude Brochu, met the asking price after the provincial government lent them $17 million Canadian ($15 million U.S.), and the city agreed to invest $15 million Canadian ($13 million U.S.) as part owner.   Kendal Windeyer

See also **Canada; Quebec.** In *World Book,* see **Montreal.**

A Mohawk stands on a police car near the Montreal suburb of Oka in protest against a proposed golf course expansion on what the Indians regard as ancestral land.

Morocco. Morocco's economy continued its downturn in 1990, threatening to destroy the political consensus that had muted opposition to the government since the mid-1980's. By late 1989, economic growth had fallen to only 20 per cent of its 1988 level, and the trade deficit had doubled. The economic picture worsened in 1990, as tourism, a primary source of revenue, fell. Morocco's foreign debt reached $22 billion.

Under pressure from international lending agencies, King Hassan II announced austerity measures. Government agencies were ordered to cut spending, and many projects were postponed or canceled. The government also officially devalued Morocco's currency for the first time, hoping to make the country's trade goods more competitive on world markets.

Political consequences. The austerity program aroused heated debate, both in and out of government. Many officials opposed the wide-ranging measures, arguing that Moroccans were already under considerable economic pressure. Unemployment, for example, averaged 35 per cent in 1990. Officials feared that further hardship might lead to an increase in political activity by Islamic fundamentalists, who have been strongly critical of the government.

Hassan also appeared to be worried about the effects of his program. To ease pressures on ordinary citizens, the government announced that taxes on trade goods would be levied on importers, rather than exporters. Officials also promised that food prices

Morocco

would remain stable and that no new taxes would be imposed. In addition, Hassan announced a literacy campaign to train 200,000 people yearly. At least 40 per cent of Moroccans are illiterate.

Political unrest. Morocco's economic problems led to increasing criticism of the government by young politicians. Many of these politicians were already disappointed by Hassan's decision, approved by a *referendum* (popular vote) in December 1989, to postpone elections for Morocco's parliament for two years. Hassan said the delay was needed to give the United Nations (UN) more time to organize a referendum in Western Sahara, over which Morocco has sought control. Since 1976, Polisario Front guerrillas have been fighting for independence for Western Sahara. The referendum will determine whether the region will become independent or a part of Morocco. Many politicians, however, argued that Hassan was using the referendum as an excuse not to hold elections.

In March 1990, Morocco and the Polisario Front agreed to a cease-fire. In June, the UN approved a peace plan, proposed in 1988, for Western Sahara.

Embargo support. Morocco supported an embargo imposed on Iraq for invading Kuwait in August 1990. Hassan contributed several thousand troops to an international force to deter an Iraqi invasion of Saudi Arabia.   Christine Helms

See also **Africa** (Facts in brief table). In *World Book,* see **Morocco.**

Motion pictures. The two most popular films in the United States in 1990, *Ghost* and *Pretty Woman,* were surprise hits. Both were romantic motion pictures with wide appeal to female audiences. Both unexpectedly outgrossed such male-oriented action movies as *Die Hard 2, Total Recall, Dick Tracy, The Hunt for Red October, Another 48 HRS.,* and *Days of Thunder.*

Ghost, which grossed in excess of $206 million in the United States, told of a love interrupted by the murder of the hero, who returns in ghostly form to protect his lover and solve his murder. The hit restored Patrick Swayze, Demi Moore, and Whoopi Goldberg (playing a phony medium) to prominence. *Pretty Woman,* with a $178-million gross in the United States, related a Cinderella-style romance between a corporate raider and a prostitute. It made a star of Julia Roberts and revived the career of Richard Gere.

Ghost and *Pretty Woman* were two of the few films in 1990 that featured substantial roles for women. A study released by the Screen Actors Guild on August 1 showed that employment and earnings for actresses in motion pictures had reached a new low. Parts for women had shrunk to 29 per cent of screen roles in 1989, while actresses' earnings totaled $296 million, compared with $644 million for male actors.

Movies from best sellers. A number of 1990 motion pictures were based on best-selling novels. Alan Pakula's *Presumed Innocent,* from Scott Turow's 1987 novel about an attorney accused of murdering a col-

Ghost—1990's biggest hit—stars Patrick Swayze, left, as a dead man who returns to watch over his lover, played by Demi Moore, center.

league, drew critical and public endorsement. Brian De Palma's screen version of Tom Wolfe's best seller from that same year, *The Bonfire of the Vanities*, was riskier. The casting of Tom Hanks, Bruce Willis, and Melanie Griffith proved controversial to fans of the book, which traces the downfall of a Wall Street high roller. Director Fred Schepisi's film version of John le Carré's *The Russia House* (1989), starring Sean Connery and Michelle Pfeiffer, opened in mid-December.

Other hits. Warren Beatty's highly touted *Dick Tracy* earned generally favorable reviews and qualified as a blockbuster with a box-office gross of $103-million. Yet that amount was disappointing compared with the $235-million take of *Batman* in 1989. Critics praised *Dick Tracy* for its mellow wit and vivid color.

The well-received *Dances with Wolves* won praise for its sympathetic and respectful attitude toward Native Americans. Kevin Costner directed and co-produced the film and also starred in it, playing a disillusioned Union Army lieutenant who becomes involved with a harmonious Sioux tribe just after the Civil War (1861-1865).

The year's most completely unexpected smash was *Teenage Mutant Ninja Turtles*, a children's film based on a popular television cartoon series. It grossed $133-million, doubling the box-office record of 1987's *Dirty Dancing* to become the most financially successful film released by a nonmajor Hollywood studio.

Home Alone, starring 9-year-old Macaulay Culkin, was the breakaway hit of the holiday season. Released on November 16, it grossed more than $152 million by year-end. Its slapstick story of an 8-year-old who must defend his home against robbers had strong appeal for both children and parents.

Whit Stillman made an auspicious directing debut with the low-budget *Metropolitan*, a study of wealthy young New Yorkers. Critics found the film's mixture of satire and compassion to be impressive.

Cops and robbers. Ironically, films depicting both police bravery and organized crime were common on motion-picture screens in 1990. Such films as *Dick Tracy*, *Robocop 2*, *Another 48 HRS.*, *Kindergarten Cop*, *Internal Affairs*, *Blue Steel*, *The Rookie*, *Die Hard 2*, *Miami Blues*, *Hard to Kill*, and *The First Power* featured police heroics. And such movies as *The Godfather Part III*, *State of Grace*, *Miller's Crossing*, *King of New York*, and *The Krays* fed the public's continued fascination with the mob underworld. Martin Scorsese's *GoodFellas*, about Mafia life as seen through the eyes of a young recruit into organized crime, was a particular hit with both critics and moviegoers.

Animation continued its resurgence during 1990. *The Little Mermaid*, released in December of 1989, played to large audiences throughout the first half of 1990, and *The Rescuers Down Under*, released in November 1990, won critical praise. In the Special Reports section, see **Once Again, "Toons" Are Tops.**

Year-end films. One of the most eagerly awaited films of 1990 was Francis Ford Coppola's *The Godfa-*

Warren Beatty plays the title role in *Dick Tracy*, a film version of the comic-strip cop's exploits, which Beatty also directed and produced.

ther Part III, the continuation of 1972's *The Godfather* and 1974's *The Godfather Part II*. The 1990 film reunited Al Pacino, Diane Keaton, and Talia Shire as members of the Corleone family, with the addition of Andy Garcia and Bridget Fonda.

Several other films from top directors were released late in 1990. Franco Zeffirelli's version of *Hamlet* had a strong cast, including action star Mel Gibson in the title role, Glenn Close as Gertrude, and Alan Bates as Claudius. Bernardo Bertolucci's first film since 1987's Oscar winner *The Last Emperor* was *The Sheltering Sky*, from Paul Bowles's acclaimed 1949 novel. *The Sheltering Sky* starred Debra Winger and John Malkovich as a troubled couple finding despair rather than redemption in North Africa. Joanne Woodward gave one of the finest performances of her career as a repressed Midwestern housewife in James Ivory's *Mr. & Mrs. Bridge*, which also featured her husband and frequent co-star Paul Newman. The film was based on two novels, *Mrs. Bridge* (1959) and *Mr. Bridge* (1969), by Evan S. Connell, Jr. Woody Allen's *Alice* starred Mia Farrow in the role of another repressed housewife.

Robert De Niro and Robin Williams co-starred in *Awakenings*. The movie was based on a true story about patients recovering from a brain disorder.

Films from other countries. The most successful import of 1990 was director Jean-Paul Rappeneau's adaptation of French dramatist Edmond Rostand's 1897 play *Cyrano de Bergerac*. Gérard Depardieu tri-

Kevin Costner stars as an Army officer in the 1860's who befriends the Sioux Indians in *Dances with Wolves,* which he also directed and co-produced.

umphed as the gallant long-nosed guardsman who helps an inarticulate friend court the woman he himself loves. At a cost of $20 million, the film was the most expensive French-language movie ever.

Among other imports that gained large audiences was Peter Greenaway's controversial *The Cook, the Thief, His Wife & Her Lover*, a literate film with a mixture of sadism and bathroom humor that some viewers found tasteless. Giuseppe Tornatore's *Cinema Paradiso*, which won the 1989 Academy Award for best foreign film, was more universally liked. It told the touching story of the friendship between a movie-mad youngster and an aging projectionist. *Cinema Paradiso* became the highest-grossing Italian film in American theaters since Federico Fellini's *La Dolce Vita*, released in the United States in 1961.

New rating. The Motion Picture Association of America (MPAA) in September 1990 inaugurated a new rating of NC-17, intended to deny admission to viewers under 17 years of age. It replaced the controversial X rating, which had come to be synonymous with pornographic films lacking any artistic merit.

During 1990, the MPAA gave X ratings to a number of films, released by independent distributors, that featured explicit sex or violence but that were, in the opinion of many critics, serious artistic efforts. Among them were *The Cook, the Thief, His Wife & Her Lover; Tie Me Up! Tie Me Down!; Henry: Portrait of a Serial Killer;* and *Life Is Cheap . . .But Toilet Paper Is Expen-*

sive. Many independent distributors felt that the MPAA's X rating would change when challenged by a major studio, and such proved to be the case.

Universal Pictures bemoaned the X rating given to its film *Henry & June*, the story of a bisexual triangle between author Henry Miller, his wife, June, and writer Anaïs Nin. *Henry & June* was directed by Philip Kaufman, who made such acclaimed films as *The Right Stuff* (1983) and *The Unbearable Lightness of Being* (1988). Universal would not release a film with an X rating, and the MPAA introduced the NC-17 rating in time for the October 5 release of *Henry & June.*

Film preservation and restoration continued to be a major concern to filmmakers during 1990. On May 1, eight producers and directors announced the formation of The Film Foundation, whose initial goal was to raise $30 million for joint restoration projects by studios and film archivists. Involved in the organization were not only Coppola and Scorsese but also Woody Allen, Stanley Kubrick, George Lucas, Sydney Pollack, Robert Redford, and Steven Spielberg.

In October, the Library of Congress announced the second group of 25 films chosen for the National Film Registry by Librarian of Congress James H. Billington. The films, selected for cultural or artistic importance, must be labeled if they are colorized or otherwise altered. Coppola's original *The Godfather* was one of the films so honored. The others were *All About Eve* (1950), *All Quiet on the Western Front* (1930), *Bring-*

ing Up Baby (1938), Dodsworth (1936), Duck Soup (1933), Fantasia (1940), The Freshman (the Harold Lloyd 1925 silent comedy, not the 1990 film with Matthew Broderick), The Great Train Robbery (1903), Harlan County, U.S.A. (1976), How Green Was My Valley (1941), It's a Wonderful Life (1946), Killer of Sheep (1977), Love Me Tonight (1932), Meshes of the Afternoon (1943), Ninotchka (1939), Primary (1960), Raging Bull (1980), Rebel Without a Cause (1955), Red River (1948), The River (1937), Sullivan's Travels (1941), Top Hat (1935), The Treasure of the Sierra Madre (1948), and A Woman Under the Influence (1974). The first group of 25 films was selected in 1989.

The world scene was dominated by American films in 1990. In the Netherlands, for example, 80 per cent of the released films were produced or released by major U.S. studios. Hollywood distributors also made inroads in South Korea, which in 1990 was the second-biggest market for American films in Asia, exceeded only by Japan.

The trend toward multiplex theaters, which show several motion pictures at once, began to reach other countries in 1990. In New Zealand, for example, the country's first six-screen multiplex theater opened to tremendous business in the university city of Palmerston North.   Philip Wuntch

See also **Awards and prizes** (Arts awards); **Day-Lewis, Daniel; Lynch, David; Tandy, Jessica.** In *World Book,* see **Motion picture.**

Mozambique. Peace talks were held in Rome and in the African nation of Malawi in 1990 in an effort to end the civil war in Mozambique, which has raged since 1975. The talks were sponsored by four Western nations—Great Britain, Italy, Portugal, and the United States—and by four African countries: Kenya, Malawi, South Africa, and Zimbabwe. Mozambique's President Joaquím Alberto Chissano, head of the nation's governing party—the Front for the Liberation of Mozambique (Frelimo)—and Afonso Dhlakama, who leads the rebel Mozambique National Resistance (Renamo), both sent delegations to the talks.

An end to one-party rule. Optimism that a settlement would be reached rose in late July when President Chissano agreed to hold multiparty elections in 1991. He said Renamo candidates could appear on the ballot if the rebel group laid down its arms. Frelimo also agreed to move away from its former Marxist rhetoric and permit private ownership of property and the sale of government-owned businesses to private investors. Proposed democratic reforms also included guarantees regarding human rights and a free press.

On Nov. 30, 1990, the nation adopted a new Constitution, and the next day Frelimo and Renamo agreed to a limited cease-fire. Renamo said it would stop attacking two important railroad lines. In return, the government promised to place tight restrictions on some 7,000 troops from neighboring Zimbabwe who have been helping Frelimo's forces protect the rail-

ways. But fighting continued in some parts of the country.

The terrible toll of war. During the year, as battles raged and Renamo disrupted the famine-relief efforts of foreign donor agencies, casualties in Mozambique continued to mount. An estimated 900,000 people have died in the civil war since 1975. In addition, more than 5 million Mozambicans have been displaced from their homes. Some 800,000 of those people are refugees in Malawi, straining that impoverished country's limited resources. The civil war has also affected Zimbabwe, which has been spending $500,000 a day to maintain the troops stationed in Mozambique to guard the rail lines.

Improved economic outlook. The possibility that peace and democracy may finally be coming to Mozambique aroused the interest of foreign investors in 1990. Among them was a coalition of South African, British, and Brazilian investors that pledged $1.5-billion for the renovation of war-damaged coal-mining facilities in Mozambique and for explorations to locate new coal deposits. The Frelimo government's policy of moving from a centralized Marxist economy to private enterprise has encouraged foreign business interests to look at a broad range of agricultural, business, and mining opportunities in Mozambique.   J. Gus Liebenow and Beverly B. Liebenow

See also **Africa** (Facts in brief table). In *World Book,* see **Mozambique.**

Mulroney, Brian (1939-   ). In 1990, support for Prime Minister Brian Mulroney's Progressive Conservative (PC) Party fell to the lowest ever registered for a governing party in the 49-year history of the Gallup poll in Canada. According to the poll, only 15 per cent of decided voters backed Mulroney and the PC's in October. The opposition Liberals were favored by 31 per cent; the New Democratic Party, by 38 per cent. Two parties that had strong regional support—the Bloc Québécois and the Reform Party (RP)—surprised political analysts by winning 16 per cent in the poll.

A number of initiatives by Mulroney's government—including free trade with the United States, the Meech Lake constitutional accord, and the goods and services tax—proved highly unpopular. Nevertheless, Mulroney sought to make a virtue of his political difficulties. He had made, he said, the right decisions "to strengthen and modernize the Canadian economy." He seemed content to have his record judged at the next general election, in 1992 or 1993.

Political analysts agreed that the popularity of the Bloc Québécois and the RP threatened an alliance between Quebec nationalists and western province conservatives. The PC won electoral victories in 1984 and 1988 based on that alliance.   David M. L. Farr

See also **Canada.** In *World Book,* see **Mulroney, Brian.**

Music. See **Classical music; Popular music.**

Myanmar. See **Burma.**

Namibians in the capital city of Windhoek celebrate their nation's day of independence—March 21, 1990—from South African rule.

Namibia.

Namibia. After 75 years of South African rule, Namibia on March 21, 1990, became the last African colony to achieve independence. As the South African flag was lowered, the reins of government passed to a 72-member National Assembly—whose members were chosen in November 1989 elections—and to President Sam Nujoma. Nujoma was elected on Feb. 16, 1990, by a unanimous vote of the Assembly.

Although Nujoma had little formal education, he demonstrated great administrative and diplomatic skills during his nearly 30 years as leader-in-exile of the South West Africa People's Organization (SWAPO). That rebel group—now a political party—fought a war with South Africa for 23 years until a 1989 cease-fire brought peace. In a spirit of reconciliation, Nujoma chose a cabinet that included members of other political parties and of various ethnic and racial groups, including five whites.

New constitution. Although SWAPO held 41 of the 72 seats in the National Assembly, it was short of the two-thirds majority needed to dictate the terms of the new constitution. Hence, the Constitution, adopted on Feb. 9, 1990, lacks any reference to SWAPO's earlier commitment to Marxist one-party rule.

The document is one of the most liberal constitutions that has been adopted by any African nation. It establishes a multiparty democracy with a president restricted to two five-year terms and an Assembly with proportional representation. The Constitution also contains provisions guaranteeing fundamental human rights, a court system free of partisan political control, respect for private property, limits on the use of emergency powers, and equal rights for women.

Economic development. Acknowledging the decline of socialism in Africa, Asia, and Europe, Nujoma rejected Marxist dogma for Namibia. Instead, he expressed support for a mixed economy that would include both public and private ownership of the nation's economic enterprises. Beyond that goal, however, Nujoma will have to address the issue of expanded education for Namibia's blacks, a vital step if they are to fully participate in the economy. Considerable revenues will be needed to meet SWAPO's goal of compulsory education for all children under 16.

Nujoma must take several other factors into account as he seeks to formulate an economic plan for Namibia. One of those factors is protecting the interests of the nation's whites, who hold most of Namibia's wealth and who have the technical skills needed for growth. Another consideration is how to attract foreign investment, essential for the development of Namibia's vast mineral wealth. A third factor is maintaining good relations with South Africa. Many Namibian enterprises are controlled by South Africans, and the South African rand is still Namibia's currency.   J. Gus Liebenow and Beverly B. Liebenow

See also **Africa** (Facts in brief table); **Nujoma, Sam.** In *World Book,* see **Namibia.**

Nebraska. See **State government.**

Nepal changed from an absolute monarchy to a constitutional monarchy in 1990 after up to 500 people died in demonstrations against King Birendra Bir Bikram Shah Dev's system of government. On February 18, worsening economic conditions caused in part by a trade dispute with neighboring India stimulated the banned Nepali Congress Party and a Communist front to begin demonstrations for democracy. The protests peaked on April 6 with a huge march on the king's palace. The army shot and killed at least 50 marchers.

With foreign donors threatening to cut off aid to the impoverished country, the king agreed on April 8 to lift the ban on political parties. On April 16, the king fired his prime minister and dissolved parliament. He named as interim prime minister Congress leader Krishna Prasad Bhattarai, a former political prisoner.

A special commission wrote a new constitution that vested power in the people rather than the king, established basic public rights, and provided for a multi-party government with a two-chamber parliament. When the king resisted accepting this document, demonstrators renewed their protests. The king finally accepted the new constitution on November 7.

India ended its virtual halt to trade with Nepal in June. Relations between the two nations remained troubled, however.   Henry S. Bradsher

See also **Asia** (Facts in brief table). In *World Book,* see **Nepal.**

Netherlands. The environment continued to shape political debate in the Netherlands during 1990. The year before, the government had fallen in a dispute over financing an antipollution program that was to cost $7.5 billion per year by 1994. After parliamentary elections in September 1989, Prime Minister Ruud Lubbers, who campaigned on a program of environmental cleanup, formed a new center-left government.

Cleaning up the environment. In September 1990, the States-General (parliament) passed a plan that gives the Netherlands one of the most far-reaching environmental programs of any country in the world. Among its goals is a reduction in emissions of carbon dioxide, a gas thought to add to global warming. The Netherlands and other low-lying lands would be flooded in the event that global warming melted polar icecaps and raised the sea level.

In March, The Hague, the seat of government, hosted the Third North Sea Conference, attended by eight nations that border the North Sea. The eight seek to halt the dumping of industrial wastes in the North Sea and to reduce the amount of phosphates and other chemicals reaching the North Sea from rivers. The heavily polluted Rhine River empties into the North Sea near Rotterdam in the Netherlands.

In December, the Netherlands Electricity Generating Board announced plans to plant forests in the tropics and help clean up the air in Poland. A spokesperson said that power plants in the Netherlands were al-ready removing 92 per cent of the sulfur from their emissions. Further investment at home would achieve only slight improvement. But the same investment in Poland, where power stations burn sulfur-rich coal, could remove a significant amount of sulfur dioxide from the polluted air. (Sulfur dioxide is a major source of acid rain.) The Dutch pledged $35 million to Poland and $300 million to help restore forests, which absorb carbon dioxide, in tropical areas.

The giant Dutch electronics firm, N. V. Philips, announced in July that it expected a loss of about $1-billion in 1990 and planned to eliminate about 10,000 jobs as a result. Among the reasons for Philips' losses was a failure of its computer division to compete with rivals in Japan and the United States. Philips had invested in developing minicomputers while purchasers had shifted to smaller personal computers.

Schengen treaty. On June 19, the Netherlands and four other members of the European Community (EC or Common Market) signed an agreement to eliminate border formalities. The agreement, known as the Schengen treaty, will permit free movement of people and goods between Belgium, France, Germany, Luxembourg, and the Netherlands. It was expected to take effect in 1992 after ratification by parliaments in the five nations.   Karin C. Rosenberg

See also **Europe** (Facts in brief table). In *World Book,* see **Netherlands.**

Nevada. See State government.

New Brunswick. Premier Frank J. McKenna and his Liberal Party continued in 1990 to control New Brunswick's Legislative Assembly, the only one-party legislature in Canada. The party has held all of the 58 seats in the Assembly since the October 1987 election. A poll in January 1990 showed that 58 per cent of decided voters—enough to sweep another election—supported the Liberals.

On March 27, Finance Minister Allan Maher introduced a budget in which revenues exceeded expenditures by $3.7 million Canadian ($3.1 million U.S.). By August, however, an economic slowdown in Canada had resulted in lower sales tax receipts. Overall, the slowdown helped turn the expected surplus into an estimated $19.6-million Canadian ($16.8-million U.S.) deficit. In addition, the province spent more than expected on job training and on fighting forest fires.

In an attempt to cut health-care costs, which amount to one-third of New Brunswick's expenditures, the government on April 26 announced immediate fee capping for the province's physicians. The government also announced plans to replace 300 hospital beds with community-based care over the next five years.   David M. L. Farr

In *World Book,* see **New Brunswick.**

New Hampshire. See State government.
New Jersey. See State government.
New Mexico. See State government.
New York. See New York City; State government.

New York City

New York City experienced a fiscal crisis in 1990 as the budget went into a severe deficit. During the year, the city raised taxes and reduced many services to stop the flow of red ink, but it was not enough. Mayor David N. Dinkins announced on November 8 that 5,400 city jobs would go unfilled and spending would be further reduced to close a $388-million budget gap for the 1991 fiscal year and a $1.6-billion deficit projected for fiscal year 1992.

The budget crisis evoked memories of 1975, when the city nearly went bankrupt. That emergency was overcome with the help of a $2.3-billion federal loan, paid back in 1978. The events of 1975 also led to a mandated balanced budget and the creation of a powerful agency, the Financial Control Board, to monitor city finances. In 1990, the control board, composed of the mayor, New York Governor Mario M. Cuomo, and several other government officials and business leaders, was once more overseeing the budget.

Crime on the increase. Crime in the streets, long a major concern in New York City, rose to new levels in 1990. The homicide rate was up about 18 per cent, and by year-end more than 2,000 people had been murdered. One of the most publicized crimes was the fatal stabbing of a tourist, Brian Watkins of Provo, Utah, in a subway station. Watkins, in town with his family during the Labor Day weekend to see the United States Tennis Open, was attacked by youths as he tried to stop them from mugging his mother.

Watkins' death and other violent crimes—including a succession of random shootings of children in neighborhoods infested by drug dealers—prompted the mayor on October 2 to propose a $1.8-billion plan to add 7,931 more uniformed officers to the police department. The staffing increase, the largest in the department's history, would be financed by a payroll tax and a surcharge on lottery tickets.

Racial friction. The mayor's inauguration pledge on Jan. 1, 1990, to unite the multiethnic city was tested during the year. Later in January, black activists began a boycott of a Brooklyn supermarket owned by Korean Americans after a black customer charged that an employee of the store had assaulted her. The boycott was soon expanded to a second Korean-American store on the same block.

After remaining neutral in the controversy for eight months, Dinkins finally responded to widespread criticism by visiting the market on September 21 and buying a small amount of fruit and vegetables. The mayor also directed the police to enforce a court decree ordering pickets to stay at least 50 feet (15 meters) from the store's entrance.

About three weeks earlier, on August 30, a special mayoral panel concluded that the boycott was not racially biased and that the mayor was right to remain aloof. But on November 7, a committee of the City Council criticized that report as biased, weak, and self-serving. At year-end, the boycott continued.

Preparing for the 1992 Democratic convention in New York City are, from left, Governor Cuomo, party Chairman Ronald Brown, and Mayor Dinkins.

A bitter newspaper strike began on October 25 after a worker at a New York *Daily News* plant refused an order to stand instead of sit at his machine. A union official who intervened was removed from the plant, as were about 30 drivers. Management said it was a strike; the union said it was a lockout. Other unions then joined the walkout.

The *News* continued to publish with replacement workers, though its usual circulation of 1.1 million copies was drastically reduced, in part because of a labor boycott. Some newsstand dealers—reported to be coerced by strikers—refused to sell the newspaper. Union contracts had expired on March 31, and negotiations stalled. At year-end, the strike continued.

In mid-September, the money-losing *New York Post* worked out a deal with its unions. Union members agreed to a 20 per cent cut in pay, a four-day workweek, and $20 million in contract adjustments to keep the publication solvent.

Arson fire tragedy. One of the worst arson fires in U.S. history killed 87 people on March 25 at a social club in the borough of the Bronx. See Crime.

Commodities exchanges stay. New York City's four major commodities exchanges agreed on November 7 not to move to New Jersey. City and state authorities enticed the exchanges to stay with $145 million in incentives, including grants and rent subsidies for a new headquarters in Manhattan.   Owen Moritz

See also **Courts**. In *World Book,* see **New York City**.

New Zealand. The government of New Zealand changed hands in 1990, when the National Party won the October 27 elections, ending six years of Labour Party control.

Prime Minister Michael K. Moore's Labour government was swept from power in a landslide election that gave 67 of the 97 parliamentary seats to the conservative National Party. Only two months before the election, Moore had replaced Geoffrey Palmer, who had resigned rather than face a leadership challenge in Parliament. James B. Bolger, leader of the National Party and a member of Parliament for 18 years, became the third prime minister to serve in 1990 (see **Bolger, James Brendan**).

Economic performance was poor in 1990. Government policy gave the highest priority to reducing inflation (4.1 per cent for the September quarter) at the expense of economic growth. *Gross domestic product* (the total value of goods and services produced within the nation's boundaries) was down 0.6 per cent over the previous three years, according to the New Zealand Trade Development Board. Forecasters said it would barely grow 1 per cent in 1990.

Unemployment figures released in November showed 207,000 out of the 3.4 million population were jobless or on government work schemes. This translated into a 7.9 per cent unemployment rate.

The incoming government in December announced sweeping cuts in social spending to reduce a projected budget deficit by $NZ 2 billion (about $1.2 billion U.S.) in fiscal 1991.

Foreign affairs. Some improvement was evident in relations with the United States. Relations between the two countries were soured by New Zealand's ban in 1985 on nuclear-powered and nuclear-armed ships entering its ports. Prime Minister Bolger supported the nuclear ban, but he said he wanted to improve ties with the United States.

Treaty celebrations. New Zealand celebrated in February the 150th anniversary of the signing of the Treaty of Waitangi. The treaty granted the British Crown sovereignty over Maori lands and made New Zealand a crown colony.

Since its signing in 1840, however, the treaty has been interpreted in different ways, because words in the Maori translation do not have exactly the same meaning as the English version. Some Maori groups protested the treaty celebrations, saying that successive governments had failed to honor guarantees that the treaty conferred on them.

Other events celebrating the nation's founding included an outdoor concert for 140,000 people by New Zealand operatic soprano Dame Kiri Te Kanawa. About 3,300 competitors and officials attended the January Commonwealth Games, similar to the Olympic Games.   Gavin Ellis

See also **Asia** (Facts in brief table). In *World Book,* see **New Zealand**.

Newfoundland. Gloomy prospects for the fishing industry were balanced in 1990 by hope for offshore oil development in Newfoundland, Canada's most economically troubled province. On January 2, the federal government announced a 16 per cent reduction in cod quotas for 1990 to conserve fish stocks. The news came at a time when fishing companies in Newfoundland and Nova Scotia were already closing plants. A long-range review of cod stocks in March stated that cod quotas would have to be slashed by one-half over the next two years.

A September 14 agreement among Newfoundland, the federal government, and four companies paved the way for the Hibernia offshore oil project. The project, costing $5.2 billion Canadian ($4.5 billion U.S.), would be the largest energy development undertaking in Canadian history. A consortium led by Mobil Oil Canada will develop the Hibernia field, which officials hope will produce 110,000 barrels per day by 1996. A 1988 plan to develop the field had been frustrated by low oil prices and by disputes over the allocation of construction work.

On September 19, the province disclosed that it faced a $120-million Canadian ($103-million U.S.) deficit, caused by a shortfall in federal funds and in sales tax revenues. Finance Minister Hubert Kitchen made up for the loss in federal grants by imposing a payroll tax on large corporations.   David M. L. Farr

See also **Canada**. In *World Book,* see **Newfoundland**.

Newsmakers of 1990

Newsmakers of 1990 included the following:

Donald Trump, of course. Billionaire developer Donald J. Trump never fails to make plenty of headlines—which is the way he seems to like it—but in 1990 he was on the front pages for reasons he would not have chosen. In December, his 12-year marriage to Ivana Trump ended in divorce after he admitted having a relationship with Marla Maples, a model. Earlier in the year, it came out that Trump, despite his public image as a man swimming in cash, was teetering on the brink of bankruptcy. A group of banks came to his aid in late June, but as part of the deal Trump was forced to give up control of his real estate empire—temporarily at least. And in November, Trump was forced to give creditors a 50 per cent share of his Trump Taj Mahal casino in Atlantic City, N.J. As though tempting fate, Trump came out with a book during the year titled *Trump: Surviving at the Top.*

Giving up the struggle. Every few years, a Japanese soldier from World War II is found hiding in an Asian jungle, usually unaware that the war has been over since 1945. In 1990, not one but two Japanese soldiers laid down their arms and returned to civilization. Shigeyuki Hashimoto and Kiyoaki Tanaka, both in their 70's, surrendered to authorities in Thailand in January and were flown back to Japan. Hashimoto and Tanaka apparently knew that Japan had been vanquished in the war, but they had refused to accept the defeat. For 45 years, they lived in the Thai jungle as part of a Communist rebel group opposing the government of nearby Malaysia. In December 1989, when the Malaysian Communists voted to end their fight, the two soldiers decided that enough was enough.

Hail to the ex-chief. Former President Jimmy Carter was the 1990 recipient of the Philadelphia Liberty Medal, an award established in 1988 by a group called We the People. Carter received the medal and a $100,000 cash award at a July 4 ceremony at Philadelphia's Independence Hall. Since leaving office in 1981, Carter has jetted around the world as America's unofficial ambassador of good will. Working through the Carter Presidential Center in Atlanta, Ga., he has promoted agriculture and health programs in Africa and helped monitor elections in countries that are groping their way toward democracy.

Feeding the homeless—in style. Kathleen Gooley of Norwalk, Conn., had her wedding plans set: a June 23 wedding ceremony followed by a dinner reception for 150 friends and relatives at the Canongate, a Norwalk catering hall. But then her fiance backed out, and she was stuck with the reception reservation. So Gooley invited 150 homeless people from Norwalk, Stamford, and Bridgeport to the Canongate, where they feasted on hors d'oeuvres, garden salad, fruit cup, stuffed chicken breast, baked potato, cake, and ice cream. Said Gooley as she mingled with her appreciative guests: "This is better than a wedding."

Checkpoint Charlie, a famous crossing point in the Berlin Wall, is lifted from its moorings in June as the Germanys prepare for unification.

A hiding place Down Under. Seven-year-old Hilary Foretich, whose whereabouts had been a mystery since August 1987, resurfaced in February 1990—in the New Zealand city of Christchurch with her maternal grandparents. Hilary was sent into hiding in 1987 by her mother, Elizabeth Morgan, after a Washington, D.C., judge ruled that Morgan's former husband, Eric Foretich, could not be prevented from having unsupervised visits with the child. The judge said there was insufficient evidence to support Morgan's charge that Foretich had sexually molested his daughter in 1985 when she was 2½ years old. For defying the judge's ruling, Morgan spent 25 months in a Washington, D.C., jail. In November, Foretich said he was abandoning his fight for custody of Hilary after a New Zealand judge ruled that the girl must remain with her mother in New Zealand.

More fun in Orlando. The city of Orlando, Fla.—already a tourist mecca as the home of Disney World and the Disney-MGM Studios Theme Park—became even more of a vacation magnet in 1990. In June, Orlando struck up the band for the opening of Universal Studios Florida, a $630-million attraction that includes an amusement park and a working film studio. One of the most gut-wrenching rides in the park is an aerial tramway on which passengers find themselves in a face-to-face confrontation with an angry King Kong, complete with banana breath.

A triumphant tour for Mandela. Antiapartheid leader Nelson R. Mandela, released from a South African prison in February after 27 years, was given a hero's welcome in North America in June. Mandela addressed a committee of the United Nations and met with Canadian Prime Minister Brian Mulroney and U.S. President George Bush. He also spoke before joint sessions of the Canadian Parliament and the U.S. Congress and was honored in several cities in both countries. See also **Mandela, Nelson; South Africa.**

They forgot to say abracadabra. The Coca-Cola Company, creator of the ill-starred New Coke five years back, found itself wishing again in 1990 that things *would* go better with Coke. In May, the company introduced MagiCans, selected cans of Coke that ejected a rolled-up piece of currency—from $1 to $500—or a coupon redeemable for a prize. To make the MagiCans indistinguishable from ordinary cans of Coke before opening, they were filled with a harmless but foul-smelling water solution. Although the liquid was sealed off from the spring-operated mechanism that pushed the money or coupon through the tab opening, at least one person drank some of it.

The entire campaign went downhill from there. Many consumers did not understand the MagiCan idea, and many of the cans did not work properly. In an effort to remedy the situation, Coca-Cola ran a full-page ad in a number of newspapers explaining how MagiCans were supposed to function and warning people not to drink the solution. A few days later, the promotion was, um, canned.

A joining of the clans. Two powerful political families, the Kennedys and the Cuomos, were united by marriage on June 9. In a ceremony at St. Matthew's Cathedral in Washington, D.C., Andrew Cuomo, the eldest son of New York Governor Mario M. Cuomo, exchanged wedding vows with Kerry Kennedy, a daughter of the late Senator Robert F. Kennedy (D., N.Y.). "It's like they say in baseball," commented a former aide of Senator Kennedy's as he surveyed the many prominent Democrats in attendance, "it's one of those trades that helps both clubs."

Actress buys some property—a whole town. Movie star Kim Basinger wanted to do something nice for her home state of Georgia, so in January she plunked down $20 million to buy the town of Braselton. The actress, whose roles include the female lead in the 1989 hit *Batman*, called the 1,728-acre (699-hectare) hamlet "a perfect place for filming." She said she planned to build a motion-picture studio in Braselton, as well as an industrial park and a recording studio. In March, Basinger was named an Outstanding Georgia Citizen.

The great white way. Six bone-weary explorers arrived at a Soviet base on Antarctica's eastern coast on March 3, ending a grueling seven-month trek across the frozen continent. The 3,800-mile (6,100-kilometer) journey, by dog sled and ski, was the longest-ever unmechanized crossing of Antarctica. The expedition team represented China, France, Great

Mary Alice, a tiger cub born at the Henry Doorly Zoo in Omaha, Nebr., in April, is the first tiger conceived in a test tube ever to survive.

Behind her steaming huskies, sledder Susan Butcher speeds to her fourth win in the Iditarod race from Anchorage to Nome, Alaska, in March.

Britain, Japan, the Soviet Union, and the United States.

Zsa Zsa tells it like it is. Celebrity Zsa Zsa Gabor, ordered in 1989 to do 120 hours of community service for slapping a Beverly Hills, Calif., police officer, got another 60 hours added to her sentence in May 1990. The judge ruled that Gabor had been cheating on the time that she was devoting to fund-raising for a Los Angeles homeless shelter and was using the activity to promote herself. "Why should I try to promote myself," said Gabor as she left the courtroom. "Darlings, I am so damn famous, it's sickening."

Leaning Tower shuts its doors. The Leaning Tower of Pisa in Italy, which engineers have been warning could become the Falling Tower of Pisa, was closed to tourists in January. The tower, completed in 1372, has been increasing its tilt by about 1/20 inch (1.25 millimeters) a year in this century. Its top is now more than 14 feet 6 inches (4.4 meters) away from the vertical. City authorities said the landmark might be off-limits for several years until it is stabilized.

Winning the union way. It probably wasn't an easy thing for her to do, but Pamela Richards of Toledo, Ohio, turned down a $17,600 Honda Accord she won on a television game show and accepted a $1,000 cash award instead. The reason? Richards has been a member of the United Automobile Workers (UAW) union since 1967, and the car she won was manufactured at a nonunion plant. American Federation of Labor and Congress of Industrial Organizations President Lane Kirkland thought such loyalty deserved to be rewarded. On August 16, he presented Richards with a union-made Dodge Dakota pickup truck as a gift on behalf of all U.S. unions.

A happy ending for Buchwald. A judge in Los Angeles ruled in January that Paramount Pictures owed humor columnist Art Buchwald a share of the profits from the 1988 Eddie Murphy movie *Coming to America*. The judge said the film was based on a story idea submitted by Buchwald to the studio in 1983. He rejected the assertion that Murphy and his co-star in the movie, television personality Arsenio Hall, developed the script for *Coming to America* independently. In Buchwald's outline, as in the movie, a prince from a mythical African country comes to the United States to seek a bride, works for a while in a fast-food restaurant, and meets and marries a young black woman. Paramount planned to appeal the decision.

Japanese Cinderella. A real prince of a real country—Prince Aya of Japan—took a bride in 1990. Aya, the second son of Japan's Emperor Akihito and Empress Michiko, married Kiko Kawashima on June 29 in a ceremony on the grounds of the Imperial Palace in Tokyo. They met at Tokyo's Gakushuin University, where she is a graduate student in social psychology.

Pottygate! That's what *The Houston Post* dubbed the Denise Wells affair, but you might just call it a case of illegal parking. While attending a pop music concert in July, Wells, a Houston paralegal, went to use the rest room but was forced to take her place at the end of a long line. Unable to wait, she ducked into the men's room. When she came out a few minutes later, a police officer gave her a ticket carrying a $200 fine and ejected her from the concert. The incident caused a furor in Houston and called attention to the issue of inadequate bathroom facilities for women at many public places. In November, a Houston jury acquitted Wells.

Bert's back, sort of. He wasn't the host of the show, but there he was—Mister Miss America, Bert Parks. Parks appeared on the 70th annual Miss America pageant on September 8, singing its theme song, "There She Is," to a group of former Miss Americas. Parks was emcee of the pageant from 1955 through 1979. The winner of the 1990 competition was Marjorie Vincent of Oak Park, Ill., a third-year law student at Duke University in Durham, N.C. She was the fourth black to win the Miss America title.

Man resuscitates dog—that's news. When a Dalmatian with a squash ball lodged in its throat was taken to the Shelton, Conn., police station in December 1989, fast action was needed to save the dog's life. Officer Michael Fusco extracted the ball and revived the animal by giving it mouth-to-mouth resuscitation. Having done it once, Fusco agreed—albeit somewhat reluctantly—to do it again, this time for television. In August 1990, the officer reenacted the rescue for the cameras of the CBS show "Rescue 911." The rescued dog was played by a trained Dalmatian named Jackie.

Barr bombs, but the flag was still there. Actress and comedian Roseanne Barr learned the hard way that Americans take their national anthem very seriously. On July 25 at the San Diego Padres' ball park, Barr sang "The Star-Spangled Banner"—screeched it, actually—at the start of a double-header between the Padres and the Cincinnati Reds. Heartily booed by the crowd as she finished her rendition, Barr then grabbed her crotch and spat on the ground before walking off the field. Barr's performance was replayed on newscasts around the country and elicited comments from many public figures, including President Bush, who pronounced it "disgraceful." Barr was unapologetic about the incident, explaining that she is no singer and that her gestures on the field had been meant simply as a parody of ballplayers' mannerisms. Informed of Bush's remark, she responded, "I'd like to hear him sing it."

Rooney gets grounded. Andy Rooney, resident grouch on the popular CBS TV show "60 Minutes," also got himself into hot water during the year. Accused of making remarks offensive to blacks and homosexuals, Rooney on February 8 was suspended from the program without pay. Although the suspension was supposed to last for three months, Rooney got his job back in early March after viewers bombarded the network with protests and the ratings of "60 Min-

Cartoonist Mort Walker, flanked by characters from his comic strip "Beetle Bailey," receives a Pentagon citation for civilian service in June.

utes" began to drop. Rooney denied making statements that were attributed to him in a national gay magazine. Nonetheless, he expressed gratitude at being reinstated and promised to tread carefully.

A city pays a ransom. On July 2, Scott Heimdal returned home to Peoria, Ill.—the city that freed him from Colombian kidnappers. Heimdal, 27, grew up in Peoria but left after completing high school to join the Army and, later, to seek his fortune. His quest took him to Colombia, where he went to work for a mining company dredging river bottoms for gold. In April 1990, he was captured by guerrillas, who demanded $60,000 for his release. Heimdal's family, unable to raise that much cash, appealed to the people of Peoria for help. The community responded, taking up collections, holding bake sales, opening lemonade stands—anything to bring in the needed money. After receiving the $60,000 in late June, the guerrillas released Heimdal to authorities in Ecuador.

Those bad bees have arrived. The first swarm of Africanized "killer" bees crossed the Rio Grande from Mexico into Texas in October. The bees, hybrids descended from African honey bees that escaped from a Brazilian laboratory in 1957, are called killers because of their aggressive stinging behavior. Although the Texas swarm was quickly trapped and destroyed, many more of the bees are expected to enter the Southwest in coming years and to spread through much of the United States.   David L. Dreier

Newspaper

Newspaper publishers worried about the future in 1990. Even before the economy soured in midyear, newspapers generally suffered from stagnant circulations and losses in advertising revenues. With the decline in advertising, such large newspapers as *The New York Times, Los Angeles Times*, and *The Wall Street Journal* cut back on the space given to articles.

Hard times. Many publishers worried in 1990 that newspapers faced even grimmer futures over the long term. The chief reason: fewer teen-agers and young adults read newspapers regularly. According to one study, the number of people aged 18 to 29 who read a daily paper plummeted by 35 per cent from 1967 to 1989. Nor do many young people take an interest in news events, according to another survey. The study found, for example, that only 42 per cent of those under age 30 were interested in the opening of the Berlin Wall. Just 19 per cent were interested in the overthrow of Romania's Communist dictator.

A few newspapers did not survive 1990. The *St. Louis (Mo.) Sun*, a tabloid launched on Sept. 25, 1989, folded on April 25, 1990, because of financial problems. Another innovative new tabloid in Missouri, the *Kansas City Evening News*, lasted only from May 14 to June 20. Publisher Stephen F. Rose said the paper, which was sold only on the street and not delivered to homes, was making money. He blamed its demise on laws in several towns forbidding teen-agers to sell the paper along busy commuter roads.

In Scranton, Pa., two much older papers—the 134-year-old *Scrantonian Tribune* and the Sunday *Scrantonian*—were shut down without warning on May 21. Owner John Buzzetta blamed the region's deteriorating economy for the papers' death. The *New York Post*, a New York City tabloid founded in 1801, narrowly escaped closing in September 1990. It survived when 11 unions agreed to $27 million in cutbacks hours before the paper was to shut down.

The New York *Daily News* battled unions in late 1990, leaving its future uncertain. A breakdown in contract negotiations finally ended in walkouts by nine unions, starting in October. The paper's management had been trained to bring out the paper in the event of a strike, but sales and advertising fell.

Despite the hard economic times, *The National*, a newspaper devoted entirely to sports news, was launched on Jan. 31, 1990. It was the first all-sports daily in the United States.

Joint operating agreement. Some newspapers attempt to stay alive through a joint operating agreement (JOA) that allows two rival papers to combine production and business operations while keeping separate newsrooms. A JOA, which requires a Department of Justice exemption from antitrust laws, was granted on Feb. 21, 1990, to the *York (Pa.) Daily Record* and the *York Dispatch*.   Mark Fitzgerald

See also **Awards and prizes** (Journalism awards). In *World Book,* see **Newspaper.**

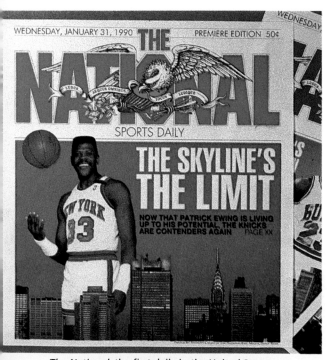

The National, the first daily in the United States devoted entirely to sports, was launched in New York City, Chicago, and Los Angeles in January.

Nicaragua. On April 25, 1990, Violeta Barrios de Chamorro of the National Opposition Union was inaugurated for a six-year term as Nicaragua's president. Her center-right administration replaced a leftist Sandinista regime that had left the nation deeply divided along ideological lines.

"This is the dawn of a new republic," Chamorro declared at her inauguration, where supporters cheered and opponents booed, setting the stage for continued political infighting. In a gesture of reconciliation, Chamorro retained General Humberto Ortega Saavedra, a Sandinista and brother of the outgoing president, as armed forces commander.

The appointment, however, disturbed many in the diverse coalition that came together to elect Chamorro, including her vice president, Virgilio Godoy Reyes, and United States-backed *contra* rebels who had fought to topple the previous regime. Reyes, a conservative member of the coalition, spent much of the ensuing year criticizing Chamorro's moderate policies on a wide array of issues, making it more difficult for Chamorro to win support for her programs.

The new government found the treasury nearly empty. Cash reserves amounted to only $3 million—about the same figure the Sandinistas inherited when they toppled dictator Anastasio Somoza Debayle in 1979. With foreign debt standing at $11 billion, the Chamorro administration was forced to impose an austerity program.

Nicaragua's new president, Violeta Barrios de Chamorro, receives the official sash from outgoing President Daniel Ortega at inaugural ceremonies in April.

Sandinista strikes. Out of power, the Sandinistas mounted a highly effective opposition by leading strikes. On May 16, 1990, Chamorro was able to end a weeklong walkout by public employees only by agreeing to their demands for a 100 per cent pay raise. On July 12, a general strike by the National Workers' Front also ended in a victory for the strikers.

The strikers adopted the same tactics the Sandinistas had successfully employed in routing Somoza. They erected barricades of paving stones, burned vehicles at major intersections, and generally disrupted life in Managua, the capital. Before riot police quelled street fighting between strikers and opponents of the Sandinistas on July 9, 4 people were reported killed and more than 40 wounded.

Contra demobilization. United Nations troops disarmed some 20,000 contras in a two-month period ending on June 27. Each contra became eligible to receive civilian clothing, rice and bean rations until December, and a $50 start-up grant—paid for by the United States government. There was considerable grumbling among former contras, who said the compensation was scarcely adequate for the sacrifices they had made during years of combat service. Many of them complained that promised grants of land failed to materialize.   Nathan A. Haverstock

See also **Chamorro, Violeta Barrios de; Latin America** (Facts in brief table). In *World Book,* see **Nicaragua.**
Niger. See **Africa.**

Nigeria. A failed coup by a group of military officers in Lagos on April 22, 1990, highlighted the serious religious and ethnic divisions afflicting Nigeria. The central issue in the rebellion was a long-standing conflict between the Muslim-dominated government in the north and the predominantly Christian regions of central and southern Nigeria. President Ibrahim Babangida aggravated that rift in December 1989 when he dropped two Christian officials from his cabinet.

The rebels in the April 1990 uprising, led by an army major named Gideon Ngwozor Oka, attempted to take over army headquarters as a prelude to seizing the government. Their goal was to expel five largely Muslim states of the north from the 21-state federation that makes up Nigeria. After an 11-hour battle with loyal government troops, Oka surrendered. He and other leaders of the uprising were executed on July 27.

Return to civilian rule. The unsuccessful coup did not interrupt plans for a return to civilian rule in December 1992. Hoping to avoid the religious, ethnic, and regional factions that doomed Nigeria's previous civilian governments, the Babangida regime in October 1989 reduced the number of would-be political parties from 15 to just 2. Moreover, it has ruled that anyone who held elective office in previous governments—roughly 70,000 people—will be barred from running in the next national election, which is scheduled for 1992.

Nobel Prizes

In July 1990, the two authorized parties held elections to select party leaders. The outcome of the balloting indicated that the parties might reflect and perpetuate the Christian-Muslim split in Nigerian society. The socialist-leaning Social Democratic Party received most of its support in the Christian south, whereas the more conservative National Republican Convention was more popular in the Muslim north.

Hoping to stabilize the next civilian government, Babangida announced in July that the size of the military would be cut and that soldiers would receive civic education supporting civilian rule. Babangida also announced plans to conduct a national census in 1991—important for fairly allocating seats in parliament and federal funding to the 21 states.

The economy. Nigeria's efforts to pay off a foreign debt of more than $32 billion were aided in March and July 1990 when Western creditors agreed to accept repayment at a lower rate of interest. The increase in oil prices resulting from Iraq's 1990 invasion of Kuwait also gave an economic boost to Nigeria, a major exporter of oil. During the year, the Babangida regime took steps to stimulate the economy, such as offering inefficient government companies to private buyers. But its easing of price controls led to riots over the higher costs of food and transportation.　　　J. Gus Liebenow and Beverly B. Liebenow

See also **Africa** (Facts in brief table). In **World Book,** see **Nigeria.**

Nobel Prizes in peace, literature, economics, and the sciences were awarded in 1990 by the Norwegian Storting (parliament) in Oslo and by the Royal Academy of Science, the Karolinska Institute, and the Swedish Academy of Literature in Stockholm, Sweden. Each prize was worth about $710,000 in United States currency.

The peace prize was awarded to Mikhail S. Gorbachev, president of the Soviet Union and the first Communist head of state to receive a Nobel Prize, in recognition of his contributions to the "peace process." Among the contributions cited were Gorbachev's role in allowing the nations of eastern Europe to obtain political freedom, withdrawing Soviet troops from Afghanistan, and pursuing arms control and an end to the Cold War with the United States.

"During the last few years," the Nobel Committee said in announcing the peace prize, "dramatic changes have taken place in the relationship between East and West. Confrontation has been replaced by negotiation. Old European nation-states have regained their freedom," and "the arms race is slowing down." The committee said that several factors were responsible for these changes, but that in 1990, they wanted to honor Gorbachev for his contributions.

The literature prize was given to Octavio Paz, a poet and essayist and the first Mexican to receive a Nobel Prize. It was the second year in a row that a Spanish-language writer had won the prize.

Octavio Paz won the Nobel Prize for literature in October, becoming the first Mexican to win a Nobel and the second Spanish-language writer in two years.

Paz is probably best known for *The Labryinth of Solitude: Life and Thought of Mexico* (1950), an analysis of modern Mexico and the Mexican personality. The work of poetry that established his reputation was the long poem "Sunstone," inspired by an Aztec calendar stone and included in *The Collected Poems of Octavio Paz: 1957-1987* (1987).

The economics prize was shared by Harry M. Markowitz of Baruch College at the City University of New York in New York City, Merton H. Miller of the University of Chicago Graduate School of Business, and William Sharpe of Stanford University in California. The three men were credited with developing theories that have widely influenced how money is invested in stocks, bonds, and mutual funds.

Markowitz developed the idea that investing in a diverse range of assets reduces risk, and he showed how to measure risk in relation to certain assets. Sharpe pioneered the theory that the merits of certain investments are linked to their volatility in relation to the rest of the market. Miller was instrumental in fashioning the theory that the profitability of a company is a far more important consideration to investors than how the company funds its activities.

The physics prize was divided among Canadian-born physicist Richard E. Taylor of Stanford University, and Jerome I. Friedman and Henry W. Kendall, both of the Massachusetts Institute of Technology in Cambridge. The three physicists were honored for experiments conducted between 1967 and 1973 that proved the physical existence of quarks, the basic units that make up the neutrons and protons in the nucleus of an atom.

The existence of quarks was first proposed in 1964 by physicist Murray Gell-Mann of the California Institute of Technology in Pasadena, but quarks were not actually detected until Friedman, Kendall, and Taylor carried out a series of experiments at the Stanford Linear Accelerator Center in Palo Alto, Calif. The experiments involved accelerating beams of electrons into neutrons and protons and studying the scatter patterns caused by the resulting collisions.

The chemistry prize was awarded to Elias James Corey of Harvard University in Cambridge, Mass., for developing a method to synthesize complex molecules, thereby revolutionizing the manufacture of drugs. Corey has produced more than 100 drugs. The Nobel Committee particularly cited his synthesis of a natural chemical found in the ginkgo tree that is widely used to treat blood circulation problems and asthma.

Corey pioneered *retrosynthetic analysis*, a technique for synthesizing drugs. This technique greatly reduced the number of steps and the costs involved in duplicating the molecular structure of chemicals found in nature and known to have medicinal properties.

The physiology or medicine prize was shared by transplant specialists Joseph E. Murray of Brigham and Women's Hospital in Boston and E. Donnall Thomas of the Fred Hutchinson Cancer Research Center in Seattle. The Nobel Assembly at the Karolinska Institute said the work of the two doctors in learning how to transplant organs and bone marrow was "crucial for those tens of thousands of severely ill patients" for whom other treatment methods are unsuccessful.

Murray, a surgeon, performed the first successful organ transplant in 1954 at what was then Peter Bent Brigham Hospital, transplanting a man's healthy kidney to the body of his twin brother, who was dying of kidney failure. Murray went on to perform transplants involving unrelated donors, using drugs to suppress the patient's immune system and prevent it from attacking the donor organ. Thomas performed the first human bone marrow transplant on a patient without an identical twin in 1970. His procedure is now standard treatment for leukemia patients.

1989 winners of Nobel Prizes were Tibet's Dalai Lama for peace; Spain's Camilo José Cela for literature; Trygve Haavelmo of Norway for economics; U.S. physicists Norman F. Ramsey, Jr., and Hans G. Dehmelt and West German physicist Wolfgang Paul for physics; U.S. chemist Thomas R. Cech and Canadian-born chemist Sidney Altman for chemistry; and U.S. cancer researchers J. Michael Bishop and Harold E. Varmus for physiology or medicine.   Rod Such

In *World Book,* see **Nobel Prizes.**

North Carolina. See State government.
North Dakota. See State government.

Northern Ireland. The outlawed Irish Republican Army (IRA) intensified its campaign of violence on the British mainland in 1990, attacking what it claimed were military and political targets.

Bombings. On July 30, the IRA killed Ian Gow, a senior Conservative member of the House of Commons and close adviser of British Prime Minister Margaret Thatcher. Gow died in a bomb blast in his car at his home in the village of Hankham, about 40 miles (60 kilometers) southeast of London. In November 1985, he had resigned as a junior treasury minister to protest the Anglo-Irish Agreement, which gave Ireland an advisory role in Northern Ireland's government. As an outspoken opponent of the IRA, he was on the IRA's list of top 100 targets. Despite police warnings, he had refused security measures on his behalf.

On June 25, 1990, the IRA bombed the Carlton Club in London, injuring eight people, including Lord Kaberry, a former vice chairman of the Conservative Party. Thatcher belonged to the club, described by the IRA as "the rest and recreation center for the British government." On July 20, the IRA bombed the London Stock Exchange, but no one was hurt.

Shooting. On September 18, Sir Peter Terry was shot nine times, but not killed, when an IRA gunman fired on him from outside a window of his home in Milford, near Derby. Terry had been governor of the British dependency of Gibraltar when three IRA suspects were shot dead there by British commandos in 1988.

Overturned IRA convictions. On April 27, the convictions against three Irish citizens known as "The Winchester Three," were set aside by a London appeals court. They had been given 25-year sentences for conspiracy to murder Tom King, Britain's secretary of state for Northern Ireland, in 1987. The court ruled that public comments by King at the time of the 1988 trial had prevented a fair hearing. King had drawn a link between terrorists and suspects who refused to answer police questions; two of the defendants had refused to answer when questioned.

On June 14, 1990, Home Secretary David Waddington announced that the convictions of "The MacGuire Seven," who had served long sentences for running an IRA bomb factory at their London home, could not stand. On July 11, he referred the case to the Court of Appeal. Tests casting doubt on the prosecution's case had been concealed at the trial. Six of the seven had been released in the mid-1980's. The seventh died in prison.

Most controversial was the case of the "Birmingham Six," who had been sentenced to life imprisonment for the IRA bombing of two public houses in Birmingham in 1974; 21 people were killed. Waddington ordered an inquiry into claims that police had altered statements. On Aug. 29, 1990, he ordered the case to be reheard for the second time.   Ian J. Mather

See also **Ireland.** In *World Book,* see **Northern Ireland.**

Northwest Territories. Protection of the fragile Arctic environment was a main concern in the vast Northwest Territories in 1990. An environmental review panel made up of federal and Inuit (Eskimo) appointees issued a harsh indictment of the federal government's ability to deal with a possible major oil spill in the Beaufort Sea. The panel stated that further drilling in the sea should be halted until nine new guidelines for oil exploration had been put into effect. This stopped plans by Gulf Canada Resources Limited to drill an exploratory well north of the mouth of the Mackenzie River. In the eastern Arctic, the territorial government put on hold a proposal for a uranium mine near Baker Lake.

The federal government and native peoples worked out agreements in principle on two major land claims in April 1990. One agreement was negotiated with the 17,000 Inuit. If formally approved, it would transfer control of 663,000 square kilometers (256,000 square miles) of land to the Tungavik Federation of Nunavut Settlement. The second settlement was offered to the 13,000 Dene Indians and *métis*, people of mixed Indian and white blood, inhabiting the Mackenzie River Valley. It would transfer 181,000 square kilometers (70,000 square miles) of land to the Dene and métis and grant them compensation of $500 million Canadian ($430 million U.S.). A joint native assembly rejected the agreement on July 18.   David M. L. Farr

In *World Book,* see **Northwest Territories.**

Norway in 1990 debated whether to apply for membership in the European Community (EC or Common Market). The issue, which had simmered for years, boiled up during the year as the other Scandinavian countries demonstrated growing interest in seeking EC membership.

On October 29, the dispute brought down the center-right coalition government led by Prime Minister Jan P. Syse. Syse, a Conservative, resigned after he lost the support of the two small parties in his three-party coalition. The two opposed his moves to permit more foreign investment in Norway and to relax immigration laws. Both moves were intended to bring Norway closer to EC policies.

A center-left government was formed by Gro Harlem Brundtland, who began a third term as prime minister on November 3. Her Labor Party lacked a parliamentary majority. But she was able to win support for a minority government because Norwegian law permits the parliament to be dissolved—and new elections to be held—only once every four years. In the last elections, in 1989, the Labor Party had fared poorly, and Brundtland's government had fallen.

While serving as prime minister from 1986 to 1989, Brundtland had become Norway's best-known politician abroad, largely because of her concern for such environmental problems as global warming and inter-country pollution. But her international popularity seemed unlikely to help her narrow the rift among Norwegians about how closely their country should be integrated with the rest of Europe.

EC or not. Brundtland was thought to favor EC membership. But her party was largely opposed to it because some of Norway's income from petroleum exports would be diverted to poorer EC nations, jeopardizing Norway's high standard of social services. Politicians were anxious to postpone a showdown on the EC question, mainly because of the divisive debate that had surrounded a 1972 national referendum in which EC membership was narrowly rejected. Pockets of resistance to EC membership remained among groups that feared opening Norwegian society to greater immigration and other outside influences. Some Norwegians also appeared reluctant to see a larger international role thrust upon their country.

Government leaders had hoped to get around the problem by creating an enlarged trading area made up of the 12-nation EC and the 6-nation European Free Trade Association, of which Norway is a member. But that approach ran into trouble in 1990, as eastern European nations sought their own EC links.

As national debate quickened, a key shift occurred in the spring when the right wing Progress Party came out in favor of EC membership. Its new policy increased pressures on the government to adopt a stronger pro-EC attitude.   Joseph Fitchett

See also **Europe** (Facts in brief table). In *World Book,* see **Norway.**

Nova Scotia. Premier John Buchanan resigned on Sept. 12, 1990, to accept an appointment to the Canadian Senate. Some political analysts said that Prime Minister Brian Mulroney gave the seat to Buchanan, a Progressive Conservative, as a reward for support of the failed Meech Lake constitutional accord (see **Canada [Close-Up]**).

At the time of the appointment, the Royal Canadian Mounted Police were investigating Buchanan's government for allegedly having illegally given government contracts to political allies. Buchanan was succeeded by the province's deputy premier, Roger S. Bacon. Bacon agreed to serve until the Conservatives chose a new leader at their February 1991 party convention. See **Bacon, Roger Stuart.**

A provincial Royal Commission harshly criticized the Nova Scotia judicial system on Jan. 26, 1990, for discriminating against Indians and blacks. The commission had been called to review the amount of compensation offered Donald Marshall, Jr., a Micmac Indian, whom an earlier trial showed had been imprisoned for 11 years for a murder he did not commit. The Nova Scotia government apologized to Marshall for his mistreatment, awarded him more than $700,000 Canadian ($600,000 U.S.) in compensation, and promised to implement 82 changes to the judicial system recommended by the commission.   David M. L Farr

See also **Canada.** In *World Book,* see **Nova Scotia.**

Nuclear energy. See Energy supply.

Nujoma, Sam (1929-   ), a former rebel leader who spent nearly 30 years in exile from his native Namibia, was elected that African nation's first president on Feb. 16, 1990. He was sworn in on March 21, the day that Namibia officially became independent of South Africa, which had ruled the country since seizing it during World War I (1914-1918). Although Nujoma had long been a Marxist, he promised that Namibia would combine state and private enterprise.

Nujoma was born on May 12, 1929, in a village in the northern part of South West Africa, as Namibia was then called. After finishing his primary education at a mission school, he moved to Windhoek, the capital city, and worked as a clerk in a railway office. While there, he became an opponent of South African rule. He organized protests against the government and was a leader of a nationwide strike in 1959.

Government authorities ordered Nujoma banished in 1960, but he fled into exile before the order was carried out. He was elected in absentia to head the South West Africa People's Organization (SWAPO), a rebel group. Nujoma launched a SWAPO guerrilla war for Namibian nationhood in 1966, directing military activities from outside the country. Hostilities ended with a cease-fire in April 1989, and Nujoma returned to Namibia the following September.

Nujoma and his wife, Kovambo, whom he married in 1956, have four children.   David L. Dreier

Nutrition. See **Food.**

Ocean. Oceanographers launched their largest scientific effort ever in January 1990, after more than seven years of planning. The World Ocean Circulation Experiment (WOCE) will combine the efforts of scientists from some 40 nations to conduct the first comprehensive survey of the physical properties of the ocean. The 10-year program will employ several satellites, dozens of ships, hundreds of floating platforms, and thousands of instruments to profile the circulation of heat, water, and chemical compounds in the ocean.

WOCE is expected to be a boon to future ocean research. In the past, oceanographers have been greatly hampered in their understanding of large-scale ocean processes because they lacked uniform, consistent data on the world oceans. Previous measurements were taken at widely scattered places and times. For many regions, data are nonexistent.

As part of the World Climate Research Program, WOCE will gather data important to understanding the world's climate patterns. The information will first be used in developing improved computer models of the ocean. These models will then be coupled with models of the atmosphere to simulate—and, it is hoped, to predict—how the ocean and atmosphere interact to influence climate change over the course of seasons, years, and decades.

Another international investigation concerning the global climate became fully operational in summer 1990. The program, the Joint Global Ocean Flux

A Japanese government researcher unveils an experimental robot designed to inspect building sites on the ocean floor.

Ohio

Study, was designed to improve understanding of the role marine organisms play in the cycling of carbon dioxide between the ocean and the atmosphere. This knowledge will help researchers determine how the ocean will moderate increases in the concentration of carbon dioxide in the atmosphere.

Both programs were stimulated in part by international concern about global warming. The burning of fossil fuels such as coal, oil, and natural gas increases the levels of carbon dioxide and other gases that trap heat in the atmosphere. Scientists predict that the build-up of these gases may eventually lead to a worldwide increase in average temperatures.

Deep-sea drilling. During a spring 1990 expedition, scientists aboard the Ocean Drilling Program's research vessel, the *JOIDES Resolution*, drilled cores in the Pacific Ocean's Ontong Java Plateau. The Ocean Drilling Program is an international project operated by Texas A&M University in College Station.

The Ontong Java Plateau straddles the equator due east of New Guinea. Scientists believe that the formation was created from volcanic outpourings in the South Pacific that slowly shifted north during the course of more than 100 million years. As the plateau moved, it accumulated the skeletons of microorganisms that once thrived near the ocean's surface and settled onto the plateau after they died.

The Ocean Drilling Program researchers removed fossil-laden sediment cores that chronicled the changes in sea level, sea chemistry, organic productivity, and bottom- and surface-water temperatures. The sediment record thus documents how climates have changed over long periods of time.

Drift nets in the Atlantic. Huge fishing nets of the kind that ignited international protest in the Pacific Ocean were spotted for the first time in the western Atlantic and Caribbean in summer 1990. The nets, used by Asian fishing ships, extend more than 30 miles (48 kilometers) behind fishing vessels and hang vertically to a depth of 30 feet (9 meters). Conservationists blame use of the nets for depleting commercial fish stocks and indiscriminately killing porpoises and large migratory fish. A United Nations resolution adopted in December 1989 had called for a worldwide moratorium on the use of drift nets after June 1992 and an immediate halt to expansion of the practice.

Treasure. On Aug. 14, 1990, a U.S. district judge in Norfolk, Va., awarded the richest sunken treasure ever found—worth more than $1 billion—to a group of treasure hunters from Columbus, Ohio. Since September 1989, the group had been retrieving gold bars and coins from the wreck of the *Central America*, sunk off the Carolinas in 1857. Nine insurance companies and New York City's Columbia University had claimed a share of the treasure.   Arthur G. Alexiou

In *World Book,* see **Ocean.**

Ohio. See **State government.**

Oklahoma. See **State government.**

Old age. See **Social security.**

Olympic Games. After five secret ballots, the International Olympic Committee (IOC) on Sept. 18, 1990, chose Atlanta, Ga., to host the 1996 Summer Olympic Games. In previous years, the IOC selected Barcelona, Spain, for the 1992 Summer Games; Albertville, France, for the 1992 Winter Games; and Lillehammer, Norway, for the 1994 Winter Games.

Atlanta won over Athens, Greece; Toronto, Canada; Melbourne, Australia; Manchester, England; and Belgrade, Yugoslavia. Atlanta officials projected raising $1.4 billion from private sources, such as television rights and commercial sponsorships, and spending $1.2 billion to hold the games. The officials said any profits would go to fund sports programs.

The Goodwill Games, an Olympic-type competition, were held from July 20 to Aug. 5, 1990, in Seattle and nearby cities. The competition attracted 2,500 athletes from 52 nations in 21 sports, including full teams from the United States and the Soviet Union. Soviet athletes led the Americans in gold medals (66 to 61) and total medals (188 to 161).

When these games were first held in Moscow in 1986, they lost $26 million. The 1990 version lost $44-million. The Turner Broadcasting System, however, which co-owned rights to the games with Soviet television, said they would be held again in 1994 in Moscow and Leningrad.   Frank Litsky

In *World Book,* see **Olympic Games.**

Oman. See **Middle East.**

Ontario voters removed the Liberal Party from its majority position and elected Robert K. Rae as the province's first-ever New Democratic Party (NDP) premier on Sept. 6, 1990. The NDP increased its strength in Ontario's Legislative Assembly from 19 to 74 of 130 seats. Rae succeeded David Peterson, who resigned as Liberal leader. Peterson, who had been premier since 1985, headed a government backed by 93 seats. The election reduced that number to 36. The Progressive Conservatives, campaigning under recently chosen leader Michael Harris, gained 3 seats in 1990, for a total of 20 seats in the legislature.

The NDP platform called for a redistribution of wealth in the province and a revamping of the tax system. Its tax proposals included a minimum 8 per cent tax on business profits, as well as a tax on individual incomes earned from real estate speculation and on inheritances of more than $1 million Canadian ($860,000 U.S.). The NDP proposed programs to limit rent increases, to provide reduced-interest loans to small businesses, and to establish government-managed automobile insurance.

Many political commentators believed that the election results represented dissatisfaction with older traditional political parties rather than approval of NDP policies. Some voters felt Peterson called the election two years early to avoid fallout from a forthcoming investigation into alleged party irregularities. The trial of former Liberal fund-raiser Patricia Starr, a key fig-

A plane drops fire-retardant chemicals on a blaze near Hagersville, Ont., in February, when millions of tires burned for more than two weeks.

ure in allegations of misuse of campaign funds, was to begin just after the elections. In calling the early vote, Peterson also was thought to be avoiding the consequences of a predicted recession in the province.

On a wider level, analysts believed the vote went against Peterson for supporting Prime Minister Brian Mulroney on the unpopular Meech Lake constitutional accord (see **Canada [Close-Up]**).

Rae, who took office on October 1, had served in the federal Parliament before being chosen head of the Ontario NDP in 1982. His 25-member cabinet included an unprecedented number of women—11—in such high-profile ministries as environment, health, and education. See **Rae, Robert Keith.**

The new government was faced with high interest rates, record numbers of bankruptcies, and slow growth in the manufacturing sector. Many experts felt the deteriorating economy would make it difficult for the NDP to implement its proposed social legislation.

Sunday closings. Legislation prohibiting Sunday shopping, except in designated tourist areas and in consenting municipalities, was declared unconstitutional by the Ontario Supreme Court on June 22. The court held that the legislation violated the rights of those people who did not observe Sunday as a religious holiday.   David M. L. Farr

See also **Canada; Toronto.**
Opera. See **Classical music.**
Oregon. See **State government.**

Pacific Islands. Political developments in Fiji and Papua New Guinea were the most significant events in the Pacific Islands during 1990.

The Fiji islands in 1990 remained under the control of an interim government established in 1987, after two military coups ousted the elected government of Timoci Bavadra and revoked the Constitution. Ratu Sir Kamisese Mara continued in 1990 as interim prime minister, saying he would step down when new general elections are held under a new constitution.

The new Constitution became effective on July 25. It was a modification of an earlier draft that coup leader Major General Sitiveni Rabuka said did not sufficiently safeguard the political interests of the country's ethnic Fijians. Fijians comprise about 48 per cent of the population of 781,000; another 46 per cent are Fiji-Indians, the descendants of people brought to Fiji from India as laborers.

The Constitution renamed the island the Sovereign Democratic Republic of Fiji. It calls for a 70-seat House of Representatives, with 37 seats reserved for Fijians, 27 for Fiji-Indians, 5 for other groups, and 1 for the island of Rotuma. Candidates for these seats will be listed by ethnic groups, each on a separate ballot.

A 34-member Senate of Chiefs, most of whom will be Fijians, will be appointed by the president, who is head of state. The prime minister must be a Fijian who has the support of a majority of the Fijian members of the House of Representatives. The president must be

Facts in brief on Pacific Island countries

Country	Population	Government	Monetary unit*	Foreign trade (million U.S.$) Exports†	Imports†
Australia	16,930,000	Governor General Bill Hayden; Prime Minister Robert Hawke	dollar (1.29 = $1)	43,200	48,600
Fiji	781,000	President Ratu Sir Penaia Ganilau; Prime Minister Ratu Sir Kamisese Mara	dollar (1.45 = $1)	312	454
Kiribati	71,000	President Ieremia Tabai	Australian dollar	5	22
Nauru	9,000	President Bernard Dowiyogo	Australian dollar	93	73
New Zealand	3,404,000	Governor General Dame Catherine Tizard; Prime Minister James B. Bolger	dollar (1.66 = $1)	8,900	7,500
Papua New Guinea	4,112,000	Governor General Sir Serei Eri; Prime Minister Rabbie Namaliu	kina (0.95 = $1)	1,400	1,200
Solomon Islands	340,000	Governor General Sir George Lepping; Prime Minister Solomon Mamaloni	dollar (2.54 = $1)	80	102
Tonga	98,000	King Taufa'ahau Tupou IV; Prime Minister Prince Fatafehi Tu'ipelehake	pa'anga (1.29 = $1)	9	60
Tuvalu	9,000	Governor General Tupua Leupena; Prime Minister Bikenibeu Paeniu	Australian dollar	1	3
Vanuatu	170,000	President Fred Timakata; Prime Minister Walter Lini	vatu (114 = $1)	16	58
Western Samoa	177,000	Head of State Malietoa Tanumafili II; Prime Minister Tofilau Eti Alesana	tala (2.26 = $1)	10	52

*Exchange rates as of Dec. 7, 1990, or latest available data. †Latest available data.

appointed by the Fijian Great Council of Chiefs to ensure that a Fijian will be chosen.

In publicizing the Constitution, President Ratu Sir Penaia Ganilau said Fiji had tried to build a multiethnic society since its independence from Great Britain in 1970. But the main ethnic groups had not assimilated. He said the general election would be held within 18 months.

Adi Kuini Bavadra, widow of the ousted prime minister and leader of the multiethnic coalition in opposition, attacked the Constitution as "racist and feudalistic." She called for an election boycott.

Papua New Guinea. The rebellion on the island of Bougainville, which began in 1988, continued in 1990. The rebellion began when a militant group called the Bougainville Revolutionary Army and a number of traditional landowners demanded the closing of a big copper mine operated by Bougainville Copper Limited. The rebels also demanded that $12 billion be paid to Bougainville residents for environmental damage caused by mining operations and that the island be given independence from Papua New Guinea.

The mine was shut down in May 1989 because of the violence, and it remained closed in 1990, greatly reducing the government's income from royalties and exports. When it was operating, the mine produced 45 per cent of the government's export income and 20 per cent of the government's revenues.

Prime Minister Rabbie Namaliu, frustrated in his ef-

forts to negotiate a peace settlement, in early January ordered a major offensive against the rebels. More than 100 rebels and soldiers died. In April, the government withdrew its forces, and in early May, it began an economic blockade of the island.

On May 17, one of the rebel leaders, Francis Ona, declared independence for Bougainville and established himself as interim president of the "Republic of Bougainville." Prime Minister Namaliu rejected the declaration and promised to continue to search for a solution to the revolt.

On August 5, talks were held between the government and the rebels aboard a New Zealand warship. The government agreed to end the blockade and restore services to Bougainville. The rebels agreed not to press their declaration of independence. More talks would be scheduled to discuss Bougainville's future. No talks, however, had been held by year-end.

The Republic of Nauru continued its legal claim in 1990 against Australia to finance the rehabilitation of phosphate lands mined before July 1, 1967. That was the date when the republic took over the phosphate monopoly from the Australian-managed British Phosphate Commissioners. The claim states the damaged lands comprise one-third of Nauru's land area.

Nauru gave Australia notice in 1989 that it would proceed with the action unless the two countries came to an agreement. On April 20, 1990, the republic filed an outline of its arguments in the International Court of Justice. Australia denied responsibility and must present a defending statement by Jan. 21, 1991.

New Caledonia. After several years of violence, New Caledonia was peaceful in 1990. Under the terms of the 1988 Matignon Accord, a referendum in 1998 will determine the future system of government for this French territory. The agreement was made between the *Kanaks*, descendants of the original Melanesian inhabitants, and the ethnic French citizens. Kanaks favor independence from France, and the ethnic French prefer to remain a territory.

At the annual meeting of the South Pacific Forum in Port-Vila, Vanuatu, in August, a committee was set up comprised of ministers from Fiji, Nauru, and the Solomon Islands to ensure that the French government implements the Matignon Accord. Forum members are leaders of all the independent island nations.

Palau. On Feb. 6, 1990, a Palau referendum to endorse the Compact of Free Association between Palau and the United States failed to pass for the seventh time in seven years. Under the compact, the United States would give $1 billion in aid over 50 years in return for defense rights, but the United States wants an antinuclear clause in Palau's Constitution removed. The Constitution states that its provisions cannot be overridden without the approval of three-fourths of the voters.   Stuart Inder

In *World Book,* see **Pacific Islands.**
Painting. See Art.

Pakistan. Prime Minister Benazir Bhutto lost power in 1990, and Nawaz Sharif succeeded her as prime minister on November 6. On August 6, President Ghulam Ishaq Khan had dismissed Bhutto's government, accusing the regime of corruption, abuse of power, and overall incompetence. He named as caretaker prime minister Ghulam Mustafa Jatoi, a former member of Bhutto's Pakistan People's Party (PPP) who had become an opposition leader. Ishaq Khan also dissolved the National Assembly and called for elections to be held on October 24.

Bhutto called the actions a "constitutional coup" by a military and bureaucratic establishment that had resented her since she came to power 20 months earlier. During her tenure, Bhutto had sharp disagreements with the armed forces over the government's policies toward India, Afghanistan, and internal disturbances.

After Bhutto's ouster, the new government filed corruption charges against her and her Cabinet ministers. Bhutto's husband, Asif Ali Zardari, a wealthy businessman, was imprisoned on October 10 on charges of kidnapping, extortion, and loan fraud. But many Pakistani newspapers questioned the fairness of the government's campaign to discredit Bhutto, given the nation's long history of widespread corruption.

In the October elections, the PPP won only 45 of the 207 contested seats in the National Assembly. Bhutto charged the opposition, the Islamic Democratic

In a shower of flower petals, Nawaz Sharif campaigns before Pakistan's October elections. He became prime minister after his coalition's victory.

Paleontology

Alliance (IDA), with widespread vote-rigging and the theft of ballot boxes. But a 40-member team of foreign observers found no evidence to substantiate her claim.

The IDA, which won 105 Assembly seats, was a coalition of right wing parties including the Pakistan Muslim League and Jatoi's National People's Party. By forming an alliance, the two parties avoided splitting the vote; in the 1988 elections, they had competed, giving the PPP the largest bloc in the Assembly with less than 40 per cent of the popular vote.

Elections for provincial assemblies, held on October 27, were the most violent in Pakistan's history, with more than 33 people killed. The IDA won 208 of 240 seats in the nation's most populous province, the Punjab, while the PPP won only 10. The PPP fared poorly even in Bhutto's home province, Sind.

On November 6, the National Assembly elected Sharif—who was president of the IDA—prime minister. He was sworn in the same day. See **Sharif, Nawaz.**

The economy suffered after the United States on October 1 cut off some $580 million in foreign aid because of its suspicion that Pakistan was developing nuclear weapons. Iraq's August 2 invasion of Kuwait cost Pakistan about $1 billion more, due to higher oil costs and the lost earnings of Pakistani workers in the Persian Gulf region.   Henry S. Bradsher

See also **Asia** (Facts in brief table). In *World Book,* see **Pakistan.**

Paleontology. Some of the most ancient birds were good fliers and not gliders or land dwellers, an analysis of a 135-million-year-old bird fossil found in China has revealed. The bird, whose discovery was reported in October 1990, is 10 million years older than the oldest previously known modern-looking bird.

The finding has provided new support for the theory that birds evolved from small, feathered dinosaurs that walked upright. According to paleontologist Paul Sereno of the University of Chicago, who helped reconstruct the fossil, the sparrow-sized bird looked like—and could fly like—most living birds but had some characteristics of dinosaurs, such as teeth.

The fossilized bird is only 10 million years younger than *Archaeopteryx*, a creature believed to have been an evolutionary link between birds and dinosaurs. This suggests that birds developed the ability to fly early in their history.

Whale legs. Fossil bones discovered in an ancient seabed in Egypt are the first direct evidence that primitive whales had functional hind legs and feet, according to a report published in July. Paleontologists had long theorized from anatomical studies of ancient and modern whale skeletons that the direct ancestors of whales lived on land and walked on four legs.

The newly discovered leg fossils belong to a species of whale called *Basilosaurus isis*, which had a serpentlike body about 50 feet (15 meters) long. It lived about 40 million years ago, 10 million years after

A newly found 135-million-year-old fossil of one of the most ancient birds, shown in the drawing above, revealed that the bird was a good flier.

whales first appear in the fossil record. By that time, whales' front legs had evolved into flippers, similar to those of modern whales.

A team of paleontologists headed by Philip D. Gingerich of the University of Michigan at Ann Arbor reported that the fossilized hind leg measured about 24 inches (60 centimeters) from the top of the upper limb bone to the tip of the longest of three toes. The leg was probably always flexed at the knee and, when not in use, folded back against the whale's body.

The scientists concluded that *Basilosaurus'* hind legs were too small to have been used in swimming. They speculated that the legs may have helped the animals remain stable during mating.

Armored "slugs." The discovery of the first complete fossils of some of the oldest known animals, reported in June, may reveal new information about the development of external skeletons. The fossils, found in Greenland, belong to a group of animals called *halkieriids*, which lived about 550 million years ago.

The scientists who discovered the fossils reported that halkieriids were sluglike animals about 2 inches (5 centimeters) long covered with scales that served as armor. The scientists also found that the animals had a circular shell at either end of their body. The halkieriids may have lived in U-shaped burrows and used their shells as shields to protect the exposed ends of their body.   Carlton E. Brett

In *World Book,* see **Paleontology.**

Panama. For Panamanians, 1990 began on a high note, as people surged into the streets on January 3 to celebrate the surrender of dictator Manuel Antonio Noriega to United States authorities. There were hopes of massive U.S. assistance to rebuild the ailing Panamanian economy and of a new democratic future under President Guillermo Endara. Endara, who won the May 1989 elections only to see the results voided by Noriega, was sworn in as president on Dec. 20, 1989, as U.S. forces massed to invade.

But as 1990 progressed, there was less cause for cheer. Panamanians became increasingly angry at delays in receiving promised U.S. assistance. To protest the delays, Endara began a hunger strike that lasted 13 days, ending on March 13. Not until April did the U.S. Congress approve $43 million to rebuild neighborhoods destroyed during the invasion, a tiny sum in Panamanian eyes. And it was not until May 25 that Congress approved, with strings attached, $420 million of the $1 billion in aid that U.S. President George Bush had requested in January.

Body count. Panamanian claims for damages and loss of life resulting from the U.S. invasion continued to be a source of controversy. Officials of the former Noriega government said 8,000 Panamanian civilians were killed. An Independent Commission of Inquiry, headed by former U.S. Attorney General Ramsey Clark, said that more than 3,000 Panamanians died. And Clark charged that there was a "conspiracy of si-lence" to cover up the actual death toll. Another source, Fernando Guardia, vicar of the Roman Catholic archdiocese of Panama, called such estimates "irresponsible and baseless." Americas Watch, a U.S.-based human-rights group, estimated about 300 deaths, while the United States Southern Command, which led the invasion, reported 314 Panamanian soldiers and 202 civilians killed.

On December 5, U.S. military forces still In Panama assisted in recapturing Colonel Eduardo Herrera Hassán, a disgruntled former police chief, who mounted a small rebellion with about 100 followers. Herrera, who escaped from prison to lead the revolt, said its purpose was to obtain better working conditions and higher salaries for police officers.

Drug trade. By midyear, there were numerous reports that despite Noriega's ouster, Panama's drug-trafficking network was back in action. "The size of the problem is really frightening," said Rodrigo Arosemena de Roux, head of Panama's customs agency. "I don't think we . . . had any idea how much drug traffic is going through here."

Noriega trial. Noriega was arraigned on drug-trafficking charges in Miami, Fla., on January 4. During his 20-minute appearance at a U.S. federal courthouse, he responded politely to a judge's questions, while refusing to enter a plea. Noriega's lawyers argued that he was a "political prisoner" immune from prosecution in the United States.

United States drug agents escort deposed Panamanian dictator Manuel Antonio Noriega onto a plane that flew him to Miami, Fla.—and jail—in January.

For much of 1990, Noriega's lawyers sought compensation for his defense. The freezing of his assets following the invasion, they said, had made this impossible. On May 5, U.S. District Court Judge William M. Hoeveler agreed with them. He ruled that the U.S. government had no right to seize Noriega's assets without first proving that he had obtained them illegally. The judge said Noriega should be able to use for his defense any money he earned legally from his dealings with the U.S. government.

Noriega's lawyers then issued a subpoena to obtain records of the estimated $11 million Noriega allegedly earned during the years when he was a paid informant of the U.S. Central Intelligence Agency (CIA). The CIA's reluctance to provide a record of those payments led to a deal whereby the U.S. government offered to pay Noriega's legal bills if Noriega's lawyers agreed to withdraw the subpoena. On May 24, however, Judge Hoeveler ruled that the deal was illegal because the U.S. government is limited by law to pay no more than $75 per hour; Noriega's lawyers reportedly expected as much as $300 per hour.

According to a newspaper report, Noriega was being held in a comfortable three-room suite—complete with color television, copying machine, safes, and paper shredder—in a separate building of a Florida prison. After the story of his preferential treatment broke in *The Miami Herald* on October 24, 72 members of Congress sent an angry letter to the director of the Bureau of Prisons.

The Cable News Network on November 8 aired portions of secret U.S. government tape recordings of conversations between Noriega and his lawyers. The Supreme Court of the United States upheld the network's right to broadcast the tapes. On December 8, Hoeveler made public a transcript of the recordings.

Banking secrecy. United States authorities and the new government of Panama quarreled during 1990 over the issue of Panama's liberal banking laws, which have long made Panama a haven for U.S. tax evaders and drug traffickers. In August, the two countries reached a preliminary agreement whereby Panama would provide the United States with access to evidence needed to prosecute such offenders.

The agreement had to be approved by Panama's National Assembly, but it ran into trouble with legislators who saw it as a violation of Panama's national sovereignty. Many high-level Panamanian officials who either are or have been directors or owners of banks tied to the laundering of drug profits opposed the measure. The release of about $84 million of the $420 million in U.S. aid was contingent on Panama's ratification of the agreement and further inflamed the issue.   Nathan A. Haverstock

See also **Endara, Guillermo; Latin America** (Facts in brief table). In *World Book,* see **Panama.**
Papua New Guinea. See **Asia; Pacific Islands.**
Paraguay. See **Latin America.**
Pennsylvania. See **Philadelphia; State government.**

Peru. Alberto Fujimori, the son of Japanese immigrants, was sworn in for a five-year term as Peru's president on July 28, 1990. An expert in farm management and a former university official, Fujimori beat the favored candidate, novelist Mario Vargas Llosa, in a runoff election on June 10. In 1988, Fujimori had helped found the Cambio 90 (Change 90) party, which made him its candidate in the 1990 election. During the campaign, he promised a fight against corruption and accused former government officials of enriching themselves while in office.

As president, Fujimori faced serious problems: a treasury that was $100 million in the red, an annual inflation rate of more than 3,500 per cent, and a foreign debt of $17.5 billion for the highest per capita debt in South America. Fujimori moved boldly. Amid tight security on the day of his inaugural, he replaced the commanders of the navy and air force. The former was reputedly involved in a coup attempt against Fujimori; the latter was accused of corruption.

Before assuming office, Fujimori met on June 29 and 30 in New York City with officials of the International Monetary Fund (IMF), an agency of the United Nations. He succeeded in hammering out an agreement whereby Peru could "rejoin the world economy," reversing the policy of his predecessor, Alan García Pérez, who angered the IMF by refusing to make debt payments.

Fujimori lost little time in making good on his commitments to the IMF. On August 8, he imposed the most drastic austerity program in Peru's history. It included a 3,000 per cent increase in the price of gasoline, a tripling of the cost of bread, and an end to subsidized prices for energy and transportation.

The stern measures proved traumatic for many Peruvians, especially the more than 33 per cent of the population mired in poverty. Their immediate concern was how to get enough to eat. In Lima, the capital, the number of soup kitchens increased from 1,000 at the beginning of August to 7,000 by the end of August. Some hungry slumdwellers took matters into their own hands and sacked food markets.

Terrorism and drugs. On August 14, guerrillas detonated a bomb at the presidential palace, while Fujimori, who was unhurt, was inside. It appeared that rebels were renewing their 10-year-old uprising following a pause for elections. Their terrorist actions had left 700 dead, including a former defense minister, in the first three months of 1990.

In September, Fujimori turned down $35 million in United States military aid for the fight against drugs because of his opposition to a purely military solution to the problem. On October 26, he proposed an alternative strategy for coping with the drug problem by encouraging peasants to switch from growing coca to growing legal crops.   Nathan A. Haverstock

See also **Fujimori, Alberto; Latin America** (Facts in brief table). In *World Book,* see **Peru.**
Pet. See **Cat; Dog.**

Petroleum and gas. The price of crude oil and of gasoline and other products made from petroleum soared after Iraq invaded Kuwait on Aug. 2, 1990, and seized control of its oil fields. Oil prices, which stood at about $22 per barrel on August 1, climbed to more than $40 per barrel on October 9—the highest price since 1980. In an effort to force Iraq to withdraw from Kuwait, the United Nations imposed an embargo on oil exports from the two countries (see **Middle East**).

Before the invasion, Iraq and Kuwait produced about 4.4 million barrels of oil per day. During the first half of 1990, world oil production averaged 61 million barrels per day. Kuwait's crude oil reserves totaled about 97 billion barrels, or 9.7 per cent of known world oil reserves.

After reaching their October high, oil prices fluctuated widely for the rest of the year, rising when war seemed imminent, declining when a peaceful settlement of the crisis seemed possible. At year-end, the average price of oil was about $28 per barrel.

Gas price jump. Although the United States had obtained only about 9 per cent of its imported oil from Iraq and Kuwait, domestic gasoline prices soared after the invasion. Prices rose from a nationwide average of $1.07 per gallon (3.8 liters) on August 1 to almost $1.40 by mid-October.

The price hikes led to sharp criticism of U.S. oil companies by Congress and consumer groups. But oil industry executives, called before Congress on August 7 to explain the higher prices, claimed that higher world oil prices forced the increases. They said that the cost of the petroleum to U.S. companies was determined at the time of its delivery to refineries, not at the time the oil was contracted for in the Middle East. As a result, they said, prices could rise steeply in a short time.

OPEC boosts output. Fears of a world oil shortage eased somewhat on August 29 when the Organization of Petroleum Exporting Countries (OPEC) suspended its production quotas and authorized members to pump to capacity during the Persian Gulf crisis. Three members of the 13-nation oil cartel—Iraq, Iran, and Libya—opposed the move. The action raised OPEC's production by about 4 million barrels per day, nearly replacing the oil lost because of the embargo.

OPEC's decision to suspend quotas came only a month after the cartel's ministers agreed to halt overproduction and raise the price of oil immediately from $18 to $21 per barrel. On July 17, Iraq's President Saddam Hussein had threatened to take military action against Kuwait and the United Arab Emirates unless they quit exceeding their oil production quotas. Hussein said that continual cheating by the two countries had led to falling oil prices and lower oil revenues for all OPEC members.

Oil reserve sale. United States President George Bush on September 26 approved the sale of 5 million barrels of oil from the Strategic Petroleum Reserve (SPR). The SPR, located in underground caverns along the coasts of Louisiana and Texas, held 590 million

A gas station attendant raises pump prices to reflect the jump in the cost of oil that followed Iraq's invasion of Kuwait in August.

barrels of oil in 1990, enough to meet U.S. oil needs for 73 days. Government officials said, however, that the sale was a test of the SPR's pumping system, rather than an effort to stabilize oil and gas prices.

Crude oil production in the United States continued to decline during 1990, the Department of Energy (DOE) reported on September 26. The United States produced an average of 7.3 million barrels per day during the first eight months of 1990, compared with 7.6 million during the same period in 1989. Crude oil imports continued to rise, averaging 6.3 million barrels per day during the first eight months of 1990, compared with 5.8 million during the same period in 1989.

Domestic natural gas production rose slightly in 1990. The DOE said that 10.2 trillion cubic feet (288 billion cubic meters) of gas was produced during the first seven months of 1990, compared with 10.1 trillion cubic feet (286 billion cubic meters) in 1989. About 848 billion cubic feet (24 billion cubic meters) was imported during the period, up from 765 billion cubic feet (21.7 billion cubic meters) in 1989.

Saudi oil find. The Arabian American Oil Company, Saudi Arabia's state-owned oil company, announced on Oct. 14, 1990, the discovery of extensive new oil fields that could increase the kingdom's reserves by more than 50 billion barrels. Before the oil strike, Saudi Arabia had 257.5 billion barrels of *proven reserves,* more than any other country and about 25 per cent of the world's total. Proven reserves consist of known oil that can be recovered economically with existing technology.

Double-hulled tankers. Conoco, Incorporated, on April 10 became the first oil company to announce that all its new oil tankers would be built with double hulls to help prevent oil spills. Double-hulled tankers have an outer hull separated by an air space from the body of the tanker in which the oil is stored. Such vessels are said to be less likely to rupture and spill their oil if they run aground or are involved in a collision. Oil companies had resisted adopting the design because of the vessels' higher costs and concerns about their stability during accidents. In August, Congress passed a law requiring most tankers and barges to have double hulls by 2015.

Cleanup plan. The oil industry on Sept. 6, 1990, announced a five-year, $800-million program to improve its ability to clean up major offshore oil spills. Under the plan, the industry would establish response centers on the East, West, and Gulf coasts, where cleanup equipment and personnel would be located. The centers would be activated during a major oil spill. The new program replaces a less comprehensive emergency response program announced by the oil industry in 1989, after the oil tanker *Exxon Valdez* hit a submerged reef in Alaska's Prince William Sound, causing the largest oil spill in U.S. history.

Drilling ban. President Bush on June 26, 1990, announced a ban on offshore oil drilling in environmentally sensitive areas of the East and West coasts. The ban placed about 99 per cent of the California coast off-limits to oil and natural gas production until at least the year 2000. It also curtailed drilling in Georges Bank, a fertile fishing area off Boston, and in areas off Florida, Oregon, and Washington state.

Canadian development. A group of oil firms headed by Mobil Oil Canada Limited on September 14 signed a $4.5-billion agreement with the governments of Canada and Newfoundland to develop Canada's largest offshore oil project. Under the agreement, drilling was to begin in 1996 in the huge Hibernia oil field, about 200 miles (320 kilometers) southeast of St. John's, Nfld. Production was expected to continue for about 20 years, with a peak output of 110,000 barrels per day. The Canadian government agreed to contribute about $2.3 billion in cash and loan guarantees. Most of the oil would be shipped to refineries in the Northeastern United States.

The project was to include the construction of a gigantic $1.4-billion oil pumping platform in an area off Canada's eastern coast known as "Iceberg Alley" because of the many icebergs that pass through. The platform reportedly will be able to withstand direct hits by even massive icebergs.

The Soviet Union remained the world's largest oil producer in 1990, with an average output of 11 million barrels per day. But shortages of drilling equipment and economic problems forced the Soviets to seek foreign help to expand production. As a result, several U.S. oil companies gained access to some of the Soviet Union's richest oil reserves.

In May, the Soviets gave Chevron Corporation exclusive rights to drill for oil in a huge, newly discovered field near the Caspian Sea. Geologists believe the field contains 20 billion to 25 billion barrels of oil. In August, Texaco Incorporated won exploration and development rights to one of the world's largest undeveloped oil fields, located in the far northwestern Soviet Union near the Arctic Circle. The area may contain 5 billion barrels of oil.

Flushing oil. Scientists from Texaco on August 28 reported the development of a more economical means of *chemical flooding* to recover billions of additional barrels of petroleum from existing oil fields. Chemical flooding involves injecting detergentlike chemicals into underground oil reservoirs.

The chemicals wash oil out of rock in much the same way that laundry detergents remove oil and grease from fabric. The use of chemical flooding had been limited by the high cost of the chemicals. But Texaco scientists said they had developed a process for producing the chemicals cheaply, using wood by-products from the manufacture of paper. They predicted that the widespread use of chemical flooding could increase U.S. oil reserves, estimated at 26.8 billion barrels, by 150 billion barrels.   Michael Woods

In **World Book,** see **Gas; Gasoline; Petroleum.**

Philadelphia found itself tottering toward insolvency in 1990. The cash crisis was the result of a shrinking tax base caused by the flight of middle-class Philadelphians to the suburbs combined with soaring costs of social services and a sharp decrease in federal assistance. Although those trends had been going on for years, by 1990 they had come to pose a serious threat to the city's continued well-being.

With the city's treasury rapidly running out of money, the administration of Mayor W. Wilson Goode spent much of the year seeking a solution to the predicament. City officials said that to balance the budget for fiscal 1991, which began on July 1, 1990, the city would need $206 million more than could be raised from taxpayers, state and federal aid, and other sources of income. Without the additional money, they said, city services would have to be curtailed.

Many businesses and universities, including some of the largest employers in Philadelphia, agreed to prepay about $50 million in wage taxes—the taxes that they deduct from their employees' paychecks—to help the city through its budget crisis. The City Council also debated such proposals as imposing a local sales tax and borrowing money from municipal unions. Normally, the city sells short-term loan notes to get through tight periods, but because its financial problems in 1990 were more severe than usual, investors would not buy the notes. In September, an attempt to sell $375 million in notes collapsed.

A bequest from Ben Franklin. The city got a bit of help with its money woes in 1990 from the most famous Philadelphian of them all, Benjamin Franklin. Franklin left 2,000 British pounds—equivalent to about $1 million in today's money—in trust when he died in 1790. His will stated that the money should be divided equally and, with accrued interest, should go to the states of Massachusetts and Pennsylvania and the cities of Boston and Philadelphia to help young people get started in business or to pay for public works. Some of the money was to be dispensed after 100 years and the remainder after 200 years. In 1990, the trust funds, containing about $6.5 million, were paid out. The Pennsylvania-Philadelphia trust, consisting of about $2 million, was less than half as large as the Boston account because the trustees in Massachusetts reportedly handled their portion more wisely.

Mayor Goode appointed a panel to decide how the city's share of the money—about $520,000—should be used. In August, he approved a proposal to spend part of it to help young people learn crafts or trades. Another share of the money will be awarded to people who have demonstrated excellence in the practice of their craft.

Subway crash. On March 7, a subway train carrying morning rush-hour passengers derailed below Market Street, one of the city's major thoroughfares, killing 4 people and injuring more than 160. The crash was the worst subway accident in the city's history.

The six-car train dropped a motor from underneath the third car, tripping a switch on the tracks and causing three cars to derail. The most heavily damaged car, the fourth, slammed broadside into a steel beam that supports the underground train line.

New orchestra conductor. The board of directors of the Philadelphia Orchestra announced in September that Wolfgang Sawallisch will become the orchestra's new music director, beginning with the 1993-1994 season. Sawallisch, who currently holds the same position with the Bavarian State Opera in Munich, Germany, will succeed Riccardo Muti, the Philadelphia Orchestra's music director since 1980. Muti said he would resign in 1992 to have more time for himself.

Sawallisch first led the Philadelphia Orchestra as a guest conductor in 1970. Since then, he has returned often, and many members of the orchestra named him as their first choice to replace Muti.

Renovation completed on landmark tower. On Aug. 22, 1990, the last piece of scaffolding was removed from the tower atop City Hall, as a five-year renovation of the Philadelphia landmark was concluded. Workers replaced most of the tower's corroding iron plates and gave the structure four thick coats of gray paint. The tower is itself topped by Philadelphia's preeminent statue—of William Penn, the founder of Pennsylvania. The cost of the project was $25 million, about what it cost to build the entire City Hall in 1871, when construction began.   Howard S. Shapiro

See also **City.** In *World Book,* see **Philadelphia.**

Philippines. The threat of an uprising by rebellious soldiers loomed over the Philippines throughout 1990. The nation also suffered a severe earthquake and economic troubles. For many citizens, the belief that President Corazon C. Aquino was indecisive and ineffective in dealing with such problems created apprehension about the future.

Army revolt. On October 4, Colonel Alexandre Noble, a former senior officer in Aquino's presidential guard, led a take-over of two army bases on Mindanao island. Noble had been a leader of the most serious previous rebellion, which the government put down in December 1989. Other military rebel groups failed to support Noble's 1990 attempt, and he surrendered to loyal troops on October 6.

The other rebel groups accused the government of representing the interests of the nation's social and political elite rather than the increasingly poor masses. But observers said the rebels were bandits more interested in their own welfare than that of the public. More than 40 terrorist bombings in Manila, the capital, in August and September were attributed to the groups' efforts to destabilize Aquino's government.

Communist guerrillas, long considered the chief threat to the government, had by 1990 become less dangerous than military rebels, Defense Secretary Fidel V. Ramos said on August 30. According to the government, internal purges and pressure from the Philippine army had apparently demoralized the Communist New People's Army (NPA), whose fighting force declined from 25,600 in 1988 to about 19,000 in 1990.

As the NPA's hold on rural areas weakened, it began campaigns of urban terrorism, assassinating government officials. In May, the NPA murdered two United States airmen on the eve of talks between U.S. and Philippine officials on the future of U.S. military bases in the Philippines. The NPA also kidnapped an American Peace Corps volunteer and a Japanese aid worker on the island of Negros. The hostages were held for two months and released on August 2.

An earthquake on July 16 killed more than 1,650 people. The quake destroyed the mountain resort city of Baguio and heavily damaged other towns north of Manila. Army officers were accused of stealing relief supplies, and news media said Aquino's government inadequately responded to the tragedy.

Economic downturn. On October 1, Finance Secretary Jesus P. Estanislao blamed the earthquake for a ballooning government budget deficit. He said the deficit forced the government to abandon a fiscal reform program to improve economic conditions and enable the repayment of foreign debt.

After the Iraqi invasion of Kuwait, remittances from Filipinos working in the Persian Gulf region were sharply reduced, and the cost of imported oil soared. As a result, officials cut their expectations of economic growth in 1990 from 6 per cent to just 3.2 per cent. Such a level would not be enough to improve living standards for the quickly growing population.

Costumed as skeletons, Philippine protesters in May call for the removal of United States military bases from the Philippines.

The 1992 presidential election was the focus of much political activity in 1990. With Aquino saying she would not enter the race, Vice President Salvador H. Laurel and former Defense Minister Juan Ponce Enrile jockeyed for position. Aquino's cousin, Eduardo (Danding) Cojuangco, Jr., also prepared to run despite facing some 20 civil and criminal charges linked to his service in the government of former President Ferdinand E. Marcos.

Courts. On July 2, a jury in New York City acquitted Marcos' widow, Imelda, of fraud and other charges. The prosecution had accused Marcos of robbing the Philippine treasury during her husband's presidency.

In the Philippines, a special court on September 28 convicted 16 soldiers of the 1983 murder of Aquino's husband, Benigno S. Aquino, Jr., who had been the main political opponent of Marcos. The soldiers, who were also convicted of killing the man initially blamed for Aquino's murder, were sentenced to life imprisonment. Twenty other defendants were acquitted. The trial failed to determine who ordered the murder.

American military withdrawal. Aquino said on September 17 that her government would work with the United States to arrange an orderly withdrawal of U.S. military forces from bases in the Philippines. In negotiations that began the next day, U.S. officials sought a 10-year phase-out.   Henry S. Bradsher

See also **Asia** (Facts in brief table). In *World Book*, see **Philippines**.

Physics. A long-standing mystery deepened in 1990: Why does the sun seem to produce fewer neutrinos than scientists think it should? New neutrino detectors have so far uncovered few clues about these elusive subatomic particles, but they have focused attention on an important problem in physics.

Neutrinos have no electric charge and little or no mass and travel at or near the speed of light. Nuclear fusion reactions deep inside the sun generate neutrinos. In these reactions, four hydrogen nuclei fuse in several steps to form a helium nucleus. This leads to the emission of heat, light—and neutrinos. From the rate at which the sun radiates energy, scientists can estimate how many neutrinos should reach the earth every second. But neutrinos interact so feebly with other forms of matter that nearly all of them pass through the earth without reacting with anything. Unless a neutrino reacts, it cannot be detected.

The Homestake detector. Since 1968, a team of scientists headed by Raymond Davis, Jr., now at the University of Pennsylvania, has monitored neutrinos using a huge tank of perchloroethylene, a dry-cleaning fluid, far below ground in the Homestake Gold Mine in South Dakota. Every few days, a nucleus of chlorine 37 in the tank absorbs a neutrino and is converted into radioactive argon 37. The team measures argon from the tank every few months. Year after year, the experiment has detected less than one-third of the number of argon atoms expected.

The Homestake detector works quite simply and has been carefully tested, and so errors in the experiment are unlikely to explain the neutrino deficit. This leaves two possibilities: Either the sun does not produce neutrinos at the rate expected, or something happens to neutrinos on their way to the earth.

Energy production at the heart of the sun may rise and fall in cycles, even though the sun's radiant energy—the heat and light emitted at its surface—remains nearly constant. Yet it seems impossible to account for so many missing neutrinos by a lowered energy production, and so speculation centers on what might happen to the neutrinos. One possibility is that solar neutrinos are converted into other neutrinos that Homestake cannot detect. The sun produces electron neutrinos, one of three kinds of neutrino. (The others are muon neutrinos and tau neutrinos.)

To complicate matters further, the Homestake team has found hints of a correlation between neutrino production and the cycle of *sunspots*—dark regions on the sun that reach a maximum number every 11 years. The fewest neutrinos are observed when sunspot activity peaks. This puzzles scientists because sunspots are a surface phenomenon, akin to weather on the earth, and should have little effect on neutrino production deep in the sun's interior.

The Kamiokande detector —an enormous tank of water deep in a lead mine in Japan—has provided data on solar neutrinos since 1987. As neutrinos collide with electrons in the water molecules, they trigger a tiny flash of light. Light-sensitive tubes on the tank's inner wall detect these flashes.

Kamiokande estimates a neutrino rate about 60 per cent higher than Homestake's but still less than half the expected rate. The detector also has observed no drop in neutrino rates, though sunspot activity has risen. By April 1990, however, Kamiokande had observed only 128 collisions, and so deviations from the Homestake results may not be statistically significant.

Less than 10 per cent of solar neutrinos have high-enough energies to be detected at Homestake. The number is less than 1 per cent for Kamiokande. In contrast, more than half of the solar neutrinos can trigger a reaction that turns the rare element gallium into radioactive germanium.

Two gallium detectors began operation in 1990. The Soviet-American Gallium Experiment (SAGE) is located in an underground laboratory in Soviet central Asia. In August 1990, preliminary results from SAGE suggested an even lower neutrino rate than Homestake found. GALLEX—a joint effort of Italy, France, the United States, Germany, and Israel—operates in an underground laboratory in central Italy. The group spent 1990 tuning and testing its detector. The first results from GALLEX were expected early in 1991.

More sensitive neutrino detectors now on the drawing boards may solve the mystery before the year 2000.   Robert H. March

In *World Book*, see **Neutrino; Physics.**

Poetry. Anthony E. Hecht and Mark Strand, both among the half dozen best active American poets, each brought out a new collection in 1990.

The Transparent Man displays Hecht's virtues—wit touched with sadness, unexpected rhyme, and delicate flow of line and meter. The highlight of this new collection is a stunning long poem about the breakup of a marriage, "See Naples and Die." The poem concludes with a playful-seeming but apt and powerful flourish: "Crabs limping in their rheumatoid pavane."

The Continuous Life showcases Strand's variety: prose poems, comic ballads, and slices of life. This poetry combines a conversational swing with an easygoing intellectual quality, praising and echoing such past writers as Franz Kafka, Anton Chekhov, and Virgil. The poems provide something for every taste. Many of Strand's poems tell stories, such as "One Winter Night," which opens, "I showed up at a party of Hollywood stars/Who milled about, quoted their memoirs, and drank." In that poem, things quickly get rowdy. Such down-to-earth poetry resulted in Strand's appointment as United States poet laureate in 1990.

Charles Simic received the Pulitzer Prize in 1990 for his 1989 collection of prose poems, *The World Doesn't End*. In 1990, his *The Book of Gods and Devils* came out in traditional verse marked by the same gentle wit and winsomeness in its representations of life in New York City. Outstanding in the new collection is a long poem that opens with a moving tribute to British lyric

Mark Strand, author of eight books of poetry, became the fourth poet laureate, or official poet, of the United States in 1990.

Poetry

poet Percy Bysshe Shelley, "Poet of the dead leaves driven like ghosts."

In *Distance from Loved Ones*, James Tate writes funny poems with images that might have come from dreams: "On another planet, a silvery starlet is brooding/on her salary" (from "Trying to Help"). They prove amusing to read, though sometimes elusive in sense.

House of Light by Mary Oliver explores in simple, clear lines the pleasures and paradoxes of nature. *The Mail from Anywhere* displays Brad Leithauser's much talked-about skill in poems on such diverse topics as tropical sunsets and Chinese firecrackers. A poem on Icelandic glaciers begins, with impressive sound effect, "The sheerly steadied stubborn tons of it."

Stephen Dobyns writes novels as well as poetry, and several of the best poems in *Body Traffic* tell stories. One begins, "I was driving to pick up my daughter from day care." It goes on to discover a moment of understanding and serenity, surprisingly, when a fat, clumsy man sings an old rock song.

In other notable new works of 1990, Amy K. Clampitt's *Westward* offers her beautifully lush verse, forcing words and images to their limits. J. D. McClatchy's *The Rest of the Way* reveals in his "An Essay of Friendship" and in a sequence of sonnets about terrorism in the Middle East that the skills of this poet have been underestimated. Poems in Michael Ryan's *God Hunger* range from an account of a burglary to a tale of losing contact lenses while swimming. Li-Young Lee's *The City in Which I Love You* reflects on life in Indonesia and the United States.

Collections of past work. *In the Western Night: Collected Poems 1965-90* combines Frank Bidart's first two autobiographical collections with later work, in which he favors dramatic recitations. Bidart's verse looks raggedy on the page—he uses many capital letters—and his poems mix free verse, half lines, and straight prose. A long, almost Miltonic new poem is "The First Hour of the Night."

Several other retrospective volumes stood out in 1990, including the collected poems of the late James Wright; Cid Corman's *Of;* and Charles Wright's *The World of the Ten Thousand Things: Poems 1980-1990*. Wright's recent work shows him thinking seriously about everything from the Southern United States to the Chinese poet Li Po.

Translations. Much of the best U.S. poetry of recent years has come to readers as translations. Robert Fagles' 1990 version of Homer's *Iliad* is easy flowing, faithful to its Greek original, and modern. So, too, is Allen Mandelbaum's translation of Homer's *Odyssey*.

Anthologies. The 1990 edition of *The Best American Poetry* (Macmillan), edited by Jorie Graham and David Lehman, gives a first-rate overview of the year in poetry. McClatchy's *The Vintage Book of Contemporary American Poetry* offers brief selections from poets active since 1945.   Michael Dirda

In *World Book*, see **Poetry.**

Poland took another big stride toward democracy on Nov. 25, 1990, when it held its first popular election for president. No candidate received the 50 per cent majority needed for election, though Lech Walesa, leader of the labor union Solidarity, outran all rivals with nearly 40 per cent of the vote. In the December 9 runoff, Walesa defeated Stanislaw Tyminski, a wealthy businessman, 75 per cent to 25 per cent.

The new president took office on December 22 and became the first non-Communist to hold the office since World War II (1939-1945). Walesa succeeded Wojciech Jaruzelski, an army general who had led the country since 1981. In September 1990, Jaruzelski announced he would step down to clear the way for an election.

The leading candidates for the office could hardly have been more different. Walesa had little formal education but extraordinary political instincts. As founder of the Solidarity movement that had overthrown the Communist government in 1989, he presented himself as a man with the "moral right" to be president. Tyminski, hitherto unknown, emerged as a dark horse in the last days of the campaign. He had lived outside Poland from 1969 until a few weeks before the election and had made his fortune running businesses in Canada and Peru. Claiming it was time for a change, Tyminski won support from frustrated Poles. His showing dismayed backers of Prime Minister Tadeusz Mazowiecki, Walesa's adviser in Solidarity,

Angry farmers blockade major roads in Poland on July 11 to protest government reforms that eliminated price supports on farm products.

Lech Walesa, the first popularly elected president in Poland's history, greets supporters shortly before winning the December 9 runoff election.

who came in third. An intellectual with an unassuming manner, Mazowiecki rejected Walesa's promise of easy solutions to Poland's economic woes.

Tyminski benefited from the split between the two former allies in Solidarity. Walesa had moved from support for Mazowiecki's government to opposition, complaining that political reform was moving too slowly.

Sweeping economic reforms instituted on January 1 gave Poland the most market-oriented economy in eastern Europe. The measures eliminated price controls and devalued Poland's currency, the zloty, by 32 per cent. Thus, the year began with the first in a grim round of price hikes. The International Monetary Fund (IMF), an agency of the United Nations, had promised aid if Poland restructured its economy. To tide Poland over until it received IMF aid, the leading industrial nations established a $1-billion emergency fund.

The reforms caused economic hardships for many, as prices soared. *Real income*—that is, wages adjusted for inflation—dropped by almost one-third. Long-scarce goods suddenly became available, but most people lacked money to buy them. Unemployment, virtually unknown under the Communists, rose as companies streamlined their work forces and inefficient firms were shut down. By year's end, more than 1 million Poles were jobless. Inflation, however, fell below 2 per cent in August, though it rose later in the year as a result of higher oil prices.

The government, buoyed in August by an IMF rating of "excellent" for its performance, remained confident that its policies were on course. It showed a record trade surplus of $3.4 billion for the first nine months of 1990.

Adding to the economic difficulties were cuts in Soviet oil deliveries announced for 1991, along with reduced Soviet purchases of Polish coal. The official government newspaper said in September that oil deliveries in the next year would fall by 21 per cent and that making up the shortfall would cost Poland about $500 million. Because of its own cash shortage, the Soviet Union was also expected to curtail purchases of Polish machinery and clothing.

German unification stirred anxiety among Poles as some German leaders seemed to question the location of Poland's western border with Germany. For that reason, Poland did not rush to join Czechoslovakia and Hungary in seeking an early withdrawal of Soviet troops from its soil. West German President Richard von Weizsäcker, however, assured Poles on May 2, 1990, that the current border was "irrevocable." On November 14, following unification, Germany and Poland signed a treaty guaranteeing the current border. In the meantime, the Soviet Union agreed to complete the withdrawal of some 40,000 soldiers from Poland early in 1991.   Eric Bourne

See also **Walesa, Lech.** In *World Book*, see **Poland.**
Pollution. See **Environmental pollution.**

New Kids on the Block, a top group in 1990, perform one of their hit songs during their May concert at Giants Stadium in East Rutherford, N.J.

Popular music. A legal controversy over whether the lyrics of some popular music are obscene erupted almost immediately as 1990 began. Guidelines set by the Supreme Court of the United States say an artistic work can be judged obscene if it lacks serious artistic merit, patently offends local community standards, and appeals primarily to lustful interests.

In January, Florida attorney Jack Thompson began a campaign against the album *As Nasty as They Wanna Be* by the rap group 2 Live Crew. Thompson considered the album obscene because of its descriptions of sexual organs and activities and because he believed it promoted violence against women. He sent copies of the album to 65 Florida sheriffs and to the governor, who publicly denounced it as obscene. The recording company then filed suit against the Broward County sheriff, charging that he had violated its First Amendment rights against prior restraint of publication. The sheriff had threatened to bring criminal actions against stores attempting to sell the album.

After months of hearings, U.S. District Judge Jose A. Gonzalez, Jr., ruled on June 6 in Fort Lauderdale, Fla., that the lyrics were obscene, though he upheld the complaint against the sheriff. Many record stores pulled the album from their shelves. Charles Freeman, however, a Fort Lauderdale record store owner, was arrested on June 8 after he sold a copy of the album. He was convicted in October and in December was fined $1,000 plus court costs.

The leader of 2 Live Crew, Luther Campbell, and two band members were arrested on June 10 in a Hollywood, Fla., nightclub for performing songs from *As Nasty as They Wanna Be*. At the October trial, the jury declared them not guilty of obscenity charges stemming from the performance. The jury foreman said that the tape recording of the performance, the key piece of evidence, was difficult to understand.

Labeling lyrics. In response to growing concern about obscenity in popular music lyrics, the Recording Industry Association of America, a trade organization, instituted in July an advisory sticker policy. The label reads "Parental Advisory—Explicit Lyrics" and is placed on recordings that deal with sex, violence, suicide, drug use, bigotry, and satanism. Record companies and artists will decide if a new release should carry the label.

Subliminal messages. A state court in Reno, Nev., addressed the issue of *subliminal*, or subconscious, messages in rock lyrics in July 1990. The families of two dead young men claimed the two shot themselves after listening to a record by the heavy-metal rock group Judas Priest. The judge was asked to determine if alleged subliminal messages on the album, *Stained Class*, led to a suicide pact by the two youths. Some of the messages were said to be clearly audible only when the record was played backward. The messages allegedly included the repeated phrase "Do it." On Dec. 23, 1985, the young men, aged 18 and 20, smoked marijuana and drank beer while listening to songs by Judas Priest, such as "Beyond the Realms of Death." After agreeing to a suicide pact, they went to a churchyard and shot themselves. One died instantly; the other recovered, but died in 1988. Judge Jerry Whitehead ruled on August 24 that Judas Priest was not responsible for the deaths. He said there was no proof that the messages had caused the two youths to shoot themselves.

Grammy taken away. Milli Vanilli was stripped of its 1989 Grammy Award for best new artist on Nov. 19, 1990, because the two performers did not sing on their album *Girl You Know It's True*. This was the first time the National Academy of Recording Arts and Sciences withdrew an award. The performers, Rob Pilatus and Fab Morvan, merely mouthed the words at concerts. The actual singers on the album were Johnny Davis, Brad Howell, and Charles Shaw.

Causes. A star-studded July performance of Pink Floyd's "The Wall" drew 320,000 to a Berlin benefit for a worldwide disaster fund. A June concert in England at Knebworth enlisted such superstars as Paul McCartney, Eric Clapton, and Phil Collins in funding programs for handicapped children and a school for performing arts. In April, Earth Day festivities in New York City's Central Park to promote awareness of dangers to the environment featured performances by the B-52's and Hall & Oates before a crowd of 750,000. Also in April, Farm Aid IV in Indianapolis raised more than $1.3 million.

Mainstream artists. Sinéad O'Connor from Ireland, Alannah Myles from Canada, and Mariah Carey from the United States hit the number-one spot on the pop singles charts. O'Connor's "I Do Not Want What I Haven't Got" was her second hit to reach the top spot. The trio Wilson Phillips was a rookie chart-topper; its debut album sold 3 million copies.

New Kids on the Block's number-one album *Step by Step* sold more than 3 million copies. George Michael's single "Praying for Time" struck a timely chord as it topped the charts in August 1990 during the crisis over Iraq's invasion of Kuwait. Another huge hit was Madonna's "Vogue," which paved the way for her appearance in the motion picture *Dick Tracy* (1990) and her spectacular "Blond Ambition" concert tour. *Janet Jackson's Rhythm Nation 1814* album continued to yield hits for Jackson, whose first concert tour, with the same name, was also a hit.

Revising the rankings. Grammy winner Bonnie Raitt's album *Nick of Time* became that highly respected artist's first number-one album in April; she has had 20 years of only modest sales. The title also made history by being the last release to rank number one on *Billboard* magazine's Top Pop Compact Discs (CD) list. Beginning in April, the publication merged CD's with its regular categories to reflect "the complete integration of the CD into mainstream sales."

Alternative artists were led by the B-52's, whose *Cosmic Thing* album reached *double-platinum*

Born in Ireland, Sinéad O'Connor captured the American spotlight and number one on the 1990 charts with "Nothing Compares 2 U."

status—that is, 2 million albums sold. Depeche Mode also finally enjoyed mainstream acceptance, and independent label hard rock group Sonic Youth became a major act. Jane's Addiction soared with *Ritual de lo Habitual*, aided, perhaps, by a controversial album cover. Record stores could choose between two covers, a solid white one with the band's name across it or one with three nude figures, two female and one male, realistically made of papier-mâché.

Hard rock and heavy metal. Jon Bon Jovi's solo debut, *Blaze of Glory*, reached number one. *Family Style*, the first studio collaboration by brother guitarists Stevie Ray Vaughan and Jimmie Vaughan, was acclaimed at its release shortly after Stevie Ray's tragic death in a helicopter crash in August. Making big comebacks on albums and tours were AC/DC, Judas Priest, and ZZ Top.

Rap acts. M. C. Hammer had hit singles, videos, and sneaker commercials and dominated the pop album chart all summer with *Please Hammer Don't Hurt 'Em*. Vanilla Ice became the first rap artist to have a number-one pop single with his "Ice Ice Baby." Other smash rap singles included Digital Underground's "Humpty Dance" and Mellow Man Ace's bilingual "Mentirosa."

Rhythm and blues. Luther Vandross's pop crossover single "Here and Now" brought him his greatest recognition. Other prominent adult-oriented black artists included Anita Baker, Regina Belle, and Dianne

Population

Reeves, whose second album, *Never Too Far*, topped the contemporary jazz album chart.

Dance music was highlighted by albums featuring dance remixes by Paula Abdul and Bobby Brown. The genre also yielded successful female groups, including Seduction, Expose, and Cover Girls, as well as the breakthrough acts Snap and Deee-Lite.

Country music. Newcomers galore invigorated the country scene, including Alan Jackson, Mary Chapin Carpenter, Travis Tritt, and Doug Stone. Garth Brooks had the fastest-rising country album on the pop charts with his *No Fences*. The Kentucky HeadHunters scored unexpectedly high with its hard rock thrust.

Madonna video. In November, the cable channel MTV refused to play a clip of Madonna's sexually suggestive music video *Justify My Love*. But it was an immediate hit in stores when released for sale as a single in December.

Jazz. Harry Connick, Jr., with three albums on the pop chart, led a young generation of jazz musicians with traditional roots. Saxophonist Branford Marsalis, whose music was featured in Spike Lee's 1990 film *Mo' Better Blues*, pianist Marcus Roberts, trumpeter Roy Hargrove, saxophonist Christopher Hollyday, and keyboardist Joey DeFrancesco were among the top names in jazz.   Jim Bessman

See also **Awards and prizes** (Arts awards). In the World Book Supplement section, see **Rock music**. In *World Book*, see **Country music; Jazz; Popular music**.

Population. The world's population reached approximately 5.3 billion in 1990, according to the United Nations (UN) Fund for Population Activities, whose annual population survey was released in May. The UN statisticians estimated that the global population will increase at a yearly rate of 1.7 per cent—or about 90 million people—until at least 1995. The population is expected to exceed 6.2 billion by 2000 and to level off by 2100 somewhere between 11.3 billion and 14 billion.

Birth rates. Fertile women in the developing world give birth to an average of 3.9 children each during their childbearing years—appreciably less than the average of 6 children in the early 1960's, but still far above the rate in industrialized nations. There, women give birth to an average of 1.9 children each. In some Western European countries, the rate is as low as 1.58.

Life expectancies remained highest in industrial nations. A child born in the United States in 1989 is likely to live 75.2 years, according to a 1990 estimate by Metropolitan Life Insurance Company. This is more than 25 years longer than the average life expectancies in some nonindustrialized nations, including Afghanistan, Guinea, and Sierra Leone. The highest life expectancies in the world are in Japan—about 79 years—and in Iceland—about 77 years.   Jinger Hoop

See also **Census**. In *World Book*, see **Life expectancy; Population**.

Portugal. Prime Minister Aníbal Cavaço Silva shuffled his cabinet on Jan. 2, 1990. Deputy Prime Minister and Defense Minister Eurico de Melo resigned, and Cavaço Silva replaced four other ministers and appointed Fernando Ferreira Real to the newly created post of minister of the environment.

Among those replaced was Finance Minister Miguel Ribeiro Cadilhe, who was considered largely responsible for policies increasing the private sector's involvement in the economy. In 1989, Cadilhe had been accused of evading taxes, but an investigation cleared him of the charge. He was succeeded by Miguel Beleza, director of the Bank of Portugal.

The cabinet reorganization followed the governing party's poor showing in local elections two weeks earlier, on Dec. 17, 1989. The Social Democratic Party (PSD) won only 31.5 per cent of the vote—compared with 50.2 per cent in Portugal's 1987 general election. The opposition Socialist Party (PS) won the largest share of the vote, 32.3 per cent.

The PSD's declining popularity was partially attributed to Portugal's economic problems. After Portugal joined the 12-nation Economic Community (EC or Common Market) in 1986, the government began encouraging private enterprise and selling state-owned industries to private investors. Foreign investment soared, and the nation experienced rapid economic growth and low unemployment. But Portugal remained the poorest nation in the EC, and inflation was a continuing problem.

Inflation. In 1989, Portugal's inflation rate was about double the average of western European nations. In early 1990, Portugal's annualized inflation rate was more than 13 per cent, chiefly due to a sharp rise in February. The government's efforts to combat inflation in part by rejecting wage increases for workers in the public sector led to labor strikes. Railroad engineers staged partial work stoppages in January, February, and March. Harbor pilots declared work stoppages in March as well.

As eastern European nations undertook their own economic reforms in late 1989 and 1990, many Portuguese officials became concerned that the EC would divert investment and aid from Portugal to eastern Europe. In a March meeting with French Prime Minister Michel Rocard, Cavaço Silva said that the EC should create a south European development program to ensure aid for the relatively poor nations of southern Europe.

Presidential election. On April 30, the PSD announced that it would not nominate a candidate to run against President Mário Alberto Soares—a member of the PS—in the presidential election scheduled for 1991. Three other candidates entered the race, but in the January balloting, Soares won reelection by a wide margin. Preliminary results gave him more than 70 per cent of the vote.   Jinger Hoop

See also **Europe** (Facts in brief table). In *World Book*, see **Portugal**.

Postal Service, United States. The United States Postal Service on March 6, 1990, requested an increase in mailing rates in 1991. Postmaster General Anthony M. Frank called for a 5-cent hike in the price of a first-class stamp, raising it from 25 to 30 cents. For all categories of mail, the increase would be about 20 per cent. Frank said the increases were necessary because the Postal Service was threatened with its biggest deficit ever in fiscal year 1990—as high as $1.6 billion. When the fiscal year ended on September 30, that projection was found overblown, but the deficit still approached $1 billion. The postmaster said the higher rates would generate an estimated $7 billion a year in added revenue. The independent Postal Rate Commission, which approves and sets rate hikes, was expected to act on the request by February 1991.

Cost-cutting moves. The Postal Service has spent more than $1 billion in recent years to automate mail handling, but the resulting savings in labor costs have been offset by higher outlays elsewhere, such as for employee health insurance. In an effort to improve service and gain new sources of revenue, the Postal Service made several customer-oriented changes in 1990. In February, the agency installed automated teller machines in selected post offices, and in May it started a 24-hour telephone line for ordering stamps. Also in May, postal officials introduced a pressure-adhesive plastic stamp that was to be tested for consumer acceptance for six months. But to further reduce operating costs, the Postal Service in July announced a slight reduction in the number of non-local overnight mail deliveries.

Moving to save $10 and $12 an hour per worker, the Postal Service announced a tentative plan on July 9 to contract out more than 12,000 new mail-sorting jobs by 1995. Assistant Postmaster General Peter A. Jacobson said the latest bar coding technology would allow workers at remote locations to process letters viewed on video screens. He said a remote letter-sorting system could save the Postal Service as much as $4.3 billion over 10 years. But many postal union members opposed the venture.

Contract talks. Negotiations on a new three-year contract for unionized postal workers began on August 24. Under the expiring contract, which ran through November 20, letter carriers received a starting salary of $24,381, and the average wage of all postal workers was $20 an hour, or $41,600 a year, not counting overtime pay. Glenn Berrien, president of the 50,000-member Mail Handlers Union, said workers deserved raises because layoffs in recent years forced many employees to do the work of two people. The contract talks were sent to binding arbitration on November 21 after negotiators failed to reach agreement.   William R. Cormier

In *World Book,* see **Post office; Postal Service, United States.**

President of the United States. See **Bush, George H. W.; United States, Government of the.**

Prince Edward Island. The dream of a fixed link between this island province and the Canadian mainland faded on Aug. 15, 1990, when a federal environmental review panel concluded that a proposed 13-kilometer (8-mile) bridge should not be built. The panel stressed the danger of the bridge blocking ice movement in the strait and damaging commercial fishing and the lobster catch. The panel recommended improved ferry service as an alternative to the bridge. Premier Joseph A. Ghiz said his government would continue to support a fixed link if strict environmental standards could be met.

The Canadian Forces air base at Summerside, P.E.I.—scheduled to close in early 1992 as a result of military cutbacks—was slated to be turned over to a locally controlled corporation promoting the base's future economic use. On May 3, 1990, Prime Minister Brian Mulroney announced a decision that will help offset the expected loss of jobs. He said that a processing center for the new federal goods and services tax (GST) will be in Summerside. Scheduled to be in operation by late 1992, the center will create 500 jobs.

The Liberal Party government of Premier Ghiz presented its second surplus budget on March 13, 1990. The surplus was to be achieved by small increases in taxes on tobacco, liquor, and gasoline and diesel fuels; and a $1-a-night room tax at hotels and tourist facilities.   David M. L. Farr

In *World Book,* see **Prince Edward Island.**

Prison. Crowding continued to plague federal and state prisons in the United States in 1990 as the number of inmates swelled by 42,862—from 712,563 to 755,425—in the first six months of the year. The inmate population of federal institutions rose by 8 per cent, compared with a 5.8 per cent increase in the number of state prisoners; the overall increase was 6 per cent. The number of women held in U.S. prisons rose 7.1 per cent in the first six months of 1990, bringing their total to 43,541. Male inmates increased by 5.9 per cent to 711,884. To keep pace with the flood of new inmates, the already crowded prison system had to add about 1,650 beds a week.

On October 27, Congress passed a major crime bill that will provide $2 billion for federal, state, and local law enforcement and correctional facilities. President George Bush signed the bill into law on November 29. The new law will allocate at least $300 million in grants to states and municipalities for the development of alternatives to imprisonment, such as short-term "boot camp" programs, community work programs, and "home jailing" enforced by electronic monitoring of prisoners. The law also authorizes the armed forces to transfer four unused military installations a year to public agencies for use as correctional institutions.

Black men and the law. In February 1990, The Sentencing Project, a nonprofit organization that monitors the sentencing of criminals in the United

Many states have begun sending offenders to military-style "boot camps," such as the Moriah Shock Incarceration Correctional Facility in New York, *above*.

States, released a report on the number of black males in prison. Based on a study of U.S. Bureau of Justice Statistics figures, the report, *Young Black Men and the Criminal Justice System: A Growing National Problem*, generated considerable attention in the media. It revealed that 23 per cent of black American males between the ages of 20 and 29—almost 1 out of 4—were in prison or on parole or probation. By way of comparison, 6 per cent of white males and 10 per cent of Hispanic males in the same age group were serving time or under correctional supervision.

Death penalty. Twenty-three death-row inmates at American prisons were executed in 1990, bringing the number of executions to 143 since 1976, when the Supreme Court of the United States reinstated capital punishment.

Debate about the constitutionality of the death penalty—the U.S. Constitution prohibits "cruel and unusual punishments"—was fueled by the execution in May 1990 of a Florida inmate, Jessie J. Tafero. Tafero had been sentenced to die in the electric chair for killing two police officers in 1976. Three jolts of electricity were required to kill Tafero, and the apparatus attached to his head gave off flames and sparks.

As of Dec. 31, 1990, more than 2,400 offenders were awaiting execution in state and federal prisons in the United States.   Linda R. Acorn

See also **Crime**. In *World Book,* see **Prison.**
Prizes. See **Awards and prizes; Nobel Prizes.**

Protestantism. Protestants sought to adjust in 1990 to the vast changes in the countries of eastern Europe. Some Protestant clergy who had taken leading roles against the Communist regime in East Germany gained high positions in the government after German reunification on October 3. The Protestant churches (Lutheran and Reformed) in the two Germanys had maintained contact during the four decades that the governments of the two countries were on opposite sides in the Cold War.

As the Soviet Union faced economic and political chaos in 1990, American evangelicals collected funds to carry on missions and distribute Bibles there. Veteran evangelical mission leaders expressed reservations, criticizing many for uncoordinated and hasty forays into the country; they called for more considered and responsive action.

Turmoil in South Africa. The release of black activist Nelson R. Mandela from a prison in South Africa on February 11 seemed to signal a change in the government's policy of *apartheid*, or strict racial segregation. But bloody battles broke out between followers of Mandela's African National Congress and the rival Zulu Inkatha forces led by Mangosuthu Gatsha Buthelezi. Buthelezi is a black Anglican church lay reader who publicly identifies himself with Christian causes.

On July 8, Allan Boesak, a Dutch Reformed minister and president of the World Alliance of Reformed

Churches (WAR), resigned his ministry after acknowledging that he was having an extramarital affair with the niece of a former South African Cabinet minister. Boesak was a leader in the antiapartheid movement. He subsequently resigned as president of the WAR and was succeeded by Jane Dempsey Douglass, a Princeton Seminary church historian.

Namibia's independence from South Africa on March 21 was celebrated by Namibia's many Protestant churches, including the Lutheran majority. Namibia was Africa's last colony. Protestant churches there had been rebelling against South Africa's apartheid policy almost since South Africa first seized Namibia from Germany in 1916.

Chinese tightrope. Bishop K. H. Ding, a Protestant who led the China Christian Council, walked a difficult path in China during 1990. He had supported the prodemocracy demonstrations in 1989, but to help ensure his church's survival in 1990, he had to muffle attacks on the government. He was criticized by some Western church leaders for his moderating stand and, at the same time, was under suspicion by the government for his actions.

In Guatemala, the evangelical right supported one of their own, retired General Efraín Ríos Montt, an evangelical preacher, for president. He had been president for 16 months in the early 1980's, after leading a military coup. His government was accused of some of the worst human-rights violations in Guatemala's history, and he was deposed in another coup in 1983. Before the Nov. 11, 1990, presidential election, the Guatemalan Court of Constitutionality ruled that Ríos Montt was ineligible to run as a candidate because the Constitution bans anyone who came to power as a dictator from being elected president. Another evangelical Christian, Jorge Serrano Elías, appeared to capture the votes of Montt's supporters, but not enough to win the election on the first round. Serrano did, however, win a runoff election on Jan. 6, 1991. He took office on January 14.

Abortion issue. Protestants in the United States remained divided on the abortion issue in 1990. Protestant prolife movements stepped up activities as politicians repositioned themselves, often in response to polls, for voting on abortion laws in state legislatures. In 1990 church conventions, some mainstream Protestant denominations moderated their prochoice positions. Yet these churches were still far from lining up in support of restrictive antiabortion legislation.

Conservative shifts. The old religious right, which saw many setbacks in recent years, put energies into family issues and campaigns against obscenity. James Dobson drew national attention with his Focus on the Family movement and strong stands against child pornography. Donald E. Wildmon and his American Family Association also gained prominence for supporting legislators who wanted to limit funding of the National Endowment for the Arts (NEA). A small number of NEA grants had subsidized exhibits and events that

Washington Cathedral's final stone was set on Sept. 29, 1990, exactly 83 years after the Episcopal church's first stone was laid.

Psychology

dren often gave first mention, in testing at the later intervals, to items that they had the most trouble remembering in the earlier tests. This was reported in July by a team of University of Arizona psychologists under the direction of Charles J. Brainerd. This finding contradicts the widely accepted psychological theory that items first recalled are those with a strong foothold in memory. It now appears, said Brainerd, that unconscious memory processes ensure the survival of weakly remembered items by calling them up first.

Brainerd and his associates studied the responses of nearly 1,000 children between the ages of 6 and 13. These children viewed a list of 12 to 24 items, such as nouns or simple pictures, and after a short break, they were asked to name as many items on the list as they could remember. This procedure was repeated up to five times for the same list. The children were tested again with the same lists two weeks later. They first recalled several "weak" items, those they had forgotten most often in previous trials, followed by "strong" items, those they had recalled most often in earlier tests. Finally, they remembered still other weak items. The same memory pattern appeared when these researchers analyzed responses from recall tests taken previously by 2,000 adults.

Brainerd suggested that this study has some practical implications for students taking school examinations. They might pull the maximum amount of information from their memories by answering the most difficult questions first. In the Special Reports section, see **Why Do We Forget? What Can We Do About It?**

Measuring beauty. Women and men may not be considered attractive because they have rare facial features. Instead, good-looking faces apparently represent the mathematical average of all faces of the same sex in a particular population. This was the conclusion reported in March by Judith H. Langlois of the University of Texas at Austin and Lori A. Roggman of the University of Arkansas at Fayetteville.

The two psychologists scanned two groups of photographs of college students, 300 male and 300 female, with a video lens connected to a computer, and selected 96 photos of each sex at random. The computer converted each of the 192 selected pictures into a series of tiny digital facial units with different numerical values. Each group of digitized pictures was divided into three sets of 32 faces. From each set, the computer then randomly chose two faces, mathematically averaged the two sets of facial units, and created a composite face of the two individuals. Composite faces were then generated from 4, 8, 16, and 32 digitized pictures from each set.

Groups of student judges attributed the most beauty to the 16- and 32-face composites and rated the composites as more attractive than virtually all of the individual faces. Even composites fashioned from both unattractive and attractive individual faces were rated as good-looking.   Bruce Bower

In **World Book**, see **Psychology.**

Public health. A major United States government report, issued on Feb. 27, 1990, urged for the first time that virtually all Americans adopt low-fat, low-cholesterol diets. Previously, federal health experts believed that such diets would be of the greatest benefit to people already at risk for heart disease because of high blood cholesterol levels. In its report, the National Cholesterol Education Program (NCEP) recommended that everyone over age 2 should substantially reduce consumption of fat and cholesterol. Americans should get no more than 30 per cent of their total calories from fat. This would be a decrease of about 15 per cent from the amount of fat most adults currently consume.

The report also recommended that Americans eat less than 300 milligrams of cholesterol a day. There are about 220 milligrams of cholesterol in an egg yolk. The NCEP estimated that the incidence of heart disease would decline by about 20 per cent if all Americans reduced their cholesterol levels by 10 per cent. About 6 million Americans have *atherosclerosis*, a narrowing of blood vessels in the heart that causes most heart attacks. About 1¼ million Americans have heart attacks each year.

The NCEP is a nationwide effort to inform the public and doctors about the health risks of high blood cholesterol. The new report was endorsed by 38 federal agencies and health groups, including the Food and Drug Administration (FDA) and the American Medical

Antonia C. Novello took office in March as the first woman and the first Hispanic surgeon general, the chief public-health officer of the United States.

Association. Officials said that no previous dietary guidelines had such broad support, and this was the first time the FDA endorsed such recommendations.

Measles cases up sharply. The U.S. Centers for Disease Control (CDC) in Atlanta, Ga., announced on Oct. 5, 1990, that there were 18,193 cases of measles reported for 1989. This was more than four times the number of cases in 1988 and more than any other year since 1978. The outbreaks led to 41 deaths, the most since 1971. The CDC said 6,650 cases occurred among preschool children and another 8,368 cases occurred among youths through age 19.

Syphilis. The CDC reported on Sept. 18, 1990, that the number of reported cases of syphilis increased 34 per cent between 1981 and 1989. Syphilis is a serious disease spread by sexual contact. The 1989 rate, 18 cases in every 100,000 people, was the highest since 1949.

Agent Orange study. A long-awaited CDC study of the herbicide Agent Orange, released on March 29, 1990, concluded that Vietnam veterans were at increased risk of developing only one rare form of cancer, non-Hodgkin's lymphoma. But, the CDC said, there is no evidence that this risk stems from exposure to Agent Orange. Veterans' groups criticized the study, insisting that it did not resolve questions about the health effects of exposure to Agent Orange during the Vietnam War, when the weedkiller was used to reveal Communist hiding places in the jungle and to destroy food crops. The Department of Veterans Affairs said, however, that it would honor disability claims from Vietnam veterans relating to non-Hodgkin's lymphoma, claims it had previously denied.

Smoke hazards to nonsmokers. On June 25, the U.S. Environmental Protection Agency (EPA) declared secondhand smoke to be a human *carcinogen*, a cancer-causing substance. The EPA concluded that passive smoking causes 2,500 deaths from lung cancer each year among American nonsmokers and 1,500 deaths each year among Americans who formerly smoked. Experts predicted that the findings would reinforce efforts to prohibit smoking in offices and public places.

Cancer death rates. Death rates from certain forms of cancer increased substantially between 1968 and 1987 in six industrialized countries, U.S. and British researchers reported on Aug. 25, 1990. In France, Great Britain, Italy, Japan, the United States, and West Germany, death rates rose from cancers of the breast, skin, brain, kidney, lymphatic system, and bone marrow. Increases were sharpest among people aged 75 to 84, rising by at least 15 per cent in all six countries. Increases for some cancers were dramatic, with brain cancer rates more than doubling and bone marrow death rates rising by 80 per cent. Researchers could not explain the increases, but they said the jumps were too great to result from improved diagnosis alone.   Michael Woods

See also **AIDS.** In *World Book,* see **Public health.**

Puerto Rico. Puerto Ricans focused their attention in 1990 on the United States Congress, where legislation that would permit them to vote on their future political status took a sizable step forward. On October 10, the U.S. House of Representatives approved a bill that would enable Puerto Ricans to decide the island's status in a referendum.

Under the terms of the House bill, the Puerto Rican legislature would determine if Puerto Ricans living in the United States could also vote in the referendum. The referendum would offer Puerto Ricans four options: a new commonwealth relationship with the United States, statehood, independence, or the choice of "none of the above." Puerto Rico currently is a commonwealth. The "new" commonwealth option would give Puerto Ricans somewhat more control over the island's affairs.

Hopes for an early 1991 referendum were dashed when the U.S. Senate failed to pass a companion bill because of the priority of other legislation and the opposition of key senators. Some senators complained that the House bill was too vague. The House passage, however, seemed to make it inevitable that Puerto Ricans would eventually decide their future by themselves.   Nathan A. Haverstock

In the Special Reports section, see **Puerto Rico—The 51st State?** See also **Latin America** (Facts in brief table). In *World Book,* see **Puerto Rico.**

Pulitzer Prizes. See **Awards and prizes.**

Quayle, Dan (1947-   ), 44th Vice President of the United States, often served as an overseas emissary of President George Bush in 1990. In January, Quayle represented the United States at the inauguration of Rafael Leonardo Callejas as president of Honduras and also visited Jamaica and Panama. United States troops had invaded Panama in December 1989 and ousted strongman Manuel Antonio Noriega. One purpose of Quayle's trip was to reassure Latin-American leaders that the Panama invasion would not set a precedent for similar action elsewhere. Mexico, Venezuela, and Costa Rica refused Quayle's offer of a January visit, fearing anti-American demonstrations. The Vice President, however, later visited Mexico and Venezuela.

On March 11, Quayle went to Chile for the inaugural of President Patricio Aylwin Azócar, who succeeded former dictator Augusto Pinochet Ugarte. Quayle drew criticism for being the only visiting democratic leader to meet with Pinochet. Quayle also traveled to Barbados, Paraguay, Argentina, Brazil, and Haiti in 1990.

In May, Quayle and his wife, Marilyn, headed a delegation that visited western Europe to mark the 100th anniversary of the birth of President Dwight D. Eisenhower.

On April 12, the Quayles reported they paid $25,479 in federal income taxes on a 1989 adjusted gross income of $133,696.   Frank Cormier and Margot Cormier

In *World Book,* see **Quayle, Dan.**

Residents of Quebec celebrate the failure of a proposed constitutional accord intended to keep the French-speaking province as part of Canada.

Quebec. The failure of the Meech Lake constitutional accord in 1990 brought political difficulties to Premier Robert Bourassa and his Liberal government (see **Canada [Close-Up]**). Committed to a working federal system, Bourassa faced supporters of a sovereign Quebec who argued that federalism was no longer a suitable option for the province. The premier responded to the question of Quebec's future in vague terms, describing a new "superstructure" for Canada, a loosened form of federation based on the western European model.

Bourassa met on June 29, 1990, with Jacques Parizeau, leader of the Parti Québécois (PQ), the party favoring independence, to set up a nonpartisan legislative commission entrusted with recommending a course for Quebec. The 35-member commission, drawn from the legislature and various sectors of Quebec society, was asked to report in March 1991. A September public opinion poll gave Bourassa's Liberal Party the support of 35 per cent of decided voters; Parizeau and the PQ, 43 per cent.

Finances. On August 30, Bourassa announced that Quebec would fall in line with the federal government's new 7 per cent goods and services tax (GST), due to take effect on Jan. 1, 1991—the first province to make this offer. The province's retail sales tax is to be broadened during 1991 and 1992 to tax all goods and services. For 1991, exemptions on clothes, shoes, and books will be ended. In 1992, services covered by the GST will be taxed. The province's own sales tax, at 9 per cent in 1990, will drop to 7 per cent by 1992. Quebec also agreed to collect the GST for Ottawa by 1992, a cost-saving measure for both governments.

On Sept. 12, 1990, Yves Séguin, minister of revenue and labor, resigned from the Bourassa cabinet in protest against the decision to support the GST. On October 5, Bourassa shuffled his cabinet, demoting two ministers who had been at the center of the summer's 11-week armed stand-off between the Mohawk Indians and the Canadian Army (see **Montreal**). Veteran minister Claude Ryan was appointed to the troubleshooting role of minister of public security, with responsibility for the provincial police, who had been criticized for their role in the Indian troubles.

The budget, announced on April 26, primed the slumping economy through increased support for public works and business ventures. The surtax on corporate profits was raised, though the extra revenue did not prevent the budget deficit from growing by $150 million Canadian ($130 million U.S.) to $1.75 billion ($1.5 billion U.S.). Quebec's allowances for newborn children were made more generous by raising payments for third and subsequent children from $4,500 to $6,000 ($3,900 U.S. to $5,200 U.S.). The payment for the first child is $500 ($430 U.S.); for the second, $1,000 ($860 U.S.).   David M. L. Farr

See also **Canada; Montreal.** In *World Book,* see **Quebec.**

Rae, Robert Keith (1948-   ), was sworn in as premier of the Canadian province of Ontario on Oct. 1, 1990. He is the first member of the New Democrats, Canada's socialist party, in that post. See **Ontario.**

Rae was born on Aug. 2, 1948, in Ottawa, Ont. His father was Canada's ambassador to Mexico and the United Nations. Rae moved around the globe with his family, attending schools in Ottawa; Washington, D.C.; and Geneva, Switzerland. While in Washington in the 1960's, Rae took on a paper route that included the house of future United States President Richard M. Nixon. As a college student, Rae led demonstrations against the Vietnam War. He received a law degree from the University of Toronto. After obtaining a graduate degree in politics from Oxford University, he worked in a housing and legal aid clinic in the slums of London, England.

Returning to Ottawa, Rae practiced law until 1978, when he was elected to Canada's House of Commons. He resigned his seat in 1982 when he became a member of the provincial legislature and was elected party leader. In 1989, after his brother had been diagnosed as having cancer, Rae donated bone marrow for a transplant in an attempt to save his brother's life. After the brother's death, Rae turned his energies toward seeking the post of premier.

One of Rae's favorite activities is watching Toronto Blue Jays baseball. He also plays guitar. Rae and his wife have three daughters.   Margaret Anne Schmidt

Railroad. Despite an unstable economy in the United States during 1990, particularly in the fourth quarter, traffic for the nation's major railroads increased. Railroads posted 967.8 billion ton-miles through the first 11 months of 1990, nearly 3 per cent better than for the same period in 1989. (A ton-mile is 1 short ton of freight carried a distance of 1 mile.) *Intermodal services* (the use of more than one mode of transportation to move goods) continued to grow in 1990 with several North American carriers adding terminals and equipment.

Fuel costs up. Railroads paid higher prices for fuel after the Persian Gulf crisis began in August. In October, most railroads raised their rates about 4 per cent in an attempt to offset escalating fuel prices.

Accidents. According to figures from the Federal Railroad Administration (FRA), between January and July 1990, there were 3,200 accidents at grade crossings, in which 394 people were killed and 1,303 people were injured. During that same period, there were 1,702 train accidents, in which 2 people were killed and 168 others injured.

Clean Air Act. On October 27, Congress passed the Clean Air Act of 1990 aimed at reducing smog, toxic emissions, and acid rain. The act could have a substantial effect on railroads because many coal users might switch to less polluting fuels to comply with the new law. And hauling coal is the railroad industry's largest source of revenue.

Combating truck competition. The Association of American Railroads geared up to fight government approval of longer and heavier trucks. The trucking industry could seek such vehicles as part of the 1991 bill for federal highway funds. Of concern are so-called longer combination vehicles (or truck-trains), double- and even triple-trailer vehicles with total lengths of more than 100 feet (30 meters) and weights possibly greater than 135,000 pounds (61,000 kilograms). The current federal limit is 80,000 pounds (36,000 kilograms).

Safety. The FRA collected more than $8.3 million in fines during the fiscal year that ended on Sept. 30, 1990. It was the highest amount collected in 10 years from railroads and shippers for violations of federal rail safety laws. Federally mandated random drug testing of employees of major railroads began in January, of medium-sized railroads in July, and of small railroads in November.

New technology. The FRA reported to Congress in June on the potential use of magnetic levitation (maglev) transportation in the United States. The report concluded that development of commercial maglev systems within 20 years, and even in 10, was economically and technically possible. Maglev vehicles can travel safely at high speeds—up to 300 miles (480 kilometers) per hour—suspended above a guideway by magnetic fields.   Kathy Keeney

In *World Book,* see **Railroad.**

Religion. The great political changes in the countries of eastern Europe during 1990 had implications for religion in the region. In October, the Soviet Union reversed previous restrictions on organized religion by passing a new law promising "freedom of conscience and religious organizations."

The law stated that all religious organizations are on an equal basis and that the state cannot interfere in religious affairs. It also said that Soviet citizens may study religion at home or in private schools; religious organizations may send students abroad for religious studies; and religious groups may establish societies or other organizations for the public profession of faith. The law also stated that the government is prohibited from promoting any religion or atheism, though atheism remained the Communist Party's policy.

Meeting with Pope John Paul II in the Vatican on December 1, Soviet President Mikhail S. Gorbachev assured the pontiff that church-state relations under the law would be handled "in a spirit of democracy and humanism and within the framework of *perestroika*" (political restructuring). Gorbachev admitted that Soviet leaders had changed their attitude toward religion and now realized that freedom of conscience should be respected.

The new freedom of religion in the Soviet Union affects all religious traditions in the country. It is estimated that more than 50 million Soviet citizens are Muslims, and they appealed for the right to visit

One of about 1,000 Buddhist worshipers in a May ceremony at Tokyo's Nishichisan Temple walks on flaming sticks to burn out evil passions.

Mecca, their holy city in Saudi Arabia. On April 23, the Soviet government announced that it would charter special direct flights to Mecca from Moscow and other Soviet cities. *Mullahs* (experts in Islamic doctrine) openly conducted meetings. The Koran, the holy book of the Muslims, was printed and distributed legally. In Tashkent, capital of the Uzbek Soviet Socialist Republic in heavily Islamic central Asia, Muslim leaders began regular publication of an Arabic newspaper for religious instruction.

The new democratic atmosphere, however, could not prevent violence stemming from religious and ethnic differences. In the Azerbaijan Soviet Socialist Republic, a predominantly Islamic republic in southeastern Europe, violence erupted on January 13 between Muslims and Armenian Christians over control of a region inside the republic. This unrest spread in February to the Tadzhik Soviet Socialist Republic in central Asia, where local Muslims set fire to cars, buses, and the Communist Party headquarters to protest the giving of scarce housing to Armenian Christians fleeing from Azerbaijan.

Adjustments in the new Germany. Christians in both West and East Germany had to accommodate their views to realities created by German reunification on October 3. For example, abortion had been restricted in West Germany. In East Germany, it was not. The reunification treaty allowed many local statutes to stand, including abortion laws, which were to be retained for at least two years. Reunification also meant that Roman Catholics, a majority in West Germany, became a minority in the united Germany.

Arrests for Jesuit murders. In January, eight Salvadoran soldiers were arrested for the murders on Nov. 16, 1989, of six Jesuit priests, their housekeeper, and her teen-aged daughter in San Salvador. But the investigation stalled, and evidence that could link top military officers to the killings was lost or destroyed.

Shinto rites. Shinto religious rites were used in the *Daijosai*, or Great Festival of Food Offering, on Nov. 22, 1990, as part of the enthronement ceremonies for Emperor Akihito of Japan. The religious rites followed Akihito's public enthronement on November 12. Political and religious figures criticized the Shinto ceremony, saying that it violated the separation of church and state required by Japan's 1947 Constitution. During the rite, the emperor meets with the gods as a shaman, or chief priest. Prior to World War II (1939-1945), the intent of the ceremony was to raise the emperor to the status of a god.

Donations increase. According to the American Association of Fund-Raising Counsel, charitable giving in the United States rose 10.43 per cent in 1989 to $114.7 billion; $54.32 billion of that amount was given to churches.   Owen F. Campion

See also **Eastern Orthodox Churches; Jews and Judaism; Protestantism; Roman Catholic Church.** In *World Book,* see **Religion.**

Religious groups with 150,000 or more members in the United States*

African Methodist Episcopal Church	2,210,000
African Methodist Episcopal Zion Church	1,220,260
American Baptist Association	250,000
American Baptist Churches in the U.S.A.	1,548,573
Antiochian Orthodox Christian Archdiocese of North America	350,000
Armenian Apostolic Church of America	180,000
Armenian Church of America, Diocese of the	450,000
Assemblies of God	2,137,890
Baptist Bible Fellowship, International	1,405,900
Baptist Missionary Association of America	229,315
Christian and Missionary Alliance	265,863
Christian Church (Disciples of Christ)	1,052,271
Christian Churches and Churches of Christ	1,070,616
Christian Methodist Episcopal Church	718,922
Christian Reformed Church in North America	225,699
Church of God (Anderson, Ind.)	199,786
Church of God (Cleveland, Tenn.)	582,203
Church of God in Christ	3,709,661
Church of God in Christ, International	200,000
Church of Jesus Christ of Latter-day Saints	4,175,400
Church of the Nazarene	561,253
Churches of Christ	1,626,000
Conservative Baptist Association of America	210,000
Coptic Orthodox Church	165,000
Episcopal Church	2,433,413
Evangelical Free Church of America	165,000
Evangelical Lutheran Church in America	5,238,798
Free Will Baptists	204,489
General Association of Regular Baptist Churches	216,468
Greek Orthodox Archdiocese of North and South America	1,950,000
International Church of the Foursquare Gospel	203,060
International Council of Community Churches	250,000
Jehovah's Witnesses	825,570
Jews	5,944,000
Liberty Baptist Fellowship	200,000
Lutheran Church—Missouri Synod	2,609,025
National Baptist Convention of America	2,668,799
National Baptist Convention, U.S.A., Inc.	5,500,000
National Primitive Baptist Convention	250,000
Orthodox Church in America	1,000,000
Polish National Catholic Church	282,411
Presbyterian Church in America	217,374
Presbyterian Church (U.S.A.)	2,886,482
Progressive National Baptist Convention, Inc.	521,692
Reformed Church in America	330,650
Reorganized Church of Jesus Christ of Latter Day Saints	190,183
Roman Catholic Church	57,019,948
Salvation Army	445,566
Seventh-day Adventist Church	701,781
Southern Baptist Convention	14,907,826
Unitarian Universalist Association	182,211
United Church of Christ	1,625,969
United Methodist Church	8,979,139
United Pentecostal Church, International	500,000
Wisconsin Evangelical Lutheran Synod	419,312

*A majority of the figures are for the years 1989 and 1990. Includes only groups with at least 150,000 members within the United States itself.
Source: National Council of the Churches of Christ in the U.S.A., *Yearbook of American and Canadian Churches* for 1991.

Republican Party. Going into 1990 from a position of strength, the Republican Party (GOP) was thrown into disarray by President George Bush's June 26 decision to abandon his winning 1988 campaign pledge of "no new taxes." Bush shifted gears to fashion a deficit-cutting agreement with congressional Democrats but, in the process, lost the support of many conservative Republicans on the issue. The party's woes were made worse by the illness of Chairman Lee Atwater of the Republican National Committee (RNC), stricken with brain cancer. And in the November 6 election, the GOP saw the Democrats win small increases in both houses of Congress (see **Elections**).

Big hopes. On January 19, before his illness was discovered, Atwater told an RNC meeting in Washington, D.C., that if congressional redistricting in the wake of the 1990 census was done fairly, then "in 1992, the combination of the reelection of George Bush, realignment, and reapportionment may give us a real opportunity to win a majority in both the Senate and the House [of Representatives]."

Republican optimism was fueled by Bush's continued popularity and by what party leaders saw as ongoing political realignment in favor of the GOP. On April 10, in Jackson, Miss., for example, four state legislators announced they were changing party affiliation from Democratic to Republican, giving the GOP 26 seats in the 174-member body. During the first 15 months of Bush's term, 2 members of Congress and more than 200 state and local elected officials switched to the Republican Party. More than three-fourths of those who switched lived in the South, where the party had been slowly but steadily gaining victories. By 1990, 25 per cent of all state legislative seats there were Republican, up from 15 per cent in 1975.

In Raleigh, N.C., on March 31, plans were unveiled at a meeting of the Southern Republican Leadership Conference for yet another attempt to bolster GOP strength in the South and elsewhere. The RNC planned to join civil rights groups in bringing court cases aimed at creating dozens of new black and Hispanic congressional and state legislative seats in post-census redistricting. Party operatives said the goal was to make GOP candidates more competitive in remaining districts by reducing the districts' proportion of minority voters, who tend to vote Democratic.

David Duke. But perhaps more important to the future of the Republican Party in the South was a strong showing in the October 6 U.S. Senate primary in Louisiana by David Duke, a former Ku Klux Klansman with ties to the American Nazi Party. Duke voiced a message of racial resentment that helped win him 44 per cent of the total vote and 60 per cent of the white vote.

Duke probably would have forced the winner, three-term Democratic Senator J. Bennett Johnston, into a runoff had not the regular Republican candidate, Ben Bagert, withdrawn two days before the primary in an effort to stop Duke. Political observers said that Duke's strong showing established him as an important, if unwanted, force—and a major embarrassment—within the GOP.

GOP revolt. Republican political optimism received another blow in October as Bush's willingness to accept higher taxes as well as spending restraints as part of a deficit-reducing package produced open revolt within party ranks. GOP conservatives, preferring to rely on spending curbs, scuttled Bush's initial "bipartisan" agreement with congressional Democrats. The President needed Democratic votes to enact a subsequent compromise accord.

Campaigning for GOP candidates in New England on October 23, Bush experienced GOP disarray firsthand. One candidate appeared with him but announced he disagreed with Bush on taxes and the expected veto of a major civil rights bill. A second said he was too busy in Washington, D.C., to appear with the President, and a third simply failed to show up.

Political analysts felt that Bush was humiliated by the GOP civil war. House Republican Whip Newt Gingrich of Georgia, who led the revolt on taxes, escaped any overt retaliation, though he squeaked in by fewer than 1,000 votes out of 156,000 cast on November 6. But the President reportedly sought the firing of Edward J. Rollins, cochairman of the National Republican Campaign Committee (NRCC), an arm of the House Republican leadership that works for the election of Republicans to the House. Rollins had sent a memo to all GOP congressional candidates urging them to oppose Bush on taxes and to take an independent course on any other issues that might help their campaigns.

Atwater's illness. Atwater's brain tumor was discovered in March after the 39-year-old chairman collapsed while making a speech in Washington, D.C. In April, doctors at a New York City hospital implanted radioactive isotopes in the right frontal lobe of Atwater's brain to deliver direct doses of radiation to the tumor. Further treatment confined Atwater to George Washington University Hospital in Washington, D.C. A successor to Atwater was to be formally elected at an RNC meeting in January 1991. Atwater was to become general chairman. William J. Bennett had turned down the regular chairmanship in December.

Senate posts. In November, Republican senators elected congressional leaders for 1991 who, analysts said, were mainly conservatives expected to counter some of Bush's moderate positions. Those elected included Republican Senate Conference Chairman Thad Cochran of Mississippi and Conference Secretary Robert W. Kasten, Jr., of Wisconsin. Two moderate Republicans reelected to congressional leadership posts, however, were Robert J. Dole of Kansas, minority leader, and Alan K. Simpson of Wyoming, Republican whip.   Frank Cormier and Margot Cormier

See also **Democratic Party.** In *World Book,* see **Republican Party.**

Rhode Island. See **State government.**

Roman Catholic Church. Political and social changes in eastern Europe were the backdrop for many events important to the Roman Catholic Church in 1990. Throughout the region, governments relaxed restrictions imposed on the Catholic Church by Communist regimes. Formal diplomatic ties were restored between the Vatican and Hungary in February, Czechoslovakia in April, Romania in May, and Bulgaria in December. The Vatican also reestablished limited ties with the Soviet Union in March, while waiting for a more clearly defined law on freedom of religion. The Soviet government enacted such a law, called the Freedom of Conscience law, on October 1. The new law banned government interference with religious activities and gave citizens the right to study religion in their homes and in private schools.

The new freedom in eastern Europe allowed information to surface about the underground practice of religion under the Communists. Many priests had celebrated Mass in hiding, and bishops were even ordained in secret. Also made public were arrests, torture, and long imprisonment of many people on the grounds that they were religiously active.

Catholics in the Ukraine continued to seek legalization from the Soviet government for their church, forced to merge with the Russian Orthodox Church in 1946. On Sept. 5, 1990, Ukrainian Catholic leaders said that they were repossessing 30 of their churches taken from them during the rule of dictator Joseph Stalin, from 1929 to 1953. The transfer was not official, however, until the government approved it.

Environmental concerns. On Jan. 1, 1990, in his message for world peace, Pope John Paul II called ecological responsibility a moral concern and urged wide cooperation and education about ecology and its moral dimensions. He warned that developing nations are especially vulnerable to environmental abuse.

New ambassador. The pope on June 13 named Archbishop Agostino Cacciavillan as the Vatican City's new ambassador to the United States, replacing Archbishop Pio Laghi.

Canadian saint. On December 9, Pope John Paul II proclaimed Marguerite d'Youville as the first Roman Catholic saint born in Canada. In 1737, she founded the Sisters of Charity of Montreal, an order better known as the Grey Nuns.

Papal travels. Pope John Paul II visited Czechoslovakia April 21-22 in a triumphant tour celebrating the country's new democracy. Czechoslovak President Václav Havel hailed the pontiff as a great champion of human rights and friend of the countries of eastern Europe in the days of Communist rule.

Pope John Paul II consecrated the largest Christian church in the world on September 10. The church, Our Lady of Peace in Yamoussoukro, Ivory Coast, was built in only three years at an estimated cost of hundreds of millions of dollars. Its dome is higher than that on St. Peter's Church in Vatican City. Ivory Coast President Félix Houphouët-Boigny was criticized for spending such huge amounts when his people live in poverty. He said he spent his own money, and he views the church as a pilgrimage center for the l00 million Catholics living in Africa.

Concern for children's rights. On April 20, Archbishop Renato R. Martino, the Vatican's permanent observer at the United Nations (UN), signed the UN's Convention on the Rights of the Child. He told the executive board of the United Nations Children's Fund (UNICEF) that the church has great concerns about using UNICEF programs to advocate abortion.

Public dissent banned. On June 26, Joseph Cardinal Ratzinger, head of the Congregation for the Doctrine of the Faith, issued *An Instruction on the Ecclesial Vocation of the Theologian*, the Vatican's strongest and most comprehensive statement on public dissent from official church teachings. The instruction said that Catholic theologians, both priests and laypeople, must submit to stated church beliefs and not debate controversial theological issues in public. It acknowledged the importance of freedom of conscience for the individual, but it denied that scholars had the right to dissent from church authorities, except in private. Cardinal Ratzinger said the statement was a response to a "climate of conflict" created by dissenting theologians.

Charges of clergy misconduct. On August 3, it was confirmed that Archbishop Eugene A. Marino had resigned on July 10 as archbishop of Atlanta, Ga., because for two years he had had an "intimate relationship" with a woman. Local news media identified her as Vicki Long, a 27-year-old singer and lay minister, who claimed she and Marino had been married in a ceremony over which he presided. When named archbishop in 1988, Marino became the first black archbishop in the United States. He cited the need for "spiritual renewal, psychological therapy, and medical supervision" as reasons for his resignation. The pope appointed Bishop James P. Lyke, auxiliary bishop of Cleveland, to serve as apostolic administrator in Atlanta until a permanent replacement could be named.

On August 3, officials of Covenant House in New York City announced that their private investigation of allegations of sexual and financial misconduct by the facility's founder and director, Bruce Ritter, supported the allegations. Ritter had resigned on February 27 after accusations by several former male residents of Covenant House that he had lured them into sexual relationships with him. Covenant House is the largest shelter system for runaway youths in the United States. Ritter was also accused of loaning money to two board members from a nearly $1-million secret fund that he had set up in 1983.

Ritter, who denied the allegations, is a member of the Franciscan Order but has not lived with the order since he founded Covenant House in 1968. An investigation by the Franciscan Provincial Council ended on March 29, 1990, when Ritter was directed to return to daily living with the Franciscan Minor Conventual

Dancers in Mali welcome Pope John Paul II in January. He toured five African nations to focus world attention on the neglected poor.

community. On July 10, Sister Mary Rose McGeady, the senior official of Catholic Charities for the New York City borough of Queens, was named president of Covenant House.

In August, A. W. Richard Sipe, a former priest who is now a psychotherapist, released a 25-year celibacy study of 500 priests whom he had counseled, 500 other priests whom he had interviewed, and 500 people said to be lovers of priests or to have been sexually abused by priests. The study, conducted from 1960 to 1985, found that at any given time 20 per cent of priests are intimately involved with women, 10 to 13 per cent are active homosexuals, and 6 per cent are sexually involved with adolescents or children, mostly in homosexual relationships. Church officials said the survey was distorted by the fact that so many of the people interviewed were in treatment for, or had been affected by, sexual misconduct by priests.

Catholic schools close. On January 21, Joseph Cardinal Bernardin of Chicago announced that 13 parishes, 6 primary schools, and 2 missions would be closed by June 30 to reduce a $28-million budget deficit. His later revision said that 28 parishes and 8 schools would be closed by mid-1991. Chicago's two high school seminaries were combined, and budgets for many church programs were cut.

Interfaith center at Auschwitz. Ground was broken on February 19 for the Center for Information, Dialogue, Education, and Prayer at Auschwitz (Oś-

Romanian protesters demanding the resignation of Interim President Ion Iliescu break into the government's headquarters in Bucharest in February.

więcim) in Poland. One section of the building will house a new convent for the Carmelite nuns who were the center of a controversy in 1989 when they continued to occupy a building overlooking the former Nazi concentration camp at Auschwitz. Jewish groups had complained that the place where so many Jews were killed was inappropriate for a convent.

The center will occupy a 9-acre (4-hectare) site and will house meeting rooms, exhibition halls, a library, and accommodations for nearly 100 people.

Excommunication. On Feb. 5, 1990, the Catholic archdiocese of Washington, D.C., excommunicated George A. Stallings, a black pastor who in 1989 established the Imani Temple, an independent African-American Catholic church. Excommunication means a person may not participate in any of the church celebrations or rites. The archdiocese also said that anyone who becomes a full, active member in Stallings' church would be excommunicated automatically.

This action came in response to Stallings' announcement the previous week that he was breaking all ties with the Vatican. On Feb. 4, 1990, he said his church would allow ordination of women, birth control, and abortion. Members of his church who are divorced or remarried would be permitted full communion without having to go through annulment. Priests also could be married.   Owen F. Campion

See also **Religion.** In *World Book,* see **Roman Catholic Church.**

422

Romania. Romania's euphoria at the December 1989 fall of Communist dictator Nicolae Ceauşescu reached new heights early in 1990, as relative plenty replaced two decades of severe shortages and strict rationing. In the first post-Ceauşescu weeks, the provisional government hastily made available food and other basic items. Soon, however, public enthusiasm turned to distrust—both of the ruling National Salvation Front's Communist makeup and of its actual commitment to democratic reform.

Anxiety gave way to anger when the Front backed down on a pledge to rule only until elections and in January proclaimed itself a political party. More disenchantment surrounded elections on May 20. The Front won nearly 70 per cent of the seats in the legislature. Its chairman and the country's interim president, former Communist Party official Ion Iliescu, was elected president with 85 per cent of the vote.

The opposition parties called the election unfair—a not surprising charge considering the great advantage held by the Front: the resources and organization of the former Communist Party. The opposition's poor showing, however, had as much to do with confused programs, Romania's lack of democratic tradition, and the total repression of dissent under Ceauşescu. Dissenting ideas had fueled the emergence of multiparty democracies elsewhere in eastern Europe.

Prime Minister Petre Roman, 44, appointed a new cabinet in June comprised chiefly of political newcomers of his own generation who had not served the Communist regime. This was meant to calm fears at home of a Communist resurgence and to impress Western leaders with his seriousness about reform.

Antigovernment protests and strikes proliferated during the year. In June, the government's violent breakup of a demonstration in Bucharest, the capital, prompted sharp protests from countries in the west. Demonstrators again took to the streets when the government hiked prices of nonessential goods on November 1 and warned that food prices would rise on Jan. 1, 1991. The government had earlier raised fuel costs to industry by about one-third and scrapped subsidies to inefficient state enterprises. Unemployment rose as many factories shut down.

A drought-afflicted harvest and Iraq's August invasion of Kuwait brought new economic troubles. A government official said in September 1990 that compliance with United Nations sanctions against Iraq had cost Romania's petroleum industry more than $3 billion. On November 12, Romania's parliament voted Roman emergency powers to manage the economy by decree. A year after Ceausescu's fall, Romania was still struggling to find direction.   Eric Bourne

See also **Europe** (Facts in brief table). In *World Book,* see **Romania.**

Rowing. See Sports.
Russia. See Union of Soviet Socialist Republics.
Rwanda. See Africa.

Ryan, Nolan (1947-   ), a pitcher for the Texas Rangers baseball team, won his 300th major league game on July 31, 1990, against the Milwaukee Brewers in Wisconsin's County Stadium. During the season, Ryan also broke his own major league record for no-hit games, with his sixth, against the Oakland Athletics. At 43, Ryan—the oldest pitcher in the major leagues—had set more than 40 league records.

Lynn Nolan Ryan, Jr., was born on Jan. 31, 1947, in Refugio, Tex. The New York Mets scouted Ryan while the right-hander pitched for his high school team in Alvin, Tex. Drafted in 1965, Ryan played briefly in the majors in 1966 and moved up permanently in 1968. In 1971, the Mets traded Ryan to the California Angels.

While with the Angels, Ryan began impressing fans and statisticians. He pitched his first four no-hitters in three seasons and in 1973 broke Sandy Koufax's season record for strikeouts, with 383. In 1979, Ryan signed with the Houston Astros as a free agent, becoming the first baseball player to earn $1 million per year. Two years later, Ryan broke Koufax's career no-hitter record with his fifth. Ryan signed with the Rangers in 1988. During the 1989 season, he became the first major league pitcher to record 5,000 career strikeouts and the first to strike out 300 batters per season six times.

Ryan and his wife, Ruth, have a daughter and two sons. The family lives in Fort Worth, Tex., during the season and in Alvin the rest of the year.   Jinger Hoop

Safety. In a departure from usual patterns in the United States, safety hazards in the workplace drew more attention than motor-vehicle accidents in 1990. In August, the National Safe Workplace Institute, a research organization in Chicago, reported that nearly 100,000 Americans died of work-related injuries or diseases in 1987. The study indicated that work-related diseases and mishaps may cause more than twice the fatalities that motor-vehicle accidents do.

Industrial accidents were of particular concern. On July 6, 1990, a disastrous explosion at an Arco Chemical Company petrochemical plant near Houston killed 17 people. The accident came on the heels of an October 1989 explosion at a Phillips Petroleum Company plant in nearby Pasadena, Tex. In that mishap, 23 workers died, and 130 were injured.

An investigation by the U.S. Department of Labor's Occupational Safety and Health Administration (OSHA) determined in April 1990 that Phillips safety personnel and consultants had ignored some unsafe conditions at the plant. OSHA levied penalties of more than $5 million on the company and fined a maintenance contractor $724,000.

According to OSHA data, injury rates at all U.S. manufacturing plants increased 21 per cent from 1985 to 1988, while rates for injuries at industrial organic chemical plants increased 100 per cent. Injuries at plants producing synthetic rubber went up by 82 per cent, and those at petroleum refineries increased by 64 per cent. OSHA proposed that employees at some 28,000 chemical plants in the United States conduct regular "hazard analyses" as preventive measures. In August, the agency announced a special inspection program for the petrochemical industry.

In July, the federal Mine Safety and Health Administration imposed its largest-ever fine for a mining accident. The $507,000 penalty was charged to Pyro Mining Company, whose Wheatcroft, Ky., coal mine was the site of a September 1989 methane explosion that killed 10 people. The agency cited 121 safety violations contributing to what it called the worst mine accident in five years.

Motor-vehicle safety. Scheduled airlines had eight fatal accidents in 1989—the most since 1973. But motorists achieved their lowest recorded fatality rate, 2.2 deaths per 100 million miles (160 million kilometers) of travel, down from 3.3 deaths per 100 million miles in 1980, according to the National Highway Traffic Safety Administration (NHTSA), a federal agency. Alcohol-related motor-vehicle deaths declined, while the use of safety belts increased.

The NHTSA predicted an "even more dramatic" decline in the death rate in the future. The agency said the projected drop would be partially attributable to stricter state laws for drunken driving and to a federal law requiring all new cars to have automatic safety belts or a driver's-side airbag.

The NHTSA also became more active in pursuing vehicle safety problems, setting records in 1989 for the

Two cars lie wrecked in Virginia in March after a head-on collision, one of the first involving two cars with airbags, that left the drivers almost unhurt.

number of investigations and for the percentage of vehicles recalled because of its investigations. The agency was praised for its October 1990 requirement that automakers reduce the danger of side-impact crashes. But some consumers said the agency downplayed the safety problems of light trucks and sport vehicles such as minivans in a June report.

Meanwhile, auto manufacturers scrambled to get on the airbag bandwagon in 1990, as this safety feature became a selling point for automobiles. Chrysler Corporation took the lead by offering driver's-side airbags as standard equipment in nearly all 1990 models sold in the United States. Ford Motor Company responded in January with a plan to install airbags for the driver and front-seat passenger in all of its cars by the mid-1990's. In August, General Motors Corporation said it would put driver's-side bags in its 1996 models. By September 1990, several large foreign manufacturers hopped aboard with similar plans.

But public concern for auto safety collided in the U.S. Senate with demands for more fuel-efficient cars. A bill to require manufacturers to boost fuel efficiency 20 per cent—including by reducing the weight of vehicles—by 1995 was defeated in September after officials claimed that lighter vehicles would result in more fatalities.   Arthur E. Rowse

See also **Aviation; Consumerism; Food. In** *World Book,* see **Safety.**

Sailing. See Boating.

Sampras, Pete (1971-   ), won the men's singles title in the United States Open tennis tournament on Sept. 9, 1990, at Flushing Meadow in New York City. At the age of 19 years 28 days, he became the youngest player to win this tournament, replacing Oliver S. Campbell, who was 19 years, 6 months, and 9 days old when he won in 1890. See **Tennis.**

In a match that took 1 hour and 42 minutes, Sampras defeated Andre Agassi 6-4, 6-3, 6-2 to collect the $350,000 prize and his first grand-slam singles title. He won 92 per cent of the points on his first serve, which has been consistently clocked at 120 miles (190 kilometers) per hour. He served 13 aces.

Sampras was born on Aug. 12, 1971, in Potomac, Md. He has one brother and two sisters. As a 10-year-old in his parents' home in Rancho Palos Verdes, Calif., Sampras spent hours watching films of Rod Laver, the Australian tennis star who won the U.S. Open in 1962 and 1969.

Sampras completely revised his tennis game in 1985 when he learned a one-handed backhand and a serve-and-volley style of playing. His game now revolves around his powerful serve and his ability to place the ball accurately in his opponent's court.

His United States Open victory put Sampras in the number six computer-ranked position among world tennis players, and his championship match with Agassi was the first played at the Open between two Americans since 1979.   Carol L. Hanson

San Diego. One of the biggest scandals in San Diego history came to a close on Sept. 24, 1990, with the sentencing of Richard T. Silberman, a financier and onetime aide to former California Governor Edmund G. (Jerry) Brown, Jr., for Silberman's part in a "money laundering" conspiracy. Silberman was sentenced to 46 months in federal prison and ordered to pay a $50,000 fine for taking part in a scheme to disguise the source of $300,000 that he believed to be drug money. The supposed drug dealer involved in the laundering arrangement, however, was actually an agent of the Federal Bureau of Investigation.

Silberman is the husband of San Diego County Supervisor Susan Golding. Golding had been considered a contender in the 1990 race for lieutenant governor, but she put her political plans on hold when her husband was arrested in April 1989. Despite Silberman's conviction, Golding remained active on the Board of Supervisors, and she may be a candidate in the 1992 mayor's race.

Perjury convictions lifted. On Sept. 6, 1990, the state Supreme Court reversed 12 of 13 felony counts against former Mayor Roger Hedgecock. In 1985, a superior court jury convicted Hedgecock on 1 count of conspiracy and 12 counts of perjury in connection with the illegal funding of his 1983 mayoral campaign. The Supreme Court reversed the perjury convictions because, it said, the judge in the 1985 trial gave faulty instructions to the jury. On Dec. 31, 1990, a Superior Court judge reduced the conspiracy conviction to a misdemeanor and then dismissed the misdemeanor.

Problems with the police. San Diegans were angry and concerned about the number of shootings by San Diego police officers during the year. As of late September, officers had shot 9 suspects fatally and wounded 13 others. A televised forum on the subject and a critical report by a Citizens Review Board on Police Practices fed the controversy.

Meanwhile, police officials defended their record. They argued that the number of serious or fatal police shootings in recent years has been far smaller than the number of assaults on police officers—more than 1,500 since 1985. Furthermore, they said, the district attorney's office had found that all but 1 of the 200 police shootings since 1980 were justified.

In another police department controversy in 1990, a law enforcement task force was investigating suspicions of corruption within the department. Part of the probe centered on the murders of 43 prostitutes and female transients in San Diego since 1985. The task force was examining the possibility that several current and former police officers were involved in some of those killings, perhaps because the victims had informed against the officers or could have done so.

The murder investigations focused primarily on the first of the victims, Donna Gentile, a prostitute who was found dead in June 1985 shortly after she testified that she had been sexually involved with two police officers. The task force was also looking into the disappearance of another prostitute, Cynthia Maine. Maine vanished in February 1986 after telling police internal-affairs investigators that other police officers were also involved with prostitutes.

The economy. The San Diego area's economic picture was less than bright in 1990. From July 1989 to July 1990, 8 of San Diego County's 15 biggest locally based corporations moved their headquarters elsewhere, were acquired by other companies, or were faced with the threat of a take-over. In mid-July, there was another major loss: San Diego's Great American Bank. After posting a $107.9-million loss in the second quarter of the year, Great American sold its 130 California branches to Wells Fargo Bank of San Francisco for $492 million. Great American retained its 81 branches in Washington state, Arizona, and Colorado.

Water woes. San Diego adopted a water-conservation policy in 1990 as the city struggled through its fourth consecutive year of drought. Although water-saving measures were voluntary, compliance was good. Usage dropped 11.3 per cent.

A new downtown. Work was completed in 1990 on a massive new convention center overlooking San Diego Bay. The center crowns a decadelong downtown redevelopment project. Other new additions to downtown include shopping centers, a historic Gaslamp Quarter, a park, and a trolley line running south to Tijuana, Mexico.   Sharon K. Gillenwater

In *World Book,* see **San Diego.**

Saskatchewan, which has almost 40 per cent of the farmland in Canada, faced bleak prospects during an agricultural depression in 1990. A bumper wheat crop could not be sold because of a worldwide glut and prices too low to cover production costs. One-third of Saskatchewan's farmers were believed to be facing severe debt, driving many from the province to seek other work.

Premier Grant Devine, leader of a Progressive Conservative administration in office since 1982 and himself a farmer, faced a constitutionally required election in 1991. With public revenues stagnant, Devine was able to offer only limited aid to farmers through low-interest loans for spring planting. He also initiated a request to the federal government for large-scale assistance and explored ways to diversify the province's economy. As part of the diversification effort, plans were announced on Feb. 7, 1990, for a massive nitrogen fertilizer plant, the first in Saskatchewan, to be built at Belle Plaine.

The federal government halted construction of a controversial $152-million Canadian ($130-million U.S.) dam on the Souris River on January 26 in order to carry out environmental impact studies. In October, claiming that it had approval from Ottawa, the provincial government resumed work on the dam, intended to irrigate large sections of southeastern Saskatchewan.   David M. L. Farr

In *World Book,* see **Saskatchewan.**

Saudi Arabia

Saudi Arabia began 1990 with good prospects for economic growth and a relatively quiet political environment. Then, on August 2, Iraq invaded Kuwait. United States President George Bush announced on August 8 that, at the invitation of Saudi Arabia, he was sending 50,000 American troops to defend the kingdom against a possible Iraqi attack. By November, U.S. troops in Saudi Arabia totaled 230,000. They were supported by smaller contingents from other countries. On November 8, Bush said he would increase U.S. forces to ensure an "offensive military option."

Peace initiative. Saudi Arabia in mid-December 1990 became the only Arab country to reject a peace initiative by Algeria's President Chadli Bendjedid, the latest proposed by Arab leaders. The Saudi leadership, however, announced it was unwilling to meet with Bendjedid unless he carried a promise from Iraq to withdraw unconditionally from Kuwait.

Some political analysts said that the Saudis' rejection of the initiative increased the perception that the United States was controlling Saudi Arabia's foreign policy. They said such a perception could lead to popular unrest within Saudi Arabia and condemnation by other Arab and Islamic countries. Saudi aircraft took part when the multinational force launched an air strike against military targets in Iraq and Kuwait on Jan. 17, 1991.

Gains. The crisis provided Saudi Arabia with several benefits. It eased the way for purchases of U.S. arms, which had previously met considerable resistance in the U.S. Congress. In September 1990, Bush said he would seek congressional approval to sell some $20 billion in military equipment to Saudi Arabia over the next several years.

The Saudis also stood to reap enormous financial gain from the crisis. They increased their oil production from an average of 5 million barrels per day to more than 8 million barrels to help compensate for the oil lost from Iraq and Kuwait because of an embargo imposed by the United Nations. Higher production and soaring oil prices boosted Saudi oil revenues in 1990 to between $80 billion and $100 billion, twice the amount Saudi Arabia normally earns annually.

Problems. The crisis also created serious dilemmas for the kingdom. Some Arab and Muslim leaders harshly criticized Saudi Arabia for allowing a foreign, non-Muslim military force into the country where the cities of Mecca and Medina—Islam's two holiest sites—are located. Some Saudis also became increasingly concerned that a long-term foreign presence would lead to greater demands for social freedom and for greater participation in government.

Tunnel disaster. Saudi Arabia drew strong criticism in July, after about 1,420 Muslims died in a tunnel stampede during the annual pilgrimage to Mecca. The victims suffocated when severe congestion in a tunnel linking Mecca with the tent city of Mina created panic.

A camel seems oblivious to a United States tank, part of the multinational force deployed in Saudi Arabia in August after Iraq invaded Kuwait.

The Saudi government, which initially denied that a large number of pilgrims had been killed, reportedly buried the victims in a mass grave. King Fahd bin Abd al-Aziz Al-Saud later called the disaster "God's will." Saudi Arabia's handling of the disaster provoked bitter and unusual criticism from many Muslim leaders and government officials from such countries as Turkey and Indonesia.

Relations with Kuwait. Before the invasion, relations between Saudi Arabia and Kuwait were strained. In September 1989, Kuwait had angrily protested Saudi Arabia's execution of 16 pro-Iranian Shiite Muslims, all of them Kuwaiti citizens, accused of sabotage in Mecca earlier that year.

In February 1990, the Saudis refused to participate in the annual Gulf Cup soccer tournament in Kuwait. The Saudis were angry because the Kuwaitis had chosen as their emblem an image of two horses that symbolized a 1919 battle in which Kuwaiti warriors had defeated a Saudi attack. The Saudis had also expressed irritation at Kuwait for attempting to improve relations with Iran and exceeding its oil quota set by the Organization of Petroleum Exporting Countries and because of increased activity by Kuwait's prodemocracy movement.   Christine Helms

See also **Middle East** (Facts in brief table). In *World Book,* see **Saudi Arabia.**

School. See Education.

Senegal. See Africa.

Sharif, Nawaz (1949-   ), president of a right wing Pakistani coalition, was sworn in as prime minister of Pakistan on Nov. 6, 1990. The National Assembly elected him by 153 votes to 39 votes earlier that day.

Sharif came to power after Pakistani President Ghulam Ishaq Khan dismissed the government of Prime Minister Benazir Bhutto in August and called for National Assembly elections to be held on October 24. In the balloting, Sharif's coalition, the Islamic Democratic Alliance (IDA), defeated Bhutto's Pakistan People's Party by a 2 to 1 margin. See **Pakistan.**

An industrialist, Sharif appeared primarily concerned with spurring Pakistan's economic growth and reducing its dependence upon foreign aid. He was born on Dec. 25, 1949, in the city of Lahore in the Punjab, Pakistan's most populous and most politically important province. After receiving a law degree from Lahore's Punjab University Law College, Sharif began a career working for a group of industries controlled by his family.

In 1981, the government of President M. Zia-ul-Haq appointed Sharif to be Punjab's finance minister. Sharif won election as the province's chief minister in 1985, and he was reelected to the post in 1988 after joining the IDA. He gained national attention through disputes with Bhutto in 1989 and 1990.   Jinger Hoop

Sierra Leone. See Africa.

Singapore. See Asia.

Skating. See Hockey; Ice skating; Sports.

Skiing. Pirmin Zurbriggen of Switzerland said farewell to competitive skiing in 1990 after winning his fourth World Cup overall championship. Petra Kronberger of Austria became the women's overall champion. It was another disappointing season for the United States, though Diann Roffe and Kristi Terzian showed signs of challenging the women's leaders.

The Swiss no longer dominated the competition, as they had since 1984. And after the season, three of their best skiers retired. They were the 28-year-old Zurbriggen, the World Cup men's overall champion in 1984, 1987, 1988, and 1990; 24-year-old Michela Figini, the women's overall champion in 1985 and 1988; and 26-year-old Maria Walliser, the women's overall champion in 1986 and 1987.

Alpine. The World Cup season started in the summer of 1989 with two races for men in Australia and two for women in Argentina. The main part of the season ran from November 1989 to March 1990 in the United States, Canada, and 10 European nations.

Zurbriggen's fourth overall title matched the record by Gustavo Thoeni of Italy in the 1970's. Zurbriggen finished with 357 points to 234 for second-place Ole-Christian Furuseth of Norway.

Furuseth won the season title in giant slalom. Zurbriggen won in super giant slalom, Armin Bittner of West Germany in slalom, and Helmut Höflehner of Austria in downhill.

The women's overall leaders were Kronberger with 341 points and Anita Wachter, also of Austria, with 300. Wachter took the season title in giant slalom, Carole Merle of France in super giant slalom, Vreni Schneider of Switzerland in slalom, and Katrin Gutensohn-Knopf of West Germany in downhill.

In the overall standing for women, Roffe of Williston, Vt., placed 10th with 130 points, and Terzian of Salt Lake City, Utah, 17th with 93. The leading U.S. men were A. J. Kitt of Rochester, N.Y., and Felix McGrath of Shelburne, Vt., tied for 51st with 22 points.

No American won a World Cup race all season. The best finishes were two second-place finishes by Roffe and one by Terzian in women's giant slalom. No American has won a World Cup race since Tamara McKinney in 1987.

McKinney, from Olympic Valley, Calif., broke her left leg in a training crash in October 1989. She missed the entire season and announced in November 1990 that she was retiring from ski competition. A crash also wiped out the season of Marc Girardelli of Luxembourg, the World Cup men's overall champion in 1988 and 1989.

Nordic. The World Cup series winners included Vegard Ulvang of Norway in men's cross-country; Larisa Lazutina of the Soviet Union in women's cross-country; and Ari Pekka Nikkola of Finland in jumping. The 36-year-old Audun Endestad of Fairbanks, Alaska, swept the four men's races in the U.S. cross-country championships.   Frank Litsky

In *World Book,* see **Skiing.**

Andreas Brehme celebrates his winning penalty kick, which gave West Germany a 1-0 victory over Argentina in the World Cup title game in Rome in July.

Soccer. West Germany won the 1990 World Cup, for most nations the most important of all sports events. The United States, playing in its first World Cup finals in 40 years, was eliminated in the first round.

The quadrennial competition had 24 national teams playing 52 games from June 8 to July 8 in 12 Italian cities. Regional eliminations in 1988 and 1989 qualified 22 teams to join Argentina, the defender, and Italy, the host.

U.S. team. American officials were especially pleased that their team had qualified for the 24-team finals because the United States is to be the host for the next World Cup, in 1994. The U.S. team was outmanned, however. The average age of its players was 23.3, making it the youngest team in the finals. The team had little experience playing together, and no other nation had reached the finals without a national program that included major league play.

In its opening game, the United States was routed by Czechoslovakia, 5-1. Next, it lost to Italy, 1-0; the low and close score, however, gained the U.S. team respect if nothing else. Then, the United States lost to Austria, 2-1, and was eliminated.

Eliminations. The finals started with six 4-team round-robins, with 16 teams advancing to direct eliminations. There were early surprises. Cameroon won an upset victory over Argentina, 1-0; Costa Rica upset Scotland, 1-0; Ireland tied England, 1-1; and Egypt tied the Netherlands, 1-1.

In the second round, Cameroon defeated Colombia, 2-1, and became the first African team ever to reach the quarterfinals. Argentina eliminated Brazil, the South American champion, 1-0, and West Germany's team eliminated the Netherlands, the European champion, 2-1.

There were no upsets in the quarterfinals. In the semifinals, Argentina defeated Italy, and West Germany eliminated England. In each game, the score was 4-3 on tie-breaking penalty kicks after the teams had finished 90 minutes of regulation and 30 minutes of overtime still tied 1-1. Italy had won its five previous games by shut-outs, and its goalkeeper, Walter Zenga, set a World Cup record of 517 consecutive scoreless minutes.

In the championship game in Rome, West Germany beat Argentina, 1-0, on Andreas Brehme's penalty kick past Sergio Goycochea, the Argentine goalkeeper. West Germany, in its third consecutive championship game, held Argentina to one shot on goal and kept the Argentine star, Diego Maradona, closely checked.

Despite careful planning by the police, rowdyism erupted often during the tournament. The main offenders were supporters of the English, Dutch, and West German teams. The police expelled 246 English supporters after one incident and 45 West Germans after another.

U.S. soccer. Werner Fricker, the president of the U.S. Soccer Federation, was expected to be a key member of the 1994 World Cup organizers. The Fédération Internationale de Football Association, soccer's world governing body, was unhappy with Fricker and encouraged Alan Rothenberg, a Los Angeles lawyer, to run against him for the federation presidency. Rothenberg won and also succeeded Fricker as the chairman of the 1994 organizing committee.

The Major Indoor Soccer League held its regular season from October 1989 to April 1990, followed by play-offs. The San Diego Sockers won their sixth championship in seven years. After the season, the league changed its name to the Major Soccer League. Although it planned to continue indoors, the league sought to become part of a projected U.S. professional outdoor league.

Europe. Italian teams won the three major European competitions. A.C. Milan won the European Champions Cup, Sampdoria won the European Cup Winners Cup, and Juventas won the Union of European Football Associations (UEFA) Cup. Manchester United won the English Football Association Cup. Liverpool won its 10th English League title in 15 years.

On July 10, UEFA lifted the ban on English teams competing on the Continent, though Liverpool remained banned for three more years. No English team had been allowed to play on the Continent since a 1985 riot in Brussels, Belgium—instigated by Liverpool supporters—left 39 dead.   Frank Litsky

In *World Book,* see **Soccer.**

Social security. The trustees of the United States Social Security Administration warned on April 8, 1990, that the Medicare trust fund will go broke sometime during the years 2003 to 2005 unless it receives additional financing. Addressing the issue in their annual report, the trustees attributed the problem to soaring medical costs and the intensity of the health care administered to many older patients.

The board said the social security combined trust funds for old age and disability should be able to pay benefits until the year 2043 without tax hikes beyond those already authorized. The trustees said the trust funds were running annual surpluses that will total $9.2 trillion by the end of 2025. Starting then, they said, benefits paid out to retiring members of the baby boom generation will quickly deplete the funds.

Taxable earnings, benefits hiked. The maximum wage subject to the social security payroll tax will rise from $51,300 to $53,400 on Jan. 1, 1991. As a result, the maximum tax paid by an individual worker will rise from $3,924.45 in 1990 to $4,085.10 in 1991. Also to take effect in 1991 is a 5.4 per cent increase in social security benefits, the largest in eight years under the cost-of-living adjustment (COLA) program.

The effects of employee cuts. In a memorandum made public in mid-April 1990, Deputy Social Security Commissioner Herbert R. Doggette, Jr., said staff reductions were seriously eroding the agency's level of service. The Social Security Administration's work

force had declined from 80,000 full-time employees in 1984 to 63,000 in early 1990. Doggette warned that despite streamlining provided by computerization, the volume of checks to be processed could overwhelm the agency. He said a minimum of 70,000 workers was needed to guarantee good service to the 40 million people who receive monthly checks.

Social Security Commissioner Gwendolyn S. King said on April 20 that 500 new employees would be hired during the year. In May, the Senate Special Committee on Aging called on King to defend her agency. She told the committee that the Social Security Administration had improved its operations in the past year. In response to a charge that the agency's employees often gave out wrong information, King said a study showed that a majority of social security recipients found the agency helpful and accurate.

Budget plan raises Medicare taxes. On October 27, Congress approved a five-year, $492-billion deficit-reduction plan containing higher Medicare assessments among its more than $140 billion in new tax revenues. The tax package will increase Medicare recipients' monthly premiums from $28.60 to $46.20 by 1995 and raise the deductible they must pay from $75 to $100 in 1991. The maximum wage subject to Medicare deductions will rise in 1991 from $51,300 to $125,000.   William R. Cormier

In *World Book,* see **Social security.**

Somalia. See **Africa.**

Souter, David Hackett (1939-   ), a federal appeals court judge, took his seat as an associate justice of the Supreme Court of the United States on Oct. 9, 1990. President George Bush nominated Souter on July 23 to replace Justice William J. Brennan, Jr., who resigned. Legal scholars described Souter's judicial approach as conservative, but many of his views on controversial issues were unknown. Souter had written only one published article aside from court opinions and had ruled on few cases concerning abortion or civil rights, two major issues of the day. His nomination was confirmed in the Senate, 90 to 9.

Souter was born on Sept. 17, 1939, in Melrose, Mass. In 1961, he received a bachelor's degree from Harvard University in Cambridge, Mass. He attended Oxford University in England as a Rhodes scholar from 1961 until 1963. Upon his return to the United States, he enrolled in Harvard Law School, where he received a law degree in 1966. After two years of private law practice, Souter in 1968 became assistant attorney general of New Hampshire. In 1976, he was appointed attorney general. Souter began his judicial career in 1978, first as a state trial judge, then as a member of the New Hampshire Supreme Court. He was appointed to the First Circuit Court of Appeals in May 1990. He heard federal appeals cases for one day before being nominated to the U.S. Supreme Court.

Souter has never been married.   Jinger Hoop

See also **Supreme Court of the United States.**

Zulus near Johannesburg, South Africa, go on a club-wielding rampage in August as the nation is torn by violence between rival black factions.

South Africa. In a historic policy reversal announced on Feb. 2, 1990, the white minority government of State President Frederik Willem de Klerk lifted long-standing bans on the African National Congress (ANC) and 33 other opposition groups. Even more dramatic was the release from prison of Nelson R. Mandela on February 11. The ANC leader had been imprisoned since 1962 (see **Mandela, Nelson**).

In another important development, on March 21, 1990, South Africa formally ended 75 years of rule over its colony Namibia, which thereupon became the continent's newest independent nation. See **Namibia.**

A busy year for Mandela. Despite fragile health, Mandela embarked on a tour of South Africa and neighboring countries. In March, exiled ANC leaders in Zambia made him their deputy president, standing in for the organization's ailing president, Oliver Tambo. Mandela later made triumphal visits to 13 European countries, the United States, Canada, and Australia.

Mandela advocated full representation in Parliament for blacks on a one-person, one-vote basis, with constitutional safeguards to protect the rights and property of whites and other minorities. Sensing the fears of South African business people and foreign investors, he and other ANC leaders muted their call for the nationalization of mines and industries and the redistribution of the nation's wealth. Mandela emphasized economic growth as the road to improving the lot of all racial groups. In August, the ANC suspended the use of guerrilla tactics against the government in favor of nonviolent forms of protest.

The dismantlement of apartheid proceeded in 1990. During the year, the government opened public hospitals, parks, beaches, and other public facilities to all races, and it announced that in 1991 blacks will be allowed to enroll in previously all-white schools.

In June 1990, the four-year-old state of emergency was ended for all but violence-torn Natal Province, and de Klerk began a phased release of the nation's approximately 3,000 remaining political prisoners. The government also offered amnesty to many returning exiles—including ANC President Tambo, who reentered the country in December—suspended the death penalty for all but major crimes, and relaxed its censorship of the news.

Substantial changes also occurred in South Africa's security forces. Police officers took part in training sessions aimed at making them more sensitive to black rights, and the government initiated probes of alleged police brutality. The military, which long had worked with the police to enforce apartheid, was also reined in, and a secret army "death squad" was dissolved.

The government held talks with the ANC in May, August, and October. De Klerk rejected the ANC's demands for a multiracial interim government that would choose an assembly to draft a new constitution. He proposed instead the enactment of a bill of rights to protect the liberties of individual citizens and the transfer of many government powers to newly created regional governing units.

Mixed reactions among whites. De Klerk's efforts to end apartheid were supported by the ruling National Party (NP) majority in Parliament and by several important white groups that had long supported racial separation. Not all whites supported de Klerk, however. Former State President Pieter W. Botha resigned from the NP in protest, and 39 deputies of the rival Conservative Party walked out of Parliament in February and later joined a rally of 50,000 protesters in Pretoria. Extremist white groups were alleged to be organizing vigilante patrols and raiding state armories.

Black politics were also divided. The South African Communist Party and many other antiapartheid groups and black leaders continued to work closely with the ANC. The principal rival of the ANC, most of whose members belong to the Xhosa ethnic group, was the Inkatha Party, made up largely of Zulus. In 1990, clashes between the two groups escalated. The violence resulted in more than 3,000 deaths. Mandela and Inkatha's leader, Chief Mangosuthu Gatsha Buthelezi, agreed in October to meet to curb the bloodshed.   J. Gus Liebenow and Beverly B. Liebenow

See also **Africa** (Facts in brief table). In *World Book,* see **South Africa.**

South America. See Latin America.
South Carolina. See State government.
South Dakota. See State government.
Soviet Union. See Union of Soviet Socialist Reps.

Space exploration. Fuel leaks grounded the United States space shuttle fleet for much of 1990. Nevertheless, astronauts launched the largest telescope ever put into orbit and sent a spacecraft to the polar regions of the sun. A probe launched in 1989 reached Venus in 1990 and returned spectacular pictures of that cloud-shrouded planet.

Satellite retrieved. A five-person crew lifted off aboard the shuttle *Columbia* on January 9 and launched a communications satellite, *Syncom 4,* for the U.S. Navy the next day. The astronauts then maneuvered *Columbia*'s robot arm to retrieve the *Long Duration Exposure Facility* (LDEF), a satellite 30 feet (9 meters) in length. The National Aeronautics and Space Administration (NASA) had launched the LDEF in 1984 to test the effects of the space environment on materials and systems used in spacecraft. The crew returned to Earth on Jan. 20, 1990, ending the longest shuttle mission to date—10 days 21 hours.

***Hubble* troubles.** The shuttle *Discovery* sent the $1.5-billion *Hubble Space Telescope* into orbit 381 miles (613 kilometers) above Earth on April 25. Launching of the telescope, named for U.S. astronomer Edwin P. Hubble, had been repeatedly postponed over eight years. Soon after the launch, controllers on the ground began having troubles with the instrument. The most serious problem turned out to be an incorrectly made mirror, which blurred the space telescope's images. Despite the flawed mirror, the tele-

The *Hubble Space Telescope,* an orbiting observatory, is released from the payload bay of the United States space shuttle *Discovery* on April 25.

Japan's Muses-A rocket lifts off on January 24 as Japan becomes the third nation, after the United States and the Soviet Union, to send a spacecraft to the moon.

scope has provided detailed images of such distant objects as the core of a galaxy and an area where new stars are forming.

In November 1990, a panel appointed to investigate the flaws in the telescope criticized both the mirror's manufacturer and the management climate at NASA. That climate discouraged people from reporting problems, the panel said. NASA planned to send a shuttle in 1993 to install lenses that would compensate for the mirror's flaw.

NASA's problems multiplied with the discovery of fuel leaks on the *Columbia* and *Atlantis*, grounding all three U.S. shuttles from late June into fall 1990. The failures prompted Vice President Dan Quayle, who chairs the interagency National Space Council, to order an outside review of NASA's operations and goals. The panel recommended in December that NASA build a new fleet of unmanned rocket boosters and abandon its near-total reliance on the shuttles.

NASA's problems caused Congress to question plans announced by President George Bush to build a U.S. base on the moon and to land astronauts on Mars by 2020. In addition, a program to build an orbiting space station came under heavy criticism.

Fuel leaks delayed the launch of the *Astro* observatory in *Columbia*'s payload bay until Dec. 2, 1990. Then the mission was hampered by problems with the computerized system that pointed *Astro*'s four telescopes at objects in the sky.

Venus unveiled. Troubled space officials got some good news when the *Magellan* space probe, launched in May 1989, began to orbit Venus on Aug. 10, 1990. Radar signals sent from *Magellan* penetrate the thick clouds that cover Venus. The signals, which reflect from the surface of Venus, are relayed to Earth and used to produce images of features as small as 300 feet (90 meters) across.

Despite losing contact with *Magellan* on two occasions in August, ground controllers started mapping Venus' surface in September. Scientists were amazed by the early results: clear images of volcanoes, fault patterns, valleys, and craters.

Sun explorer. Another success came on October 6, when astronauts on *Discovery* sent the *Ulysses* probe on a mission to the sun. *Ulysses*, a project of NASA and the 13-nation European Space Agency (ESA), should provide scientists with their first look at the sun's north and south poles. The probe will travel first to Jupiter to receive a gravitational push that will sling it toward the sun. *Ulysses* is due to reach the sun's south pole in 1994 and its north pole in 1995.

Soviet problems. The Soviet Union meanwhile encountered problems with the space station *Mir*. Two cosmonauts, Anatoly Solovyev and Alexander Balandin, narrowly escaped death after accidentally damaging an airlock during a seven-hour spacewalk on July 17, 1990. The cosmonauts used up most of their oxygen supply before they managed to reenter *Mir* through a secondary airlock and connect themselves to an emergency life support unit. Solovyev and Balandin returned to Earth on August 9.

Japan goes to the moon. In January, Japan became the third nation to launch an unmanned rocket to the moon, after the United States and the Soviet Union. The Muses-A blasted off on January 24, sending two satellites into an Earth orbit that brought them close to the moon on March 19. The smaller satellite, which carried instruments, went into lunar orbit. Ground controllers soon lost contact with it, however, and have not heard from it since. The larger satellite entered an elliptical orbit intended to carry it past the moon and then back toward Earth.

Unmanned U.S. launches. Shuttle failures caused NASA to launch more payloads with *expendable launch vehicles* (ELV's). Unlike shuttle boosters, ELV's are not recovered and reused. The *Roentgen Satellite*, known as *Rosat*, had originally been slated to fly aboard a shuttle but was modified to fit on a Delta 2 rocket. On June 1, *Rosat* rode into orbit. This X-ray observatory—named after the discoverer of X rays, Wilhelm Roentgen—was a cooperative effort of the United States, West Germany, and Great Britain. *Rosat* carries instruments to study objects in space that generate X rays. It orbits above the atmosphere, which blocks X rays and prevents them from reaching Earth.

NASA on April 5 successfully tested a system to launch small satellites from high-flying aircraft. A B-52 bomber flew to an altitude of 43,000 feet (13,000 meters), carrying a 50-foot (15-meter) Pegasus rocket under one wing. After release, the rocket ignited and sent into orbit a satellite for measuring Earth's magnetic field. That satellite, in turn, released a smaller Navy communications satellite. This system can orbit small satellites at a cost of about $6,000 per pound (0.45 kilogram), compared to $20,000 per pound for ground-launched rockets.

China sought to become a player in the commercial launching business with a refurbished U.S.-built communications satellite first launched in 1984. At that time, the satellite failed to reach the proper orbit. A shuttle mission later retrieved the satellite, and it was sold to the Asia Satellite Telecommunication Company. On April 7, 1990, China put the satellite into orbit, where it was to relay telephone and television signals to Asian nations.

Ariane explosion. The ESA and its commercial counterpart, Arianespace, attempted to launch two Japanese communications satellites with an Ariane-4 rocket on February 22. But the rocket exploded shortly after take-off from Kourou, French Guiana. The failure was blamed on a discarded rag that blocked a valve in the rocket's cooling system. Arianespace got back on track with successful launches on July 24 and October 12.   William J. Cromie

See also **Astronomy.** In the Special Reports section, see **A Hitchhiker's Current Guide to the Planets.** In *World Book,* see **Communications satellite; Space travel.**

Spain. The governing Socialist Workers' Party suffered continuing blows to its popularity in 1990. The party's troubles came on the heels of its disappointing showing in October 1989 parliamentary elections.

One of the party's problems was an influence-peddling scandal involving the brother of Deputy Prime Minister Alfonso Guerra González. In January 1990, Juan Guerra González was accused of running a private business from government offices and using his influence to enrich himself through real estate transactions. Under fire, Juan Guerra on January 20 temporarily gave up his party membership. As investigations continued throughout the year, the public and the press attacked the deputy prime minister for his alleged role in the scandal.

An economic slowdown also shook faith in the government. In 1988 and 1989, Spain's economy grew at 5 per cent per year, but the rate for 1990 appeared certain to slip below the target of 4 per cent. The 1991 growth rate was expected to be only 2 per cent.

The public also reacted negatively to a decision by Prime Minister Felipe González Márquez to send three warships with crews that included draftees to the Persian Gulf in late August. After Iraq invaded Kuwait on August 2, many nations sent troops to the Persian Gulf region to enforce a United Nations embargo against Iraq. But González' decision was unpopular in Spain, which has a long history of isolationism. According to one opinion poll, 59 per cent of the population disapproved of the deployment.

The Basque separatist organization Basque Homeland and Liberty (ETA) on February 17 offered to negotiate a truce with the Spanish government. But the minister of the interior said that talks would not begin unless the ETA halted its violence for six months.

With no truce in sight, the ETA continued a campaign of terror throughout 1990 to further its efforts to achieve independence for the Basque provinces in the north. In March, the ETA claimed responsibility for sending letter bombs that injured two postal workers and the judge who presided over the court in which terrorism cases are tried. Although the government later arrested about 20 ETA members, including the group's second-in-command, bombings continued, with at least 5 people killed and more than 50 injured.

To strengthen ties to Mexico, King Juan Carlos I and Queen Sofía visited the former Spanish colony for six days in January. During the visit, the two nations signed a treaty of economic cooperation, with Spain pledging to give Mexico loans and private investment.

Judaism and Protestantism were officially accorded the same religious privileges as Roman Catholicism when a government agreement was signed on Feb. 21, 1990. Although the Spanish government granted Jews and Protestants freedom of religious expression in the 1960's, those faiths had not qualified for tax exemptions and other benefits.   Jinger Hoop

See also **Europe** (Facts in brief table). In *World Book,* see **Spain.**

Sports

Sports. The structure of major-college football conferences in the United States began to change in 1990, largely due to present and projected income from television. Teams moved from one conference to another, and more new alliances were discussed.

Most major colleges tried to finance their athletic programs from football or basketball income, or both. All major colleges belonged to the National Collegiate Athletic Association (NCAA). Except for the members of the Big Ten and the Pacific Ten conferences, the 64 remaining major football schools also belonged to the College Football Association (CFA).

In 1990, the most important CFA games were televised by the American Broadcasting Companies (ABC), and major Big Ten or Pacific Ten games by CBS Inc. Several cable networks televised other games.

Instead of staying with CBS, the Big Ten and the Pacific Ten signed a new contract with ABC, starting in 1991. The CFA also negotiated a five-year contract with ABC paying $210 million from 1991 through 1995. The Federal Trade Commission, a government agency that enforces antitrust laws, then filed a complaint against the CFA and ABC, charging that their new contract was monopolistic.

Notre Dame defection. The most attractive team for television was Notre Dame because of its national popularity. In February 1990, Notre Dame, a CFA member, broke away from the TV plan by signing a five-year, $37.5-million contract with the National Broadcasting Company to televise six home games a year from 1991 through 1995. ABC, smarting at the loss of Notre Dame from its package, trimmed its $210-million contract with the CFA to $175 million.

The defection of Notre Dame set off alarms among conferences and colleges. Conferences feared their stature and TV income would suffer. Colleges, both conference members and independents, feared they would lose some of the money they were receiving and opportunities to get more. Weaker colleges feared they would be left out.

The shuffling began with these moves:

■ The Big Ten added Penn State, long the leading Eastern independent, as its 11th member.

■ The Southeastern Conference added Arkansas (a member of the Southwest Conference for 76 years) and South Carolina.

■ The Atlantic Coast Conference, known for its basketball, added Florida State, a football power.

■ The Big East added Miami of Florida for basketball. It then moved to create a football conference involving West Virginia, Temple, Rutgers, and Virginia Tech joining its football-playing members.

■ Metro's eight members unsuccessfully tried to add eight more (Miami, Pittsburgh, Syracuse, Boston College, Penn State, West Virginia, Temple, and Rutgers), some for football only. Instead, it lost two members (Cincinnati and Memphis State) to a new Great Midwest basketball conference,

which also included DePaul, Marquette, St. Louis, and Alabama-Birmingham.

■ In addition, Big Eight members were wooed—Nebraska by the Big Ten, Colorado by the Pacific Ten, and Oklahoma by the Southwest Conference. The Southeastern Conference wanted Texas and Texas A&M from the Southwest Conference.

■ The Southwest Conference and the Big Eight held merger talks. The Big East and others talked about forming an Eastern football conference.

Awards. Janet Evans, an 18-year-old swimmer from Placentia, Calif., was voted the James E. Sullivan Memorial Award as the outstanding amateur athlete in the United States in 1989. During 1989, she broke one world record and two American records. In the 1988 Olympic Games, she won three gold medals.

The United States Olympic Committee voted Evans as Sportswoman of the Year and Roger Kingdom of Pittsburgh, Pa., as Sportsman of the Year. Kingdom won gold medals in 1984 and 1988 Olympic track and field. In 1989, he set a world record of 12.92 seconds for the 110-meter hurdles.

Among the winners in 1990 were:

Cycling. For the second consecutive year, Greg LeMond of Wayzata, Minn., won the Tour de France, which ended on July 22 in Paris. Before that, because of illness and inadequate training, he had finished 78th in the Tour de Trump and 105th in the Tour of Italy.

Diving. Gao Min of China, a 1988 Olympic champion, swept the three women's medals in the Asian Games in Beijing, held from Sept. 22 to Oct. 7, 1990, and both springboard titles in the Goodwill Games, held from July 20 to August 5 in Seattle. Of the 12 United States championships indoors and outdoors, Krista Wilson, Wendy Lucero, Wendy Lian Williams, Mark Bradshaw, and Pat Evans won 2 each.

Fencing. West Germany and Italy won three titles each in the world championships, held from July 7 to 16 in Lyon, France. The best placing by an American was 23rd in men's foil by Michael Marx of Portland, Ore. Marx won the United States title in men's foil for a record seventh consecutive year.

Gymnastics. Fourteen-year-old Kim Zmeskal of Houston won the women's all-around in the McDonald's American Cup, the most important international competition in the United States, held on March 3 and 4 in Fairfax, Va. Otherwise, Soviet men and women won the major all-around titles, including Valery Belenky and Tatyana Lisenko in the World Cup, held on October 27 and 28 in Brussels, Belgium.

Rowing. The West German men and the Romanian women won the eight-oared titles in the world championships, held from October 29 to November 3 on Lake Barrington in Australia. The only gold-medal winners from the United States were Steve Peterson of Wakefield, R.I., and Robert Dreher of Durham, N.H., in the men's lightweight double sculls. The Wisconsin men won the United States collegiate championship.

Wrestling. The Soviet Union won the team titles in the world freestyle championships, held from September 6 to 9 in Tokyo, and the world Greco-Roman championships, held from October 19 to 21 in Rome. John Smith of Stillwater, Okla., won the 62-kilogram (136.5-pound) freestyle title and became the first American to take four consecutive world-level titles.

Other champions

Archery, U.S. champions: men, Ed Eliason, Stansbury Park, Utah; women, Denise Parker, South Jordan, Utah.
Badminton, world team champions: Thomas Cup (men), China; Uber Cup (women), China.

Biathlon, world champions: men's 10-kilometer, Mark Kirchner, East Germany; men's 20-kilometer, Valery Medvedsev, Soviet Union; women's 7.5-kilometer, Anne Elvebakk, Norway; women's 15-kilometer, Svetlana Davidova, Soviet Union.

Billiards, world three-cushion champion: Ludo Dielis, Belgium.

Bobsledding, world champions: two-man, Gustav Weder, Switzerland; four-man, Gustav Weder.

Canoeing, world 500-meter champions: canoe, Mikhail Slivinsky, Soviet Union; men's kayak, Sergei Kalesnik, Soviet Union; women's kayak, Josefa Idem, Italy.

Court tennis, world champion: Wayne Davies, New York City.

Cross-country, world champions: men, Khalid Skah, Morocco; women, Lynn Jennings, Newmarket, N.H.

Curling, world champions: men, Tommy Stjerne, Denmark; women, Dordi Nordby, Norway.

Equestrian, world champions: jumping, Eric Navet, France; dressage, Nicole Uphoff, West Germany; three-day, Blyth Tait, New Zealand; endurance, Becky Har, Los Gatos, Calif.

Field hockey, World Cup champions: men, Netherlands; women, Netherlands.

Handball, U.S. four-wall champions: men, Naty Alvarado, Hesperia, Calif.; women, Anna Engele, St. Paul, Minn.

Horseshoe pitching, world champions: men, Jim Knisely, Bremen, Ohio; women, Tari Powell, Rankin, Ill.

Judo, U.S. heavyweight champions: men, Douglas Nelson, Englewood, N.J.; women, Carol Scheid, Nevada, Iowa.

Lacrosse, world men's champion: United States.

Luge, world champions: men, Georg Hackl, West Germany; women, Susi Erdmann, East Germany.

Modern pentathlon, world champions: men, Gianluca Tiberti, Italy; women, Eva Fjedllerup, Denmark.

Motorcycle racing, world 500-cc champion: Wayne Rainey, Downey, Calif.

Parachute jumping, world combined champions: men, Sergei Razomazov, Soviet Union; women, Denise Bar, East Germany.

Platform tennis, U.S. doubles champions: Rich Maier, Scarsdale, N.Y., and Steve Baird, Harrison, N.Y.

Racquetball, U.S. champions: men, Cliff Swain, Boston; women, Lynn Adams, San Diego.

Racquets, U.S. Open champion: James Male, Great Britain.

Rhythmic gymnastics, U.S. all-around champion: Tracey Lepore, Miami, Fla.

Rodeo, U.S. all-around champion: Ty Murray, Odessa, Tex.

Shooting, world champions: free rifle, Glenn Dubis, Fort Benning, Ga.; air rifle, Hans Riederer, West Germany.

Softball, world women's champion: United States. U.S. fastpitch champions: men, Penn Corporation, Sioux City, Iowa; women, Raybestos Brakettes, Stratford, Conn.

Surfing, world champion, Tom Curren, Carpenteria, Calif.

Synchronized swimming, U.S. champion: Kristen Babb, Walnut Creek, Calif.

Table tennis, World Team Cup champions: men, Sweden; women, China.

Tae kwon do, U.S. heavyweight champions: men, Paris Amani, Highland Park, Ill.; women, Kathy Wagner, Colorado Springs, Colo.

Triathlon, Ironman champions: men, Mark Allen, Cardiff, Calif.; women, Erin Baker, New Zealand.

Volleyball, world champions: men, Italy; women, Soviet Union.

Water polo, U.S. champions: men, Harvard Foundation, Los Angeles; women, Beach, Long Beach, Calif.

Water skiing, U.S. Open overall champions: men, Carl Roberge, Orlando, Fla.; women, Deena Brush Mapple, Windermere, Fla.

Weightlifting, world superheavyweight champion: Leonid Taranenko, Soviet Union.　　Frank Litsky

See also articles on the various sports. In *World Book,* see articles on the sports.

Curtis Hibbert won five gold medals, a silver, and a bronze—the best performance ever by a Canadian at the Commonwealth Games, held in January.

Sri Lanka

Sri Lanka. A separatist guerrilla force ended its yearlong cease-fire with the government on June 11, 1990, and began a savage war that raged for the rest of the year. The group, the Liberation Tigers of Tamil Eelam, was seeking an independent state in the north and east for the Tamil ethnic minority.

In 1989, with the help of army troops from India, Sri Lanka had held provincial elections in an effort to satisfy the demands of the separatists. Although the Tigers agreed to a cease-fire, they boycotted the elections, which were won by a rival Tamil group, Eelam People's Revolutionary Liberation Front (EPRLF).

On March 24, 1990, India withdrew the last of its troops, and Tiger guerrillas moved into some of their positions. On June 11, the Tigers shelled government army camps and, in surprise attacks on 20 police stations, executed about 100 surrendering police officers. One week later, 13 EPRLF leaders were murdered in Madras, India, a haven for Tamil separatists. The Tigers were blamed.

In the most savage fighting of the war thus far, more than 3,350 people had died by mid-August. Many of the victims were Muslim or Buddhist villagers, whom the predominantly Hindu Tamils suspected of aiding the government. On August 3, the Tigers killed 120 men and boys praying at two Muslim mosques. A few days later, 127 Muslims were slain in their homes. On August 14, some 85 Tamil villagers were hacked to death with knives and axes, apparently by Muslims seeking revenge.

The Tigers took control of the largest city in the north, Jaffna, and on June 11 began a siege of Sri Lankan army troops stationed at a 300-year-old fort in the city. An army assault force broke the siege on September 13, but within two weeks the army had abandoned the area and nearby islands.

A separate civil war in Sri Lanka appeared to have ended after taking at least 20,000 lives. The government had been fighting guerrillas in the Marxist People's Liberation Front, which sought to take over the regions dominated by the Sinhalese ethnic group. In November 1989, police killed the Front's leaders, and the group stopped its activities.

But the government was accused of terrorist acts against the Marxist People's Liberation Front in 1990. On September 19, the London-based human-rights organization Amnesty International claimed that Sri Lankan security forces had killed tens of thousands of people and that death squads linked to the ruling political party had murdered young people suspected of Front activities.

Economy. The resumption of war against the Tigers forced the government of Sri Lanka to increase its deficit spending. The economy also suffered from trade sanctions against Iraq—a major market for Sri Lankan tea—following Iraq's August 2 invasion of Kuwait.   Henry S. Bradsher

See also **Asia** (Facts in brief table). In **World Book,** see **Sri Lanka.**

Stamp collecting. The United States Postal Service unveiled designs for four Creatures of the Sea stamps at the National Aquarium in Baltimore on Oct. 3, 1990. The 25-cent stamps, a joint issue between the Postal Service and the Soviet Union's Ministry of Posts and Telecommunications, depict marine animals common in U.S. and Soviet waters. Pictured are a killer whale, a dolphin, a northern sea lion, and a sea otter.

Other stamps issued by the Postal Service in 1990 included a 25-cent commemorative booklet of five different lighthouse stamps, a 25-cent folk-art booklet depicting the headdresses of five American Indian tribes—the Cheyenne, Comanche, Shoshone, Flathead, and Assiniboine—and 25-cent commemoratives honoring the statehood centennials of Idaho and Wyoming and the bicentennial of Rhode Island. As the 1990 addition to its Black Heritage series, the Postal Service issued a 25-cent stamp honoring Ida Bell Wells-Barnett, a journalist and civil rights activist of the late 1800's and early 1900's.

Among other 1990 stamps was a block of four 25-cent stamps commemorating four classic Hollywood films of 1939: *Beau Geste,* starring Gary Cooper; *Gone with the Wind,* starring Clark Gable and Vivien Leigh; *Stagecoach,* one of John Wayne's most famous movies; and *The Wizard of Oz,* the film that made Judy Garland a star.

The annual poll conducted by *Linn's Stamp News* named a block of four 25-cent stamps depicting forms of classic mail transportation as the most popular stamps issued in 1989. A $2.40 stamp commemorating the 1969 moon landing was the runner-up.

A plastic stamp designed to be dispensed by automatic teller machines (ATM's) was introduced by the Postal Service in May 1990. The 25-cent stamps, which were the first plastic stamps ever issued by the United States, picture a stylized American flag. They were being test-marketed in Washington state and were also available at post offices throughout the United States that have special sales facilities for stamp collectors. The "self stick" stamps, sold in sheets of 12 for $3, are made of an extremely thin polyester coated with a pressure adhesive. The sheets are the same size as a dollar bill so an ATM machine can handle them just as it does currency.

Counterfeit stamps. Increasing numbers of people are defrauding the Postal Service by using counterfeit stamps produced with the aid of color photocopying machines, postal authorities reported in 1990. They said that most of the color copiers now in use can accurately reproduce any of the multicolored photogravure and engraved stamps printed by the Postal Service. When perforated, the fakes are difficult for postal employees to spot. The Postal Service is now looking into ways of printing stamps so that photocopiers will be unable to match their colors.

Foreign stamps. Canada in 1990 issued a 39-cent stamp celebrating the 25th anniversary of its maple leaf flag and a set of four 39-cent stamps depicting fossils of prehistoric life. New Zealand issued an 80-cent stamp commemorating the 50th anniversary of Air New Zealand, picturing the national airline's planes through the years. The British Post Office issued five 20-pence stamps, depicting Great Britain's highest decorations for bravery, to pay tribute to the civilians and military personnel who helped Britain prevail in World War II (1939-1945). Australia and the Soviet Union jointly issued a pair of stamps saluting international scientific cooperation in Antarctica.

Auctions. A unique 1855 Swedish 3-skilling banco stamp with a color error—it was printed orange-yellow instead of green—sold for 1.9 million Swiss francs (about $1.35 million U.S.) on May 20, 1990, at an auction in Zurich, Switzerland. That was a new record price for an individual stamp. The previous record was $935,000 paid in 1980 for the famous 1856 British Guiana 1-cent magenta stamp.

A 1965 Falkland Islands 6-pence stamp with a printing error at its center sold for $15,000 at a May 25 auction in Chicago. The stamp was part of a four-stamp series issued in 1964 to commemorate the 50th anniversary of the Battle of the Falkland Islands, a naval engagement in World War I (1914-1918). The correctly printed 6-pence stamp pictures the British cruiser H.M.S. *Kent.* One sheet of 60 stamps was accidentally printed with H.M.S. *Glasgow,* a cruiser depicted on the 2½-pence stamp.   Paul A. Larsen

In *World Book,* see **Stamp collecting.**

State government. The big issues for state governments in 1990 were schools, crime, health care, and the tax dollars needed to pay for basic services. As legislatures raised taxes to balance budgets, tax revolts began to brew in several states.

Education. The Kentucky legislature completely restructured the state's education system in 1990 in response to a 1989 order by the Kentucky Supreme Court. The court had ruled the old system was unconstitutional, chiefly because of gaps in spending between rich and poor school districts. The legislature granted more authority to local school districts and planned to reward schools financially for improving academic performance. It also guaranteed $2,305 in spending for each child. In addition, grade levels from first through fourth were to be eliminated, allowing schools to group children by ability. All school districts were ordered to offer preschool programs for disadvantaged 4-year-olds by fall 1991. To fund the reform, the state increased its sales tax and corporate taxes.

Legislatures in Texas, Montana, and New Jersey also raised taxes in 1990 to meet court orders to close the spending gap among school districts. Texas raised $548 million for education by hiking sales and cigarette taxes. In September, however, poor school districts won a lower court challenge that claimed the Texas reforms had not gone far enough. The state supreme court was expected to hear the case in 1991.

The New Jersey legislature approved Governor

L. Douglas Wilder, the first black to be elected governor in the United States, is sworn in as governor of Virginia in Richmond on January 13.

437

State government

James J. Florio's request for higher sales, income, and excise taxes to meet a court ruling that ordered equal funding for rich and poor school districts. Taxes were hiked by a total of more than $2 billion, both to provide more aid to schools and to avoid a budget deficit. Citizens massed in protest rallies at the State Capitol and signed petitions objecting to the tax increases.

Idaho and Washington in 1990 joined the handful of states that allow parents to pick the public school their children attend. In addition, Wisconsin approved a voucher system under which the state may pay the tuition at private, nonreligious schools for up to 1 per cent of the students in Milwaukee public schools. The voucher system is intended for students from low-income families.

Taxes and finance. In addition to tax hikes for improving education, many states increased taxes just to pay for ongoing programs and avoid budget deficits. Nearly half the states raised taxes. The biggest increases came in Florida, Kentucky, Massachusetts, New Jersey, New York, and Texas.

Massachusetts voters rejected a proposal to reduce income taxes and eliminate a new 5 per cent sales tax on services, fearing that the $2-billion tax cut would deal a devastating blow to human services. Measures to reduce taxes or limit spending also failed on November ballots in Colorado, Nebraska, and Utah.

Although the budding recession hit the Northeast and Midwest hardest, even California faced a multibillion-dollar revenue shortfall. Many governors reacted to news that tax revenues would not meet expectations by ordering cuts in spending.

Crime. States continued their war on drugs by stiffening penalties for those who use or sell illegal drugs. Georgia passed the most far-reaching legislation. Under the new laws, the state can take away the occupational license or suspend the driver's license of drug offenders. It also can tax drug transactions and thus prosecute drug dealers for tax offenses. A U.S. district court, however, struck down one Georgia law that required all applicants for state jobs to be tested for drug use. The court said that the law violated the workers' constitutional protection from unreasonable searches under the Fourth Amendment.

Indiana, Maine, Virginia, and Wyoming also introduced laws suspending the driver's license of drug offenders. In 15 of the more than 20 states with such laws, the suspension applies only to people under 21.

More states adopted laws that severely punish drug dealers for selling near schools. The addition of Colorado, Idaho, and Kansas brought to 42 the number of states with mandatory jail sentences for people who sell drugs within 1,000 feet (300 meters) of a school.

The growing number of arrests and convictions for drug offenses has filled prisons to overflowing. At least 37 states have been ordered by courts to improve prison conditions. Some states are trying alternatives to imprisonment, such as military-style "boot camps." These minimum-security facilities seek to teach young offenders discipline and responsibility. In 1990, at least 23 states were operating boot camps.

Gun control. New Jersey became the second state—after California—to ban the sale of military-type assault rifles. California, Connecticut, and Rhode Island extended the waiting period required between purchasing a gun and receiving it. Florida voters approved a mandatory three-day waiting period.

Health. Few states moved to restrict abortions, despite the leeway they received under a 1989 ruling by the Supreme Court of the United States. Legislatures in Idaho and Louisiana passed bills that would ban abortions except when a woman's life was endangered or in rape cases that were reported within a week. The governors of both states vetoed the measures. Oregon voters defeated a measure to restrict abortions, and voters in Nevada made it impossible for the legislature to change the state's current, liberal law without a popular vote. A new Connecticut law guarantees women the right to an abortion even if the U.S. Supreme Court were to overturn its 1973 ruling, which established the right to an abortion under certain conditions.

The U.S. Supreme Court upheld Minnesota and Ohio laws that require minors to tell their parents before having an abortion. The high court said that parental consent and parental notification laws were legal as long as teen-agers could instead obtain court permission for an abortion. Kentucky and South Carolina in 1990 passed laws requiring minors to get the consent of at least one parent for an abortion. They joined 30 other states with similar laws.

The abortion debate figured in several gubernatorial races, but the results were mixed. Voters in Iowa, Kansas, Michigan, and Pennsylvania elected governors who oppose abortion. Candidates who support abortion rights were elected in Florida and Texas.

Connecticut and Kentucky attempted to expand health care for poor people without insurance. The Connecticut measure was aimed at making insurance more affordable for small businesses. Kentucky moved to expand rural health care by offering financial incentives to rural clinics and tax credits to employers who provided worker coverage.

Environment. The year's biggest environmental story at the state level was the defeat of the "Big Green" proposition by California voters on November 6. The wide-ranging measure would have changed laws in many areas. For example, it would have phased out the use of pesticides and set reductions in automobile and power plant emissions. Voters seemed to view the proposal as too complex and too costly.

With memories still fresh of the 1989 oil spill off the coast of Alaska, several states passed tougher regulations on oil tankers. They included California, Florida, Louisiana, Maryland, New Jersey, and Rhode Island. California levied a tax of 25 cents per barrel on petroleum to create a $100-million trust fund to pay for cleanups of future oil spills.

Selected statistics on state governments

State	Resident population*	Governor†	House (D)	House (R)	Senate (D)	Senate (R)	State tax revenue‡	Tax revenue per capita‡	Public school expenditures per pupil§
Alabama	4,062,608	Guy Hunt (R)	82	23	28	7	$ 3,663,000,000	$ 890	$3,194
Alaska	551,947	Walter J. Hickel (I)	24	16	10	10	1,410,000,000	2,670	7,151
Arizona	3,677,985	**	27	33	17	13	4,061,000,000	1,140	3,632
Arkansas	2,362,239	Bill Clinton (D)	91	9	31	4	2,172,000,000	900	3,146
California	29,839,250	Pete Wilson (R)	48	32	25	13#	41,214,000,000	1,420	4,303
Colorado	3,307,912	Roy Romer (D)	27	38	12	23	2,904,000,000	880	4,315
Connecticut	3,295,669	Lowell P. Weicker, Jr. (I)	89	62	20	16	4,808,000,000	1,480	7,249
Delaware	668,696	Michael N. Castle (R)	17	24	15	6	1,130,000,000	1,680	5,478
Florida	13,003,362	Lawton Chiles (D)	74	46	23	17	12,456,000,000	980	4,699
Georgia	6,508,419	Zell Miller (D)	145	35	45	11	6,347,000,000	990	4,125
Hawaii	1,115,274	John Waihee (D)	45	6	22	3	2,217,000,000	1,990	4,238
Idaho	1,011,986	Cecil D. Andrus (D)	28	56	21	21	1,011,000,000	1,000	2,935
Illinois	11,466,682	Jim Edgar (R)	72	46	31	28	11,761,000,000	1,010	4,571
Indiana	5,564,228	Evan Bayh (D)	52	48	24	26	5,903,000,000	1,060	3,883
Iowa	2,787,424	Terry E. Branstad (R)	55	45	28	22	3,158,000,000	1,110	4,483
Kansas	2,485,600	Joan Finney (D)	63	62	18	22	2,496,000,000	990	4,482
Kentucky	3,698,969	Wallace G. Wilkinson (D)	68	32	27	11	4,038,000,000	1,080	3,575
Louisiana	4,238,216	Charles E. (Buddy) Roemer III (D)	84	18††	33	6	3,969,000,000	910	3,435
Maine	1,233,223	John R. McKernan, Jr. (R)	97	54	22	13	1,590,000,000	1,300	4,932
Maryland	4,798,622	William Donald Schaefer (D)	118	23	38	9	6,196,000,000	1,320	5,545
Massachusetts	6,029,051	William F. Weld (R)	121	38‡‡	24	16	9,071,000,000	1,530	6,001
Michigan	9,328,784	John Engler (R)	61	49	18	20	11,124,000,000	1,200	4,778
Minnesota	4,387,029	Arne H. Carlson (R)	80	54	46	21	6,398,000,000	1,470	4,789
Mississippi	2,586,443	Ray Mabus (D)	108	14	43	9	2,312,000,000	880	2,923
Missouri	5,137,804	John Ashcroft (R)	98	65	23	11	4,685,000,000	910	3,923
Montana	803,655	Stan Stephens (R)	61	39	29	21	728,000,000	900	4,176
Nebraska	1,584,617	Ben Nelson (D)	(unicameral) 49 nonpartisan				1,450,000,000	900	3,849
Nevada	1,206,152	Robert J. Miller (D)	22	20	11	10	1,340,000,000	1,210	3,833
New Hampshire	1,113,915	Judd Gregg (R)	128	269§§	11	13	613,000,000	660	4,624
New Jersey	7,748,634	James J. Florio (D)	43	36##	23	17	10,501,000,000	1,360	7,571
New Mexico	1,521,779	Bruce King (D)	49	21	26	16	1,890,000,000	1,240	3,940
New York	18,044,505	Mario M. Cuomo (D)	97	53	26	35	26,576,000,000	1,480	7,717
North Carolina	6,657,630	James G. Martin (R)	81	39	36	14	7,369,000,000	1,120	4,085
North Dakota	641,364	George A. Sinner (D)	48	58	27	26	665,000,000	1,010	3,662
Ohio	10,887,325	George V. Voinovich (R)	61	38	12	21	10,814,000,000	990	4,273
Oklahoma	3,157,604	David Walters (D)	69	32	37	11	3,312,000,000	1,030	3,333
Oregon	2,853,733	Barbara Roberts (D)	29	31	20	10	2,586,000,000	920	4,904
Pennsylvania	11,924,710	Robert P. Casey (D)	107	96	24	26	12,629,000,000	1,050	5,329
Rhode Island	1,005,984	Bruce Sundlun (D)	90	10	44	6	1,159,000,000	1,160	6,085
South Carolina	3,505,707	Carroll A. Campbell, Jr. (R)	80	42#	36	9##	3,716,000,000	1,060	3,556
South Dakota	699,999	George S. Mickelson (R)	25	45	17	18	468,000,000	650	3,197
Tennessee	4,896,641	Ned Ray McWherter (D)	57	42	20	13	4,066,000,000	820	3,304
Texas	17,059,805	Ann W. Richards (D)	93	57	23	8	13,974,000,000	820	3,856
Utah	1,727,784	Norman H. Bangerter (R)	31	44	10	19	1,546,000,000	910	2,579
Vermont	564,964	Richard A. Snelling (R)	73	75***	15	15	634,000,000	1,120	5,115
Virginia	6,216,568	L. Douglas Wilder (D)	59	39***	30	10	6,621,000,000	1,090	4,645
Washington	4,887,941	Booth Gardner (D)	58	40	24	25	6,511,000,000	1,370	4,280
West Virginia	1,801,625	Gaston Caperton (D)	74	26	33	1	1,913,000,000	1,030	3,747
Wisconsin	4,906,745	Tommy G. Thompson (R)	58	41	19	14	6,408,000,000	1,320	5,309
Wyoming	455,975	Mike Sullivan (D)	22	42	10	20	582,000,000	1,230	5,244

*1990 census (source: U.S. Bureau of the Census).
†As of January 1991 (source: state government officials).
‡1989 figures (source: U.S. Bureau of the Census).
§1988-1989 figures for elementary and secondary students in average daily attendance (source: National Education Association).
**Election undecided at publication.

#One independent; one vacancy at publication.
††One independent; two vacancies at publication.
‡‡One independent.
§§Two independents; one vacancy at publication.
##One vacancy at publication.
***Two independents.

439

Steel industry

King holiday. Arizona voters defeated two initiatives that would have established a holiday for state workers in honor of slain civil rights leader Martin Luther King, Jr. Montana and New Hampshire were the only other states without a state holiday marking King's birthday.

Election rules. Several states adopted measures to limit the terms of elected officials. California voters imposed a lifetime limit of six years on members of the state Assembly and eight years on state senators and people elected to statewide offices. Colorado voters limited the time served in the U.S. Congress to 12 years and placed a lid of 8 consecutive years in state elected offices. Oklahoma voted to limit state legislators to a total of 12 years in office.

Proponents of limits on terms say that incumbents' advantages in fund-raising eliminate competition for public office. Opponents say that limiting terms unfairly restricts the voters' choice of candidates.

Although voters across the nation returned most incumbents to state legislative and executive offices, six incumbent governors lost reelection bids on November 6. Ten incumbents chose not to run, and three were barred by law from succession. In all, 19 new governors were elected in the 36 states with governor's races.   Elaine S. Knapp

See also **Education; Elections.** In *World Book,* see **State government** and articles on the individual states.

Steel industry. United States steel production during the first nine months of 1990 fell by about 1 per cent from 1989 levels, the American Iron and Steel Institute (AISI) reported on July 24, 1990. The AISI, the chief association of U.S. steel producers, said that 73.9 million short tons (67 million metric tons) of steel were produced in the first half of 1990, compared with 74.7 million short tons (67.8 million metric tons) during the same period in 1989.

Lower production resulted partly from reduced sales to the U.S. automobile industry, which used about 10 per cent less steel during the first half of 1990 because of falling domestic car sales. The decline was also due to increased efficiency in steel production, which allows firms to produce more "finished" or salable steel from raw steel. Sales of steel pipe and other products to the oil and gas industry, in contrast, increased by 60 per cent.

Steel imports, a major factor in the severe economic problems that plagued the U.S. steel industry in the 1980's, declined in 1990. The AISI reported in August that 7.9 million short tons (7.2 million metric tons) of steel were imported during the first half of 1990, about 9 per cent less than the amount imported during the first half of 1989.

Recycling success. Recycled automobiles, appliances, food cans, and other steel scrap were used to make about 77 per cent of the finished steel produced in the United States in 1989, the AISI reported on April

2, 1990. The institute said that about 72 million short tons (65 million metric tons) of steel scrap were recycled. This total exceeded the amount of recycled glass, paper, plastic, or other scrap metals.

South Africa imports. Officials of the U.S. Department of Commerce acknowledged in April that they had allowed South Africa to ship $350 million worth of steel to the United States despite a 1986 law that specifically forbids such imports. The U.S. Congress passed the law in an attempt to pressure South Africa to dismantle its system of *apartheid* (racial segregation). About 900,000 short tons (820,000 metric tons) of steel were allowed into the United States because the Department of the Treasury defined the term *steel* to exclude fabricated steel products such as beams and girders used in construction. Commerce officials claimed that the law did not explicitly prohibit such imports.

High-tech mill. The most advanced steel finishing plant in the United States began production in April 1990. The $450-million mill, located in New Carlisle, Ind., is a joint venture of Japan's Nippon Steel Corporation, the world's largest steel firm, and Inland Steel Industries, based in Chicago.

At the plant, sheets of steel intended for use in such products as automobiles and appliances are subjected to a process called *cold rolling*. This process makes the steel resistant to corrosion and imparts other special properties.

In the past, the cold-rolling process was done in several stages, often with equipment located in different buildings, and took up to 10 days. The production line at the new plant, which uses computerized technology developed by Nippon, can complete the entire finishing process in less than one hour. The quality of the steel produced by the new process is also higher than that of steel finished by the traditional method. The new process eliminates nearly all of the surface defects that result from traditional cold rolling. Officials said the plant would have a capacity of 1 million short tons (910,000 metric tons) of cold-rolled steel per year.

Research group. The Department of Energy and 10 U.S. firms that produce high-performance steel and other specialty metals agreed on July 17 to establish the first industrywide research and development program. Specialty metals include alloys used in nuclear reactors, high-speed drills, aircraft, satellites, and weapons systems.

The new organization, the Specialty Metals Processing Consortium, Incorporated, will conduct research on new alloys and production technology. One of its goals is to improve the ability of United States companies to compete with foreign firms. Energy Department officials noted that in recent years U.S. steel firms have cut back their research and development programs while steel companies in Japan have emphasized the development of new products and processes.   Michael Woods

In *World Book,* see **Iron and steel.**

440

Stocks and bonds. In the summer of 1990, everything changed in the United States financial markets. Although the U.S. economy had begun to stumble after nearly eight years of expansion, the first seven months of the year were fairly good for the stock market. Most stock indexes set record highs in mid-July.

But Iraq's August 2 invasion of Kuwait sent oil prices and inflation soaring. Jitters about a possible war with Iraq and the sluggish economy kept many investors from the stock market. The market lost more than 20 per cent of its value from August to mid-October.

The securities industry continued to lay off workers. By late 1990, nearly 50,000 had lost their jobs since the October 1987 stock market crash. In November 1990, a seat on the New York Stock Exchange sold for $250,000, the lowest price in eight years.

The Dow. For the first time since 1984, the Dow Jones Industrial Average (the Dow) was lower at the end of the year than at the beginning. The Dow, the best-known stock market average, comprises 30 large, publicly held U.S. companies. At the close of the first day of trading in 1990, the Dow reached 2,810.50—a record high. In mid-July, the index closed at 2,999.75 twice and on three days briefly shot above 3,000. But the Dow started to fall even before the Iraqi invasion, as investors worried that the faltering U.S. economy would cut corporate profits. The Dow's low for the year was 2,365.10 on October 11, and it closed on December 31 at 2,633.66.

The Standard & Poor's 500 Composite Index, a more comprehensive average that many stock market watchers consider a better indicator than the Dow, also had a mixed year. The index opened 1990 at 353.40, rose to a record high of 368.95 on July 16, and closed the year at 330.22, down 6.5 per cent for the year.

Most foreign stock markets also declined during 1990. The Japanese market suffered the most, with the seemingly invincible Nikkei Index of 225 large Japanese companies losing nearly 40 per cent of its value. The Nikkei stood at a record high 38,915.87 as 1990 began. By October 1, it had dropped to 20,221.86, and it ended 1990 at 23,848.71.

London's Financial Times-Stock Exchange Index of 100 stocks hit a record high of 2,463.70 on January 3. During the year it dropped as low as 1,990.20 and on December 31 was 2,143.50. In Canada, the Toronto Stock Exchange Index lost 24 per cent of its January value by mid-October, when it recovered slightly. The Toronto index of 300 stocks opened the year at 3,969.79 and closed 1990 at 3,256.75. Australia's All Ordinaries Index ended the year at 1,279.80, down nearly 23 per cent from its 1990 opening, 1,654.70.

The bond market. In January, the yield on 30-year U.S. Treasury bonds—an indicator of long-term interest rates—was just under 8 per cent. The yield rose to 8.25 per cent one day before Iraq invaded Kuwait, then soared above 9 per cent as higher oil prices and inflation rates seemed likely. Foreign investors' lack of

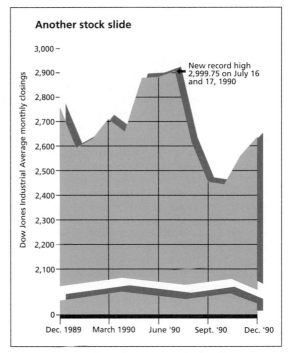

Another stock slide

New record high 2,999.75 on July 16 and 17, 1990

Dow Jones Industrial Average monthly closings

The Dow Jones Industrial Average—the best-known stock market index—hit a record high in July but ended 1990 lower than it began.

interest in U.S. bonds also kept bond rates high. For many of these investors, their home country's bond yields had become competitive with those in the United States.

Junk bonds. The market for so-called junk bonds continued to shrink in 1990. These high-yield, high-risk bonds are used to finance corporate take-overs or for leveraged buy-outs. As the junk-bond market collapsed and bankers became reluctant to make risky loans, financing for mergers, leveraged buy-outs, and take-overs virtually dried up.

The difference between yields on 10-year U.S. government bonds and junk bonds was more than 10 percentage points at the end of 1990. As recently as spring 1989, the difference had been less than 4 percentage points. The wider spread reflected the higher risk debt-laden companies face in a shaky economy.

In April 1990, Michael R. Milken pleaded guilty to six felony charges linked to his activities as junk-bond manager for Drexel Burnham Lambert Incorporated. He was fined $600 million and sentenced in November to 10 years in prison, the most severe penalty levied in the government's five-year investigation of violations of securities law. Drexel, the investment banking firm Milken and junk bonds made rich in the 1980's, filed for bankruptcy protection from its creditors in February 1990.   Pat Widder

In *World Book,* see **Bond; Investment; Stock, Capital.**

Sudan

Sudan. Civil war, turmoil within the central government, and famine dashed any hopes in 1990 for political stability and economic prosperity in Sudan, despite the country's rich water and oil resources.

Political unrest escalated as the government of Prime Minister Umar Hasan Ahmad al-Bashir, who seized power from a civilian government in a 1989 coup, ruthlessly suppressed any opposition. Hundreds of people were jailed in 1990 on charges of disloyalty to the government. Among those detained were physicians who had led antigovernment strikes in late 1989. Several of them reportedly died during 1990 of injuries sustained during interrogations.

Coups. In March, the government arrested some 20 people for plotting a coup. In late April, 28 military officers were executed for their involvement in another alleged coup attempt. The number of executions and the speed with which they were carried out were unprecedented in Sudanese history. Some opposition groups claimed that the regime had used reports of an alleged coup as a pretext for eliminating political opponents.

Many of the executed officers had reportedly opposed the strong influence exerted on the government by the National Islamic Front, a fundamentalist party that has sought to impose Islamic law throughout Sudan. The imposition of Islamic law is a key issue fueling the civil war between northern Sudanese, who are predominately Muslim, and southern Sudanese, who practice Christianity or local religions.

The civil war raged on in 1990, with little hope for a negotiated settlement or a decisive win by either side. An estimated 500,000 people had been killed by war and famine in Sudan since 1986. To increase pressure on the rebels, the government in July 1990 began forcing tens of thousands of refugees, who had fled war and famine in the south, to return home.

Sudan's economy was in a shambles in 1990. The country's foreign debt totaled more than $10 billion. Despite rich oil reserves in the south, Sudan experienced serious energy shortages. During 1990, however, Western and Arab governments refused to pledge new development aid to Sudan because of the regime's economic mismanagement and its failure to make payments on foreign loans.

Famine. United States relief officials warned in November that starvation of "apocalyptic proportions" threatened 11 million of Sudan's 24½ million people. The officials also accused Sudan's government of ignoring the danger.

Despite the desperate situation, Sudan received little humanitarian aid. Donor countries charged the government with blocking efforts to ship food and medical supplies to the south and repeatedly bombing rebel-held towns while relief operations were underway. The regime was also accused of selling donated food to obtain military supplies.   Christine Helms

See also **Africa** (Facts in brief table). In *World Book,* see **Sudan.**

Supreme Court of the United States. The 1989-1990 term of the Supreme Court of the United States, which ended on June 28, 1990, marked the continued ascendancy of the court's conservative members. The conservative shift was especially apparent in decisions involving abortion and criminal procedure. Yet the court's elderly liberal wing was able to muster enough votes for significant victories in decisions affecting affirmative action, political patronage practices, and school desegregation. The court also handed down a much-awaited decision on the right of a hospitalized person to die—rather than be kept alive indefinitely by artificial means—when there is no hope of recovery.

After the end of the term, the court got a new member, Associate Justice David H. Souter. Souter, a federal appeals court judge from New Hampshire, succeeded Justice William J. Brennan, Jr., who retired because of declining health. See **Souter, David Hackett.**

The right to die. The court issued its first ruling on the so-called right to die on June 25. The 5 to 4 decision upheld a Missouri law prohibiting the withdrawal of life support from a comatose patient unless there is "clear and convincing evidence" that the patient had approved such a step before becoming incapacitated. The ruling, confirming an opinion by the Missouri Supreme Court, blocked efforts by the parents of Nancy Cruzan to remove a feeding tube that has sustained her life. Cruzan had been unconscious since suffering brain damage in a 1983 car wreck.

After it became clear that Cruzan would not recover from her injuries, her parents obtained permission from a state court to stop the artificial feeding. That court based its decision on the parents' assertion that their daughter had indicated prior to the accident that she would not want to be kept alive as a "vegetable." The Missouri Supreme Court ruled, however, that the woman's statements had been too vague to be used as a guide to her true feelings.

Following the Supreme Court ruling, Cruzan's parents requested a new hearing. After witnesses testified that Cruzan had said she would rather die than live in a coma, a state judge ruled that "clear and convincing evidence" existed and gave permission to remove the feeding tube. Cruzan died on Dec. 26, 1990.

Affirmative action upheld. On June 27, the court upheld, 5 to 4, the right of Congress to enact affirmative action programs aimed at giving a boost to minority groups. At issue were policies of the Federal Communications Commission (FCC) giving minorities, even when they are not the proven victims of discrimination, advantages in obtaining broadcast licenses. In 1989, the court had limited the use of affirmative action by state and local governments.

Court no patron of patronage. On June 21, 1990, the Supreme Court struck a major blow to political patronage systems in a case challenging the employment policies of Illinois Governor James R. Thompson. The 5 to 4 ruling held that a state cannot use

After taking his seat on October 9, new Supreme Court Associate Justice David H. Souter, center, gets acquainted with his colleagues.

political-party affiliation as the basis for promotions, transfers, or hiring for jobs that are not at a policy-making level. The ruling stemmed from a 1986 civil rights suit against Thompson and other Republican officials charging that only those with Republican Party support could be hired or promoted.

Taxation for desegregation. In another 5 to 4 decision, the court on April 18 upheld the power of federal courts to force school districts to raise property taxes to ensure continued funding for classroom desegregation. The state of Missouri had challenged a federal appeals court decision requiring Kansas City to raise its property taxes from $2.05 to $4 for every $100 of assessed valuation.

Since 1985, the U.S. District Court in Kansas City has issued a series of remedial orders designed to attract nonminority students from private schools and the suburbs to the city's public schools. The tax increase was aimed at financing the development of *magnet schools* in Kansas City. Magnet schools are open to students from an entire school district, not just from a neighborhood. Many offer special training.

Abortion rules tightened. For the second consecutive year, the court approved increased state regulation of abortion. Ruling on cases from Ohio and Minnesota, the court on June 25 upheld state laws requiring parental notification before an abortion is performed on an unmarried minor. The Ohio law, approved by a vote of 6 to 3, requires abortion providers

to give at least 24 hours notice to a parent before terminating a pregnancy. Minnesota's law, upheld by a 5 to 4 margin, is more stringent: It says that both parents must be notified at least 48 hours beforehand.

Justice Sandra Day O'Connor cast the key fifth vote for the Minnesota statute. She said the state's requirement that both parents be notified was "unreasonable," and she was voting to support the law only because it provided the alternative of a judicial hearing for pregnant girls who are unwilling to have their parents notified. In a separate opinion on Minnesota law, she and four other justices said that without that provision, the Minnesota law would be unconstitutional. The Ohio law also allows a girl to petition a judge rather than tell her parents.

Flag burning upheld again. For the second time in a year, the high court ruled, 5 to 4, that a law making it a crime to burn the American flag violates the free-speech rights of political protesters. At issue in the June 11 decision was the constitutionality of the Flag Protection Act of 1989. That law was enacted in response to the court's controversial decision in 1989 invalidating a Texas law that had prohibited the desecration of the American flag.

Church and state. In a June 4 decision, the high court upheld, 8 to 1, the federal Equal Access Act. That 1984 law requires public high schools to make their facilities available to student religious groups if those facilities are open to other groups whose activi-

443

ties do not relate to the school's curriculum. The case was brought by the Westside Community Board of Education in Omaha, Nebr. Students at Westside High School had successfully sued the board for denying them permission to organize a Christian Bible club at the high school. Justice O'Connor declared in the court's opinion that the 1984 federal law granted "equal access to both secular and religious speech" and took no stand on religion.

Defendants' rights. The high court issued a number of decisions during the 1989-1990 term affecting the rights of criminal defendants in such areas as child abuse and drunken driving.

On February 20, in an opinion written by Justice O'Connor, the court ruled, 7 to 2, that parents or guardians may not refuse to disclose the whereabouts of a child who is under court protection because of abuse or neglect. That decision resulted from the appeal of a Baltimore woman, Jacqueline Bouknight, jailed for refusing to reveal the whereabouts of her baby son, whom authorities suspected she had killed. Bouknight based her defiance on the Fifth Amendment's protection against self-incrimination.

Justice O'Connor also wrote the court's opinions in two 5 to 4 rulings on June 27 that, in child abuse cases, created exceptions to the Sixth Amendment right of a defendant "to be confronted with the witnesses against him." In appeals from Maryland and Idaho, the court held that defendants in child abuse cases have no absolute right to face their accusers in court and that the victims may testify through closed-circuit television and out-of-court statements.

Law enforcement officials' battle against drunken driving received a boost from two rulings. On June 14, the court upheld, 6 to 3, the constitutionality of "sobriety checkpoints"—temporary roadside stops set up by the police to detect drunken drivers among motorists. And in an 8 to 1 decision on June 18, the court ruled that police officers may videotape drunken-driving suspects without first warning them of their rights. Such tapes, the justices said, may be used as evidence in court against the defendants.

Exit Brennan, enter Souter. On July 20, after suffering a small stroke, Justice Brennan, 84, the undisputed leader of the court's liberal wing, announced his retirement in a letter to President George Bush. On July 23, Bush nominated David H. Souter to fill the vacancy. The 50-year-old Souter was widely viewed as a conservative. During five days of hearings before the Senate Judiciary Committee in September, however, he took pains to present himself as a moderate. On October 2, Souter was confirmed by the Senate by a 90 to 9 margin. He took his seat on the court on October 9.   Glen R. Elsasser

See also **Courts.** In *World Book,* see **Supreme Court of the United States.**

Surgery. See Medicine.

Suriname. See Latin America.

Swaziland. See Africa.

Sweden. In 1990, Sweden's Social Democratic government began paring back the programs that have made the nation a welfare state, proposing sharp cuts in benefits and state jobs to stop the country's economic decline. Prime Minister Ingvar Carlsson emphasized the need for cutbacks when he resigned on February 15. Parliament had rejected his plan to impose a wage, rent, and price freeze and to restrict strikes.

At the time Carlsson left office, Sweden's banks had been shut down by a strike that ultimately lasted three weeks, hurting retail business and causing major supply problems for industry. The strike was settled when bank employees won a 13 per cent pay increase. Strikes were also threatened by municipal engineers, preschool teachers, and nurses.

On February 26, the Riksdag (parliament) voted to return the Social Democratic government to office. Carlsson, again prime minister, submitted an altered economic plan that abandoned the wage freeze and the strike ban but imposed price controls. It also called for increased taxes on alcohol and tobacco.

Economic indicators showed that Sweden's economy was in trouble. In the period 1987-1989, salaries rose by 28 per cent while production grew by only 2 per cent. In 1989, the balance of payments deficit doubled. In 1990, inflation reached as high as 11.5 per cent. By October 1990, financial speculators were expecting Sweden to devalue its currency in an effort to improve the country's balance of trade.

In addition, Swedish morale seemed low. Citizens had been voicing growing complaints about personal income taxes—as high as 72 per cent in the upper bracket. And, business leaders worried about rising employee absenteeism and what some called an erosion of the Swedish work ethic.

Austerity measures. In October, Carlsson gave the Riksdag plans to slash $2.65 billion from the national budget and to eliminate 10 per cent of the country's 185,000 civil service jobs over the next three years. He also proposed cuts in sick pay, defense, education, and price subsidies. The Riksdag approved these austerity measures in December. Their passage touched off a dispute among the Social Democrats that brought the party to its lowest level of support in decades in public opinion polls—about 30 per cent.

By year-end, the Carlsson government had enacted tax reforms to take effect in January 1991. Personal income taxes were lowered, so that the maximum rate fell to 50 per cent of taxable income. An already existing value-added tax was increased and extended to the purchase of all goods and services.

New cabinet members. On January 9, Carlsson for the first time appointed a labor leader, Rune Molin, as industry minister. Molin was known for opposing the nation's plan to phase out all nuclear power plants. On February 27, Carlsson named Allan Larsson as finance minister.   Margaret Anne Schmidt

See also **Europe** (Facts in brief table). In *World Book,* see **Sweden.**

Australian Hayley Lewis, a 15-year-old from Brisbane, slices through the water at the Commonwealth Games en route to her fifth gold medal.

Swimming. The United States, preparing for the 1991 world championships, looked impressive in 1990. The best U.S. swimmers won most of the honors in the Goodwill Games, and a U.S. team missing many stars beat the best Europeans and Canadians in the League of European Nations Cup competition.

The best performance of the year came from Mike Barrowman, a junior at the University of Michigan in Ann Arbor. The world's best female swimmers were Janet Evans of Placentia, Calif., and Summer Sanders of Roseville, Calif., who were about to become team-mates at Stanford University in that state.

International. In the Goodwill Games, held from July 20 to August 5 near Seattle, the United States won 20 gold medals, East Germany 5, and the Soviet Union 3. Barrowman won the men's 200-meter breast-stroke in 2 minutes 11.53 seconds, breaking his 1989 world record of 2:12.89. Matt Biondi of Moraga, Calif., won 4 gold medals in men's events; Evans and Sanders, 3 each in women's events.

In the League of European Nations Cup meet, held from Aug. 9 to 12, 1990, in Rome, the United States won 6 of the 16 events for men and 10 of the 16 for women. Anders Holmertz of Sweden won 3 men's freestyle finals.

In the Commonwealth Games, held from January 25 to 30 in Auckland, New Zealand, Australia won 21 of the 31 gold medals. Hayley Lewis, a 15-year-old Australian, took 5 gold medals in women's finals.

East Germany's domination of women's events ended with the political changes in that nation as the government stopped supporting the sport. Chinese women swam the year's fastest times in three events and the second fastest in three.

Stars. The year's only world-record breaker, in addition to Barrowman, was Tom Jager of Topanga, Calif. On March 24 in Nashville, Tenn., he lowered the men's 50-meter freestyle record to 21.81. Adrian Moorhouse of England twice equaled his 1989 world record of 1:1.49 for the men's 100-meter breaststroke.

Evans enjoyed another outstanding year in 1990. She won six finals in the Mission Viejo (Calif.) Meet of Champions, three in the Goodwill Games, three in the United States long-course championships, and three in the National Collegiate Athletic Association championships. The latter two were held in Austin, Tex. For the first time since 1986, Evans lost in the 400-meter individual medley, first to Sanders at the Goodwill Games and then to Erika Hansen of King of Prussia, Pa., at the long-course championships.

The year's new crop of American women included Sanders; 17-year-old Nicole Haislett of St. Petersburg, Fla.; 17-year-old Jenny Thompson of Dover, N.H.; 17-year-old Mary Ellen Blanchard of Norcross, Ga.; and 16-year-old Janie Wagstaff of Mission Hills, Kans. All won national titles and qualified for the U.S. team for the world championships.　　Frank Litsky

In *World Book,* see **Swimming.**

Men in Appenzell Inner Rhoden, a Swiss half-canton, refuse in April to give women the vote. The Swiss Supreme Court later granted women that right.

Switzerland. The Kopp affair continued in 1990 to shed light on Swiss banking and police practices. Elisabeth Kopp, a former justice minister, was cleared on February 23 of charges of divulging official secrets. Kopp admitted to alerting her husband in 1988 that a company of which he was an officer was being investigated for *laundering* (hiding the illegal origins of) drug profits. Her defense was that she believed the information she was passing on had come from banking circles, not from her own ministry.

Protests mounted, however, about secret files kept on Swiss citizens and foreigners, which had come to light during the Kopp inquiry. On March 7, 1990, the government promised new legislation to improve parliamentary supervision of security authorities.

New laws against money-laundering took effect on August 1 as part of Switzerland's effort to cooperate with international efforts to curb drug trafficking. In April, Swiss banks gave United States investigators the records of bank accounts thought to belong to a major Colombian cocaine-trafficking cartel.

Jean and Barkev Magharian, Lebanese brothers convicted of laundering millions of dollars of drug money through Swiss accounts, were sentenced on October 20 to 4½ years in prison. They had come to Switzerland in 1983 to work with a firm of which Kopp's husband had been a codirector.   Joseph Fitchett

See also **Europe** (Facts in brief table). In *World Book,* see **Switzerland.**

Syria. Iraq's invasion of Kuwait in August 1990 gave Syria's President Hafez al-Assad an opening to improve his country's badly damaged international relations and consolidate his position in Lebanon. During the 1980's, Syria's backing of terrorist groups, its military involvement in Lebanon's civil war, and its support for Iran during the eight-year Iran-Iraq war left Syria isolated from both Western and other Arab countries.

Political opportunism. In August 1990, Syria deployed 4,000 soldiers to the multinational force stationed in Saudi Arabia to deter an Iraqi invasion of that country (see **Middle East**). Assad has long regarded Iraq's President Saddam Hussein, who had supported anti-Syrian factions in Lebanon, as a bitter rival for leadership in the Arab world.

By taking action against Iraq, however, Assad risked triggering domestic unrest. Hussein's call for economic development, the redistribution of oil wealth among Arab states, and Arab unity found some support among Syrians unhappy with poor economic conditions in their country and the presence of foreign troops in the Middle East.

Action in Lebanon. In mid-October, while the international community was preoccupied with the Persian Gulf crisis, Assad ordered his troops in Lebanon to move against the headquarters of Lebanese General Michel Awn (also spelled Aoun). Awn, a Christian and the commander of Christian units in Lebanon's army, had considered himself Lebanon's only legitimate leader since 1988. Syrian forces quickly overran Awn's headquarters, and Awn fled to the French Embassy in Beirut. Assad's victory made Syria the chief power broker in Lebanon.

Egyptian visit. One sign of Assad's attempts to improve regional relations was his visit to Egypt in July 1990, his first in 13 years. Egypt had broken off relations with Syria in 1977. The two nations restored diplomatic ties in December 1989.

Economic developments. Foreign aid and foreign investments declined sharply during 1990 because of Syria's diplomatic isolation and economic inefficiency. A population growth rate of 3 per cent—among the world's highest—and heavy military expenditures in Lebanon also hampered economic development.

Lower-than-normal rainfall and a diminished waterflow in the Euphrates River reduced agricultural output. In January, Turkey cut the flow of water in the river, upon which Syria depends, by about 75 per cent for one month in order to fill a reservoir behind its new Atatürk Dam.

Terrorism. In April, the United States again included Syria on its annual list of countries accused of supporting international terrorism. In November, however, U.S. President George Bush met with Assad during a tour of the Middle East to seek Arab support for military action against Iraq.   Christine Helms

See also **Middle East** (Facts in brief table). In *World Book,* see **Syria.**

Taiwan. President Li Teng-hui was elected without opposition to a six-year term on March 21, 1990. Li, a former vice president, had become president upon the death of Chiang Ching-kuo in 1988. Li took office on May 20, 1990, as did Vice President Li Yuan-zu.

In the president's inaugural speech, he promised that within two years the Constitution would be revised to move the government toward a more democratic system. He also restored the civil rights of some outspoken critics of the government and the ruling party, the Kuomintang (KMT). But inaugural festivities were canceled to avoid trouble with thousands of hostile demonstrators.

The demonstrators sought democratic reforms and protested the influence of elderly conservatives holding lifetime appointments to the National Assembly. Public demonstrations had gathered force in December 1989, when the KMT won only 53 per cent of the popular vote in national elections. Although the KMT swept local elections in January 1990, students continued to lead the call for reform. Under fire, members of the National Assembly in mid-March attempted to increase their own power as well as their salaries. A few days later, on March 20, more than 6,000 students rallied in Taipei, the capital, in the nation's largest-ever student-led demonstration.

New premier. Protests turned more heated—with fire bombs thrown and the windows of government buildings broken—after President Li in May named Hao Po-ts'un to succeed Li Huan as premier. The appointment of Hao, Taiwan's defense minister and only four-star general, drew the anger of those who saw the military's involvement in government as a threat to reform.

According to the president, Hao's firm hand was needed to control Taiwan's crime problem. Indeed, by August Hao was getting credit for acting decisively to reduce crime and for choosing well-qualified officials for key jobs. According to one poll, 86 per cent of the population approved of his performance.

National Affairs Conference. In an effort to disarm his critics, Li called a National Affairs Conference to debate Taiwan's future. The attendees—including former political prisoners and exiles as well as administrators of martial law—on July 4 issued a nonbinding recommendation that the nation's president be elected by popular ballot in the future.

The economy of Taiwan—one of Asia's wealthiest countries—suffered in 1990. The stock market dropped 80 per cent from February to October, wiping out small investors and hurting many big companies. After oil prices began to soar following Iraq's August 2 invasion of Kuwait, Taiwan's economic growth rate fell from 7 per cent to about 5 per cent. Environmental complaints forced Taiwanese businesses to build new facilities in foreign countries—including China—instead of at home.   Henry S. Bradsher

See also **Asia** (Facts in brief table); **China.** In *World Book,* see **Taiwan.**

Tandy, Jessica (1909-   ), won the Academy of Motion Picture Arts and Sciences Award for best actress on March 26, 1990, for her portrayal of a proudly independent Southern matron in *Driving Miss Daisy* (1989). Tandy's Oscar nomination for *Miss Daisy* was a first for the actress, whose reputation rests mainly on her acclaimed stage performances.

Tandy was born on June 7, 1909, in London. She made her stage debut in London in 1927 and her Broadway debut the following year. Her performance as Blanche DuBois in the 1947 Broadway premiere of Tennessee Williams' *A Streetcar Named Desire* established her as a theatrical star and earned her the first of three Antoinette Perry (Tony) awards for best actress. She won her second Tony in 1978 for her performance in *The Gin Game* (1977), one of a number of stage plays and films in which she has appeared with her husband, actor Hume Cronyn. She received her third Tony for her role in *Foxfire* (1983). In 1988, Tandy won an Emmy Award for her performance in the 1987 television production of *Foxfire*.

Tandy's films include *A Woman's Vengeance* (1948), *The Light in the Forest* (1958), *The Birds* (1963), *The World According to Garp* (1982), and *Cocoon* (1985).

Tandy's marriage to British actor Jack Hawkins ended in divorce in 1940. She married Cronyn in 1942. She has a daughter by her first marriage and two children by her marriage to Cronyn.   Barbara A. Mayes

Tanzania. See **Africa.**

Taxation. The United States government adopted its largest budget deficit reduction bill ever in 1990. With a majority of Republicans voting no, Congress on October 27 authorized $164.6 billion in tax increases over the next five years. The increases were part of a plan worked out with President George Bush to pare $492 billion from the nation's deficit during that period. In 1991, the plan provided for a $40-billion reduction, about half from tax increases and half from spending cuts.

Income tax changes. The plan increased the top tax rate from 28 per cent to 31 per cent. The 31 per cent tax bracket applies to individuals earning more than $49,300 in 1991 and to couples filing jointly earning more than $82,150. The plan limited deductions that can be claimed by individuals and couples with incomes of more than $100,000. It gradually eliminated the personal exemption for individuals whose incomes exceed $100,000 and couples whose incomes top $150,000. Analysts expect these changes to offset the deficit by about $29 billion over five years.

Congress gave tax breaks to families with incomes of less than $20,000—the so-called working poor—in the form of an expansion of the earned income credit. And, Congress granted $2.5 billion in breaks to independent oil and gas developers.

Other budget changes. The largest single budget change contained in the plan was a 1991 increase in the wage base for the 1.45 per cent Medicare payroll

Taxation

tax. The tax for 1991 applies to salaries up to $125,000. The old figure was $51,300. The increase offsets the deficit by an estimated $26.5 billion.

Congress also voted in a new luxury tax of 10 per cent on the portion of a purchase price exceeding $250,000 for private planes not used by businesses; $100,000 for boats; $30,000 for automobiles; $10,000 for furs; and $5,000 for jewelry.

Excise-tax increases enacted by Congress will offset the federal deficit by more than $56 billion over five years. The deficit-reduction plan increased the federal gasoline tax from 9 cents to 14 cents a gallon (3.8 liters). It raised the tax on cigarettes from 16 cents a pack to 20 cents in 1991 and to 24 cents in 1993. A 3 per cent tax on local and long distance telephone service—due to expire—was permanently extended. And, the tax on airline tickets was renewed and increased from 8 per cent to 10 per cent.

Congress also hiked alcoholic beverage taxes. The tax on a six-pack of beer was doubled to 32 cents. The tax on wine was boosted from 3 cents to 21 cents per 750-milliliter bottle. The tax on 100-proof liquor was increased from $12.50 a gallon to $13.50—about 20 cents a fifth. Members of Congress said other measures to reduce the deficit would be forthcoming, including scaled-down spending and tightened tax-collection efforts.   Frank Cormier and Margot Cormier

See also **State government.** In *World Book,* see **Taxation.**

Television. The return of animated cartoons to evening programming; the introduction of an innovative, brooding, and often confusing murder-mystery soap opera; and the use of amateurs' home videos to get laughs. Those were three of the trendsetting highlights on television in the United States in 1990.

"The Simpsons." The animated program was "The Simpsons," a satiric family comedy created by cartoonist Matt Groening that ran on the Fox network. The lowbrow Simpsons became a weekly Sunday-night attraction in January 1990, and the impudent statements of the family's young son, Bart, were repeated on playgrounds across the country.

"The Simpsons" became such a big hit that Fox programming executives decided to move it in late summer to an 8 p.m. Eastern Standard Time (EST) time slot on Thursdays. That shift, which put the program opposite the highly rated "The Cosby Show" on the National Broadcasting Company (NBC) network, was aimed at giving Fox a Thursday-night foothold in viewers' homes. But because Fox had contracted for only 13 "Simpsons" episodes, it was forced to broadcast reruns of the show into the fall before new episodes were ready. "The Cosby Show" continued to dominate Thursday night's ratings until mid-October, when the new "Simpsons" episodes started appearing. After nearly matching the ratings of its more established opponent for several weeks, the Fox entry settled into a strong second place.

The Fox network's animated family comedy "The Simpsons," created by Matt Groening, was one of the big hits of the 1990 television season.

"Twin Peaks" was another show that drew critical praise and a loyal, if somewhat smaller, audience. This eccentric mystery series, which aired on the American Broadcasting Companies (ABC) network, was created by two top Hollywood talents: avant-garde film director David Lynch and TV scriptwriter Mark Frost.

"Twin Peaks" was set in a fictional town of the same name in the Northwestern United States and centered around the question "Who killed Laura Palmer?" The series followed Federal Bureau of Investigation agent Dale Cooper as he probed the murder of Palmer, a student at the local high school. But the program was multilayered, also giving viewers a behind-the-blinds look at the town's oddball assortment of residents.

"Twin Peaks" debuted with a two-hour pilot episode on Sunday, April 8. The large audience that tuned in to the aggressively promoted pilot diminished when ABC moved the show for the rest of its spring run to Thursdays opposite NBC's popular comedy "Cheers." Moreover, the show's continuing failure to identify Palmer's killer frustrated many viewers. Although the program still had a dependable core audience when it returned in the fall in a Saturday night slot, the show had fallen into the ratings basement by the time the crime was finally solved on November 10. (Just for the record, the killer was Laura's father.)

Home videos. "America's Funniest Home Videos," presented on the ABC network, was the highest rated, if least praised, of the three 1990 trendsetters. Based on a Japanese show, this wildly popular program was rushed into production after the success of a home-videos special and debuted in mid-January. The half-hour show featured amateur videotapes of amusing incidents. The tapes, submitted by viewers at the invitation of the program, were augmented at the TV studio with sound effects and comic narration. Although the show was the ratings winner in its 8 p.m. EST Sunday time slot, ABC was still unable to win the overall ratings battle for that night because most of the "Home Videos" audience turned their dials to "The Simpsons" at 8:30.

Unconventional is in. The success of "The Simpsons," "Twin Peaks," and "America's Funniest Home Videos" seemed to encourage the networks to experiment. Several innovative first-run series were offered for summer viewing by the three dominant networks —ABC, NBC, and CBS Inc.— in an effort to stem a severe loss of viewership that occurred at the end of the regular TV season. None of those shows attracted a large audience, but at least two did well enough to survive in the fall. Those two programs, both on CBS, were "Top Cops," a realistic dramatization of actual police cases; and "Northern Exposure," a whimsical drama about a New York City doctor practicing in a small town in Alaska that was offered as a midseason replacement.

New fall shows. The fall season, too, had more than its share of unconventional shows. ABC tried a

FBI agent Dale Cooper (Kyle MacLachlan) shares a quiet moment with new-found friend Audrey Horne (Sherilyn Fenn) in ABC's offbeat "Twin Peaks."

weekly musical police drama, "Cop Rock," and NBC presented "Hull High," a musical set in a high school. Other NBC offerings included two situation comedies —"American Dreamer" and "Ferris Bueller"— in which the main characters at times talked directly to the audience, and "Fresh Prince of Bel Air," a comedy starring rap artist Will Smith. CBS's fall line-up included "Evening Shade," a sitcom starring Burt Reynolds as a high school football coach in a small town.

But none of the new shows was able to generate much excitement among viewers. "Hull High" was among the first shows canceled, and "Cop Rock" soon followed. The highest-rated newcomer was ABC's "America's Funniest People," a spin-off of "America's Funniest Home Videos," featuring the antics of amateur comedians. By late fall, the ratings trophy had been claimed by a nine-year-old show: NBC's "Cheers."

Other network news. During the year, ABC, CBS, and NBC all challenged the People Meter system—a method of gauging viewership devised by the A. C. Nielsen Company. The networks refused to accept data that showed a steep decline in the network audience. In November, the Nielsen company said its measurements had been leaving out some 20 million viewers, mainly in bars, waiting rooms, and other such places. But whatever the actual numbers involved, there was little doubt that network viewership was diminishing. As a result, nervous network executives kept a close eye on their budgets.

Top-rated U.S. television series

The following were the most-watched television series for the 31-week regular season—Sept. 18, 1989, through April 22, 1990—as determined by the A. C. Nielsen Company.

1. "Roseanne" (ABC)
2. "The Cosby Show" (NBC)
3. "Cheers" (NBC)
4. (tie) "A Different World" (NBC)
   "America's Funniest Home Videos" (ABC)
6. "The Golden Girls" (NBC)
7. "60 Minutes" (CBS)
8. "The Wonder Years" (ABC)
9. (tie) "Empty Nest" (NBC)
   "Wings" (NBC)
11. "Chicken Soup" (ABC)
12. "NFL Monday Night Football" (ABC)
13. "Unsolved Mysteries" (NBC)
14. "Who's the Boss?" (ABC)
15. "Grand" (NBC)
16. "Murder, She Wrote" (CBS)
17. "L.A. Law" (NBC)
18. (tie) "Dear John" (NBC)
   "In the Heat of the Night" (NBC)
20. "Coach" (ABC)
21. "Matlock" (NBC)
22. "Carol & Company" (NBC)
23. (tie) "Full House" (ABC)
   "Growing Pains" (ABC)
25. "Designing Women" (CBS)

In management changes, Jeff Sagansky, former president of Tri-Star Pictures, was named CBS entertainment president in January. At NBC, Brandon Tartikoff, after a decade as entertainment president, was promoted in July to head the larger entertainment group, where he appeared to control programming.

At year-end, the three-network ratings race was closer than it had been in years, though NBC retained a slight lead. NBC had problems on other fronts, however. Its nightly news show slipped to third place—ABC's "World News Tonight" was leader of the pack in the ratings race—and NBC's "Today" show, rocked by the departure of cohost Jane Pauley, lost its morning lead to ABC's "Good Morning America" despite the return to "Today" of Joe Garagiola and the addition of Faith Daniels from CBS. The executive in charge of "Today," Dick Ebersol, soon resigned, though he remained head of NBC sports.

NBC also stirred up a controversy when comedian Andrew Dice Clay, who specializes in foul-mouthed put-downs of women, homosexuals, and minorities, was named guest host of the "Saturday Night Live" show of May 12. To protest Clay's appearance, "Saturday Night Live" cast member Nora Dunn and musical guest Sinéad O'Connor boycotted the program. Predictably, the flap resulted in one of the highest "Saturday Night Live" ratings of the season.

Among network shows that ended their run in 1990 were two on CBS: the cult favorite "Beauty and the Beast," quickly canceled by Sagansky, and "Newhart," after its star, Bob Newhart, decided to end it.

A big hit on public TV. The most praised show of the fall television season was *The Civil War,* an 11-hour documentary presented on five consecutive nights in September on Public Broadcasting Service (PBS) stations. The series mixed old photographs, interviews with historians, and readings of Civil War documents and letters by well-known actors and other personalities. The series won critical acclaim and the highest ratings of any series in PBS history.

Cable TV. Most of the audience gains in 1990 were posted by basic-cable channels, those that are included in the flat monthly rate for cable service. Two competing all-comedy channels—The Comedy Channel and HA!—agreed in December to merge into a single channel to be known as Comedy TV. Despite extensive negotiations with large cable systems, neither channel had made much of a national impact.

The U.S. cable industry, which at the local level is essentially a monopoly, protected its financial interests once again in 1990. For another year, cable system owners were able to stave off congressional action aimed at regulating the rates they charge their subscribers. Michael Hill

See also **Awards and prizes; Groening, Matt; Lynch, David.** In the Special Reports section, see **Once Again, "Toons" Are Tops.** In *World Book,* see **Television.**

Tennessee. See **State government.**

Tennis. For teen-agers Jennifer Capriati and Pete Sampras, the 1990 tennis season produced a wonderful start to championship careers. For such veterans as Ivan Lendl, Boris Becker, Stefan Edberg, Martina Navratilova, and even Steffi Graf, it was a year of alternating success and frustration.

For the first time since 1966, no man or woman won more than one grand-slam title. The men's champions were Sampras of Rancho Palos Verdes, Calif., in the United States Open; Edberg of Sweden at Wimbledon; Lendl of Greenwich, Conn., and Czechoslovakia in the Australian Open; and Andrés Gómez of Ecuador in the French Open. Among the women, Navratilova of Fort Worth, Tex., won a record ninth Wimbledon; Gabriela Sabatini of Argentina the U.S. Open; Graf of West Germany the Australian Open; and Monica Seles of Yugoslavia the French Open.

In the computer rankings, Edberg replaced Lendl as the men's leader, and Graf stayed atop the women's list for the third consecutive year. Sampras, 81st at the start of the year, moved up to 5th. The 14-year-old Capriati, starting from scratch, advanced to 10th among women.

The leading money winners included Edberg; Andre Agassi of Las Vegas, Nev.; Becker; and Lendl among the men and Graf, Seles, and Navratilova among the women. Each earned more than $1 million in prize money and much more than that in exhibitions and endorsements.

Pete Sampras returns a volley en route to winning the U.S. Open in September at the age of 19, the youngest man ever to win the tournament.

Men. For the first time, the men's tour was conducted by the Association of Tennis Professionals, the players' union. The tour comprised 78 tournaments worth $40 million in prize money.

The first of the four grand-slam tournaments, the Australian Open, ended on January 28 in Melbourne. Lendl led Edberg in the final, 4-6, 7-6, 5-2, when Edberg quit because of an injured abdominal muscle. In the French Open final on June 10 in Paris, Gómez defeated Agassi 6-3, 2-6, 6-4, 6-4.

The $6.4-million Wimbledon championships outside London ended on July 8. For the third consecutive year, Edberg met Becker of West Germany in the final. Edberg, who won in 1988, won again, 6-2, 6-2, 3-6, 3-6, 6-4.

In the $6.3-million U.S. Open in New York City, John McEnroe of New York City, a four-time champion, reached the semifinals. The 12th-seeded Sampras defeated Lendl in the quarterfinals and McEnroe in the semifinals. In the final on September 9, Sampras upset Agassi, 6-4, 6-3, 6-2. Sampras, at 19 years, 28 days, was the youngest man ever to win this title. Sampras also won the year-ending $6-million Grand Slam Cup and its record winner's purse of $2 million.

Women. In the Australian Open final, Graf defeated Mary Joe Fernandez of Miami, 6-3, 6-4. In the French Open final, the much-improved Seles upset Graf, 7-6, 6-4, and at age 16 became the youngest winner of this title.

Seles also won the Italian and German opens before Zina Garrison of Houston upset her in the Wimbledon quarterfinals. Garrison then upset Graf in the semifinals before losing in the final to the 33-year-old Navratilova, 6-4, 6-1.

In the U.S. Open, Manuela Maleeva-Fragniere of Bulgaria and Switzerland upset Navratilova in the round of 16. Graf, trying for her third consecutive title in these championships, was upset in the final by Sabatini, 6-2, 7-6.

Capriati, an eighth-grader from Wesley Chapel, Fla., lost to Seles in the French semifinals and to Graf in the fourth round at Wimbledon and at the U.S. Open.

International team. The United States won the Davis Cup for men by defeating Mexico (4-0), Czechoslovakia (4-1), Austria (3-2), and Australia (3-2). Michael Chang of Placentia, Calif., and Agassi played singles for the United States against Austria from September 21 to 24 in Vienna, Austria, and against Australia from November 30 to December 2 in St. Petersburg, Fla. Rick Leach of Laguna Beach, Calif., and Jim Pugh of Rancho Palos Verdes won the doubles in all four competitions. Among the women, Capriati helped the United States defeat the Soviet Union, 2-1, in the Federation Cup final, held on July 28 and 29 in Norcross, Ga.   Frank Litsky

See also **Capriati, Jennifer; Sampras, Pete.** In *World Book,* see **Tennis.**

Texas. See **Houston; State government.**

Thailand. A political duel between the prime minister and a rival with ties to the military disturbed Thai political waters in 1990. After four years as army commander in chief, General Chaovalit Yongchaiyut resigned the post on March 30 to become deputy prime minister and defense minister in the cabinet of Prime Minister Chatchai Chunhawan (sometimes spelled Chatichai Choonhavan).

Rumors of a coup. Chaovalit, who had been a vocal critic of government corruption, soon found himself under attack for corruption in the armed forces. Fuming over the attacks, Chaovalit quit his cabinet posts on June 11, hours before Chatchai was scheduled to leave for a trip to the United States. Military rallies in support of Chaovalit during the day fed rumors of an impending coup. Chatchai hastily traveled to a provincial palace to talk with King Bhumibol Adulyadej, Thailand's widely respected monarch and a symbol of political stability. Chatchai returned to Bangkok, the capital, flanked by Thailand's three most senior military officers, who promised that there would be no trouble while he was out of the country.

Even so, the armed forces appointed Chaovalit as their special adviser while the prime minister was gone. When he returned, Chatchai named Chaovalit his personal adviser on national security, foreign affairs, and narcotics.

Cabinet shakeup. On July 20, Chatchai's coalition government defeated a no-confidence motion in par-

451

Union of Soviet Socialist Republics

Mikhail S. Gorbachev, the president of the Soviet Union and general secretary of the Communist Party, struggled through 1990 to keep his reform policies alive and hold the country together. For much of the year, he steered a middle course between conservatives, who wished to see the Communist Party restore order, and radicals, who wished to see the pace of reform quicken. But at year's end, fears that Gorbachev was trying to satisfy conservatives were strengthened by the surprise resignation of his reform-minded foreign minister, Eduard A. Shevardnadze. In resigning on December 20, Shevardnadze warned that a dictatorship was approaching.

Gorbachev's standing abroad continued to outstrip his reputation at home. In October, he was awarded the Nobel Peace Prize. The Nobel Committee said the award recognized Gorbachev's "many and decisive contributions" to a new East-West order, and Gorbachev confessed to being very moved by the award.

Disorder within. The peace prize struck some observers as ironic in light of Gorbachev's valiant but largely vain efforts to cope with the disorder inside the Soviet Union. There, unrest mounted and ethnic conflict seethed, further frustrating *perestroika*— Gorbachev's policy of political and economic restructuring. But serious as these problems were, they paled by comparison to the steadily deteriorating economy. Nor did it help when economic reformers failed for four months to agree on a plan. Those who favored a gradual shift to a market economy, including Gorbachev, locked horns with the strategists of a rapid break from central planning. The latter group lined up behind the 500-day program drafted chiefly by economist Stanislav S. Shatalin.

In an effort to bridge the gap, Gorbachev presented a compromise plan. It favored a middle course, instituting only modest price hikes and keeping price controls an extra year—until 1992. The compromise also called for the gradual privatization of industry, as opposed to Shatalin's plan to transfer 70 per cent of state-owned enterprises to the private sector in little more than a year. While conceding that economic power must pass to the republics, the Gorbachev plan stipulated that the central government retain control over such key exports as petroleum and gold. Arguing against continued control by Moscow were the 15 republics that make up the Soviet Union.

Finally, on October 19, the Supreme Soviet (parliament) agreed by a vote of 333 to 12 on the compromise plan. The very next day, economic statistics for the first nine months of 1990 were released. They provided a grim picture of declining production, mounting inflation, and growing unemployment.

The situation deteriorates. The economy fared even worse in 1990 than it had in 1989, a disastrous year that produced the country's first trade deficit in 14 years. Productivity dropped because of repeated strikes. And what promised to be a record grain harvest seemed doomed by shortages of labor, fuel, and machinery. The distribution of goods also became a major problem as the central government's control weakened.

As winter approached, Soviet shoppers faced shortages of nearly all goods. Moscow, Leningrad, and other cities introduced food rationing. Disturbed by worsening food shortages and growing public unrest, the Supreme Soviet in November demanded that Gorbachev report on the state of the union. Gorbachev quickly responded with a plan to restructure the government and give new emergency powers to the president. He dissolved the Presidential Council of Advisers, created earlier in the year, and downgraded the position of Prime Minister Nikolay I. Ryzhkov. Ryzhkov, who remained committed to a slow reform tempo, had become increasingly unpopular.

Gorbachev also announced that he would turn an advisory body comprised of the heads of the 15 republics into the country's chief executive agency, the Council of the Federation. By offering the republics greater power, Gorbachev hoped to gain their cooperation in averting political and economic chaos.

Gorbachev's plan for restructuring the government was endorsed by the Supreme Soviet in November. Nearly all of his proposals also received the approval of the Congress of People's Deputies, the country's chief lawmaking body, when it met in December. The Congress voted to expand the president's powers by giving him direct authority over a cabinet of ministers and the power to legislate by decree. But it refused to create a special police force to enforce presidential decrees. In addition, the Congress added representatives from smaller regions to the Council of the Federation, despite Gorbachev's objections that the body would become unwieldy.

Gorbachev's greatest setback at the Congress came from his foreign minister's abrupt resignation. Shevardnadze had actively pursued Gorbachev's policies for forging improved relations with the West. Gorbachev was dealt a further blow when the Congress rejected his candidate for the newly created post of vice president, Gennady I. Yanayev. The choice of Yanayev, a conservative who earlier opposed a radical "shock" reform program, stunned liberal members of the Congress. Yanayev was finally approved in a second round of voting on December 27.

Boris N. Yeltsin, the president of the Russian republic and Gorbachev's chief rival, warned that the government restructuring served only to strengthen the

A Moscow crowd demands an end to the Communist Party monopoly on power just before the party's Central Committee met in February.

Will the Center Hold?

Is central government possible in a land populated by a far-flung multitude of different ethnic groups? This question confronted Soviet leader Mikhail S. Gorbachev in 1990 when one Soviet republic after another sought greater self-government. As the economic situation worsened, opposition to the central government in Moscow grew stronger. By December, all 15 of the country's republics had declared that their own laws took precedence over federal laws—in other words, that legislation enacted by the Soviet parliament in Moscow did not apply unless the republic's own lawmakers approved it.

The moves had been fostered by Gorbachev's own policies of *perestroika* (economic and political restructuring) and *glasnost* (openness). Both policies unleashed strong nationalist ambitions among the Soviet Union's non-Russian population, and even among Russians. With glasnost and the free exchange of ideas, long-standing resentments toward the central government and the Communist Party surfaced. At the same time, simmering tensions between ethnic groups erupted in riots. Perestroika led to elections in which voters openly rejected the federal government's policies. Many of the demonstrations against the government turned anti-Russian.

Many Westerners think of Russia and the Soviet Union as much the same thing. But it became clear that they are not the same when Russia—by far the largest and most populous of the republics—itself talked about seceding from the Soviet Union in June.

Russia lies at the heart of a sprawling empire built by the czars, who ruled from the 1500's until the Bolsheviks (later called Communists) came to power in 1917. For centuries, the czars added lands in eastern Europe and in Asia to the original Russian territory surrounding Moscow.

To give the country's non-Russian ethnic groups some measure of self-government, Bolshevik leader V. I. Lenin called for the creation of a federation—the Union of Soviet Socialist Republics (U.S.S.R.). It was formally established in 1922 and eventually came to include 15 republics.

Most republics carry the name of the region's dominant ethnic group—for example, the Ukrainian Soviet Socialist Republic (S.S.R.). Within these republics are a number of smaller republics, regions, and areas, also based on ethnic identity—that is, a shared language and culture. Altogether the Soviet census recognizes more than 90 ethnic groups called *nationalities*.

Although the Soviet Constitution proclaims all the republics equal, the Russian republic has always been the most powerful. Yet ethnic Russians today make up only half the total Soviet population, and that proportion is dwindling. At present growth rates, ethnic Russians will constitute only 40 per cent of the population by the mid-2000's. Muslims—of many nationalities—who comprise only 16 per cent of the population today, should jump to at least 32 per cent.

Soviet governments have followed contradictory policies toward the many nationalities in the U.S.S.R. On the one hand, the government has officially recognized local languages and customs. On the other hand, Russian has remained the official language, and languages once written in Latin, Arabic, or other scripts have had to use the Cyrillic alphabet of Russian. The government has encouraged ethnic Russians to move to non-Russian republics, where they often acquire the top jobs in government and industry. And the supreme central authority—the Communist Party—rules from Russia's largest city, Moscow.

Russia's empire nearly came apart in the early 1900's. Soon after the Bolshevik Revolution of 1917, several regions declared their independence. They included the Baltic States of Estonia, Latvia, and Lithuania; Azerbaijan on the border with Turkey; Georgia to the south; and the Ukraine, which borders Poland. The Soviet Army soon recaptured all but the Baltic States. They, too, however, were reannexed in 1940.

The Baltic republics predictably led the clamor for independence in 1990, after they elected parliaments with non-Communist majorities. All three republics claimed that they had been illegally incorporated into the Soviet Union in 1940. In March 1990, Lithuania became the first Soviet republic to try to secede.

Gorbachev ordered the rebellious republic to reconsider or face economic retaliation. When Lithuania refused to retreat, the Soviet government cut off its fuel supplies. Because Lithuania depends on low-priced Soviet petroleum and natural gas, the republic backed down in June. It suspended its declaration without actually repealing it. The Soviet Union lifted the sanctions and, after prolonged haggling, offered to begin negotiations on independence.

Latvia and Estonia took a more moderate approach. Their declarations avoided an actual break with the Soviet Union by calling for a period of transition prior to independence.

Gorbachev claimed that moves toward immediate independence violated the Soviet Constitution. He agreed that any republic had the right to secede under the Constitution, but only if it followed procedures set by the Soviet parliament.

These procedures require that the republic hold a referendum in which at least three-fourths of the republic's adults vote. Independence must receive a two-thirds majority in the referendum, followed by a waiting period of five years and the approval of the Soviet parliament.

As Gorbachev struggled to stay on top of the situation, separatist movements gained strength in many republics. Local Communist parties broke with the parent party and backed *sovereignty* (self-rule). In June, the Russian republic declared that its laws took precedence over federal laws. The Ukraine soon followed suit. So did Byelorussia. In December, Kirghizia became the last Soviet republic to declare sovereignty.

To prevent complete disintegration, Gorbachev proposed a new confederation of Soviet republics. He spoke of transforming the U.S.S.R. into a new, looser union of sovereign states voluntarily joined under a treaty. Such a federation would transfer local affairs to the republics, while the central government retained control over currency, energy, defense, and other key functions. In November, Gorbachev proposed giving broad powers to a Federation Council made up of the heads of the 15 republics.

Gorbachev insisted that the Soviet Union needed what he termed "an efficiently working center." The center would, in his vision, have only those rights that the republics agreed to. This proposal deviated sharply from the current structure, in which the central government determines which powers the states can exercise.

A draft of a new union treaty was presented in December to the Congress of People's Deputies, the country's highest legislative body. But the plan failed to satisfy those who insisted upon full political and economic sovereignty for the republics. Although the Congress endorsed the plan for a new federation, the treaty still needed approval from the republics.

Yet hope remained that some compromise was possible. There seemed little doubt that economic reform—the switch to a market economy—had its best chance of success if accompanied by political reform and support from sovereign governments in the republics.

Perhaps the future structure of the U.S.S.R. will resemble that proposed more than 100 years ago by George Hume, a remarkable Scottish businessman and author. Hume introduced the reaper to farmers in southern Russia in the mid-1800's and lived there for 35 years. Russia, he wrote, had such a diversity of nationalities, climates, languages, and customs that centralized government no longer made any sense. Russia should, Hume concluded, become a United States of Russia on the American pattern.   Eric Bourne

Lithuanians rally for independence from the Soviet Union early in the year. In March, Lithuania became the first Soviet republic to try to secede.

Union of Soviet Socialist Republics

presidency and would not help the republics. Despite the added powers, it was unclear whether Gorbachev could regain control over the spreading chaos. As the economic situation deteriorated, feuding with the central government escalated. On December 27, the Russian republic voted to slash its contribution to the central government's budget.

The increasingly rebellious republics challenged the central government throughout the year. The Lithuanian republic led the revolt by declaring its independence on March 11. The Latvian and Estonian republics followed in May, though they avoided a complete break with Moscow by not specifying a date for independence.

In a tough confrontation, Moscow demanded that Lithuania invalidate the declaration and halted fuel shipments in an effort to force the republic to back down. Because of Lithuania's reliance on Soviet fuel, its parliament voted in June to suspend the declaration pending the start of talks with Moscow over the republic's future status. After lengthy preliminary talks, formal negotiations opened in October.

Gorbachev meanwhile began a general discussion with the leaders of all the Soviet republics about a looser confederation that would, he said, combine *sovereignty* (self-rule) of equal republics with "an efficiently working center." In December, the Congress of People's Deputies approved the draft of a new union treaty, which proposed a voluntary federation.

Movements to separate from the Soviet Union had spread during the year. In June, even the Russian republic proclaimed its right to secede from the Soviet Union. By December 11, all 15 republics had set their sights on autonomy and declared that their laws took precedence over laws enacted by the federal government. See **Close-Up.**

Armed warfare continued in the Azerbaijan republic over Nagorno-Karabakh, a region largely populated by Armenians that lies within Azerbaijan. Armenians want the region to belong to the Armenian republic. In the Ukraine, student protesters who backed independence forced the republic's prime minister, an old-time party member, to resign in October. Earlier in the month, Gorbachev warned that the failure to contain separatist movements could turn the Soviet Union into another Lebanon, referring to the civil war that has torn that country apart.

The authority of the Communist Party steadily broke down during 1990, and movements advocating greater democracy sprang up. In February, the party's Central Committee voted to drop the article of the Constitution that guaranteed the party a "leading role" in public life. The Congress of People's Deputies endorsed this decision in March, in theory paving the way for a multiparty system.

The Constitution was further amended in April amid internal party strife and calls for a new party from Yeltsin, Gorbachev's main rival for power. The amend-

Moscow residents line up to buy bread in November as the Soviet Union faces its worst shortages of food and other basic goods since World War II.

A smiling Boris Yeltsin lifts his arms in victory after his election as president of the Russian republic by the republic's legislature on May 29.

ment permitted the formation of political parties for the first time in 70 years and legalized the Democratic Platform, an umbrella organization of reform groups.

At its March session, the Congress of People's Deputies expanded the powers of the presidency. The new president would assume the policymaking role that had belonged to the Politburo, the party's executive committee. Gorbachev was elected president with 1,329 of the 2,250 deputies voting for him. The nearly 500 "nyet" (no) votes and many abstentions were attributed to fears that a strong presidency could lead to the kind of dictatorship that the country had suffered under Joseph Stalin, who ruled from 1929 until 1953. After Gorbachev's five-year term ends, Soviet citizens were to elect a president directly.

Before the 28th Congress of the Communist Party opened on July 2, Gorbachev conceded that the party could in the future operate only in a multiparty environment. The two-week congress was widely seen as Gorbachev's most significant political victory since proclaiming *perestroika* at the last congress, in 1986.

Gorbachev succeeded in enlarging the Politburo from 12 to 24 members, bringing in the party chiefs of all 15 republics and significantly expanding the power base of the reform bloc. Only two members remained from the previous Politburo. Gorbachev was reelected party chairman by a 3-to-1 majority. But the quickening pace of departures from the party limited his victory in holding the party together.

Yeltsin criticized the cautious pace of Gorbachev's reforms. To fulfill his responsibilities as president of the Russian republic, Yeltsin announced he was leaving the Communist Party. Other radical reformers said they would also leave.

Shifts in Soviet foreign policy during 1990 matched internal political change in significance. Despite reservations about German unification, Gorbachev bowed to Western insistence on the principle of self-determination, ensuring that East German elections on March 18 became a vote on German unity. In April, the Soviets dropped their demand that a united Germany remain neutral. In July, Gorbachev agreed to Germany's joining the North Atlantic Treaty Organization (NATO), the Western security alliance.

West German Chancellor Helmut Kohl sought to reassure Gorbachev about German goals on a visit to Moscow in July. On November 9, the first anniversary of the 1989 opening of the Berlin Wall, Gorbachev and Kohl signed a treaty of cooperation and nonaggression.

Moscow also joined the United Nations in condemning Iraq, a former Soviet ally, for its August 1990 invasion of Kuwait. In addition, the Soviets supported the use of sanctions against Iraq and the build-up of Western forces in the Persian Gulf.

Superpower talks on defense became virtually "routine" in 1990, as Gorbachev remarked in October when he met with United States Secretary of Defense

465

Union of Soviet Socialist Republics

Richard B. Cheney in Moscow. Gorbachev and Bush reached accord in June on the major elements of the strategic arms reduction treaty (START). That treaty would reduce each side's arsenal of long-range nuclear weapons by about one-third over seven years. In November, an agreement on limiting conventional forces in Europe was signed. See **Armed forces.**

Churches, mosques, and synagogues—which had long been closed by the government—reopened during the year. On October 1, the Supreme Soviet approved a law guaranteeing freedom of worship. The new law ended the official policy of atheism, gave equal status to all religions, and forbade state interference in religious activities.

Government relations with the Roman Catholic and Russian Orthodox churches continued to improve. In mid-March, Moscow and the Vatican announced they would exchange envoys. It was the first step toward a restoration of ties that were broken after the Communist revolution in 1917. In October, the patriarch of the Russian Orthodox Church celebrated the first full religious service in Moscow's St. Basil's Cathedral in 70 years. A midyear opinion poll indicated that the Orthodox Church had become the country's most respected institution by a 2-to-1 majority over the Communist Party.   Eric Bourne

See also **Eastern Orthodox Churches; Europe** (Facts in brief table); **Yeltsin, Boris N.** In *World Book,* see **Union of Soviet Socialist Republics.**

United Nations (UN) played a leading role in international diplomatic efforts to force Iraq to end its occupation of Kuwait following an invasion in August 1990. The UN also worked at preventing war between Iraq and a multinational military force sent to the Persian Gulf region. The United States provided the bulk of that force. On November 29, however, the UN Security Council authorized the use of force if Iraq failed to withdraw from Kuwait by Jan. 15, 1991.

Persian Gulf crisis. Iraqi troops at the order of Iraqi President Saddam Hussein invaded Kuwait on Aug. 2, 1990. The day before, talks between the two countries had collapsed. The talks stemmed from Iraqi charges that Kuwait had been pumping too much petroleum, thereby weakening oil prices. See **Iraq; Middle East.**

The invasion triggered an international outcry, in large part because the economies of so many countries depend on petroleum exports from the region. The UN Security Council reacted immediately, voting 14 to 0 on August 3 to condemn Iraq and demand the withdrawal of Iraqi forces from Kuwait. The resolution was approved by all 5 permanent members of the Council: China, France, Great Britain, the Soviet Union, and the United States. In addition, 9 of the 10 nonpermanent members voted for it. They were Canada, Colombia, Cuba, Ethiopia, Finland, Ivory Coast, Malaysia, Romania, and Zaire. Yemen abstained.

Iraq refused to withdraw. On August 6, the Council

The UN Security Council, meeting in November against a backdrop of photos that Kuwait claims show Iraqi atrocities, authorized use of force against Iraq.

imposed sanctions, prohibiting trade with Iraq except for certain humanitarian aid in the form of food and medical supplies. Even that aid needed authorization from the Council's sanctions committee. (Twenty countries later demanded UN assistance because of huge economic losses suffered as the result of suspending trade with Iraq.)

Iraq annexed Kuwait on August 8, and the Security Council voted unanimously the next day to declare the annexation "null and void." On August 18, the Council demanded that Iraq release all foreigners it had detained and cancel an order closing diplomatic embassies in occupied Kuwait. To strengthen the embargo, the Council authorized a naval blockade of Iraq in the Persian Gulf. A new UN measure on September 25 expanded the embargo to prohibit all air traffic with Iraq and occupied Kuwait, except for humanitarian purposes.

On October 27, the Council voted 13 to 0 to hold Iraq responsible for war damages and human-rights violations in Kuwait. Yemen and Cuba abstained. From August 3 to year-end, the Security Council adopted 12 resolutions against Iraq for its occupation of Kuwait and refusal to release foreign hostages. Hussein released the hostages on December 6.

UN authorizes use of force. The Security Council won praise for taking in hand its responsibility as the keeper of international peace and security as it dealt forcefully with the explosive situation in the Persian Gulf. With the Cold War ending, the five permanent members of the Council began working together.

On November 20, U.S. President George Bush met with Soviet President Mikhail S. Gorbachev in Paris to urge Soviet support for a resolution on the use of force against Iraq. Although Gorbachev withheld immediate consent, the Soviet Union on November 29 backed a Security Council resolution authorizing military action against Iraq unless it ended the occupation of Kuwait by Jan. 15, 1991. The resolution carried by a vote of 12 to 2. China abstained, and Yemen and Cuba voted against it. This was the first time the United Nations had authorized force since 1950, when it approved intervention in Korea during the Korean War.

Namibia, the last colony in Africa, gained independence on March 21, 1990, ending 75 years of rule by South Africa. A UN peacekeeping force had been sent to Namibia in April 1989 to supervise the transition and ensure free and fair elections. UN Secretary-General Javier Pérez de Cuéllar said independence was achieved "in dignity and with great rejoicing" after UN member states had striven so long for it. Namibia, formerly known as South West Africa, was admitted to the UN on April 17, 1990. See **Namibia.**

Central America. In another peacekeeping operation, the UN Observer Group in Central America disarmed some 22,000 Nicaraguan rebels, known as *contras*, and destroyed their weapons. The contras, backed by the United States, had been fighting since the early 1980's to overthrow the leftist government

A candlelight vigil is held as the leaders of more than 70 nations gather for the UN's World Summit for Children in New York City in September.

headed by Daniel Ortega. After Ortega lost to Violeta Barrios de Chamorro in a February presidential election, the contras agreed to dismantle their armies under a peace plan worked out by the presidents of five Central American countries. The five were Costa Rica, El Salvador, Guatemala, Honduras, and Nicaragua. The demobilization operation, the first in UN history, lasted from April 16 to June 29. See **Nicaragua.**

Next on the agenda for the five Central American presidents was El Salvador. The five hoped to end a decade of civil war in that country through UN-supervised negotiations. Pérez de Cuéllar's senior aide, Alvaro de Soto, served as a mediator in the peace talks between the Salvadoran government and leftist rebels. After several rounds of negotiations, the two sides failed to agree on a cease-fire. On July 26, they did agree on establishing a UN commission to investigate human-rights abuses in El Salvador. But under the agreement, the commission can begin its work only after a cease-fire takes effect. See **El Salvador.**

Other peacekeeping actions. The five permanent members of the Security Council on August 28 completed a peace plan intended to settle conflicts among factions in Cambodia. The plan would end two decades of fighting and place the country under UN supervision until elections could be held to form a new government. See **Cambodia.**

The Council afterward turned its attention to the Arab-Israeli conflict. On October 12, it condemned the use of excessive force by Israeli security forces, who fired on Palestinian demonstrators, killing at least 17. The shootings took place on October 8 during a violent confrontation on the Temple Mount in Jerusalem, where two of the most sacred Islamic mosques are located. The Security Council ordered an investigation of the deaths. But the Israeli government rejected the investigation as interference in its internal affairs. The Council condemned Israel a second time on October 24 for refusing to cooperate with the investigation. On December 20, the Council adopted a resolution that called the occupied West Bank and Gaza Strip "Palestine territories" and criticized Israel for its deportation of four Palestinians. The United States supported all three resolutions, breaking with its longtime policy of backing Israel. See **Israel.**

The world's children received new attention in September 1990 when the presidents and prime ministers of more than 70 countries attended a World Summit for Children at UN Headquarters in New York City. The countries committed themselves to halting the deaths of 40,000 children every day from preventable diseases, including pneumonia, measles, and malaria. The UN Children's Fund (UNICEF) organized the summit, along with Canada, Egypt, Mali, Mexico, Pakistan, and Sweden.

The meeting ended with the signing of a declaration that pledged to offer "every child a better future." A plan for carrying out the declaration included such goals as having more governments ratify the Convention on the Rights of the Child. This document, adopted by the General Assembly in 1989, sets minimum standards for the survival, health, and education of children. It also states that children have a right to protection from abuse and exploitation. The convention took effect on Sept. 25, 1990, after 20 governments ratified it. The United States signed the convention, but at year's end Congress had not ratified it.

A World Conference on Education for All was held in Jomtien, Thailand, from March 5 to 9, 1990. It was organized by three UN agencies—UNICEF, the United Nations Educational, Scientific and Cultural Organization (UNESCO), and the United Nations Development Program. The purpose was to improve current teaching methods and find ways of educating 100 million children in areas without primary schools as well as some 900 million illiterate adults. The conference recommended using modern technology—such as transistor radios, television, and videotape recorders—to complement standard instruction.

Special sessions. The General Assembly held two important special sessions in 1990. The first, from February 20 to 23, approved a program of action against drug abuse and declared that the years from 1991 to 2000 are to be the UN Decade Against Drug Abuse. The program includes providing economic and technical assistance to developing countries that grow poppies, from which opium comes, and coca shrubs, used to produce cocaine. It is hoped that this aid will en-

courage these countries to switch to other crops, such as coffee beans.

A second special session was held from April 23 to May 1 to discuss the economic plight of developing countries. The 136 countries that participated in the session pledged to realize the "basic right of all human beings to a life free from hunger, poverty, ignorance and fear." The participants called for greater international economic cooperation, increased aid by rich nations, the protection of the environment, an open trading system, and stable commodity prices.

The General Assembly's 45th session opened on September 18. Guido de Marco, the foreign minister of Malta, was elected as its president. During the first three weeks of debate, 27 presidents, 15 prime ministers, and 86 foreign ministers addressed the world organization. Their speeches warned of the devasting economic and political consequences of war in the Persian Gulf. They also spoke of the economic difficulties of developing countries and called for action to stop the deterioration of the environment.

The General Assembly on November 11 elected five nonpermanent members of the Security Council to replace the five that were to leave on December 31. The five new members were Austria, Belgium, Ecuador, India, and Zimbabwe. They replaced Canada, Finland, Colombia, Malaysia, and Ethiopia. Nonpermanent members serve for two years.   J. Tuyet Nguyen

In *World Book,* see **United Nations.**

United States, Government of the. The federal government's staggering budget deficits became a major issue in 1990, placing tax policy on the front burner and affecting the fortunes of the two major political parties and President George Bush. In the end, Bush and congressional Democrats agreed to a $492-billion, five-year "big fix" deficit-paring program that included $164.6 billion in added tax revenues. But a majority of Republicans in Congress opposed Bush on the issue, decrying the President's decision to abandon his vote-winning 1988 campaign pledge of "no new taxes." As Bush negotiated with the Democrats, taking first one stance on taxes and then another, his ratings in the national polls plummeted.

The budget picture, gloomy enough as 1990 began, worsened after Bush in August sent troops to Saudi Arabia to protect it from a possible invasion by Iraq. On August 2, Iraq had seized Saudi Arabia's neighbor Kuwait—an act of aggression that Bush promised "will not stand." See **Armed forces; Middle East.**

Moynihan gets the ball rolling. Senator Daniel P. Moynihan (D., N.Y.) touched off the tax debate in December 1989, proposing a two-year, $62-billion cut in scheduled social security payroll taxes. He contended that social security taxes were higher than necessary and that receipts were being used to mask the true size of the mounting federal deficit.

Moynihan's move caused dismay and disarray among Republicans, who felt they had established a monopoly on tax cutting. But many Democrats also opposed the plan, believing it would be irresponsible to reduce federal revenue at a time of massive red-ink spending. In January 1990, Senator Ernest F. Hollings (D., S.C.) proposed a 5 per cent national sales tax to offset losses that would result from cutting both social security taxes and the capital gains tax. A reduction in the tax on capital gains—the profit realized from the sale of stocks or certain other assets—was an idea that Bush had been pushing.

In the House of Representatives, Congressman Dan Rostenkowski (D., Ill.), chairman of the House Ways and Means Committee, weighed in with a bolder proposal in March. Rostenkowski submitted a $510-billion plan to balance the budget by 1995. He wanted to freeze much government spending—including social security outlays—for one year, cut defense expenditures by $150 billion over five years, and raise taxes by $30 billion in the first year. Although the White House called it "comprehensive and thoughtful," the plan died—as did those of Moynihan and Hollings.

The budget battle begins. On January 29, Bush sent Congress a $1.23-trillion budget for the 1991 fiscal year (Oct. 1, 1990, to Sept. 30, 1991) that included $14 billion in tax hikes. About $4 billion of that total consisted of "user fees"—higher fees for the use of some federal services and property.

Relying on optimistic economic assumptions, the President forecast a deficit of less than $64 billion. But events at home and abroad conspired against him. The cost of bailing out the savings and loan industry soared, and a recession seemed near. Another factor was a dramatic increase in interest rates in Japan and Germany. Able to get a higher return on their money at home, the Germans and Japanese were less disposed to invest in U.S. government securities.

Richard G. Darman, director of the Office of Management and Budget, invited congressional Democrats to join in talks on writing a new, bipartisan budget. But the Democrats backed off, preferring first to fashion their own budget as a take-off point for negotiations. On May 1, the House approved a Democratic budget plan that cut more from military spending than the Bush budget while allocating more for social programs. On May 6, Bush and congressional leaders of both parties agreed to budget talks with "no preconditions," which Democrats interpreted to mean that tax hikes would be considered. Darman said the alternative to a budget accord would be $100 billion in across-the-board spending cuts mandated by the Gramm-Rudman deficit-reduction law.

Bush makes it official—yes, taxes. The President stunned fellow Republicans on June 26 by scrapping his promise of "no new taxes." He agreed that "tax revenue increases" would be needed as part of a deficit-reducing package. On July 18, angry House Republicans met privately and, by a 2 to 1 margin, adopted a resolution repudiating Bush's position.

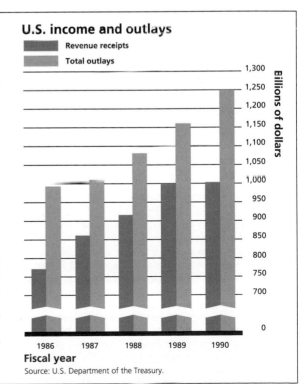

Federal spending

United States budget for fiscal 1990*

	Billions of dollars
National defense	299.3
International affairs	13.8
General science, space, technology	14.4
Energy	2.5
Natural resources and environment	17.0
Agriculture	12.0
Commerce and housing credit	67.5
Transportation	29.5
Community and regional development	8.5
Education, training, employment, and social services	37.5
Health	58.1
Social security	248.6
Medicare	97.7
Income security	148.3
Veterans' benefits and services	29.1
Administration of justice	10.1
General government	10.8
Interest	183.8
Undistributed offsetting receipts	–36.6
Total budget outlays	**1,251.9**

*Oct. 1, 1989, to Sept. 30, 1990.

Source: U.S. Department of the Treasury.

U.S. income and outlays

Revenue receipts

Total outlays

Fiscal year

Source: U.S. Department of the Treasury.

United States, Government of the

What followed were weeks of partisan "budget summit" wrangling, not only among party leaders, none of whom wanted to be first to propose higher taxes, but also among rank-and-file Republicans.

On September 30, Bush and a majority of congressional leaders agreed to a five-year, $500-billion package that emphasized spending restraint but also included $133.8 billion in higher taxes. Led by House Republican Whip Newt Gingrich of Georgia, conservative Republicans trumpeted their opposition to the tax hikes. Liberal Democrats were also opposed, charging that the proposed higher taxes on gasoline, liquor, beer, and cigarettes would hit the poor hardest. The Democrats also complained that Medicare cuts in the plan would be too drastic.

Early on October 5, the House rejected the budget agreement, 254 to 179, with a majority from both parties voting no. It was a crushing defeat for Bush. After the vote, the President shut down many government services for the Columbus Day weekend rather than sign legislation to temporarily finance federal agencies while budget talks continued.

During tense negotiations that followed, Bush stumbled badly. He first seemed to agree with Democrats that more of the tax burden should be borne by the rich. Then he met with Republican lawmakers—who disagreed strongly with that viewpoint—and backed off. The Democrats depicted him as a friend of the rich, particularly because he continued to argue for a lower capital gains tax.

The House approved a Democratic-sponsored budget on October 16, and the Senate adopted a competing plan three days later. Compromising, they adopted a $492-billion deficit-reduction blueprint on October 27. It raised the highest tax bracket, for the wealthiest taxpayers, from 28 to 31 per cent, and put a top tax rate on capital gains (which had been taxed at the same rate as ordinary income) of 28 per cent. Although the package did contain some Medicare cuts, they were smaller than in the original, rejected plan. The measure passed the House by a vote of 228 to 200 and by the Senate 54 to 45. A Republican majority in both houses opposed the accord. Bush signed the bill on November 5.

New Supreme Court justice. On July 20, William J. Brennan, Jr., a justice on the Supreme Court of the United States since 1956, resigned at age 84 after suffering a minor stroke. The departure of the liberal Brennan gave Bush a chance to enlarge the court's 5 to 4 conservative majority and perhaps affect future decisions on such major issues as abortion and affirmative action. Within three days, the President named his choice: David H. Souter, a federal appeals court judge from New Hampshire. Souter won Senate confirmation, 90 to 9, on October 2. See **Souter, David.**

The environment. On June 26, Bush, who promised to be an "environmental President," blocked—for a few years at least—the planned sales of undersea oil drilling rights off the coasts of southern California and Florida. A few days earlier, the President dropped his opposition to a proposed $100-million international fund to help reduce chemical depletion of the ozone layer that protects the earth from ultraviolet rays.

Secretary of the Interior Manuel Lujan, Jr., angered environmentalists in May by commenting that he questioned the need to "save every subspecies" of endangered plant and animal life. The nation's top conservation official said the 17-year-old Endangered Species Act was "too tough" and should be revised. See **Conservation; Environmental pollution.**

Cabinet. There were two changes in the Bush Cabinet in 1990. Elizabeth H. Dole announced on October 24 she was resigning as secretary of labor to become president of the American Red Cross. On December 14, Bush nominated Representative Lynn M. Martin (R., Ill.) to succeed her. And on December 12, Secretary of Education Lauro F. Cavazos announced his resignation. On December 17, Bush named former Tennessee Governor Lamar Alexander to the post.

HUD investigation. A scandal involving the management of the Department of Housing and Urban Development (HUD) during the Administration of President Ronald Reagan was pursued in 1990. Attorney General Richard L. Thornburgh recommended on February 1 that an independent counsel be named to investigate whether former HUD Secretary Samuel R. Pierce, Jr., engaged in a criminal conspiracy to reward loyal Republicans with hundreds of millions of dollars in federal housing subsidies. On April 30, a former Pierce assistant, DuBois L. Gilliam, told a House subcommittee that Pierce several times ordered him to award housing grants on a purely political basis—a charge Pierce had denied under oath. At the time he gave his testimony, Gilliam was serving an 18-month federal prison sentence for accepting payoffs from people seeking HUD grants.

Pentagon contracting scandal. Prosecutions in the two-year-old Pentagon weapons-procurement scandal continued in 1990, bringing to about three dozen the number of individuals and corporations convicted of or pleading guilty to criminal offenses. Some big-name defense contractors paid heavy fines. The penalized firms included Northrop Corporation, fined $17 million; General Electric Company, $10 million; and RCA Corporation, $2.5 million.

S&L bailout. One of the government's biggest headaches in 1989—bailing out the stricken savings and loan (S&L) industry—grew even worse in 1990 as the cost of the rescue mounted. Treasury Secretary Nicholas F. Brady told Congress on May 23 that outlays might eventually total nearly $300 billion. By some estimates, the final bill, including long-term interest on the money borrowed to cover S&L losses, could top $500 billion. See **Bank (Close-Up).**

On September 11, the General Accounting Office (GAO), an investigative arm of Congress, raised a new financial alarm. GAO Comptroller General Charles A.

Selected agencies and bureaus of the U.S. government*

Executive Office of the President
President, George Bush
Vice President, Dan Quayle
White House Chief of Staff, John H. Sununu
Presidential Press Secretary, Marlin Fitzwater
Assistant to the President for National Security Affairs, Brent Scowcroft
Assistant to the President for Science and Technology, D. Allan Bromley
Council of Economic Advisers—Michael J. Boskin, Chairman
Office of Management and Budget—Richard G. Darman, Director
Office of National Drug Control Policy—Bob Martinez†, Director
U.S. Trade Representative, Carla A. Hills

Department of Agriculture
Secretary of Agriculture, Clayton K. Yeutter

Department of Commerce
Secretary of Commerce, Robert A. Mosbacher
Bureau of Economic Analysis—Allan H. Young, Director
Bureau of the Census—Barbara E. Bryant, Director

Department of Defense
Secretary of Defense, Richard B. Cheney
Secretary of the Air Force, Donald B. Rice
Secretary of the Army, Michael P. W. Stone
Secretary of the Navy, H. Lawrence Garrett III
Joint Chiefs of Staff—
General Colin L. Powell, Chairman
General Merrill A. McPeak, Chief of Staff, Air Force
General Carl E. Vuono, Chief of Staff, Army
Admiral Frank B. Kelso II, Chief of Naval Operations
General Alfred M. Gray, Jr., Commandant, Marine Corps

Department of Education
Secretary of Education, Lamar Alexander†

Department of Energy
Secretary of Energy, James D. Watkins

Department of Health and Human Services
Secretary of Health and Human Services, Louis W. Sullivan
Public Health Service—James O. Mason, Assistant Secretary
Centers for Disease Control—William L. Roper, Director
Food and Drug Administration—David A. Kessler, Commissioner
National Institutes of Health—Bernadine P. Healy†, Director
Surgeon General of the United States, Antonia C. Novello
Social Security Administration—Gwendolyn S. King, Commissioner

Department of Housing and Urban Development
Secretary of Housing and Urban Development, Jack F. Kemp

Department of the Interior
Secretary of the Interior, Manuel Lujan, Jr.

Department of Justice
Attorney General, Richard L. Thornburgh
Bureau of Prisons—J. Michael Quinlan, Director
Drug Enforcement Administration—Robert C. Bonner, Administrator
Federal Bureau of Investigation—William S. Sessions, Director
Immigration and Naturalization Service—Gene McNary, Commissioner
Solicitor General, Kenneth W. Starr

Department of Labor
Secretary of Labor, Lynn M. Martin†

Department of State
Secretary of State, James A. Baker III
U.S. Representative to the United Nations, Thomas R. Pickering

Department of Transportation
Secretary of Transportation, Samuel K. Skinner
Federal Aviation Administration—James B. Busey IV, Administrator
U.S. Coast Guard—William J. Kime, Commandant

*As of Dec. 31, 1990. †Nominated but not yet confirmed.

Department of the Treasury
Secretary of the Treasury, Nicholas F. Brady
Internal Revenue Service—Fred T. Goldberg, Jr., Commissioner
Treasurer of the United States, Catalina Vasquez Villalpando
U.S. Secret Service—John R. Simpson, Director
Office of Thrift Supervision—T. Timothy Ryan, Jr., Director

Department of Veterans Affairs
Secretary of Veterans Affairs, Edward J. Derwinski

Supreme Court of the United States
Chief Justice of the United States, William H. Rehnquist
Associate Justices
Byron R. White
Thurgood Marshall
Harry A. Blackmun
John Paul Stevens
Sandra Day O'Connor
Antonin Scalia
Anthony M. Kennedy
David H. Souter

Congressional officials
President of the Senate pro tempore, Robert C. Byrd
Senate Majority Leader, George J. Mitchell
Senate Minority Leader, Robert J. Dole
Speaker of the House, Thomas S. Foley
House Majority Leader, Richard A. Gephardt
House Minority Leader, Robert H. Michel
Congressional Budget Office—Robert D. Reischauer, Director
General Accounting Office—Charles A. Bowsher, Comptroller General of the United States
Library of Congress—James H. Billington, Librarian of Congress
Office of Technology Assessment—John H. Gibbons, Director

Independent agencies
ACTION—Jane A. Kenny, Director
Agency for International Development—Ronald W. Roskens, Administrator
Central Intelligence Agency—William H. Webster, Director
Commission on Civil Rights—Arthur A. Fletcher, Chairman
Commission of Fine Arts—J. Carter Brown, Chairman
Consumer Product Safety Commission—Jacqueline Jones-Smith, Chairman
Environmental Protection Agency—William K. Reilly, Administrator
Equal Employment Opportunity Commission—Evan J. Kemp, Jr., Chairman
Federal Communications Commission—Alfred C. Sikes, Chairman
Federal Deposit Insurance Corporation—L. William Seidman, Chairman
Federal Election Commission—Lee Ann Elliott, Chairman
Federal Emergency Management Agency—Wallace E. Stickney, Director
Federal Reserve System Board of Governors—Alan Greenspan, Chairman
Federal Trade Commission—Janet D. Steiger, Chairman
General Services Administration—Richard G. Austin, Administrator
Interstate Commerce Commission—Edward J. Philbin, Chairman
National Aeronautics and Space Administration—Richard H. Truly, Administrator
National Endowment for the Arts—John E. Frohnmayer, Chairman
National Endowment for the Humanities—Lynne V. Cheney, Chairman
National Labor Relations Board—James M. Stephens, Chairman
National Railroad Passenger Corporation (Amtrak)—W. Graham Claytor, Jr., Director
National Science Foundation—Walter E. Massey†, Director
National Transportation Safety Board—James L. Kolstad, Chairman
Nuclear Regulatory Commission—Kenneth M. Carr, Chairman
Peace Corps—Paul D. Coverdell, Director
Securities and Exchange Commission—Richard C. Breeden, Chairman
Selective Service System—Robert William Gambino†, Director
Small Business Administration—Susan S. Engeleiter, Administrator
Smithsonian Institution—Robert McC. Adams, Secretary
U.S. Arms Control and Disarmament Agency—Ronald F. Lehman II, Director
U.S. Information Agency—Bruce S. Gelb, Director
U.S. Postal Service—Anthony M. Frank, Postmaster General

United States, Government of the

Bowsher disclosed that the fund used to insure the deposits of regular commercial banks could run dry if the United States goes into a recession.

NASA. The National Aeronautics and Space Administration (NASA) also had a rocky time of it in 1990. Although Bush on May 11 predicted a manned mission to explore Mars by the year 2020, the space agency was having problems with less venturesome projects. On June 27, NASA officials said that at least one mirror on the $1.5-billion *Hubble Space Telescope,* put into orbit on April 25 by the space shuttle *Discovery,* had been improperly ground. The defect prevented the telescope from performing up to the standard that astronomers had expected of it. A space shuttle crew was tentatively scheduled to make repairs on the instrument in 1993.

But the space shuttle itself was in trouble. On May 29, the discovery of a fuel leak in the shuttle *Columbia* forced its launch to be postponed. On June 29, a similar leak found in the shuttle *Atlantis* caused NASA to ground all three shuttles in its fleet. Shuttle flights resumed on October 6 with the launching of *Discovery*. See **Space exploration.**

Federal pay rates. On April 1, the Bush Administration sent Congress a long-promised plan to overhaul the federal pay system. Congress approved its own version of the proposal, eliminating automatic and uniform nationwide pay increases for federal workers. The measure also called for wages and salaries for government jobs to be set at the local level at rates competitive with similar, nonfederal positions. Some 2.4 million civilian employees of the federal government were, however, to receive an across-the-board nationwide pay hike of 4.1 per cent on Jan. 1, 1991. Bush recommended a 3.5 per cent increase on Aug. 24, 1990, but Congress raised it.

U.S. trade policy. The issue of trade between the United States and Japan continued to be a source of friction in 1990. On June 28, the two nations signed an agreement aimed at revising each side's economic practices and paring the $49-billion U.S. trade deficit with Japan. Japan agreed to increase its spending on public works by more than $2.7 trillion during the 1990's, an action that U.S. trade experts thought would create opportunities in Japan for many American companies, such as contractors and suppliers of construction materials. The United States pledged to increase tax revenues to slash its budget deficits—a factor behind Bush's shift on tax policy.

On June 11, Bush and visiting Mexican President Carlos Salinas de Gortari agreed to work toward the elimination of all barriers to the movement of goods, services, and money between the United States and Mexico. Canada, which has a free-trade agreement with the United States, would be invited to join the arrangement.   Frank Cormier and Margot Cormier

See also **Bush, George H. W.; Congress of the United States; Supreme Court of the United States.** In *World Book,* see **United States, Government of the.**

Uruguay. Luis Alberto Lacalle of the center-right National Party, also known as the Blanco Party, was sworn to a five-year term as Uruguay's president on March 1, 1990. A lawyer and rancher, Lacalle pledged to balance the budget, to improve the efficiency of social-welfare programs, and to cut the soaring inflation rate in half—to 50 per cent.

The promises had a familiar ring to the residents of a country where a work force of 1 million supports 650,000 retirees, most of them living on government pensions. But when Lacalle moved to cut government spending by a modest 15 per cent and raise taxes, there were protests from the nation's powerful labor unions. Similar opposition developed to his efforts to privatize some inefficient state-run enterprises, including a telephone company that has been unable to provide more than 90,000 people with service.

While Lacalle pushed for what he called "maximum austerity," Tabaré Vásquez, the newly elected mayor of Montevideo, the country's capital, moved in the other direction. A Socialist, Vásquez pushed through a program that included highly subsidized bus fares and pay increases for municipal workers. To pay for the subsidies, Vásquez imposed higher taxes on real estate and automobiles.   Nathan A. Haverstock

See also **Latin America** (Facts in brief table). In *World Book,* see **Uruguay.**

Utah. See **State government.**

Vanuatu. See **Pacific Islands.**

Venezuela. Higher oil prices resulting from the Persian Gulf crisis and new discoveries beneath old Venezuelan oil fields gave promise in 1990 of better times ahead for Venezuela. Public outrage over an austerity program imposed in 1989 waned in 1990 due to the good news related to oil.

Venezuela depends on oil for about three-fourths of its income. Following the United Nations-imposed trade embargo against Iraq and Iraqi-occupied Kuwait, President Carlos Andrés Pérez announced on August 23 that Venezuela would boost its daily production by 25 per cent, by December.

Citing what he called the "inevitability of confrontation" in the Middle East, Pérez urged foreign oil companies to help develop reserves estimated at 270 billion barrels of extra heavy oil recoverable through new technology in the Orinoco Belt, an area north of the Orinoco River in eastern Venezuela.

In October, authorities announced the largest oil field discovery since 1965—rich crude oil reserves beneath old wells in eastern Venezuela that had begun to dry up in the 1960's. To tap them, companies must employ new technology, drilling four times deeper than for wells previously drilled in the area.   Nathan A. Haverstock

See also **Latin America** (Facts in brief table). In *World Book,* see **Venezuela.**

Vermont. See **State government.**

Vice President of the U.S. See **Quayle, Dan.**

Vietnam. The Communist Party Central Committee, which sets Vietnamese policy, argued inconclusively during 1990. At issue was the moderation of Vietnam's rigid Marxist political and economic system.

Hard-liners won in the first round, a Central Committee session from March 12 to 27 in Hanoi, the capital. The committee denied that Communism had failed in eastern Europe, blaming the changes there on "imperialist and reactionary" forces. The committee called for more "political and ideological indoctrination to overcome what it said was Vietnam's own "socio-economic crisis."

Conservatives arranged the first known dismissal of a member of the party's steering committe, the Politburo. He was Tran Xuan Bach, a recent advocate of political reforms. Bach, once considered a future top leader, was accused of violating party discipline. Despite his ouster, Bach was given a good job and was allowed to keep his Politburo benefits. According to some observers, this indicated that Bach was being kept available for a comeback if public opinion forced the party to liberalize.

The Central Committee met again from August 16 to 28. The committee discussed the second political program in the party's history, set to be adopted in 1991. Despite having made 10 revisions in the program, the committee could not agree on basic principles. A new economic plan was not so heavily revised, but its details were kept secret.

One of Vietnam's economic problems was that the Soviet Union, which supplied all of Vietnam's fuel and cotton and most of its steel and fertilizer at subsidized rates, planned to put such sales on a cash basis at international prices in 1991. A delay in fertilizer shipments in 1990 was blamed for the year's small rice crop, which caused Vietnam to default on some rice export contracts. The economy was also burdened by the return home of workers from the countries of eastern Europe and the Soviet Union—where their earnings had helped pay off wartime debts—and from the Middle East.

Le Duc Tho died of cancer on October 13. He had negotiated the 1973 United States withdrawal from Vietnam with U.S. Secretary of State Henry A. Kissinger. Tho, who had refused to accept a Nobel Peace Prize for his actions, was a leader of the conservative bloc in the Communist Party leadership.

U.S. relations. Vietnamese Foreign Minister Nguyen Co Thach and U.S. Secretary of State James A. Baker III held the nations' first high-level meeting since the 1970's on Sept. 29, 1990, in New York City. They discussed the two main obstacles to establishing normal diplomatic relations: Vietnam's involvement in Cambodia and the U.S. servicemen missing since the Vietnam War.　　Henry S. Bradsher

See also **Asia** (Facts in brief table); **Cambodia.** In *World Book,* see **Vietnam.**
Virginia. See **State government.**
Vital statistics. See **Census; Population.**

Walesa, Lech (1943-　　　), on Dec. 9, 1990, won a landslide victory in Poland's first presidential election by popular vote. In January, Walesa (pronounced *vah WEHN sah*) gave the money he had won for the 1983 Nobel Peace Prize to a relief fund in Poland.

Walesa was born in Popow, north of Warsaw, on Sept. 29, 1943. The son of a carpenter, he attended a state vocational school and became an electrician at the shipyards in Gdańsk.

In 1970, after watching the militia gun down workers rioting over food shortages, Walesa joined the workers' rights movement. Later, he founded the organization that became Solidarity, Poland's first labor union independent of the Communist government. His negotiations led the government to recognize Solidarity as a legitimate voice of the workers.

In 1981, Poland's Communist government cracked down on dissent and imposed martial law. In 1982, it outlawed Solidarity. Walesa remained Solidarity's leader through years of underground struggle. During that time, he was held for 11 months in prison.

In 1989, faced with economic collapse, the Communists permitted Solidarity to hold seats in a new legislature. In elections for parliament, the Communist regime was peacefully turned out of office.

Walesa and his wife, Danuta, were expecting a ninth child in 1991.　　Margaret Anne Schmidt

See also **Poland.** In *World Book,* see **Walesa, Lech.**
Washington. See **State government.**

Washington, D.C. The trial of Mayor Marion S. Barry, Jr., for cocaine possession and perjury dominated the news in Washington, D.C., in 1990. The mayor was arrested on January 18 at the Vista International Hotel in downtown Washington, D.C. Barry had gone there to meet a former girlfriend, Hazel Diane (Rasheeda) Moore. Moore cooperated with federal authorities in videotaping the meeting, when Barry allegedly smoked crack. A federal grand jury on February 15 and May 10 indicted Barry on 14 counts of both cocaine possession and perjury.

The Vista sting followed years of federal investigation of allegations of drug use by the mayor. The probe had escalated in December 1988, when police went to the Washington, D.C., Ramada Inn to investigate alleged drug activity by former city employee Charles Lewis, a friend of Barry's. When the police learned that Barry was in Lewis' hotel room, they broke off the investigation. On Dec. 29, 1988, the U.S. Department of Justice said it would investigate whether Barry had committed a crime during visits to the hotel room. Lewis eventually testified that he had used drugs with the mayor in Washington, D.C., and earlier on trips to the Virgin Islands—charges the mayor denied.

After a 10-week trial, Barry was found guilty on Aug. 10, 1990, on one misdemeanor count of cocaine possession in a 1989 incident. Barry was found not guilty on a second charge of drug possession in 1988.

Washington, D.C.

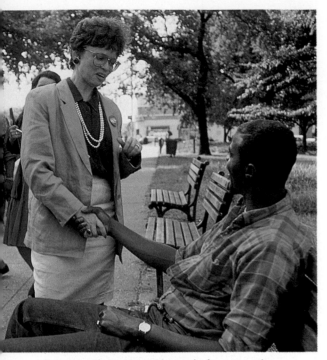

Democrat Sharon Pratt Dixon asks for support in her successful quest to become Washington's mayor and the first black woman to head a major U.S. city.

The jury deadlocked on the other 12 counts. On Oct. 26, 1990, United States District Judge Thomas Penfield Jackson sentenced Barry to six months in prison and fined him $5,000. Barry appealed both the verdict and the sentence.

Barry announced on June 13 he would not seek reelection to a fourth term as mayor. He did, however, run as an independent for a seat on the City Council and lost that race decisively.

Elections. Most of the top political offices in Washington, D.C., changed hands as a result of the 1990 general elections on November 6. Democrat Sharon Pratt Dixon, a lawyer, former treasurer of the Democratic National Committee, and former vice president of Potomac Electric Power Company, won the mayoral election. In her first bid for elective office, Dixon—with 86 per cent of the vote—defeated her Republican opponent, former Police Chief Maurice T. Turner, Jr. On September 11, Dixon had won the Democratic primary—the key contest in this overwhelmingly Democratic city—with 35 per cent of the vote. See **Dixon, Sharon Pratt.**

Eleanor Holmes Norton, a Georgetown University law professor and former chief of the United States Equal Employment Opportunity Commission, was elected the city's delegate to Congress. She succeeds Walter E. Fauntroy, who stepped down to run for mayor. In the general election, she defeated Republican Harry M. Singleton with 62 per cent of the vote despite disclosures that Norton and her husband had not filed city income tax returns for seven years.

Civil rights activist Jesse L. Jackson had been expected to run for Barry's post. Instead, Jackson ran for and won one of Washington, D.C.'s two new positions for "shadow senators." The City Council authorized the positions in March. Shadow senators are expected to lobby Congress and the White House, supporting Washington, D.C., statehood. The position brings no salary and no official legislative responsibility. Analysts said the post was important to Jackson, however, as a showing with voters.

In races for the 13-member City Council, voters elected council member John A. Wilson as the new chairman. The two at-large City Council races went to Linda Cropp, the Democratic nominee, and incumbent Hilda Mason, the Statehood Party candidate. Others reelected were Frank Smith, Jr., Jim Nathanson, and Harry L. Thomas, Sr.—all Democrats. Harold Brazil, who had defeated four-term council member Nadine P. Winter in the Democratic primary, won election to the council with 93 per cent of the vote.

Homicides. For the third year in a row, the District of Columbia set a new homicide record. There were 483 killings in 1990—about 41 per cent of them classified by the police as drug-related. The number of homicides increased from 434 in 1989, and 148 in 1985.   Sandra Evans

See also **City.** In *World Book,* see **Washington, D.C.**

Water. A drought in California and the Southwestern United States continued to cause shortages and restricted water use in 1990 along with questions about the region's ability to preserve its comfortable life style. The drought began in 1986 and was one of the longest since 1895, exceeded in extent and persistence only by droughts in the 1930's and 1950's.

The drought remained serious in California, where conditions have been most severe along the central California coast from Monterey to Los Angeles. Rainfall there was less than one-half normal. Santa Barbara, a resort city with 80,000 residents, was one of the hardest hit areas. The tinder-dry condition of natural vegetation and landscaping in the region contributed to a devastating fire that destroyed more than 500 homes and businesses on July 27-28.

The Santa Barbara area is dependent on local reservoirs and water wells. The city pays for the right to tap into the California Aqueduct, which brings water from northern to southern California. In 1979, however, voters rejected the construction of a connecting pipeline, saying that increased water supply would result in too-rapid urban growth.

In 1990, Santa Barbara's Gibraltar Reservoir was completely dry, while another major reservoir, Lake Cachuma, was filled to less than 25 per cent of its capacity. In response to the low water reserves, the city and other local water agencies adopted strict water rationing. Lawn watering was banned. Special "water cops" enforced the rationing rules and levied fines of up to $250.

In May 1990, the city of Santa Barbara decided to build a desalinization plant to produce fresh drinking water by removing salt from seawater. This plant, which could provide one-third of the city's water by 1992, will produce water at a cost of about 60 cents for 100 gallons (380 liters). In contrast, reservoir water costs about 1 cent for 100 gallons.

Drought-related fires in places other than Santa Barbara were reported in a wide area ranging from the Los Angeles suburb of Glendale to San Diego County, as well as in Arizona, Colorado, Utah, and Montana. Particularly severe was a fire in the Tonto National Forest of Arizona, north of Phoenix.

In response to the drought, the Phoenix City Council imposed a 30 per cent surcharge on each household's water use in excess of a base amount in times of water emergency. In times of water crisis, the city has the right to raise the surcharge as high as necessary to get people to cut back. And in Los Angeles, the Metropolitan Water District used a *Landsat* satellite circling 450 miles (720 kilometers) above the earth to spot areas of excessive water use.

Perrier recall. In early February, routine testing of well water in Mecklenburg County, North Carolina, revealed unsafe amounts of benzene, a cancer-causing chemical, in bottles of Perrier mineral water used in the test. Investigators also discovered benzene-laden Perrier in Europe, prompting a worldwide recall of 160 million bottles. The contamination was caused by not replacing charcoal filters used in processing Perrier water at its source in an underground spring.

Cancer-fluoride study. The United States Public Health Service in April announced the results of a two-year study on a possible link between sodium fluoride and cancer. Many cities add fluoride to drinking water to reduce tooth decay. The study found no persuasive evidence that the fluoridation of drinking water created a significant risk of cancer.

Worldwide water supply crisis. In September, experts from 115 nations met in New Delhi, India, to discuss an impending crisis in the supply of safe water worldwide. Already, water officials testified, 80 countries suffer from serious water shortage. By the year 2000, another 10 countries would be added to the list. Of the 15 million child deaths that occur worldwide each year, one-third stem from diarrhea, which is often related to unsafe drinking water.

Zebra mussels were multiplying rapidly in the Great Lakes, various cities reported. A mussel is a water animal that has a soft body inside a hard shell. Officials feared the animals would clog water intake pipes and shut down water treatment plants, power plants, and factories dependent upon lake water. Since arriving in Lake St. Clair near Detroit on a European tanker in 1986, zebra mussels have spread as far east as Cornwall, Canada.   Iris Priestaf

In *World Book,* see **Water.**

A "water cop" may impose a fine of up to $250 while enforcing the water rationing rules in drought-troubled Santa Barbara, Calif.

Workers search for survivors in the wreckage of an apartment complex
in Crest Hill, Ill., after a deadly tornado struck on August 28.

Weather. Above-average temperatures continued to dominate the United States weather pattern for most of 1990. In January 1991, scientists at the National Climatic Data Center in Asheville, N.C., announced that 1990 was the seventh warmest year in this century. Precipitation averaged above normal in the southern Great Plains, causing major spring flooding in Texas and Arkansas. Drier than normal conditions, however, were found in the Southeast and in a broad band from the Northern Plains to southern California and the interior of Oregon and Washington. Severe storms in North America, Europe, and Asia claimed high tolls in both property and lives.

Severe storms. There were numerous thunderstorms and tornadoes, especially in the Southeastern United States and in the Northern Plains. During the first six months of 1990, there were a record 935 tornadoes. In March, 130 tornadoes were recorded—the second-highest number in 37 years of recordkeeping —and in June, 412 tornadoes were reported.

On June 2, more than 100 tornadoes killed 14 people in the Ohio River Valley. Indiana was the worst hit with 10 dead and about 150 injured.

Then, on August 28, there was an outbreak of 255 severe weather events, including 10 tornadoes. The worst of these touched down at Plainfield and Crest Hill, Ill., suburbs of Chicago, killing 29 people and injuring 300 more. Several hundred homes and a high school were destroyed or severely damaged.

As is usual in the summer, many other severe weather events occurred in July and August. On July 11, softball-sized hail and two tornadoes struck Edmonton, Canada. In July, hail in the Denver area caused an estimated $345 million in damage to cars and roofs of buildings. Heavy rains poured down on Fairbanks and Nome, Alaska, and a funnel cloud—unusual for that area—was reported at Nome on July 26.

On August 7, Nome, where there is typically a lag of three years between thunderstorms, reported its ninth thunderstorm of the year.

Record highs. Much of the severe spring and summer weather resulted from unusually warm temperatures. Record-setting warm weather conditions began in January and persisted throughout the year. For the first time in the almost 100 years during which weather records have been kept, Rochester, Minn., did not have a single reading below 0°F. (-18°C) during the month of January. January temperatures across all of the northern Great Plains averaged up to 18 Fahrenheit degrees (10 Celsius degrees) above normal. This was because winter cyclones in Canada tracked far to the north of their usual paths, causing above-average precipitation across Canada and record-high temperatures and below-normal precipitation in the northern Great Plains of the United States.

A heat wave from March 11 to 17 set hundreds of records in the United States and central Canada. In Columbus, Ohio, high temperatures broke records for

476

five days in a row. Baltimore had 95°F. (35°C) on March 12, and Moosonee, Ont., at the southern tip of Hudson Bay recorded 35°F. (2°C) on March 14.

The high temperatures continued in April throughout most of the United States, except in the Southeast and lower Mississippi Valley. Fairbanks had its warmest April ever, and Anchorage, Alaska, had 21 days of temperatures reaching 50°F. (10°C) or higher.

Summer heat waves. Hot, dry summer weather resulted in record-high temperatures in the West, especially on June 26. That day, temperatures reached 122°F. (50°C) in Phoenix; 117°F. (47°C) in Tucson, Ariz.; and 112°F. (44°C) in Los Angeles.

The heat wave then moved eastward, setting more record-high temperatures: 105°F. (41°C) in Grand Junction, Colo., on June 27; 108°F. (42°C) in Pueblo, Colo., on June 29; and 102°F. (39°C) in Denver, tying the record for three days in a row. For the nation as a whole, June was the third driest in 95 years.

More record heat descended between August 5 and 11. California and Oregon averaged up to 11 Fahrenheit degrees (6 Celsius degrees) above normal. Sacramento, Calif., had seven days with temperatures at or above 105°F. Medford, Ore., recorded 10 days in a row with temperatures at or above 100°F. (38°C).

Alaska also shared in the extreme heat. Barrow reached 71°F. (22°C) on June 25, 8 Fahrenheit degrees (4 Celsius degrees) higher than the previous June record. July continued hot and dry, setting up conditions that resulted in many forest fires.

Heavy rains and flooding. Heavy spring rains caused flooding in the Southern Plains states, and, in late March, floods forced thousands of people to flee their homes in Alabama, Georgia, and Florida. Between April 15 and May 19, up to 24 inches (61 centimeters) of rain fell over northern Texas, eastern Oklahoma, and western Arkansas. Hot Springs, Ark., was deluged with 12 inches (30 centimeters) of rain in one 24-hour period on May 18—9.5 inches (24.1 centimeters) of it in seven hours.

Flooding stranded many cars and people in Texas and Arkansas. In northeast Texas, the Trinity River by the end of May had swelled to its highest crest since 1921. Flooding along rivers in Arkansas prompted disaster declarations for more than one-third of the state's 75 counties and caused millions of dollars in damage to farmland and homes. Flooding was also widespread in southern Illinois and Indiana.

Much flooding again occurred early in June over a wide area from Nebraska to West Virginia. The worst disaster struck on June 14 at Shadyside, Ohio, where 5.5 inches (14 centimeters) of rain fell in 3½ hours. Witnesses described a wall of water 10 to 15 feet (3.0 to 4.6 meters) high churning with motorcycles, cars, trailers, trees, toolsheds, telephone poles, and houses, and carrying everything away in its path. After the disaster had run its course, 26 dead were counted along with 70 homes that were obliterated and 30 more that were badly damaged.

Surrounded by a hastily erected earthen dike, a ranch home near Dayton, Tex., forms an island amid Trinity River floodwaters in May.

In Canada on June 14 and 15, high temperatures and rainfall up to three times normal produced the worst flooding in 20 years in the Peace River and Athabasca River valleys of Alberta. Mud slides and washed-out bridges killed nine people and caused $10 million in property damage.

From August 19 to 24, a front advanced slowly through the Ohio Valley and New York, bringing 13.5 inches (34.3 centimeters) of rain to Dividing Creek, Va.; 12.0 inches (30.5 centimeters) to Nassawaddox, Va.; 6.8 inches (17.3 centimeters) to Islip, N.Y.; and 4.5 inches (11.4 centimeters) to Chichester, N.H.

On September 11 and 12, torrential rains of 15 inches (38 centimeters) or more in 24 hours soaked Seoul, South Korea. More than 200 persons were reported dead or missing as a result of flooding, and property damage was estimated at $15 million.

Alaskan cold. On December 1, a record low of -47°F. (-44°C) was set in Fairbanks. Early in the year, Alaska also experienced record cold. In late January and early February, an intensely cold air mass built up over Alaska. Nome, Anchorage, and Kotzebue experienced their coldest February ever.

Southern portions of Alaska in February had heavy snowfalls. At Valdez, a total of 461 inches (1,170 centimeters) was recorded for the month.

On February 13, the huge air mass burst out of its boundaries and quickly covered the lower United States from coast to coast. Numerous low-temperature

Weightlifting

records were shattered in California, and snow fell at Laguna Beach, south of Los Angeles.

Winter storms in Europe. On January 25, Great Britain was lashed by a cyclone with winds reported at up to 110 miles (177 kilometers) per hour. At least 45 deaths in Great Britain were blamed on this storm, which left another 47 dead as it moved through the Netherlands, Belgium, France, and West Germany. On February 27, a second intense storm swept through western Europe, leaving 65 dead in 12 countries.

At least 12 people were killed by a storm on December 9 that brought snow and ice to Britain and northern Europe and torrential rains to southern Europe.

Tropical storms. There were 14 Atlantic hurricanes in 1990. Most of these formed in the eastern Atlantic Ocean and curved up into higher latitudes before menacing East Coast areas of the United States.

India and Asia were less fortunate. On May 9 to 11, a fierce tropical cyclone moved over southeast India with high winds and torrential rains. Maximum sustained winds were estimated at 120 miles (193 kilometers) per hour. More than 400 people were killed. On November 13, Typhoon Mike devastated Cebu and surrounding areas of the central Philippines, killing at least 188 people. Philippine President Corazon C. Aquino declared 30 of the nation's 73 provinces disaster areas.   Alfred K. Blackadar

In *World Book,* see **Weather.**

Weightlifting. See Sports.

Welfare. The United States Bureau of the Census reported in September 1990 that the poverty rate in the United States had inched downward in 1989 for the sixth straight year. The 1989 rate, 12.8 per cent of the population, compared with 13.1 per cent in 1988. Census Bureau officials said that this decline was so slight that 1989 family incomes remained about the same as in 1988. The slowness of the decline indicated that poverty remained a persistent problem.

Poverty. The Census Bureau said 31.5 million Americans had 1989 incomes below the poverty line, defined by the U.S. government as an annual income of $12,675 or less for a family of four. The poverty line is based on the amount of money needed to buy basic necessities and determines eligibility for a variety of welfare benefits.

The National Commission on Children, a federal fact-finding group, on April 26 said that 20 per cent of the nation's children were living in poor families, up from 15 per cent in 1970. The commission said that poverty places young Americans at risk for poor health, drug abuse, academic failure, teen-age pregnancy, and other problems.

A private study released on April 15, 1990, said 5 million American children under the age of 6—or nearly 1 in every 4 children—lived in families with incomes below the poverty line. The report, issued by the Columbia University National Center for Children in Poverty, called for universal health insurance coverage and expanded child care to help poor families with children.

Teen-aged parents. The Center for Population Options, a private research group, reported in September that the U.S. government spent more than $21.5 billion in 1989 on welfare programs for families headed by teen-aged parents. The amount was $1.7-billion higher than in 1988 because of an expansion in welfare benefits and an increase in births to parents under the age of 20. The report concluded that greater efforts are needed to prevent teen-age pregnancies, including sex education and contraception.

Food stamps. The U.S. Department of Agriculture reported in August 1990 that 44 states had increased enrollment in the food stamp program. The number of people on the food stamp rolls rose by 1.3 million from May 1989 to May 1990. Food stamps are a form of welfare that do not require that recipients be unemployed. Therefore, welfare experts say, an increase in the food stamp rolls often signals an oncoming increase in demands on other welfare programs such as unemployment insurance. The year 1991, they said, could be one in which more people apply for all forms of welfare. The report noted that many states also had an upturn in the number of aid recipients in various welfare programs. New Hampshire, for example, showed a 38 per cent increase in welfare recipients overall.   William R. Cormier

In *World Book,* see **Welfare.**

West Indies. A bizarre coup attempt unfolded in Port-of-Spain, the capital of the island nation of Trinidad and Tobago, from July 27 to Aug. 1, 1990. Iman Yasin Abu Bakr, leader of an Islamic sect, attempted to overthrow the government with support from more than 100 members of his Society of Muslims.

The rebels blew up the capital's police headquarters and stormed the Parliament building and the state-run television station, taking hostages at both locations. Among the hostages were Prime Minister Arthur Napoleon Raymond Robinson and a number of Cabinet members.

Abu Bakr, a former policeman and a convert to Islam who boasted that he was a "personal friend" of Libyan leader Muammar Muhammad al-Qadhafi, went on television and demanded Robinson's resignation and new elections. In polls taken before the coup attempt, Robinson's popularity had plummeted due to austerity measures he had imposed on the economy. An oil-producing country, Trinidad and Tobago has been in a recession since 1985 when world oil prices declined. Unemployment was estimated at 22 per cent, and food prices rose 25 per cent during 1990.

By the time the coup attempt ended with the surrender of the Muslims and their release of 46 hostages, 30 people had been killed and 300 wounded. Among the wounded was the prime minister, who was shot in the leg. Although the residents of Port-of-Spain did not revolt, as Abu Bakr apparently had hoped, they took out their frustration over hard times during three days of rioting and looting. Peace was finally restored with the help of troops from Jamaica, Barbados, and Guyana.

The surrender of the rebels apparently came after government negotiators had assured them of Robinson's resignation, new elections, and an offer of amnesty. The rebels were immediately taken into custody, however, upon their surrender.

Dominican elections. On August 16, Joaquín Balaguer Ricardo was sworn in for a second consecutive four-year term as president of the Dominican Republic. It had taken nearly two months to certify his electoral victory in one of the closest contests in Dominican history. Balaguer's chief opponent, Juan Bosch, charged fraud.

On August 8, Balaguer announced an unpopular austerity plan that doubled the price of some food staples and fuel. Violent protests against the plan broke out during a general strike on August 13 and 14, leaving at least 14 people dead. Sharp rises in fuel prices, due to the Persian Gulf crisis and reduced earnings from a shortfall in the sugar crop, added to the country's woes.   Nathan A. Haverstock

See also **Latin America** (Facts in brief table). In *World Book,* see **West Indies.**

West Virginia. See **State government.**
Wisconsin. See **State government.**
Wyoming. See **State government.**

Yeltsin, Boris Nikolayevich (1931-   ), was elected president of the Russian Soviet Federative Socialist Republic of the U.S.S.R. on May 29, 1990. The Russian republic is the largest of the 15 Soviet republics, containing three-fourths of the country's land, more than half of the population, and many of the natural resources. Yeltsin received 535 votes, 4 more than he needed for the required majority in the 1,060-member parliament. Yeltsin's campaign for office promised rapid change, including greater self-government for the Russian republic, creation of a separate currency, and a switch to a market economy. See **Union of Soviet Socialist Republics.**

Yeltsin was born on Feb. 1, 1931, in Sverdlovsk, the industrial capital of Siberia, located in the Ural Mountain region of European Russia. He earned an engineering degree from the Urals S. M. Kirov Polytechnic Institute in Sverdlovsk and worked on various construction projects from 1955 to 1968. In 1961, when he was 30, he joined the Communist Party.

Yeltsin has held various posts in the Communist Party, including that of *candidate* (nonvoting) member of the Politburo, the policymaking body of the party. Increasingly, he was viewed as the most important political rival of President Mikhail S. Gorbachev because of his views promoting self-government of Soviet republics. He resigned from the Communist Party on July 12, 1990, to concentrate on running the Russian republic.   Carol L. Hanson

Yemen. Yemen (Sana), also known as North Yemen, and Yemen (Aden), also known as South Yemen, merged into a single country, known as the Republic of Yemen, on May 22, 1990. Previous unification agreements between the two countries had collapsed because of political differences that had led to border clashes and other violence.

Ali Abdallah Salih, the president of North Yemen, was elected president of the new nation by the parliaments of the two countries. He was to rule for a transition period lasting 2½ years, after which elections were to be held.

Economic blow. Yemen's abstention from an Arab League vote condemning Iraq for its invasion of Kuwait in August proved costly. In October, Saudi Arabia, which accused Yemen of being pro-Iraq, suspended residency permits for the approximately 2 million Yemenis working in that country. Money sent home by these workers—an estimated $2 billion yearly—was one of Yemen's largest sources of income. Saudi Arabia also ordered all Yemeni business owners to find Saudi partners and obtain residency permits within one month. Failure to do so forced many Yeminis to sell at a great loss. By December, an estimated 750,000 Yemenis had returned home from Saudi Arabia, straining the new republic's already battered economy.   Barbara A. Mayes

See also **Middle East** (Facts in brief table). In *World Book,* see **Yemen (Aden)** and **Yemen (Sana).**

Yugoslavia. The federation of six republics that make up Yugoslavia came dangerously close to breaking apart in 1990. Conflict deepened between Serbia, the largest and most populous republic, and the more Westernized and prosperous republics of Slovenia and Croatia. Serbs dominated the Communist Party and the federal government in Belgrade, and Serbia argued that a strong party and a strong central government were needed to hold the country together. Slovenia and Croatia pressed for multiparty elections and for less federal control over the republics. Amid the turmoil, Yugoslavia lagged behind the rest of eastern Europe in economic and political reform—an area in which for decades it had led the Communist world.

The lack of unity among the republics was evident at a congress of Yugoslavia's Communist Party, which began on January 20. After three days of wrangling, the congress fizzled out. The Communists did, however, vote to give up their monopoly on power, paving the way for a multiparty system. Delegates from Slovenia walked out at the end, protesting the failure of the congress to approve more specific democratic reforms. Such changes were blocked chiefly by Serbian hard-liners.

Federal Executive Council President (prime minister) Ante Marković said that Yugoslavia would continue to function whether the Communist Party was unified or broke up into different parties. He said the government planned to provide a constitutional guarantee

479

Ethnic Albanians in Yugoslavia's Kosovo province protest in January against efforts by the republic of Serbia to extend its control over Kosovo.

of free elections and to grant the Federal Assembly greater powers. Many observers felt that Marković was the only leader capable of governing the entire country since the 1980 death of Josip Broz Tito. On June 29, 1990, Marković announced the formation of a new national party, the Alliance of Reformist Forces.

An anti-inflation program instituted by Marković met with initial success, reducing inflation from 65 per cent per month in December 1989 to nearly zero by mid-1990. But by September, retail prices were rising twice as fast as expected. According to government figures, industrial output for the first nine months of 1990 fell 10.4 per cent from the same period in 1989.

In Slovenia and Croatia, the Communists were routed in spring 1990 elections for local assemblies. In Slovenia, a seven-party coalition won 55 per cent of the assembly seats. The Communists came in second with 17 per cent. Nevertheless, a former Communist Party boss, Milan Kucan, took 58 per cent of the vote in a runoff election to become president of the republic. In Croatia, the center-right Democratic Union won a majority of seats in the assembly.

In October, the governments of both Slovenia and Croatia proposed a far looser confederation that would make each republic virtually independent. In a December 23 *referendum* (direct vote), 89 per cent of Slovenia's voters favored independence. The republic's assembly was to decide whether Slovenia would try to secede from Yugoslavia.

In Serbia, on the other hand, the conservative leadership continued to block moves toward greater autonomy by other republics. The ruling Communists, renamed Socialists, were victorious in December elections. Serbia also responded with violence to unrest in Kosovo, a province within Serbia.

Ethnic Albanians make up a large majority of Kosovo's population. Most of them want Kosovo given equal status with the six republics. During nine bloody days in January, Serbian paramilitary riot police clashed with demonstrators in Kosovo, leaving a number of ethnic Albanians dead. The demonstrators demanded the release of their leaders, who had been held in custody since 1989 for alleged "counterrevolutionary activities." In April 1990, a Kosovo court acquitted former regional Communist Party leader Azem Vlasi and 13 others.

The conflict escalated on July 5, when Serbian authorities dissolved Kosovo's assembly, took over its government, and shut down its Albanian-language news media. After Kosovo workers went on strike in protest, Serbian police again responded with force.

Amid the mounting tension, Marković insisted that the best chance of keeping the country together lay in open multiparty elections and in constitutional changes that would grant greater authority to the Federal Assembly.   Eric Bourne

See also **Europe** (Facts in brief table). In *World Book,* see **Yugoslavia.**

Yukon Territory. A final agreement on land claims was initialed on April 1, 1990, the culmination of 17 years of on-and-off talks between representatives of the 6,500 Yukon Indians and the federal and territorial governments. The agreement gave Indians title to 16,000 square miles (41,000 square kilometers) of land, about 8.6 per cent of the Yukon's area. The pact also guaranteed the Indians' participation in the management of lands, forests, and wildlife throughout the Yukon. Compensation was set at $232 million Canadian ($200 million U.S.). For the first time in land negotiations, the settlement did not require the Indians to give up their claim to original title. The agreement must still be ratified by the 14 Yukon Indian bands and by the territorial and federal governments.

Budget. In spite of reduced transfer payments— such as welfare and other aid—from the federal government, the Yukon budget for 1990-1991 forecast a surplus of $6.8 million ($5.8 million U.S.) on revenues of $351.5 million ($300 million U.S.). Mineral production was stagnant because of low metal prices and high costs of financing exploration.

Fires. In July, Alaskan fire fighters helped battle 28 forest fires menacing the remote Indian village of Old Crow north of the Arctic Circle. Most of the 250 residents were evacuated to the town of Inuvik for about 10 days.   David M. L. Farr

In *World Book,* see Yukon Territory.

Zaire. See Africa.

Zambia. President Kenneth David Kaunda in 1990 faced the greatest threat he had ever confronted in his 26-year presidency. For four days in late June, Zambians outraged at increased food prices rioted in several cities. The violence, which left at least 23 people dead, was followed on June 30 by a coup attempt against Kaunda by a group of junior military officers. Although the uprising failed, it revealed the depth of the hostility to many of Kaunda's policies.

The crisis was sparked by the government's decision on June 19 to double the price of corn meal, which is Zambia's staple food. The price hike was part of an austerity program launched in February to reduce foreign debt and stimulate economic growth.

The June crisis also resulted from opposition to the 17-year single-party rule of Kaunda's United National Independence Party. On June 29, Kaunda agreed to let the people vote in October on whether Zambia should have a multiparty system, but he later tried to put the vote off until August 1991. An angry public reaction to that proposed delay forced Kaunda on Sept. 24, 1990, to consent to hold multiparty elections in 1991 for both the parliament and the presidency. Kaunda also pardoned many political prisoners, including the leaders of the June coup. On December 17, he signed constitutional amendments legalizing opposition political parties.   J. Gus Liebenow and Beverly B. Liebenow

See also **Africa** (Facts in brief table). In *World Book,* see **Zambia**.

Zimbabwe. Going against a growing democratic trend in Africa, President Robert Mugabe in August 1990 reaffirmed his plan to establish a one-party Marxist government in Zimbabwe. The near monopoly of Mugabe's political organization, the Zimbabwe African National Union (ZANU), had been further strengthened by election results in March. ZANU won all but 4 of the 120 contested seats in Parliament, and Mugabe defeated the opposition presidential candidate, his former comrade Edgar Tekere, by a 5-to-1 margin. Only 54 per cent of eligible voters took part in the elections, and Mugabe's opponents charged that the voting had been rigged. Nonetheless, Mugabe called the lopsided election results a mandate for his policies.

During the year, the Mugabe regime continued its tight control of the press. In a concession to dissenters, Mugabe in July lifted the state of emergency that had been imposed by the colonial regime in 1965. The state of emergency gave the government many dictatorial powers to deal with unrest and maintain order. To reassure nervous foreign investors, the government in July 1990 announced that it was committed to a market economy and would sell many government-owned businesses to private buyers. Also in July, the government launched a long-delayed land reform program.   J. Gus Liebenow and Beverly B. Liebenow

See also **Africa** (Facts in brief table). In *World Book,* see **Zimbabwe**.

Zoology. West German primatologist Bernhard Meier reported in a scientific journal in 1990 the rediscovery of the hairy-eared dwarf lemur, a tiny primate that scientists had feared was extinct. Meier had found three of the dwarf lemurs in a burrow in April 1989 after an arduous three-day hike to reach a rain forest in Madagascar, a large island off the east coast of Africa.

The dwarf lemur, the world's second-smallest primate, had never been seen alive by scientists, and its existence was known only from five preserved specimens in museums. The last reported sighting of the tiny lemur, which is only 5¼ inches (14 centimeters) long, was in 1964. Meier, of Ruhr University, photographed one lemur and kept it under observation until releasing it back into the wild.

The hairy-eared dwarf lemur is the only surviving species of an entire genus of lemurs. Primatologists place great value on the study of lemurs because, on the isolated island of Madagascar, the animals evolved separately from other primates, such as monkeys, apes, and human beings.

Rare monkey find. In June 1990, two Brazilian zoologists reported discovering what they say is a new species of tamarin. The tamarin is a rare type of small monkey that lives in tropical rain forests in Central and South America. The monkey is in danger of extinction because those forests are disappearing. The black-faced lion tamarin was discovered on Superagui,

The hairy-eared dwarf lemur, formerly believed to be extinct, was rediscovered in a Madagascar rain forest by a German primatologist.

a small island 160 miles (260 kilometers) south of São Paulo, Brazil.

Vanessa Guerra Persson and Maria Lucia Lorini of the Natural History Museum in Curitiba, Brazil, went looking for the monkeys after finding a description of them written in 1850 and hearing accounts of their existence from local inhabitants. In February 1990, they spotted about 24 of the reported new species. The tamarin has a black face and golden body, with a thick mane around its face. The finding was considered remarkable because the island where the monkeys live is also inhabited by people and is near popular resorts on the mainland.

Some scientists view all types of lion tamarins as members of a single species. It was uncertain whether these scientists agreed that the black-faced lion tamarin represented a new species.

Long-distance traveler. A humpback whale has traveled farther than any other mammal except human beings, going more than 5,200 miles (8,400 kilometers), three oceangoing scientists reported in August 1990. The whale was seen first in April 1986 off Antarctica, according to researcher Gregory S. Stone of the National Ocean and Atmospheric Administration. It was then spotted off the coast of Colombia in late August 1986. The scientists recognized the whale from photographs that showed distinctive markings on the underside of its tail.   Elizabeth J. Pennisi

In *World Book,* see **Zoology.**

Zoos and aquariums throughout the world in 1990 opened some of the most ambitious exhibits ever conceived. Aquatic displays were among the most spectacular, especially the Osaka Aquarium, which opened in Japan in mid-July. The $133-million facility occupies 286,000 square feet (27,000 square meters). Its tanks hold 2.9 million gallons (11 million liters) of water, and it houses more than 300 species of fish, birds, mammals, reptiles, and *invertebrates* (animals without backbones, such as shellfish).

Visitors tour nine representations of locales along the "Ring of Fire," the volcanic region that encircles the Pacific Ocean along the west coasts of North and South America and the east coasts of Australia and Asia. The exhibits depict Japan's own Seto inland sea, the Aleutian Islands, California's Monterey Bay, the Gulf of Panama, the South American coast, Antarctica, New Zealand's Tasman Sea, and Australia's Great Barrier Reef. Each locale is populated by wildlife found at the actual site.

The ninth exhibit, the core of the building, represents an open expanse of the Pacific Ocean, with a 1.4-million-gallon (5.3-million-liter) tank that is 90 feet (27 meters) tall. It is home to various fish, including the whale shark, the largest fish species on earth.

American aquariums. The Texas State Aquarium opened in Corpus Christi on July 6, focusing on species native to the Gulf of Mexico and the Caribbean Sea. Visitors can travel through representations of marshland, shoreline, barrier islands, and the open sea. The grand finale simulates the Flower Gardens Coral Reef, the northernmost coral reef on North America's continental shelf.

On September 1, the Aquarium of the Americas opened on the Mississippi riverfront in New Orleans. Visitors can view some 7,500 aquatic animals representing 395 species native to the Western Hemisphere. They can explore a Caribbean reef by walking "underwater" through a transparent tunnel, where they encounter bonnethead sharks, angelfish, and butterfly fish. Under a canopy of moss-draped trees, a Mississippi bayou habitat is home to large fish called *alligator gar*, sturgeon, paddlefish, and snapping turtles. A Gulf of Mexico display features the underpinnings of an oil rig populated by sand bar and sand tiger sharks, tarpon, and barracuda, fish that are attracted to the legs of rigs in the gulf. An Amazon rain forest features colorful parrots called *macaws*, 15-foot (5-meter) anaconda snakes, poison-arrow frogs, and piranhas.

Africa in America. The Wilds of Africa, a 25-acre (10-hectare) first phase of a $100-million expansion and modernization, opened at the Dallas Zoo on April 21. A 1,500-foot (460-meter) trail through wooded and rocky areas like those in east Africa leads to a reserve that is a re-creation of a rain forest in central Africa. Along the trail, there are seven rare okapis, the closest living relatives of the giraffe.

The reserve is a forest and clearing that is home to a troop of lowland gorillas. Researchers are studying them by using hidden cameras, tracking devices, and other sophisticated electronic equipment.

New York City's Bronx Zoo re-created another part of Africa in its Baboon Reserve, which premiered on July 10. In the nearly 5-acre (2-hectare) reproduction of Ethiopia's high, grassy mountains, the stars are two troops of *geladas* (baboons) led by mature males who have long, capelike manes flowing over their shoulders. Their behavior and vocal sounds rank as some of the most complex in the primate world. Visitors can wander along pathways that offer several vantage points to view the geladas, *Nubian ibexes* (big-horned wild goats), and African ducks and geese.

Domed desert. In July, the Indianapolis Zoological Park opened its Living Deserts of the World, a transparent domed observatory 80 feet (24 meters) in diameter, containing animals and plants adapted to hot, dry habitats. This *biome*, a natural community of plants and animals controlled mainly by climatic conditions, contains 210 plant species, including many desert palms, cacti, and 8-foot (2.4-meter) boojum trees. Many of the 30 arid-climate animal species are free-flying, such as sand grouse and scaled quail, or free-ranging, such as iguanas and rare radiated tortoises from Madagascar.

Mist and mystery permeate the Miami Metrozoo's $1.2-million Asian River Life exhibit that opened on August 4. The sounds of chanting monks, drums, insects, and animals provide an eerie, but realistic, at-mosphere to a winding southeast Asian river setting. In the water are Asian small-clawed otters, which can be seen from above and below the water surface. A Malayan water monitor, a lizard that can grow 7 feet (2.1 meters) long, shares a pool with the rarely seen fly river turtle. Clouded leopards, small deer called *muntjacs* or *barking deer*, and Burmese mountain tortoises each occupy their own territory.

Test-tube tigers. On April 27, at the Henry Doorly Zoo in Omaha, Nebr., three Bengal tiger cubs were delivered from a 9½-year-old Siberian tiger.

The cubs were produced through *in-vitro* (test-tube) fertilization and embryo transfer. A research team from the Omaha zoo, the National Zoological Park in Washington, D.C., and the Minnesota Zoological Gardens in Minneapolis worked together for 10 years to achieve this successful birth. The team removed eggs from two Bengal tiger females and fertilized them with sperm collected from a Bengal male. The fertilized eggs were inserted into the Siberian female tiger's uterus, and she gave birth 109 days later.

Only one of the cubs survived. The others died of respiratory and kidney problems. This experimental procedure was the first step toward a long-range goal of providing strong, new stock to wild animal populations weakened by inbreeding. The plan is to freeze fertilized embryos from zoo animals and transfer them to animals in the wild.   Eugene J. Walter, Jr.

In *World Book,* see **Zoo.**

A monorail transports visitors along a 1-mile (1.6-kilometer) track through The Wilds of Africa, a new habitat at the Dallas Zoo.

1890

Gibson girl
Nellie Bly
Electric chair

Peanut butter
Wounded Knee

The World Book Year Book looks at some of the political developments and popular culture of 100 years ago and, in a special section, casts a backward glance at events of 50 years ago as reported in **The World Book Encyclopedia Annual for 1940.**

See page 489 ▶

JEANS

BY JOSEPH ARTHUR
— AUTHOR OF —
"THE STILL ALARM"

By Sara Dreyfuss

1890: What Was News 100 Years Ago

More than 200 Sioux Indians died at the Battle of Wounded Knee, and a melodrama called Blue Jeans, with an exciting sawmill scene, became a hit.

W MILL SCENE

The Ghost Dance religion spread like a prairie fire among the Plains Indians in 1890. "Within a few months the belief in this new religion has spread from tribe to tribe with marvellous rapidity," *Harper's Weekly* magazine reported. "The Arapahoes, the Shoshones, the great Sioux tribes, the Cheyennes, both North and South, and many other tribes, have been taught the faith." A Paiute Indian named Wovoka, also called the Paiute Messiah, had started the Ghost Dance religion in 1889. While sick with a fever, Wovoka dreamed that he was lifted into heaven. There, God told him to teach the Indians to stop fighting, to love others, and to perform a special ceremonial dance that white people called the ghost dance. If the Indians obeyed, God promised, the white settlers would disappear and the buffalo and all the Indians who had died in the past would return to life.

The Ghost Dance religion brought new hope to the Indians, who suffered from hunger, poverty, and disease. The vast buffalo herds had disappeared, leaving the Indians without their chief source of food, clothing, and other necessities of life. The government had moved many tribes onto reservations, where the Indians lived in near starvation, supported by meager rations from the government. In their unhappiness, they listened eagerly to Wovoka's preaching. "No man longs so much for a Messiah," *The Nation* magazine said, "as a man whose stomach is seldom effectually filled." *Harper's Weekly* reported, "It seems generally believed that the Indians will all fall into a trance, and when they awake they will find that the whites will have been buried,…and the Indians, with all the dead restored to life, will remain upon the earth—renewed and made many times more beautiful….The prairies will be covered with grass waist-deep; the forest and mountains alike will abound in buffalo, elk, deer, and antelope, more abundant then ever."

Buried at Wounded Knee

White settlers and Army leaders feared that the Ghost Dance would lead to an Indian uprising. *Harper's Weekly* said, "The delusion of the coming of the Messiah among the Indians of the Northwest, with the resulting ceremony known as the ghost dance, is indicative of greater danger of an Indian war in that region than has existed since 1876." On Dec. 15, 1890, the Army sent Indian police officers to arrest the Sioux chief Sitting Bull, who had settled on the Standing Rock Reservation in South Dakota. The chief resisted arrest, and one of the Indian police shot and killed him. Some of Sitting Bull's followers fled the reservation and joined a band of Sioux led by a chief named Big Foot, near the Cheyenne River. The Army then ordered that Big Foot be arrested, calling him a "fomenter of disturbances."

Four troops of cavalry caught up with Big Foot's band late in December and took the Indians to an Army camp near Wounded Knee Creek in South Dakota. When the soldiers surrounded the

The author:
Sara Dreyfuss is Associate Editor of *The World Book Year Book*.

The Ghost Dance ends in death

Arapaho Indians in 1890 perform rituals of a new faith called the Ghost Dance religion, *above*. The Ghost Dance increased hostilities between whites and Indians, leading to the deaths that year of Sioux chiefs Sitting Bull, *left*, and Big Foot, *below*, who died with some 200 of his followers at the Battle of Wounded Knee.

Sioux and began to disarm them, someone shot off a rifle. The soldiers opened fire on the Indians, who were almost entirely unarmed and outnumbered nearly 3 to 1. Big Foot and more than half of his band were killed. The cavalry massacred over 200 Indian men, women, and children. About 30 soldiers were killed, many by their comrades' bullets. *Frank Leslie's Illustrated Newspaper* commented, "In the annals of American history there cannot be found a battle so fierce, bloody, and decisive as the fight at Wounded Knee Creek between the Seventh Cavalry and Big Foot's band of Sioux." It was the last major battle between the Plains Indians and the whites. The Ghost Dance religion died out quickly after the massacre at Wounded Knee because many Indians lost faith in Wovoka's preaching.

With almost all Indian resistance gone, white settlement spread westward faster than ever. The way of life that characterized the Western frontier vanished rapidly. "The reign of the cow-boy in the Indian Territory is over," *Leslie's* newspaper reported in July 1890. "With the final round-up, which has just been completed, the ranchmen have been banished from the Territory and from Kansas, and all stock that is held in that part of the West will be close herded within fences." Two Western states, Idaho and Wyoming, entered the Union in 1890 as the 43rd and 44th states.

The "billion-dollar Congress"

The Republican-controlled Congress pushed government expenditures to new heights in 1890. The lawmakers had inherited a surplus of more than $100 million from their tight-fisted

Higher tariffs boost prices
The McKinley Tariff Act of 1890 levied stiff new taxes on imports, raising prices of food, clothing, and other goods. An advertisement for a ladies' clothing store boasts that its prices have not been affected by the new tariffs.

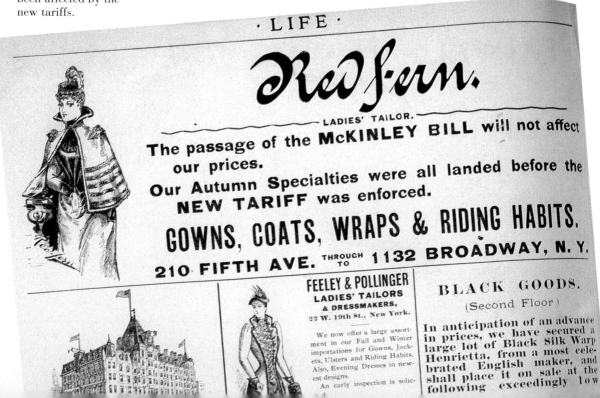

· LIFE ·

Redfern.

— LADIES' TAILOR. —

The passage of the McKINLEY BILL will not affect our prices.

Our Autumn Specialties were all landed before the NEW TARIFF was enforced.

GOWNS, COATS, WRAPS & RIDING HABITS.

210 FIFTH AVE. THROUGH TO 1132 BROADWAY, N.Y.

FEELEY & POLLINGER
LADIES' TAILORS
& DRESSMAKERS,
22 W. 19th St., New York.

We now offer a large assortment in our Fall and Winter importations for Gowns, Jackets, Ulsters and Riding Habits. Also, Evening Dresses in newest designs.
An early inspection is solic-

BLACK GOODS.
(Second Floor)

In anticipation of an advance in prices, we have secured a large lot of Black Silk Warp Henrietta, from a most celebrated English maker, and shall place it on sale at the following exceedingly low

predecessors and seemed determined to spend every cent.
Congress voted lavish appropriations for river improvements,
new federal buildings, and other projects.

Harper's Weekly said, "The demoralizing effect of a surplus is
shown by recent legislation in the House of Representatives,
which in two days appropriated more than three millions of dollars for public buildings....A little scrutiny shows the foolish
waste of many of these grants." The Democrats accused
Congress of wastefulness and nicknamed it "the billion-dollar
Congress." Speaker of the House Thomas B. Reed, a Maine Republican who was called Czar Reed because of his strong control
of the House, replied, "Yes, but this is a billion-dollar country."

The McKinley tariff

The free spending by Congress was partially offset by the
McKinley Tariff Act of 1890. This act pushed *tariffs* (taxes on
imports) higher than ever before, increasing the average rate
to almost 50 per cent. Representative William McKinley (R.,
Ohio)— who later became President of the United States—supported the bill to protect American industries from foreign competition. "Let England take care of herself," he cried, "let
France look after her own interests, let Germany take care of
her own people, but in God's name let Americans look after
America."

There were great differences of opinion about the tariff bill.
Leslie's called it "a wise and patriotic measure," but *The Nation*

491

Feminine ideals

Girls and women who make news in 1890
include Wilhelmina, *above*, 10-year-old
new queen of the Netherlands; reporter
Nellie Bly, who receives a golden globe,
right, after completing a record trip
around the world; the Gibson girls drawn
by Charles Dana Gibson, who grace the
pages of *Life* magazine, *below*; and singer
Lillian Russell, *below right*, who stars in
the light opera *The Grand Duchess*.

described it as "monstrous" and a "fool of a bill." Representative Richard P. Bland (D., Mo.) thundered, "The whole thing is a steal and a robbery of the great American people."

The tariff resulted in higher prices for textiles, foods, and many other consumer goods, including, *The Nation* declared, "tin plate, worsted cloth, carpet wool, pearl buttons, and a thousand other things that enter into the food and raiment of the people." *Harper's Weekly* complained, "Consequently, the burden of the tariff will fall on farmers, wage earners, and salaried men and women." And although farmers and workers had to pay higher prices for household goods, their earning power remained the same. Workers earned an average of about $500 per year for more than 50 hours of work per week.

Public unhappiness with congressional extravagance and with the high prices caused by the McKinley tariff contributed to a Republican setback in the elections of 1890. The Democrats won control of the House of Representatives, and the Republican majority in the Senate shrank to six. *The Nation* blamed the tariff for the Republican defeat, declaring, "The main cause of the cyclone which has emptied seventy Republican seats in Congress, is the wicked and unprincipled measure which that party devised."

The Sherman Antitrust Act

By 1890, monopolies called *trusts* had become common in oil refining and other industries. "The Sugar Trust [was] the first in the field," *The Nation* reported. "Then came the Lead Trust, followed by the Cotton-Bagging, the Binding-Twine, the Plate-Glass, the Linseed-Oil, the Window-Glass, and ever so many more." The trusts eliminated most competition by buying up smaller firms or forcing them out of business, and then limited production and raised prices.

The trusts increased in number and power until public opposition led to the Sherman Antitrust Act of 1890, the first antitrust legislation in the United States. This law, named for Senator John Sherman (R., Ohio), bans any business combination or practice that interferes with free competition or promotes monopoly or any "conspiracy in restraint of trade or commerce." The Sherman Act eventually became a cornerstone of the United States free-market economy.

The little princess

A 10-year-old girl, Princess Wilhelmina of the Netherlands, became queen in 1890 after the death of her father, King William III. *Harper's Weekly* told how, while her father lay ill, the child "watched with round, wondering eyes many strange proceedings—constant comings and goings...huge bundles of papers brought for her mother to sign, and frequent conferences of grave-faced men." When the child was told that she would be queen, her first question was, "Shall I have to write my name on all those papers every day as mamma does?"

At that time, the king of the Netherlands also served as the grand duke of the tiny country of Luxembourg. Luxembourg's laws did not permit a female ruler. As a result, Luxembourg broke away from the Netherlands and named its own ruler after Wilhelmina took the throne.

Around the world in 72 days

A 23-year-old New York City newspaper reporter named Elizabeth Cochrane Seaman, who used the pen name Nellie Bly, captured much attention in 1890. Her paper, *The World*, sent her on a trip around the world. Her mission was to outdo Phileas Fogg, hero of Jules Verne's 1873 novel *Around the World in Eighty Days*.

The brave young woman left New York by ship in November 1889 and made the trip—by ship, train, *jinrikisha* (handcart), and burro—in a record 72 days 6 hours 11 minutes. She arrived in triumph in Jersey City, N.J., on Jan. 25, 1890. *The World* boasted, "Without guide or escort; speaking no language but her mother tongue; with but a single gown and an outfit which the ordinary woman would consider inadequate for one day's visit to Newark, this frail, slender, plucky young woman has traveled over 23,000 miles, has demonstrated the perfection and simplicity of modern methods of travel, and has established a record which within her own lifetime would have been regarded as chimerical as a journey to the mountains of the moon."

Ideal women

If the resourceful Nellie Bly represented one ideal of American femininity, another was the Gibson girl, created by illustrator Charles Dana Gibson. The Gibson girl—a tall, poised, attractive, and outdoorsy woman—came to life in Gibson's drawings in *Life* magazine in 1890 and went on to become the symbol of the Gay Nineties.

Another role model for American women was actress and singer Lillian Russell. Her blond hair, lovely face, and statuesque figure made her the feminine ideal of her time. In May 1890, Russell became the first person to speak over the new long-distance telephone line linking New York City and Washington, D.C. From her New York dressing room, she sang a song from the light opera *The Grand Duchess* to a group of Washington notables including President Benjamin Harrison. "But still more impressive than the musical part," said *Scientific American* magazine, "is the remarkable clearness of the long distance transmission. Although we are all accustomed to ordinary local telephone transmission, the mind can yet hardly grasp the reality of the enormous progress which permits persons hundreds of miles apart to maintain perfect oral intercourse."

Lines from a dead poet

Another woman who made news in 1890 was Emily Dickinson, now honored as one of the greatest American poets. Dickinson had spent most of her life hidden away on the second story of her parents' home in Amherst, Mass. She never married and seldom saw anyone outside her own family. *Poems by Emily Dickinson* was finally published in 1890, four years after her death at age 55. A review in *Life* magazine described the poet as "a refined and gentle woman, who wrote these verses with absolutely no thought of publication, but simply to give expression to her deepest feelings." The review added, "The volume will delight thoughtful people as the poetic expression of a rare and shy intelligence."

Novels published in 1890 included *The Picture of Dorian Gray* by Oscar Wilde, describing a man whose portrait grows old and ugly as a reflection of his moral corruption while his face remains youthful; *The Light That Failed* by Rudyard Kipling, the story of a young man facing oncoming blindness; and *The Sign of the Four*, the second novel by Arthur Conan Doyle featuring master detective Sherlock Holmes. *The Illustrated London News* said the Holmes story "maintains a high average of excitement."

Other important books published in 1890 included the first volume of *The Golden Bough*, a 12-volume study of mythology and religion by anthropologist Sir James G. Frazer, and *The Principles of Psychology* by William James. Dramatist Henrik Ibsen wrote one of his greatest plays, *Hedda Gabler*, about a woman who has great wealth but can achieve none of her desires. One of the year's hit plays, a melodrama called *Blue Jeans*, thrilled audiences with a scene in which a deadly buzz saw threatened to cut the hero in two.

Execution by electricity

In 1890, New York became the first state in the United States to electrocute a criminal. At the Auburn, N.Y., state prison, in the presence of several doctors, electricians, lawyers, and reporters, convicted murderer William Kemmler became the first criminal to die in the electric chair. *Scientific American* reported, "He was strapped to a stout chair, electrodes were placed so as to make contract with top of head and base of spine, an alternating electrical current from a powerful Westinghouse machine

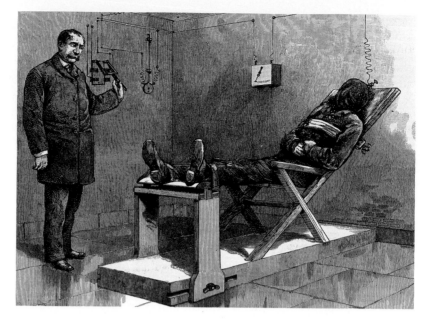

The first electric chair

Prison officials demonstrate the operation of the electric chair, hailed as a modern and humane method of capital punishment. New York in 1890 became the first state to use the electric chair to execute a criminal.

was joined, a switch was moved, and the criminal was struck dead—instantly killed by lightning. The apparatus employed was sure and effective."

The electric chair was widely hailed as an example of progress. *Scientific American* called it "a more humane and scientific method of executing criminals," and *Harper's Weekly* said, "While hanging is undeniably cruel, execution by electricity is instantaneous, painless, and less revolting to the spectator than the present system." *Leslie's* exclaimed, "In no recent change of methods is modern enlightenment more visible....It is in harmony with the human sentiments of an age which shudders at brutality." The method of execution was so new that there was no verb in the English language to describe it. A humorist in *Life* magazine had a proposal: "To meet the demand for a new verb to fit the new legal method of capital punishment, it is suggested that criminals executed by electricity shall be said to be 'elected.' Would that do?"

The "killer current"

In 1890, engineers, scientists, and the general public were still hotly debating the advantages of the two types of electric current—direct current (DC), which flows in only one direction, and alternating current (AC), which regularly reverses direction. DC was safer to use in homes, but AC was easier to transmit. The great inventor Thomas A. Edison used DC for his electric lighting system, but another top inventor, George Westinghouse, favored AC. Edison and his supporters attacked Westinghouse's AC system as a "killer current." Several cities even passed ordinances forbidding AC transmission. In a master publicity stroke, Edison and his associates sold three Westinghouse AC generators to New York state prisons for use in executions. Alternating current overcame any bad publicity stemming from its use in executions, and it soon became the standard form of electricity in the United States and Canada.

Two inventors, one sticky spread

Peanut butter, one of today's most popular sandwich spreads, was invented by a physician in 1890 as a health food. That much seems certain, but historians are not sure which of two doctors should get the credit. An unknown physician in St. Louis, Mo., ran some roasted peanuts through a kitchen food grinder to make a nutritious, high-protein food for his toothless patients. He turned the product over to food maker George A. Bayle, Jr., who sold the spread under the name Bayle Peanut Butter.

At about the same time, physician John Harvey Kellogg of Battle Creek, Mich., created a similar concoction. Kellogg operated a medical center called the Battle Creek Sanitarium (now the Battle Creek Adventist Hospital), which he defined as "a place where people learn to stay well." He advocated a diet of nuts, fruits, and whole grains, and maintained a laboratory where he worked to develop new health foods. According to Kellogg Company archives, Kellogg and his younger brother, W. K.—later a pioneer in the breakfast cereal industry—made peanut butter together in 1890. The brothers bought 10 pounds (4.5 kilograms) of peanuts, roasted and shelled them, and put the nuts through rollers in their food laboratory to make a spreadable paste.

Scandal topples Parnell

A scandal erupted in 1890 that ruined the career of Irish political leader Charles Stewart Parnell. At that time, Ireland and Northern Ireland formed a single country that was united with Great Britain and ruled by the British. Irish nationalists, including many Irish members of the British Parliament, wanted independence for Ireland. Parnell had united the Irish nationalists in Parliament and, as chairman of the Irish Parliamentary Party, greatly increased the movement's power.

A supporter of Parnell's named Captain William O'Shea filed divorce proceedings against his wife, Katharine—nicknamed Kitty—because

Parnell appeals to the people
Irish nationalist leader Charles Stewart Parnell, his career threatened by scandal because of an affair with a married woman, addresses his supporters in 1890 in Cork, Ireland. Parnell's party elected a new chairman to replace him.

The World Book Encyclopedia Annual 50 Years Ago

News of World War II, which had begun in 1939, dominated *The World Book Encyclopedia Annual for 1940*. Germany won swift victories in 1940 over Denmark, Norway, Belgium, the Netherlands, France, and Romania. Germany then attempted to bomb Great Britain into surrendering, beginning the air raids known as the Blitz. Almost every page of the annual reflected the impact of the war. But, as the foreword to the book said, "In spite of World War II and its effects on every phase of civilian life, the year saw great advances in wide-ranging fields." Excerpts from the annual are printed here in boldface type. The words in lightface type did not appear in the annual but are included here to help identify or explain the events described.

CHEMISTRY. Nylon, long heralded as the first synthetic textile, made its bow to the public. Dealers had difficulty in maintaining stocks. Nylon quickly replaced silk as the most common fiber for hosiery.

FRANCE. Perhaps never in history has a great nation collapsed with the tragic suddenness of the Third French Republic....Before the might, the paralyzing terror, and the dazzling speed of the German war machine, France was crushed like an eggshell.

GREAT BRITAIN. In his first public utterance as Prime Minister, [Winston] Churchill said he had "nothing to offer but blood, toil, tears, and sweat." This was the stark truth....As the fall and winter nights grew longer, the nocturnal attacks [German air raids on civilian targets in Britain] **grew in length and severity. London had them nearly every night....These attacks put the civilian population "in the front line trenches," and made urban life more dangerous than that in the army....But the new occupants of the front line were not defeated or driven to panic or surrender. They met danger with a poise and courage, an ability to "take it" and to "stand it" that won the unbounded admiration of the outside world.**

LITERATURE. The book which in the opinion of many led the fiction list for the year was...Ernest Hemingway's *For Whom the Bell Tolls*, a moving and vivid portrayal of a band of Spanish Loyalists who carried on a guerrilla action against [General Francisco] **Franco's men under the leadership of** an American who had enlisted for their cause....**In many ways the most distinguished American novel of the year was the posthumous *You Can't Go Home Again* by Thomas Wolfe, whose death removed from American literature one of its brightest talents....One of the outstanding books of the year was by a Negro, Richard Wright. His *Native Son*, which was a Book-of-the-Month Club selection, is a grim, exciting, and tragic tale, bitter in its realism but escaping melodrama by the sincerity of its emotion.**

MOTION PICTURES. The adaptation of John Steinbeck's novel, *The Grapes of Wrath*, was a fine screen account of farmers straggling into California from the Dust Bowl....The chief events of the year were probably Charlie Chaplin's long-awaited film, *The Great Dictator*, and Walt Disney's new blend of music and comic cartoons, *Fantasia*....*Rebecca* and *The Philadelphia Story* were escapist screen dramas, but vastly entertaining offerings. *Rebecca* received the 1940 Academy Award for best picture.

NORWAY. Occupation in the south was practically accomplished within twenty-three days, and the whole country was under the Nazi heel in less than two months....Major Vidkun Quisling and his friend Colonel Konrad B. H. Sundlo, in command at Narvik, were the prime traitors. The surname of the former came into common usage as an apt term to apply to persons or actions of treasonable character. The word *quisling*, standing for *traitor*, is still used today.

RADIO. Quiz programs were 1940 favorites with "Information Please" leading the field, but with numerous other question-mark programs in its wake, namely, the Quiz Kids, Kay Kyser's College, Dr. I.Q., "Take It or Leave it," and Professor Quiz.

TELEVISION. Although experimental programs were on the air for several hours daily, it was obvious that no great progress could be made in television for the general public until such time as the broadcasters can sell time on the air, as is regularly done with sound broadcasting; in other words, a way must be found to pay the high cost of transmission.

UNION OF SOVIET SOCIALIST REPUBLICS. In a year of spreading war, the Soviet Union in 1940 terminated its conflict with Finland, but absorbed without resort to force Bessarabia, North Bucovina [two regions then controlled by Romania], and the three Baltic states of Lithuania, Latvia, and Estonia....Thus some 23,000,000 people were added to the population of the Union. Five new independent republics came into the Soviet Union....In these newly acquired areas Soviet political institutions were immediately introduced.

UNITED STATES. The first peacetime selective service act in the history of the United States was accepted as a...necessity....

WORLD WAR II. On May 25 King Leopold [Leopold III of Belgium], believing that the situation was hopeless and that further resistance meant useless shedding of blood, decided to surrender the Belgian Army [to Germany]. His pocketed British and French Allies thought otherwise. They continued to fight desperately while retreating toward Dunquerque [also spelled *Dunkerque*, a French seaport on the English Channel]. From this port and its flat sandy beaches more than 300,000 of these soldiers were rescued by British vessels of all sizes, ranging from cruisers to small private yachts and fishing boats....This evacuation from Dunquerque, from May 29 to June 4, under fire from German guns in the rear, from German planes in the air, and from German ships in the Channel, was one of the most remarkable amphibious operations in the history of warfare, and did much to hearten the British in the hour of disaster. The evacuation of Dunkerque saved most of Britain's army. But the army left behind all of its tanks and equipment.   [S.D.]

London's financial district, The City, lies in ruins after German air raids in 1940.

she was living with Parnell. The case came to court in November 1890, and the charges—which Parnell did not deny—were proved.

Despite widespread calls for his resignation, Parnell refused to step down. "Surely the crime of which Mr. Parnell has been guilty stamps him as a man utterly unfit to lead a great political and national cause," scolded *Leslie's*. "He was not only weak, he was wicked. He was not only frail, he was false. He entered the house of a friend to despoil it." *Life* magazine, however, urged tolerance. "It is perfectly possible," *Life* said, "to combine intellectual qualities of the highest values, and creditable political, or even spiritual aspirations, with too warm a regard for another man's wife." Andrew Carnegie, the Scottish-born steel millionaire, supposedly cabled Parnell: "Resign, marry, return."

Parnell married Kitty O'Shea after the divorce, but his reputation and influence had been ruined. In December, a majority of members of the Irish Parliamentary Party declared Parnell's leadership at an end and elected a new chairman. Parnell died the next year.

Baseball news

In 1890, Denton True Young, a 23-year-old right-hander from Gilmore, Ohio, tried out as a pitcher for the Chicago White Stockings (now the Cubs) of the National League. Chicago's Cap Anson rejected Young as "just another big farmer," but the Cleveland Spiders (now the Indians) hired him. A catcher compared Young's fast ball to a cyclone and gave him the nickname Cyclone, soon shortened to Cy. Cy Young went on to win 511 major league games, more than any other pitcher in history. The Cy Young Award, given annually to the best pitcher in each league, was established after his death.

Starlings arrive in the United States

The first starlings, songbirds with glossy black feathers and long pointed beaks, arrived in North America from Europe in 1890. On March 16, a group of Shakespeare lovers released about 60 starlings in Central Park in New York City. The group planned to introduce into the United States all the birds mentioned in the works of playwright William Shakespeare. About 40 more starlings were set free in 1891. Those first 100 birds multiplied so rapidly that there are millions of starlings in the United States today, and huge flocks of them have become a nuisance in many cities.

And so began a decade that would be remembered nostalgically as the Gay Nineties. Probably few people living in 1890, however, considered the period one of unusual happiness or prosperity. To many, it brought worry over Indian uprisings, high prices, and the gulf between the rich and the poor. Others took cheer from the year's scientific progress and industrial growth, and looked forward hopefully to the new decade.

Dictionary Supplement

1990

Baby bust
Dweeb
Hip-hop
Neo-Geo
Rambo

WYSIWYG
Wussy

An informative essay on how we shorten our language—and, perhaps, make it more colorful—by using such acronyms as *dinks*, *SWAT*, and *Yuppie* leads off this section. Following the essay is a list of words added to the 1991 edition of **The World Book Dictionary** because they have been used enough to become a permanent part of our ever-changing language.

Whether or not you agree with the way the English language is developing, there can be no doubt that it is flowing faster. More people have more to say in English than ever before, and their messages are being spread faster and farther by fax and satellite. But even though it is becoming easier to convey our thoughts, we are still continually striving to condense our language.

We can see this shortening process at work as it spreads from one aspect of our lives to another. This year *dinks* (double income no kids) has found its way into *The World Book Dictionary*, continuing a social shorthand that builds on the earlier *yuppie* (young urban professional) and *WASP* (white Anglo-Saxon Protestant). This phenomenon is not limited to American English. British English has made numerous contributions, one of the more curious being *quango* (quasi-autonomous national governmental organization, of which the British Post Office is an example).

Speakers of English seem to have started using pronounceable abbreviations a long time ago. These forms are usually called *acronyms*, a word apparently coined about 1943. It is patterned on the much older *homonym*, *synonym*, and *antonym* from which *acronym* takes *-onym*, with the sense "name," from the Greek *onyma*. To this was added the Greek *ákros* meaning "tip" or "end."

Acronyms are coined in English in almost every field. For example, computer technology added this year's *WYSIWYG* (what you see is what you get) to the earlier *GIGO* (garbage in, garbage out) and *ROM* (read-only memory) and *RAM* (random-access memory). Law enforcement contributed *PINS* (person in need of supervision) and *SWAT* (special weapons attack team). Two important scientific devices, *radar* (radio detection and ranging) and *laser* (light amplification by stimulated emission of radiation) originated as acronyms. Medicine added its own shorthand for two dreaded diseases, *AIDS* (acquired immune deficiency syndrome) and *SIDS* (sudden infant death syndrome). Politics and world affairs contributed such acronyms as *PAC* (political action committee), *COLA* (cost of living adjustment), and *OPEC* (Organization of Petroleum Exporting Countries). Even the field of extraterrestrial exploration has contributed the now accepted *SETI* (search for extraterrestrial intelligence).

The popularity of acronyms is so widespread that organizations seeking a name often think first of a catchy and relevant word and then form their organization around it. Good examples of this are *MADD* (Mothers Against Drunk Driving), *ASH* (Action on Smoking and Health), and *CARE* (originally, Cooperative for American Relief to Europe, later changed to the less euphonious "Everywhere" in order to preserve the spelling CARE).

Although an acronym can serve as a convenient code for a particularly long name, the indiscriminate use of acronyms is sometimes decried by commentators on English usage. But as long as this language process remains popular, usage conservators will be facing an ever-increasing wave of acronyms, even unto their own doorstep: DOTEL (Defenders of the English Language), an organization of language preservation.   *Robert K. Barnhart*

A a

ab|zyme (ab′zīm), *n.* an antibody that is chemically modified to function as an enzyme: *Enzymatic antibodies, or abzymes, . . . perform a range of chemical jobs such as making or breaking specific bonds between the amino acids that make up proteins* (Science News). [< *ab-*[1] + (en)*zyme*]

a|cute-care (ə kyüt′ kãr′), *adj.* designed for the care of patients with serious diseases of relatively short duration; equipped to treat nonchronic diseases: *Citing a "drastically eroded" financial situation, the head of the city's Health and Hospitals Corporation has recommended reducing from 15 to 11 the number of acute-care municipal hospitals* (New York Times).

ADD (no periods), attention deficit disorder: *ADD children reported significantly more symptoms of depression and anxiety than the comparison group* (Science News).

a|dip|sin (ə dip′sin), *n.* a chemical substance found primarily in adipose tissue and associated with various types of obesity, such as those due to defects in genes or metabolism: *Some forms of obesity . . . may be tied to a lack of adipsin* (Gina Kolata). [< Latin *adip(i)s* fat + English *-in*[2]]

am|bu|lette (am′byə let′), *n.* a small bus, van, or similar vehicle designed to carry elderly or handicapped people: *The Holmes Ambulance service . . . operates the so-called ambulette vans to transport as many as four wheelchair or ambulatory patients* (New York Times).

AOR (no periods) adult-oriented rock; classic rock: *Sales are helped by Zeppelin's status as the backbone of AOR and classic-rock radio* (Rolling Stone).

attention deficit disorder, a neurological or psychological disorder of children, characterized by excessive restlessness and an inability to concentrate on a single subject or activity; hyperactivity: *The use of Ritalin and other stimulants to treat attention deficit disorder (ADD), commonly called hyperactivity, . . . has been a controversial issue* (Jenny Tesar).

au|ric|u|lin (ô rik′yə lin), *n.* a hormone produced by the heart that dilates blood vessels, decreases the rate of heart contractions, and stimulates the excretion of sodium in the urine: *A lack of . . . auriculin could play an important role in causing some forms of hypertension* (John H. Laragh). [< Latin *auricul(a)* auricle + English *-in*[2]]

B b

baby bust, a sharp decrease in the birth rate of a population: *The baby bust . . . has meant a shrinking pool of college-age youngsters* (Time).

back-chan|nel (bak′chan′əl), *adj., n.* —*adj.* secret; clandestine: *Mr. Kelly had been engaged in back-channel discussions with Lieut.-Col. Oliver North . . . on hostage releases* (Manchester Guardian Weekly). —*n.* the person or means by which something is carried on secretly.

bean count, *U.S. Informal.* a tally or reckoning by numbers; statistical analysis: *The Pentagon's bean count . . . ig-*nores French and Spanish forces because these do not come under direct NATO command (Time). —**bean counting.**

bean counter, *U.S. Informal.* someone who compiles statistical records or accounts, as of business or sales.

beltway, *n.* **2 the Beltway**. Washington, D.C., considered as the seat of the U.S. government and all of the people concerned with the functioning of the government: *There's a life beyond the Beltway, a whole country out there . . .* (Rolling Stone).

bipolar disorder, a mental disorder characterized by alternating periods of mania and depression; manic-depressive psychosis: *Bipolar disorder . . . is marked by extreme mood swings and by alternating episodes of depression and intense activity* (Lewis L. Judd).

C c

chill out, *U.S. Slang.* to take it easy; calm down; cool it: *I said angrily, "You messing with my high." "Chill out," he said. "You can't get too deep into this or it will take you out, man"* (Vanity Fair).

classic rock, rock music, especially of the 1960's and 1970's, considered to be the original or traditional form of this music: *a concert of classic rock.*

Clay|ma|tion (klā mā′shən), *n.* Trademark. animation of clay figures filmed in action, especially for use in cartoons and commercials: *The television commercials featured Claymation (clay animation) raisins, dressed in sunglasses, white gloves, and sneakers, who sang and danced* (Bonnie B. Reece).

cold fusion, the fusion of the nuclei of hydrogen atoms at normal temperature, resulting in a release of heat energy, attempted in various experiments, especially one in which an electric current is passed between two electrodes immersed in heavy water at room temperature: *Whether cold fusion proves to be a nearly endless supply of cheap energy or one of the greatest scientific delusions of recent times, it is . . . the hottest of scientific topics* (New York Times).

col|lid|er (kə līd′ər), *n.* a particle accelerator used to identify and study subatomic particles by striking together two beams of protons at great speed and energy to cause subatomic particles to be released: *The future holds the exciting prospect of very large . . . colliders* (New Scientist).

compatible, *adj., n.* —*n.* a computer program or equipment that can be used in different models or systems without adaptation: *The current family of I.B.M. personal computers and compatibles uses an operating system called MSDOS, for Microsoft Disk Operating System* (Peter H. Lewis).

cook|ie-cut|ter (kùk′ē kut′ər), *adj. U.S. Informal.* cast from the same mold; identical in form, nature, or character: *At Bush headquarters . . . there are so many beautiful blond cookie-cutter interns it looks like the student union at Princeton* (Vanity Fair).

core[1], *n., v.,* **cored, cor|ing,** *adj.* —*adj.* central; basic: *Deterring such an attack has been the core reason for NATO's* existence (Time). *The Fed decided the core questions of regulating the money supply* (New Yorker).

critical mass, **2** *Figurative.* the point where conditions or opinions combine to produce change (of focus, direction, policy, or the like): *. . . that critical mass of public pressure necessary for effective, vigorous public policies* (Thomas B. Edsall).

D d

dime, *n.* **3** *U.S. Slang.* ten dollars' worth of a narcotic drug: *There I was repeatedly accosted by dealers chanting, "Jumbos, dimes, crack"* (Dennis Watlington).

dinks or **DINKS**, *n.pl. U.S. Slang.* a childless couple with a double income: *They have wooed the busy yuppie couples known to market researchers as dinks . . .* (Economist). [< *d(ouble) i(n-come), n(o) k(ids)*]

ditz (dits), *n. U.S. Slang.* a flighty, confused, or eccentric person: *A nurse . . . inadvertently administers a fatal overdose to a patient—and catches all kinds of flak for being such a ditz* (Rolling Stone). [< *ditzy*]

done deal, *U.S. Informal.* an accomplished fact; fait accompli: *The 50 per cent raise [for members of Congress] is a done deal (barring miracles)* (Sarasota Herald-Tribune).

dweeb (dwēb), *n. U.S. Slang.* a foolish or inept person. [origin uncertain]

dweeb|y (dwē′bē), *adj. U.S. Slang.* foolish or inept: *. . . the dweeby high-school principal played by Jeff Daniels in the puppyish new movie "Sweet Hearts Dance"* (Vanity Fair).

E e

edit down, to shorten by or as if by editing: *The last 20 minutes [of "Deaches," a motion picture] could have been edited down* (Washington Times).

en|try-lev|el (en′trē lev′əl), *adj.* of or for a basic level at which one begins to learn a skill or use: *an entry-level job. . . . the latest version of a very popular entry-level laptop* (Connoisseur).

eth|no|as|tron|o|my (eth′nō ə stron′ə mē), *n.* the study of astronomy as used by different cultures and civilizations: *Ethnoastronomy . . . includes prescientific astronomy . . . [and] the astronomy of modern peoples who have not been influenced by advanced scientific culture* (Science News). —**eth′no|as|tron′o|mer,** *n.*

F f

feeding frenzy (fē′ding), *U.S. Informal.* the frantic pursuit of anything, as of profit, markets, art, or the like: *Charles Saatchi . . . was soon buying Chia [paintings], and other collectors quickly went into a feeding frenzy* (Anthony Haden-Guest).

G g

greenhouse, *n., adj.* —*adj.* of or having to do with the greenhouse effect: *There* is still major uncertainty about the magnitude of greenhouse warming (Science News).

gridlock, *n., v.* —*v.t.* to subject to a gridlock: *The phones were also gridlocked at Stanford, in Palo Alto* (Rolling Stone). —**grid′locked**, *adj.*

H h

herd immunity, immunity acquired by unvaccinated individuals through exposure to the weakened virus spread by recently vaccinated individuals: *Herd immunity is a great public health benefit, since even in the United States large numbers of individuals remain unvaccinated* (Rick Weiss).

high-end (hī′end′), *adj.* **1** including or comprising the high-income consumers; upscale: *the high-end segment of the housing market.* **2** most advanced or expensive of its kind: *Some systems available on the PC [personal computer] could go up as far in resolution as you can get on a high-end workstation today* (Microage Quarterly).

high profile, **2** a person who attracts attention or notoriety: *Such high profiles as Mariel Hemingway . . . and Sigourney Weaver were flashed by paparazzi* (Vanity Fair).

high-profile (hī′prō′fīl), *adj.* attracting much notice; conspicuous: *Progress on nuclear-arms reduction . . . could yield a high-profile political victory* (Atlantic).

hip-hop (hip′hop′), *adj. U.S. Slang.* of, having to do with, or characteristic of music intended for dancing, with a rap or Latin beat: *the hip-hop scene. Public Enemy's [a rock music group] hip-hop rage, however wrenching and reactionary, better reflects the street-level spirit of 1988* (Rolling Stone).

-holic, *combining form.* a person who is obsessed with or has a strong craving for something; a _____ addict: *Chocoholic = a person who has a strong craving for chocolate.* [variant of *-aholic*]

I i

im|mu|no|com|pro|mised (i myü′nō kom′prə mīzd), *adj.* made vulnerable to disease or opportunistic infection by a deficiency in the immune system: *The [Epstein-Barr] virus is a causative cofactor of some cancers . . . in patients who are profoundly immunocomprised, e.g. by AIDS* (Allen D. Allen).

infect, *v.t.* **6** to insert a computer virus into (a computer operating system or program): *Whenever the infected computer comes in contact with an uninfected piece of software, a fresh copy of the virus passes into the new program* (Time).

J j

jockette, *n.* **2** *Slang.* a woman athlete: *Here it [the Olympics] is capsulized into less than two hours, focusing on the most central concerns of myriad wonderful jocks and jockettes* (National Review).

jour|no (jėr′nō), *n. Especially British Informal.* a journalist: *Lunch tends to be in a wine bar or pub with fellow journos, talking shop* (Sunday Times).

504

K k

kiss-and-tell (kis′ən tel′), *adj. U.S.* revealing confidential or private matters: *kiss-and-tell books. The talk of the business right now is former ABC exec Jim Spence's kiss-and-tell memoir* (Sports Illustrated). [< the idiom *kiss-and-tell*]

knowledge base or **representation**, the basic store of information required by a computer to solve a problem or perform a task: *Until they acquire . . . a knowledge base or knowledge representation, computer systems are going to miss . . . many common, and seemingly simple, writing problems* (Atlantic).

L l

LBO (no periods), leveraged buyout: *In LBOs, often 90% or more of the purchase price is borrowed money* (Wall Street Journal).

life-care (līf′kãr′), *adj.* of or designating a housing complex for elderly people which provides residents with an apartment unit and services for the rest of their lives: *Almost every life-care development offers a beauty salon, a doctor's office, and places for social activities* (Philip Langdon).

lip, *n.*

read my lips, *U.S. Informal.* pay close attention to my words; watch what I say: *"I could play . . . love scenes! She'll gaze up at me longingly . . ." "4′11″. Read my lips. You're 4′11″."* (Washington Post).

low-end (lō′end′), *adj.* **1** including or comprising the low-income consumers; downscale: *[On tap . . . were additional] new models in the high-end and low-end segments of the import market* (Maynard M. Gordon). **2** least complicated or expensive of its kind: *Consumers are shifting away from the low-end game machines to the higher-priced, higher-capability personal computers* (New York Times).

M m

mantra, *n.* **2** any often-repeated, formulaic phrase: *. . . transition mantras . . . may even contain traces of truth. But . . . they are as dulling to the mind as New Age music* (Time).

mon|key-wrench (mung′kē rench′) *adj.* of or designating an action, policy, or other effort designed to throw something into disorder: *We are already in the age of monkey-wrench politics in which a few terrorists can transform a comfortable way of life* (New York Times Magazine).

multiplex, *adj., v., n.* —*n.* **1** a multiplex system or signal. **2** Also, **multiplex theater**. a cinema with smaller theaters within it showing several motion pictures at the same time: *He prefers multiplex theaters. That way, if the movie he sets out to see isn't riveting, he can . . . walk over to watch another movie that's playing* (Vanity Fair).

N n

Ne|o-Ge|o (nē′ō jē′ō), *n.* a completely abstract form of art of the late 1980's,

characterized by the use of geometric forms: *Neoexpressionism, suddenly rather vieux chapeau [old hat], was being replaced on the assembly line by Neo-Geo* (Anthony Haden-Guest).

nickel, *n.* **3** *U.S. Slang.* five dollars' worth of a narcotic drug: *His cargo: "loose joints" (single joints) and "nickel bags" and "dime bags" (plastic bags holding $5 and $10 worth of marijuana)* (New York Times Magazine).

O o

obsess, *v.i.* to be obsessed; have an obsession: *One can't obsess too long about the café-au-lait mark near one's cheekbone . . . when one's porch is being hacked off* (James Gorman).

obsolesce, *v.t.* to make obsolescent: *Academic America . . . obsolesces whole literature departments (English, French, German, all those pipe-and-tweed fogies)* (Washington Times).

office park, *U.S.* a cluster of office buildings set in a parklike setting: *While office parks have . . . been categorized by critics as architectural graveyards, suburban developers are now showing a new-found aesthetic ambition* (Daralice D. Boles).

off-load, *v.* **2** to dispose of; unload; sell: *The Government is also thought to be planning to off-load its 49 per cent holding in British Telecom* (Manchester Guardian Weekly).

o|meg|a-3 fatty acid (ō meg′ə thrē′; -mē′gə, -mā′-), a polyunsaturated fatty acid, found in fish or fish oil, that lowers the levels of cholesterol and triglycerides in the blood and decreases blood coagulation: *The omega-3 fatty acids in fish reduce the likelihood of getting heart disease* (Science News).

P p

panic attack, a sudden feeling of intense anxiety for no apparent reason, which can recur and increase in severity: *Panic attacks typically involve unexpected periods of fear or terror, combined with physical symptoms such as shortness of breath, dizziness, palpitations* (Bruce Bower).

plain-va|nil|la (plān′və nil′ə), *adj. U.S. Informal.* ordinary; without embellishment; run-of-the-mill: *Academic America . . . obligates with-it deans to create jobs (feminist, structuralist, post-structuralist, . . . even plain-vanilla theoretical)* (Washington Times).

protocol, *n.* **6** set procedures that permit communication between two or more computer systems: *He points out that the asynchronous protocol used by most personal-computer communications packages has a higher potential of interference errors than synchronous . . . protocols* (Personal Computing).

Pronunciation Key: hat, āge, cãre, fär; let, ēqual, tėrm; it, īce; hot, ōpen, ôrder; oil, out; cup, pùt, rüle; child; long; thin; ᴛнen; zh, measure; ə represents **a** in about, **e** in taken, **i** in pencil, **o** in lemon, **u** in circus.

Q q

queue, *n.* **4** a group of messages, data, or other items waiting to be processed by a computer.
—*v.t.* **2** to arrange (messages, data, or other items) into a sequence: *You control, queue, prioritize, or view spooled data at any time using the pop-up PrintQ . . . display* (Global Computer).

R r

Ram|bo (ram′bō), *n.*, *pl.* **-bos**, *v.*, **-boed**, **-boing.** —*n.* an extremely aggressive male: *The Rambo of commercial theater directors, Nunn is renowned for being able to surmount any obstacle* (Vanity Fair).
—*v.i.* to act in an extremely aggressive manner: *I think cowardice is much more the common experience than Ramboing all over the place* (American Film).
[< *Rambo,* macho hero of a series of motion pictures]
rap[4], *v.i.* **3** to play or perform rap music; talk in rhyme to the beat of rap music: *The Beastie Boys . . . rap to a couple of Zeppelin riffs in their album and in their concerts* (Rolling Stone).
rapper[2], *n.* **2** a person who plays, performs, or talks in rhymes to the beat of rap music: *Black rappers could also benefit from the expanding audience for hard rhythms and catchy rhyme* (John Milward).
riff, *n.* **1** a melodic phrase or distinctive rhythm in jazz or rock, especially as a recurring statement of the theme, performed by individual instrumentalists. **2** *U.S. Slang.* a standard speech, act, or piece of stage business; routine; bit: *Schwartz [is] known for his . . . urbane on-air riffs about Sinatra, the Red Sox, and Palm Springs* (New York Magazine).

S s

scent strip, a paper strip impregnated with a brand of perfume and inserted as part of a magazine advertisement or brochure: *Giorgio of Beverly Hills placed scent strips of its brash new fragrance in up-scale women's magazines like Vogue and Harper's Bazaar* (Atlantic).
skinhead, *n.* **2** a type of young American tough, usually the member of a gang, who wears closely cropped hair and follows ideas and practices derived from the Nazis: *American skinheads are as likely to be middle-class as working poor. But in other respects they are typical gang members. They tend to come from broken homes and . . . are creatures of dysfunction* (Jeff Coplon).
sniffer dog, a dog trained to discover by scent the presence of illegal drugs, explosives, casualties trapped in debris, or other specific odors: *Police with sniffer dogs were seen searching the surrounding hedgerows* (Manchester Guardian Weekly).
spelling checker, a computer program that checks typed words against a list of words stored in the computer memory and identifies errors in spelling.

squat, *v.i.* **4b** to occupy illegally an abandoned building.
—*n.* **3a** the illegal occupation of land or of an uninhabited building, as by a squatter: *This is the biggest squat ever, a serious attempt to house homeless people* (London Times). **b** a place, especially a building, occupied illegally: *"I been living in a squat"—an abandoned building—"making money by various means"* (New York Magazine). **c** a person who occupies a place illegally, often as a form of protest: *. . . a spectrum which spans the insurgent squats of Hamburg and the often respectable ecologists and reformers* (Manchester Guardian Weekly).

T t

tear-down or **tear|down**, *n.* **2** *U.S.* **a** the act or practice of demolishing a house in order to build a larger house in its place: *Teardowns are rampant on almost every one of its fashionable streets* (Vanity Fair). **b** a house bought to be demolished and replaced by a larger one: *In pricier Bel-Air, speculators are paying up to $3 million for teardowns on one-acre lots* (Atlantic).
tell-all (tel′ôl′), *adj. U.S.* revealing everything, including damaging or confidential information: *a tell-all memoir. The tell-all tome implicated several of [his] Hollywood friends and associates for condoning . . . his self-destructive behavior* (Time). *[He] published a tell-all memoir that revealed further dissonance between appearance and reality in Washington* (Spy Magazine).
touch|y-feel|y (tuch′ē fē′lē), *adj. U.S. Informal.* characterized by or emphasizing sensitivity and emotion rather than reason: *. . . the whole touchy-feely smorgasbord of group-gropers, anxiety-studiers, and fruit-juice drinkers who believe that the purpose of education is emotional adjustment* (Harper's).
trap door or **trap|door** (trap′dôr′, -dōr′), *n.* **3** a gap left intentionally in a computer program or operating system to facilitate access for later alteration or improvement: *Intruders sometimes use trapdoors, too, as happened in the . . . well-publicized virus attack on a Department of Defense computer network, Arpanet* (Atlantic Constitution).

U u

urban village, *U.S.* a small, self-contained community within or near a large metropolitan area: *The suburban office boom has had a powerful impact on the exurban landscape, creating what some authors call "urban villages" or concentrated nodes strung out along interstate highways* (Daralice D. Boles).

V v

vaccine, *n.* **3** = vaccination program: *A typical vaccine will surround those memory locations with the equivalent of a burglar alarm. If something tries to*

alter the contents of one of those cells, the vaccine program is supposed to stop everything and alert the operator (Time).
video, *n.* **3a** a videotaped recording or videocassette: *The BBC recognised early on that there was money to be made from selling archive programmes on video* (New Scientist). **b** the showing of videotaped recordings: *The VCR . . . gives the individual the temporal power over video* (New York Times). **c** a videocassette recorder: *We are the only family in our street who haven't got a video* (S. Townsend).

W w

wait state, a condition in which a computer processor must stop functioning between instructions: *A wait state is one indicator of the overall speed and performance of a computer system* (New York Times). *A machine with zero wait state has something like 80-nanosecond chips, which can keep pace with the processor* (Atlanta Journal/Constitution).
wan|na-be (won′ə bē′, wôn′-), *n. U.S. Informal.* a person who aspires to a position; aspirant or candidate: *We didn't even try to get the presidential wannabes to tell us . . . what they'd do* (Rolling Stone). *Now coming to bat: the veteran catcher on his last leg, . . . the Willie Mays wanna-be* (Time). [< contraction of *want to be*]
Western blot, a test for confirming the presence of the AIDS virus by spreading a blood sample on blotting paper that contains AIDS virus proteins of different sizes. If AIDS antibodies are present in the blood, they will stick to the particular proteins. *The existing combination of antibody tests—the so-called Elisa test, backed by the Western blot—will continue to be the best tool for large-scale testing* (New York Times).
wus|sy (wus′ē), *adj.*, **-si|er**, **-si|est.** *U.S. Slang.* of a weak and unassertive sort; timid and ineffectual: *. . . a wussy editorial decrying boxing* (James Wolcott). *Field of Dreams is the male weepie at its wussiest* (Time). [< *wussy, n.* old slang for an effeminate man]
WYSIWYG (wiz′ē wig, wis′-), *adj.* (of a computer screen display) displaying a text or image exactly as it will appear in printout: *. . . integrated WYSIWYG word processing* (Global Comuter). [< *W*(hat) *Y*(ou) *S*(ee) *I*(s) *W*(hat) *Y*(ou) *G*(et)]

Y y

yo|ko|zu|na (yō′kə zü′nə), *n.* a sumo wrestler of the highest rank: *To be yokozuna in Japan is to be a Babe Ruth or Willie Mays* (New York Times). *Atisanoe, who hails from Hawaii, . . . moved within one ranking of the top—yokozuna (grand champion)* (Jay Myers). [< Japanese *yokozuna*]
yup[2] (yup), *n.* = Yuppie: *It's a loosely joined series of sketches about . . . rich twits, pushy yups, and the working poor* (New Yorker).

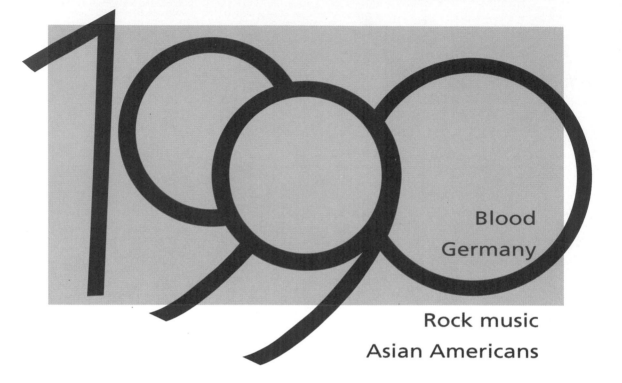

World Book Supplement

1990

Blood
Germany

Rock music
Asian Americans

To help **World Book** owners keep their encyclopedias up to date, the following articles are reprinted from the 1991 edition of the encyclopedia.

See page 509 ▶

© B. Bisson, Sygma

Unification of East Germany and West Germany took place on Oct. 3, 1990. Millions of Germans celebrated throughout the country, including these people at the Brandenburg Gate in Berlin.

Germany

Germany is a large country in central Europe. From 1949 to 1990, it was divided into the German Democratic Republic (East Germany) and the Federal Republic of Germany (West Germany). On Oct. 3, 1990, East and West Germany were unified into a single nation, also called the Federal Republic of Germany. Berlin is Germany's official capital and largest city.

For hundreds of years, Germans lived in many separate states, one of the most powerful of which was the kingdom of Prussia. During the late 1800's, Otto von Bismarck, the prime minister of Prussia, united most of these states and cities under Prussian leadership. After

James J. Sheehan, the contributor of this article, is Dickason Professor of Humanities at Stanford University.

Bismarck, German leaders tried to expand their influence in Europe and overseas. These policies helped trigger World War I in 1914. When the war ended in 1918, Germany had been defeated and a period of political and economic crises followed.

In 1933, Adolf Hitler—leader of the Nazi Party, an extremely militaristic and nationalistic political movement—established his dictatorship and began to rebuild Germany's military power. In 1939, Hitler started World War II. Germany was defeated in 1945 and was divided into zones that, in 1949, became West Germany and East Germany. Berlin, the old capital, was also divided. West Germany became a parliamentary democracy with strong ties to Western Europe and the United States. East Germany became a Communist dictatorship closely associated with the Soviet Union.

Picture Finders from Bavaria-Verlag

The beautiful Rhine River, made famous in song and legend, has come to symbolize Germany. Picturesque towns line the river, which is also one of Europe's most important waterways.

After World War II, the West Germans and East Germans rebuilt their shattered industries and made them more productive than ever. West Germany became one of the leading industrial nations. Although East Germany's economic development was not as rapid, the country ranked as one of the most economically advanced of the nations that adopted Communism. Yet dissatisfaction led millions of East Germans to flee to West Germany between 1946 and 1961, the year that East Germany built the Berlin Wall to cut off the major escape route.

In 1989, reform movements swept through the Communist nations of Europe. In East Germany, political protests and massive emigration set in motion the chain of events that ended in the unification of East and West Germany. In November 1989—in response to the protests—the East German government allowed its citizens to travel freely for the first time. The end of travel restrictions included the opening of the Berlin Wall. Also for the first time, non-Communist political parties were permitted to organize and form their own policies in late 1989. In March 1990, East Germany held free parliamentary elections, and non-Communists gained control of the government.

With the end of Communist control in East Germany, many Germans, both East and West, began considering unification. In July 1990, East Germany and West Germany united their economies into a single system. In August, both nations signed a treaty that would finalize unification. The treaty took effect on October 3. Germany scheduled its first national elections after unification for December 1990.

Germans are famous for being hard-working and dis-

© David Pollack, The Stock Market

Neuschwanstein Castle in Bavaria was begun in 1869 by King Louis II, known as Mad King Ludwig. The "fairy-tale" castle is one of Germany's popular tourist attractions.

Germany in brief

General information

Capital: Berlin.
Official language: German.
Official name: *Bundesrepublik Deutschland* (Federal Republic of Germany).
National anthem: Third stanza of "Deutschland-Lied" ("Song of Germany").
Largest cities: (1985 official estimate)

Berlin (3,062,979)	Frankfurt am Main (595,348)
Hamburg (1,579,884)	Dortmund (572,094)
Munich (1,266,549)	Düsseldorf (561,686)
Cologne (916,153)	Stuttgart (561,628)
Essen (619,991)	Leipzig (554,595)

H. E. Harris & Co.

The German flag represents the German Confederation and the Weimar Republic.

Coat of arms. The eagle emblem has been used since the ancient Romans introduced it into Germany.

Land and climate

Land: Germany lies in central Europe. It borders France, Switzerland, Austria, Czechoslovakia, Poland, Denmark, Netherlands, Belgium, and Luxembourg, and it has a short coastline on the North and Baltic seas. The northern part of the country is mostly flat; the terrain is hilly in central and southern Germany. The Alps run along the border with Austria; the rugged Black Forest lies in the southwest; the Bohemian Forest is along the Czech border. Major rivers include Rhine in the west, Danube in the south, Elbe and Weser in the north, and Oder in the east.

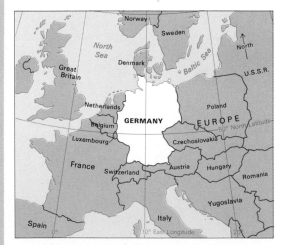

Area: 137,772 sq. mi. (356,829 km²). *Greatest distances*—north-south, 540 mi. (869 km); east-west, 390 mi. (628 km). *Coastline*—574 mi. (924 km).
Elevation: *Highest*—9,721 ft. (2,963 m) at Zugspitze, in the Alps. *Lowest*—sea level along the coast.
Climate: Mild summers, cool winters. Typical summer daytime highs are in low 70's F. (20's C). In winter, typical daytime high is a few degrees above freezing. The Rhine Valley is generally the warmest part of the country; the

coastal areas are usually milder than the inland areas. Moderate rainfall in all seasons.

Government

Head of state: Federal president.
Head of government: Federal chancellor.
Legislature: Parliament of two houses—the Bundestag (663 members) and the Bundesrat (up to 69 members). The Bundestag is more powerful than the Bundesrat.
Executive: Federal chancellor (elected by Bundestag). Chancellor selects Cabinet ministers.
Judiciary: Highest court is the Federal Constitutional Court.
Political subdivisions: 16 states.

People

Population: *1991 estimate*—77,454,000. *1996 estimate*—77,030,000.
Population density: 562 persons per sq. mi. (217 per km²).
Distribution: 84 per cent urban, 16 per cent rural.
Major ethnic/national groups: 95 per cent German, 5 per cent other Europeans.
Major religions: 45 per cent Protestant (chiefly Lutheran); 40 per cent Roman Catholic; 2 per cent Muslim.

Population trend

Millions

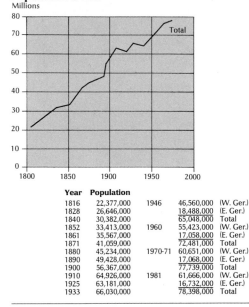

Year	Population			
1816	22,377,000	1946	46,560,000	(W. Ger.)
1828	26,646,000		18,488,000	(E. Ger.)
1840	30,382,000		65,048,000	Total
1852	33,413,000	1960	55,423,000	(W. Ger.)
1861	35,567,000		17,058,000	(E. Ger.)
1871	41,059,000		72,481,000	Total
1880	45,234,000	1970-71	60,651,000	(W. Ger.)
1890	49,428,000		17,068,000	(E. Ger.)
1900	56,367,000		77,739,000	Total
1910	64,926,000	1981	61,666,000	(W. Ger.)
1925	63,181,000		16,732,000	(E. Ger.)
1933	66,030,000		78,398,000	Total

Economy

Chief products: *Agriculture*—milk, hogs, wheat, potatoes, barley, sugar beets, beef cattle. *Manufacturing*—processed foods and beverages, motor vehicles, chemicals and pharmaceuticals, machinery, electrical equipment, steel. *Mining*—coal.
Money: *Basic unit*—Deutsche mark. For value in U.S. dollars, see **Money** (table: Exchange rates).
Gross national product: *1988 total GNP*—$1,327,000,000,000. *GNP per capita*—$17,100.
Foreign trade: *Major exports*—machinery, motor vehicles, electrical equipment, chemicals. *Value of exports*—$324,000,000,000 (1987). *Major imports*—petroleum and petroleum products, food products, electrical machinery, clothing. *Value of imports*—$259,000,000,000 (1987). *Main trading partners*—France, Netherlands, United States, Italy, Great Britain, Soviet Union.

ciplined, but they are also known for their love of music, dancing, good food, and fellowship. Germans also enjoy vacations in their world-famous scenic areas. The Bavarian Alps, for example, are a popular winter sports region. The beautiful Rhine River winds through valleys with grand castles overlooking the river.

The German people have made many important contributions to culture. Johann Sebastian Bach and Ludwig van Beethoven composed some of the world's greatest music. Johann Wolfgang von Goethe and Thomas Mann wrote masterpieces of literature. German scientists have made breakthroughs in chemistry, medicine, and physics.

Government

Germany is a federal republic in which the people elect their representatives by secret ballot. The government's main bodies and offices include a Parliament, a federal chancellor, and a Cabinet. The government was established after the unification of East and West Germany in 1990. It was based on the democratic government system of West Germany. East Germany had operated under a dictatorial Communist government system until shortly before unification, when a democratic system was established.

Parliament of Germany has two houses, the *Bundestag* (Federal Diet) and the *Bundesrat* (Federal Council). The Bundestag passes the laws and chooses the head of government. The Bundestag has 663 deputies elected by the voters to four-year terms.

The Bundesrat has up to 69 members appointed by the state governments. Each state has 3 to 6 votes in the Bundesrat, depending on the population of the state. Each state may appoint up to as many members as it has votes. Some laws passed by the Bundestag require approval of the Bundesrat. They include laws that relate directly to the states' responsibilities, such as matters dealing with education and local government. The Bundesrat can raise objections to other laws. Its objections can be overridden by a majority vote of the Bundestag.

Executive. The Bundestag elects a member of the strongest political party in that house to be federal chancellor, the head of the government. The Bundestag can remove the chancellor from office by electing a replacement. The chancellor selects the ministers who make up the Cabinet and head government departments.

The federal president is the head of state, but the powers of the office are largely ceremonial. Bundestag deputies and an equal number of electors selected by German state legislatures elect the president to a five-year term.

State government. Germany has 16 states. Each state has a legislature. Members of most of the legislatures are elected to four-year terms. In most of the states, the legislature elects a minister president to head the state government. In Berlin, Bremen, and Hamburg, which are cities as well as states, a mayor heads the state government.

Politics. The Christian Democratic Union (CDU) and the Social Democratic Party are Germany's largest political parties. The CDU's branch in Bavaria is the Christian Social Union. Traditionally, both large parties support close ties to other Western nations. The Christian Demo-

cratic Union has conservative economic and social policies. The Social Democratic Party supports more social welfare programs and greater regulation of the economy.

In most national elections, neither major party gains enough votes to control the Bundestag. In such cases, the political party with more votes must form a *coalition* (alliance), usually with the liberal Free Democratic Party (FDP), in order to gain a majority of seats in the Bundestag.

The Party of Democratic Socialism—the Communist Party that formerly controlled East Germany—has maintained some of its membership since unification. Germany also has a number of smaller parties. These include the Green Party, which represents environmental causes, and the extremely conservative Republican Party. During the 1960's, the National Democratic Party won the support of former Nazis. Germans must be at least 18 years old to vote.

Courts. Germany's highest court is the Federal Constitutional Court. It interprets the Constitution and settles disputes between the executive and the legislature and between federal and state governments. The court's 16 judges are appointed for 12-year terms. Half of the judges are appointed by the Bundestag and half by the Bundesrat. The regular court system tries civil and criminal cases, which can be reviewed by regional and national appellate courts. Judges in all these courts are appointed for life. Administrative courts decide disputes between individuals and government agencies. There are special courts for disputes about labor issues, taxes, and social security payments.

Armed forces. After World War II, the Allies planned to keep Germany disarmed. But by the 1950's, the Western Allies wanted West Germany's help against possible Communist expansion. West Germany joined the North Atlantic Treaty Organization (NATO) in 1955, and began to build up its armed forces under NATO command. After unification, Germany remained in NATO. The East German armed forces were dissolved, but some of its personnel joined the unified German armed forces. The German armed forces have about 500,000 men, but plan to reduce it to about 370,000 by the mid-1990's. German men must serve at least one year in the armed forces after reaching the age of 18.

People

Unification brought many changes to the German people. For many years, the people were divided by the heavily guarded 858-mile (1,381-kilometer) border that split their land between East and West. Many relatives and friends were separated from one another. The East German government restricted travel between East and West Germany.

Until 1961, millions of East Germans fled to West Germany through Berlin. In August 1961, the Communists closed off this escape route by building the high, heavily guarded Berlin Wall between eastern and western sectors of the city. Although some East Germans were allowed to resettle in West Germany, most people could not even visit there.

In 1989, thousands of East Germans fled to West Germany by way of neighboring countries. In response to these departures and popular protests, the East German

Germany map index

States

Name	Population	Area In sq. mi.	In km²	Map key
Baden-Württemberg	9,241,100	13,804	35,751	I 3
Bavaria	10,973,700	27,238	70,546	H 5
Berlin	3,062,970	341	883	D 6
Brandenburg*	2,600,000	10,811	28,000	E 6
Bremen	659,900	156	404	C 3
Hamburg	1,579,900	289	748	C 4
Hesse	5,532,000	8,152	21,113	G 3
Lower Saxony	7,156,900	18,308	47,418	D 3
Mecklenburg-Western Pomerania*	1,900,000	9,189	23,800	C 5
North Rhine-Westphalia	16,674,100	13,154	34,069	E 2
Rhineland-Palatinate	3,615,000	7,660	19,839	G 1
Saar	1,045,900	994	2,574	H 1
Saxony*	5,000,000	7,066	18,300	F 6
Saxony-Anhalt*	2,900,000	7,876	20,400	E 5
Schleswig-Holstein	2,614,200	6,065	15,709	B 3
Thuringia*	1,600,000	6,255	16,200	F 5

Cities and towns

Name	Population	Map key
Aachen	238,587	F 1
Aalen	63,195	I 4
Ahlen	52,405	E 2
Albstadt	45,870	I 3
Alfeld	22,453	E 4
Alsdorf†	45,896	F 1
Altenburg	54,659	F 6
Amberg	43,523	H 5
Andernach	26,520	G 2
Anklam	20,202	C 6
Annaberg-Buchholz	26,211	G 6
Ansbach	37,395	H 4
Apolda†	28,535	F 5
Arnsberg	74,970	F 2
Arnstadt	29,830	F 4
Aschaffenburg	59,240	G 3
Aschersleben	34,231	E 5
Aue	28,398	G 6
Augsburg	245,193	I 4
Aurich	35,005	C 2
Bad Homburg	50,905	G 3
Bad Kreuznach	39,813	G 2
Bad Oeynhausen†	43,207	E 3
Bad Salzuflen	50,819	E 3
Baden-Baden	48,684	I 3
Balingen	29,917	I 3
Bamberg	69,920	G 4
Bautzen	51,615	F 7
Bayreuth	71,848	G 5
Bensheim	33,311	H 3
Berchtesgaden	8,345	J 6
Bergheim†	54,061	F 1
Bergisch Gladbach	101,112	F 2
Bergkamen†	47,747	E 2
Berlin	3,062,970	D 6
Bernau	19,713	D 6
Bernburg	40,826	E 5
Bielefeld	299,727	E 3
Bingen	22,138	G 2
Bitburg	10,309	G 1
Bitterfeld†	21,068	E 5
Bocholt	66,105	E 1
Bochum	382,041	E 2
Bonn	290,769	F 2
Borna†	23,384	F 6
Bottrop†	112,487	E 2
Brandenburg	95,021	D 6
Braunschweig	248,001	E 4
Bremen	526,377	D 3
Bremerhaven	133,521	C 3
Bruchsal	36,602	H 3
Brühl†	40,723	F 1
Burg	28,633	E 5
Buxtehude	32,453	C 3
Castrop-Rauxel†	76,430	E 2
Celle	70,482	D 4
Coburg	44,244	G 5
Coesfeld	31,508	E 2
Cologne	916,153	F 1
Coswig	28,209	E 6
Cottbus	123,898	E 7
Crimmitschau†	24,881	F 6
Cuxhaven	56,504	C 3
Dachau	32,682	I 5
Darmstadt	134,181	G 3
Delitzsch	28,094	E 5
Delmenhorst	70,546	D 3
Dessau	103,748	E 5
Detmold	66,403	E 3
Dinslaken†	61,032	E 1
Döbeln	27,115	F 6
Dormagen†	57,293	F 1
Dorsten†	72,945	E 2
Dortmund	572,094	E 2
Dreieich†	37,936	G 3
Dresden	519,860	F 6
Duisburg	518,260	E 1
Düren	84,272	F 1
Düsseldorf	561,686	F 1
Eberswalde	54,032	D 6
Einbeck	27,440	E 4
Eisenach	50,949	F 4
Eisenhüttenstadt	48,463	E 7
Eisleben†	26,869	F 5
Elmshorn	41,192	C 3
Emden	49,686	C 2
Erding	24,555	I 5
Erftstadt†	44,738	F 1
Erfurt	215,499	F 5
Erkrath†	44,626	E 1
Erlangen	99,628	H 5
Eschweiler	52,786	F 1
Essen	619,991	F 2
Esslingen	87,467	I 3
Euskirchen†	45,309	F 1
Falkensee	23,471	D 6
Finsterwalde	23,965	E 6
Flensburg	86,779	B 3
Forst	26,331	E 7
Frankenthal	43,941	H 2
Frankfurt (am Main)	595,348	G 3
Frankfurt (an der Oder)	85,185	D 7
Frechen†	42,424	F 1
Freiberg	50,098	F 6
Freiburg	184,230	J 2
Freising	36,061	I 5
Freital	43,968	F 6
Freudenstadt	20,058	I 2
Friedrichshafen	51,665	J 3
Fulda	54,780	G 3
Fürstenfeldbruck	31,476	I 5
Fürstenwalde	35,083	D 7
Fürth	97,331	H 5
Garbsen	57,249	D 3
Gelsenkirchen	285,002	E 2
Gera	131,537	F 5
Giessen	71,104	G 3
Gifhorn	34,133	D 4
Gladbeck†	76,592	E 2
Glauchau†	29,095	F 6
Göppingen	51,471	I 4
Görlitz	79,506	F 7
Goslar	49,636	E 4
Gotha	57,583	F 4
Göttingen	133,394	E 4
Greifswald	64,661	B 6
Greiz	35,601	F 5
Grevenbroich	57,049	F 1
Gronau	39,769	E 2
Guben	34,594	E 7
Gummersbach†	48,373	F 2
Gustrow	39,065	C 5
Gütersloh	79,001	E 2
Hagen	206,408	F 2
Halberstadt	46,915	E 4
Halle	235,858	E 5
Halle-Neustadt	92,168	E 5
Hamburg	1,579,884	C 4
Hameln	55,580	E 3
Hamm	166,379	E 2
Hanau	84,672	G 3
Hanover	508,298	D 4
Hattingen†	55,051	F 2
Heidelberg	134,724	H 3
Heidenheim	47,584	I 4
Heilbronn	111,338	H 3
Hennigsdorf	27,254	D 6
Herford	59,640	E 3
Herne	172,150	E 2
Herten†	69,004	E 2
Herzogenrath†	43,274	F 1
Hilden†	53,413	F 2
Hildesheim	100,864	E 4
Hof	51,035	G 5
Homburg	41,295	H 2
Höxter	31,579	E 3
Hoyerswerda	69,969	F 7
Hürth†	50,741	F 1
Ibbenbueren	42,447	E 2
Idar-Oberstein	34,258	H 2
Ilmenau	29,504	F 4
Ingolstadt	91,836	I 5
Iserlohn	89,539	F 2
Itzehoe	32,072	C 3
Jena	107,241	F 5
Kaiserslautern	97,664	H 2
Kamen†	44,393	E 2
Karl-Marx-Stadt	316,361	F 6
Karlsruhe	268,211	H 2
Kassel	184,466	F 3
Kaufbeuren	41,365	J 4
Kempten	56,705	J 4
Kerpen†	54,769	F 1
Kiel	245,682	B 4
Kleve	44,548	E 1
Koblenz†	110,843	G 2
Köln, see Cologne		
Konstanz	69,852	J 3
Köthen	34,507	E 5
Krefeld	216,833	F 1
Kreuztal	28,989	F 2
Lahr	34,594	I 2
Landau	35,482	H 2
Langenfeld†	48,357	F 1
Langenhagen†	46,520	D 4
Lauchhammer	24,304	E 6
Lauf	22,217	H 5
Leer	30,075	C 2
Leipzig	554,595	F 6
Leverkusen	155,077	F 1
Limbach-Oberfrohnat†	22,247	F 6
Limburg	28,905	G 2
Lingen	45,433	D 2
Lippstadt	60,032	E 3
Lörrach	40,862	J 2
Lübbenau	21,256	E 7
Lübeck	210,318	C 4
Luckenwalde	26,845	E 6
Lüdenscheid	73,292	F 2
Ludwigsburg	76,973	I 3
Ludwigshafen	153,654	H 2
Lüneburg	59,645	C 4
Lünen†	84,532	E 2
Magdeburg	288,914	E 5
Mainz	188,571	G 2
Mannheim	294,984	H 3
Marburg	75,092	F 3
Marl†	87,449	E 2
Meerane†	21,134	F 5
Meerbuscht†	49,037	F 1
Meiningen	25,890	G 4
Meissen	38,137	F 6
Memmingen	37,370	J 4
Menden†	37,034	F 2
Merseburg	48,002	F 5
Merzig	29,228	H 1
Minden	75,511	E 3
Moers†	97,760	E 1
Mönchengladbach	254,495	F 1
Mühlhausen	43,403	F 4
Mülheim	171,948	F 1
München, see Munich		
Munich	1,266,549	I 5
Münster	270,102	E 2
Naumburg	32,491	F 5
Neubrandenburg	84,017	C 6
Neumarkt	31,780	H 5
Neumünster	78,280	B 4
Neunkirchen	49,759	H 1
Neuruppin	26,755	D 6
Neuss	143,512	F 1
Neustadt (am Ruebenberge)	37,918	D 3
Neustadt (an der Weinstrasse)	48,463	H 2
Neustrelitz	27,276	C 6
Neu-Ulm†	46,253	I 4
Neuwied	58,471	G 2
Norderstedt	67,232	C 4
Nordhausen	47,219	F 4
Nordhorn	47,921	D 2
Northeim	31,033	E 4
Nuremberg	465,255	H 5
Nürnberg, see Nuremberg		
Nürtingen	35,681	I 3
Oberammergau	4,664	J 4
Oberhausen	222,664	E 1
Oberursel	38,857	G 3
Offenbach	107,090	G 3
Offenburg	50,207	I 2
Oldenburg	138,773	D 2
Oranienburg	28,443	D 6
Osnabrück	153,202	E 2
Osterode	26,990	E 4
Paderborn	109,906	E 3
Parchim	23,350	C 5
Pasewalk	15,883	C 7
Passau	52,523	I 6
Peine	45,707	E 4
Pforzheim	104,184	I 3
Pirmasens	46,526	H 2
Pirna	47,387	F 7
Plauen	77,733	G 5
Potsdam	138,737	D 6
Prenzlau	23,997	C 6
Pulheim†	47,353	F 1
Quedlinburg†	29,488	E 5
Radebeul	34,356	F 6
Radolfzell	25,016	J 3
Rastatt	37,337	I 2
Rathenow	31,630	D 5
Ratingen†	88,718	F 1
Ravensburg	42,911	J 3
Recklinghausen†	117,897	E 2
Regensburg	124,480	H 5
Reichenbach†	24,855	G 5
Remscheid	124,204	F 2
Rendsburg	30,970	B 3
Reutlingen	97,030	I 3
Rheine	70,662	E 2
Riesa	49,744	F 6
Rosenheim	52,743	J 5
Rostock	242,729	B 5
Rottenburg	32,934	I 3
Rudolstadt	32,485	F 5
Rüsselsheim	57,579	G 3
Saalfeld	33,592	G 5
Saarbrücken	186,229	H 1
Salzgitter	105,958	E 4
Salzwedel	23,201	D 5
Sangerhausen	33,388	F 5
Schmallenberg	24,429	F 2
Schönebeck	45,093	E 5
Schwabach	35,437	H 5
Schwäbisch Gmünd	56,117	I 4
Schwäbisch Hall	30,913	H 4
Schwedt	51,700	D 7
Schweinfurt	51,016	G 4
Schwerin	127,065	C 5
Schwertet†	48,138	F 2
Senftenberg	32,211	E 7
Siegen	107,421	F 2
Sindelfingen	55,501	I 3
Singen	41,531	J 3
Sinsheim	27,716	H 3
Solingen	157,923	F 2
Sömmerda	23,417	F 5
Sondershausen	23,807	F 4
Sonneberg	28,368	G 5
Sonthofen	20,781	J 4
Speyer	43,923	H 2
Spremberg	24,460	E 7
Stade	42,988	C 3
Stadtallendorf	20,412	F 3
Stassfurt	27,302	E 5
Stendal	46,380	D 5
Stolberg	56,435	F 1
Stralsund	75,408	B 6
Straubing	41,632	I 5
Strausberg	26,727	D 7
Stuttgart	561,628	I 3
Suhl	53,933	G 4
Templin	14,500	D 6
Torgau	21,717	E 6
Trier	93,472	H 1
Troisdorf†	60,981	F 2
Tübingen	75,825	I 3
Uelzen	35,518	D 4
Ulm	99,936	I 4
Unna†	58,778	E 2
Varel	23,859	C 2
Velbert†	88,403	F 2
Viersen†	78,489	F 1
Villingen-Schwenningen	76,303	J 3
Völklingen	43,413	H 1
Waiblingen†	44,570	I 3
Waren	24,300	C 6
Weiden	42,073	H 5
Weimar	63,438	F 5
Weinheim	40,655	H 3
Weissenfels	36,606	F 5
Weisswasser	35,341	E 7
Wernigerode	36,168	E 4
Wesel	54,791	E 1
Wetzlar†	50,063	F 3
Wiesbaden	266,623	G 2
Wilhelmshaven	95,570	C 2
Wismar	57,662	C 5
Witten†	102,259	F 2
Wittenberg	54,190	E 6
Wittenberge	30,675	D 5
Wittstock	14,400	D 6
Wolfen	42,414	E 5
Wolfenbüttel	48,641	E 4
Wolfsburg	121,703	D 4
Wolgast	16,923	B 6
Worms	71,827	H 2
Wunstorf	37,368	D 3
Wuppertal	376,579	F 2
Würzburg	127,997	G 4
Zeitz	43,467	F 5
Zittau	40,040	F 7
Zweibrücken	33,018	H 1
Zwickau	120,101	F 6

*1990 estimates.
†Does not appear on map; key shows general location.
Sources: 1985, 1986 and 1988 official estimates.

Germany political map

International boundary	
State boundary	
Expressway	
Other road	
Rail line	
⊛	National capital
★	State capital
•	Other city or town

WORLD BOOK map

Population density

More than 80 per cent of the German people live in urban areas. The area surrounding the Rhine and Ruhr rivers is one of the most densely populated parts of Europe.

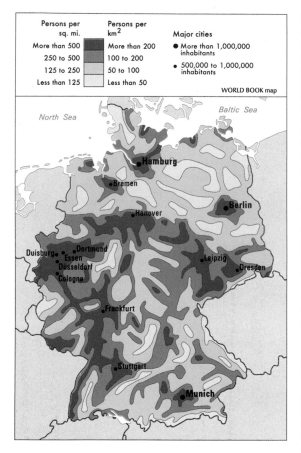

Persons per sq. mi.	Persons per km²	Major cities
More than 500	More than 200	● More than 1,000,000 inhabitants
250 to 500	100 to 200	
125 to 250	50 to 100	● 500,000 to 1,000,000 inhabitants
Less than 125	Less than 50	

WORLD BOOK map

government lifted all restrictions on travel. East Germans were permitted to travel to West Germany or any other country. In addition, West Germans were permitted to visit East Germany without any restrictions. After unification, all Germans were granted complete freedom of travel.

Population and ancestry. In 1991, about 77 million people lived in Germany. Among all the countries of Europe, only the Soviet Union had more people.

Almost all the people living in Germany were born there. Germans are descended from many ancient tribes, including the Cimbri, Franks, Goths, and Teutons. Most non-Germans who live in the country are foreign workers called *guest workers.* Guest workers came mostly from Turkey, Yugoslavia, and Italy to work in the cities of western Germany. A small group of Slavic people called *Sorbs* live in eastern Germany.

Language. Two main forms of the German language have long been spoken in Germany—High German in the south and center and Low German in the north. In addition, there are many dialects associated with particular regions or cities. Today, schools, businesses, newspapers, and radio and television broadcasts use a standardized form of High German called Standard German.

For more detailed information about the language, see **German language.**

Way of life

Before unification, the people of West Germany had a higher standard of living than the people of East Germany. West Germans generally dressed better, were more likely to own a car, and had access to more luxury goods. But East Germany was one of the most prosperous countries in Eastern Europe. Government-controlled businesses provided jobs, and the government regulated prices. Medical care was free. Unification brought about a free enterprise economy for all of Germany, opening up new economic opportunities for East Germans. But the changes also resulted in some problems. Some East Germans lost their jobs because their companies or factories closed when they could not compete in the new economy. Also, the cost of many goods rose, and medical care is no longer free. However, Germans still enjoy one of the highest standards of living in Europe.

City life. About 84 per cent of Germany's people live in urban areas. Berlin, with more than 3 million people, is the largest German city. Hamburg and Munich both have more than a million people. Eleven other German cities have populations of more than 500,000.

Many German cities were destroyed during World War II. In some of them, such as Munich, the old city center has been restored. Most cities, however, have buildings dating from the postwar construction of the 1950's and 1960's.

German cities face the problems of pollution and congestion that affect urban areas everywhere. Many German cities also have housing shortages.

Rural life. About 6 per cent of German workers are farmers. In western Germany, most farms are small and owned by families that live on them. In eastern Germany, most farms were large collective farms formerly controlled by the East German government. The German government planned to take steps after unification to return these farms to private ownership.

Food and drink. Germans are known for enjoying good food in large quantities. They usually eat their main meal at noon, a heavy meal often featuring veal, pork, beef, or chicken. The main meal also includes such vegetables as beets, carrots, onions, potatoes, or turnips. Breakfast usually consists of rolls and jam with coffee or milk. In the afternoon, especially on Sunday, many Germans enjoy a snack of fancy pastries. They generally eat a light supper of bread, cheese, and sausage. German beer and wine are internationally famous for their high quality. Immigrants from Germany started many of the United States breweries, especially in Milwaukee, Wis.

Many world-famous German dishes were created hundreds of years ago to prevent foods from spoiling. Sauerkraut, perhaps the best-known German food, was developed to preserve cabbage. To preserve meat, German cooks soaked it in vinegar and spices—and created sauerbraten. The Germans also preserved meats by making such sausages as bratwurst and frankfurters. They developed many kinds of cheeses, including Limburger, Münster, and Tilsiter, which were named for the regions where they were first made.

© Owen Franken, German Information Center

Shopping malls in German cities carry a great variety of goods. The mall shown above is in Stuttgart.

© Lala Wille

Picturesque old buildings are preserved in many towns. This photograph shows Wernigerode, in central Germany.

Recreation. Germans enjoy hiking, reading, gardening, swimming, and watching television. Many young people take bicycling, hiking, or hitchhiking trips. They carry knapsacks and spend the night in the open or at inexpensive inns called youth hostels (see **Youth hostel**). Germany has many lakes and rivers for canoeing, rowing, sailing, and swimming. The country's high, snow-covered mountains help make skiing a favorite winter sport.

Soccer is the most popular organized sport in Germany. There are thousands of soccer teams, most of which represent various towns or cities. Gymnastics, tennis, and track are also popular. Some Germans belong to sharpshooting clubs.

Religion. The Reformation began in Germany during the early 1500's. This religious movement brought about the establishment of Protestantism. By 1600, most people in northern and central Germany had become Protestants. Most of those in the south remained Roman Catholics. These religious groups are about the same today. For more information, see **Reformation.**

About 45 per cent of Germans are Protestants, mostly Lutherans. About 40 per cent of the people are Roman Catholics. About 2 per cent are Muslims.

About 560,000 Jews lived in Germany when the Nazis came to power in 1933. By the end of World War II, most Jews had been killed by the Nazis or had fled the country. Today, about 40,000 Jews live in Germany.

© Messerschmidt, Bavaria-Verlag

Oktoberfest is a lively festival held in Munich each autumn. People fill beer halls for food, beer, and music. Oktoberfest began in the 1800's after a royal wedding celebration.

Shops and cafes line the Kurfürstendamm, a famous boulevard in Berlin. At its east end, the bombed-out Kaiser Wilhelm Memorial Church, *left,* serves as a reminder of World War II.

Picturesque Heidelberg includes the ruins of Heidelberg Castle, *center background.* The castle dates from the Middle Ages and overlooks the old city and a square called the *Kornmarkt.*

Education. The German states were among the first in the world to set up a public education system for all children. Prussia established a system during the early 1800's. The other German states developed their own systems by the mid-1800's. By the 1900's, almost all Germans over the age of 15 could read and write. Germany also developed one of the finest university systems in the world. In the late 1800's and early 1900's, students came from many countries to study in Germany. Such German universities as the University of Berlin (now Humboldt University) and the University of Leipzig (now Karl Marx University) were especially famous for scientific research. Between 1900 and 1933, German scientists won more Nobel Prizes than those from any other country.

Education in Germany is controlled by the individual states. All children must go to school full time for at least 9 or 10 years, starting at the age of 6.

Swimmers crowd the beaches on Germany's seacoast during the warm summer months.

© Muhlberger, Bavaria-Verlag

Soccer is the most popular organized sport in Germany. Thousands of teams represent towns and cities. The photo above shows a game between clubs from Munich and Stuttgart.

In the states that made up West Germany, children attend elementary school for four years. The nine-year gymnasium, from 5th to 13th grade, is the traditional junior and senior high school. The gymnasium prepares students for entrance into a university. Vocational schools provide students with various types of job training, as well as some academic subjects. There are also some comprehensive schools in Germany, which offer the curricula of both the gymnasium and the vocational schools.

In the states that were part of East Germany, children attend a 10-year polytechnical school that stresses technical training, mathematics, sciences, and languages. After graduation from 10th grade, students may take a three-year continuation course to fulfill university entrance requirements.

Germany has about 60 universities and many special-

© Owen Franken, German Information Center

Schools in Germany are famous for the quality of their education. Students must attend school for at least 9 or 10 years. These students are watching their teacher conduct an experiment.

ized and technical colleges. These universities and colleges have about 2 million students. About 6 per cent of German adults have a university education. The University of Heidelberg, founded in 1386, is Germany's oldest university. See **Heidelberg, University of.**

Arts

Many of the world's greatest artists, musicians, writers, and thinkers have been German. During the Middle Ages and Renaissance, German architects, painters, and sculptors produced great works, mostly with religious subjects. During the 1700's, many German writers and thinkers were part of the European Enlightenment, which focused on rational thinking and the order of nature. In the late 1700's and early 1800's, Germans helped create the Romantic movement. More recently, Germans were among the pioneers in modern art, motion pictures, literature, and music. This section mentions only some of the most important German contributions to the arts. For more detailed information, see the separate articles on **Architecture; Classical music; Drama; German literature; Opera; Painting; Sculpture;** and **Theater.**

Literature and philosophy. The greatest period of German literature lasted from about 1750 to 1830. During these years, Johann Wolfgang von Goethe, Gotthold Ephraim Lessing, Friedrich Schiller, Friedrich Hölderlin, Heinrich von Kleist, and many other German novelists, poets, and dramatists produced works of lasting importance. The most important German philosopher during this period was Immanuel Kant, who wrote three influential works in the 1780's. During the early 1800's, Georg Wilhelm Friedrich Hegel produced a philosophy of history that would have a lasting impact on Western thought. Hegel's work greatly influenced Karl Marx, who used Hegelian ideas as the basis for his revolutionary theories.

From the mid 1800's on, German writers and philosophers often focused on the political and cultural situations in their own land. Poet Heinrich Heine produced works that were critical of the German political establishment. Theodor Fontane wrote gently ironic novels about Prussian society in the late 1800's. Friedrich Nietzsche wrote a series of poetic philosophical works on the nature of language and culture. Between 1890 and 1920, Max Weber created a series of studies about modern society. During the 1900's, novelist Thomas Mann and dramatist Bertolt Brecht wrote about the problems of German politics and culture. After the collapse of Nazi Germany, Günter Grass, Heinrich Böll, and many other writers tried to come to terms with the burden of the Nazi past.

Music. The great tradition of German music was established during the early 1700's by Johann Sebastian Bach and George Frideric Handel. Later in the 1700's, one of the greatest musical geniuses of all time, Wolfgang Amadeus Mozart, carried on this tradition in Austria, which was historically connected to the other German states. In the early 1800's, Ludwig van Beethoven invented new and powerful forms of symphonic expression and then reached new heights of creative power with his last quartets. Felix Mendelssohn became the most famous composer of his time, with his own classical works and by reviving interest in the works of Bach.

Saint James the Greater (1510); Öffentliche Kunstsammlung Basel, Kunstmuseum (© Colorphoto Hans Hinz)

Porcelain figurine (1746) by Johann Kändler; Wadsworth Atheneum, Francis G. Mayer Art Color Slides, Inc.

Sculpture and ceramics have long traditions in German art. A carving by Tilman Riemenschneider, *left,* is a masterpiece of late medieval sculpture. The Meissen factory created beautiful ceramic figurines, *right,* in the 1700's.

© Wilhelm Rauh, Bayreuther Festspiele

Richard Wagner's opera *Lohengrin,* first performed in 1850, is based on a medieval German legend. Wagner's music dramas established a new style in opera and influenced many composers. His operas are performed each year at a special festival in Bayreuth, *above.*

Film Stills Archive, The Museum of Modern Art

German filmmaking has excelled in portraying psychological themes. The silent film *Metropolis* (1926), *above,* was directed by the famous German director Fritz Lang. The film depicts a city of the future that has been corrupted by mad scientists.

Giraudon/Art Resource

The interior of the Wies church near Oberammergau is a masterpiece of rococo decoration. The interior was intended to give visitors a vision of heaven. The church, designed by Dominkus Zimmermann, was built between 1745 and 1754.

Oil painting on canvas (1911); Collection Walker Art Center, Minneapolis, gift of the T. B. Walker Foundation, Gilbert M. Walker Fund, 1942

German expressionism was one of the most important art movements of the 1900's. In 1911, Franz Marc helped found a school of expressionism in Munich called *Der Blaue Reiter* (The Blue Rider). Marc's *The Large Blue Horses, above,* is one of his best-known paintings.

Franz Schubert and Robert Schumann achieved greatness by composing the romantic German art songs called *lieder* (see **Lieder**).

In the mid-1800's, Richard Wagner established a new style in opera with his *music dramas,* which sought to combine music, poetry, and theatrical design. In the late 1800's and early 1900's, Richard Strauss and Arnold Schoenberg wrote important music in different styles.

During the 1920's, Kurt Weill broke new musical ground with his innovative music for the stage.

Painting and sculpture. German artists created some outstanding works during the Renaissance. Albrecht Dürer and Hans Holbein the Younger produced great paintings and engravings. They are especially famous for their portraits. Matthias Grünewald painted masterpieces of religious art, and sculptor Tilman

© Scholz, Bavaria-Verlag

The Dresden Opera House was built between 1871 and 1878. The building shows the influence of the baroque architectural style of the 1700's. It was damaged by bombs in 1945, during World War II. But it was restored to its original appearance.

© F. Karsten, London from Bauhaus-Archive, Berlin

The Bauhaus was an internationally important school of design founded by German architect Walter Gropius in Weimar in 1919. This photograph shows the buildings Gropius designed for the school when it moved from Weimar to Dessau in 1925.

Riemenschneider made beautiful woodcarvings.

In the early 1800's, Caspar David Friedrich was an important romantic painter. In the late 1800's and early 1900's, Max Beckmann and other German painters developed the expressionist style. They sought to express unconscious emotions and dreamlike states.

Architecture. During the Middle Ages, magnificent cathedrals in the Romanesque and Gothic styles were built in such cities as Bamberg, Cologne, Regensberg, Ulm, and Worms. In the 1700's, German princes built palaces modeled on the magnificent French palace at Versailles. At the same time, Germans built great baroque and rococo churches, especially in the predominantly Roman Catholic southern German states. During the 1800's, such German architects as Friedrich Schinkel built museums and other public buildings in the neoclassical style. After 1900, Walter Gropius and his famous Bauhaus group developed a basic style of modern architecture.

The land

Germany has a varied landscape made up of five main land regions. From north to south, they are (1) the North German Plain, (2) the Central Highlands, (3) the South German Hills, (4) the Black Forest, and (5) the Bavarian Alps.

The North German Plain, the largest land region in Germany, is low and nearly flat. Almost the entire plain lies less than 300 feet (91 meters) above sea level. The region is drained by broad rivers that flow northward into the North Sea or the Baltic Sea. These rivers include the Elbe, Ems, Oder, Rhine, and Weser, all of which are important commercial waterways. Large ports and industrial centers are located on them.

The wide river valleys, as well as land along the seacoasts, have soft, fertile soil. Between the valleys are large areas covered with sand and gravel. These areas are called *heathlands.* The sand and gravel were deposited by glaciers that moved across much of Europe thousands of years ago. The glaciers also formed many small lakes in the North German Plain. The soil of the heathlands is not suitable for farming, and trees have been planted in many to provide timber.

The southern edge of the North German Plain has highly fertile, dustlike soil called *loess.* This area is heavily cultivated and thickly populated. Many of Germany's oldest cities, including Bonn and Cologne, are located in this area.

The Central Highlands are a series of plateaus that range from nearly flat to mountainous. They are covered with rock and poor soil. Most of the plateaus lie from 1,000 to 2,500 feet (300 to 760 meters) above sea level. Two of them—the Harz Mountains and the Thuringian Forest—have peaks that rise more than 3,000 feet (910 meters).

Rivers in the Central Highlands have cut steep, narrow valleys. These rugged gorges, especially that of the Rhine River, are among the most beautiful sights in Germany. In some areas, the valleys broaden into small, fertile basins. See **Rhine River.**

The South German Hills include a series of long, parallel ridges, called *escarpments,* that extend from southwest to northeast. Sheep are raised on these rocky ridges. Lowlands between the ridges have fertile clay soil. Some of these lowlands are among the best farmlands in Germany. Along the southern edge of the hill region are large areas covered with sand and gravel. This soil was deposited by ancient glaciers that spread northward from the Alps. Most of the South German Hills rise from 500 to 2,500 feet (150 to 762 meters).

Much of the region is drained by the Rhine River and two of its branches, the Main and Neckar rivers. The

© K. W. Gruber, Bavaria-Verlag

The North German Plain is a low, flat region that covers all of northern Germany. Fertile lands are found in the river valleys and along the seacoast of the plain.

Danube River drains the southern part. The Danube is the only major river in Germany that flows eastward. See **Danube River.**

The Black Forest is a mountainous region. Its name comes from the thick forests of dark fir and spruce trees that cover the mountainsides. The region consists of granite and sandstone uplands with deep, narrow valleys. It averages between 2,500 and 3,000 feet (762 and 910 meters) above sea level. Some peaks rise more than 4,000 feet (1,200 meters). The Black Forest is the scene of many old German legends and fairy tales. It is also known for its mineral springs. Many famous health resorts are located near them. See **Black Forest.**

The Bavarian Alps are part of the Alps, the largest mountain system in Europe. The majestic, snow-capped Bavarian Alps rise more than 6,000 feet (1,800 meters).

Physical features

Germany terrain map

WORLD BOOK map

International boundary

Land region boundary

• City or town

+ Elevation above sea level

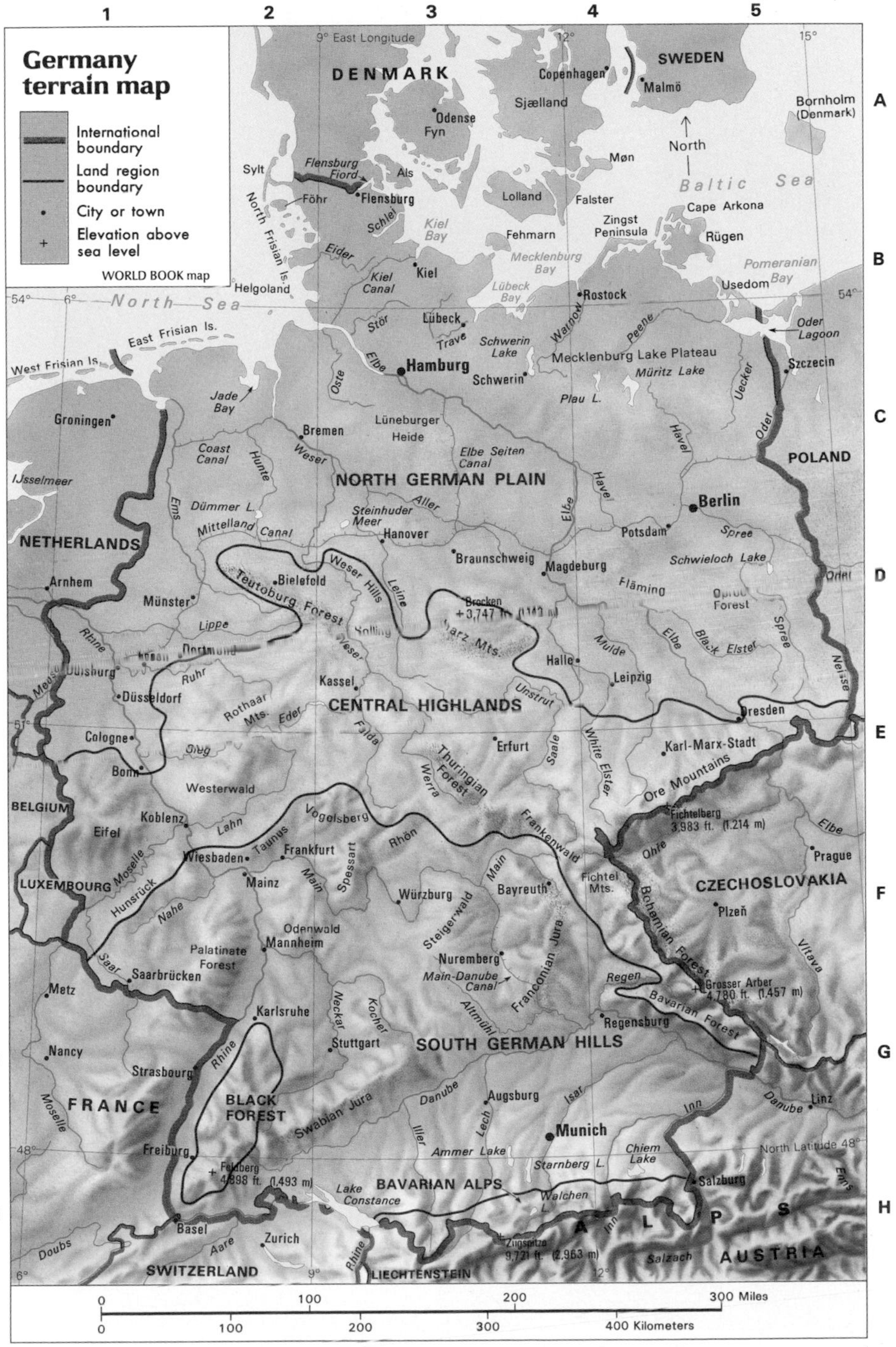

© Marvullo, The Stock Market

The Central Highlands are a series of flat to mountainous plateaus. Many rivers, including the Rhine, *left,* one of Europe's most important rivers, flow through the region.

© M. u. H., Bavaria-Verlag
© L. H. Mantell, The Stock Market

The Black Forest is a mountainous region of southwestern Germany. It is named for the dark fir and spruce trees that cover its slopes. Many German legends are set in the Black Forest.

The Bavarian Alps, forming part of Germany's southern boundary, are part of Europe's highest mountain chain. Their scenic beauty makes them a popular year-round vacation destination.

The highest point in Germany, the 9,721-foot (2,963-meter) peak Zugspitze, is in this region. The beauty of the Bavarian Alps has made them a year-round vacation-land. The region has many lakes formed by the ancient glaciers from the Alps. It is drained by mountain streams that flow into the Danube River. See **Alps.**

Climate

Germany has a mild climate, largely because the land is near the sea. In winter, the sea is not so cold as the land. In summer, it is not so warm. As a result, west winds from the sea help warm Germany in winter and cool it in summer. Away from the sea, in southern areas, winters are colder and summers are warmer.

Average monthly weather

	Berlin					**Munich**				
	Temperatures				**Days of rain or snow**		**Temperatures**			**Days of rain or snow**
	F°		**C°**				**F°**		**C°**	
	High	**Low**	**High**	**Low**			**High**	**Low**	**High**	**Low**	
Jan.	35	26	2	−3	10	Jan.	33	23	1	−5	10
Feb.	38	27	3	−3	8	Feb.	37	25	3	−4	9
Mar.	46	32	8	0	9	Mar.	45	31	7	−1	10
Apr.	55	38	13	3	9	Apr.	54	37	12	3	13
May	65	46	18	8	8	May	63	45	17	7	13
June	70	51	21	11	9	June	69	51	21	11	14
July	74	55	23	13	10	July	72	54	22	12	14
Aug.	72	54	22	12	10	Aug.	71	53	22	12	13
Sept.	66	48	19	9	8	Sept.	64	48	18	9	11
Oct.	55	41	13	5	8	Oct.	53	40	12	4	10
Nov.	43	33	6	1	8	Nov.	42	31	6	−1	9
Dec.	37	29	3	−2	11	Dec.	36	26	2	−3	11

The average temperature in January, the coldest month in Germany, is above 30° F. (−1° C). Cold winds from eastern Europe sometimes reach Germany in winter, and the temperature may drop sharply for short periods. In July, the hottest month in Germany, the temperature averages about 64° F. (18° C).

Most of Germany receives from 20 to 40 inches (50 to 100 centimeters) of *precipitation* (rain, melted snow, and other forms of moisture) a year. Some hilly and mountainous areas receive more precipitation. The moisture-bearing west winds first reach Germany in the northwest. In that area, rain falls almost evenly throughout the year, with a little more in autumn and winter than in spring and summer. Inland, most rain falls in summer, often in heavy thunderstorms. Deep snow covers some mountainous areas throughout the winter.

Economy

In 1945, at the end of World War II, Germany's economy lay almost in total ruin. Both West and East Germany had to be rebuilt by the controlling Allied powers. West Germany's postwar recovery was greatly helped by aid that the United States began to send in 1948 under the Marshall Plan (see **Marshall Plan**). The West German economy recovered at an amazing rate in the 1950's. This recovery is described as West Germany's "economic miracle."

In East Germany, the Soviet Union set up a strong Communist state where the government controlled the economy, including production, distribution, and pricing of almost all goods. Under this system, East Germany grew to be one of the wealthiest Communist countries, though it lagged well behind West Germany.

Average January temperatures
January is Germany's coldest month. Winds from the sea warm the northern part of Germany during winter.

Average July temperatures
July is Germany's hottest month. But German summers are mild, thanks to sea winds that cool the land.

Average yearly precipitation
Precipitation levels vary throughout Germany. Mountainous areas in the south receive the most rain and snow.

WORLD BOOK maps

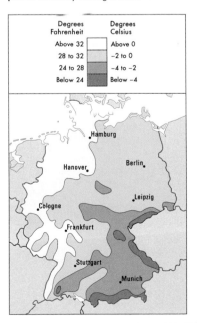

Degrees Fahrenheit	Degrees Celsius
Above 32	Above 0
28 to 32	−2 to 0
24 to 28	−4 to −2
Below 24	Below −4

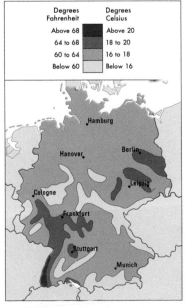

Degrees Fahrenheit	Degrees Celsius
Above 68	Above 20
64 to 68	18 to 20
60 to 64	16 to 18
Below 60	Below 16

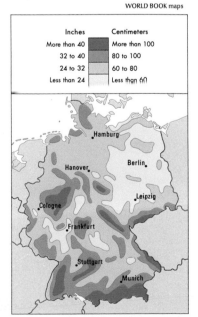

Inches	Centimeters
More than 40	More than 100
32 to 40	80 to 100
24 to 32	60 to 80
Less than 24	Less than 60

Steel mills in the Ruhr region help make Germany one of the world's leading steel producers. Most of the country's steel is used to manufacture automobiles, machinery, and ships.

© Cameramann International, Ltd.

In 1989, popular protests forced the East German government to make political and economic reforms. As part of these reforms, free, multiparty elections were held in 1990. East Germans elected officials who favored unification with West Germany. One of the first steps taken toward unification was the union of the economies.

Germany began economic unification on July 1, 1990. East Germans traded their money, called *DDR marks,* for West German money, called *Deutsche marks.* The Deutsche mark became the unit of currency throughout Germany. East Germany began to operate under a free enterprise system. The East German government started to sell government-owned businesses.

Economic unification had several results. Goods that had been scarce in East Germany became readily avail-

able. But the cost of many goods in the free market was higher than they had been when the government controlled prices. Economic unification also caused problems for East German businesses. Many companies could not operate without the government's financial support. Many businesses closed or operated on shorter hours, causing increased unemployment.

Before unification, West Germany had one of the world's strongest economies. Many economists believe the united German economy will remain strong, but will require several years of adjustment. West Germany joined the European Economic Community (EEC) in 1957. This economic union, also called the European Common Market, helped strengthen the economy through increased trade. United Germany remained in the EEC (see **European Community**).

BMW of North America, Inc.

Automobiles built in Germany are shipped worldwide, making motor vehicles one of the nation's chief exports. Germany is the world's third largest producer of cars.

Manufacturing, Germany's fastest-growing industry, has been the basis of the nation's rapid economic recovery. Germany has several major manufacturing regions, and there are factories almost everywhere. The Ruhr is the most important industrial region, and one of the busiest in the world. It includes such manufacturing centers as Dortmund, Duisburg, and Düsseldorf. This region has more than 8 million people. It produces most of the nation's iron and steel, and has important chemical and textile industries. See **Ruhr.**

Much of Germany's steel is used to make automobiles and trucks, industrial and agricultural machinery, ships, and tools. The country is the world's third largest manufacturer of automobiles, after Japan and the United States. Germany also produces large quantities of cement, clothing, electrical equipment, and processed foods and metals. The chemical industry produces large quantities of drugs, fertilizer, plastics, sulfuric acid, and artificial rubber and fibers. Other important products include cameras, computers, leather goods, scientific instruments, toys, and wood pulp and paper.

Service industries are those economic activities that produce services, not goods. Service industries account for about half of the value of Germany's economic production. The most important group of service industries

in Germany is community, government, and personal services. Community services include such economic activities as education and health care. Personal services consist of such activities as advertising and data processing, and the operation of cleaning establishments, repair shops, and beauty salons. Government includes both public administration and defense. Other service industries are finance and insurance, trade, transportation and communication, and utilities.

Agriculture. About a third of Germany's food must be imported. Germany is the world's largest importer of agricultural goods. Potatoes are the only food produced in large enough quantities so that they do not have to be imported. The chief grains include barley, oats, rye, and wheat. Sugar beets, vegetables, apples, grapes, and other fruits are also important crops. Fine wines are made from grapes grown in vineyards along the Rhine and Moselle (or Mosel) rivers. Livestock and livestock products are important sources of farm income. Large numbers of farmers raise beef and dairy cattle, hogs, horses, poultry, and sheep.

Many German farms are 25 acres (10 hectares) or less in size. Most of these small farms are operated part-time by farmers who have other jobs. In eastern Germany, the government planned to break up the large farms for-

Economy of Germany

This map shows the economic uses of land in Germany. It also shows the main farm and mineral products, and it includes German cities that are important manufacturing centers.

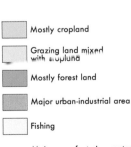

Mostly cropland

Grazing land mixed with cropland

Mostly forest land

Major urban-industrial area

Fishing

• Major manufacturing center

• Mineral deposit

WORLD BOOK map

© Müller-Güll, Bavaria-Verlag

Farms in western Germany are mostly small. German farmers produce only about two-thirds of the nation's food. Germany is the world's largest importer of agricultural goods.

merly controlled by the East German government and sell them to individuals.

Mining. Germany has large supplies of potash and rock salt. It also has some lead, copper, petroleum, tin, uranium, and zinc. In the 1800's, coal deposits near the Ruhr River helped German industries grow. But by the 1970's, most of the high-quality deposits had been exhausted. Eastern Germany produces large quantities of a low-quality coal called *lignite.*

Foreign trade. Only the United States outranks Germany in the value of its foreign trade. Germany exports more than it imports, even though it must import great amounts of food and industrial raw materials. Its major exports include automobiles, chemicals, iron and steel products, and machinery. Germany trades with countries in all parts of the world. More than half its trade is with European Common Market nations. The United States and the Soviet Union are also important trading partners.

Energy sources. Coal is still a major source of electrical power in Germany, but its use has declined since 1970 as oil-burning and nuclear-powered generating plants have become more common. In southern Germany, mountain streams are used to generate hydroelectric power. Germany has some gas fields, but must import most of its natural gas. The nation also depends on imported oil, mainly from the Middle East.

Transportation and communication. Railroads and highways connect all parts of Germany. Germany has one of the most extensive railroad networks in the world, providing excellent passenger and freight service. Germany's fine highway system includes about 6,500 miles (10,500 kilometers) of four-lane highways called *autobahns.* Adolf Hitler began building the autobahns in the 1930's. Germans own almost 35 million cars. In 1990, there was about 1 car for every 2 people in what had been West Germany and 1 car for every 4 people in what had been East Germany.

The Rhine River and its branches carry more traffic than any other European river system. Canals connect the major rivers of Germany. The chief seaports are Hamburg, Wilhelmshaven, and Bremen.

The government-owned airline, Deutsche Lufthansa, flies to all parts of the world. Major airports operate at many cities, including Berlin, Düsseldorf, Frankfurt am Main, Hamburg, Leipzig, and Munich.

Germany has about 400 daily newspapers. The largest is the *Bild Zeitung* of Hamburg. Several other large newspapers circulate throughout the country. The press is free from government censorship.

Nearly all German homes have one or more radios, and most homes have a TV set. Three major channels, all produced by public corporations, are broadcast nationwide. Local programs are also broadcast. Commercials may be broadcast at only a few times a day. The public corporations receive money from license fees paid by owners of radios and TV sets. The government owns and operates the postal, telegraph, and telephone systems.

History

Ancient times. Fossils discovered in what is now Germany indicate that the area was home to primitive human beings as early as 650,000 years ago. The Neanderthal people, who lived throughout Europe between 100,000 and 35,000 years ago, are named for a fossil discovery in Germany's Neander Gorge, near Düsseldorf.

But the history of the German people really began sometime after 1000 B.C., when warlike tribes began to migrate from northern Europe into what is now Germany. These tribes wandered the area, and lived by hunting and farming. In the 100's B.C., they moved south to the Rhine and Danube rivers, the northern frontiers of the Roman Empire. The Romans called the tribes *Germani,* though that was the name of only one tribe. Other tribes included the Cimbri, Franks, Goths, and Vandals. The Romans called the tribes' land *Germania.*

In A.D. 9, the Romans tried to conquer the tribes, but Germanic warriors crushed the Roman armies in a decisive battle at the Teutoburg Forest. The Romans built a wall, called the *limes,* between the Rhine and Danube rivers to protect their lands to the south from attacks by Germanic tribes. By the late A.D. 300's, Roman power had begun to collapse. In the 400's, Germanic tribes moved south, plundered Rome, and eventually broke up the western portion of the empire into tribal kingdoms. The kingdom of the Franks became the largest and most important. See **Rome, Ancient** (Decline and fall).

Kingdom of the Franks. In 486, Clovis, a Frankish king, defeated the independent Roman governor of Gaul (now France). Clovis extended the boundaries of his territory by defeating other Germanic tribes in Gaul and parts of what is now western Germany. He became an orthodox Christian, and also introduced other Roman ways of life into his kingdom (see **Clovis I**). The greatest Frankish ruler, Charlemagne, came to power in 768. He established his capital in Aachen. Charlemagne expanded his kingdom east to the Elbe River and, in some places, beyond the river. In 800, Pope Leo III crowned him emperor of the Romans. See **Charlemagne.**

The breakup of Charlemagne's empire. In 843, the Treaty of Verdun divided Charlemagne's empire into three kingdoms, one for each of his grandsons. Louis II (called the German) received lands east of the Rhine River, most of which later became what is now Germany. The western part, later called France, went to Charles I (the Bald). Lothair I received the middle kingdom, a narrow strip that extended from the North Sea to central Italy. He also kept the title of emperor.

In 911, the German branch of the Frankish royal family died out. By then, the German kingdom had been divided into five powerful *duchies* (territories ruled by a duke)—Bavaria, Lorraine, Franconia, Saxony, and Swabia. The dukes elected Conrad I of Franconia as king. In 919, Conrad was succeeded by Henry I (the Fowler) of Saxony, whose family ruled until 1024. With the founding of the Saxon *dynasty* (a series of rulers from the same family), the lands given to Louis II became permanently separated from the French parts of Charlemagne's empire.

Henry's son, Otto I (the Great), drove invading Hungarians out of southern Germany in 955, and extended the German frontier in the north. Otto also won control over most of the old middle Frankish kingdom, including Italy. This gave him the right to claim the title of emperor. In 962, Otto was crowned emperor in Rome. This marked the beginning of what later was called the Holy Roman Empire. See **Otto** (I, of Germany).

The Holy Roman Empire. Under the Saxon emperors, the Holy Roman Empire was a powerful combination of territories, each with a separate ruler. The Salian dynasty (1024-1125) included several strong emperors. In 1075, Pope Gregory VII disputed the right of Emperor Henry IV to appoint bishops. Many German princes sided with the pope and a series of civil wars began. See **Henry** (IV, of Germany); **Gregory VII, Saint.**

The Hohenstaufen emperors (1138-1254) reestablished order. But after the dynasty died out, disorder returned. By the 1300's, the emperors were almost powerless. The last Hohenstaufen died in 1254. The German princes did not elect another emperor until 1273. He was Rudolf I of Habsburg (or Hapsburg). Rudolf seized Austria and made it his main duchy. After Rudolf, emperors of various families reigned. Starting in 1438, the Habsburgs reigned almost continuously until 1806. See **Habsburg, House of; Holy Roman Empire.**

Drawing (1457) by Hektor Muelich; Archiv für Kunst und Geschichte

Otto I (the Great) drove the Hungarians out of southern Germany in the battle of the Lech River, *above,* in A.D. 955. In 962 he was crowned emperor of what became the Holy Roman Empire.

The Holy Roman Empire was never fully a German territory. Some Germans lived outside its borders, while some non-German areas were part of the empire. For a time, the empire included parts of Italy, as well as Slavic areas in eastern Europe, and part of what are now Belgium and the Netherlands. The empire also was made up of independent territories. A strong emperor could make their rulers cooperate. But often the emperor could not force them to do what he wanted.

The rise of cities. Before the fall of the West Roman Empire in 476, Roman towns stood along and near the Rhine and Danube rivers. These towns were centers of

Important dates in Germany

c. 1000 B.C. Tribes from northern Europe began to arrive in what is now Germany.

A.D. 486 Clovis, a Germanic king, defeated the Roman governor of Gaul (now France).

800 Charlemagne's empire was established.

843 The Treaty of Verdun divided Charlemagne's empire.

962 Otto I was crowned emperor of what later became the Holy Roman Empire.

1438 The Habsburg family of Austria began almost continuous rule of the Holy Roman Empire.

1517 The Reformation began in Germany.

1618-1648 The Thirty Years' War devastated much of Germany.

1740-1786 Frederick the Great made Prussia a great power.

1806 The Holy Roman Empire came to an end.

1815 The German Confederation was established at the Congress of Vienna.

1848 Revolution broke out, but it failed.

1866 Prussia forced Austria out of German affairs.

1867 Prussia established the North German Confederation.

1870-1871 Germany defeated France in the Franco-Prussian War, and the German Empire was founded.

1914-1918 The Allies defeated Germany in World War I, and the German Empire ended.

1919 The Weimar Republic was established.

1933 Adolf Hitler began to create a Nazi dictatorship.

1939-1945 The Allies defeated Germany in World War II, ending Hitler's dictatorship. They divided Germany into four military occupation zones in 1945.

1948-1949 A Soviet blockade failed to force the Western Allies out of Berlin.

1949 East and West Germany were established.

1953 The Soviet Union crushed an East German revolt.

1955 East and West Germany were declared independent, and joined opposing Cold War military alliances.

1961 The East German Communists built the Berlin Wall to prevent East Germans from escaping to West Berlin.

1973 East and West Germany ratified a treaty calling for closer relations between the two nations. Both nations joined the United Nations (UN).

1989 East Germany opened the Berlin Wall and other border barriers, and allowed its citizens to travel freely to West Germany for the first time since World War II.

1990 East Germany held free elections in March, resulting in the end of Communist rule there. In October, East and West Germany were unified and became the single nation of Germany.

trade. They included what are now Bonn, Cologne, Regensburg, Trier, and Vienna. After the fall of Rome, these towns almost disappeared. Trade gradually resumed under the Saxon and Salian emperors. Some of the old towns grew again, and new ones appeared around the castles of princes and bishops. Many cities became so large and rich that they gained self-rule.

When the emperors began losing power, the cities could not rely on outside help in case of attack. The more prosperous cities banded together into leagues and formed their own armies for protection. The strongest league was the Hanseatic League, which began to develop in the late 1100's. It included Cologne, Dortmund, and the major ports of Bremen, Hamburg, and Lübeck. The Hanseatic League became a great commercial and naval power in the North and Baltic seas during the 1300's. See **Hanseatic League.**

Serfdom in Germany. By the 700's, most peasant farmers in western Germany had become serfs. Each serf worked on land that was owned by a powerful person or by the church. In return for their work, the serfs received protection and a share of the harvest. Generally, serfs were not free to leave the land they worked. Beginning in the 1100's, some serfs gained their freedom by escaping to towns. In the western parts of Germany, serfdom gradually died out as peasants were allowed to substitute monetary payments for labor. In eastern Germany, serfdom did not begin to develop until the 1300's. It lasted until the early 1800's.

The Reformation. In 1517, Martin Luther, a German monk, began to attack many teachings and practices of the Roman Catholic Church. Nobles, peasants, and townspeople joined this movement, called the Reformation, and it spread quickly. Its followers became known as *Protestants,* meaning *those who protest.*

Some princes were sincere reformers, but others became Protestants in order to gain church property. Many peasants hoped the Protestant movement would free them from their lord's control. The peasants revolted against the lords in the Peasants' War of 1524-

1525, but were brutally crushed. See **Luther, Martin; Peasants' War.**

Neither the pope nor Emperor Charles V could stop the Protestant movement. In 1555, Protestant princes forced Charles to accept the Peace of Augsburg. This treaty gave each Lutheran and Roman Catholic prince the right to choose the religion for his own land. It also established a division of church lands between the two religions. See **Reformation.**

During the 1500's and 1600's, the Roman Catholic Church underwent its own reform, called the *Counter Reformation* or *Catholic Reformation.* In this movement, the church won back many Protestants by peaceful means or by force. By 1600, relatively few Protestants were left in Austria, Bavaria, and parts of Bohemia and the Rhineland. The rest of Germany remained chiefly Lutheran. See **Counter Reformation.**

The Thirty Years' War. By 1600, the German lands were divided by many political and religious rivalries. In 1618, a Protestant revolt in Bohemia set off a series of wars that lasted for 30 years. The wars were partially religious struggles between Protestants and Catholics, but they were also political struggles between certain princes and the emperor. In addition, the kings of Denmark, Sweden, and France entered the wars to gain German lands and to reduce the Habsburgs' power.

The Peace of Westphalia ended the Thirty Years' War in 1648. Under this treaty, France and Sweden received some German lands. The wars had been hard on German trade and farming. Large parts of Germany were ruined, and some towns had nearly disappeared. The emperor's already limited power had been further weakened by the wars. Germany was a collection of free cities and hundreds of states. See **Thirty Years' War.**

The rise of Prussia. During the 1600's, the Hohenzollern family began to expand its power in eastern Germany. The Hohenzollerns ruled the state of Brandenburg. Berlin was their capital. In 1618, the ruler of Brandenburg inherited the duchy of Prussia. The Peace of Westphalia added part of Pomerania and some terri-

German Information Center

Martin Luther, whose teachings helped start the Reformation, was summoned before the emperor in the city of Worms in 1521. There, Luther refused to retract his beliefs.

tories on the lower Rhine River to the Hohenzollern holdings. See **Hohenzollern.**

The Hohenzollerns' rise to power began with Frederick William (the Great Elector), who became ruler of Brandenburg in 1640. He began to unite and expand his lands after the Thirty Years' War. In 1701, his son, Frederick I, was given the title king of Prussia. The Hohenzollerns' power continued to grow under the next two kings, Frederick William I and Frederick II (the Great). See **Frederick II (of Prussia); Frederick William (of Brandenburg and of Prussia); Prussia.**

The Hohenzollerns built a large, well-trained professional army and a strong civil service to defend and rule their scattered territories. Through their civil service, they improved farming and industry, and filled their treasury with tax money. They built canals, schools, and roads, and promoted the arts and learning.

After Frederick the Great became king in 1740, he seized Silesia, a rich province of Austria. This invasion led to fighting between Prussia and Austria in two wars, the War of the Austrian Succession (1740-1748) and the Seven Years' War (1756-1763). Many other nations fought in these wars. Some sided with Frederick, and others with his enemy, Empress Maria Theresa of Austria. Under the final peace treaty, Silesia remained under Prussian rule. Prussia was now recognized as a great power. See **Maria Theresa; Seven Years' War; Succession wars** (The War of the Austrian Succession).

During the 1770's, Prussia, along with Austria and Russia (the name for the Soviet Union before 1922), began to seize parts of Poland. By the end of 1795, Poland had been divided among these states.

Conflicts with France. The French Revolution, which began in 1789, caused many changes throughout Europe. France built huge armies made up of citizens inspired by patriotism. Germany's old-fashioned professional armies were not prepared for the new age.

From 1792 until 1815, France was almost continually at war with other European states. Much of the fighting involved German states and took place on German soil. By the end of 1800, Napoleon—who had seized control of France in 1799—had taken parts of western Germany, set up dependent states, and destroyed the Holy Roman Empire. Some German states became members of the Confederation of the Rhine, which Napoleon had established in 1806 and which was allied with France.

Between 1795 and 1806, Prussia stayed out of the wars. But Napoleon's threats became too great. In 1806, Prussia declared war on France. Napoleon crushed the Prussian army at the battles of Jena and Auerstädt that same year. As a result, Prussia lost its territories west of the Elbe River and had to pay war damages to France. To recover from this defeat, the Prussian government introduced reforms, including laws that freed the serfs and gave some self-government to the cities. In the army, reformers fired incompetent officers and improved training.

After the failure of Napoleon's Russian campaign in 1812, Prussia, Austria, Russia, and Great Britain joined against him. The reformed Prussian army helped defeat Napoleon at Leipzig in 1813 and at Waterloo in 1815. For the story of the Napoleonic wars, see **Napoleon I.**

The Congress of Vienna. The victorious powers met in Vienna from late 1814 to early 1815 to restore order to Europe. They left intact most of the middle-sized states created in the Confederation of the Rhine. But their treaty divided the rest of Napoleon's lands among themselves. Prussia received lands including the Rhineland, Westphalia, and much of Saxony, greatly increasing its power in northern and western Germany. Austria gave up its territories in southern Germany and the lands that are now Belgium and Luxembourg, and it took territories in Italy. Austria, Prussia, and Russia again divided Poland. See **Vienna, Congress of.**

The German Confederation. The Congress of Vienna also set up the German Confederation, a union of 39 independent states. An assembly called the *Bundestag* was established. Members were appointed by the rulers of the states. Austria appointed the president.

Except for four self-governing cities, the German states were ruled by kings or princes. Each state had its own laws, collected its own taxes, and was responsible for its own defense. Several states had constitutions and parliaments, but even in these states the people had little voice in their government. Though the king of Prussia had promised to grant a constitution during the war against Napoleon, he did not keep his word.

During the early 1800's, the German population was growing faster than the economy. Some regions prospered, but most areas were still poor. Cities were small, and most people still lived by farming. In the 1840's, popular discontent increased. Business and professional people wanted more opportunities for political involvement. Farmers and craftworkers suffered from poor harvests and economic depression.

The Revolution of 1848. In February 1848, the people of Paris rebelled against their king. When this news reached the Germans, they also rebelled. In Austria, rioting and demonstrations forced the chancellor to resign. In Berlin, people defied the army and forced the Prussian king to appoint new ministers and to promise a constitution. Similar rebellions occurred in most other German capitals. Many Germans hoped that they could replace the Confederation with a more unified nation. In May, an elected assembly met in Frankfurt to write a new constitution.

However, some people began to lose interest in the revolution. Others disagreed about its goals. Meanwhile, the governments began to recover. In October 1848, Austrian troops recaptured Vienna. In December, the new Prussian assembly was dissolved by troops.

The Frankfurt Assembly was divided on many issues, especially on whether Catholic Austria or Protestant Prussia should be the leading power in the new German nation. In March 1849, members compromised on a constitution that called for an emperor and a two-house parliament. The Prussian king Frederick William IV was invited to be emperor but he refused. The assembly then broke up. The revolution was defeated in the spring of 1849. The German Confederation of 1815 was reestablished.

The unification of Germany. In the early 1860's, a conflict about army reforms caused a constitutional crisis in Prussia. The Prussian king, Wilhelm I, appointed Otto von Bismarck prime minister in 1862. Bismarck hoped he could resolve the constitutional crisis with foreign triumphs. He also wanted to establish Prussia as the leading German power.

Between 1864 and 1870, Bismarck had the German states fight three short, victorious wars. In the first, Austria and Prussia, in the name of the German Confederation, took the duchies of Schleswig and Holstein from Denmark. In 1866, Bismarck picked a quarrel with Austria. His army easily defeated Austria at Königgrätz in what was called the Seven Weeks' War (see **Seven Weeks' War**). Bismarck then dissolved the German Confederation, annexed some territory to Prussia, and established the North German Confederation under Prussian leadership. The four German states south of the Main River remained independent, but made military alliances with Prussia. Austria's defeat left it greatly weakened. In 1867, the Austrian emperor was forced to give equal status to his Hungarian holdings, creating the Dual Monarchy of Austria-Hungary. Austria was never again a power in Germany.

To complete the unification of Germany, Bismarck knew that he needed to overcome the opposition of France. In 1870, he encouraged a Hohenzollern prince to accept the throne of Spain. As Bismarck expected, France objected. Although the prince withdrew as a candidate, Bismarck used the dispute to start the Franco-Prussian War. This conflict pitted France against the North German Confederation and its south German allies. After several battles, the Germans defeated the main French armies at Sedan in September 1870. The German army captured Paris in January 1871. Under the peace treaty, France gave up almost all of Alsace and part of Lorraine. See **Franco-Prussian War.**

During the Franco-Prussian War, the four south German states agreed to join a united German nation under Prussian leadership. On Jan. 18, 1871, Wilhelm I was crowned the first *kaiser* (emperor) of the new German Empire. Wilhelm appointed Bismarck chancellor and head of government. See **Bismarck, Otto von; Wilhelm (I).**

The German Empire. The German constitution provided for a two-house parliament. Members of one house, the Reichstag, were popularly elected. Members of the other house, the Bundesrat, were appointed by the state governments. The empire had 26 member states. Most states were very small, and several were completely surrounded by Prussia. The emperor, who was also the king of Prussia, controlled foreign policy, commanded the army, and appointed the chancellor. The parliament approved all laws and taxes, but could not force the chancellor to resign.

Bismarck allowed all men over 25 to vote, thinking that most Germans would support the government. He won support from the growing class of business people and the traditional Prussian landowners and nobles. But Bismarck faced opposition from Roman Catholics and Socialists. Catholics did not trust the Protestant-led empire and organized their own political party. Socialism was growing popular among city dwellers and the workers in the developing industries. Bismarck tried to wreck the Catholic and Socialist parties, but failed.

Foreign policy. After 1871, Bismarck tried to avoid conflicts so the newly united empire could develop. He particularly feared a combined attack from east and west. He tried to keep Germany allied with Russia and Austria-Hungary so they would not form alliances with France. But Russia and Austria-Hungary had opposing interests in the Balkans, which made it difficult to keep an alliance with both of them.

Germany, Austria-Hungary, and Russia formed a loose alliance in 1873, but it soon broke up over the Balkan problem. In 1879, Bismarck established a military and political alliance with Austria-Hungary. Italy joined in 1882, and the alliance became known as the Triple Alliance. During the 1880's, Germany also established colonies in Africa and on islands in the Pacific Ocean.

In 1888, Wilhelm I died. He was succeeded by his ter-

German unification was completed in 1871 under the leadership of Otto von Bismarck, prime minister of Prussia. By maneuvering the German states to fight three wars, Bismarck unified them to form the German Empire.

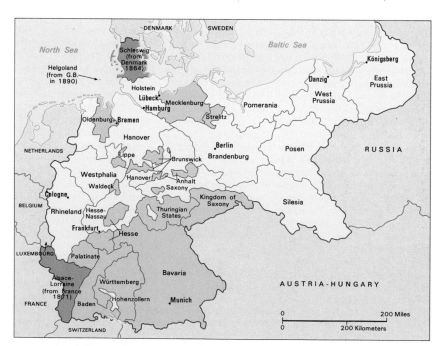

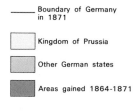

— Boundary of Germany in 1871

Kingdom of Prussia

Other German states

Areas gained 1864-1871

minally ill son Frederick III, whose reign lasted only 99 days. The crown then passed to Frederick's son, Wilhelm II, who was eager to establish his own authority. In 1890, he forced Bismarck to resign. Wilhelm demanded that Germany have influence throughout the world. He also wanted to build a modern navy to defend German interests and challenge British naval supremacy. Wilhelm's ambitions, which he often expressed in an aggressive manner, frightened other powers. In 1894, Russia allied itself with France. Great Britain felt its control of the seas threatened and established the *Entente Cordiale* (cordial understanding) with France in 1904. In 1907, Britain and Russia signed a similar agreement. Under these agreements, the three countries formed the Triple Entente. Europe was divided into two armed camps, with the Triple Alliance on one side and the Triple Entente on the other. See **Triple Alliance; Triple Entente; Wilhelm** (II).

World War I started in the Balkans. On June 28, 1914, Archduke Francis Ferdinand of Austria-Hungary and his wife were murdered in Sarajevo, Bosnia. Bosnia was an Austrian territory claimed by Serbia, a little Balkan country where the murder had been planned. Austria-Hungary decided to punish Serbia, and Germany promised to support these efforts. Austria-Hungary declared war on Serbia on July 28, 1914. Russia prepared for war to support Serbia. Germany then declared war on Russia. After France called up its troops to support Russia, Germany went to war against France. In an effort to reach Paris quickly, German troops invaded neutral Belgium. Great Britain then declared war on Germany.

Germany won the opening battles of the war, but France, Britain, and Russia continued to fight. Germany, Austria-Hungary, and their allies were called the Central Powers. The nations opposing them were called the Allies. As the war dragged on, other countries became involved. Almost all of them joined the Allies. In 1915, Italy joined the Allies, hoping to gain Austrian land. In 1917, the United States entered the war on the Allied side.

Despite the size and strength of the Allies, Germany seemed close to winning the war. After 1914, German troops held Luxembourg, most of Belgium, and part of northern France. In 1917, Germany won on the Eastern

WORLD BOOK map

Germany in World War I drove deep into eastern Europe, overwhelming the old-fashioned Russian army. But continued battles along the western front eventually defeated the Germans. Germany gave up some of its territory in the peace agreement.

Front as the Russian war effort collapsed. But by 1918, Germany's armies were exhausted. Supplies were running low and there was social unrest at home. Meanwhile, an increasing number of fresh American troops were arriving to reinforce the Allies. In the summer of 1918, American troops helped stop the last great German offensive in the west. On November 11, Germany signed an armistice. For the story of Germany in World War I, see **World War I.**

Under the Treaty of Versailles, which was signed after World War I, Germany lost its colonies and some of its European territory. Alsace and the German part of Lorraine were returned to France, Poland was reestablished, and it received Posen (now Poznan), some of Silesia, and part of West Prussia. France got control of the Saar region for 15 years. The treaty also placed the Rhineland under Allied occupation for 15 years. Germany's army was reduced to 100,000 men, and the nation was forbidden from having an air force. Germany was also required to pay the Allies *reparations* (payments for war damages), which were later set at about $33 billion.

The Weimar Republic. Before the armistice was signed in November 1918, German workers and troops had revolted in protest against continuing the war. This revolution began in Kiel, and spread quickly from city to city. On November 9, Germany was declared a republic. Emperor Wilhelm II fled to safety in the Netherlands.

In January 1919, the German voters, including women for the first time, elected a national assembly to write a constitution. The assembly met in Weimar, and the new republic became known as the Weimar Republic. The constitution established a democratic federal republic in August 1919. It provided for a parliament of two houses—the Reichstag and the Reichsrat—and a popularly elected president. The chancellor and the cabinet members were appointed by the president, but could be removed from office by the Reichstag.

The Weimar Republic was weak from the start. Many important Germans remained loyal to the empire. Ger-

Bettmann Archive

The powerful German army won early victories in World War I. These German forces fought Russian troops in trenches along the Eastern Front during 1914.

Burning money for fuel became a symbolic gesture in Germany in the 1920's. Runaway inflation in 1922 and 1923 made German money almost worthless and ruined the economy.

man army officers claimed that Germany had been defeated by the revolution, not by Allied armies. The terms of the Treaty of Versailles were harsher than the Germans had expected.

In 1922 and 1923, the economy collapsed when inflation ruined the value of German money. By 1923, the republic appeared doomed. Communists rebelled in some areas. In Munich, the National Socialist German Workers Party—better known as the Nazi Party—attempted an armed rebellion under its leader, Adolf Hitler. But despite these events, the republic survived.

Gustav Stresemann became chancellor and then foreign minister. Under his leadership, order was restored. A new money system was set up to end the inflation. In 1924, the Allies made it easier for Germany to pay its reparations. At the Locarno Conference in 1925, Stresemann signed a security pact with France and Belgium. The pact was also guaranteed by Great Britain and Italy (see **Locarno Conference**).

The republic's prospects looked much brighter by the late 1920's. But in 1929, a worldwide economic depression began. Millions of Germans lost their jobs. The government appeared powerless and political violence increased. The voters increasingly supported groups that promised a new system of government. After the 1930 elections, political parties in the Reichstag failed to agree on a program. Between 1930 and 1933, President Paul von Hindenburg and his chancellors ruled largely by issuing laws without the approval of parliament.

Nazi Germany. During the political confusion of the early 1930's, the Nazi Party made rapid gains in German elections. The Nazi Party had been founded in 1919.

After his 1923 revolt failed, Hitler decided to gain power by lawful means rather than by revolution. From 1924 to 1929, the republic was prosperous and stable, so the Nazis attracted few voters. After the Great Depression struck, more Germans were attracted to Hitler's promises to improve the economy, defy the hated Treaty of Versailles, and rebuild Germany's military power. In 1932, the Nazis emerged as the strongest party in the Reichstag. In 1933, Hindenburg appointed Hitler chancellor. See **Hitler, Adolf; Nazism.**

Soon after he became chancellor, Hitler began to destroy the constitution and build a dictatorship. He permitted only one political party—the Nazis. The party seized control of the nation's courts, newspapers, police, and schools. People who opposed the government were murdered, imprisoned in concentration camps, forced to leave Germany, or beaten up by the Nazis' private army called *storm troopers*. After Hindenburg died in 1934, Hitler declared himself *der Führer* (the leader) of Germany. The Nazis called their government the *Third Reich* (Third Empire). The first was the Holy Roman Empire, and the second was the German Empire.

Many Germans approved of Nazism. Many others objected to some features of Nazi rule, but supported Hitler's efforts to improve the economy and rebuild the military. Some Germans opposed Hitler but remained silent. Only a very few resisted.

Hitler pursued two goals. He wanted to assert German superiority over what he believed to be inferior races, including Jews, Slavs, and other non-German peoples. He also wanted to gain territory—*Lebensraum* (living space)—for Germany, especially in eastern Europe. In 1933, Hitler removed all German Jews from government jobs. In 1935, he took away the rights of Jewish citi-

Adolf Hitler's Nazi Party controlled most aspects of German life from 1933 to 1945. Large rallies, like this one at Nuremberg, glorified Hitler and encouraged loyalty to the Nazi cause.

zens. Faced with this persecution, more than half of Germany's 500,000 Jews left the country. On Nov. 9, 1938, Nazi crowds burned down synagogues and broke the windows of Jewish businesses in an event later called *Kristallnacht* (Crystal Night). In English, the event is known as the Night of Broken Glass.

At the same time Hitler was acting against the Jews, he was also preparing for war. In 1936, German troops reoccupied the Rhineland. Also in 1936, Germany formed an alliance with Italy and signed an anti-Communist agreement with Japan. The three countries became known as the *Axis* powers. In March 1938, Germany occupied Austria and made it part of the Third Reich. In September, Britain and France consented to Hitler's demands to take over the German-speaking areas of Czechoslovakia (see **Munich Agreement**). The next year, Germany seized the rest of Czechoslovakia.

In August 1939, Germany and the Soviet Union agreed to remain neutral if the other became involved in a war. They also secretly agreed to divide Poland and much of Eastern Europe between them. On September 1, Germany invaded Poland and World War II began.

World War II. On Sept. 3, 1939, Great Britain and France declared war on Germany to help defend Poland. But Poland fell quickly under the German, and later, Soviet attacks. In the spring of 1940, German forces captured Denmark, Norway, the Netherlands, Belgium, and Luxembourg. The Allied forces that opposed the Germans had been unprepared for Germany's *blitzkrieg* (lightning war) methods. Hitler used fast-moving tanks and infantry supported by dive bombers.

In May 1940, the German army moved around France's eastern defenses and overwhelmed the French army. France fell by the end of June.

The German advance stopped at the English Channel. After a series of desperate air battles over Britain in the summer and fall of 1940, the Germans failed to gain the air superiority they needed to invade England. Hitler now turned to the east and the south. He conquered the Balkans, occupied Crete, and sent an army to northern Africa. In June 1941, a huge German force invaded the Soviet Union and drove deep into Soviet territory.

At the end of 1941, Nazi Germany dominated the continent. Hitler used his power as proof of his theory that the Germans belonged to a "master race." The Nazis ruthlessly murdered about 6 million European Jews and about 5 million Poles, Gypsies, and others. Many of these people died in the Nazi concentration camps.

Despite his army's initial success, Hitler could not defeat the Soviet Union. The Soviets continued to resist and slowly pushed the invaders back. Japan's attack on Pearl Harbor on Dec. 7, 1941, brought the United States into the war. The tide turned against Germany in 1943. The Soviets counterattacked in the east. American and British troops drove the Germans out of North Africa and invaded Italy from the south. In June 1944, the Allies invaded France. After the failure of the last German offensive in December 1944, Allied troops poured into Germany. As Soviet troops closed in on Berlin from the east, Hitler committed suicide on April 30, 1945. On May 7, Germany surrendered. For the story of Germany in World War II, see **World War II.**

Occupied Germany. The war left most of Germany in ruins. The Allied bombing and invasion had de-

UPI/Bettmann Newsphotos

Nuremberg, *above,* like cities throughout Germany, lay in ruins after the Nazis' defeat in World War II.

stroyed cities, farms, industries, and transportation. Supplies of food, fuel, and water were very low. People were half starved, and many lived in ruined buildings.

In June 1945, the Allied Big Four—the United States, Great Britain, France, and the Soviet Union—officially took over supreme authority in Germany. The country was divided into four zones of military occupation, with each power occupying a zone. Berlin, located deep in the Soviet zone, was also divided into four sectors of military occupation.

In July and August 1945, leaders of the United States, Great Britain, and the Soviet Union met in Potsdam, Germany. They agreed to govern Germany together and to rebuild it as a democracy. They also agreed to stamp out Nazism and to settle German refugees from Eastern Europe in Germany. Under the agreement, the Soviet Union also was granted northern East Prussia, which it claimed. The rest of that region, and German territory

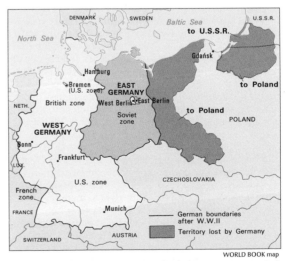

WORLD BOOK map

After World War II, Germany was divided into zones occupied by the victors—the United States, Great Britain, France, and the Soviet Union. These zones later became East and West Germany. Other German lands were lost to Poland and the Soviet Union.

east of the Oder and Neisse rivers, were placed under Polish control. As a result, Germany lost about a fourth of its land. See **Potsdam Conference.**

Many of the most important Nazi leaders had committed suicide or had disappeared. The Allies brought to trial those remaining. A number of these Nazis were hanged or imprisoned. The most important trials took place in Nuremberg (see **Nuremberg Trials).**

The division of Germany. Almost immediately after their victory over the Nazis, the Allies began to quarrel among themselves. The Soviet Union began to establish Communist governments in the Eastern European countries its army had occupied at the end of the war. The Western powers tried to block Communist expansion in the areas under their control. The Soviets imposed barriers against communication, trade, and travel between East and West. Extreme mistrust and tension grew on each side, a condition that came to be called the Cold War. See **Cold War.**

The outbreak of the Cold War affected Germany immediately. When the Soviet Union and the Western Allies could not agree on a common policy in Germany, each side began to organize its own occupation zones in Germany overall and in Berlin. Great Britain, France, and the United States combined the economies of their zones and prepared to unite the zones politically. The Soviet Union imposed Communist rule on its zone.

In June 1948, the Western Allies moved to rebuild the economy of their occupation zones in Germany. They reorganized the German monetary system and issued new money, replacing the virtually worthless existing currency. Under the Marshall Plan, U.S. aid began to pour into the Western zone, and economic recovery got underway (see **Marshall Plan).** The Soviets responded by stopping all highway, rail, and water travel between Berlin and the Western zone. The Soviets hoped that they could force the Allies out of Berlin. But the Allies set up the huge Berlin airlift and flew about 8,000 short tons (7,300 metric tons) of supplies into the city every day. The Soviets lifted the blockade in May 1949, realizing it had failed. See **Cold War** (The Berlin blockade).

West Germany. The Western Allies turned over increasing authority to German officials. As the division between the Eastern and Western zones grew, the Allies arranged for a German council to write a federal constitution, which they approved in May 1949. On Sept. 21, 1949, the three Western zones were officially combined as the Federal Republic of Germany. The military occupation ended, and the Allied High Commission, a civilian agency, replaced the military governors. Military occupation continued in West Berlin, because treaties uniting Germany had not been signed. On May 5, 1955, the Allied High Commission was dissolved, and West Germany became completely independent.

The new West German parliament met for the first time in Bonn, the country's capital, in September 1949. It elected Konrad Adenauer chancellor. Under him, West Germany helped found the Council of Europe and the European Economic Community (EEC). In 1955, West Germany joined the North Atlantic Treaty Organization (NATO) and began to establish its armed forces.

By 1955, West Germany had made an amazing economic recovery. The value of goods produced there was greater than that for all Germany in 1936. This "economic miracle" helped West Germany absorb more than 10 million refugees from Eastern Europe, and more than a million workers from the rest of Europe.

West Germany's prosperity helped the republic gain the support of its citizens. Also, Adenauer was a strong leader, though he was criticized in his later years for ignoring the views of others. He retired in 1963. Ludwig Erhard succeeded Adenauer as chancellor and served until 1966. Kurt Georg Kiesinger was chancellor from 1966 to 1969. Adenauer, Erhard, and Kiesinger were members of the Christian Democratic Union.

Willy Brandt of the Social Democratic Party, who had been vice chancellor since 1966, became chancellor in 1969. He resigned in 1974 after it was discovered that one of his aides was an East German spy. Helmut Schmidt, also a Social Democrat, succeeded Brandt. In 1982, Schmidt was forced from office by a vote of no confidence from the Bundestag. The small Free Democratic Party, which had supported the Social Democrats, switched its parliamentary support to the Christian Democratic Union. The Bundestag elected Christian Democratic leader Helmut Kohl chancellor. Kohl remained chancellor following the 1983 and 1987 elections, in which the Christian Democratic coalition with the Free Democrats won majorities in the Bundestag.

In the 1980's, many Germans, especially young people, expressed concern for the environment and opposition to the placement of U.S. missiles in West Germany. Mass protests occurred. The Green Party, an organization devoted to environmental issues, gained popularity and won seats in the Bundestag. In 1989, the Green Party gained support in local elections. The party formed coalitions with the Social Democratic Party in several states and participated in state governments.

East Germany. After World War II, the Soviet Union appointed German Communists to local offices and set up a system much like that of the Soviet Union. Banks, farms, and industries were seized and reorganized. People suspected of opposing Communism were thrown into prison camps. In 1946, the Communists forced the Social Democratic Party to join them in forming the Socialist Unity Party. The party came under control of the Communist leader Walter Ulbricht. Ulbricht became first secretary, or head, of the Socialist Unity Party. The first secretary (later general secretary) was the most powerful leader in East Germany.

A Communist-prepared constitution was adopted in May 1949. On October 7, the Soviet zone became the German Democratic Republic, with East Berlin its capital. Ulbricht held the real power, though he did not head the government. In October 1955, East Germany became officially independent from the Soviet Union, but Soviet influence continued. Also in 1955, East Germany joined the Warsaw Pact, an Eastern European military alliance under Soviet command (see **Warsaw Pact).** East Germany's armed forces were established officially in 1956, though special "police" units had been given tanks as well as other heavy weapons as early as 1952.

The East German economy recovered after 1945, but the standard of living remained much lower than West Germany's. In 1953, Ulbricht tried to increase working hours without raising wages. Strikes and riots broke out in East Berlin and other cities. Soviet tanks and troops crushed the revolt. Living and working conditions slowly improved, but many people remained dissatisfied. Every week, thousands of East Germans fled to West Germany. Almost 3 million East Germans left, and the labor force fell sharply. Most refugees fled through Berlin, because the Communists had sealed off the East-West border. In August 1961, the Communists built the Berlin Wall between East and West Berlin. They also strengthened barriers around the rest of West Berlin. See **Berlin Wall.**

In 1971, Ulbricht resigned as head of East Germany's Socialist Unity Party. Erich Honecker, a member of the party's Central Committee, succeeded him. Under Honecker, East Germany improved its relations with many non-Communist nations. Before 1960, only the Soviet Union and several other Communist countries had diplomatic relations with East Germany. But eventually, East Germany established relations with other nations.

East Germany experienced major changes in 1989. In many Eastern European nations, people demonstrated for more freedom from their Communist governments. Communist Hungary removed its barriers on its border with non-Communist Austria. Thousands of East Germans went to Hungary, crossed into Austria, and then moved to West Germany. Throughout East Germany, citizens protested for more freedom. In October, the growing pressure forced Honecker to resign as head of the party and from government positions he held. He was succeeded in all his positions by another Communist, Egon Krenz.

In a dramatic change in policy, the East German government announced on Nov. 9, 1989, that it would open its borders and permit its citizens to travel freely. The opening of the Berlin Wall, long a symbol of the East German government's control of its citizens, was part of this policy change. Thousands more East Germans moved to West Germany.

Throughout this time, protests continued. Thousands of East Germans continued to move to the west. Non-Communist political parties and organizations were started and began forming new policies. In early November, the East German cabinet, called the Council of Ministers, resigned. Hans Modrow, a Communist leader from Dresden, became the new chairman of the Council of Ministers. In December, continued demands for reforms forced the Socialist Unity Party to reorganize. Krenz resigned as party head and from his government positions. Modrow then took control of the government, even though he was not the party head. Modrow's government participated in discussions with opposition leaders and church organizations. These discussions helped prepare East Germany for free elections. During this time, freedom of speech and the press were guaranteed in East Germany.

On March 18, 1990, East Germans voted in free parliamentary elections for the first time. The Christian Democratic Union, a non-Communist party, won the most seats in parliament. Together with the Social Democrats and some smaller parties, the Christian Democrats formed a government with CDU leader Lothar de Maizière as its head. The Socialist Unity Party, which had been renamed the Party of Democratic Socialism, won only about 17 per cent of the seats.

East-West relations. Throughout the 1950's and 1960's, relations between East Germany and West Ger-

© DPA from Photoreporters

East Germans flocked into West Germany when reforms gave them freedom to travel in 1989. Many crossed at Checkpoint Charlie, a border station along the Berlin Wall, *above.*

many were strained. Little travel was permitted between the two nations. Following the construction of the Berlin Wall in 1961, many East Germans were killed trying to flee to the west. Relations improved slightly during the 1970's. Nevertheless, the governments of East and West Germany continued to view each other with suspicion and hostility. In 1973, both countries joined the United Nations.

The unification of East and West Germany. With the move toward a more democratic government in East Germany, many people began to consider the idea of a unified Germany. In February 1990, East German leader Modrow announced that he favored unification with West Germany. In their March elections, most East Germans voted for candidates who favored rapid unification. Most West Germans also supported unification, but they wanted to keep their strong ties with western Europe and their position in NATO. At first, the Soviet Union objected to united Germany remaining in NATO. However, in July, it agreed that united Germany could be a member of NATO.

In mid-1990, East Germany began selling many government owned businesses. In May, East Germany and West Germany signed a treaty providing for close economic cooperation. In July, the economies of East and West Germany were united. The West German Deutsche mark became the unit of currency throughout Germany.

Between May and September, talks about unification were held among the foreign ministers of the two German states and the four Allied powers of World War II—France, Great Britain, the Soviet Union, and the United States. The Allied powers still held some occupation rights in Berlin and in East and West Germany, including certain rights to oversee Berlin and to approve Germany's borders. In a treaty signed on September 12, the Allied powers agreed to give up these rights. The treaty, called the Treaty on the Final Settlement With Respect to Germany, made it possible for the Germans to complete the unification of East and West Germany.

On August 31, representatives of East Germany and

West Germany signed their own treaty for unification. The treaty detailed the major aspects of unification, including the merging of the social and legal systems. The treaty took effect on Oct. 3, 1990, marking the official date for the unification of East and West Germany. West German Chancellor Helmut Kohl continued to serve as chancellor of Germany after unification. The first national elections of unified Germany were scheduled for December 1990.   James J. Sheehan

Related articles in *World Book* include:

Rulers

Charles (IV, Holy Roman emperor)
Frederick I (Holy Roman emperor)
Frederick II (of Prussia)
Frederick III (of Prussia)
Frederick William
Frederick William I (of Prussia)
Henry (kings of Germany)
Louise of Mecklenburg-Strelitz
Otto (kings of Germany)
Wilhelm (emperors of Germany)

Political and military leaders

Adenauer, Konrad
Bismarck, Otto von
Blücher, Gebhard von
Bormann, Martin
Brandt, Willy
Clausewitz, Karl von
Doenitz, Karl
Eichmann, Adolf
Goebbels, Joseph
Goering, Hermann W.
Hess, Rudolf
Himmler, Heinrich
Hindenburg, Paul von
Hitler, Adolf
Honecker, Erich
Jodl, Alfred
Keitel, Wilhelm
Kohl, Helmut
Ludendorff, Erich F. W.
Luxemburg, Rosa
Mengele, Josef
Moltke, Helmuth Karl von
Papen, Franz von
Ribbentrop, Joachim von
Rommel, Erwin
Rosenberg, Alfred
Schmidt, Helmut
Speer, Albert
Virchow, Rudolf
Wallenstein, Albrecht

Cities and towns

Aachen
Augsburg
Baden-Baden
Bayreuth
Berchtesgaden
Berlin
Bonn
Bremen
Cologne
Dresden
Duisburg
Düsseldorf
Essen
Frankfurt
Hamburg
Hanover
Heidelberg
Karl-Marx-Stadt
Koblenz
Leipzig
Lübeck
Mainz
Mannheim
Munich
Nuremberg
Oberammergau
Potsdam
Rostock
Stuttgart
Trier
Wiesbaden
Worms

History

Alsace-Lorraine
Augsburg Confession
Axis
Berlin, Congress of
Berlin Wall
Brunswick (family)
Dawes Plan
Europe, Council of
European Community
Feudalism
Franco-Prussian War
Franks
Free city
Guelphs and Ghibellines
Habsburg, House of
Hanseatic League
Hohenstaufen
Hohenzollern
Holy Alliance
Holy Roman Empire
Kaiser
Krupp
Locarno Conference
Munich Agreement
Nazism
Peasants' War
Prussia
Reformation
Revolution of 1848
Rhineland
Schmalkaldic League
Seven Weeks' War
Seven Years' War
Succession wars
Teutons
Thirty Years' War
Triple Alliance
Vandals
Verdun, Treaty of
Versailles, Treaty of
Vienna, Congress of
Warsaw Pact
World War I
World War II

Physical features

Alps
Black Forest
Danube River
Elbe River
Helgoland
Kiel Canal
Lake Constance
Moselle River
Oder River
Rhine River
Weser River

States and regions

Bavaria
Brandenburg
Hanover
Palatinate
Pomerania
Ruhr
Saar

Other related articles

Air force (The world's major air forces)
Army (The West German army)
Biedermeier
Bonhoeffer, Dietrich
Christmas (In Germany)
Deutschland über Alles
Doll (The history of dolls; pictures)
Europe (pictures)
Flag (picture: Historical flags)
Food (Customs)
Geopolitics
German language
German literature
Heidelberg, University of
Motion picture (Filmmaking in Europe)
Reichswehr
Swastika
Theater (Germany)
Volkswagen
Wine (Where wine comes from)

Outline

I. **Government**
II. **People**
   A. Population and ancestry
   B. Language
III. **Way of life**
   A. City life
   B. Rural life
   C. Food and drink
   D. Recreation
   E. Religion
   F. Education
IV. **Arts**
   A. Literature and philosophy
   B. Music
   C. Painting and sculpture
   D. Architecture
V. **The land**
   A. The North German Plain
   B. The Central Highlands
   C. The South German Hills
   D. The Black Forest
   E. The Bavarian Alps
VI. **Climate**
VII. **Economy**
   A. Manufacturing
   B. Service industries
   C. Agriculture
   D. Mining
   E. Foreign trade
   F. Energy sources
   G. Transportation and communication
VIII. **History**

Questions

Why was sauerkraut created?
What conditions led to the rise of Adolf Hitler and the Nazis?
What is Germany's leading industrial region?
What was called West Germany's "economic miracle"?
Why did the Communists build the Berlin Wall in 1961?
What two German states were rivals for German leadership during the 1800's? Which state won?
What events in East Germany helped bring about the unification of East and West Germany?
What are Germany's main land regions?
What nations occupied Germany after World War II?

Reading and Study Guide

See *Germany* in the Research Guide/Index, Volume 22, for a *Reading and Study Guide*.

Additional resources

Asmus, Ronald D. "A United Germany." *Foreign Affairs* (Spring 1990): 63-76.
Fodor's Germany. McKay. Published annually.
Hoffmeister, Gerhart, and Tubach, F. C. *Germany: 2000 Years.* 3 vols. Ungar, 1979-1986.
Pfeiffer, Christine. *Germany: Two Nations, One Heritage.* Dillon Press, 1987. For younger readers.
Turner, Henry A., Jr. *The Two Germanies Since 1945.* Yale, 1987.

Asian Americans are Americans of Asian descent. They or their ancestors came to the United States from such Asian countries as Cambodia, China, India, Indonesia, Japan, Korea, Laos, Pakistan, the Philippines, Thailand, and Vietnam. Today, about $6\frac{1}{2}$ million people of Asian descent live in the United States. Asian Americans make up the country's third largest minority group. Only blacks and Hispanic Americans form larger minorities.

Asian Americans make up a wide variety of ethnic and cultural groups. Although most Asian Americans speak English, many also speak such languages as Chinese, Hindi, Japanese, Korean, Punjabi, Tagalog, and Vietnamese. Religions practiced by Asian Americans include Buddhism, Islam, Christianity, and Confucianism.

A majority of Asian Americans live in the Western United States. Numerous Asian Americans also live in New York, Illinois, and Texas.

Immigration from Asia. The first wave of Asian immigration consisted of hundreds of thousands of Chinese who came to the United States between 1850 and 1882. Many of these people came to California to mine gold. Numerous others were recruited as laborers to help build U.S. railroads.

Thousands of Japanese came to Hawaii in the late 1800's to work as contract laborers on sugar plantations. Others immigrated to California, Oregon, and Washington. There, many Japanese opened small businesses, joined fishing crews, or worked as miners, railroad workers, or farm laborers.

Like other Asian Americans, Japanese Americans faced racial hostility from many whites. But hostility against Japanese Americans grew especially strong during World War II. After Japan attacked Pearl Harbor in 1941, the U.S. government confined about 110,000 Japanese Americans to detention camps. In 1944, the U.S. Supreme Court ruled such confinement unconstitutional.

In the early 1900's, numerous Koreans came to Hawaii to work on the sugar plantations. A number of Indian Americans also came to the United States during these years. The Indian Americans had immigrated first to Vancouver, Canada, and later moved south to California, where they worked as farm laborers.

Filipinos began to come to America in large numbers after the United States gained the Philippines from Spain in 1898. This wave of immigration continued until the mid-1930's. Many of the immigrants worked on Hawaii's sugar plantations. Others settled in California, where they worked on vegetable farms.

Since 1965, millions of Asians have immigrated to the United States. Many of these people have come from China, India, the Philippines, and South Korea. Numerous Vietnamese, Cambodians, and Laotians came to the United States after U.S. troops withdrew from Vietnam in 1973.

Restrictions on immigration from Asia were imposed by Congress at numerous points in U.S. history. The restrictions resulted in part from fears that Asian workers would compete with Americans for jobs. In addition, some Americans argued that Asians could not be *assimilated* (incorporated) into American society.

One of the first important laws restricting immigration was the Chinese Exclusion Act of 1882. This law prohibited all Chinese laborers from immigrating to the United States. In 1908, the U.S. government completed its negotiation of the Gentlemen's Agreement with Japan to restrict Japanese immigration to the United States. In 1917, Congress passed a law that excluded immigrants who came from an area known as the Asiatic Barred Zone. This area covered most of Asia and a majority of the islands in the Pacific Ocean. The Immigration Act of 1924 went into effect in 1929. It denied even more Asians the right to immigrate to the United States.

Easing of restrictions. During World War II, China became an ally of the United States, and in 1943 the U.S. government ended its ban against Chinese immigrants. In 1952, the Immigration and Nationality Act, also called the McCarran-Walter Act, established limited quotas for Asian countries from which immigrants were excluded. The law, for the first time, also made citizenship available to people from all countries of Asia. But according to the law, no more than 100 people could immigrate to the United States each year from each independent country in Asia. In 1965, Congress enacted a bill to repeal all discriminatory immigration laws against nonwhite people. Since then, millions of Asians have become U.S. citizens.   Robert H. Kim

Asian Americans contribute to many aspects of life in the United States. Americans of Asian descent, such as the Japanese-American engineer at the far left, play an important role in the U.S. economy. In the photograph at the left, Chinese Americans take part in a colorful celebration of their cultural heritage.

© Dave Benett, Gamma/Liaison

Rock music's energetic style is captured by Mick Jagger, *left,* and Ron Wood, *right,* of the Rolling Stones. Formed in 1962, the "Stones" have been one of rock's most enduring groups.

Rock music

Rock music is one of the world's most popular and adaptable musical forms. When it originated in the United States in the early 1950's, rock music was known as *rock 'n' roll* (also spelled *rock and roll*). From the start, it was party music, dance music, and music that appealed to young listeners. It often celebrated the joys of being young, and it occasionally expressed the frustrations of youth.

Many adults dismissed rock 'n' roll as a passing fad or condemned it as a threat to society. By the mid-1960's, however, rock 'n' roll had earned wide respect as a legitimate art form. The music's popularity spread internationally and among older listeners as well. By the end of the 1960's, the music had moved far from its roots in blues and country music, and it became known simply as *rock*.

In the 1970's, rock became a bigger business than ever. It not only dominated the music industry, but also influenced everything from film to fashion to politics. As rock music became increasingly accepted, it lost much of the rebelliousness that had originally given it its power.

Since the early 1980's, rock music has continued to defy musical barriers and has drawn much of its strength from international musical influences. Today,

rock music is no longer only the music of young Americans. It is music of the world.

Characteristics of rock music

At first, rock music generally followed a $\frac{4}{4}$ beat and used only two or three chords in its melody. The songs were simple, repetitive, and easy to remember. Most of them were only two or three minutes long. The simplest rock continues to rely on a basic beat and a few chords. But some rock songs are more complex and sophisticated. Rock music has also expanded to include international influences. Traditional musical elements from Africa, Ireland, South America, and other places have become more widely used in rock music.

Rock lyrics express a wide range of emotions and ideas. Early rock songs dealt with such themes as cars, girls, boys, dances, and the joy of being young. Later, rock songwriters broadened their range to include everything from world politics to highly personal poetry.

Early rock music featured electric guitar or a blues-style boogie-woogie piano and drums. Today, musicians may use computers and electronic instruments called *synthesizers* as well as guitars, pianos, and drums. Some recordings include electronic drum machines instead of human drummers. Musicians also use electronic devices to manipulate the pitch, tempo, and duration of digitally recorded sounds. Today, many studio recordings are produced entirely by computer.

Many rock groups feature a vocal soloist, with other group members performing as a chorus. When groups

---

Don McLeese, the contributor of this article, is Pop Music Critic for the Chicago Sun-Times.

perform, they usually use huge amplifiers and dozens of speakers. The music may be soft, but it is often extremely loud. Many groups also specialize in highly theatrical concert performances. Some rock performers wear wild costumes and makeup. They may also add unusual stage effects, such as clouds of smoke or laser light shows.

Beginnings of rock music

Musical roots. Rock developed from a variety of different popular music styles. The roots of rock can be heard in the lyrics and electric guitar of the blues, in the rhythms of a form of blues known as *rhythm and blues,* and in the spirit of American country music. The squawking saxophone of dance-band jazz, and the melodies, choruses, and harmonies of popular (pop) music also added to the rock sound.

Many of the elements of rock music had been around long before rock developed as a musical form. In the 1950's, musicians combined these musical elements and created the revolutionary form of music called rock 'n' roll. It was louder and faster than the forms from which it drew. Its lyrics contrasted sharply with the sentimental lyrics of earlier pop songs. And it was generally performed in a wild and spontaneous manner with a more primitive and raw display of emotions.

The emergence of rock 'n' roll. Before rock 'n' roll became a musical category, such rhythm and blues hits as "Rocket '88'" (1951) by Jackie Brenston had the spirit of rock 'n' roll. This and other similar records became increasingly popular with both black rhythm and blues audiences and white country music audiences.

The major rock 'n' roll explosion began with Elvis Presley. Although he was white, he had the style commonly associated with increasingly popular black music. The popularity of his black sound combined with his hip-shaking live performances and frequent radio play

UPI/Bettmann

Chuck Berry helped define the rebellious spirit of rock 'n' roll in the 1950's. His rocking guitar rhythms and vivid lyrics effectively expressed the feelings and problems of youth.

quickly made Elvis a superstar. His first major success came with his 1956 recording of "Heartbreak Hotel" for RCA Victor.

Another important influence on rock music was St. Louis blues artist Chuck Berry. He was the first of the great rock songwriters. His lyrics effectively expressed the feelings and problems of youth. Berry's first hit record was a country-styled tune titled "Maybellene" (1955). Berry was a major influence on later rock performers, including the Beatles and the Rolling Stones.

Richard Penniman, known as Little Richard, helped influence rock performance styles. His vigorous and flamboyant stage performances provided a model for performers who followed. His first major success came in 1955 with "Tutti Frutti."

Bill Haley and the Comets became the first famous rock band. Their recording of "Rock Around the Clock" was the first international rock hit. It was used as the theme song for *The Blackboard Jungle,* a 1955 motion picture about juvenile delinquents. The song contributed to rock 'n' roll's reputation as music of rebellion.

Growing popularity. Radio played an important role in spreading rock music during the mid-1950's. Television had replaced radio as the chief producer of drama and variety entertainment, and many radio stations began to play rock to capture an audience. Disc jockeys who played the records became powerful forces in promoting the popularity of rock performers. Disc jockey Alan Freed helped popularize the name rock 'n' roll with his radio program, "Moondog Rock 'n' Roll Party."

Though the United States was racially divided, some people sensed a spirit of racial equality in rock 'n' roll. It featured black artists, such as Chuck Berry, who were influenced by white country music. It also presented white

Bettmann

Elvis Presley, *center,* became rock's first superstar. His tough, rebellious manner and suggestive movements are apparent in this scene from the movie *Jailhouse Rock* (1957).

artists, such as Presley and songwriter-guitarist Buddy Holly, who adopted styles based on black rhythm and blues. In earlier times, the recordings of such Southern black artists as Bo Diddley and Fats Domino would have been categorized as "race records" and sold primarily to black customers. With the rise of rock 'n' roll, these artists appealed to black and white audiences alike.

Most important for its young listeners, rock 'n' roll was the first music that was all their own. Rock 'n' roll proclaimed that being a teen-ager was special. Although rock 'n' roll was extremely popular, its lyrics and the performance style that went with it were still considered indecent by many adults.

Artistic decline. As rock 'n' roll continued to grow in popularity, the major record companies and professional songwriters who had ignored the music started to recognize rock 'n' roll's profitability. By the late 1950's, much of what record companies released as rock 'n' roll was no longer wild, spontaneous, and rebellious. While rock continued to sell well, the music was much tamer than it had been just a few years earlier. Such popular artists as Frankie Avalon and Pat Boone had toned down the volume and the feel of the music. As a result, rock 'n' roll became just another form of popular music.

Rock 'n' roll also lost many of its stars and creative forces toward the end of the 1950's. In 1958, Elvis Presley was drafted into the United States Army and rocking pianist Jerry Lee Lewis caused a scandal by marrying his 13-year-old cousin. Then in 1959, Chuck Berry was arrested, Buddy Holly and singer-guitarist Richie Valens died in an airplane crash, and Little Richard left music to study for the ministry.

British Invasion and rock's revival

The Beatles and the British Invasion. The Beatles, a group from Liverpool, England, returned excitement to rock 'n' roll in the early 1960's. They made the music more popular than ever and more respected artistically. Their witty and sophisticated music made the sentimental rock of the time seem tame and old-fashioned.

The Beatles consisted of George Harrison, John Lennon, Paul McCartney, and Ringo Starr. Their first British hit was "Love Me Do" in 1962. Their American breakthrough came with "I Want to Hold Your Hand" in 1964. Both hits were written by Lennon and McCartney, who eventually established themselves as the most popular songwriting team in rock's history.

Beatlemania was the term generally used to describe the excitement generated by the Beatles. It affected society in a number of ways. Teen-age boys began growing their hair longer to copy the Beatles. Teen-age girls screamed so loudly during the band's concerts that it was impossible to hear the music. At first, many parents feared the effects of Beatlemania. But the personal charm and musical appeal of the band soon conquered older listeners.

The Beatles turned rock 'n' roll from an American-dominated musical style into an international phenomenon. Soon after the Beatles hit the United States, popular music charts became filled with songs by British bands that wrote and played their own music. The British bands replaced American solo singers, such as Fabian and Frankie Avalon, who relied primarily on outside songwriters and musicians.

The Rolling Stones were the most significant of the British groups that followed the Beatles in the so-called "British Invasion" of the United States. They represented a scruffier, more rebellious alternative to the more widely accepted Beatles. Their music also was more faithful to its roots in the blues. Other British bands that became popular in the United States after the Beatles included The Who, the Kinks, the Animals, the Dave Clark Five, and Herman's Hermits.

Expanding styles and sounds. In addition to the Beatles and the Rolling Stones, the third major force in the rock of the 1960's was Bob Dylan. The strong social message of Dylan's songs influenced many musicians. Dylan helped swing the balance of popularity away from the British and back to American musicians.

Dylan began his musical career in the early 1960's as a solo folk singer and follower of American folk singer Woody Guthrie. His popularity began among many fans of early rock 'n' roll who had dismissed the music of the early 1960's as uninspired. They began listening to folk music for its social significance. Folk music fans turned to Dylan for his "protest songs." These songs protested what many people considered the wrongs of society, such as racial prejudice, poverty, and war. Some Dylan songs, such as "Blowin' in the Wind" (1962) and "A Hard Rain's A-Gonna Fall" (1963), achieved wider popularity through versions by such artists as Peter, Paul, and Mary and Joan Baez. They helped make Dylan the leading writer of protest songs.

Following the example of the Beatles, Dylan began

The Beatles, shown here at a 1965 press conference, earned a huge international following with their witty, sophisticated songs and whimsical humor. Their sensational popularity—called *Beatlemania*—resulted in mobbing fans, Beatle fashions, and tremendous media coverage of the band.

© Dan McCoy, Black Star

The 1969 Woodstock Music and Arts Festival was a huge rock concert that celebrated the "hippie" culture. The event drew over 300,000 people and lasted for three days. Woodstock showed that rock music had become a focal point for social issues.

playing his material on electric guitar with a band that used electrically amplified instruments. Gradually, his songs became less political and more poetic and personal. Dylan had one of his first and biggest rock hits in 1965 with "Like a Rolling Stone." Dylan's ambitious, poetic lyrics set to a rock beat produced a style known as *folk rock.* Folk rock was the first major challenge to rock's domination by the British.

The mid-1960's became a time of peak creativity for rock music. Rock artists explored new possibilities in lyrical content and form. Some began to examine the meaning of dreams in their lyrics. Others began to use *free-verse* poetry that did not rhyme. Some musicians also began to produce *concept albums,* which linked their songs together by story line or theme. One such album was *Sgt. Pepper's Lonely Hearts Club Band* (1967) by the Beatles. In addition, rock was featured in a number of popular stage works, including *Hair* (1967).

The 1960's also found instrumentalists exercising more creative freedom. American guitarist Jimi Hendrix extended the range of the electric guitar by manipulating its switches and pedals to create new sounds. In addition, such instrumentalists as Hendrix and British guitarist Eric Clapton began stretching a single song to about 10 or 20 minutes. Their extended solos were inspired by blues and jazz traditions. The music played by such bands as the Jimi Hendrix Experience and Clapton's Cream were sometimes categorized as *progressive rock.* Some of their music was also called *acid rock,* after the illegal drug LSD, or "acid," which was popular among some rock fans.

Another popular musical style of the 1960's was the California sound called *surf music.* The Beach Boys became the most popular surf music group. They sang of surfing, hot rods, and teen dreams. The Beach Boys be-

came well known for their fine vocal harmonies, as well as the experimental production techniques of the band's Brian Wilson.

The 1960's was also the peak period for *soul music.* Soul music developed from the gritty, emotional rhythm and blues style, but it had a smoother sound and more widely pleasing melodies. It was recorded primarily by black artists, but it found wide popularity among both black and white listeners. Detroit's Motown label was the most popular and successful soul label. Leading Motown artists included Marvin Gaye, Diana Ross and the Supremes, and Stevie Wonder. The gritty soul styles of Otis Redding, Sam and Dave, and others from the Stax label in Memphis were also popular.

Growing social significance. The growing influence and popularity of rock music affected society in a number of ways. It produced new fashions, such as Beatle boots and longer hairstyles. Some rock music encouraged the use of illegal drugs. Other rock music inspired public protest against such social and political problems as racial prejudice and the Vietnam War.

Toward the end of the 1960's, rock's various styles came together at massive outdoor rock festivals. These festivals showed how popular and diverse the music had become. The most significant rock festival was the 1969 Woodstock Music and Arts Festival in upstate New York. Woodstock was a musical, communal celebration of the alternative "hippie" culture. It was dedicated to world peace. The event drew more than 300,000 fans and featured three days of top rock talent. It included such performers as the Grateful Dead, Jimi Hendrix, Jefferson Airplane, and blues singer Janis Joplin.

Rock music in the 1970's

Rock goes pop. Throughout the 1970's, almost all popular music contained elements of the rock style. The music's audience spanned from preteens to middle-aged adults. As the audience for rock grew, a variety of new musical categories developed. *Country rock* featured such groups as Poco and the Eagles, which emphasized country music roots. Musicians such as Chick Corea and the members of the group Chicago blended rock with the improvisation techniques of jazz to create a form called *jazz rock. Heavy metal rock* groups, such as Led Zeppelin, stressed screaming electric guitars. The *glitter rock* of David Bowie and others popularized flamboyant onstage visuals. Musical groups including King Crimson and Emerson, Lake, and Palmer combined a rock beat with the more complex melodies of classical music in a form called *art rock.* James Taylor, Joni Mitchell, and others popularized an acoustic singer-songwriter tradition by composing music with thoughtful, often autobiographical, lyrics.

The early 1970's found rock more profitable than ever. In terms of musical quality, however, the period was generally considered rock's lowest point since the pre-Beatles 1960's. Through its attempt to appeal to a wide audience, rock lost much of the youthful energy and spirit of rebellion that had once powered it.

By the mid-1970's, the music started to reclaim some of the inspiration and energy associated with earlier rock. Bruce Springsteen and the E Street Band attracted an enthusiastic following with "Born to Run" (1975). Springsteen's music reflected the energetic rock 'n' roll and rhythm and blues music of the 1950's. He showed how rock might find a future by drawing from its past. The *reggae* music of Jamaica's Bob Marley and the Wailers injected fresh inspiration into the sounds of the mid-1970's with its slow, pulsing rhythms and soulful singing.

Disco and punk. Probably the most popular musical style of the mid-1970's was *disco*. Disco often combined Latin rhythms and elements of *funk*, a type of earthy blues, to produce a strong, steady dance beat. It was created primarily for dance clubs called *discotheques*, or *discos*. It was rarely performed live. Instead, discotheques played records and tapes of the music. Popular disco artists of the 1970's included Donna Summer and Chic. Although many people considered disco to be mindless formula music, disco returned dancing and the spirit of fun to popular music. At a time when many white rock radio stations were giving little exposure to black artists, disco appealed to a diverse audience with dance music recorded by both black and white artists.

The *punk rock* of the mid-1970's attempted to launch a rock revolution. Such British bands as the Sex Pistols and the Clash returned to the raw energy of earlier rock. They were fueled by an anger at the materialism of society and the lack of inspiration in much of the early 1970's rock music. Punk was not a big commercial success, but it had a number of important effects on rock music. It proved that new styles could develop outside the established rock industry. It also showed that young musicians could express themselves without expensive equipment and years of practice. Punk rock influenced many nonpunk musicians to make their music simpler, faster, and more energetic.

Such New York bands as Talking Heads and the Patti Smith Group took an artier approach to punk rock. Their music was more poetic and conceptually original than punk. These groups became categorized as punk's *new wave* of rock. The music of punk and new wave bands represented an aggressive alternative to the more established musicians who dominated the rock industry.

At first, disco and punk were considered opposites. But they came together toward the end of the 1970's. Blondie, and other musical groups, enjoyed hits that combined disco rhythms with the spirit of new wave rock.

Rock music in the 1980's and 1990's

New directions and old. The most popular new music to emerge from the 1980's was *rap music*. Rap is spoken rather than sung. Electronic rhythms and sounds of records being scratched provide background music. Rap's streetwise rhymes and chants reflect the concerns of urban youths living in a tough world. Public Enemy became one of the most successful rap groups.

Music from the 1960's inspired some of rock's most popular musicians of the 1980's. Among these musicians was the American band R.E.M., which drew heavily from 1960's folk rock. In addition, many artists who had begun their careers in the 1960's, such as singer Tina Turner, achieved greater popularity than ever before. Some bands from the 1960's, such as the Rolling Stones, Pink Floyd, and the Grateful Dead, were among the leading concert attractions of the 1980's. These bands remained popular not only with their original fans from the 1960's but with new and younger listeners as well.

Rock videos. During the 1980's, many rock performers began to feature their music in short films called *rock videos*. In addition to music, these films included acting, dancing, striking visual images, and sometimes excerpts from rock concert performances. Rock videos were shown on commercial and cable television stations and at many dance clubs. Cable television's Music Television (MTV) network played rock videos 24 hours a day. The rise of rock video and MTV brought widespread exposure and massive popularity to a number of artists. Among them were the Eurythmics, Madonna, and George Michael. Many songs became as popular for the visual element of the video as for the music. The popularity of rock videos continued into the 1990's.

The American singer and dancer Michael Jackson starred in several highly successful videos and became one of the most popular performers in the history of rock music. His *Thriller* (1982) became the largest-selling record album of all time.

Technological changes. Since 1980, rock has continued to reflect an ongoing technological revolution. Computers and synthesizers have often replaced guitars and drums. Rhythm machines, synthesizers, and computers have also been widely used with rap and dance music. These instruments have influenced the recording of more traditional rock as well. Even in concert, musicians have mixed live music with preprogrammed computer and synthesizer backing. As a result, it has become difficult to distinguish "live" music from "canned," or taped, music.

Rock and society. During the 1980's, rock extended its importance as a force for social change through a broadening interest in international concerns and a reawakening of its social idealism. Several artists, including Peter Gabriel, Talking Heads, and Paul Simon, incorporated the music of Africa into their music. Such albums as Springsteen's *Born in the U.S.A.* (1984) and U2's *The Joshua Tree* (1987) dealt with socially relevant themes.

Rock's idealism and internationalism came together in such events as Live Aid, an all-day concert held in July 1985. Money raised by the event went to help feed starv-

Rock videos combine music with acting, dancing, and striking visual images. Rock star Peter Gabriel appears above in the video for his song "Sledgehammer."

© Patrick Harbron, Sygma

Rock musicians have worked to promote social change around the world. The musicians at left, *from left,* Peter Gabriel, Tracy Chapman, Youssou D'Nour, Sting, Joan Baez, and Bruce Springsteen, were part of the Amnesty International concerts designed to help raise awareness of human rights issues.

ing people in Africa. The concert was held in both Philadelphia and London. It was televised throughout the world. Live Aid featured many of the biggest stars in rock, including Mick Jagger, Madonna, and U2.

Various artists—including the heavy metal band Guns n' Roses and rap groups 2 Live Crew and Public Enemy—sparked controversy in the late 1980's and early 1990's with their rebellious lyrics, aggressive music, and anti-social stance. Concerned parents in such groups as the Parents' Music Resource Center (PMRC) called for record companies to attach warning labels to albums with lyrics that might be objectionable.

Rap and heavy metal moved closer to the mainstream of rock culture in the early 1990's. At the same time, rock musicians continued to explore international music as a source of inspiration.   Don McLeese

Related articles in *World Book* include:

Beatles	Jackson, Michael	Reggae
Berry, Chuck	Jazz (Jazz today)	Rolling Stones
Blues	Lennon, John	Simon, Paul
Country music	McCartney, Paul	Springsteen,
Dylan, Bob	Popular music	Bruce
Electronic music	Presley, Elvis	Synthesizer
Hendrix, Jimi	Radio (Broadcasting	Who, The
Holly, Buddy	today)	Wonder, Stevie

Outline

I. **Characteristics of rock music**
II. **Beginnings of rock music**
  A. Musical roots
  B. The emergence of rock 'n' roll
  C. Growing popularity
  D. Artistic decline
III. **British Invasion and rock's revival**
  A. The Beatles and the British Invasion
  B. Expanding styles and sounds
  C. Growing social significance
IV. **Rock music in the 1970's**
  A. Rock becomes pop   B. Disco and punk
V. **Rock music in the 1980's and 1990's**
  A. New directions and old   C. Technological changes
  B. Rock videos   D. Rock and society

Questions

What kinds of rock music emerged during the 1970's?
Who were the Beatles? How did they affect rock music?
What is *rap music*?
Why was Elvis Presley popular?
What are the characteristics of early rock 'n' roll?
Why was Bob Dylan an important force in the music of the 1960's?
How did rock music contribute to social causes in the 1980's?
What are the roots of rock music?
Why was rock music seen as music of racial equality in the 1950's? In the 1970's?
What did Chuck Berry contribute to rock 'n' roll? Who did he influence?

Additional resources

Clifford, Mike, and others. *The Harmony Illustrated Encyclopedia of Rock.* 6th ed. Harmony, 1988.
Hanmer, Trudy J. *An Album of Rock and Roll.* Watts, 1988. Suitable for younger readers.

© John Roca, LGI

Madonna, one of rock's superstars of the 1980's and 1990's, gained fame for her recordings, videos, and live performances.

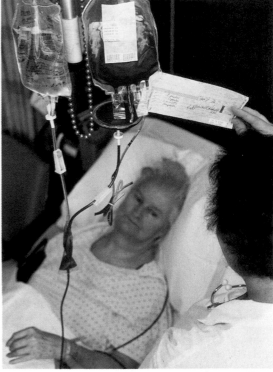

Granger Collection

The importance of blood has been appreciated since ancient times, but knowledge of blood's role in health and disease has changed significantly. For thousands of years, people believed that bloodletting would allow illness to flow out of a sick person. The woodcut above shows a physician bleeding a patient during the 1500's. Today, doctors know that giving blood—not removing it—can save lives. The photo at the right shows a patient receiving a blood transfusion.

© Patrick Watson, Medichrome

Blood

Blood is the river of life that flows through the human body. We cannot live without it. The heart pumps blood to all our body cells, supplying them with oxygen and food. At the same time, blood carries carbon dioxide and other waste products from the cells. Blood also fights infection, keeps our temperature steady, and carries chemicals that regulate many body functions. Finally, blood even has substances that plug broken blood vessels and so prevent us from bleeding to death.

When oxygen combines with certain cells—the red blood cells—the blood takes on its characteristic red color. Thus, blood that escapes from the body through a broken vessel appears bright red because of the oxygen in the air. Blood carrying oxygen to body cells has that same brilliant red color. But it turns a dark brownish-red after delivering oxygen.

The amount of blood in your body depends on your size and the altitude at which you live. An adult who weighs 160 pounds (73 kilograms) has about 5 quarts (4.7 liters) of blood. An 80-pound (36-kilogram) child has about half that amount, and an 8-pound (3.6-kilogram) infant has about $8\frac{1}{2}$ ounces (250 milliliters). People who live at high altitudes, where the air contains less oxygen, may have up to 2 quarts (1.9 liters) more blood than peo-

ple who live in low regions. The extra blood delivers additional oxygen to body cells.

This article discusses the blood of human beings. Blood also circulates through the bodies of dogs, cats, birds, insects, and most other kinds of animals. Only such simple animals as jellyfish and sponges do not need blood to live. For information about blood in some types of animals, see **Circulatory system** (The circulatory system in other animals). See also **Mammal** (Internal organ systems); **Insect** (Circulatory system).

The composition of blood

Blood consists of cells that move about in a watery liquid called *plasma*. The cells are known as *formed elements* because they have definite shapes. Three types of cells make up the formed elements: (1) red blood cells, (2) white blood cells, and (3) platelets. A microliter ($\frac{1}{30,000}$ of an ounce) of blood normally contains about 4 million to 6 million red blood cells, 5,000 to 10,000 white blood cells, and 150,000 to 500,000 platelets. The red and white blood cells are also called *corpuscles*.

Plasma is the liquid, straw-colored part of blood. It makes up about 50 to 60 per cent of the total volume of blood. The formed elements account for the rest.

Plasma consists of about 90 per cent water. Hundreds of other substances make up the balance. They include proteins that enable blood to clot and to fight infection; dissolved *nutrients* (foods); and waste products. Plasma also carries chemicals called *hormones,* which control

---

G. David Roodman, the contributor of this article, is Professor of Medicine at the University of Texas Health Science Center at San Antonio and Chief of Hematology at the Audie L. Murphy Memorial Veterans Hospital.

Here are your
1991 Year Book
Cross-Reference Tabs

To help update your World Book set

Put these Tabs in the appropriate volumes of your **World Book Encyclopedia** now. Then, when you later look up some topic in **World Book** and find a Tab near the article, you will know that one of your **Year Books** has newer or more detailed information about that topic.

How to use these Tabs

First, remove this page from **The Year Book.**

Begin with the first Tab, **AN-IMATION.** Take the A volume of your **World Book** set and find the **Animation** article in it. Moisten the **ANIMA-TION** Tab and affix it to that page.

Go on to the other Tabs. Your set may not have articles on some of the topics— **ASIAN AMERICANS,** for example. In that case, put the Tab in the correct volume and on the page where it would go if there *were* an article. The **ASIAN AMERI-CANS** Tab should go in the A volume on the same page as the **Asia Minor** article.

growth and certain other body functions.

Red blood cells, also called *erythrocytes* (pronounced *ih RIHTH roh sytz*), carry oxygen to body tissues and remove carbon dioxide. A red blood cell has a flat, disklike shape. It is thinner in the middle than at the edges—somewhat like a doughnut without the hole.

Red blood cells consist mainly of *hemoglobin* (*HEE muh GLOH buhn*), an oxygen-carrying protein that gives them their red color. The cells also contain chemicals, particularly *enzymes.* Enzymes enable the cells to carry out necessary chemical processes more effectively. A flexible membrane surrounds each red blood cell. The membrane is so flexible the cells can squeeze through the tiniest blood vessels. Most kinds of cells have a *nucleus,* a central structure that controls many cell activities. But mature red blood cells have no nuclei.

White blood cells, also called *leukocytes* (*LOO kuh sytz*), fight infections and harmful substances that invade the body. Most of the cells are round and colorless. They have several sizes, and their nuclei vary in shape. Some kinds of white blood cells kill bacteria by surrounding and digesting them. Other kinds produce *antibodies,* proteins that destroy bacteria, viruses, and other invaders or make them harmless.

Platelets (*PLAYT lihtz*), also known as *thrombocytes* (*THRAHM buh sytz*), are disklike structures that help stop bleeding. They are the smallest formed elements. If a blood vessel is cut, platelets stick to the edges of the cut and to one another, forming a plug. They then release chemicals that react with *fibrinogen* (*fy BRIHN uh juhn*) and certain other plasma proteins, leading to the formation of a blood clot.

What blood does in the body

The major jobs of blood are to transport oxygen and nutrients to body tissues and to remove wastes. To accomplish those tasks, blood must flow to all parts of the body. It does so by means of our circulatory system, which consists of the heart, a vast network of blood vessels, and the blood itself.

The heart pumps blood to all the body tissues. Blood leaves the heart through arteries and returns through veins. Within the tissues, the arteries become smaller and smaller. The smallest blood vessels are the *capillaries.* They connect the tiniest arteries and the tiniest veins. Oxygen, food, and other substances pass from the blood through the thin capillary walls into the tissues. Carbon dioxide and other wastes from the tissues also pass through the capillary walls and enter the bloodstream. Blood returns to the heart through ever-larger veins. For more information about how blood moves through the body, see **Circulatory system; Heart.**

Carrying oxygen and carbon dioxide. All living cells in your body continuously absorb oxygen and give off carbon dioxide. Oxygen is carried to your body tissues mainly by hemoglobin in the red blood cells. Each molecule of hemoglobin binds easily with four molecules of oxygen.

When you inhale, air enters the *alveoli* (air sacs) of your lungs. Oxygen from the air passes through the walls of the capillaries that surround each alveolus and binds with hemoglobin. Some oxygen also dissolves in the plasma. The bonds that hold hemoglobin and oxygen molecules together react to oxygen levels in the

Blood cells

Blood contains three types of cells, which perform many vital tasks. (1) Red blood cells carry oxygen to body tissues. (2) White blood cells help the body fight infection and disease. (3) Platelets plug leaks in blood vessels and help begin the process leading to the formation of a blood clot.

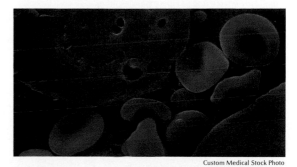

Custom Medical Stock Photo

Red blood cells

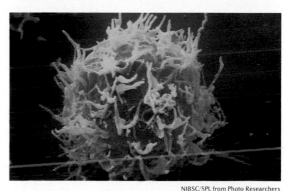

NIBSC/SPL from Photo Researchers

White blood cell

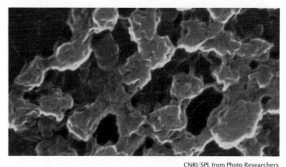

CNRI/SPL from Photo Researchers

Platelets

cells. If the oxygen levels are low, the bonds break easily, releasing oxygen.

Your cells use oxygen to produce energy. The process creates carbon dioxide, which passes from the cells through the capillary walls. Most carbon dioxide enters the plasma, but some attaches to hemoglobin. When the blood reaches the capillaries in your lungs, the carbon dioxide enters the alveoli and is exhaled. See **Hemoglobin; Lung; Respiration** (Internal respiration).

Transporting nutrients and wastes. Food reaches

What blood does in the body

Blood serves as a fluid highway, carrying food, oxygen, disease-fighting cells, and *hormones* (chemical messengers) throughout the body. It also carries away wastes for disposal. The diagram below shows some areas of the body where important exchanges or activities involving the blood take place.

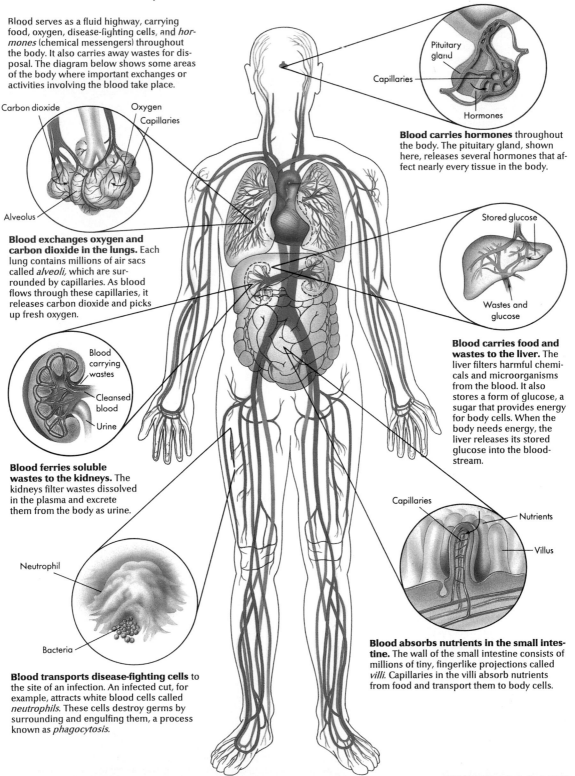

Blood carries hormones throughout the body. The pituitary gland, shown here, releases several hormones that affect nearly every tissue in the body.

Blood exchanges oxygen and carbon dioxide in the lungs. Each lung contains millions of air sacs called *alveoli,* which are surrounded by capillaries. As blood flows through these capillaries, it releases carbon dioxide and picks up fresh oxygen.

Blood carries food and wastes to the liver. The liver filters harmful chemicals and microorganisms from the blood. It also stores a form of glucose, a sugar that provides energy for body cells. When the body needs energy, the liver releases its stored glucose into the bloodstream.

Blood ferries soluble wastes to the kidneys. The kidneys filter wastes dissolved in the plasma and excrete them from the body as urine.

Blood absorbs nutrients in the small intestine. The wall of the small intestine consists of millions of tiny, fingerlike projections called *villi.* Capillaries in the villi absorb nutrients from food and transport them to body cells.

Blood transports disease-fighting cells to the site of an infection. An infected cut, for example, attracts white blood cells called *neutrophils.* These cells destroy germs by surrounding and engulfing them, a process known as *phagocytosis.*

WORLD BOOK illustration by Charles Wellek

your body tissues by means of the blood. After food passes through your stomach, it enters the small intestine, where digestion is completed. The wall of the small intestine has millions of tiny, fingerlike projections called *villi.* The villi absorb digested food molecules, which enter the capillary network of each villus and pass into the blood. Many nutrients bind with the plasma protein *albumin,* which carries them to body tissues.

Your cells use nutrients to produce the energy needed for cell growth, reproduction, and other functions. In producing energy, the cells create waste products. Like nutrients, wastes enter the bloodstream through the capillary walls. Many wastes bind with albumin or dissolve in the plasma, which transports them to the liver. The liver filters wastes and other harmful substances from the blood. It converts some wastes into a compound called *urea.* The blood carries urea to the kidneys, which remove it in urine. See **Digestive system; Intestine; Liver; Kidney.**

Protecting against disease. White blood cells play an important role in your *immune system,* which helps your body resist disease-causing substances. The invasion of a harmful substance activates the white blood cells. They then work to destroy it. Some proteins in the plasma also help fight disease. There are five main groups of white blood cells.

Three kinds of white blood cells attack and destroy germs, especially bacteria, in a process called *phagocytosis* (FAG *uh sy TOH sihs*). In phagocytosis, a white blood cell surrounds a germ and then kills it with enzymes. Such white blood cells are called *phagocytes.*

Neutrophils (NOO *truh fihlz*) are the most numerous phagocytes. They fight mainly bacterial infections. When bacteria invade the body, neutrophils leave the bloodstream and travel to the infected area. *Monocytes* (MAHN *uh sytz*), like neutrophils, leave the bloodstream and migrate to infected tissues, where they mature and become *macrophages* (MAK *ruh fayj uhz*). Macrophages not only kill germs but also destroy cancer-causing cells. In addition, they help begin antibody production. *Eosinophils* (EE *uh SIHN uh fihlz*), a rare third kind of phagocyte, defend the body against parasites.

Members of a fourth group of white blood cells, *lymphocytes* (LIHM *fuh sytz*), do not perform phagocytosis. Instead, they have a key part in the body's immune system by recognizing and responding to specific viruses, bacteria, and other invaders. There are two major kinds of lymphocytes—*B cells* and *T cells.* B cells produce antibodies and release them into the plasma, where they circulate in the form of *globulin proteins.* Such proteins, especially *gamma globulin,* fight infection (see **Globulin; Gamma globulin**). T cells release substances that control B-cell activity. They also produce substances that activate monocytes and so help destroy harmful organisms.

The chief function of a fifth group of white blood cells, *basophils* (BAY *suh fihlz*), is uncertain. Like eosinophils, they are rare blood cells.

To learn more about how white blood cells help us fight disease, see **Immunity.**

Carrying hormones. Organs called *endocrine glands* produce hormones and release them directly into the blood. The hormones enter the plasma and act as "chemical messengers." When a hormone reaches a

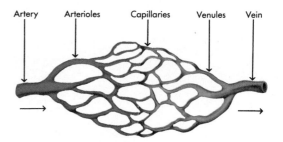

Capillaries form an "exchange system" for the blood. Blood, carrying food and oxygen, flows from the arteries, through the smaller arterioles, into the capillaries. In the capillaries, the blood exchanges food and oxygen for waste materials that are given off by the body cells. The blood returns the wastes to the heart by way of venules and veins. Then the heart pumps the wastes to such organs as the liver, lungs, and kidneys, where the wastes are removed.

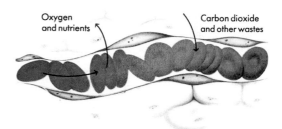

Most capillaries are so small that blood cells must pass through them in single file. Food and oxygen needed by the cells of the body ooze out through the thin capillary walls. Carbon dioxide and other waste materials from the body cells squeeze back through the walls into the bloodstream. The blood then returns these waste materials to the heart.

part of the body it regulates, it may affect growth, reproductive processes, how the body uses food, or some other function. See **Hormone; Gland.**

Distributing body heat. All cell activities produce heat. But some cells, particularly those in muscles and glands, create more heat than others. The heat enters your bloodstream and travels throughout your body. Excess heat escapes through your skin. If blood did not distribute heat, some body areas would become extremely hot while others would remain extremely cold. Thus, blood circulation helps keep your body temperature steady and safe.

How the body maintains its blood supply

You cannot live without a proper supply of healthy blood. In addition, the amounts of the various blood *components* (parts) must change constantly as the needs of your body change. Substances called *hematopoietic growth factors* govern the production of the red cells, white cells, and platelets. Your body maintains its blood supply by (1) regulating the volume of blood components, (2) controlling bleeding, and (3) replacing worn-out blood components.

Regulating the volume of blood components. The volume of each blood component continuously adjusts to meet the body's needs. The plasma proteins, especially albumin, control the movement of plasma be-

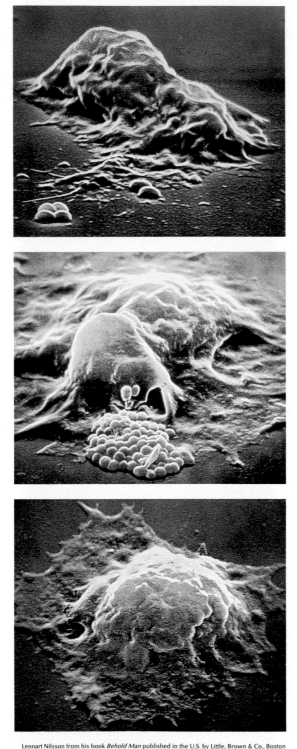

Lennart Nilsson from his book *Behold Man* published in the U.S. by Little, Brown & Co., Boston

The destruction of bacteria by a macrophage—a kind of white blood cell—is shown above. In the top photo, the macrophage approaches a cluster of bacteria. In the middle photo, the macrophage has begun to surround the germs. In the bottom photo, the macrophage has engulfed the bacteria, which it will destroy with enzymes.

tween the capillaries and the cells. Normally, only dissolved substances, such as nutrients, pass from the plasma through the capillary walls. But if the amount of albumin falls below normal, plasma may escape into tissues. In contrast, if the concentration of albumin is high, water from the tissues enters the plasma.

The volume of red blood cells depends on how much oxygen body tissues require. The kidneys produce a hormone called *erythropoietin* that stimulates output of the cells. When the tissues need oxygen, the kidneys produce increased amounts of erythropoietin, causing red-cell production to rise. When oxygen need falls, erythropoietin output drops. Certain diseases also may reduce the production of red blood cells.

Other hematopoietic growth factors control the number of white blood cells and platelets, which also increase and decrease according to the condition of the body. For example, an infection leads to a rise in the number of germ-fighting white blood cells. Similarly, severe bleeding can cause an increase in the number of platelets, thus improving the blood's ability to clot.

Controlling bleeding. You would bleed to death from a small cut if your blood did not *coagulate* (clot). An injured blood vessel causes platelets to stick to the damaged surface and to one another, forming a plug.

The plasma contains proteins called *clotting factors.* They normally circulate in an inactive form in the blood. But if a blood vessel suffers damage, the platelet plug and the injured vessel give off chemicals that react with the clotting factors. Eventually, the plasma protein fibrinogen changes into sticky strands of *fibrin.* The strands crisscross one another, creating a mesh that holds red blood cells and the platelet plug tightly to the site of bleeding. The fluid is squeezed out, and a solid plug— the clot—forms. A clot on the skin surface is a scab.

Occasionally, a clot may occur in an undamaged vessel that has no bleeding. Such a clot, called a *thrombus,* may block the flow of blood to tissues beyond the clot and cut off food and oxygen to those tissues. If a clot blocks an artery that nourishes the heart, a *coronary thrombosis* results, which may cause a heart attack (see **Coronary thrombosis**). If a clot blocks an artery to the brain, a stroke may occur (see **Stroke**).

Blood contains substances that dissolve clots as well as produce them. The clot-dissolving substances circulate in an inactive form until clotting occurs. They are then activated to control the extent and duration of the clotting.

Replacing worn-out blood components. Each formed element can live only a particular length of time, and so your body must continuously replace worn-out cells. Red blood cells live about 120 days, and platelets about 10 days. The life span of white blood cells varies greatly. For example, neutrophils live only a few hours, dying soon after they perform phagocytosis. But some lymphocytes live many years, thus providing long-term immunity against certain diseases.

Destruction of worn-out blood components. Two body organs—the liver and the spleen—remove worn-out red blood cells from the bloodstream and break them down. The liver uses coloring matter from the old cells in producing a digestive liquid called *bile.* The iron from hemoglobin is reused by the body to make new red blood cells. Worn-out white blood cells migrate to

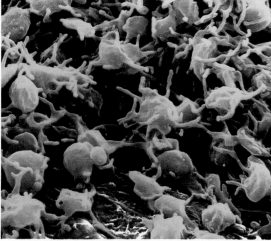

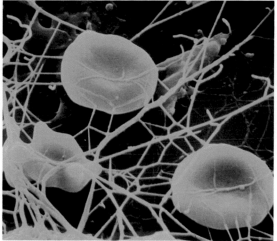

Clotting helps prevent blood loss from an injured vessel. Platelets immediately stick to the surface of a damaged blood vessel, forming a temporary plug at the site of injury, *above left.* A series of chemical reactions then takes place. Eventually, sticky strands of a substance called *fibrin* form a mesh that traps red blood cells, creating a clot, *above right.*

body tissues, where they die. Platelets probably wear out plugging tiny leaks in blood vessels.

Formation of new blood components. The core of human bones is filled with a soft red or yellow substance called *marrow.* In adults, the red bone marrow produces millions of blood cells per second. Red marrow occurs mostly in flat bones, such as the vertebrae, sternum, ribs, and skull. All blood cells begin in the marrow as *stem cells.* They develop into more mature *precursor cells,* each of which forms many red blood cells, white blood cells, or platelets.

As red blood cells develop in the marrow, they make hemoglobin. They also shrink and lose their nuclei. At maturity, they enter the bloodstream through tiny blood-filled cavities, called *sinuses,* in the marrow.

Although all white blood cells originate in the red bone marrow, lymphocytes—the T cells and B cells—mature elsewhere in the body. T cells enter the bloodstream through the sinuses and move to the *thymus,* a gland near the base of the neck, where they complete their development. The mature T cells then travel to structures called *lymph nodes,* which occur in many areas of the body. B cells complete their maturation in the lymph nodes and spleen.

Platelets develop in the red marrow into large precursor cells called *megakaryocytes* (MEHG *uh KAR ee uh sytz*). They eventually split into fragments, each of which becomes a platelet and enters the bloodstream.

Blood groups

The membranes of red blood cells contain proteins called *antigens.* More than 300 red-cell antigens have been identified. Based on the presence or absence of particular antigens, scientists have classified human blood into various groups.

The significance of blood groups. Blood-group classifications have extreme importance in certain medical procedures. Information about blood groups has also been used in law and anthropology.

In medicine, the chief use of blood groups is to determine whether the blood of one person, called a *donor,* can be transfused into the body of a patient without rejection or serious reaction. In almost every person, the plasma contains antibodies that react to certain antigens not present on the surface of that person's own red blood cells. During a transfusion, dangerous clumping of the red blood cells may occur if antibodies in the patient's plasma bind to antigens on the donor's red blood cells. The clumping can block small blood vessels and result in severe illness or even death. No one's plasma normally contains antibodies that bind with the person's own red-cell antigens.

The most serious transfusion reaction is the rapid destruction of the transfused red blood cells. This may lead to shock, kidney failure, and sometimes death. Other reactions may include fever, shaking, and chills.

Before a patient has a blood transfusion, hospitals always perform a *cross-match,* a test in which a sample of the donor's red blood cells is mixed with a sample of the patient's plasma. If clumping occurs, the patient does not receive blood from that donor. Cross-matching thus reduces the possibility of dangerous transfusion reactions.

The membranes of white blood cells carry proteins called *HLA antigens.* Physicians use the presence of those antigens to help determine whether an organ or tissue from a certain donor can be safely transplanted into a patient (see **Tissue transplant**).

In law. Law enforcement officials have used blood groups to help uncover the identity of criminals. For example, a blood specimen from the scene of a crime can be compared with that of a suspect. Such comparison cannot positively identify a criminal, but it might eliminate an innocent suspect.

The antigens on red blood cells are inherited, and so blood tests have been used in *paternity cases,* in which a man is accused of being a child's father. The tests cannot prove that a certain man fathered a certain child, but

Transfusion reactions between ABO blood types

Safe combinations		
Blood type of donor	**Blood type of patient**	
Type AB	→ Type AB	→
Type A	→ Type AB or A	→
Type B	→ Type AB or B	→
Type O	→ Type AB, A, B, or O	→

Unsafe combinations		
Blood type of donor	**Blood type of patient**	
Type AB	→ Type A, B, or O	→
Type A	→ Type B or O	→
Type B	→ Type A or O	→

Normal reaction

Clumping reaction

© Martin M. Rotker, Phototake

Before a blood transfusion, doctors mix samples of the donor's red blood cells and the patient's plasma to make sure no unsafe reactions will take place. Combining certain blood types causes red cells in the donor blood to *clump* (stick together). Clumping may block small blood vessels and cause the patient to become seriously ill or even die.

they can sometimes prove that he did not. The use of blood groups in paternity and other parenthood cases has been largely replaced by studies of the *DNA molecules* in blood cells. DNA carries hereditary information in all the body cells, and such tests are almost 100 per cent accurate in determining parenthood.

In anthropology. Many anthropologists have used blood-group frequencies to separate people into races and subraces. But that method of racial identification has not been successful. Blood-group antigens apparently do not differ among races, possibly because the races have intermarried throughout the ages.

The ABO blood groups make up the leading system of blood classification. The system classifies human blood into four main types, or groups. The types are based on the presence or absence of two antigens, called *A* and *B,* on the surface of red blood cells. (1) If the cells have only antigen A, the blood is *type A.* The plasma contains *anti-B* antibodies, which clump cells having antigen B. (2) If the red cells have only antigen B, the blood is *type B.* The plasma contains *anti-A* antibodies, which clump cells having antigen A. (3) If the cells have both antigens A and B, the blood is *type AB.* The plasma contains neither anti-A nor anti-B antibodies. (4) If the red cells have neither antigen A nor antigen B, the blood is *type O.* The plasma contains both anti-A and anti-B antibodies. Worldwide, type O blood is the most common, followed by type A. Relatively few people have type B, and even fewer have type AB.

Doctors prefer to use donor blood of the same ABO type as that of the patient to avoid clumping during a transfusion. But in an emergency, type O blood may be transfused into patients of any blood type. Similarly, type AB patients may be able to receive any ABO blood in an emergency because they have no antibodies to A or B antigens. But even then, hospitals perform a cross-match to ensure that no clumping will occur. Type A patients should never receive type B blood, and type B patients should never receive type A blood.

In most cases, it does not matter if the donor's plasma contains antibodies that clump the patient's red blood cells. The plasma dilutes rapidly in the patient's blood, making the risk of clumping slight.

Rh blood types form the second major blood-group system. People who have Rh antigens on their red blood cells are *Rh positive.* The antigen itself is called the *Rh factor.* People who lack the factor are *Rh negative.* Most people are Rh positive.

Plasma has no natural antibody to the Rh antigen. But Rh-negative people may build up antibodies called *anti-Rh* if they receive a transfusion of Rh-positive blood. The donor blood usually dilutes quickly, and so the antibodies create no problems. But clumping will occur later if an Rh-negative patient receives another transfusion of Rh-positive blood, which causes the anti-Rh to attack the Rh-positive blood. A mixing of Rh-negative and Rh-positive blood can also happen if an Rh-negative woman becomes pregnant with an Rh-positive baby. If some of the baby's red blood cells enter the woman's blood, anti-Rh may build up in her plasma. The situation can cause serious problems if the mother later becomes pregnant with another Rh-positive baby. See **Rh factor.**

Other blood groups. Many other systems for classifying blood have been developed. They include the Duffy, Kell, Kidd, Lewis, Lutheran, MNS, and P systems. But natural antibodies to the antigens in those systems occur rarely. Aside from the A and B antigens of the ABO system and the Rh factor, most red-cell antigens do not produce strong or dangerous reactions.

Medical uses of blood

Blood transfusions. The ability to transfuse blood or blood components into sick or injured people has saved countless lives and revolutionized patient care. If an adult suddenly loses more than 1 quart (0.9 liter) of blood, death may occur unless the person receives a transfusion. Transfusions can also help patients whose bone marrow does not produce enough blood cells. In addition, transfusions replace blood lost during surgery.

Blood banks collect blood from donors and store it in sterile bags with a preservative and a chemical to help prevent clotting. Generally, patients need only one blood component, such as red blood cells. For that reason, blood banks separate most whole blood into components before storage. Whole blood can be refrigerated and stored for 21 to 49 days. Plasma, red blood cells, and certain other components can be frozen and stored up to several years.

Some diseases may be transmitted from a donor to a patient through a transfusion. Laboratory workers therefore screen all donated blood for the presence of hepatitis, AIDS, and certain other infectious diseases. In addition, a cross-match must ensure that no dangerous reactions will result. See **Blood transfusion.**

Blood tests. Doctors use two main types of blood tests: (1) screening tests and (2) diagnostic tests.

Screening tests help physicians detect unsuspected problems in patients. For example, a *blood count* calculates the number of red and white cells and the amount of hemoglobin in a sample of blood (see **Blood count**). A *hematocrit* measures the volume of red blood cells compared with other blood components. Abnormalities revealed by either test may indicate a disease or a defect in blood-cell production.

Doctors use various other blood tests to detect certain diseases. For instance, a test that shows a high level of *glucose* (sugar) in the blood may indicate diabetes, a disease in which the body does not use sugar normally (see **Diabetes**). A blood test that reveals a high level of the waste product urea may indicate a disorder of the kidneys, which filter urea from the blood. Physicians also screen patients' blood for high levels of cholesterol, which has been associated with an increased risk of heart disease (see **Cholesterol**).

Diagnostic tests help doctors discover the causes of some conditions. For example, *anemia* (an abnormally low number of red blood cells) may result if the diet does not include enough iron, vitamin B$_{12}$, or folic acid. The size of a patient's red blood cells can reveal which nutrient the body needs. If the anemia results from too little iron, for example, the red cells are unusually small. But if it results from not enough vitamin B$_{12}$, the cells are unusually large.

A *differential white count test* tells a doctor the percentage of each type of white blood cell in a patient's blood. An extremely high number of white blood cells may mean *leukemia,* a form of cancer. On the other hand, a low neutrophil count may indicate an inability to fight infections effectively.

Such diagnostic tests as a *platelet count* and a *clotting test* help physicians learn of certain bleeding disorders. The tests may also be performed before an operation to determine if the patient might bleed excessively during surgery.

Blood disorders

Disorders of the blood involve overproduction, underproduction, or excessive destruction of blood cells. Certain infections also can affect the blood.

Anemia results from abnormally low levels of red blood cells or hemoglobin. A severely anemic person's blood carries too little oxygen to meet the needs of body tissues.

Various conditions may cause anemia. One main cause is insufficient production of red blood cells by the bone marrow. The underproduction may stem from nutritional deficiency, disease, or infection. In addition, blood loss from an injury often results in anemia. Excessive *hemolysis* (destruction of red blood cells) may also cause anemia. Two hereditary diseases—*sickle cell anemia* and *thalassemia*—involve hemoglobin abnormalities. Physicians use diet therapy, drugs, or transfusions to treat anemia, depending on its cause. See **Anemia; Hemolysis; Sickle cell anemia; Thalassemia.**

White-cell abnormalities. Leukemia arises from uncontrolled and excessive production of immature or mature white blood cells. Physicians do not know exactly what causes the cancer. They use drugs, radiation, and blood transfusions to treat it. See **Leukemia.**

The blood has an unusually low number of white

© Will McIntyre, Photo Researchers

Donated blood is tested by a laboratory worker for the presence of certain infectious diseases. Such screening helps prevent transmission of hepatitis and AIDS during transfusions.

blood cells in a disorder called *leukopenia.* It can result from exposure to certain drugs, diseases, or infections. In *neutropenia,* the most common type of leukopenia, the number of neutrophils is sharply reduced. People with neutropenia have an increased risk of infection because their blood lacks enough neutrophils to defend the body against harmful bacteria.

Bleeding disorders come from a disruption of the blood's ability to clot. Most such disorders result from abnormally low levels of clotting factors in the plasma or from an abnormality of the platelets.

A lack of some clotting factors causes *hemophilia,* a hereditary condition in which the blood coagulates extremely slowly. Hemophiliacs risk sudden, unexplained bleeding; severe bleeding from minor injuries; and bleeding of the joints and internal organs. Physicians treat the disorder by injecting the patient with the missing clotting factor. See **Hemophilia.**

Platelet abnormalities also affect the blood's clotting ability. People with *thrombocytopenia*—that is, an unusually low number of platelets—risk dangerous episodes of bleeding. The low platelet count may be caused by certain drugs, infections, or increased platelet use by the body. People with *thrombocythemia*—that is, an excessive number of platelets—may also risk abnormal bleeding as well as abnormal clotting. A shortage of iron or the presence of cancer or certain other diseases may produce the high platelet count. Treating the causes of both conditions usually corrects them.

Infections. Various infections can attack the blood. For example, infectious organisms can poison the blood and spread throughout the body (see **Blood poisoning**). In *malaria,* a parasite destroys the red blood cells (see **Malaria**). In *mononucleosis,* a virus infects the B cells (see **Mononucleosis**). In AIDS, one of the most serious infections carried by the blood, a virus infects the T cells, thereby blocking the immune system's ability to fight germs. See **AIDS.**

History of blood research

Scientific interest in blood probably began with the Greek physician Hippocrates, who lived during the 400's and 300's B.C. He proposed that all diseases resulted from an imbalance of four *humors* (body fluids)—black bile, blood, phlegm, and yellow bile. The theory led to bloodletting—the drawing of blood from a vein of a sick person so the disease would flow out with the blood. For many centuries, bloodletting was standard medical treatment. Barbers performed the procedure during the Middle Ages. In the late 1700's and early 1800's, a number of doctors, especially the American physician Benjamin Rush, prescribed bloodletting to treat most illnesses. Reckless use of the procedure caused some patients to die of excessive blood loss.

In 1628, the English physician William Harvey described how blood circulates through the body. His work became the basis for later discoveries about the functions of blood. See **Harvey, William.**

In 1882, Élie Metchnikoff, a Russian biologist, discovered phagocytosis. His achievement helped explain how white blood cells kill germs. Also in 1882, an Italian biologist named Giulio Bizzozero was the first to correctly describe the function of platelets and relate them to the clotting of blood.

As knowledge of blood components grew, interest in transfusions increased. Physicians first transfused blood directly from donors into patients. Most of the attempts failed. Then in the early 1900's, Karl Landsteiner, an Austrian-born American physician, discovered the ABO blood types. Cross-matching blood types of donors and patients led to a dramatic increase in successful transfusions. In 1940, Landsteiner and Alexander S. Wiener, an American scientist, discovered the Rh factor.

The storage of blood became possible in 1914 with the addition of nutrients and of chemicals that checked clotting. In 1937, Bernard Fantus, an American physician, set up the first blood-bank program. Another American physician, Charles Drew, organized many such programs during World War II (1939-1945). Drew also urged the use of plasma, which at that time could be stored longer than whole blood, for battlefield and other emergency transfusions.

Scientists today are working to develop blood substitutes or artificial blood that could replace human blood in transfusions. Such research is very important because, even with strict precautions, transfusions involve risk of reactions and the transmission of viruses and other infections through transfused blood.

Other current research involves producing and testing the hematopoietic growth factors responsible for the formation of all blood cells. Many of the growth factors are available in large quantities for testing in patients. They are being used in patients who lack enough red blood cells, white blood cells, or platelets. Such research offers hope of a better life for countless people.

G. David Roodman

Related articles in *World Book* include:

Blood circulation

Artery	Capillary	Heart
Blood pressure	Circulatory system	Vein

Blood diseases and defects

Anemia	Hemolysis	Leukemia
Bends	Hemophilia	Mononucleosis
Bleeding	Hypertension	Sickle cell anemia
Blood poisoning	Hypoglycemia	Thalassemia
Blue baby	Hypothermia	Von Willebrand's
Embolism	Leukocytosis	disease

Blood in diagnosis and treatment

AIDS	Blood transfusion
Antitoxin	Races, Human (Blood-group
Blood count	differences)

Blood researchers

Drew, Charles R.	Metchnikoff, Élie
Harvey, William	Osler, Sir William
Landsteiner, Karl	

Parts of the blood

Albumin	Globulin	Iron
Anticoagulant	Glucose	Plasma
Coagulant	Hemoglobin	Rh factor
Fibrin	Interleukin	Serum
Gamma globulin		

Other related articles

Bloodletting	Hormone (Blood	Spleen
Blushing	composition	Temperature,
Cholesterol	hormones)	Body
	Lymphatic system	

Outline

I. **The composition of blood**
   A. Plasma
   B. Red blood cells   D. Platelets
   C. White blood cells
II. **What blood does in the body**
   A. Carrying oxygen and carbon dioxide
   B. Transporting nutrients and wastes
   C. Protecting against disease
   D. Carrying hormones
   E. Distributing body heat
III. **How the body maintains its blood supply**
   A. Regulating the volume of blood components
   B. Controlling bleeding
   C. Replacing worn-out blood components
IV. **Blood groups**
   A. The significance of   C. Rh blood types
      blood groups   D. Other blood groups
   B. The ABO blood groups
V. **Medical uses of blood**
   A. Blood transfusions   B. Blood tests
VI. **Blood disorders**
   A. Anemia   C. Bleeding disorders
   B. White-cell   D. Infections
      abnormalities
VII. **History of blood research**

Questions

What does a *hematocrit* measure?
How does blood deliver oxygen to body cells?
Why do hospitals cross-match the patient's and donor's red blood cells before performing a transfusion?
How much blood does an 80-pound (36-kilogram) child have?
How do the ABO blood types differ from one another?
What is *leukemia*? *Hemophilia*? *Anemia*?
How does blood help keep body temperature steady and safe?
Where in the body do all blood cells begin?
What is *phagocytosis*?
How does blood circulate through the body?

Additional resources

Asimov, Isaac. *The Bloodstream: River of Life.* Rev. ed. Collier, 1961. First published as *The Living River.*
Hackett, Earle. *Blood.* Saturday Review Press, 1973.

Index

How to use the index
This index covers the contents of the 1989, 1990, and 1991 editions of *The World Book Year Book.*

There are two basic kinds of index entries. One kind of entry has a key word or words between it and the edition year, as: **General Motors Corp.,** advertising, 91: 155. This means that information about General Motors Corporation can be found on page 155 of the **Advertising** article in the 1991 *Year Book.*

The other basic kind of entry, in capital letters, is followed immediately by an edition year and a page number, as: **GEOLOGY,** 91: 306. This means that an article on geology begins on page 306 of the 1991 *Year Book.*

An index entry followed by "WBE" refers to a new or revised World Book Encyclopedia article in the supplement section, as: **GERMANY:** WBE, 91:508. This means that a revised *World Book Encyclopedia* article on Germany begins on page 508 of the 1991 *Year Book.*

The "See" and "See also" cross-references are to other entries within the index, as: **Global warming.** See also **Greenhouse effect.** This means that additional entries related to global warming are listed in the index under **Greenhouse effect.**

Clue words or phrases are used when two or more references to the same subject appear in the same edition of the *Year Book,* as: **Grammy Awards,** awards and prizes, 91:189; popular music, 91:407. This means that information about the Grammy Awards is in two articles in the 1991 *Year Book*—Awards and prizes and Popular music.

The indication "il." means that the reference is to an illustration only, as: **Hawkins Dance Co.,** il., 91:263.

Index

A

A-12 attack jet, armed forces, 91:172
Abderemane, Ahmed Abdallah, Africa, 90:162
Abdul-Jabbar, Kareem, basketball, 90:205
Abernathy, Ralph David, deaths, 91:265
Aborigines, Australia, 90:187; Close-Up, 89:185
Abortion, Belgium, 91:203; Canada, 91:222, 89:219; Congress, 90:253; courts, 90:256; Eastern Orthodox Churches, 90:281; Jews and Judaism, 90:343; medicine, 89:369; Protestantism, 91:411, 90:419, 89:422; religion, 91:418, 90:425; Roman Catholic Church, 90:429; state govt., 91:438, 90:445; Supreme Court, 91:443, 90:449; Washington, D.C., 90:480
Abu Bakr, Iman Yasin, West Indies, 91:478
Accidents. See Disasters; Safety.
Accutane, consumerism, 89:253; drugs, 89:276
Acetaminophen, health, 90:321
Acid rain, conservation, 89:251; energy crisis, Special Report, 90:111; environmental pollution, 91:290, 90:292, 89:294
Acne, consumerism, 89:253; drugs, 89:276
Acquavella, William, art, 91:175
Acquired immune deficiency syndrome. See AIDS.
Adamec, Ladislav, Czechoslovakia, 90:260, 89:257
Adams, Randall Dale, newsmakers, 90:393
Addiction. See Drug abuse; Smoking.
Aden. See Yemen.
Adenosine deaminase (ADA) deficiency, medicine, 91:362
Adolescent, Supreme Court, 89:453; teen drug use, Special Report, 89:58; welfare, 91:478
ADVERTISING, 91:154, 90:156, 89:156; consumerism, 91:257; television, Special Report, 90:74, 84. See also Magazine.
Aerospace industry. See Aviation; Space exploration.
Afars and Issas, Territory of. See Djibouti.
Affirmative action, civil rights, 91:240, 90:237; elections, 91:285; labor, 91:342; Supreme Court, 91:442, 90:449
AFGHANISTAN, 91:155, 90:157, 89:157; Asia, 91:179, 90:179, 89:180; Saudi Arabia, 90:432; United Nations, 90:472, 89:474; U.S.S.R., 90:470, 90:470
Aflatoxin, food, 90:306
AFRICA, 91:156, 90:158, 89:158; African elephant, Special Report, 91:36; AIDS, 91:161; anthropology, 89:167; conservation, 90:253; population, 90:415
African National Congress (ANC), Africa, 91:156, 90:158; Mandela, Nelson, 91:360; South Africa, 91:430, 90:436
Afrikaners, South Africa, 89:440
Agent Orange, public health, 91:415; veterans, 90:478, 89:480
Aging, drugs, 90:280; hearing, Special Report, 89:145; medicine, 91:363; memory, Special Report, 91:128; population, 89:418
Agriculture. See Farm and farming.
AIDS, 91:161, 90:164, 89:164; Africa, 91:161; child welfare, 90:228; civil rights, 89:237; Congress, 91:277, 89:275; dentistry, 89:271; drug abuse, 91:277; prison, 89:421; psychology, 89:423; Roman Catholic Church, 89:432; teen drug use, Special Report, 89:60; Thailand, 91:452; United Nations, 89:476
Ailey, Alvin, dancing, 91:264
Air Force. See Armed forces.
Air pollution, Antarctica, Special Report, 90:130; city, 89:234; petroleum, 90:407. See also Environmental pollution.
Airbag, safety, 91:424
Aircraft crashes. See Aviation; Disasters.
Airlines. See Aviation.
AKIHITO, 90:165; Japan, 91:335, 90:339; religion, 91:418
Alabama, state govt., 91:439, 90:444, 89:448
Alar, environmental pollution, 90:293; farm, 90:301; food, 90:305; public health, 90:421
Alaska, census, 91:227; consumerism, 90:255; environment, Close-Up, 90:294; petroleum, 90:406; state govt., 91:439, 90:444, 89:448; weather, 91:477, 90:481
ALBANIA, 91:162, 90:165, 89:164; Europe, 91:295, 90:298, 89:297
Albanians, Yugoslavia, 91:480, 90:485, 89:488
Al-Bashir, Umar Hasan Ahmad, Africa, 91:157, 90:162; Sudan, 91:442, 90:448
ALBERTA, 91:163, 90:166, 89:165; Indian, American, 89:330; Olympic Games, 89:396. See also Canada.
Alcoholic beverage, drug abuse, 91:277; memory, Special Report, 91:129; state govt., 89:449; teen drug use, Special Report, 89:59

Alcoholism, health, 91:315, 89:322; homelessness, Special Report, 90:101; mental illness, 89:370
Aleksandrov, Chudomir, Bulgaria, 89:213
Aleksei II, Eastern Orthodox Churches, 91:279
Alexander, Lamar, education, 91:281
Alfonsín, Raúl Ricardo, Argentina, 90:173, 89:171
Algal blooms, environmental pollution, 89:294
ALGERIA, 91:164, 90:166, 89:165; Africa, 91:158, 90:160, 89:158; Middle East, 91:366, 90:380, 89:374; Morocco, 89:382
Algiers, Algeria, 91:164, 89:165
Al-Huss, Salim, Lebanon, 90:355, 89:353
Alia, Ramiz, Albania, 91:162
Alien. See Immigration.
Allais, Maurice, Nobel Prizes, 89:391
Allen, William Barclay, civil rights, 90:238
Allison, Gray D., Liberia, 90:357
Allison, Tropical Storm, weather, 90:481
Al-Mahdi, Al-Sadiq, Sudan, 90:448, 89:451
Alpine skiing. See Olympic Games; Skiing.
Al-Sabah, Amir Jabir al-Ahmad, Kuwait, 91:340
Al-Sayed, Refaat, Sweden, 90:451
Alternative fuels, energy supply, 90:290
Altman, Sidney, Nobel Prizes, 90:397
Alzheimer's disease, drugs, 91:278; health, 89:322; memory, Special Report, 91:129
Amal militia, Lebanon, 89:353; Syria, 89:456
Amazon region, mining, 91:371; rain forests, Special Report, 89:97. See also Rain forest.
American Ballet Theatre, dancing, 91:263, 90:262, 89:260
American Broadcasting Companies (ABC), Olympic Games, 89:397; sports, 91:434; television, Special Report, 90:73. See also Television.
American Family Association, art, 91:174
American Federation of State, County, and Municipal Employees, Philadelphia, 89:410
American Indian. See Indian, American.
American Kennel Club. See Dog.
American Library Association. See Library.
American Psychiatric Association, mental illness, 91:364
American Psychological Association, mental illness, 91:364, 89:370
American Tail, An, animation, Special Report, 91:136
American Telephone and Telegraph Co. (AT&T), communications, 90:243; Italy, 90:338; labor, 90:348
Americans with Disabilities Act, Congress, 91:249; handicapped, 91:314; transit, 91:457
America's Cup. See Boating.
"America's Funniest Home Videos," television, 91:449
Amnesia, memory, Special Report, 91:129
Amoco Chemical Co., safety, 89:346
Amphetamines, teen drug use, Special Report, 89:64
Amphibian, conservation, 91:254
Anafranil (drug), mental illness, 91:364
Andean condor, bird conservation, Special Report, 90:44
Anderson, Marian, classical music, 90:241
Andorra, Europe, 91:295, 90:298, 89:297
Andreotti, Giulio, Italy, 91:332, 90:339
Andrew, Prince, Great Britain, 90:318, 89:317
Anemia, biology, 90:207; drugs, 90:280
Angioplasty, medicine, 89:369
Anglicans. See Church of England.
ANGOLA, 91:165, 90:166, 89:166; Africa, 91:156, 90:158, 89:158; Cuba, 90:260, 89:257; Namibia, 90:387; United Nations, 89:476
Animal. See Cat; Conservation; Dog; Farm and farming; Zoology; Zoos.
Animated film, Groening, Matt, 91:313; motion pictures, 89:380, 90:375; motion pictures, Close-Up, 90:385; Special Report, 91:135
Anne, Princess, Great Britain, 90:317
Antall, Jozsef, Hungary, 91:321
Antarctica, environment, Close-Up, 89:294; environmental pollution, 91:289, 90:292, 89:294; mining, 89:376; newsmakers, 91:383; Special Report, 90:126
Anthony, Beryl F., Jr., Democratic Party, 90:272
ANTHROPOLOGY, 91:165, 90:167, 89:167
Antibiotics, hearing, Special Report, 89:149
Antibodies, biology, 90:207
Antigua and Barbuda, Latin America, 91:345, 90:353, 89:350; West Indies, 90:484
Aouita, Said, track, 89:464
Aozou Strip, Africa, 91:156; Chad, 91:229; Libya, 90:358, 89:355
Apartheid. See South Africa.
Apple Computer, Inc., computer, 91:248, 90:245, 89:242

Aquariums. See Zoos.
Aquino, Benigno S., Jr., Philippines, 91:402
Aquino, Corazon C., Philippines, 91:401, 90:409, 89:411
Arab Cooperation Council, Middle East, 90:380
Arab League, Egypt, 91:284; Lebanon, 90:355; Middle East, 90:379
Arab Maghreb Union (AMU), Algeria, 90:166; Libya, 90:358; Middle East, 90:380
Arabia. See Middle East; Saudi Arabia.
Arabs. See Middle East; Muslims; Palestinians.
Arachnids, paleontology, 90:404
Arafat, Yasir, Middle East, 90:377, 89:375; Syria, 89:456; United Nations, 89:475
Aral Sea, water, 89:483
ARCHAEOLOGY, 91:166, 90:169, 89:168; Indian, American, 90:330; Latin America, 89:352
Archery. See Sports.
ARCHITECTURE, 91:168, 90:171, 89:170. See also Awards and prizes; Building and construction.
Architecture, Computer, computer, 90:244
Arco Chemical Co., safety, 91:423
Arctic, Canada, 89:220; conservation, 89:250; newsmakers, 89:388
ARENA (political party), El Salvador, 90:289
ARGENTINA, 91:170, 90:173, 89:171; international trade, 89:332; Latin America, 91:346, 90:354, 89:350; Menem, Carlos Saúl, 90:374
Ariane (rocket), space, 91:433, 90:439, 89:442
Arias Madrid, Arnulfo, Panama, 89:407
Arias Sánchez, Oscar, Calderón Fournier, Rafael A., 91:216
Aristide, Jean-Bertrand, Haiti, 91:313
Arizona, state govt., 91:440, 90:444, 89:447
Arkansas, state govt., 91:439, 90:444, 89:448
ARMED FORCES, 91:170, 90:173, 89:172; building, 91:209; Nobel Prizes, 89:391; Reagan, Ronald W., 89:428; space program, Special Report, 89:40; U.S. govt., 90:474. See also specific continents and countries.
Armenia, disasters, 89:272; Europe, 89:298; U.S.S.R., 91:464, 90:469; U.S.S.R., Close-Up, 89:472; U.S.S.R., Special Report, 90:65
Arms control, armed forces, 91:171, 90:173, 89:172; Bush, George, 90:216; Europe, 91:294; France, 90:310; Germany, West, 90:314; U.S.S.R., 90:470, 89:470; U.S.S.R., Special Report, 90:67
Army, United States. See Armed forces.
Arpino, Gerald, dancing, 91:263, 89:258
ART, 91:173, 90:177, 89:173; Latin America, 91:347; public art, Special Report, 89:72
Art Institute of Chicago, art, 90:177
Arthritis, drugs, 89:277; health, 91:315, 90:321
Arts. See Awards and prizes and specific arts, such as Dancing.
As Nasty as They Wanna Be, popular music, 91:406
Asbestos, environmental pollution, 89:294; public health, 90:421
ASIA, 91:176, 90:179, 89:177; African elephant, Special Report, 91:36; automobile, 90:188; geology, 89:312; Pacific rim, Special Report, 91:103; population, 90:415; rain forests, Special Report, 89:90
Asian Americans, theater, 91:452; WBE, 91:537
Asian Games, China, 91:236
Aspects of Love, theater, 91:453
Aspirin, advertising, 89:157; consumerism, 89:253; drugs, 89:277; hearing, Special Report, 89:151
Assad, Hafez al-, Syria, 91:446, 90:452, 89:456
Assam state, India, 90:329
Assault weapons. See Gun control.
Astrology, Reagan, Ronald W., 89:428
Astronaut. See Space exploration.
ASTRONOMY, 91:180, 90:183, 89:181; space, Special Report, 89:50. See also Space exploration.
Atari Corp., computer, 90:245
Atatürk Dam, Turkey, 91:459
Athanassopoulos, Nikos, Greece, 91:312
Athletics. See Olympic Games; Sports; and specific sports.
Atlanta, zoos, 89:491
Atlantis (spacecraft), space, 90:437, 89:441
Atwater, Lee, Republican Party, 91:419, 90:426
Auctions and sales. See Art; Coin collecting; Stamp collecting.
Aulby, Mike, bowling, 90:209
Auroras, Antarctica, Special Report, 90:129
Auschwitz, Jews and Judaism, 90:342; Roman Catholic Church, 90:428
AUSTRALIA, 91:181, 90:185, 89:183; architecture, 89:170; Asia, 91:179, 90:182, 89:179; Hogan, Paul, 89:323; mining, 90:381, 89:376; Pacific Islands, 91:394, 90:403
Australopithecus, anthropology, 91:165, 89:167

Index

Index

560

Index

Index

568

Contributors

Contributors not listed on these pages are members of *The World Book Year Book* editorial staff.

Acorn, Linda R., B.A.; Associate Editor, American Correctional Association. **[Prison]**

Alexander, David T., B.Sc., M.A.; Executive Director, Numismatic Literary Guild. **[Coin collecting]**

Alexiou, Arthur G., B.S.E.E., M.S.E.E.; Assistant Secretary, Committee on Climatic Changes and Ocean. **[Ocean]**

Andrews, Peter J., B.A., M.S.; free-lance writer; biochemist. **[Chemistry]**

Apseloff, Marilyn Fain, B.A., M.A.; Associate Professor of English, Kent State University. **[Literature for children]**

Barber, Peggy, B.A., M.L.S.; Associate Executive Director for Communications, American Library Association. **[Library]**

Barnhart, Robert K., B.A.; Editor in Chief, Clarence L. Barnhart, Inc. Coeditor, *The World Book Dictionary.* **[Dictionary Supplement: Essay]**

Bell, James B., B.A., M.Div., Ph.D.; Senior Vice President, U.S. International Culture and Trade Center. **[Special Report: Ellis Island, Museum of Memories]**

Berman, Howard A., B.A., B.H.L., M.A.H.L.; Rabbi, Chicago Sinai Congregation. **[Jews and Judaism]**

Bessman, Jim, contributor, *Billboard* magazine; Senior Editor, *Spin* magazine. **[Popular music]**

Blackadar, Alfred K., A.B., Ph.D.; Professor Emeritus, The Pennsylvania State University. **[Weather]**

Bourne, Eric, columnist, foreign affairs, *The Christian Science Monitor.* **[eastern European country articles; Union of Soviet Socialist Republics (Close-Up)]**

Bower, Bruce, M.A.; Behavioral Sciences Editor, *Science News* magazine. **[Psychology]**

Bradsher, Henry S., A.B., B.J.; foreign affairs analyst. **[Asia and Asian country articles]**

Brett, Carlton E., B.A., M.A., Ph.D.; Professor of Geological Sciences, University of Rochester. **[Paleontology]**

Brock, Frances D., B.A., M.S.J.; Features Editor, *Adweek* magazine. **[Advertising]**

Campbell, Geoffrey A., B.J.; staff reporter, *The Bond Buyer.* **[Civil rights]**

Campbell, Linda P., B.A., M.S.L.; National Legal Affairs Correspondent, *Chicago Tribune.* **[Civil rights]**

Campbell, Robert, B.A., M.S.J., M. Arch.; architect; architecture critic, *The Boston Globe.* **[Architecture]**

Campion, Owen F., A.B.; Associate Publisher, *Our Sunday Visitor* magazine. **[Religion; Roman Catholic Church]**

Canemaker, John, M.F.A.; film animator, author. **[Special Report: Once Again, "Toons" Are Tops]**

Cardinale, Diane P., B.A.; Assistant Communications Director, Toy Manufacturers of America. **[Toys and games]**

Cormier, Frank, B.S.J., M.S.J.; former White House Correspondent, Associated Press. **[U.S. government articles]**

Cormier, Margot, B.A., M.A.; free-lance writer. **[U.S. government articles]**

Cormier, William R., M.S.J.; newsman, Associated Press. **[U.S. government articles]**

Cromie, William J., B.S., M.S.; science writer, Harvard University. **[Space exploration]**

DeFrank, Thomas M., B.A., M.A.; White House Correspondent, *Newsweek* magazine. **[Armed forces]**

Dent, Thomas H., B.S.; Executive Director, The Cat Fanciers' Association, Inc. **[Cat]**

Dirda, Michael, B.A., M.A., Ph.D.; writer and editor, *The Washington Post Book World.* **[Poetry]**

Ellis, Gavin, Assistant Editor, *New Zealand Herald.* **[New Zealand]**

Elsasser, Glen R., B.A., M.S.; correspondent, *Chicago Tribune.* **[Supreme Court of the United States]**

Evans, Sandra, B.S.J.; staff writer, *The Washington Post.* **[Washington, D.C.]**

Falk, Pamela S., Ph.D.; former Director, Puerto Rico project of the Americas Society; editor, *The Political Status of Puerto Rico.* **[Special Report: Puerto Rico—The 51st State?]**

Farr, David M. L., M.A., D.Phil.; Professor Emeritus, Carleton University, Ottawa. **[Canada; Canada (Close-Up); Canadian province articles; Mulroney, Brian]**

Fisher, Robert W., B.A., M.A.; Senior Economist/Editor, U.S. Bureau of Labor Statistics. **[Labor]**

Fitchett, Joseph, B.A., M.A.; Senior Political Correspondent, *International Herald Tribune.* **[Europe and western European country articles]**

Fitzgerald, Mark, B.A.; Midwest Editor, *Editor & Publisher* magazine. **[Newspaper]**

Friedman, Emily, B.A.; contributing editor, *Hospitals* magazine. **[Hospital]**

Garvie, Maureen, B.A., M.A., B.Ed.; Books Editor, *The* (Kingston, Ont.) *Whig-Standard.* **[Canadian literature]**

Gatty, Bob, editor, Periodicals News Service. **[Food]**

Gillenwater, Sharon K., B.A.; Assistant Editor, *San Diego Magazine.* **[San Diego]**

Goldner, Nancy, B.A.; dance critic, *The Philadelphia Inquirer.* **[Dancing]**

Graham, Timothy J., Assistant City Editor, *The Houston Post.* **[Houston]**

Harakas, Stanley Samuel, B.A., B.D., Th.D.; Archbishop Iakovos Professor of Orthodox Theology, Hellenic College, Holy Cross Greek Orthodox School of Theology. **[Eastern Orthodox Churches]**

Haverstock, Nathan A., A.B.; Affiliate Scholar, Oberlin College. **[Latin America and Latin-American country articles]**

Heartney, Eleanor, B.A., M.A.; free-lance art critic. **[Art]**

Helms, Christine, B.A., Ph.D.; free-lance writer; consultant. **[Middle East and Middle Eastern country articles; North Africa country articles]**

Higgins, James V., B.A.; auto industry reporter, *The Detroit News.* **[Automobile]**

Hill, Michael, B.A.; television critic, *Baltimore Evening Sun.* **[Television]**

Hillgren, Sonja, B.J., M.A.; Washington Editor, *Farm Journal.* **[Farm and farming]**

Inder, Stuart, former Editor and Publisher, *Pacific Islands Year Book.* **[Pacific Islands]**

Jacobi, Peter P., B.S.J., M.S.J.; Professor of Journalism, Indiana University. **[Classical music]**

Johanson, Donald C., B.S., M.A., Ph.D.; President, Institute of Human Origins. **[Anthropology]**

Keeney, Kathy, B.A.; Editor, *Modern Railroads* magazine. **[Railroad]**

Kim, Robert H., Ed.D.; Full Professor, Center for Global and Peace Education, Western Washington University. **[World Book Supplement; Asian Americans]**

King, Elliot W., M.S., M.A.; Editor, *Optical and Magnetic Report* magazine. **[Computer]**

Kisor, Henry, B.A., M.S.J.; Book Editor, *Chicago Sun-Times.* **[Literature]**

Knapp, Elaine S., B.A.; Editor, Council of State Governments. **[State government]**

Kolgraf, Ronald, B.A., M.A.; Publisher, *Adweek* magazine. **[Manufacturing]**

Larsen, Paul A., P.E., B.S., Ch.E.; member: American Philatelic Society; Collectors Club of Chicago; Fellow, Royal Philatelic Society, London; past President, British Caribbean Philatelic Study Group. **[Stamp collecting]**

Lawrence, Al, B.A., M.A., M.Ed.; Executive Director, United States Chess Federation. **[Chess]**

Lawrence, Richard, B.E.E.; International Economics Correspondent, *The Journal of Commerce.* **[Economics; International trade]**

Leff, Donna Rosene, B.S.J., M.S.J., M.P.P., Ph.D.; Associate Professor of Journalism and Urban Affairs, Northwestern University. **[City]**

Lewis, David C., M.D.; Professor of Medicine, Brown University. **[Drug abuse]**

Liebenow, Beverly B., B.A.; author and freelance writer. **[Africa and African country articles]**

Liebenow, J. Gus, B.A., M.A., Ph.D.; James H. Rudy Professor of Political Science and African Studies, Indiana University. **[Africa and African country articles]**

Litsky, Frank, B.S.; sportswriter, *The New York Times.* **[Sports articles]**

Maran, Stephen P., B.S., M.A., Ph.D.; Senior Staff Scientist, National Aeronautics and Space Administration-Goddard Space Flight Center. **[Astronomy]**

March, Robert H., A.B., S.M., Ph.D; Professor of Physics, University of Wisconsin-Madison. **[Physics]**

Marty, Martin E., Ph.D.; Fairfax M. Cone Distinguished Service Professor, University of Chicago. **[Protestantism]**

Mather, Ian J., B.A., M.A.; Diplomatic Editor, *The European,* London. **[Great Britain; Ireland; Northern Ireland]**

Maugh, Thomas H., II, Ph.D.; science writer, *Los Angeles Times.* **[Biology]**

McCarron, John F., B.S.J., M.S.J.; urban affairs writer, *Chicago Tribune.* **[Chicago]**

McGinley, Laurie, B.S.J.; reporter, *The Wall Street Journal.* **[Aviation]**

McLeese, Don, M.A.; pop music critic, *Chicago Sun-Times.* **[World Book Supplement: Rock music]**

Merina, Victor, A.A., B.A., M.S.; staff writer, *Los Angeles Times.* **[Los Angeles]**

Moores, Eldridge M., B.S., Ph.D.; Professor of Geology, University of California at Davis. **[Geology]**

Moritz, Owen, B.A.; Urban Affairs Editor, New York *Daily News.* **[New York City]**

Morris, Bernadine, B.A., M.A.; Chief Fashion Writer, *The New York Times.* **[Fashion]**

Newcomb, Eldon H., A.B., M.A., Ph.D.; Folke Skoog Professor, Department of Botany, University of Wisconsin-Madison. **[Botany]**

Nguyen, J. Tuyet, B.A.; United Nations Correspondent, United Press International. **[United Nations]**

Pennisi, Elizabeth, B.S., M.S.; Associate Editor, *The Scientist.* **[Zoology]**

Prater, Constance C., B.S.J.; City-County Bureau Chief, *Detroit Free Press.* **[Detroit]**

Priestaf, Iris, B.A., M.A., Ph.D.; Geographer and Vice President, David Keith Todd Consulting Engineers. **[Water]**

Raloff, Janet, B.S.J., M.S.J.; Policy/Technology Editor, *Science News* magazine. **[Environmental pollution]**

Roccaforte, Sharon, B.A., M.L.S.; Director, Information Service, Magazine Publishers of America. **[Magazine]**

Roodman, G. David, M.D., Ph.D.; Professor of Medicine, University of Texas Health Center, San Antonio, and Chief of Hematology, Audie L. Murphy Memorial Veterans Hospital. **[World Book Supplement: Blood]**

Rowse, Arthur E., I.A., M.B.A.; free-lance writer. **[Consumerism; Safety]**

Schooler, Jonathan W., B.A., M.S., Ph.D.; Assistant Professor of Psychology and Research Scientist, University of Pittsburgh. **[Special Report: Why Do We Forget? What Can We Do About It?]**

Shapiro, Howard S., B.S.; Editor, *Weekend Magazine, The Philadelphia Inquirer.* **[Philadelphia]**

Sheehan, James J., A.B., M.A., Ph.D.; Dickason Professor of Humanities, Stanford University. **[World Book Supplement: Germany]**

Shewey, Don, B.F.A.; contributing writer, *Village Voice* and *American Theatre.* **[Theater]**

Smerk, George M., B.S., M.B.A., D.B.A.; Professor of Transportation, School of Business, Indiana University. **[Transit]**

Stein, David Lewis, B.A., M.S.; author; journalist, *The Toronto Star.* **[Toronto]**

Terrile, Richard J., B.S., M.S., Ph.D.; planetary astronomer, Jet Propulsion Laboratory. **[Special Report: A Hitchhiker's Current Guide to the Planets]**

Thomas, Paulette, B.A.; staff writer, *The Wall Street Journal.* **[Bank; Bank (Close-Up)]**

Toch, Thomas, B.A., M.A.; Associate Editor, *U.S. News & World Report.* **[Education]**

Tuchman, Janice Lyn, B.S., M.S.J.; Executive Editor, *Engineering News-Record.* **[Building and construction]**

Unger, Danny, A.B., M.S., Ph.D.; Assistant Professor, Georgetown University. **[Special Report: Riding a Wave of Prosperity on the Pacific Rim]**

Vesley, Roberta, A.B., M.L.S.; Library Director, American Kennel Club. **[Dog]**

Vizard, Frank, B.A.; Electronics Editor, *Popular Mechanics.* **[Electronics]**

Voorhies, Barbara, B.S., Ph.D.; Professor of Anthropology, University of California at Santa Barbara. **[Archaeology]**

Walter, Eugene J., Jr., B.A.; Director of Publications and Editor in Chief, *Wildlife Conservation* magazine, New York Zoological Society. **[Conservation; Zoos; Special Report: The African Elephant: Saved from Extinction?]**

Widder, Pat, B.A.; New York Financial Correspondent, *Chicago Tribune.* **[Stocks and bonds]**

Williams, Susan, B.A.; journalist, Sydney, Australia. **[Australia]**

Windeyer, Kendal, President, Windeyer Associates, Montreal, Canada. **[Montreal]**

Woods, Michael, B.S.; Science Editor. *The* (Toledo, Ohio) *Blade.* **[Industry articles and health articles]**

Wuntch, Philip, B.A.; film critic, *Dallas Morning News.* **[Motion pictures]**

Acknowledgments

The publishers acknowledge the following sources for illustrations. Credits read from top to bottom, left to right, on their respective pages. An asterisk (*) denotes illustrations and photographs that are the exclusive property of *The Year Book*. All maps, charts, and diagrams were prepared by *The Year Book* staff unless otherwise noted.

4 © B. Bisson, Sygma; Duncan Willets, Gamma/Liaison; Jet Propulsion Laboratory
5 © Andrew Holbrooke, Black Star; Reuters/Bettmann; © Craig Aurness, Woodfin Camp, Inc.
7 © B. Bisson, Sygma
8 TM & © Twentieth Century Fox Film Corporation 1990; Dennis Brack, *Time* Magazine; © Oswald, Gamma/Liaison
9 © R. Bossu, Sygma; AP/Wide World; NASA
10 © Roger M. Richards, Gamma/Liaison; © N. Tully, Sygma
11 Focus on Sports
12 AP/Wide World; © Wesley Bocxe, Sipa Press
13 AP/Wide World
14 © Gamma/Liaison; APA from Black Star
15 © A. Tannenbaum, Sygma
16 © Michael Abramson, Sipa Press
17 © P. F. Gero, Sygma; AP/Wide World; AP/Wide World
18 © Gamma/Liaison; Canapress
19 Reuters/Bettmann
20 © Greg Smith, Sipa Press; © Eslami Rad, Gamma/Liaison
21 © Carlos Angel, Gamma/Liaison
22 Focus on Sports; © Walker, Gamma/Liaison
23 UPI/Bettmann
24 Reuters/Bettmann; Dennis Brack, *Time* Magazine
25 © J. Patrick Forden, Sygma
26 © Tony Savino, Sipa Press
27 AP/Wide World
28 © M. Milner, Sygma; © B. Bisson, Sygma
29 Focus on Sports
30 © John Arthur, Impact
31 Diana Walker, *Time* Magazine; Reuters/Bettmann
32 © De Keerle, UK Press from Gamma/Liaison; © Bill Gentile, Sipa Press
33 © Bassignac/Deville/Gaillard from Gamma/Liaison
35 NASA
36 Katharine Payne
39 Rick Weyerhaeuser, World Wildlife Fund for Nature; © Tim Davis, Photo Researchers
41 Rick Weyerhaeuser, World Wildlife Fund for Nature
43 © Mark Boulton, Photo Researchers; Greg Girard, *Time* Magazine; © Farrell Grehan, Photo Researchers
47 Duncan Willets, Camerapix from Gamma/Liaison; William Campbell, *Time* Magazine
49 Rick Weyerhaeuser, World Wildlife Fund for Nature
52 Tony Pacheco*
54-55 © Robert Frerck, Odyssey Productions
56 Wangtek Puerto Rico, Inc.; Tony Pacheco*; © Alan Hirsch, FPG
57 © Robert Frerck, Odyssey Productions
58 Granger Collection; Bettmann
59 AP/Wide World; Reuters/Bettmann; Economic Development Administration of Puerto Rico
61 © Chip Peterson and Rosa Maria de la Cueva Peterson; © Tony Pacheco, Sygma
64 © Tony Arruza
68 Jet Propulsion Laboratory
71 Roberta Polfus*
72 Jet Propulsion Laboratory
74 NASA (4); © François Colas, Pic du Midi Observatory from Starlight; Jet Propulsion Laboratory
75-78 Jet Propulsion Laboratory
79 U.S. Geological Survey; Jet Propulsion Laboratory
80 Jet Propulsion Laboratory
81 U.S. Geological Survey
83 Jet Propulsion Laboratory (3); U.S. Geological Survey
84 Bradford A. Smith, University of Arizona, and Richard J. Terrile, Jet Propulsion Laboratory
86 © Joe McNally, Sygma
89 JAK Graphics*
91 AP/Wide World
92 Bettmann; UPI/Bettmann
93 Culver; UPI/Bettmann
94 Culver; UPI/Bettmann
95 Guy Wolek*
97 © Andrew Holbrooke, Black Star; © Andrew Popper, Picture Group; © Andrew Holbrooke, Black Star
98 © Nicholas Cerulli; © Andrew Popper, Picture Group; © Andrew Holbrooke, Black Star
99 © A. Tannenbaum, Sygma; Metaform Inc.; © Andrew Popper, Picture Group
100 © Andrew Popper, Picture Group
102 © Imtek Imagineering from Masterfile
108 Cameramann International, Ltd.; © Bob Nickelsberg, Gamma/Liaison

109 © Bob Nickelsberg, Gamma/Liaison
112 Pan-Asia Newspaper Alliance; Cameramann International, Ltd.
113 Cameramann International, Ltd.; © Paul Chesley, Photographers/Aspen
116 Pan-Asia Newspaper Alliance; © Dan Lamont, Matrix
117 © Matthew Naythons, Gamma/Liaison
120-130 Scott Harris*
134 Sygma; © 1989 Warner Bros. Inc. All rights reserved; © The Walt Disney Company; © 1986 Pixar. All rights reserved.
135 Foote, Cone & Belding; © 1989 Warner Bros. Inc. All rights reserved; TM & © Warner Bros. Inc.; TM & © Twentieth Century Fox Film Corporation 1990
138 © The Walt Disney Company; © Pixar. All rights reserved.
139 TM & © Lucasfilm Ltd. (LFL) 1980. All rights reserved; Foote, Cone & Belding
141 © 1985 Fido Dido Inc., Licensed by UFF Inc., J. J. Sedlmaier, Executive Producer (Joel Gordon*)
143 © 1990 Pixar. All rights reserved.
145-146 Film Stills Archive, The Museum of Modern Art
147 © The Walt Disney Company; © The Walt Disney Company; © 1940 Turner Entertainment. The Looney Tunes characters are trademarks of Warner Bros. Inc.
148 © Hanna-Barbera Productions from Hamilton Projects, Inc.; © The Walt Disney Company
149 © 1986 Universal City Studios, Inc.; TM & © Twentieth Century Fox Film Corporation 1990
150 © 1988 Touchstone Pictures and Amblin Entertainment, Inc.
153 © J. Langevin, Sygma
154 Clarity Coverdale Rueff Advertising Agency from MADD Minnesota
156 Agence France-Presse
160 © P. Robert, Sygma
161 © John Berry, Black Star
162 © Joel Robine, Agence France-Presse
163 Chuck Stoody, Canapress
164 © Albert Facelly, Sipa Press
166 FAR SIDE CARTOON by Gary Larson is reprinted by permission of Chronicle Features, San Francisco.
167 Reuters/Bettmann
168 AP/Wide World
169 © Eric Brissaud, Gamma/Liaison
171 © J. Langevin, Sygma
172 AP/Wide World
173 Reuters/Bettmann
174 © R. Maiman, Sygma
175 © Mike Williams
176 © Richard Vogel, Gamma/Liaison
180 NASA
182 © Branco Gaica
184 © Deutsche Presse-Agentur from Photoreporters
186 Heinz Kluetmeier, *Sports Illustrated*
188 © N. Tully, Sygma
189-193 AP/Wide World
197 AUTH copyright *The Philadelphia Inquirer*. Reprinted with permission of Universal Press Syndicate. All rights reserved.
200 AP/Wide World
202 Focus on Sports
205-208 Reuters/Bettmann
210 © Deutsche Presse-Agentur from Photoreporters
211 © Bassignac/Deville/Gaillard from Gamma/Liaison
213-214 AP/Wide World
215 Reuters/Bettmann
216 © C. Thumporn, Agence France-Presse
218-221 Canapress
222 © Terry McEvoy
225 Etienne Bol
228 © Douglas Burrows, Gamma/Liaison
230 Lawrence Livermore National Laboratory
232 © Chicago Tribune Company, all rights reserved, used with permission.
234 AP/Wide World
238 © Chicago Tribune Company, all rights reserved, used with permission.
239 AP/Wide World
240 © Duane Hall, Vis-Tec
243 Reuters/Bettmann
244 © Joan Marcus
245 Jose R. Lopez, NYT Pictures
247 © Ken Kerbs
249 © P. F. Gero, Sygma
255 Greenpeace
256 Reprinted by permission: Tribune Media Services

574

Family milestones of 1990

In the preceding pages, *The World Book Year Book* reported the major events and trends of 1990. Use these two pages to record the developments that made the year memorable for *your* family.

Family members (names)	Ages	Family pets
_____	_____	_____
_____	_____	_____
_____	_____	_____
_____	_____	_____
_____	_____	_____
_____	_____	_____
_____	_____	_____

Births (name)	Date	Where born	Weight	Height
_____	_____	_____	_____	_____
_____	_____	_____	_____	_____
_____	_____	_____	_____	_____

Weddings (names)	Date	Where held
_____	_____	_____
_____	_____	_____
_____	_____	_____

Religious events

Graduations

Anniversaries

In memoriam

Awards, honors, and prizes

Sports and club achievements

Vacations and trips

Most enjoyable books

_____

_____

_____

_____

_____

Most-played recordings and tapes

_____

_____

_____

_____

_____

Most unforgettable motion pictures

_____

_____

_____

_____

_____

Most-watched television programs

_____

_____

_____

_____

_____

Paste a favorite family photograph
or snapshot here.

Date

_____

Location

_____

Occasion

_____

_____

World Book Encyclopedia, Inc. provides high quality educational and reference products for the family and school, including a FIVE-VOLUME CHILDCRAFT FAVORITES SET, colorful books on favorite topics, such as DOGS and INDIANS; and THE WORLD BOOK MEDICAL ENCYCLOPEDIA, a 1,040-page, fully illustrated family health reference. For further information, write WORLD BOOK ENCYCLOPEDIA, INC., P.O. Box 3073, Evanston, IL 60204.